A Whole World

A Whole World

Letters from James Merrill

EDITED BY LANGDON HAMMER
AND STEPHEN YENSER

ALFRED A. KNOPF
NEW YORK
2021

THIS IS A BORZOI BOOK PUBLISHED BY ALFRED A. KNOPF

www.aaknopf.com

Knopf, Borzoi Books, and the colophon are registered trademarks of Penguin Random House LLC.

LIBRARY OF CONGRESS CATALOGING-IN-PUBLICATION DATA
Names: Merrill, James, 1926–1995, author. | Hammer, Langdon, [date] editor. | Yenser, Stephen, editor.
Title: A whole world : letters from James Merrill / edited by Langdon Hammer and Stephen Yenser.
Description: First edition. | New York : Alfred A. Knopf, 2021.
Identifiers: LCCN 2020026454 (print) | LCCN 2020026455 (ebook) | ISBN 9781101875506 (hardcover) | ISBN 9781101875513 (ebook)
Subjects: LCSH: Merrill, James, 1926–1995—Correspondence. | Poets, American—20th century—Correspondence.
Classification: LCC PS3525.E6645 Z48 2021 (print) | LCC PS3525.E6645 (ebook) | DDC 811/.54 [B]—dc23
LC record available at https://lccn.loc.gov/2020026454
LC ebook record available at https://lccn.loc.gov/2020026455

Jacket photograph: James Merrill by Rollie McKenna, 1969 © Rosalie Thorne McKenna Foundation, courtesy Center for Creative Photography. Print: National Portrait Gallery, Smithsonian Institution; gift of Rollie McKenna.
Jacket design by Chip Kidd

Manufactured in the United States of America
First Edition

In memory of J. D. McClatchy

Contents

Introduction

> One day, of course, you may open one of these envelopes, and
> I myself will fall out, tiny and dry, like the Japanese flowers, for
> you to revive in a bowl of water, or clear soup. Be sure you shake
> each envelope carefully, or you may lock me away in a drawer.

So James Merrill wrote at age twenty-four to his lover. He had almost forty-five years remaining in which to slip his speculations, advice, and metaphors into envelopes posted almost daily and from all parts of the world. He wrote impressively often to many people he knew in strikingly different contexts: his family; friends from his youth (he never let relationships lapse); his lovers; new acquaintances (he was ever alert to cultivating them, especially among younger generations, partly because he was wary of losing touch with the times); and fellow writers and scholars whose views affected his poems more or less directly.

Merrill might turn out to be the last great American letter writer. His adored friend Elizabeth Bishop once proposed a seminar at Harvard on what she called "Letters! . . . Just *letters*—as an art form or something"—an art form, she opined, that was "the dying 'form of communication.'" That was in 1971, a couple of decades before email became ubiquitous, not to mention the subsequent expansion of social media. Unlike W. H. Auden, a more distant friend and influence, who asked upon his death that his correspondents burn his letters to them, Merrill wanted his to be preserved. He kept drafts and carbons, especially when he was younger, and his provident friends saved their copies, just as he usually saved their letters and cards to him—thousands of pieces of his correspondence are in the Special Collections of Olin Library at Washington University, and a substantial number are at the Beinecke Library at Yale, in addition to those at a variety of other institutions—in part because he wanted the record of his life to be as complete as possible. One early letter here to his mother records his dismay when she destroyed correspondence from some of his closest friends. His reaction, as he describes it in his memoir, *A Different Person*, verged on the corporeal: her "crippling blow" left him "in shock." The loss of some of the letters not only had dealt "an incalculable loss to posterity" but also had left him "with little evidence of having been loved by anyone, except her."

Readers of his memoir have had a glimpse of the color and density of the life he wished to record and to shape. The book's 271 packed pages establish as a *point d'appui* the period of two and a half years that he spent abroad in 1950–52. Subsequently a "different" person in two senses of that word, if he hadn't been in the first place, Merrill was an inveterate dualist. His once troublesome need "to dramatize the ambivalence I live with," he says to a correspondent, soon became "the very stuff of my art." Temperamentally inclined to contraries, he believed, he told an interviewer, that "the ability to see both ways at once isn't merely an idiosyncrasy but corresponds to how the world needs to be seen: cheerful *and* awful, opaque *and* transparent." His favorite literary devices, from pun to paradox, reflected that conviction, and so did his geographical affinities. When he left for Europe, he wanted to explore the old world new to him and yet—by means of his many letters—to strengthen his ties at home. His opposing penchants for movement and for permanence generate the paradox latent in the closely crafted opening sentence of *A Different Person*: "Meaning to stay as long as possible, I sailed for Europe."

Years later, in *The Book of Ephraim*, he quoted Peter Quennell's biography *Alexander Pope*, and, "meaning to stay as long as possible" himself, he would have known that Auden approved of Quennell's report of Pope's faith "that his letters were bound to interest posterity," that he was "establishing a link between himself and his unborn readers," and that "when he took up his pen, he assumed the vigilant attitude of the creative artist." Just such vigilance pervaded all that Merrill did. If it led him to admit in his journal that disparagement of his poetry's aversion to the social effects of politics and money could depress him, it also gave him perspective on "the pulsing N*O*W" and shored up his trust in those "unborn readers." The same faith encouraged him to shrug off criticism that his poems could be exacting and required patience to understand, let alone appreciate.

His predilection for doubling up contributed to the work's difficulty yet also, surprisingly, to its broader appeal. Beginning in the 1950s, even as he was making a life on both sides of the Atlantic, he was creating connections between this world and the realm beyond. He and his partner David Jackson (some skeptical readers would call their project a *folie à deux*) communicated with the latter by means of a Ouija board in séances that by the late 1970s provided the basis for the epic poem *The Changing Light at Sandover*. The otherworldly spirit presiding over the epic's eponymous first part, *The Book of Ephraim*, while enticing an audience largely unfamiliar with contemporary poetry, reinforced Merrill's dedication to his art. In the course of his most urgent yet solemn revelation, Ephraim instructs him as follows: "& NOW ABOUT DEVOTION IT IS I AM FORCED TO BELIEVE THE MAIN IMPETUS DEVOTION TO EACH OTHER TO WORK TO REPRODUCTION TO AN IDEAL IT IS BOTH THE MOULD & THE CLAY SO WE ARRIVE AT GOD." Merrill had determined long before that the object of his devotion was his "work." "A poet" is a person "choosing the words he lives by," he told an interviewer. His surrogate Manuel, addressing his mother in the closet drama *The Image Maker,* rephrases it: "My work, Mamá. That's *my* whole life."

While that declaration harbors its own profound contradiction, to a degree greater than any of his fellow poets Merrill came to combine and even to identify his "life" and his "work" and to incorporate the quotidian dimension of the former in the precisely turned particulars of the latter, an accomplishment all the more arresting when we remember that early in his career he seemed to embody the prototypical artificer. In that phase, his own trope for the ideal artwork was a "cold crystal" bowl whose "splendid curvings of glass artifice / Informed its flawlessness / With lucid unities"—until it broke, and even then its essential elegance was ineluctable:

> The splinters rainbowing ruin on the floor
> Cut structures in the air,
> Mark off, like eyes or compasses, a face
> Of mathematical fixity, spotlight

Within whose circumscription we may set
All solitudes of love.

His first novel, *The Seraglio*, though a *roman à clef*, had as its tutelary
genius the rarefied stylist of *The Golden Bowl*. But from the 1960s
onward, along with but different from both his debonair contempo-
raries in the New York school and the more theatrical and publicized
"confessional" poets, he mined personal experience and everyday
circumstance for aesthetic material.

Critical attention has made the shape of his career well known.
Some points in the general trajectory toward more varied, often inti-
mate subject matter would include the breakout poems "A Tenancy"
and "An Urban Convalescence" in *Water Street*, a book named notably
for his home address, beginning in 1954, in Stonington, Connecticut;
his responses, both overt and implicit, in his first daringly ambitious
volume, *Nights and Days*, to Louise Bogan's stinging criticism (in
The New Yorker) of his *First Poems* for its hermetic lucubrations; the
contretemps involving some of his good friends in Stonington when
he used them as models in the wickedly witty ballad "The Summer
People"; the award of the Bollingen Prize for Poetry and the ensuing
bickering initiated by a *New York Times* editorial over the "elitism"
of the choice; the minor scandal that followed his satiric portrayal
of local village life in a "November Ode"; and, most notoriously, his
literary use of the Ouija board transcripts.

His mature poems often demand that his readers get acquainted
with friends who turn up frequently in this selection: see, among
many others, "Kostas Tympakianákis," "Words for Maria," "Strato in
Plaster," "Manos Karastefanís," "Days of 1971," "Peter," "Tony: End-
ing the Life," "Bronze," and "Family Week at Oracle Ranch." "Days
of 1994," the last poem in the last volume he saw through press, *A
Scattering of Salts*, opens with "These days in my friend's house" and
concludes with "The laughter of old friends." Yet all of this introduc-
tion into his work of the personal and even the private, paralleled
by an increasingly experimental yet steadfast technique, occurred
without undermining his basic commitment. The point was to turn
the perishable by means of the formal into the perdurable, and the
correspondence of this man of letters was integral to the process.

Over the years, the speaking voice and the poetic style interpenetrated more and more, even as he developed the quasi-symbolist mode notable in *The Fire Screen* and *Braving the Elements*. Especially after the publication of *Water Street*, to listen to his conversation was to detect the diction and the syntax of his poems, while in reading the poems one could recognize the manner of his talk. The correspondence is an arena in which the two modes work together. As a poet he learned about subsuming the conversational in part through his experience with writing plays and novels, though he also attended closely to the poems of Elizabeth Bishop (who, like him, revered Herbert, Donne, and Marvell), in particular her hesitations and recommencements— all the self-questionings and manifest revisions the Renaissance rhetoricians knew by the terms "epanorthosis," "aporia," and "metanoia." Supplementing that practical knowledge, letters were themselves inextricable from his determination to be at once a writer who used all the means available to him and (to lift a phrase from Henry James, whose influence persisted) a person upon whom nothing was lost.

His financial inheritance notwithstanding, this scion of the founder of Merrill Lynch was a thrifty man, one of whose favorite maxims was "Waste not, want not." In his remarkably integrated experience, rocks lugged home from New Mexico as souvenirs served also as doorstops in Stonington, while his friends' personalities and his acquaintances' escapades, along with their verbal tics and bon mots, became stuff for his correspondence, which sometimes laid the groundwork for poems. One letter to friends concludes with a scene featuring details that would be crucial to his poem "Days of 1964":

> A week ago exactly I was driving to Kolonaki and saw a familiar figure trudging up into the pines of Lykabettos on her bad legs— Kyria Kleo who cleans for us. I honked + honked + finally she looked around. She is fat and sixty with the face of a Palmyra sculpture done in horsehair + guttapercha, but that day she was wearing a tight sky-blue sweater + had painted + powdered herself within an inch of her life, or mine. Was she off to a rendezvous? to sell herself? Was she "just lucky, I guess" like the Smith girl in the brothel? The memory absolutely <u>haunts</u> me.

The letters were thus at once repositories and writerly practice. They had the additional benefit of enhancing his ever-complicit daily life.

His letters to his Greek lover in his lover's native tongue led him to try out idioms he could draw on later.

Mildly graphomaniac, like Byron, Merrill registered observations and musings on the same pages as his rough drafts of poems and notes toward missives. Fond of the sturdily bound and handsomely covered notebooks from Antica Legatoria Piazzesi in Venice, he would just as quickly use a pad of graph paper made for French secondary-school students, but equally regularly he composed letters, preferably on the typewriter but often by hand. Occasionally he would draft an important letter in a casual chronicle, but he could not be a steady diarist. "But I don't *keep* a journal, not after the first week," he insisted in a letter to Irma Brandeis when he and David Jackson were circumnavigating the globe in 1956: "letters have got to bear all the burden." Writing earlier to Jackson himself about the riskiness of their incipient romance, he had asked, "Oh must the mails be asked to bear such weight?" One Mrs. Lowder, overheard by the poet in the wake of a lamentable accident, voices a version of his view when she exclaims, "I'd be crying now if I weren't writing letters."

He liked to paraphrase the mock misgiving traceable to Cicero: "I did not have time to write a short letter, so you will have to forgive a longer one." In fact, Merrill's letters are usually of modest length—one page give or take a paragraph seems to have been a formal desideratum as he got older—and while he cannot have given inordinate time to them (since he had time enough to write and rewrite everything else in spite of being caught in what he calls in one a "social or domestic web"), he set them down with an eye to style and structure as well as with a zest for entertaining his reader. Some assorted openings:

It pleased me to no end to have your letter. I've read it upside-down and held it to the light, parts of it being too well-written to make perfect sense—not that that matters, as you know. What, at this stage, does matter? Pure dull good will, attentiveness, one eye for possibilities, another eye for impossibilities—what always mattered in short.

Masses of green outside. This morning early—we had gone for the night to our beloved Morses in Bedford Hills—after one of those by now quite involuntary half-waking colloquies with you, I went out into their garden, sunny, windless, glittering with moisture: the lilacs only slightly rusted, the pink dogwood in its glory, tulips frosty with dew, and the great Chinese peonies easily a foot in diameter, their petals a dazzling crinkled white— and all of these, like those flowers that talk in the 1st song of the *Dichterliebe*, speaking to me of you; as everything does, these days.

A lovely day of sunlight and cement being poured outside; everything in Salzburg is subjected now to repairs, the facades of hotels, fountains, sidewalks, the cathedral dome. I've had such a strange impression that tomorrow morning, when the Festival begins, everyone will wake up to see a shining + perfect city. The last nail driven, the flowerpots all set out.

Although his manuscripts of verse attest to relentless revision— revision, he told an interviewer, was his "one dependable pleasure"— he forestalled that impulse in the letters, where cancellations and marginalia are rare. Their rhetorical finesse testifies to a daunting ingrained fluency and an attention to technique that had become second nature. The exercise of that technique must often have super-seded in importance the nominal subject. True, once in a while the scene's import seems about to capsize the craft. Fortunately misdi-rected one day in the Vatican Museums, he has an epiphany that can only be called—he calls it—a "vision of love"; but it includes a "vision of the absence of love" and is in sum an experience "complex and shattering and miraculous." As he relates it, the visual minutiae, the *scriptible* elements, proliferate passionately, complicate—and finally hold their own. But ordinarily the phenomena surrender more read-ily to the rendering. The accidental amputation of a small piece of his finger leads him to memorialize that digit as one "need[ed] to trill with at the piano" and to define the severed bit as a "5-carat ruby" presently "drained to the gray of a tooth." A visit to an old house in Tuscany enables him to dust off some vocabulary—and to hone his descriptive skills ("'my' room . . . boasted 2 fat white marble columns + a greenish pier-glass that made it all look like a submerged quarry" and in the stairwell nearby stood "a sedan chair battered with use").

Awkward social moments repeatedly become occasions to frame miniature set pieces replete with piquant dialogue.

He shuffles his diverse subjects dexterously. Vignettes gleaned from his daily routine, whether he is in Stonington or Athens, Key West or Venice in the course of his travel (travel so frequent that he worries about appearing to spend much of his life on a 747), might combine with estimations of art exhibits in one venue or another, or counsel about his correspondent's current plight, which in turn might fray out into opinions about Jungian or Freudian analysis. A meticulous account of a Native American ceremonial dance, or a percipient assessment of a new operatic production, or an infatuation with a puppet-theater performance given in a New York apartment, or an evaluation of a novel he has just reread gives way to a critique of the verse his friend has sent, or to a relay of some dishy gossip, or to a recipe for an omelette soufflé or to a recapping of a conversation with the hitchhiker he picks up who is going to meet a renowned poet in fact dead for decades, or with the raving crackpot seated next to him on a long flight on a 747.

Aside from the rare scathing reference, politics is one subject that does not arise. He has to ask a correspondent about the results of the 1972 presidential election won by Richard Nixon—though he had published earlier in the year a poem rich in allusions to events bearing on that election in the course of commemorating a childhood home, a Greenwich Village townhouse at "18 West 11th Street," which was blown up accidentally by the revolutionary Weathermen faction. But apart from politics, little else, depending on the recipient, is off limits, notwithstanding his preference for punctilio and "surfaces." ("*I am something of a waterbug, skating upon the depths*"—his emphasis.) He resorts to French when relating at length a pickup turned mugging and entreats his reader to keep the episode secret, but that language is intended less to signal chagrin—he does not shy from lurid particulars—than to amuse and to comport waggishly with the *malheurs* in a time-honored French children's book.

Sympathetic and supportive of his best friends, he is candid about his own foibles and will confront those friends and his relatives with theirs. "Il est trop honnête d'être sincère," Proust says of one of his letters, and Merrill might have adopted the remark as a motto. One friend's moralism, another's habitual vice, his mother's sanctimony, his own insouciance are addressed head-on, and he grits his teeth and sails right into an old friend's reproach for seeming insufficiently affected by a monumental work the friend had dedicated to him.

Though now and again he indicates the progress of his longer poems, and nuggets prized by literary critics can be picked out here and there, comments on specifics of his own work were restricted to a few correspondents—and most of those letters have not been included here because of their narrower technical interest. Ordinarily resistant to self-explication in his letters, as in person, he was wary of imposing (punctilio again) and disdained self-importance. Devoted to his craft, he was nonetheless committed to the principle that the poems, not to mention the language, knew more than he did. Scorn was foreign to his temperament, but he came near it in his contempt for puffery. He did not believe "that the artist can afford to involve himself with the views of the public," especially "the middlemen, publishers and reviewers," whose "praise and blame . . . is a worthless coin flipped in the air." He did not contribute to the literary kerfuffle sparked by the editorial about his Bollingen Prize.

Laconic as he was about his own writing, he eagerly shared insights about individual artists in other mediums. Several essays in his *Collected Prose*—on his older Greek contemporary Yannis Tsarouchis, on his young American contemporary Barbara Kassel, and especially in his "Notes on Corot"—suggest his latent talent as an art critic, a talent that produces an inspired paragraph in this selection on Vermeer's *The Artist in His Studio,* which he extols as "one of the wonders of the world." His clear-eyed appraisal of an Andrew Wyeth exhibit and its popular reception in a letter to Elizabeth Bishop is, in contrast, tinted with ironies ("everyone suddenly knew more about art + the world than ever in life before"). Appreciations of musical compositions and interpretations of them recur throughout and are often as alluring as they are illuminating, as in a running commentary on the parts of Mahler's *Das Lied von der Erde* and an excursus on *The Magic Flute.*

Merrill taught on only a few occasions and, after a year at Bard College when he was twenty-two, never for an extended period, and never to his enjoyment; but his flair for mentorship flowered in his letters to younger writers. He had a tutor's fervor for syllabi, and he would recommend lists of musical works and literary texts with ardor. Indeed, such tutelage could express and perhaps enhance deep affection. Having hoped that one correspondent will see that a course of reading he has prescribed disguises "a love letter," he nonetheless complains to him a year later that "I don't think I know how to write love letters."

We trust that these selections will disprove that last suspicion, even as they recall the "old love letters from the other world" authored by the spirits in *Sandover* (whoever the reader takes *them* to be), and that in doing so they will represent a personality and a temperament: a sensibility. At age twenty he wrote to a kindred spirit:

> It is not inconceivable that one day we shall find in ourselves that all the contradictions and desires and angers have through their quarreling created a way of life, a way of thought, an element as lucid, revealing as we had always imagined existing outside ourselves. We shall have created our own commonplace.

Over time his "commonplace," his sensibility, is notably of a piece, since Merrill's gift—like Mozart's, and unlike Beethoven's, in Northrop Frye's heuristic view of those two composers—was one that opened up rather than evolved. The six-year-old boy's request for a "flash-light" at Christmas, set down in this selection's initial item, could be taken in retrospect as the first in a series of beacons marking crucial intersections through the poet's career. Veteran readers can trace their own patterns, one of which might continue from that flashlight through the poet's well-known "bargain with— say with the source of light" in "A Tenancy" (*Water Street*) and through *The Changing Light at Sandover* itself (the spirits in the *au-delà* punningly abbreviate "source of light" as "S/O/L") to the earthy roundup of "Home Fires" in his posthumous book *A Scattering of Salts*.

Equally auspicious is the second selection—chosen, however, like the first, with no thought of the links teased out here—which summarizes the boy's seventh-birthday trip with his parents to New York. He was thrilled by the performances of "Italian marionettes" and the Broadway production of *Alice in Wonderland* based on the two novels by Lewis Carroll, and gratified at his completion of a large jigsaw puzzle. One of Merrill's most brilliantly intricate yet widely engaging, lyrically meditative poems, "Lost in Translation" (*Divine Comedies*) shapes itself, along with the life it turns out to comprise, around such a puzzle. And one might see in the ability of Carroll's White Queen to live backwards the seeds of the conclusion of the poet's "18 West 11th Street" (*Braving the Elements*). The same inversion of chronology informs the narrative of Rufus Farmetton's death (converted thereby to a rebirth) in section L of *The Book of Ephraim*. The Italian marionettes, for their part, both reflect those devised and manipulated by the boy and his governess, the beloved "Mademoiselle" in "Lost in Translation," and anticipate the poet's enchantment with The Little Players, the puppet theater of Francis Peschka and Gordon Murdock that he supported and promoted in New York, as well as the Greek shadow puppets in "Yánnina" (*Divine Comedies*) and the Japanese Bunraku in "Prose of Departure" (*The Inner Room*). The boy grew up to recommend to his friends Heinrich von Kleist's essay "On the Marionette Theater"—and to surmise, after an evening of Bunraku, that "we the living" often "feel 'more ourselves'" when we are "spoken through, or motivated by, 'invisible' forces." In *The Book of Ephraim* (section I) Merrill recalled Oscar Wilde's aperçu in "The Critic as Artist": "Man is least himself when he talks in his own person. Give him a mask and he will tell the truth."

Or the venturesome reader might begin perversely at the other end of this selection, with Merrill's last complete letter, written a few days before his unexpected death, to André Aciman, whom he had never met, in praise of his recently published *Out of Egypt*. The book is a memoir based on a family's life in Alexandria, the ancient site of both the Pharos, the magnificent lighthouse that was one of the Seven Wonders of the World, and the original Musaeum, the dwelling of the Muses. It was more important to Merrill that the eminently sophisticated, polyglot city was heir to a history commingling ancient Egyptian, Greek, Jewish, and Roman cultures with the more recent influences of Christianity and Islam. For him, the memoir recalled "the kitchen-Italian libretti of Bernard de Zogheb," the Alexandrian writer and artist whose macaronic scripts The Little Players enacted, and the poems of the venerated Cavafy, also a native of Alexandria. Aciman's pages summoned "that whole world of the trivial & the tragic, interwoven as in Chekhov, and underscored as in opera," which constituted "the very best life [had] to offer" and came "as close to a 'real' home" as Merrill had ever known. It was from such a home that he wrote these letters.

Stephen Yenser

This Edition

This selection of James Merrill's letters spans his lifetime, from one of the first pieces of correspondence preserved, a note to Santa Claus, to the last, a fan letter written four days before he died. Letters have been chosen primarily on the basis of their interest as letters; we make no attempt to tell the story of Merrill's life or show the full range of his correspondence and relationships. His letters to his mother alone would fill a long volume; yet only a few of them—telling letters, written at critical moments in their relationship—appear here.

Every letter is framed by the same information: the correspondent and the current holder of the letter are indicated; then the date (in the day-month-year format that Merrill favored but did not always follow) and the place of composition. When Merrill does not indicate the date or place of composition, we do so in brackets. Rather than give street addresses, we simplify and regularize the place of composition. Thus "107 Water Street, Stonington, Connecticut" becomes "Stonington, CT." Merrill's letters from Stonington were invariably sent from his Water Street home, as his letters from Greece were invariably sent from Athinaion Efivon 44, his home in Athens.

In every case possible, from the salutation to the signature, we give the body of these letters whole, without cuts, at the cost of occasional redundancy or the inclusion of trivia. (The rare exception is because of illegibility or a missing page.) We do so because to excise passages and then introduce ellipses would be to disrupt flow and damage transitions, and raise questions for the reader about what was cut, and because Merrill adapted his anecdotes and news for different addressees. We preserve postscripts by Merrill, or sometimes by another hand, only when they seem substantive or in some way suggestive. The same goes for marginalia. When we can identify the image on the front of postcards, and if it is significant in relation to the message, we indicate it.

In preparing the texts of Merrill's letters, we aim to preserve the eccentricities and spontaneity of the private letter while making allowances for the conventions of print and the expectations of clarity and consistency readers naturally bring to it. The conflict between those principles is eased by the legibility of Merrill's handwriting, his use of typewriters for much of his correspondence (on his around-the-world trip in 1956–57, he carried a typewriter with him), and his impressive ability to minimize routine slips of the pen, typos, grammatical errors, missing words, and the like. We silently emend incidental errors when they are inconsequential but potentially confusing to the reader (a missing s on a plural, say, or an "of" or an "and" that dropped out); we make corrections and clarifications in brackets when needed; and we let stand, without an intrusive "sic," errors that are no obstacle to the reader. When Merrill makes the same error frequently (for instance, his spelling of "cemetary"), we preserve it. We keep certain idiosyncrasies as well, such as Merrill's curious and habitual running-together of nouns and modifiers to make compounds, as in "titlepage" or "goodnatured." In the notes, we italicize the titles of books, movies, operas, and other works, following print convention, while Merrill's letters often capitalize or underline them. We retain Merrill's underlinings when they indicate his emphasis. Except for the odd instance in which Merrill uses them himself, brackets are the editors'. Inside brackets, italic type indicates the editors' words, and roman type indicates Merrill's.

Merrill's English is marbled with other languages. We make no effort to correct foreign- language mistakes or to make accents or other diacritical marks consistent; for instance, we retain Merrill's Greek accents but do not supply them when he doesn't, and we avoid Greek accents in annotations. English translations for some phrases and sentences in Greek and other foreign languages appear in the notes. One letter to Daryl Hine is composed in French; the editors' English translation follows the French text. Merrill's letters to Strato Mouflouzelis, composed in Greek, have been translated by Stathis Gourgouris.

The editors' notes, keyed to phrases in the letters and set at the end of the letter, provide clarifying information, context, and short identifications of people, works, and events. We supply dates for obscure or modern works, and we usually provide the date of publication for each reference to a book by Merrill so that the reader can gauge quickly the relationship between that work and the letter at hand. Following the letters, the Chronology outlines events in Merrill's life, while Biographies supplies fuller identifications of some of Merrill's correspondents and people who figure prominently or recurrently in the letters.

A Whole World

To Santa Claus

WUSTL
[1932?]
[Southampton, NY]

Dear Santa Clause please bring me a flash-light.

                    Jimmy Merrill

To Doris Merrill

AMHERST
March 1933
Southampton, NY

Dear Doris,

Many thanks for the lovely birthday present you sent me.

I went into New York to spend my birthday with Mummy and Daddy. And had a wonderful time. I went to see the Italian marionettes and *Alice in wonderland*. Which I enjoyed so much.

Do you like jigsaw puzzles? I love them! We have just finished one called The Lily Pond with 750 pieces. I am getting on very nicely at school. And am learning to do short-division. I am learning to ride my bicycle and roller skates very nice [*corrected*: nicely]. I hope you will have a lovely time in Bermuda.

                    Love kisses and hugs from
                    Jimmy

kisses xxxxxxxxxxxxxx
hugs oooooooooooooo

Doris Merrill Merrill's older half-sister. See Biographies.
Alice in wonderland Broadway adaptation of Lewis Carroll's tale, directed by Eva Le Gallienne.

To Doris and Robert Magowan

AMHERST
[Summer 1936]
[Southampton, NY]

Dear Dot and Bob;

Here are some names you must <u>not</u> name the coming infant;

BOYS	GIRLS
Marmaduke	Aurora
Aaron	Belinda
Abel	Dorcas
Augustus	Myra
Eli	Lydia
Asa	Salome
Oscar	Georgiana
Oswald	Huldah
Constantine	Ethelinda
Cyril	Bertha
Abijah	Ernestine
Barnaby	Ophilia
Christopher	Sabina
Duncan	Olivia
Egbert	Zenobia
Ichabod	
Isaac	
Kenelm	
Horace	
Joshua	
Levi	
Luke	
Giles	
Laurence	
Marcus	
Oliver	
Zebedee	
Valentine	
Silas	

Timothy
Reynold

Much love,
Jimmy

Robert Magowan Married Doris Merrill in 1935. See Biographies.

To Doris and Robert Magowan

AMHERST
[September 1936]
Wildwood Plantation
Greenwood, MS

Dear Doris + Bobby

I wish you all possible congratulations, you know, and all those luck, happiness and joy things. Are you glad it's a boy? How much does it weigh? What color eyes? Any hair yet? Whew! I can't tell you all my adventures so if you want to know about them ask mama.

Love
Unc. J.I.M.

it's a boy Robert Magowan Jr., known as Robin, the first of the Magowans' five sons, was born on September 4, 1936 (see Biographies). While Merrill's parents were present in San Francisco for the birth, James, with his older half-brother, Charles, was sent to Mississippi, where his father had bought an antebellum plantation called Wildwood.

To Doris and Robert Magowan

December 1936
Southampton, NY

Dear Doris + Bobby [drawing of a sailboat]

I hope this letter finds you well also "tiny Robert."

Did Daddy tell you that I bought ten shares of safeway and It has gone up almost 9 points!!!!!

I am leaving for Palm Beach Wednesday. I am enclosing something I have saved to show you for over 3 years. I think its someone you know. (is it??)

I wish you could see my album it is beautiful.

No more news now

so

Love
Jimmy

P.S. kiss the baby for Unk J.

someone you know The enclosure and the identity of "someone" have been lost.
my album Merrill, as a child, was an avid stamp collector.

To Charles E. Merrill

[March 1938]
[New York, NY]

Dear Daddy,

How are you? I hope you are having a good time with Doris + Bobby + Charles. Caught any more sailfish??

It's a pity Robin could not come. He would love it. This Saturday I am going to *Carmen* at last. It will be my 18th opera. That ends the winter season at the Metropolitan. Then I'll have to go to the Hippodrome. My first there are *Cavallieria Rusticana* + *Pagliacci*.

I got some swell stamps with the 12 dollars.

School is getting along O.K. I shot a bulls eye at shooting class.

Sunday I am going to an operatic program in commemoration of Martinelli's 25th years with the Met. (I think I told you that before.)

Much love to you, Doris, Bobby, Charles.
Jimmy

Charles E. Merrill See Biographies.
Martinelli's 25th years Giovanni Martinelli (1885–1969), Italian tenor.

To Charles E. Merrill

Dear Daddy,

Thanks so much for the stock and books. I have read *A Kiss from Cinderella* + started *Sentimental Tommy*.

Daddy, I <u>DO</u> wish you happiness because I have always felt you have never gotten your full share of it. And now, you are taking a third try at life and I hope you will be successful.

You refer to me taking this like Doris in 1925. In 1925 there were totally different proceedings, but now that the battle has worn off, I have no hard feelings toward you. I can only wish that you will at last be happy and that you will not regret anything—

Much love,
Jimmy

A Kiss from Cinderella Play by J. M. Barrie (1916).
Sentimental Tommy J. M. Barrie's novel *Sentimental Tommy: The Story of His Boyhood* (1896), Charles Merrill's favorite book.
third try Charles married his third wife, Kinta Des Mares, on March 8, 1939.
taking this Merrill's parents' divorce, finalized in February 1939. Charles had divorced his first wife, Eliza Church, in 1925, a less contentious and less well-publicized parting. Their daughter, Doris, had at first resented the replacement of her mother by Hellen Ingram but came to like and admire her.

To Frederick Buechner

Dear Freddy—

The last thing I ever expected from you was a six page letter. Here I was looking for a terse message but it was a pleasant surprise. <u>Please</u> write and tell me when you can come to New Canaan. We'd love you to stay a week at least + I'm sure you'd have a nice time not doing much tho'. Write me in N.Y. up to the 1st then to New Canaan, Conn., Mrs. Greenleaf's house (believe it or not there <u>is</u> such a person + you'd better put it on the envelope for no one knows us).

Went back to our little chain of bookstores and discovered a nice new place where I got the play—Oscar Wilde for 75¢—nice copy. At Argosy I got *Portrait of Mr. W.H.* for 1.25 limited edition in pretty good shape. The fattest plum was *Salomé* in French having searched all through 59th st for it was tipped off by a seedy little man in Argosy + went to La Librarie Française (Madison + 55th) + got one paperbound. (Dessins D'Alastair—whoever <u>he</u> may be) for $4.

Brother Charles came for dinner—he's leaving for Mexico Tuesday + friends. He said he was going to announce his engagement to a girl in Chicago sometime depending on war. Still wondering what I'm going to do when Daddy wants to see my story, think I'm going to give him the Emperor Nero one. How about it?

I practically sealed your doom socially this morning—told Mama 'bout your nice letter + she asked if there was anything personal in it + could she read it. I said no. After she had gotten 4 pages + a bit I recalled what you'd put about S.J.'s brother (male nymphomaniac) + a look came over my face that surpassed the gingerale scandale at the Jigger. Snatching the letter from her hands, trembling with interest (her hands, I mean) I said quickly, "Thereissomethingpersonalonthatpage!" + substituted your P.S. quickly while she begged me to show her the "personal" part, but I was firm. God! it makes me shudder to think of what might have happened had she read it.

I haven't heard from Tony either, but to my intense misfortune I must visit him (with an ulterior motive naturally), for he has some records of mine from school.

Went bowling this afternoon and missed you—probably just as well you weren't there it was so hot, but I lost <u>pounds</u>—you [would] never recognize me. No need to tell me about Ry-Crisp now (not because I'm sylph-like, but because I've already been told about it).

Mama went to Southampton for the Fresh Air Home annual meeting, and she can't evade it as she is chairman of the board. Miserablement, Mama has not severed <u>all</u> connections in that hotbed of decadence and illicit love.

You really must see the *Ziegfeld Girl*—I haven't enjoyed anything so much. It is really a gratifying experience to see Lana Turner collapse once but when she does it twice, it acts as cocaine on the soul. There is one marvellous song "Minnie from Trinidad" and I would see the whole extravaganza over again just to hear it. Unfortunately Judy Garland sings it, but one is inclined to overlook that. (I'll apologize if you like J.G.)

Boy, oh, boy! Have I got a juicy bit of gossip to tell you!! And it's perfectly true—Garlock swore on his ma's life, and he must have been some story teller to invent a spicy but intricate web such as this. Doubtless you recall the picture in *Life* of the woman (purse over puss) coming out of the gambling joint. Well that was La Rose + here's the whole ugly plot—Dr. G. was in Detroit or some other den of iniquity + this MAN a "friend" of La Flamme's offered to treat her to as many 50$ chips as she fancied (of course it doesn't take much imagination to guess what she did for him). Jim said: (I quote from memory): "—and she was so embarrassed that she was the first one out!" (Tony + I exchange glances)

> Jim: Well she was.
> Me: So I see.
> Jim:—(weakly) and that's how her picture got in—the first one
>   out you know.
> Tony: (chillily) Yes.

I never discovered whether Dr. G found out about it, but I have my doubts + my own opinion on the subject. Jim also told Mama (to her intense interest, you may be sure) as he was afraid I would. It was on the day school let out + he helped so much that she gave him a quarter (after he asked for it).

Well. I've tried very hard to equal your six page record but I've run out of gossip except the very trivial things such as Mrs. O. Munn's love, Peppe Russo being slapped in public by a french matron—whoever said that the French had no courage is wrong. I've gone against the rigid principles set in "On Unanswering Letters" and I hope I haven't bored you. By the way, have you got your marks yet—I haven't. Don't forget to let me know about them. Remember me to your mother + Jamie—and PLEASE let me know what week you can come to N. Canaan (anytime from 1 to Labour day).

Au revoirrr,

<u>Fishface</u>

Frederick Buechner Merrill's Lawrenceville classmate. See Biographies.
New Canaan Following her divorce, Hellen Merrill lived in the Carlyle Hotel, and then in a small townhouse on East Fifty-Seventh Street in New York. In 1940 Charles Merrill bought a house for her in New Canaan, CT, where she lived until 1950. The idea was to expose his son to sports and the countryside.
Portrait of Mr. W.H. Story by Oscar Wilde based on the speculation that Shakespeare's sonnets are addressed to a boy actor in the playwright's company. An enlarged limited edition edited by Mitchell Kennerley was published in 1921.
Salomé Wilde's tragedy was published in its original French in 1891.
a girl in Chicago Mary Klorr, who married Merrill's brother, Charles, in 1941.
gingerale scandale One afternoon at the school sweet shop, the Jigger, Buechner made Merrill laugh so hard he blew ginger ale out of his nose.
Ziegfeld Girl (1941), musical film directed by Robert Z. Leonard and Busby Berkeley.
"Minnie from Trinidad" Song by Roger Edens.
Garlock . . . Tony Lawrenceville classmates James Garlock and Tony Harwood (1926–74). Harwood remained Merrill's close friend.
Mrs. O. Munn's Lawrenceville classmate Orson Munn. Merrill used the name Orson for a character in his novel *The (Diblos) Notebook*.
Jamie Buechner's younger brother.

To Doris Magowan

AMHERST
[March 1944]
Amherst, MA

Dear Doris,

One of the most pleasant surprises I have ever had (and a revelation in that) came this fall when I discovered, quite casually, that I was <u>talking</u> to Robin and Merrill, not merely asking about school and toys and the zoo, but engaged in a genuine conversation. I don't know what I expected of children—perhaps I thought they did not blossom out as people until the age of ten, for example. I personally have no recollection of conversing on an adult plane with <u>anybody</u> when I was seven, but they were doing it and it was delightful.

You see how this is all working in. Keep having more children so they can all be as charming as their brothers and their mother, and so forth. But I am really very excited. I think the new Magowan will be rather exceptional and I shall have the pleasure of watching a fourth marvel mature. The time relationship within the family seems particularly fascinating, Robin nearly 8 years older than Mr. X, and the various other ages, Mr X will have all the advantages of his brothers put together—he will not have to learn very much but a simple "Look what happened to Merrill when he tried the same thing"—will quiet him forever. I think you are so wonderful and so lucky with your family, with you as mother, it can't help being a phenomenal success.

> All my love. Will call you Sunday,
> Jimmy

Be sure it is born on Easter!

the new Magowan Stephen (1944–2001) was the fourth of the five Magowan brothers. Merrill, following Robin, was born in 1938, Peter (d. 2019) was born on Easter in 1942, and Mark was born in 1953.

To Thomas Howkins   WUSTL
[24 June 1944]
[Camp Croft, North Carolina]
<u>Thursday</u>
FLASH!!!
GOOD AFTERNOON MR AND MRS NORTH AND SOUTH AMERICA, ALASKA, HAWAII, PHILIP EENS, AND HUDSON FALLS. IN MIAMI BEACH, CENTRE OF ALL THAT IS ORCHIDACEOUS, MRS DILLIE TANTE HAS BEEN ENTERTAINING TOMAS HOWQUINS, THE TWOFISTED SOPHISTICATE

NATURAL SON OF SIMON BOLIVAR. ISNT IT GAY TO BE
AT A TYPEWRITER AGAINE, AND ISNT THIS TYPE THE
.chSMARTEST THING YET, I MEAN, IT HAS SUCH POSITIVE
CHIC—LOOK AT THOSE C'S: WHEN ALL'S SAID AND DONE I
FEEL 50% CIVILIAN, AND THAT IS, AS THOSE FRENCH WHO
HAVE A WORD FOR EVERYTHING SAY, QUELQUE CHOSE.
MY, LOOK AT THOSE Q'S—ITS ENOUGH TO MAKE YOUR
HAIR CURL. TWO RUMOURS ARE BEING CIRCULATED. ONE
IS DELIGHTFUL—THAT THE CAMP WILL BE RUN AS INTI-
MATELY AS PÈRE BROWN'S HOTEL, WITH MANY THREE
DAY PASSES, IN WHICH CASE I COULD GET TO NEW YORK
OR PALM BEACH TO VISIT MY DYING FATHER, AND IF I
COULD GET TO PALM BEACH WHAT I WANT TO KNOW IS
COULD YOU, PROVIDING YOU WERE THERE, COME UP
AND SEE ME? IT IS ALL VERRY REMOTE. THE OTHER OLD
GREY NIGHTMÈRE IS THAT EVERYTHING IS GOING TO
BE PERFECTLY DREADFUL, THAT BLACKHEARTED GEN-
ERAL GREEN WILL LET NO ONE MISS BEDCHECK ANY
NIGHT OF THE WEEK EVEN SATURDAY (GREEN NEVER
GIVES PASSES TO MEN WHO WEAR GLASSES) AND THE
WHOLE SITUATION SEEMS TO BE A TENSER. THIS IS FAR
MORE PROBABLE THAN THE OTHER LITTLE DREAM, MAIS
ENFIN JE NE SAIS RIEN. EST-CE QUE JE T'AI DIT QUE J'AI
FAIT VISITE À FREDDI DEUX WEEKENDS DEPUIS QUE JE
SUIS ICI. IL DOIT ÊTRE À DEVONS LE DIX NOVEMBRE, CE
QUI EST ENNUYANT, MAIS NOUS AVONS CONSPIRÉ DE
NOUS ÉLOIGNER DE LA VIE MILITAIRE AVEC PLUSIEURS
INDICATIONS D'UNE SANITÉ PAS TOUT À FAIT PARFAITE,
ET DE CÉLÉBRER LE 4 JUILLET À PRINCETON AVEC UNE
BOUTEILLE DE BOURGOGNE ÉTINCELLANTE. R A T H E R
S T I L T E D F R E N C H BUT THE SENTIMENT THEREIN
IS INTENSE. O I HAVE MET THE STRANGEST PIPPLE. THERE
IS A HARRIED YOUNG PAINTER WHO SPENDS HIS WEEK-
ENDS, DRUNK, DOING STUDIES OF HIMSELF IN NICOTINE
BROWN AND 'CHATRAISE' AS HE PRONOUNCES IT: I WANT
TO SEE THEM: HE WANTS ME TO SEE THEM. DO YOU THINK
MY FAMILY WOULD OBJECT? ALSO A SGT—POET OF THE

FASHIONABLE FRUSTRATED SCHOOL, WRITER OF TERSE CURSES AND WORSE VERSES. ONE ENDED (I THOUGHT OF YOU):

SURE I'LL KISS YOU. I LIKE YOUR MOUTH.
BUT GET THIS. I DON'T LOVE YOU.
YOU DON'T LOVE ME.
THIS AIN'T THE THING.

REMINISCENT OF ALEXANDER POPE, NO? INTOXICATED BY HIS COMPANION'S SUCCESS (I SAID 'OOO, I <u>LIKE</u> THAT"). THE PAINTER REVEALED HIMSELF AS A POETASTER ALSO AND QUOTED A LINE FROM ONE OF HIS LITTLE NOCTURNES, 'THE MOON HUNG LIKE THE VAST ABORTION OF NIGHT'.

I SAID, 'LET'S HAVE ANOTHER CUP OF COFFEE.'

FREDDY COULD SING NOTHING BUT THE FIRST LINE OF THIS ENCHANTING SONG ONE OF HIS FRIENDS IN THE MERCHANT MARINE BROUGHT BACK FROM LONDON. IT GOES, CATCHILY:

"I'M A <u>NYMPHO</u>-
<u>DIPSO</u>-
EGO-
MANIAC,
A BUNDLE OF GOOD CLEAN FUN!"

BROWN COULD DO A WONDERFUL JOB ON THAT Couldn't HE. HE Hasn't WRITTEN ME AT ALL. I WONDER IF HE IS JEALOUS. I AM ALMOST JEALOUS OF MYSELF, I AM HAVING SUCH A LUXURIOUS LIFE. BREAKFAST (COOKIES) IN BED, AND ALL THOSE NEUROTICS TO HAVE LONG TALKS WITH. WELL.

FRED AND I HAVE MADE LONG PLANS FOR OUR POST WAR LIFE. AFTER COLLEGE, WE ARE GOING TO EUROPE, TO LIVE OFF SOME OF OUR FRIENDS—HIS ROOMMATE HAS A COUNTRY HOUSE IN ENGLAND, AND ANOTHER PAL HAS

A TOWN HOUSE, SO THAT IS GOOD FOR TWO MONTHS IN
ENGLAND. THEN THROUGH FRANCE TO SWITZERLAND,
WHERE HIS GREAT GRANDMOTHER AND DESCENDANTS
LIVE, THEN TO ITALY WHERE ALL WE ASK IS THE HUMBLEST
FIVE ROOM APARTMENT IN THE PALAZZA DELLATORRE,
THAT IS IF YOU AND PETEE ARE THERE. IF NOT, WE'LL
TAKE THE WHOLE BUILDING. WE WILL ACCOMPANY YOU
TO BUDAPEST FOR THE WINTER SEASON, AND THEN BACK
TO PARIS WHERE OUR WORK WILL BE CUT OUT FOR US.
MR GRIFFIS (YOU KNOW) WHO OWNS BRENTANOS NOW
WANTS TO OPEN SOME BRANCHES IN FOREIGN CAPITALS,
AND WANTS ATTRACTIVE INTERESTED YOUNG MEN TO
WORK IN THEM OR MANAGE THEM. FRED AND I THINK
WE'D BE THE ONES FOR THE JOB, BECAUSE EVEN IF WE DID
LOSE MONEY WE WOULD DO IT IN SUCH A FASCINATING
MANNER THAT IT WOULD BE WORTH THE EXPENSE JUST
TO HEAR US TELL ABOUT IT. AT LAWRENCEVILLE WE HAD
OFTEN CONTEMPLATED RUNNING A BOOKSTORE (TO BE
NAMED BOOKBINDER AND THRUSH, FREE TRANSLATIONS
OF OUR NAMES—MERRILL Really MEANS BLACKBIRD, BUT
THRUSH IS NICER DON'T YOU THINK. I DO). WE WILL BE
MAKING SO MUCH MONEY SELLING CLEAN POSTCARDS
(THEY WILL BE THE RAGE—SUCH A NOVELTY) THAT WE
WILL HAVE INCREDIBLY SPACIOUS APARTMENTS ON
THE RUE RASPAIL (GOOSING MONTPARNASSE) WITH SIX
OR EIGHT GUEST ROOMS FOR THE CERTIFIED ARABIANS
WHO HAPPEN TO BE STOPPING OVER—SEVEN ROOMS
WOULD BE BEST I THINK SO THAT WE COULD HAVE THEM
FURNISHED LIKE THE SEVEN ROOMS IN "THE MASQUE
OF THE RED DEATH" (YOU COULD HAVE THE SEVENTH
IF YOU THINK YOU'D LIKE IT). OF COURSE WE HAVEN'T
SPOKEN TO ANYONE, LEAST OF ALL MR GRIFFIS BUT
FROM ALL INWARD APPEARANCES, IT'S IN THE BAG MRS
POUCH.

WELL I HAVE CONSUMED ⅘ OF A DULL LUNCH HOUR
RATTLING THIS OFF. WHY DON'T YOU WRITE TOO FOR
A CHANGE. I WONT MAIL THIS RIGHT AWAY. I WANT TO

READ IT OVER SEVERAL TIMES, BECAUSE IT IS TYPEWRIT-
TEN AND <u>SO</u> AMUSING.

> FONDLY,
> Jimmy (Per Pvt. H.P. Jones)

Mr. Merrill left before I could type this out, and requested me to sign
it as above.

> Respectfully,
> H.P. Jones

Thomas Howkins Merrill's unconventional Amherst classmate.
PÈRE BROWN'S HOTEL Robert Brown, Merrill's friend at Amherst. The con-
text suggests a humorous allusion to Father Brown, the Roman Catholic priest in
stories by G. K. Chesterton, English writer (1874–1936).
J'AI FAIT VISITE À FREDDI Frederick Buechner. Merrill translates "Buech-
ner" below as "Bookbinder."
"THE MASQUE OF THE RED DEATH" Short story by Edgar Allan Poe.
PALAZZA DELLATORRE The Palazzo della Torre is an old hotel in Venice near
the Grand Canal.
GRIFFIS Stanton Griffis (1887–1974), American businessman and diplomat; friend
of Charles Merrill, who commissioned Griffis to write a biography of him that was
never published.

To Gerrish Thurber

WUSTL
[Winter 1946]
[Amherst, MA]

Dear Mr. T,

At last I can spare an hour or so to give you more words than post-
cards afford, but unless I switch to the red ribbon I doubt whether
you would be able to make them out. Your letter was so wonderful;
you are one of the two people who will actually make the effort to
see what I am trying to do (the other is a member of the Army fac-
ulty here) and it is highly gratifying. My burst of activity since last
October has not quite yet expired; I enclose two more poems. "The
Broken Bowl" has not yet been revised, but it is my first attempt at
combining different line lengths, a thing I have always shied away

from. I am sending the beach poems to *Harper's Bazaar* out of something close to caprice.

One thing that has worried me is the problem that Fred is involved in with his writing. He seems to have all but completely stopped writing at the barrier of semantics, the very words themselves. I really believe that this particular problem must be overlooked the moment the writer begins to write. It is a different thing to hunt for the mot juste, but to be frozen by the knowledge that the mot juste does not exist is not only horrible but a waste of time. I feel I am right in dismissing it so consciously. I should like perhaps to attempt a more surrealistic imagery, but I don't dare yet. The one dreadful thing is my ivory tower that I have worked at so hard, to the extent that I am afraid of the very simple things that will get me out of it, learning something about politics, social issues; I have thought so long of these as <u>contaminating</u> things. Well.

I have been reading much Wallace Stevens; have you read "Notes Towards a Supreme Fiction"? It is rather hard to get, but so magnificent. I'd like to bring it down to Lawrenceville with me and lend it to you if you haven't seen it; Mallarmé (and [I] saw Martha Graham—she did a Herodiade dance; I think she is a great woman; there is a dance, *Deaths and Entrances*, on the Brontë sisters, where she handles props and dances with objects, a glass, two chessmen, just the way I should like to use <u>things</u> in poetry); the *Four Quartets*, very carefully studied. Also, briefly, Lewis, David Gascoygne, John Brinnin, an Englishwoman named Kathleen Raine; they are all worth looking at. I have gotten to know Anais Nin fairly well; she is the one who prints her own books, and has the monumental diary Henry Miller writes about. She is coming to Amherst this week, as a matter of fact, to give a reading to our little club, called The Medusa, and she will read a chapter from her newest book that concerns a huge party for all the artists in Paris, a party attended by none of them because they were each obsessed with their private destinies. And like you, paintings have come over me all of a sudden; I have always spells of a mad desire to paint; I am trying to turn that craving into poetry because my painting stinks. Daddy gave me a picture for Christmas, of my own choice, and I got a wonderful little Braque in cinnamon and bottle green and ochre, and I have been haunting the galleries—in short, living as if I were the only person in the world and the world was one monstrous art-form. That is part of my thesis, also, which I must begin writing this semester—how Proust creates his aesthetic attitude and sees life as one picture after another; which requires a study of impressionism. Do you know any book that really states the impressionist theories, I have never found one. Seurat fascinates me. I went to the Maggie Teyte concert last week, and I have seldom been so thoroughly moved by anything. She was such a personality, and sang with that rare way by which all the love songs mean <u>her</u> love and the death song, <u>her</u> death. What a superb dilettante I am becoming!

And here we are. I have so much to do of actual schoolwork, but I shall do my best to get down, perhaps even around the 24th of March. We shall see. Are you well? Thank Edward for the bed in his fort. Excuse all this talk just about myself, but I've seen so little of anyone else for quite a while.

As ever,

Jim

Gerrish Thurber (1907–2000). The assistant (later the head) librarian at Lawrenceville School, he was a mentor and friend to Merrill and Frederick Buechner, and advisor to the Lawrenceville *Lit*, which Merrill and Buechner edited in their senior year.

member of the Army faculty here Kimon Friar, who taught at Amherst College as an instructor especially hired to teach demobilized GIs.

My burst of activity since last October When Friar became Merrill's unofficial poetry teacher and lover, resulting in the composition of the poems collected in Merrill's first book, *The Black Swan* (1946).

rather hard to get Merrill read Stevens's long poem *Notes Toward a Supreme Fiction* as a limited edition chapbook published by the Cummington Press, either in the 1942 or the 1943 version.

Martha Graham (1894–1991), American choreographer and dancer. Merrill refers to her dances *Deaths and Entrances* (1943), with music composed by Hunter Johnson, and *Hérodiade* (1944), with music by Paul Hindemith and sets by Isamu Noguchi.

Four Quartets T. S. Eliot's long poem (1941). Merrill was attending lectures by Friar on the modernist long poem, given at the 92nd Street YMHA, where Friar was director of the Poetry Center.

Lewis Probably Alun Lewis (1915–44), Welsh poet, who died in Burma as a British infantryman fighting the Japanese.

David Gascogyne Gascoyne (1916–2001) was an English poet associated with French surrealism.

John Brinnin (1916–98), American poet and critic, formerly Kimon Friar's protégé and lover, who served as director of the Poetry Center (1949–56), where he sponsored Dylan Thomas's readings in the United States; in the 1980s, a friend of Merrill's in Key West.

Kathleen Raine (1908–2003), English poet.
Anais Nin (1903–77), French-Cuban-American author, known as a diarist.
Henry Miller (1891–1980), American writer, author of *Tropic of Cancer* (1934) and Nin's lover.
The Medusa A circle at Amherst around Kimon Friar, who had developed an elaborate poetics based on the myth of Medusa.
Braque Georges Braque (1882–1963), French painter, with Picasso the center of cubism.
Maggie Teyte English soprano (1888–1976), a famous recitalist who specialized in French art songs.
Edward The son of Gerrish Thurber and his wife, Mary.

To Kimon Friar

WUSTL
17 July 1946
New Canaan, CT

Dear Kimon,

Things have been going very badly. I hate to bother you with it, but there was another long, quiet, strained talk last night in which I admitted I had written you simply friendly letters; that, along with your postcard which did not escape unnoticed was regarded as a serious break in the solemn compact that the three of us made at Xmas, in which we agreed that no more communication would take place, etc. The third person is frantic now, feels that someone else in the family will have to be told, probably Doris' husband, whom I dislike, nervous businessman. I tried to say more about what I thought would happen in the future, and this was greeted with complete incomprehension and the resolution that it was a matter too strong for the responsibilities of a single person, meaning of course herself. I don't know what will happen now, or what can possibly happen before or after I am 21. What is the point of going to a doctor if your mind is made up, etc. I am really frightfully depressed, and although I can probably "stand" anything, I feel there is really nothing I can do now but resist everything. She is away now for four days in Vermont, and I shall not see her till I return from Southampton a week from this Friday, nine days; I can't keep on thinking these things are "what I must expect," I don't dare expect them to be as bad as they are; I fear now chiefly, though nothing has been said about it, that something may be done to you, probably because I believe, I must believe, that nothing can be done to change me.

I don't want to write any more in such an unpleasant letter, except to reassure you that I have not changed. Will write more of other things tomorrow.

Always,

J

Here, at last, are the photographs . . .

Kimon Friar Merrill's mentor and first lover. See Biographies. Friar lived in Greece during the summer and fall of 1946.
The third person Hellen Merrill.
a matter Merrill's relationship with Friar and generally his homosexuality. Hellen Merrill arranged for her son to see a psychiatrist (here "**a doctor**") to "treat" him.

To Kimon Friar

WUSTL
22 July 1946
Southampton, NY

Dear Kimon,

With this pen, at this lemon-leather desk, with the sound of the fountain in the garden, surrounded by flowers, Chinese lamps, silver, glass; having just left the large two-storey music room with the four Florentine pillars in each corner, of peeling gilt reaching to the carven ceiling to which the portraits raise their eyes imploringly and which the two little urchins in the enormous threadbare tapestry—a skating scene—choose to ignore in favor of their stolen jam, the color of the red damask at sunset when through the stained glass windows the lawns stretch out like a rough mathematical diagram of infinity and the flowers are polite for just a little while longer; rather uncomfortably full of an elegant, withal simple, dinner in the company of my father + his doctor, both of whom have now retired, I begin my "Southampton letter" to you by assuring you of my deep and lasting love. Please forgive the two stupid letters that have preceded this— they were stupid only in as much as my fears were stupid, as this whole business of worry, conflict and deception is stupid. I should not have written them, but I was upset and still am for that matter. I had many nightmares this past week which somehow followed me with more persistence than the actual events of those days; it was a long time before I could separate the two aspects—not that I wish to discredit anything I have written you—but I am in clear air at the moment and I realize with more assurance what it is I want to have and to escape from. As I told you long ago, the only solution that I can conceive is that of some kind of break between me and the world of my mother; I still feel that strongly, and when you suggest my wearing the fez before her, etc—I feel that you have <u>never</u> understood the passion, the determination in her, how strongly she feels about you; so strongly in fact that to wear the fez would be as much to her as anything else. There is a point—and for her that point is the mention of your name—beyond which no calm distinctions can be made. You must realize this and know how it bewilders me to have you write me suggesting these impossibilities; I do not exaggerate—it <u>can</u> be accomplished gradually or reasonably I am sure of that; and, if it is, it will cost both her + me dreadfully. Do you understand? These things are serious—the fez will no doubt arrive while I am here not in Mexico—and <u>that</u> will be stored up for our next "talk"—Ah well, I don't want to be gloomy anymore. Please forgive the lapse of letters this past week, I have really been unable to write, things have been so confused.

I got your two letters, the 4th + 5 <u>th</u> this morning—Seldon and I came into New York yesterday afternoon, waited 2 hours for Harrigan, the boy from the *Bard Review* whom I had arranged to meet, but he never appeared, so we went, after dinner to see Francoise Rosay in *Portrait of a Woman*, a French movie—not too good, but Sasha's Toscanini film was also shown and it was excellent, except for the music, oddly enough, which confirmed my occasional suspicions that Verdi is the least intelligent of all famous composers, relying completely on accidental beauties that, when he is lucky, are amazingly good.

I envy you so much—not envy. I just want to be with you,—meeting all your poets, want to <u>hear</u> them say you are unique! And thank you for the pictures—although some of them are particularly like you (especially that close-up)—the moustache is/was Legaut. By all means grow it back on your return trip. I hadn't been able to place

Mrs. Roosevelt from your description, but I remember her now as looking like a wonderful person. I don't know how long the letters took—no more than 10 days on the last one, written July 12, as I got it this morning, the 22nd. There is coffee in both Shraffts boxes I sent you. Tomorrow I go to see Anaïs, if I can find her; neither she nor the woman she is staying with is in the phone book—Also I shall go to the beach + cry Θαλασσα! Θαλασσα! at the grey-blue waves. No new poems or anything yet—but something may come soon now that I am less depressed. Just got Cyril Connelly's new book, *The Condemned Playground* which is amusing + occasionally disappointing. I shall go to bed now + continue this to-morrow—goodnight. I love you, I miss you, I love you—Jimmy

Tuesday, 23rd July—

Just back from dinner with Anaïs in Easthampton. Had a long talk with her about my fears as to my mother, in very general terms of course, and she gave me such confidence and such encouragement, saying to me what you would say I am sure if you were with me, that now I am very much relieved and feel full of courage and hope and love for you. She asked after you + was very pleased to hear about Anaïs and is glad your voyage is so wonderful. It is, isn't it. I want so much to be sure that you are happy and doing what you want, especially since we are apart. Anaïs has a small room in a little cottage ("Cozy Cottage" by name) with a closet full of old toys and a fireplace painted bright red inside of which is her lamp and writing desk; there are ghastly prints on the wall and a pianola in the next room but she looks very well + is, for the moment, working happily. She will send me the ms. of the new section, to be entitled "Ladders of Fire,"also some addresses of friends in Mexico so I shall not be entirely among the philistines. I saw an ad. for Gore's book the other day, by the way—Eleanor Roosevelt calls it "Vividly engrossing."! I have still had no word from *Kenyon*—although I did write them a note as you suggested. And nothing from *Horizon*. Anaïs is writing an article on the Youth of America for *Harper's Bazaar;* she will write something about me, she said. I am really terribly grateful to her for what she said to me tonight; I feel ever so much more secure, whether she meant it or not and I see how much I have distorted many things—not exaggerated but seen them out of perspective. I think I shall stop this letter now and send it off to you tomorrow to make up quickly for those last two dread-ful ones. Everything, now, is balanced, is not what I feared. I am at peace and I love you peacefully + longingly.

Always—
Jimmy

the fez A gift from Friar, who was born on an island today controlled by Turkey.
Seldon Seldon James, Amherst student.
Portrait of a Woman (1944), originally titled *Une Femme disparaît*, directed by Jacques Feyder.
Sasha's Toscanini film *Hymn of the Nations* (1944), directed by Alexander (Sasha) Hammid, then the husband of Maya Deren.
Θαλασσα! Θαλασσα! "Thalassa! Thalassa!": the primordial Greek deity of the sea.
Anaïs Anaïs Nin.
to hear about Anaïs Merrill has written "Anaïs" when he means someone else.
"Ladders of Fire" Nin's *Ladders to Fire* (1946).
Gore's book Gore Vidal's *Williwaw* (1946).

To William Burford

AMHERST
5 August 1946
New Canaan, CT

Dear Bill,

This time tomorrow I shall be in New York (seeing a new dr., as a matter of fact); this time the next day I shall be high fathoms in the air, the nimble blue plateaus (not original) of pure escape, and I had not planned to write anybody any more letters until I was in the thin air of Mexico City, feeding marzipan to pigeons before cathedrals, and, like the foreigner who was so fabulously successful in America by learning only this one idiom, saying "Why not?" to everyone who speaks to me . . . but I have had, it seems, so many letters from you I feel obliged to send you some famous last words before sailing off into the sunset.

You are quite right about Proust; it is as though the creature one were observing through a microscope was itself possessed of a microscope and so on; it is therefore, spatially, the most enormous book ever written. Joyce breaks off pieces of his world and creates an imperfect mosaic. Proust never really gets past the first bit of enamel. The fish-skeleton of Renoir is a wonderful idea; you must use it by all means. A nude in Mrs. Rando's room, especially Renoir with glowing clear flesh, would be a wonderful psychological touch, her wish to destroy herself, etc.

I agree with you about the poem, except that it is not written about my mother who has not that arrogance or belief in tradition to that extent. I have been working with complete unsuccess on another poem which has such good closing lines that I cannot let it go:

To drown was the perfection of technique,
As one might speak of poems in a poem
Or at the crisis in the sonata quote
Five-finger exercises: a compliment
To all accomplishment.

I won't even bother to reconstruct the rest.

Yes I have at times wanted to change places with them, but they were, as they are now, glamorous only in the mirror of my own sorrows and bewilderment. I do not think these people have any conscious beauty, as a century of great peace and cultural integrity is remarkable not to itself but to the anguished years that follow it, or those who suffer within it. Those people like Mrs. Ramsay who blessedly knit socks and watch the sea and wonder about life, placed calmly on a terrace between two oblivions—to explore their minds would be like diving through clear water past charming fish and wise shells; but neither you nor I could ever <u>be</u> the water, the fish and shells, who have not the slightest emotion for or against the diver. It is not inconceivable that one day we shall find in ourselves that all the contradictions and desires and angers have through their quarreling created a way of life, a way of thought, an element as lucid, revealing as many wonders as we had always imagined existing outside ourselves. We will have created our own commonplace, and whether we drown from love of it like Narcissus or find that it is an atmosphere accessible to the entire world it will be the achievement, of all others, that is most perfect personal and liberating.

That (in case I die in a plane crash) is what I believe, what I honestly believe I believe; it explains, now, what I must do with my poem and with all poems.

And so I am prepared for my journey except for packing which I must do now. The victrola has not been repaired yet so I shall not hear Maggie Teyte sing "Les Roses d'Ispahan" before I go, which somehow saddens me more than anything else. Postcards will begin to come in from airports all over the country.

Au revoir,
Jim

William Burford (1927–2004), Merrill's fellow student poet and with him the co-editor at Amherst of the one-issue campus magazine *Medusa*, a contributor of an essay to Anaïs Nin's pamphlet *On Writing*, later a translator of Proust's *On Reading Ruskin*, and for many years a teacher of creative writing at Southern Methodist University.
nimble blue plateaus From Hart Crane, "For the Marriage of Faustus and Helen," section II.
Mrs. Rando Character in a story Burford was writing.
To drown Merrill's poem "The Drowned Poet" in *The Black Swan* (1946).
Mrs. Ramsay In Virginia Woolf's novel *To the Lighthouse*.
"Les Roses d'Ispahan" Song by Gabriel Fauré.

To Kimon Friar

WUSTL
[Summer 1946]
[New York, NY]

My dearest,

I am, at the moment, cold with rage; my father has been applying pressure, wants me to join Chi Psi this fall. I cannot help but feel, trivial as it is, that any point of disagreement with my family is now so bound up with you that I must fight it as powerfully as I can, and I have just written him, in admirable prose, a rather defiant letter which I am sending to his nurse in the hopes he [is] well enough to read it. I am going down there Thursday to spend the night, and he has already made it clear that he wishes no argument about fraternities, but relies, in so many words, upon my sympathies for his present condition. It is an impossible position, and I feel myself turning to stone, as I have so often in conversations with my mother, but I cannot give in, now, on any grounds, I cannot deny this break that has already started—otherwise all will be lost. If I were not so afraid

of becoming hardened against anything there would be no prob-
lem; I should already be, I suppose, quite callous; but <u>that</u> I will not
become, I will lose everything before I lose my love of gentleness. I
wrote you a letter, rather short, with poems in it (the old ones) last
Saturday, but the post-office was closed when I tried to mail it, and
I could get no stamps, so it had to wait until this morning; I'm very
distressed that you shall have to go a week without letters from me,
but shall wire you in between in an attempt to compensate. I found
your second letter about the islands this morning with the rest of
the forgotten lady and the big magenta flower, mailed in Naxos; it
took 14 days. I am very upset now, but chiefly about Daddy. I have
had three interviews with the Doctor, who is a gentleman, to be
sure, but denies completely, or seems to, the existence of a "poetic"
motive; which indeed may not exist, I like to think it does. He sees,
I feel, only part of things; I told him, for instance, that in a sense you
were the first father I had ever had as well as—but at that point he
exclaimed "Exactly! But one doesn't have sex with one's father, that's
incest," which seemed rather idiotic at the time, and still does. On
the whole, however, I am not alarmed, I do not expect to be shaken—
not that my attitude with him is at all defiant—but what I feel now
with a certain degree of clarity (with reference to you and my family,
disregarding as much as possible the constant awareness of what we
mean to one another) is that it is through you that I have made the
first assertion away from my family, and that, even on this rather dis-
passionate level alone, it would be fatal (just as in the fraternity case)
for me to back down, deny my only channel of escape from them,
whatever form our relationship assumes. It will be time enough later
to discover myself more fully; at the moment, all I have found out
about myself is that I love you. I cannot discover myself until I have a
chance to be myself, and that chance is what you have given me. The
doctor advised me not to talk about it too much with my mother,
which is a relief; we did have, three nights ago a very calm, clear talk,
in which she appeared to understand and accept a great deal; but
the more I think about it, the more I am convinced it was a failure,
that her calmness is worse than her frenzy, that her understanding
is falser than her misunderstanding, just as I feel a kind of scorn for
her whenever she tries to read some of the books I lend her (she is
reading Fowlie's *Rimbaud* now, with copious underlinings by me). But

I can make plans. I like to think now that I shall get out of college in February; stay in New York through part of June (Coley will be here in the spring when his novel is coming out; he is applying for a Rhodes scholarship which would begin in the fall, and I should like to have him know you) and then—simply—we will go to Europe. It is possible, it is certainly possible, and I am terribly relieved that I can even conceive of such a move; my imagination, up to now, has been so overclouded and warped by circumstances, that I had been able only to picture our life together as a sort of bright garden at the end of an impossible labyrinth; but now I begin to see the way to it, which gives me great comfort, great joy. Things are still confusing, but thanks to a number of things, perhaps the most important of which were my days with Coley, I feel renewed, restored.

Your letters mean so much to me, and I think of you constantly, wherever I am; and the strangeness of things, of events, of sunlight, of people on the street, strikes me continually. Fred and I drove in from New Canaan this morning, he on his way to Princeton, after a rather dull weekend there where I had too many martinis and slept all Sunday afternoon. Mama will be in town this afternoon. I must go to lunch now, as it is late and I have had no breakfast. I shall send this off now, as I do not anticipate anything of interest today; an afternoon with Carol listening to her rehearse *Werther*, and an evening of giving information about Mexico to two friends of ours who are going there. Will write you again before I go to Southampton, and please forgive the delay during the hectic days of my arrival home, beginning with the doctor and no stamps in New Canaan. I love you and miss you and love you "more and more."

[signature missing]

Chi Psi As a student, Charles Merrill was a member of the Amherst chapter of the fraternity Chi Psi. He later served as president of the national organization.
Fowlie's *Rimbaud Rimbaud, the Myth of Childhood* (1946) by Wallace Fowlie (1908–88).
Coley Coley Newman (d. 1982), Merrill's friend, an Amherst classmate.
Carol Carol Longone (1892–1987), Merrill's piano teacher, whose "operalogues" gave narrative synopses and musical analysis introducing works in the Metropolitan Opera season to audiences in New York.

To Kimon Friar   WUSTL
20 September 1946
[New York, NY]

My dearest,

As I told you, I received your letter about your accident on a Thursday. Last Monday evening, the day I mailed you my last letter, I was crushing ice in our mechanical grinder with the handle that makes the little blades inside revolve, and managed, by thoughtlessly inserting my finger while still turning the handle, to give myself a small, deep, jagged cut in the flesh near the nail of my second finger, left hand. So that now I too will have a scar. It bled quite a bit and I, having always doubted the existence of a shock after minor injuries, turned extremely cold for a half-hour, sweating and coming close to fainting on several occasions—not from pain, I was too cold to feel pain—it was all involved with you, with your accident with a kind of nervousness I had felt all day and which this incident cleared up completely, but I welcomed it, I now look at my bandage lovingly, because it is your bandage as well. It was a moment, far too intense for surprise, like your appearance at the New Year's party, violent yet something to be grateful for. And now, we are healing together.

Maya telephoned me yesterday, and I met her in some little cafe in the village yesterday afternoon, where we talked for about two hours about you, me, Sasha and herself. It was very good to see her, as it is to see anyone who knows you, and she, like Anaïs and Coley, underlined so many of the things I feel about us, talking a great deal about herself and her difficulties with Sasha and Anaïs (in regard to the movie). She has apparently had a very restful summer at Cape Hatteras, and is now thinking in terms of her new movie, which, she says, will take two years. She looked exceedingly well, and it did mean a lot to me to talk with her though I do not feel I understand her as well as I do Coley and Anaïs, or perhaps it is simply that now I do not need as much guidance and support as I did earlier in the summer. I shall try to see her when I come down on weekends; she is very kind and brings me very close to you.

There is no day without misfortune. I heard from Daddy's secretary that he had been given my letter, and that now he did not wish to have me come down and visit him, in fact, not to see him at all until perhaps some weekend later in the fall, perhaps not all winter. It distresses me that we should have this conflict, especially as it is so warped by his illness and as our "break" is, as far as I am concerned a realization, for <u>him</u>, of what has always existed for me—a lack of honesty and sympathy between us. I haven't really thought what I should do; perhaps write him saying I will go ahead and join the damned fraternity in order that when I tell him I shall go to Europe next summer, but not to work with the Quakers [handwritten *in the margin:* he will not have any accumulated grievances]; or adhere to my mask of defiance. I shall decide something in the next day or so.

Anaïs just telephoned me (I had written her asking to see her sometime, not having her phone number) and I am going there tonight after dinner with Huyler (who was in Florida with Fred and me) and Pete (with whom I went to New Hampshire). Princeton opens more or less tomorrow and they are rooming together, along with two other people. Everything is so crowded there. I shall be able to send you the *Medusa-Mask* airmail when I get up to Amherst, and get the copies of the magazine. I'll send you two copies and more if you want them, or save others for you. I am hoping that Burford will be able to drive me up, as I have far too much to take by train, and I don't want Mama to take me. I wired him today asking if it would be possible, and, at the same time wired you hoping it might arrive in the week's gap between letters. Don't forget to write me at Amherst from now on, as I shall cancel my box before I go up there—they will forward anything that comes after. I'll have to stop now and finish this tomorrow, as Pete and Huyler will be here soon.

It is late Thursday night; I have just returned from the theatre with Carol—a really awful Lehar operetta (I loathe operetta music) with Richard Tauber, the famous, <u>old</u> tenor. Earlier I had had tea at Joan Taylor's (you never, I believe, met her) and I am taking her to lunch today; and even earlier had dropped in on Toni Griffis for a few minutes; my days since my return are like mosaics. A very nice evening with Anaïs, Hugo and one of those awful people who were there the last time I went with you, handwriting analysis person. Her new book is all printed but not to be released till October 21. I am seeing her again today before supper. She gave me to read what she had done this summer, "Minuettes of Adolescence"—the story, real or invented, of "Stella" and the boy from Yale who spent a month with Anaïs before going into the army; it is very lovely, lyrical, young. Tonight I have dinner with Tony Harrigan of the *Bard Review*, and then taking a late train out to the country. And now the phone just rang; it was my old French governess who had six friends on that Belgian plane that crashed, and was of course frantic, and I must see her this afternoon. This is all too much. I have now to rearrange my day, or at least start doing the things I must do. I'll try to write you once more before I (this is Friday morning early now) go back to Amherst, but if not, remember that I love you and love you even when I am very busy. Anaïs wanted to know, have you met Durrell, are you going to? Darling, I miss you dreadfully, and shall probably faint on the docks from joy at seeing you tanned and scarred and beautiful.

Jimmy

in regard to the movie Deren's *Ritual in Transfigured Time* (1946).
her new movie *Meditation on Violence* (1948).
Huyler . . . Pete Huyler Held (1925–2012) and C. Peter Forcey (1925–2008) were Merrill's friends and classmates at Lawrenceville.
Medusa-Mask An essay on mythology and poetics by Kimon Friar that appeared in *Poetry* in 1940.
Hugo Hugh Parker Guiler (1898–1985), aka Ian Hugo: Nin's husband, a visual artist and experimental filmmaker.
Her new book *Ladders to Fire*.
my old French governess Lilla "Zelly" Howard (d. 1977) was Merrill's governess from 1933 to 1938. See his poem "Lost in Translation" in *Divine Comedies* (1976) and his essay "Acoustical Chambers" in *Recitative* (1986).
Durrell Lawrence Durrell (1912–90), British novelist and poet.

To Kimon Friar

WUSTL
2 January 1947
Amherst, MA

Dear Kimon,

Excuse me for being rather strange on the phone last night, but I can't help fearing someone may be listening on another phone; you see how foolish I am. One thing, I think, that bothers me: I find it very difficult to accept the language of love from you, realizing at the same time that difficulty you find in avoiding it. I want so badly not to "encourage" you falsely, and my very listening to your words when you tell me you love me is painful because I cannot for the moment return them and my silence is one of embarrassment. Until the analysis is over I cannot risk the responsibilities of love, I will not risk them. More than ever there is now for me, at the same time that I want a clarity, a great virtue in obliquity, when it comes to things that I cannot easily face. Speak to me in the way that you have taught me to admire, of everything except what you are eager to tell me. I will know what you are saying, that I assure you, but do not say it if that is possible. I will not forget anything, I will not and cannot make any final denial now, give me credit for that. But I think I will be able to be with you more gladly if you will wear a mask that will be, nevertheless, transparent to me. I hope this doesn't sound callous, I know you may think of it as deception; but I shall not be deceived, and the transformation, if it is such, may not be as necessary later as it is now. I am, as strongly as I can be, convinced of your goodness and honesty and indeed your love, but do not protest, do not entreat me as long as my only answer can be Wait.

I know how badly you want to come here, and I have no wish to prevent you if you must, but do not come asking me for what I can't give you. Do bring your work; we may work together, and talk of cabbages and kings. If you should come, wire me—

Jimmy

cabbages and kings From Lewis Carroll's poem "The Walrus and the Carpenter": " 'The time has come,' the Walrus said, / 'To talk of many things: / Of shoes—and ships—and sealing-wax—/ Of cabbages—and kings—' "

To Kimon Friar

WUSTL
3 March 1947
Amherst, MA

Dear Kimon,

Your letter came this morning, thank you for it, it is beautiful; if you will write me these things in a letter, will you not send me the poems you say you are writing? I do want to see them. There was a huge storm last night with rain and lightning, and the electricity stopped but returned in time for my midnight ritual of playing the *Rosenka-valier* waltzes to greet my birthday. Howkins, Burford and Boom Boom came over and it was all somewhat quiet, and the incredible Howkins, who goes in for that sort of thing, wept, because of my 18th birthday when the same things had happened, as I told you, and that was so very long ago. I wish you might have been there with us. And the Cookies came down (how I do love all helpless people, if you know what I mean). I suppose I should have stayed with you, as I was quite sick Saturday night. I couldn't get a doctor but took lots of aspirin and went to bed. Sunday morning I had to go out to the doctor as he is too busy with a mild flu epidemic to pay calls, and he did all sorts of things for me and gave me some splendid pills which I took all day, so that this morning I am weak but well, and will be quite well in a few more days. I shall venture out, in a closed car, this evening to have dinner with the Spragues—Mrs. S has made me a cake—and will be permitted, I am sure, to return early. I read a lot of Keats yesterday, about 40 letters, they are really wonderful; I was impressed particularly by what he says in letter 32 about "Negative Capability" which is almost a new idea as far as I am concerned and I will think about it; and "nothing startles me beyond the moment"—that is difficult but so much to be desired. They are, too, such delightful letters, comparing rocks to dancing masters, and sitting down every day to write 50 lines of *Endymion*. And tragic, as well, in the way you speak of the lightest music as being tragic, simply through perhaps the purity and the vulnerability of the form. I have also been reading some essays of Baudelaire in his *Art Romantique* volume, very measured, very exquisite, essays directing the painter of "today" to understand the beauties of his society, the peculiar beauties of the soldier, the dandy (a wonderful and I am sure very influential essay), etc; and a very touching one called "The Morality of the Toy" in which he describes a childhood experience of being taken by his mother to visit one Mme. Panckouke who received them dressed in velvet and fur and, at the end of the visit, she took him into a room reserved for nice little boys like Charles, a room filled with amazing toys, on the walls, on the floor, hanging from the ceiling, toys simple or intricate, expensive or cheap, and told him to choose one. (Of course he chose the most beautiful, and of course his mother refused to let him take it.) Mrs. Cosby has just insisted on bringing me an enormous glass of mixed fruit juices which I sip gratefully as I write. I have been reading as well Durrell's book on Corfu which is very delightful, and that seems to be all. From the way the trees are lurching about outside I presume it is still windy and probably much colder, though yesterday was very mild, and I long for Florida and the constant sun and the Gulf Stream. Unless something happens, I shall see you in 10 days and will keep writing. Thank you again for your letter; if you wrote it to make me think of you, that was not necessary, really.

Jimmy

Boom Boom Frederick Beck, Merrill's classmate from Amherst.
the Spragues Merrill's friend Rosemary Sprague (1926–2005) and her parents, Atherton (1897–1986), a professor of mathematics at Amherst, and Mary Ann Sprague (1900–90).
"Negative Capability" See Keats's letter to his brothers George and Tom, December 22, 1818.
Art Romantique L'Art romantique by Charles Baudelaire.
Mrs. Cosby Merrill's rooms were in Mrs. Cosby's house on Tyler Place, very close to Emily Dickinson's home.
Durrell's book *Prospero's Cell* (1945).

To Charles E. Merrill   AMHERST
                                                  14 June [1947]
                                                  Amherst, MA

Dear Daddy,

This little note, on the eve of Father's Day, is simply to tell you again of my love + friendship for you, + my gratitude to you for the many kindnesses of all varieties you have extended to [me] in the past years—school, college, allowance, and the more gifts of understanding, patience, and sympathy. I, for one, am very happy in the shape our relationship has assumed, and am confident that it will continue to be as pleasant and fruitful as it has been up to now.

That is really all I have to say, or can say, except to assure of my love and respect for you.

Always,
Jimmy

14 June The Amherst College class of 1947 graduated on Sunday, June 15.

To Charles E. Merrill

WUSTL
7 July 1948
Georgetown, ME

Dear Daddy,

We've been here eleven days now, and it couldn't be more wonderful. The house has been completely done over—new floors, screens, paint, wallpaper, still no plumbing—and couldn't, except for this last (there is a pump across the road + a two-holer in the barn), be more satisfactory. We are a mile + a bit from the little "town" of Georgetown—a postoffice + general store all in one; and 12 miles from Bath, where we shop twice a week—we have perhaps 25 books with us, most of which we haven't opened, we've been working so hard, and about 20 albums of records which are playing 1/3 of our waking hours. We are living on soups, salads, much fresh fruit, and occasionally, clams and lobsters—all cooked on a double hot-plate, as we don't want to tamper with the stove unless it gets very cold. The splendid thing is that in these eleven days, we have both done exactly half of what we did all last summer, from late June to mid-September: Fred has written over 20 pages of his novel, + I have done 3 poems—altogether over 100 lines. We are at our desks from 4–5 hours a day, without any strain + hardly any depression; so that the few afternoons a week we take off to lie in the sun on some neighbors' float in the river are well-earned. Even then, we are absurdly eager to get back to work. The difference from New York is really incredible—no sense of waste or urgency; it is a calm unlike anything I have experienced.

These neighbors, a New York family with two children, named

Levine (he is a sculptor) were warned of our coming by the Shains (from Princeton, who arranged for our renting the house) and have been very helpful + kind; on the 4th, we took our fireworks to their place + had a wonderful clam + lobster dinner on the shore before setting them off—the only other people we know at all well are two maiden schoolteachers who keep Angora Rabbits, which we went over the other morning to pluck in return for hot baths in their tub.

Freddy's mother is coming up for a week Sunday (which is Freddy's birthday) and we have 4 or 5 friends, coming up for a few days at a time, scattered through the summer. Bard opens almost immediately after Labor Day, so I shall drive down perhaps the Thursday before (stopping off there to leave some of my belongings), and, I think, spending a night on the road in Amherst, as it's a 12 hour drive from N.Y. here. The car, by the way, is behaving splendidly.

Amherst was so very nice at Commencement: I may not have told you often enough how much I enjoyed all of it, seeing you get your degree and the delightful meals + martinis chez Newlin. I was terribly busy the last days in N.Y. + had no chance to write—I couldn't find a suitable room off campus when I stopped at Bard, so I have taken a smallish room in a faculty house, sharing a bath; it will have to do, as it's all I could find.

Let me hear from you how you are + what the summer is bringing you; I do hope it is pleasant and restful. How is Kinta? Give her my best if she's back at the Orchard. Perhaps you could share this letter with the Magowans, as I don't want to write too many letters at this point + this is all the news up to the moment. My love to all of them, + to you + best wishes to Miss Erwin. Freddy sends you, Kinta, + the Magoogles his best.

Much love,
Jimmy.

Fred has written Buechner was writing his first novel, what would become the well-received *A Long Day's Dying* (1950).
Levine The sculptor Morris Levine (1914?–2004).
the Shains Charles Shain (1915–2003), a Princeton English professor, and his wife, Jo.
chez Newlin William Jesse Newlin (1878–1958), an Amherst philosophy professor.
Kinta Kinta Des Mares (1898–1989), Charles Merrill's third wife.
the Magoogles Magowans.

To Hellen Ingram Merrill   WUSTL
                                              August 1948
                                           Georgetown, ME

Dear Mama + Mis' Annie—

How nice to get your long letter this morn when I drove down to
the "Centaah" for staples, not daring to expect mail, but finding
5 envelopes in all! Freddy had nothing so we read it over our little
hamburgers—and I mean little. We entertained the Levines + their
two charming children (boy 13, girl 9), friends of the Shains—he is a
sculptor—who had asked us to dinner our 2nd night (Saturday)—they
have been so very nice. We aren't going to use the stove if we can
help it, a wood stove, that will, we are assured, work—But we have 2
hot plates + do very well on them—lots of salad + canned foods—not
much fruit up here—we've not yet dared do anything with sea-food.
There is an electric heater if we get chilly—we're using it now. 3 cold-
ish, cloudy days + the wonderful thing is there is nothing to do but
work + that is what we are doing: nothing much to show, but we are
getting along. I never have known such a blessed calm, of having not
so much nothing to do, but having nothing in the way of a substitute
adequately + insidiously to fill the gap—there is none of the jealousy
of time as in N.Y.—+ we can always make faces at each other when we
need to laugh. Tonight we read some 70 pages of Henry James aloud
to each other which was great fun.

Most fun probably is our sense of the natives' reaction to "the
teachers" or "the boys" as we have been told they call us. Driving the
mile of dirt road that shields us from the "main" road we passed a
house and saw 3 elderly faces pressed to the corner of their screened
porch staring at the car as it went by. There is also Mr. Todd who runs
the general store, Mrs. Davis, the postmistress, and a wonderfully
funny, tall, massive eunuch, Mistah Lewis who sells ice—all, except
Mrs. Davis (who is no chicken) quite elderly. Lots of bugs but the
house is well-screened. We're growing moustaches. Mine only grows
on one side, or seems to, + Freddy's can be felt but hardly shows at all.

I don't know about airmail as I've not received an airmail letter
yet—one delivery a day to G.town—arrives about 12:30.

I received a lease from Bard for my little room—I think I will buy

2 daybeds to replace the big double bed that's in it now. No need to bother about this till mid-August—they needn't be too elaborate—I can sleep on anything, + I'd like to have a place to put my guests. I'll want them sent right to the college, however, if that can be arranged.

Hope the move in from 164 was accomplished easily. Let me know how you all are and about all the weddings.

Love to you both, to Jonnie + of course M. + J. + the Vittis—
Jimmy

Hellen Ingram Merrill See Biographies.
Mis' Annie Merrill's maternal grandmother.
from 164 164 East Seventy-Second Street in Manhattan. Mis' Annie bought the apartment after her husband's death. It was Merrill's New York address in the 1980s and 1990s. See his poem "164 East 72nd Street" (*A Scattering of Salts,* 1995).

To Theodore Baird

AMHERST
21 October 1948
Bard College

Dear Colleague,

I am so delighted to have a letter, and a letter from you, that I can afford to turn from my first batch of papers (which speak of Jane Austen as having been written for the masses), to compare the symptoms of our occupational disease. Foremost among the things I have learned is not to listen to myself talk—the technique, I have heard, of the translators-on-the-spot at the U. N. Another thing is how hopelessly students in a Progressive College react to the word "experimental," a general favorite here: there seems to be no antonym similarly blessed. However, I do enjoy it, <u>my</u> eye at least is bright in class, and I have felt helpful on a few occasions.

In two weeks we are having a Poetry Festival, led by W. C. Williams + Louise Bogan, with Robt. Lowell, Eberhart, Dick Wilbur + Elizabeth Bishop dancing attendance. This is our major excitement for autumn.

Thank you for recommending the Grigson book. Is the "Acrobatics" essay included, or printed elsewhere? I'm particularly glad to have such a suggestion, as my private reading has suffered to the extent that I no longer am sure where to begin: so I will begin with Grigson. I read Boswell and *Anna Karenina* over the summer with great pleasure, as well as a book on Corneille, Moliere + Racine (Martin Turnell: the *Classic Moment*—New Directions, the <u>English</u> house) which inspires me to look more closely at the plays. I have no idea what other studies of these poets are like: this book, though perhaps a bit simple, is quite suggestive to me.

I'll look out for your paper in *The American Scientist*. I too have a rejection from *The American Scholar*. In fact, the greater part of my correspondence with publishers involves requests (from them) for Burford's address. This is annoying. However, *The Kenyon Review* has taken 98 lines of terza rima (perhaps the winter issue) and I am still waiting to hear from Princeton whether or not they will publish my collection. It's nearly impossible for me to write here—which is as I expected—but I'm pleased enough with my summer's work not to be too depressed by this.

If I can manage to visit Amherst before Christmas, I will by all means do so. I'm going to Europe for a month during our field period; this requires some planning in N.Y., but I'd like very much to see the fairest college, + will drop in on you.

My regards to the English department, and to your wife + mother,

Yours,
Jim

Theodore Baird (1901–96), legendary teacher of English 1–2, a two-semester composition course for freshmen at Amherst College.
the "Acrobatics" essay Geoffrey Grigson, "How Much Me Now Your Acrobatics Amaze," an attack on Dylan Thomas's "swarm of mud," in his book *The Harp of Aeolus* (1947).
98 lines of terza rima "Transfigured Bird," *The Kenyon Review*, vol. 11, no. 1 (Winter 1949), collected in Merrill's *First Poems* (1951).

To Frederick Buechner   WHEATON
15 November 1948
Bard College

As we have often agreed, old friend, few pleasures are equal to that of the Common Cold, and for three days now I have abandoned myself to just such a thing and its trappings, aspirins, Scotch, Benzedrine inhaler, fruit juice, cookies, mouthfuls of Vicks, and the like. Also quantities of reading: I finished yesterday the fourth [sic] Osbert Sitwell volumes, continued with Coleridge who promises more cumulative excitement than anything for a long time, read a little Penguin book on spiders, beginning: "Spiders are a matter of taste. There will be few so fond of them as the 'great lady still living' who, as described by the Rev. E. Topsell, in 1607, 'will not leave off eating them,'" and have embarked also on a charming book called *The Lungfish, the Dodo and the Unicorn, An Excursion into Romantic Zoology*; *Studies in Iconology* which has to do with the subject matters and motifs of Renaissance art; and finally have devoted the morning just past to Darwin's *Voyage of the Beagle*, his round-the-world diary which I have long wanted to read. Also this morning, after a six day disappearance the largest of my snails turned up in my bureau drawer, and I gave it its freedom, poor faithful thing. The other I released several days ago, it was of a more adventurous temperament and had conceived so great a passion for my blue blotter that delicate, brilliant blue bowel movements had begun to appear all over.

I can now, at a certain remove, speak to you of Dr. Edith Sitwell, whom, as I believe I said, you must exert yourself to see, if the occasion arises. She sat, at the reception at Miss Steloff's, on an early american bench. The first impression, apart from the remarkable face, was one of shapelessness—much bottle-green satin beneath something black and not smooth. Out of this her hands proposed themselves: one holding a drink, this hand largely hidden by an enormous ring, elliptical, agate or tortoiseshell, at whose extremity little more than the fingernail was visible; the other hand, weighted with something equally spreading in filigree, was at the guests' disposal. There must have been a necklace of some sort; at any rate a dappled brown orchid on her shoulder, by offering a minor contrast to the expanse of black and the shocking hands, prepared to a small extent for the shocking face. As for which, let us spend a moment looking at the palms of our hands. There. Are they very small? No they are not very small. Are they large? No, I would say they were smallish. Very well then, place your palm over your face, vertically. Do you not observe that the length of your palm is precisely that of the distance between your chin and your hairline? Keeping this in mind, along with the notion that the female hairline does not, with notable exceptions, greatly recede, my chief difficulty with the great woman may more readily be appreciated. The face was very big. Bending over it to greet her, it could not be seen all at once, as though I were even closer than I was, and on the verge of kissing her. There was so much forehead beneath the gold-and-black elaborate turban, so unbelievable a drop (whose extent was largely Nose) from that quantity to the big delicate chin, undismayed by its faintly adipose lodging. The mouth was large, the lips thin, their curve arbitrary; the eyes, though finely socketed, small and (perhaps because of the nose's prominence) close together, as though magnetized by what kept them apart. Colorless and hairless was the entire face, powdered, and in spite of the impression of great age, unwrinkled; a suggestion of thin, brownish hair at the turban's edge. The expression was one of considerable malignity; the manner was kind and restrained; I could imagine her doing many things, lecturing, sleeping, sitting on the john, playing the harp—everything, perhaps, except writing a poem. It occurred to me rather tritely later that she really is her own Collected Works, that, considering our brief span on earth, it is beyond all else remarkable and of the highest poetic order, that a single person could have achieved a bodily appearance of that quantity and quality in anything less than two hundred years. Accordingly, she can not be reproduced; forgive these tedious lines. See you in nine days,

As ever,
Jimmy

reception at Miss Steloff's Frances Steloff (1887–1989), owner of the Gotham Book Mart in Manhattan, hosted Edith and Sir Osbert Sitwell during their visit to the U.S. The reception was the occasion of a photograph of Sitwell, W. H. Auden, Marianne Moore, Elizabeth Bishop, Randall Jarrell, Delmore Schwartz, Tennessee Williams, and other authors. Merrill was directed with others to another room while the group portrait of the famous was taken. Merrill, an admirer of Sitwell's poetry, on various public occasions spontaneously recited from *Façade,* her and William Walton's 1922 musical-theatrical entertainment.

To Hellen Ingram Merrill

WUSTL

11 January 1949
Paris, France

Dear Mama and Miss Annie,

Tony is going out for tea with the Vicomtesse de Bouillabaisse, so that I have a minute or two to write you. I can't seem to keep track of what I've been doandseeing, so will report at random. Today we lunched with Martine and her little Dior mother, Mme. Hallade, after which we drove to a few nice churches, Ste. Genevieve, la patronne de Paris, and St. Severin, then to the Musée de Cluny which was closed; and this evening we are giving up *Bohème* at the Comique in favor of a simple dinner in the hotel. Isn't it exciting about the epidemic? Tony had the bug in Florence, and was deathly ill; I'm just marking time until I am stricken and, as you have read with delicious horror, the American hospital is overflowing. See Paris and die, you know. Monday we revisited the Munich pictures, inspected a beautiful Limoges casket, saw a few Tibetan scrolls at Loo's, after which I took to my bed for supper and spent an hour at the Cafe Flore later in the evening. Sunday, after a rather irresponsible performance of the *Magic Flute,* to which Ellie Forsyth accompanied me, I went with Charlie to Neuilly where one of his St. Tropez friends, a photographer who has done very well by the Greek countryside, has a studio in the shadow of the Bois, a sort of Brother-Sebastian's-done-his-cell-over-again effect, for a pleasant meal of oysters, roast beef and tangerines. On Saturday (how well this works in reverse) I had dinner with Charlie and some other people, and met a woman named Bumble Dawson; that is the important thing to remember about Saturday. Whereas Friday, Martine and Tony went with me to *Don Giovanni,* which was SO awful, I can't bear to revive the memory. All during these days I have wandered alone or with Tony through the city, chiefly the left bank, looking in shops and galleries, stopping here and there for a piece of pastry, doubtless crawling with germs. The Seine is so lovely, especially at night when it is very calm except in places where it shines and bubbles, as Freddy put it in the spring of 1941, like ornaments in a woman's hair. I have seen Matilda, whom you will recall, twice, once briefly, once for a second-rate tea. She is married to a kind of Mittel Europa student, and is great with his child, in a sprawling flat on the left bank, quite unfurnished but for a few couches and her "treasure," a huge Louis treize chair, exuding the original straw, the very sight of which brings the Black Death to mind; it unfolds into an agonized bed. I keep forgetting to call Hattie Bensen, but I will, I will. Tomorrow I am taking all the Princeton girls out to dinner, and Friday we are thinking of spending the night in Chartres, and will probably go to Rheims for a day or so next week. Martine will drive us to Versailles the first bright day. As it stands now, I shall sail on the Queen Mary, the only ship leaving at the proper time, on the 4th of Feb., I believe, which gets into NY on the 12th or thereabouts. My feet are a trifle stronger nowadays, though I dreamed the other night that I sawed both of them off so as never to have to walk again. Tony drugs me with Chinese tea and talk about Chinese furniture, and is now suggesting a trip next winter to Egypt, Arabia and Turkey, winding up in Venice by June. I tell him I will consider it, though I suspect I shall not; it's a peculiarly appropriate daydream to entertain in Paris, however.

Which just about does it for the moment. Distribute this shallow letter with many thanks for letters received.

Much love,
Jimmy

Tony Tony Harwood.
Vicomtesse de Bouillabaisse Invented rhyming name.
Martine Martine Hallade (d. 2016) later married the French diplomat Geoffroy de Courcel, became a psychotherapist, and edited *Malraux: Life and Work* (1976).
See Paris and die In the winter of 1949, a severe flu epidemic spread across Western Europe. It was estimated that as much as 20 percent of the French population was affected.
Charlie Charles Shoup, a friend of Merrill's who had recently moved to Paris and established himself as a society painter. He later moved to Athens and became a noted landscape architect.
Brother Sebastian The American cartoonist Chon Day (1907–2000) created a well-known pantomime comic character of this name.
Bumble Dawson Beatrice "Bumble" Dawson (1908–76), British costume designer.

To Frederick Buechner

Dear Freddy—

I'm damn near too puzzled to write this card, but wanted you to be the first, + for the time being only one to know that for 20 hours now I have been head over heels in love with the girl who last fall told me she loved me because we looked alike. We don't, actually, but I think she does love me, + her name is Louise + she is short + thin with brownish hair + looks like a bright, unhappy child. I am afraid to be doing the "wrong thing" for her + maybe after today she won't want to see me anymore + dear me, how does an inexperienced faculty member woo a sophomore? But mostly I am lighthearted + mostly she is mixed up and worried about herself + this will perhaps never get beyond what it has already been. I haven't been able to think of anything else all day; I love her physically also, I mean + this is a little postcard about something that is happening now and it is very wonderful. Florida on Tuesday. See you the 23rd??

> Yours ever,
> Jimmy

the girl Louise Fitzhugh, Merrill's student. See Biographies.

To Frederick Buechner

Dear Freddy,

Yours, long + newsy, of a few days ago met me at the airport, wrapped around (several times) by Miss King who was delighted to hear of your book. There's so much trash being written, she remarked elliptically. Today is a broiler. I am smeared with olive oil on Daddy's balcony. He is shaving—poor man: after his 2 operations since December he announces himself, pungently, "left with two navels and one nipple." And it's right! I've <u>seen</u> it. Colleen ("The Doll Souse" woman) + I went to see *Rope* last night + loved it. Such responsibilities as a teacher has.

The house is full of roses, massed + mounted in not large vases, and by a pool is a tree equally full of orioles + young woodpeckers maybe. On the plane I devoured the 1st of 5 volumes of *The Tale of Genji*, by Lady Murasaki, the 11th century diarist at the Japanese court + I can't wait to race through the rest of it, as it's one of the most remarkable + beautiful novels I've ever read and, on dit, a great classic in Japan. They all speak in poems, about sleeves being wet (with dew?) + the voice of the young crane among (reeds?) but you would love it + must read it. Try it and see: it's bound to be at Princeton. I must get out of the sun. My love continues, but limpingly; she loves me, she says, but doesn't want to see me. Well she is not seeing me.

I must shave before Messmore Kendall + his son come. Oh Lord it is so beautiful here. Let me know, in an idle moment, how you are, what doing, what thinking? What? +, more explicitly what I must be prepared to do at Forcey's wedding, besides screwing Janet Cottier. This sun is unbearable.

Miss you. As ever,
Jimmy

Miss King Esther King, Charles Merrill's long-serving, book-loving secretary.
his 2 operations Charles Merrill's heart surgery.
"The Doll Souse" Essay (inspired by visit to exhibit of the Queen's Doll's House) by E. M. Forster, collected in *Abinger Harvest* (1936).
Rope Film directed by Alfred Hitchcock.
Messmore Kendall (1872–1959), business leader.
Forcey's wedding C. Peter Forcey, classmate of Merrill's and Buechner's at Lawrenceville.
Janet Cottier Wife of Princeton English professor Hamilton Cottier, and mother of Pamela, whom Peter Forcey was marrying.

To Kimon Friar

Dear Kimon,

At last all this Bard business is over, and for two days now I have quite given myself over to the pleasure of living in my own place. Except for one or two inconsiderable things, it is complete and, to my mind, everything one could desire in the way of a home in the city. You will know I do not speak idly when I tell you I have an air-cooling unit in the study, so that this room is always cool, and it is here on hot nights that I sleep. I move from here to the piano in the living-room, looking at all of it, and loving all of it, and wanting to show it to my friends, to you as much as anyone.

Nothing but the tediousness of the last months at Bard kept me from answering your last letter. I more or less gave up five weeks ago, spent most of my days at a beautiful waterfall nearby the college, swimming with friends (I was nearly swept over it once), fell very much in love with a fine and charming student who, although otherwhere committed, is staying with me here until July 1st., and concentrated all my academic energies upon my final lecture on *The Wings of the Dove* which, though my mother's presence flustered me somewhat (it has been years since I've spoken intimately in her presence), was the best thing of its sort I've ever done. You should, if you haven't already, receive a bundle of clothes. It's not very much, as I found Mama had given away most of my old things to our gardener in the country, but I hope it will be helpful.

It's quite impossible that I should come to Europe this summer. I should love to, and the chances are I'd get as much done (writing) with you, if not more, than here in New York, but my circumstances (the inner ones) require, for the time being, that I be, in so many senses, chez moi. Insofar as I have any influence on your own plans, though, I'd like to suggest to you the possibility (it is not a promise, it can't be) of allowing you to prolong your stay in Greece by another year or so, if you should want it. This observation comes from me at, you must realize, a lull in the merry round of requests for help; yet it seems to me, if it can be arranged, you should not have to return at the very moment when you are giving yourself over to the fulfillment of your own work, no longer, I mean, chiefly translating or anthologizing. And I cannot imagine you have forgotten the distractions of all sorts you would have to face if you settled again in New York. I think you should have at least another year, if we count October as the end of the second year, in which really to confirm the habits and perceptions you are able to live by now. I don't doubt you have this power, but you would, I think, uselessly expose it to the familiar dangers by leaving too soon its birthplace, and yours.

It is strange you should ask particularly about the Braque. I am tired of it and think I shall sell it; it is not here. If I do sell it, I'd like to get more of the Rajput or Moghul paintings after finding three of the latter in Paris. I have become tremendously delighted by those little miniatures, in tempera or grisaille. Perhaps, if you have occasion, you would inquire of your artist friends if any good ones are available in Athens. One can always find mediocre ones, for they are only just beginning to "catch on," and in Paris they were remarkably cheap. But I would trust your taste to procure a few for me—they should not (unless extraordinarily fine) cost more than 10 or 12 dollars (this by Parisian standards), whereas in NY they are several hundreds apiece. Ghika's swan faces me, and the little 18th century boy is in the living-room.

What is the best time for me to come to Greece next year? I shall be in Europe probably from late May through October or November. One of the summer months I'll be with Tony motoring through Italy, possibly six weeks; and I do want to go to Egypt, though I'd suspect November would be the month for that. How would late August through mid-October be, or late May, when I sail, through mid-July? Let me know what you think. I am not interested in extensive touring, though I shall like to spend say two weeks or so drifting through various islands with you, and four or five days in Athens: the rest of the time it would be lovely just to rest and work at the Medusa.

I'm still tired from the last few days, and since Wayne is in the country tonight I think I'll sleep a full eleven hours.

Do write soon. This is my permanent address.

Love,
Jimmy

my own place A garden apartment on West Tenth Street in Greenwich Village.
the Braque See Merrill's letter to Gerrish Thurber, Winter 1946.
Ghika's swan Nikos Hadjikyriakos-Ghikas (1906–94), aka Nico Ghika, Greek artist whose woodcut is reproduced on the cover of Merrill's *The Black Swan* (1946).
the Medusa The name for Friar's cottage on Poros, referring to Friar's writing on the myth of Medusa.
Wayne Wayne Kerwood (1929–84), Merrill's lover, was secretary to Blanche Knopf (1894–1966), president of Knopf Publishing and wife of Alfred A. Knopf Sr.

To Irma Brandeis

WUSTL
13 July 1949
[New York, NY]

Dear Irma—

I awoke, teeth chattering in the cold, contrived air of my study, listened to Ludwig's 4th concerto over a hard-boiled egg + a cup of Hu kwa, and then down to find your postcard. It's good to know where you are, + that where you are is good, with mother, book and cat. I was on the verge of sending you a line to 12th St., as I have discovered the song you wanted me to find in Paris: it is "Le Chapelier" by Satie + has been recorded by Jennie Tourel in a new Columbia album of French songs, not too well sung. But it is a nifty song, if you'll pardon the expression.

The brown walls have not only spoken, but resounded (on different occasions, naturally) and much of the time I lisp in numbers, + am very happy and all that.

The Summers stayed here on their way to the cape + we had a nice party (Stingers) + the Hirsches were seen at a vernissage, talking to a Mrs. Rockefeller. Elliott Halpern is trying to get his own radio program, reading poetry. He ran into Louise Bogan crossing a bridge; she described me as "a-very-apt-young-man," which I cherish.

Soon I go to Maine. Tovey, in the Beethoven book, speaks of "the giant-gooseberry experience of a Boccherini cello concerto." This has haunted me for days.

Do you play your flute under trees? walk barefoot among fireflies? drink lots of buttermilk? know that we miss you badly, here in the city?

Tante belle cose alla mamma, et à toi, beau sphinx, mes plus déli-
cats sentiments, Iago.

Oh but what I have most to tell you, while it is still with me, is about
the South American woman at the cloisters, among the unicorn tap-
estries, last Sunday: an evil sort she was, with hairline merging into
eyebrows, holding on to husband + child, rouged + diamonded. "U-ni-
corn . . . u-ni-corn" she repeated slowly to her self, then (and I must
write it in Italian, as I don't know how it would look in Spanish) in a
dim, doubtful voice, the abyss opening at her feet, "Credo che non
exista . . ."

In the gothic garden they have lavender, caraway, pigweed, toad-
wort, Cretan Dittany, and Lemon Balm, not to mention Love Entan-
gle + wallflower.

J.

Irma Brandeis See Biographies.
Jennie Tourel (1900–73), Russian-born American mezzo-soprano noted for her
interpretations of French song.
I lisp in numbers From Alexander Pope's "Epistle to Dr. Arbuthnot."
The Summers Joseph (1920–2003) and U. T. Summers (1920–2015). Joseph Sum-
mers was a scholar of Renaissance poetry who taught at Bard when Merrill was on
the faculty there; U.T. was an editor at Houghton Mifflin, in which role she became
a friend of Elizabeth Bishop's.
the Hirsches Felix Edward Hirsch (1902–82), German journalist and later librarian
and professor at Bard College, and his wife, Elisabeth Feist Hirsch, also a professor
at Bard.
Louise Bogan (1897–1970), poet and poetry reviewer for *The New Yorker.*
Tovey Donald Francis Tovey (1875–1940), British musicologist and author of
Beethoven (1945) and *A Companion to Beethoven's Pianoforte Sonatas* (1931).
Tante belle . . . sentiments All the best to your mother, and to you, beautiful
sphinx, my most tender sentiments, Iago ("Iago" is a Spanish version of "James").
"Credo che non exista" I don't think it's real.

To Charles E. Merrill   AMHERST
                                          19 December 1949
                                          [New York, NY]

Dear Daddy,

For the last several years I have wanted very deeply to write a poem
that would be for you. It's something one cannot sit down to do, as

one usually, in the course of composition, comes to envisage more and more the sort of person—sometimes a friend, an acquaintance, or even a fictive person—to whom one happens to be addressing the particular poem: and over this one has no control. At times, even, one addresses oneself, and nobody else. But since October I have been working on a poem, a group of poems which, as they were being written, suggested to me with increasing vividness that they were y o u r poems. So that, for better or worse, whether or not you like or understand them, it is with the greatest pleasure and gratitude that I offer them to you with this formal dedication. Above and beyond this, there is the deep, personal dedication acknowledging the extent to which you have made not only these, but all my poems, and the life from which they come, possible and real.

The theme of the poems, a theme so far-reaching I cannot hope to have done it justice, is one I have been more and more conscious of since adolescence: the interaction of material and spiritual elements, as when one cherishes an object in part for its evident physical beauty, and even more for its having been cherished by one's grandmother. It makes all the difference, I believe, which of these points of view predominates in a man's attitude—what an object or situation is, on the one hand; or what it means, on the other. I could say much more, but would rather send you these poems. Here they are with my love,

> now and always,
> Jimmy

a group of poems Merrill dedicated "Variations and Elegy: White Stag, Black Bear" to his father in *First Poems* (1951).

To Claude Fredericks

GETTY
[January 1950]
[New York, NY]

Dearest Claude—

The fire is about to go out, following Wayne's example: I am glad to have these unexpected minutes in which to send you a little greeting—

little only in that I'm tired + it has not yet broken on me where you are. Thirty minutes ago you were received into the cold airs of Lee and now, at last, after allowing you time to gather your baggage, I'm no longer able to follow the roads you will take, in space + in speech. In a way I am impatient to know that you have left—though probably I shall not until I have your first letter—if only to establish you in my mind as a person to whom I can write letters, since that must be, for a while, our primary communion. I suspect, when I am resigned to this, the very paper will shine with the pleasure of its errand; but tonight it is sad and a bit difficult to embark on so diminished an extension of what I feel. One day, of course, you may open one of these envelopes, and I myself will fall out, tiny and dry, like the Japanese flowers, for you to revive in a bowl of water, or clear soup. Be sure you shake each envelope carefully, or you may lock me away in a drawer.

Tomorrow I have lunch with my mother and put her on the train to Jacksonville; then dinner with Meredith and Robert Drew (whom we saw coming out of the museum, de chez les Hapsbourg); finally, with these two, the Gala Performance of *Tosca* in honor of Edward Johnson—the anti-Christ of American opera.

My ring! I keep touching it and rubbing it—are not gold rings, wedding rings, thought to be medicinal? One rubs one's eyes with them, I believe, to cure styes or sharpen one's vision. I am, at any rate, encircled utterly. Dear Claude, even in your absence I can do little but rejoice; even in my fatigue there is more vigor than I have known for many a year, and more warmth than the cooling fire sent out at its brightest. Every deferred beauty, every impoverished immediacy, shine in the light I have from you.

To say "I am thinking of you" would be, as you put it, "what one would say to Walter." (I use the phrase idiomatically). But I <u>am</u> thinking of you and I <u>do</u> miss you and I love you, I love you.

Jimmy

Monday evening. The 11:00 mail (I hope).

Claude Fredericks See Biographies.
Lee Lee, MA, where Fredericks changed buses on his way home to Pawlet, VT.
Meredith The poet William Meredith (1919–2007).
de chez les Hapsbourg The Metropolitan Museum of Art's exhibition *Art Treasures from the Vienna Collections*.

Edward Johnson (1878–1959), Canadian tenor who became the general manager of the Metropolitan Opera, 1935–50.
My ring Fredericks and Merrill had exchanged rings as love pledges. The gold ring Merrill gave to Fredericks bore the Merrill crest and the initials of Merrill and his mother.

To Claude Fredericks

GETTY
3 March 1950
[New York, NY]

Dear, dear Claude,

I too resort to this machine, whose violent legibility James among others deplored, not for reasons as honorable as yours, but because I am beyond all reason exhausted. Yet I cannot let my birthday pass, this day whose importance (like that of all other days) lies only with you, or in my dedication to you, without spending part of it writing you. It has been a day only dubiously notable, except (which means everything) for having had two letters from you, letters so moving and beautiful that everywhere I have taken them out to read them, read them over, merely to touch them, my rooms here, taxis, street-corners, have witnessed my joy and my trembling. How much I love you keeps breaking over me; perhaps this is the shifting you write of, the gathering and reassembling of jewels. Alas, there is little I can say tonight by way of answer to them, except what is for me most important, that I think there was not one word in them I did not, and do not, respond to, and would not, in my own way, say to you, over and over. I feel with such keenness all that you have said: and if I loved you less it would sadden me to recognize how much more you have said than I. It seems as though the words of love in their profusion lay somewhere, just beyond my reach, or rather in the disorder in which I left them four years ago. Not that I feel a need of fluency, but it would make me happy to caress you with a language entirely my own, therefore yours, and since all language, it seems now, trails so piteously in the wake of what has happened, the words come with a special difficulty. And a special delight. I shall be glad to board the plane, to have four hours alone with my thoughts of you, and with your letters; and to look forward to the one that will reach me in Palm Beach. I doubt that I shall be able to send you more than a hurried note, if that, until I arrive there, for tomorrow and Sunday will be impossible days.

This morning was a very curious one. Wayne and I had been out quite late last night, to usher in my birthday. We talked in a surprisingly sensible way: he still loves me, he says, but it would seem that the margin in his mind is diminishing between the presumed splendors of life with me and the abysses of life alone or with another person. All our differences, or most of them, are now under display, under fire almost; we exercise them constantly in conversation, thereby actually calling into being a critical and intellectual relationship that, by its low saturation (emotionally), should soon cease to interest him. I mean, time and distance will destroy the attention I still feel I must give him; and that absence will accomplish the rest, from his point of view. It is hard to shake off a kind of sadness, that I doubt would have come about except through having found you, a sadness rising from the consideration of any life presently or prospectively less glorious than the one, with you, that is constantly before me. The image of you, in bed by the fire, the night against the windows, is a terribly stirring one; and although I would be with you in all surroundings, the ones you describe, for your very being in them, take on an overwhelming glamor. But, as for this morning, I became for two hours a French poet, probably Apollinaire. Mme. Vincent, Suzel's mother, telephoned asking me to write a menu in verse for a little supper after the reception tomorrow night. And, after a few moments of despair (I don't really enjoy that sort of thing) I began and finished the greater part of ten quatrains, with a pleasure and irresponsibility combined that I have never before experienced. For two hours I felt I was a Frenchman; when the phone rang, it was all I could do to speak English, my own language had so eluded me. Beneath all this were the effects of my night of drinking, slowly but steadily, Pernod; which prevented nearly all of my mind from operating on even the simplest levels. Not that the poem is necessarily good (I enclose it for your amusement), but the experience of writing with a conscious (if not apparent on the page) felicity in a language not my own is one I shall never forget.

Orfeo has been playing through this letter. Ever since you recognized for me the closeness of my dream to it, I have felt strangely involved with his story. Possibly it is an involvement with all dancing, as, in its way, a metaphor for the quality of our behavior towards one another, and, tremendously, towards those Others, whose gestures interposed bring a spectacular tautness into the dance, whose entire beings become, in one sense, an overpowering absence—for I feel they cannot press upon the spirit—but who equally, as in a dance, set puzzling motions in action. You say, and you are right, that we have different situations to face in terms of the Others, yet I feel so often they confirm us, how much, for enlightenment, we have had need of them. So that, while knowing hardly any of what is happening to you now in Vermont, I am aware of a continual harmony, an understanding of words you have not yet spoken, no matter to whom you speak them. I shall sleep now and, as I have no stamps, mail this in the morning. Do be thinking of where we shall meet on the 19th. Saturday the 18th Freddy has asked me to come to Princeton: I shan't see him again for ever so long, and I can't refuse him. Is there any place where they have fires in the rooms? Monday night I am in Jacksonville with my mother. Tuesday in Palm Beach. Twelve days thereafter in your arms. The Toltec charm goes with me, and the cross, and the ring, to wear at night and mornings alone on the beach.

Goodnight, my love, my dearest.
Jimmy

Mme. Vincent, Suzel's mother Merrill met Suzel Vincent Parker through Frederick Buechner and helped her financially off and on for many years. She became an art dealer in Paris.
Orfeo Early-seventeenth-century opera by Claudio Monteverdi about Orpheus and Eurydice. See Merrill's poem "Orfeo" in *The Country of a Thousand Years of Peace* (1959).

To Charles E. Merrill

WUSTL
17 March 1950
N.Y., N.H., + H.R.R.

Dear Daddy + Kinta—

I'm on the train now, for New Canaan, to wake my car from its winter sleep, and all I can find to write on is this familiar, though somewhat crumpled, piece of paper. Things have happened since my return that make it essential I use every free moment I have.

First things first: as I kept saying while I was there, I don't think there has <u>ever</u> been a lovelier visit with you. The guests were all so charming, fitted so well together: each day, each meal, each moment with one or more of your household was a genuine pleasure and I shall remember it always as a perfect ten days. It was so good of you to have Bill in spite of crowded conditions—I'm sure you could see how much he + I both appreciated it.

<u>But</u> yesterday at 3:36 P.M. I was informed that Knopf will publish my book of poems. Of course I am overjoyed and in a considerable dither about it—I have many letters to write, securing copyrights from the various magazines, thinking of a title for the book, and a few final considerations as to its form. And since there's many a slip, etc.—I wish you would wait until I have signed the contract (next Thursday) before you spread the news. When this is signed, I will wire you. They said the book would probably appear in the fall. My first thoughts, in hearing this news, was of you, Daddy—feeling, as I do, over and over again how much all this springs from the freedom and encouragement and care you have given me. At this most happy moment for me, I want to thank you again—hastily but with all my heart—for those things.

I know you will understand the brevity of this note, and I hope, under the circumstances, forgive it. Love to Jack + Stella + the others. And again, how can I ever tell you what a specially lovely visit this was.

> Always my love to you both,
> Jimmy

N.Y., N.H., + H.R.R. New York, New Haven and Hartford Railroad line.
visit with you In Palm Beach.
Bill William Meredith.
my book of poems *First Poems* (1951).

To Hellen Ingram Merrill

Dear Mama,

Quick note while the bath is running. Things are going rapidly now, of course, but, as I wired you yesterday the contract is signed. I wired Daddy also, and he telephoned me, saying I probably felt as he did on the day of his big McCrory deal. Could be. Went down to Merrill Lynch today to arrange things like rent and local bills with Tony Meyer, and have Miss Francis type several carbon copies of the completed manuscript, one of which I'll send you, or have Wayne do it if I don't have time. Then lunch with Mis' Annie, who seemed very well (though I was extremely distressed and alarmed to hear about Aunt Emma)—she talks of <u>nothing</u> now but television! Tonight, probably, the opera. Tomorrow I go to Princeton to a little party Bill is giving for me. I had a very nice evening in Princeton with Freddy last Saturday; we had a long talk about his plans (I think he will stay in Europe), and both enjoyed it a lot. I had such a reaction against the extent and complexity of my own plans that I <u>will</u> not make any for the time after Daddy has left until I see just what the possibilities are over there. I forgot all about phoning Annette—please forgive me: I just found her letter in my wallet today, and of course she has left the city by now.

Stopped at the Chase Bank this afternoon. Mrs Kelly has been retired since last November, and the man I spoke to said you would have to write a note (as a depositor) to them in NY, saying I was going to Paris and wanted to use the Bank as my permanent mailing address. There is a fee, which I shall pay there, but the man said a note from you would be necessary. Can you do this right away, so their letter to Paris, if sent air mail (request this), will get there before I do, the evening of the 7th.

I imagine the house is shaping up fairly well by now. Everyone here sounds very pleased about its progress—Maggie and Jessie, Mis' A., etc. Mis' A, hearing that, as usual, she has the nicest room in the house, has expressed no qualms at living there. I know she'll love it, once she's there—and even if she doesn't, I should think your presence and her friends' would almost completely make up for any discomfort she might feel. Of course, she feels discomfort everywhere, as we must remember. Have you <u>seen</u> Aunt Emma? You're one of the few people who can talk sense to her—do make sure she rests completely, as the doctor instructed; it's just too bad if poor little Shirley has chicken-pox.

Tell Paula how excited we were to see Kitty's picture in *Look*. Though, entre nous, from all that Paula has scribbled all over the magazine cover, I expected Kitty to appear naked inside.

I doubt that I'll be writing you again before I sail at six PM Wednesday. There will be lots of people to see me off, with champagne in the cabin. I think of the other time I went to Europe and what a lovely sendoff I had from all of you. As I say, I don't know how long I'll be away—I don't want to know, but I'll surely see you, if you don't get to come over, before you leave Florida next spring. Do keep well and take it easy. I'll miss you very much and will do my best to write as often as I can. Write me at the Vendome, 1 Place Vendome, in Paris, for your first letter or so, then to the Chase Bank, so that letters won't miss me if I should wander around much in Greece. Though, on the other hand, I should be, while in Greece, more likely to get letters quicker if sent to the island where Kimon is; that address is: The Medusa, Poros, Trizinias, Greece. 15¢ airmail is what you need.

I hope you understand completely in what an impersonal spirit I am visiting him, and be assured there is no reason whatsoever for you to be distressed about it. We have often talked about that power of memory that selects the good things in a person to recall; that does not mean one cannot recognize the bad things. After so many years, I have, naturally no <u>need</u> to see him, nor shall I develop such a need while I'm there. I go to him as I would to a person who, for better or worse, has done a lot to shape me in my knowledge of the world and my skill as a poet. There is nothing further I can learn of him now. Indeed, I go more to let him show me the ravishing Greek countryside in spring than to see <u>him</u>.

Well, enough of that. My bath is probably cold by now. But that can be remedied. Much, much love to you, my dear; don't worry about me. I expect to have a beautiful and enriching trip, and it only saddens me we are not sailing together.

Love to everyone else, Jonnie, Lalla, Paula, and the Burwells—

As ever,
Jimmy

big McCrory deal Charles Merrill was the underwriter for the expansion of McCrory's, the five-and-dime store chain.

To Hellen Ingram Merrill

WUSTL
16 April 1950
Poros, Greece

Dear Mama and Mis' Annie,

I'm here and it's so lovely. Well, from the beginning. My days in Paris were very rushed—trying to arrange things about the car, but most of the places were closed until the Tuesday after Easter, so I left Tony with most of it to do. We both have our international permits, at any rate. My last night, I had dinner with Doris, Bobby and Robin—who had not been expected until the following day, when I should have left. Bobby had to fly back to NY the next morning, for business. Saw Howkins, Jennifer, Charlie Shoup (who sent his love to you); he has very sweetly let me have his apartment for the few days I shall be in Paris in June. The flight to Greece was uneventful, except for some beautiful moments over the Alps. I spent the first night in Athens, saw the Acropolis by starlight, then, early the following afternoon, took the ship to Poros, three hours away. The weather is a bit cooler than I'd expected, and it is faintly cloudy, which I am told is very unusual. I am staying on an estate overlooking the water, close to the mainland—owned by Kimon's friend Mina Diamantopoulos, a charming and remarkable woman in her late fifties, whose husband died a year or so ago. Kimon has a little cottage to himself. I have never been so wonderfully welcomed, felt such kindness and goodwill, as by the people here—Mina, her little grandson, aged 6, the gardener and his wife. In the mornings, usually, we work, all of us writing; in the afternoon, one can go in the boat, or work in the garden: my first day I transplanted wildflowers from the abundance of them in the surrounding hills—poppies, violets, daisies. It is a very rocky land, with beautiful trees, pine, eucalyptus, cypress, fig and almond and lemon. In the evening, Mina and Kimon and I have dinner, usually by a small fire—and talk or listen to music, taking a stroll along the road overlooking the sea that mirrors the lights of the town—such calm water, azure, crystalline, with sea-urchins like black stars several feet underneath. Thursday we rowed and walked to a festival at a monastery several miles away—much dancing to old gramophones in an extraordinarily beautiful ravine, in view of the sea; we ate cheese and drank the strange resinated wine. I had a lot of candy in my pockets for the children, who clustered around me— very charming and of course quite poor: we pointed to our noses and mouths and fingers, they giving me the greek words, I giving them the english ones, and then after dark, we walked back to the rowboat singing and laughing. Today being Sunday, we are going now (late afternoon) into town, a mile or two away by water, where everyone will roam about in a party spirit.

No word yet from Daddy about Venice, but Bobby told me they had already suggested he go there—and his reaction was that he had been there before and didn't particularly care to do it again. So I can do nothing but sit tight. In a week or so we're going to see some other islands, along with more of Athens and possibly Delphi—all this might take ten days; so that I'd have another ten days here before leaving for Italy around May 15. Your letter came about young Mr. Young, who sounds charming: I hope you'll be very happy. Thank you for writing about the poems. My own feeling is that titles nowadays are <u>too</u> provocative; if I had my way I would call the book *Poems;* but I'm quite fond of the title as it stands now. A letter from Meredith contains the rumor that the book may not come out until January— but I've not heard that yet, or anything, from Knopf. Much much love to all of you.

Always,
Jimmy

Tony Tony Harwood. He and Merrill rented a car together in Europe.

To Hubbell Pierce

WUSTL
27 April 1950
Athens, Greece

Darlin' Hub:

How I have tortured myself, not to have written you that lawng, lawng lettah Ah promised wen Ah kissed you on the Wawf. (When will you have that wharf removed? It's <u>so</u> unsightly!) But, my dear, I am even now in the hospital, and this is the first time, in the past twelve days that I've felt really strong and well enough to want to be out and doing things. I have been in such pain, and so terribly <u>weak</u>; that was the worst thing. But now, after four days among Greek nuns (all so devine and so chic; my favorite changes her habit five times a day—every possible combination of black and white) eating nothing but cool rice-water, so vile, and glutinous noodles, tepid tea, and (to gild the pill) chocolate pudding, I am quite restored, had three microscopic lamb chops for lunch, have had my backside shot full of penicillin, and the veins in my arms of glucose—BULLY! I cry, like Teddy Roosevelt, I feel strong as an Ox, and out of my window I see Mt. Hymettus, and I am learning all sorts of little greek phrases about cheese and bread and dogs and good men. I trust Wayne shared my letter to him with you; if not, do call him and get hold of it—not that it was very much, but it's such a bore repeating all these things to you, when they are set down in pristine splendor for him. You might extend the same favor, and see that he reads this little note. I miss you furiously. Really you should be in this wonderful country. Everyone is so charming and friendly (you can take that in as many ways as you care) and suffering from a fatal passion for Americans. I'm as happy as I can be, without the people closest to me, and I mean to return here for a much longer stay before the summer is out. Possibly a walking tour would be the nicest thing; sort of with rucksack and a handkerchief full of wine and cheese. It was probably the octopus I ate that reduced me to my present condition.

Hubbell dear, how are you? I count on you for a long newsy letter telling me everything. How is your Boss? Have you had another raise? has he taken you to more gaudy leggy musicals? what do you hear from Tony? <u>is</u> there any chance of your coming to Europe?

You must come, you know. I can't tell you how at home I feel here, how welcomed, how wanted; in Greece, in Paris, everywhere one is greeted, by landscapes, by customs, by the whole spirit of life, the life one leads in these places. I left Tom and Jennifer planning to spend the next few months in St. Tropez, that amusing little Sodom on the Riviera. They are both so well, and so glowing, and so penniless; and foolish Timothy Hennessy with his collages . . . When I get out of the hospital (tomorrow or, at the latest Saturday) I shall spend a few quiet days in Athens, drink tea, sitting in gardens, looking at museums, meeting the writer chaps; then Kimon and I go on a truncated trip to the Cyclades, just to two or three islands, to give me a little inkling of the rest of Greece; finally, we return to Poros for the last week or so of my visit. No word yet from my father, but I plan to go to Italy around the middle of May; by mid-June Claude should have arrived, and we'll see what we'll see. I had a lovely letter from Ankey, concerning itself chiefly with telegrams and postcards she'd been receiving from Wayne. Now, what exactly is going on in my poor, bemused apartment? Do give my especial love to Sandra and Madelon and Fred and Bert. I brood over them frequently. I really can't begin to say how often I think of you, and wish for your good fortune, and wonder how you are getting along; poor struggling Atlanta boy, how could you have known what was to be demanded of you in the Wicked City? Bless you, and keep you (is somebody? oh, the lucky!) and make your face to shine. Write me do, and you'll have these foolish letters every now and then.

> Ever thine,
> James (no ink in pen)

Hubbell Pierce (d. 1980), a Southerner who performed Cole Porter songs in bars, and later made his own fabrics and wallpaper, including the "bat" wallpaper that Merrill designed for his living room in 1974. See Merrill's memorial poem "Hubbell Pierce" in *Collected Poems* (2001) and his memories of Pierce's singing in *A Different Person* (1993).
Tom Thomas Howkins.
Timothy Hennessy (b. 1925), American artist who trained in France.

To Claude Fredericks   GETTY
                                                    26 May 1950
                                                    Capri, Italy

And now only a few words before mailing this in time for it to greet
you when first you present yourself at 5 rue Christine. Today is cloudy
and I have little moments of anger with the people in Rome who are
not forwarding your last letters from New York. I told you, I think,
to use American Express (38 Piazza di Spagna) until around the 15th.
But I think, in view of the delays in forwarding, you should write
after the 9th of June to the Grand Hotel, Piazza Ognissanti, Flor-
ence; we expect to go there on the 11th, but it might have to be the
12th; anyhow you can beg them to hold the letters for my arrival. The
sun has come out suddenly, only to disappear behind the hotel. Five
more days in Capri. I think of an old Baedeker that belonged to Bill
Meredith's grandfather, which this gentleman had carried to Paris;
next to a description of something quite innocent like the Cafe de la
Paix or Rumpelmayer's he had pencilled in a spidery hand "ne jamais
encore." That goes for Capri. I had laid my wreath, as it were, on the
tomb of the Unknown Tourist . . .

Last night I dined alone with my father, and had one of those
conversations we occasionally contrive, he and I, in which what-
ever we may have had to drink has little or nothing to do with the
fountain of pure sentiment that springs between us. He has such
gentleness, such a—conscience, almost a consciousness, developed
through reflections virtually forced upon him by his illness. His
spiritual change in the past six years, or seven, since he fell ill, has
been extraordinary; I cannot think of him except in terms of that
movement towards patience and understanding and growing respon-
sibility for his own acts. We spoke of this, of the difficulty of such a
change, my own apprehension—is that what I mean? there seems to
be an unfortunate double entendre—comprehension and apprecia-
tion of it. He had described to me earlier a model for a war memorial
that is to be erected at Anzio, by the sculptor Manship (whom he
had met on the *Vulcania*), and how deeply he had been moved by it—
two young soldiers facing a woman who holds their dead comrade
in her arms; last night he said he had seen me as the dead soldier in
the woman's arms and, with tears in his eyes spoke of the loneliness

that brought us together, and of his intuition, somewhat belated, he knew, that, of his three children, it was I who had most needed him as a child—all somehow said and received, with many pauses but an utter absence, thank God, of that embarrassment, so much a part of the myth surrounding such conversations. Whatever his perceptions meant or mean to me I can't say; it is his having had them, and that they were of a certain quality, that touches me most of all and makes me happy, happy even to be his son. Granted, of course, that if we had been close when I was little, such feelings and such words would be unlikely now . . . perhaps . . . more or less unlikely. Yet it is for moments such as that, their value to me, their value to him— which is perhaps even greater—that we have asked one another for this month. I pause suddenly, wondering if what I say disturbs you. And pause again, wondering why I should think it might. And pause once more, a last time, to hold you close to me in such a quietness, as though I could hear nothing but your breathing, and could kiss your cheek by the slightest movement of my head, and to say over and over again, in all possible ways, I love you. I kiss you. I love you.

Jimmy

5 rue **Christine** Last address in Paris where Gertrude Stein and Alice B. Toklas lived together. Fredericks befriended Toklas while printing Stein's *Things as They Are* (1950) at the Banyan Press.
Manship Paul Manship (1885–1966), American sculptor.

To Claude Fredericks   GETTY
                                                                    10 June 1950
                                                                     Rome, Italy

Darling, darling,

Even the echo is gone today—Gone? at least referred to a different level of my mind, all that I have been brooding about—and the echo is gone. I feel well and happy and flowing, loosened and at ease, and shining with love. I could not feel as I do, without having had you to write to, without having you now, a little removed from this page, and although I know without having heard yet, your response to these last days, all that remains is the sorrow for the cost, the special cost of its having happened while we were apart, so that, faced with the incoherence of my letters, and only my letters, you had no other way of understanding or observing. What a vast injustice that is, that it could not have fallen, somehow, if it was to fall at all, upon us in our intimacy, in all love, without these delays, intervals between one day's letters and the next. Perhaps, of course, it would have happened so differently <u>between us</u>, without the violence of it, as something not to be apprehended as immediately, with such swift terrible and beautiful clarity. I cannot feel of no matter what experience, even a purely painful one, which this was <u>not</u>, that past a certain degree of intensity I can wish it changed in any of its parts. So that I can't truly regret, for myself, the shape this experience has taken—I can't honestly regret the solitude, the hospital, the slightest circumstance involved: <u>I</u> would not alter it. But I would alter it for you—I would have done anything in my power (there was nothing, of course, I <u>could</u> do) to have brought it differently to you, to have spared you not what was happening to me, but the means at my disposal to let you know about it. It is here that I resent the cost, and the <u>unnecessary</u> pain, that, for being at the mercy of letters, could not be avoided.

After lunch: Darling, suddenly I <u>know</u>, this minute, what I have been through. It has taken this long, and I know. I know at least the part of it that means something to me, and the meaning comes to me in a golden cloud; it is right, once again I feel, in this, the utter truth of my whole experience, and of this present intuition. There are parallel meanings: how can there help but be, in an experience as complex and shattering and miraculous. But this is what I come out with. This morning I had been to the Vatican museum for an hour, with the chauffeur, Marcello, who is truly charming and likeable. We were caught in the crowd filing in, and though I had wanted to look at Paintings, I was trapped by the current and the barricades and guided into room after room of Roman sculpture which I abhor per- haps more categorically than any other body of work of comparable quality, but it was amusing, especially the tourists who were there out of duty, plucking one another by the sleeve (Henry, we've <u>seen</u> this already), and there was a good bit too much of it, and too close together. But, following the wrong arrow, we arrived in the Egyptian rooms, low-ceilinged, a bit dusky—though I can't remember . . . First there were two mummies, lying in caskets, in the same vitrine (though a little card took pains, for some reason, to say it was mere accident that they should be so displayed, that they had been, as it were, nothing to one another back then, dans le temps). They were small, delicate, black, with teeth and rather unconvincing hair, an expression of great intensity on their faces, a crust of flesh over—whatever was beneath; the woman's hands, with fingernails, protruding simply from the folds of stained linen, her feet, too . . . It struck me then how much more, how infinitely more acceptable, as <u>representation</u> of the human spirit and condition, she was, this frail bundle, than the hysterical marbles, the smiling matrons, heroes—Venus, Diana, Hebe, she was all of these, and none. One could believe in such an image; one could kneel to it, fear it, crumple it with a blow . . . Then there were the caskets themselves, the granite tombs, that amazing curve, like a wave rising from the feet, about to break at the head—in one line to have described the splendor: and to know what lay <u>inside</u>: the painted caskets, repeating the same curve less abundantly: and inside those, the linen, and the body inside that, as though one could travel forever inward, to the first secret. Inside the wooden caskets were little paintings, so fresh, so extraordinarily moving: all saffron, green, red and white, blue—the little gods sitting, with animal heads, or human heads, the women sitting, the birds, a snake with a trumpet, the food to be eaten at the awakening, images as fresh and persistent as the colors that held them; and on the breast of the mummy a scarab, wings folded. Such a richness. And everything, in so many ways, <u>included</u>: not the transfiguration of flesh alone, but both death <u>and</u> its transfiguration, at once, forever. My love, do I need to say any more? I didn't see it <u>then</u>, I know it now, however. I feel there is nothing I do not know. One wonders always how to begin, which means where to begin. I begin there. It is a threshold. There we shall meet. Oh Claude—what this means—to know where to begin. And in such splendor. And of these past days I knew more than I needed to bring me to that threshold, how both parts of my experience are profoundly inextricable—not, as I <u>had</u> to feel yesterday, superficially so, when I was bewildered and could find no image, no image seemed possible, until I stumbled onto it this morning. And the vision of love came to me again in all its radiance, but coupled with it, the vision of the absence of love. I can't write you swiftly now, as I did before.

I get up and walk; I cannot contain my feeling. I tremble. What <u>can</u> life mean without death? or death without life? How is it possible to have a full, an overwhelming knowledge of love, as it came to me so powerfully, so beautifully on Wednesday, without having a qualitatively equal knowledge of—lovelessness, the utter evil, the total inadequacy, the most terrible counterpart of the most glorious love. How can a soul truly <u>be</u> damned until he has experienced paradise? Ah, the <u>easy</u> love, when it ends, ends in pain, in <u>disappointment</u>, a meaningless emotion, both of them. Granted it is possible for the love I speak of to end (I think it cannot), it would end in the extremes of its opposite, the ultimate destruction. And for it to end is not possible—by definition. For this love does not <u>contain</u> the evil [*in the margin:* the <u>easy</u> love <u>contains</u> its disappointment, I mean.], nor this contain the love. At terrible moments they approach one another: the love sees the evil, the evil sees the love—and they turn back shuddering with the sympathy felt, the horror endured, to what is as much as they can bear, themselves, the fresh, the eternal love, the fresh and eternal suffering . . . They are so strictly apart, so unaware, except at these moments, of one another, one can mercifully forget their relation—almost as mercifully, I mean, as it has been revealed to me. Without you, I mean, simply, having known you, the darkness would have engulfed me . . . <u>Now</u>, it cannot touch me, much as it may <u>concern</u> me—do you see? Darling, I know, I know all of this . . . I'm not a person who usually goes around talking about opposites; in as trivial a consideration as a "point of view," I find such a preoccupation uninteresting, meaningless. But this is different—At this moment I am truly exhausted, gasping on the edge of my vision; but I know it is right, I know it leaves nothing out that can approach it in significance, I am at peace, the relation has been made, my love is boundless. Now to my bath. What more can I say to you today? darling, darling,—without you, none of this. I am awake, I love you, my heart is a flower beneath your eye, I am coming to you, you to me—it is beyond beauty, virtue, truth: it is love, it is you.

Jimmy

the echo Reference unclear.
these last days Merrill was admitted to Salvator Mundi International Hospital for surgery to remove hemorrhoids under the care of Dr. Albert Simeons (1900–70), a

British endocrinologist and society doctor. During his stay Merrill was examined by Simeons and his junior colleague Thomas Detre (1924–2010), who recommended psychoanalysis. Simeons, and then Detre, would treat Merrill as an analysand.
Egyptian rooms The Gregorian Egyptian Museum in the Vatican.

To Hellen Ingram Merrill

WUSTL
29 June 1950
Cassis, France

Dearest Mama,

Your letter of last Sunday came this morning. I think I ought to scold you for having written so lightly about your courtship, for, until today, you have given me very little reason to consider seriously what is happening—I mean, I have had the impression that you were not taking it too seriously (although Lord knows he has been), so that it appeared unnecessary for me to say anything about it, more than I have up to now. First of all, I am delighted that you are taking it seriously, whatever your final decision; and I am predisposed to like the man who can awaken that seriousness in you, after the years in which you have been obliged, for one reason or another, to disclaim its possibility. Of course, there is so much I don't know, so much that I'm waiting to hear—and not from Carol, from you—that what I say today cannot carry too much weight. Yet that, in its own way, is right. If I felt that, in any but the most superficial sense, your decision were to rest on my approval, I should not be able to write you in this spirit. I feel with genuine pleasure that I have no responsibility in this matter, except the responsibility (which is no responsibility at all, but something deeper, a way of seeing things, a way of approaching you) to encourage in you whatever impulse you may feel toward happiness or love or life. It would seem to me that there is more than one occasion in a person's life when he (or in this instance, she) is ready for marriage. Perhaps the first of these comes in the flower of childhood, at that magical awakening of oneself to the knowledge that one is a child; the last might come when one is very old indeed, past all change and suffering but that of the flesh. What I'm saying is, I suppose, only this: that in all the stages of life, from childhood to second childhood, there are mirrored the movements of growth, maturity and decay which are usually recognized only in the curve of an entire life—the decay of childhood is the infancy of adolescence, which reaches its peculiar ripeness only to dwindle into a different maturity, at which stage the first marriage is most likely to occur. But it is not the first marriage (for one gives oneself completely to someone or something as a child); nor the last (for at successive maturities one gives oneself to other ideas, and the people or things that embody them). It seems to me you have reached such a maturity, one of many, now. Perhaps it has been slow in coming, and hindered by the disappointments of the last fifteen years; but there have been signs in you that point to independence (your new house) and unrest (your illness), and that may very well require, for their resolution, this act of marriage which, under any circumstance, is a beautiful act, and one that I would wish for you with my whole heart.

What your marriage would consist of, practically and emotionally, I do not know. I am glad not to know, for the time being, since that is entirely your affair, and whether you become an army wife or whether he sweeps you off to Johannesburg are such minor considerations, after all. I do not need to inquire, trusting your reasonableness, if he is a man you like, or (trusting your integrity) a man you love. The important thing is that you should be able to consider and, depending on your own considerations, take this step, make this gesture, <u>for yourself</u>, because it is something you want, and something you need. Equally important is that you should need it no more than you want it. But all this, again, is for you to answer.

If you have not done so already, do write me at length, about him, about the pros and cons. I want to know, and it may help you in your decision to express what you feel to me. I warn you, though, that I have already answered that letter, that <u>this</u> is the only answer you will have, essentially: that, in the light of what I've said, I'm "for" it, very much so; but, more, I'm "for" you. You have gone splendidly far on your own, I cannot imagine you will lack the courage to accept him. Or the courage to refuse him—but that depends on who he is and who you are, and is a courage that can proceed only from the first courage, the courage of acceptance. To be very bold, I want you to be happy, to love and be loved. I shan't, now, be surprised to hear you have said Yes; and I shall be very pleased, for you will have decided honestly and knowing, I believe, all you can know at such a moment.

I'm well + happy here. Claude comes tomorrow + we'll drive to Aix + Avignon, I think, for a day or so—leaving here July 4th or 5th—almost certain I'll see Carol—on the 8th or 9th.

> Love to everybody + to you.
> Jimmy

your courtship Hellen Merrill would soon marry William L. Plummer (1896–1969). Plummer had served with distinction as brigadier general in the U.S. Army Air Corps during World War II before going into business in Atlanta.
Claude comes tomorrow Fredericks and Merrill had been together since they met in Cassis on June 18. Merrill conceals the fact from his mother, presenting Fredericks simply as a friend he is traveling with.
Carol Carol Longone.

To Hellen Ingram Merrill

WUSTL
6 July 1950
Berne, Switzerland

Dear Mama and Mis' Annie,

A three or four day stopover in Berne is necessary, to get the visa for Austria. We arrived from Lausanne yesterday afternoon, and made our applications at once. Nothing to do but wait, write letters, explore this quite charming city, notably its bookstores, and drink beer. They speak chiefly German here, so that I can't get over the thought that I'm already in Austria or Germany, and that is amusing. We should be in Salzburg by Monday or Tuesday, however, and then to find a place pleasant enough to spend two months in will be my chief endeavor, along with getting seats for the music.

We reached Geneva, from Cassis, in about ten hours, quite easily; and went on to Lausanne the next day, stopping by Le Rosey to say hello to Robin. That was very brief, as he had just returned from the dentist in Lausanne, and was eager to play with his classmates; the school is very beautiful however, and I saw all I needed to, of it and of him. As soon as we reached Lausanne, I phoned Hans and stayed with him from four in the afternoon until nine that evening. He has leukemia, is extremely pale and weak; they are filling him with injections and he has a large transfusion every three days. Apparently he has been ill, on and off, quite seriously, for the past five months; though he has only been in Switzerland one week. His parents are there, and his sister, and Ray Daum. Although he knows he is very sick, I think he does not know <u>how</u> sick—his mother spoke very sombrely to me about it. He is blind in one eye (temporarily, he said), because a blood-vessel burst one day when he was trying to get out of bed. I don't need to say how terribly sad it struck me, particularly in view of his unflagging charm and gallant lively talk the whole time I was there. He gave me his book of poems, published last winter in Amsterdam, and showed me the very good reviews they had received. But he is too weak to write now. I stayed with him an hour or so the next morning, before moving on to Berne—yesterday, that was. According to him, he will stay in Switzerland until autumn, moving then to a warmer climate, perhaps the Italian lakes; by spring he hopes to be well enough to visit his beloved Morocco, though he does not expect to be entirely well for another year and a half. All this seems very dubious and heart-rending to me—but there is always a chance. If you would like to send him a little note, he is at the Clinique Cécil, Lausanne, Switzerland, and will be in that particular place, he expects, another month. Lodeizen is his last name. Having written this, I am almost too depressed to say anything more. I myself feel very well, as I have since Rome, and Claude is a perfect companion. The drive to Switzerland was through the most ravishing country I've ever seen; it is less beautiful in Switzerland, what I've seen of it, but mercifully cool in Berne and, Lord knows, beautiful enough. Hope all is well with you both. And my special love to Aunt Emma when she arrives, if she hasn't already by now. And to the "staff."

> As ever, all my love,
> Jimmy

Le Rosey Institut Le Rosey, a boarding school in Rolle, Switzerland.
Hans Hans Lodeizen. See Biographies.
Ray Daum Lodeizen's roommate at Amherst.
his book of poems Lodeizen's *Het Innerlijk Behang* (*The Inner Wallpaper*, 1949).

To Hans Lodeizen

WUSTL
26 July 1950
Salzburg, Austria

Dear Hans,

A lovely day of sunlight and cement being poured outside; everything in Salzburg is subjected now to repairs, the facades of hotels, fountains, sidewalks, the cathedral dome. I've had such a strange impression that tomorrow morning, when the Festival begins, everyone will wake up to see a shining + perfect city. The last nail driven, the flowerpots all set out. My first impression, in pouring rain, had been one of such embracing ugliness that it seemed folly to spend even the afternoon here. Then followed days of driving through handsome landscape, looking for a country *pensione* which, as I ought to have known, does not exist. Anyhow at last I am settled here in an apartment in the shadow of a castle +, all things considered, delighted to be where I am. The city has grown on me; in fact I quite love it—the bare, bare squares, the flat, flat facades, badly synchronized bells, leather shorts and foolish hats, all of it. I have seen Mozart's first violin, several locks of his hair, + the cottage transported from Vienna, in which he is said to have written the *Magic Flute*. I've gone four times to the marionette theatre, + thought of you there. You probably saw them in Holland: here they have done *Faust*, *Don Juan*, a terrifying *Rumpelstiltskin* + a curious little scene of the child Mozart playing before Marie-Therése + falling for Marie-Antoinette. At night the stars are small + hard; the river glistens, and a great searchlight from the Café Winkler on the hill illuminates, one by one, the upper portions of all the memorable buildings, suggesting thereby so powerfully + so mysteriously the 18th century—I can't think why. Perhaps in the 19th century all the buildings were lit from the ground. The town is crawling with opera singers + pale American girls with brand new scores. The actor who plays Jedermann is on crutches at the moment. Let us hope he recovers in time.

How are you? Do send me just a little card if you can, letting me know. I have thought so often of our hours together, hoping that you are steadily recovering your strength. It was such a great pleasure to see you and to recognize, even during such an illness, how constantly resourceful and lively you are in spirit. Thank you again + again, too, for your book of poems: I am so often moved to receive poems from friends, in letters, or in little books: it seems such an act of faith, a kind of gentle love, that has nothing to do with the poems themselves, but only that they should first have been written, then given. In time, of course, I shall learn Dutch! It touched me also, as you know, to hear from you of whatever part I played in some of the poems—to know that for you as well the strange energy we elicited from one another, always recognized, never articulated, had found an expression, in its own way.

My plans are still uncertain. One doesn't speak of the war, yet it colors so much. I continue to think of Italy in September, though I may head for Paris shortly after that—it's hard to tell. Presently I am working every morning, which delights me, and afternoons, with Claude Fredericks, who was in Lausanne with me, explore castles and hills and eat ices wherever we go.

Do give my best to your parents, to Ray, and your charming nurse— not the Picasso women. And let me hear a little from you, how you are, + where you expect to be going. I hope to see you again before long.

Yours, as ever,
Jim

26 July 1950 The day of Lodeizen's death.
the Festival The Salzburg Festival, an annual summer program of classical music and opera.
marionette theatre The Salzburg Marionette Theatre, established in 1913.
Jedermann Everyman, character in the play of that name (first performed in 1911) by Hugo von Hofmannsthal. The play has been performed at the Salzburg Festival annually since 1920.
whatever part I played in some of the poems Merrill is an important presence in Lodeizen's book of poems. Lodeizen wrote "Meeting the Merrills" about visiting Merrill and his mother, began one poem with a line by Merrill, and dedicated two poems to him.

To Mr. and Mrs. Lodeizen

WUSTL
4 August 1950
[Salzburg, Austria]

Dear Mr. & Mrs. Lodeizen,

It would be presumptuous to write you all that is in my heart at this moment. Next to your loss, and the world's loss, mine is very small. Yet I have felt no loss so deep as this one—of all my friends, none has ever embodied for me so profoundly as Hans the vigor and understanding essential to life. At moments when the world seemed, as it seems now, full of people dead or dying, dying within themselves the death of the spirit and the heart, it had always been of him that I thought, for there was none of this death in him even during the hours I spent with him in Lausanne, his charm and intellectual energy were constantly apparent, as though in his vision of life sickness had no natural place. Knowing what it means to those who knew him even as briefly as I, I can only imagine what his death must mean to you. My thoughts and deepest sympathy are with you and your family. May you face these days with his own beautiful courage.

Sincerely yours,
James Merrill

To Hellen Ingram Merrill

WUSTL
5 August 1950
Salzburg, Austria

Dear Mama, Mis' Annie and Aunt Emma,

A very very cold and wet few days these have been, the thermometer around 60 and two or three rainstorms a day. I bought an umbrella, and wear sweaters and things. About a week ago, Claude and I were dining at a fairly ritzy hotel, for Salzburg, when after a long exchange of glances and smiles with an elderly woman eating away at an omelet, we found ourselves in conversation with her. She looked like an old dancer, or soprano, with big frog's eyes, curly black hair and wonderful hands, but turned out to be a Mrs. Bohm from New York, a remnant of the Coronia's cruise. She had some extra tickets, and let us buy them, and we've been fairly thick with her ever since. At the concert the following night we met through her Frau Professor Wiesel, who seems to write up the festival for some obscure Austrian paper, and who, the following day, after sitting with us for hours in a cafe late at night, pointing out all the somewhat famous people, got us into the last half of the dress rehearsal of *Fidelio*. It was a great delight to hear Flagstad after so many years, but as her voice is not shown to its best advantage in that opera, and because the memory of it has grown so big and golden since I heard it last, it was something of a disappointment. Yesterday we went with Mrs. B. (after lunch on us, and tea on her) to a radio program, said by Mme. Wiesel to be a great treat, that was so terrible and so interminable, jazz band and arias accompanied by the piano and Oscar Karlweiss; we left because another strange little woman was getting us tickets for *Don Giovanni*, which was marvelous, and poor Mrs. Bohm stayed on, because she had been invited by one of the singers, a foolish Italian woman whom she met through La Wiesel, Emmy van Ghezzi—this is all simply to confuse you to the extent that I am confused, and it doesn't mean anything. Mrs. Bohm knows Carol, however, and they're all very sweet, which may be as much of a point as is necessary: a doctor's widow, a tiny little woman.

The music continues and is very fine. *The Magic Flute*, of which I may have written you, done in the old riding academy, a single set of plinths and sunbursts against the old arcades carved into the mossy walls; that has been the best thing so far. Welitsch and Furtwangler, the conductor, seem to have quarreled, so that her last and greatest aria in *Don Giovanni* was omitted, but otherwise it is the finest performance one could imagine. Sunday, tomorrow, if the rain lets up, I'm going to Hofmansthal's *Everyman* in the cathedral square; and later on in August comes the *Rape of Lucrece*, and *Capriccio*, Strauss' last opera which nobody has ever heard. Also the *Messiah*, Mozart's requiem, and plenty of chamber music. I've seen one or two people from Bard, but no one I enjoy seeing that I've known before, which is all right with me.

I don't quite know how to tell you that Hans died last week. I feel a tremendous sense of loss, and that the world as well has lost so much. I can't think of any of my friends who to such a degree was free of the traces of that interior death by which a man can truly perish. He was free of it, entirely, and it's a terrible thing to think of him as gone. I learned so much from him, about music, the world and myself. Mr. and Mrs. Lodeizen (I don't know his first name) live at Schouwweg 102, Wassenaar, Holland, if you want to write them. On the back is a poem about my visit to him in Lausanne.

It seems to me the only thing you can do is to write Daddy yourself, Mama, when you begin telling people; I think he should be among the first you tell; under the circumstances the only effect can be to flatter him, and he should be very touched by your gesture. As you recall, I had told him in Capri you had a beau, while reading an early letter about Billy, before I'd reached the part where you said not to mention it; and though I didn't mention it thereafter, it seemed to stick in his mind. You know how much he broods about the past and all the real or imaginary unkindnesses he is responsible for, and with this chance to write him a generous and happy note about yourself, and perhaps relieve him of some of these burdens, I don't think you'd want to pass it up.

Gas is rationed now here, but not seriously; all one has to do is go to the Travel Bureau and get coupons, as many as you want. There is no Spanish or Portuguese consul in Salzburg; or in Austria, I believe; the nearest is in Switzerland. In an emergency, I could drive to Switzerland, get my visas there and fly to Lisbon direct. I expect to be in Paris by the middle or end of October anyhow, and once there I'll feel entirely protected.

How long are you going to stay in Ponte Vedra in August? and let me know in time how to address you there.

How very nice of Billy to offer me the books. The ones I want are

Nims—*The Iron Pastoral*
Barker—*Calamiterror*
    "   *Lament and Terror*
Watkins—*Selected Poems*

Although I don't have the Fitzgerald early editions, I don't really want them; and think they should be given to someone who does. If he has no one in mind, perhaps you could get them for Freddy; it would be a lovely present, and I know he'd enjoy having them.

Received the airmail package; heavenly guava jelly; thanks ever so much.

Love to everyone, Ever,
Jimmy

THE COUNTRY OF A THOUSAND YEARS OF PEACE
   Here they all came to die,
   Fluent in death since childhood.
   But being a young man, never of their race,
   It was a madness he should lie
   Blind in one eye, and fed
   By the blood of a scrubbed face:
   It was a madness to look down
   On the toy city where
   The glittering neutrality
   Of clocks and chocolate and lake and cloud
   Made every morning somewhat
   Less than he could bear,
   And makes me cry aloud
   At the old masters of disease
   Who dangled close above him on a hair
   The name of Switzerland,
   The sword that, never falling, kills.
   There is a countryside his shut eye sees
   No man shall travel to until
   He takes the sword in his own hand.

Flagstad Kirsten Flagstad (1895–1962), Norwegian soprano.
Oscar Karlweiss Oskar Karlweis (1894–1956), Austrian actor.
Welitsch and Furtwangler Ljuba Welitsch (1913–96), Bulgarian soprano; Wilhelm Furtwängler (1886–1954), German conductor.
the *Rape of Lucrece* Benjamin Britten's *The Rape of Lucretia.*
Billy William Plummer.
Ponte Vedra Mis' Annie's home in Florida.
Nims . . . Watkins *The Iron Pastoral* (1947) by John Frederick Nims; *Calamiterror* (1937) and *Lament and Triumph* (1940) by George Barker; and Vernon Watkins's *Selected Poems* (1948).
Fitzgerald early editions Works by F. Scott Fitzgerald.
THE COUNTRY Draft of "The Country of a Thousand Years of Peace," title poem in the volume of the same name (1959).

To Herbert Weinstock

28 September 1950
Rome, Italy

Dear Mr. Weinstock,

Your letter of September 8th caught up with me yesterday afternoon in Rome, along with one from Mr. Ford. I'm delighted to hear that the proofs are on their way, and expect, as I wrote him yesterday, I shall have them from Paris in a few days. On October 9th I'm sailing from Naples to Majorca where, if I like it, I'll spend the winter, but I'll be in Rome until the 6th, and hope to get the proofs off to you before leaving Italy.

I imagine most of the people you would send proofs to are those I would suggest—Stevens, Ransom, Eliot, Marianne Moore, Blackmur, Tate, Elizabeth Bishop, Louise Bogan; and, less forcefully, Lowell, Eberhart, Berryman, etc. Perhaps William Empson. I can't think of any living novelists whose comment would seem relevant to me, but if you have an extra set I'd like Fred to have one, since in a way it is his book as well. Although I don't particularly care whom you ask for opinion, it is important to me whose opinion you use in connection with the poems, and I hope you will let me see the quotes, if not a proof of the jacket (assuming the jacket is their destination) before it is too late to alter it.

Even in Italy there is music. I've just come from Perugia where the Vienna Symphony and most of the Salzburg soloists did the B minor *Mass* and *Israel in Egypt*, very splendidly. I'm four and a half poems along on the next book, and hope to work more steadily in Majorca, where Fred writes he will come with a minimum of urging. Statesmen move so much more slowly than people that one keeps forgetting about them.

With very best wishes,
James Merrill

P.S. I just thought of Edith Sitwell.

Mr. Weinstock Herbert Weinstock (1905–71), American writer, primarily about classical music, and editor at Knopf.

Statesmen move so much more slowly Reference to escalation of the Korean War and the resulting global political crisis.

To Blanche Knopf

TEXAS
6 December 1950
Majorca, Spain

Dear Mrs. Knopf—

Everything seems to have moved so rapidly, and yesterday I received a copy of my book. I shan't even try to tell you what it means to me to see it printed and bound and on the verge of publication under so admirable an imprint as yours. But I wanted only to let you know how thoroughly I am delighted by every aspect of the book—it is all, and more than I could have hoped for; and how deeply I appreciate your faith in me.

With all good wishes,

Sincerely,
James Merrill

Blanche Knopf See note to letter of 22 June 1949.

To Theodore Baird

AMHERST
13 March [1951]
Mallorca, Spain

Dear Mr Baird,

I was extremely pleased to have your note. It means more, naturally, than all but one or two others, past or passing or to come. The Darwin poem was written not long after that course of which I still speak wonderingly, and has remained one of the few I feel proud of. No, I don't know Emma Darwin's letters, but shall remember to watch for a copy.

A few weeks ago I came across *The Nature of the Universe* by Hoyle, which seems to have made something of a splash. In its way, it is more of a rack for the imagination than *King Lear*. How distant, in the past years, the simple <u>machine</u> has become! no less mysterious perhaps, but almost as if Adams and Hart Crane were rushing from us as irrevocably as Hoyle's galaxies from one another. And the point at which the intellect boggles, or at least protests, has been a thousandfold extended. The book indicates for me, in passing, how richly you in particular have helped me read it, and others like it, as speaking directly to the sensibility, a problem set whose mere phrasing is the better part of its solution. I wonder often how your own book, also about the universe, is progressing.

Mallorca has been a quiet and lovely place these past months. I met briefly Robert Graves, full of his new book, a critical entangling of the Gospels, which ought to be quite amusing, though I'd be more interested to see a study of how (unless it is to be ignored) it will be assimilated by forward-looking clergymen the world over.

Tomorrow I leave for France—3 weeks among Romanesque buildings in the southwest, then to Paris. I've learned to work regularly, even though it's "Europe"—and find it hard to think of returning.

My best to Mrs Baird and to you.

Sincerely,
Jim Merrill

Hoyle Fred Hoyle (1915–2001), whose *Nature of the Universe* (1950) compiled a series of his broadcast lectures, was a proponent of the steady-state theory and of stellar nucleosynthesis.
Adams Henry Adams (1838–1918), American intellectual, author of the nine-volume *History of the United States* and the memoir *The Education of Henry Adams*.
your own book, also about the universe Never completed. At Amherst Merrill took Baird's course Science and Literature in the Nineteenth Century.
his new book Graves's *The Nazarene Gospel Restored* would be published in 1953.

To Hellen Ingram Plummer

Dear Mama—

Have had 2 nice letters from you in two days. I love the pictures taken at Miss Wick's—they are so good—you look so wonderfully well + girlish. Keep up the good work.

I had a wire from Betty, am expecting her now on the 4th. It's a pity she won't be here for the Caracalla opera, which opens the 8th (she leaves the 7th she said) but I'll do what I can. Probably if she wants to see Rome, she'd better stick with the tour most of the time, hectic as it is; but I imagine they let them breathe in the evening + I'll take her to the nice restaurants, as well as shops and perhaps places like the leisurely Palatine hill where—since there's not much to look at but Nature—the group probably wouldn't be going. I'm sorry she'll be here so short a time, but I'm looking enormously forward to meeting her. I'll have the gabardine ready. The best place for leather is Florence (I got a box for Billy there last week), but most of the things turn up in Roman shops.

Isn't it too bad about Daddy? You do know Mrs C, don't you? I didn't like her at all, probably it was mutual; and I don't think Doris would have in Barbados, if she hadn't been comparing her with Kinta. In fact, I think Doris has changed her opinion already.

Thank you for taking care of my apartment. I couldn't figure out—what letters + papers did you burn? There in the apartment or from 431? I hope the latter, as there are things I want to keep. Wayne is going to send for his trunk this fall.

About gloves: did you like the ones I sent Mis' Annie? Are they the kind you mean. If so, they came from Rome + aren't expensive.

Last week—I went to Florence a 2nd time (overnight) for the outdoor performance of Weber's Oberon—a beautiful opera—and marvelously put on, with bathing beauties, frogs croaking, moon rising—the works. Little Mrs Bohm has turned up in Rome (she turns up everywhere) and I've seen her a couple of times before she runs off to take the waters + revisit Salzburg. I like Rome so very much—though the heat has begun + there is more to come: far more,

I think, than Florence, and even a bit more than Paris, despite a certain deadness in the air. The treatments are going well: I had a brief respite from my strict diet, but it has begun again and the flesh is melting.

Am sending out 10 poems today, to various magazines; the first effort towards publication in well over a year. I suppose you saw the horrible review in *The New Yorker*—June 8, I believe. Louise Bogan wrote it; the pity is, I've always admired her work + judgment very much—although it was she who, at the 2nd Holyoke contest which Freddy won, said of him "This is the kind of talent that usually ends up in advertising." I've returned to the novel now—have reworked the first third of it—+ in another 2 weeks or so should embark upon Part II. The thing is, I know perfectly well the extent to which Miss Bogan is right; + would think she might have assumed I did. I don't mind as much for myself as I do for, say, Daddy who could so easily feel it's all a waste of time, what I'm doing.

So glad you saw Freddy. His book must be all but done by now. I received last week the Will Cuppy book you sent—mailed Mar 28. Thank you so much. I have found it extremely amusing—had never read his others.

Isn't it nice that Mis' A. is happy at the beach. What a terrible account of her maid's accident, coming on the heels of a letter from Doris describing her servants' misfortunes—I wonder if it isn't best really to do it all oneself . . .

Irma comes to Rome the 9th for a week, and in August Mina + Kimon, bound for America, will pass through. Kimon's Anthology is out, after so many years; with two of my poems at the end.

I'm reading Dante + have begun the Gibbon *Decline + Fall*—which seems appropriate; and the rest of the time working.

Much love to you + Mis Annie + Bill. I perfectly understand her not writing—glad only to think of her with you + eating as a growing girl should.

Ever,
Jimmy

Betty Beatrice Plummer (b. 1930), William Plummer's only daughter and Merrill's new stepsister.

too bad about Daddy Charles Merrill, married to Kinta Des Mares, had an affair with Lilian Coe, a married woman from Southampton, and was the subject of lively gossip.

what letters + papers did you burn? Merrill's mother destroyed letters from Kimon Friar, Frederick Buechner, and Claude Fredericks that she found in his New York apartment. When he confronted her about it, she told Merrill she was protecting him from vulnerability to blackmail.

The treatments Under the supervision of Dr. Simeons, Merrill was injected with the hormone hCG, touted to help him shed weight and cure him of his listlessness.

horrible review Louise Bogan called *First Poems* "impeccably written, but everything about them smells of the lamp; they are frigid and dry as diagrams."

the novel Merrill had begun a novel, parts of which were incorporated in *The Seraglio* (1957).

His book Buechner's novel *The Seasons' Difference* (1952), dedicated to Merrill.

To Hellen Ingram Plummer

WUSTL
31 August 1951
Rome, Italy

Dear Mama,

I was happy to have your letter this morning, after having had no letters from anybody for five days. Yes, the large tan box is for Bill; I got it in Florence while I was there for the opera. Glad you like the umbrella, and the rest. The gloves and boxes are all so cheap, I'm sure that all together they don't come to more than $15.

I may be crazy, I must be, but I'm nearly certain that I didn't hear of Pete Baldwin's death; and I'm <u>positive</u> I didn't hear about Frank Huckins—when did it happen? I'm terribly sorry and shocked on both accounts, knowing how much they meant to you, especially Frank. I knew Pete had been very ill, so that I'm less surprised by the news; but it is terrible, and I shall write them both, Pearl and Betty, within the next days. Perhaps I ought to wait to hear from you <u>when</u> Pete and Frank died, so that I can blame my own forgetfulness (which is probably at fault) rather than your not having told me. If the interval hasn't been too long, nothing at all needs to be said. I know how much you will miss those wonderful friends. But I never stop being glad that you have Bill, that he is there sharing your life, able to comfort you and accompany you through such sorrows, and the joys as well.

Two days ago Dr Simeons told me that <u>he</u> couldn't do anything for me. He realized (as I was beginning to) that he just wasn't the person, that we liked each other too well, that we were too "real" for one another to confront successfully these "subjective" problems. He felt the time had come for me to begin with his colleague, the young Hungarian Dr Detre—with whom Daddy talked last year. Actually, I'm enormously relieved. I hadn't known how to say it myself to him, but had felt a bit uncertain (which is fatal) about Simeons' qualifications in the field of psychoanalysis. I think he has had no professional experience as an analyst; and, while he knows an enormous amount about it, I'm sure the work will go more quickly and smoothly with a man who has made it his career. I like Detre very much, and know enough of him through Simeons, who admires him unreservedly, to feel the same faith in his ability. He has said this to me: that if within six months <u>in any case</u> there is not considerable improvement, either the patient cannot be helped, or there is a failure in the relation of patient to doctor. Furthermore he believes that any case (short of a psychotic, which I am not) can be cured within a year's time. All that can be, apparently, taken without question.

There is also the matter of money. Detre charges in proportion to what his patients can pay, in order that they feel the actual and symbolic value of what they are doing. He asks of me $30 an hour, half of which (if I can) I am to pay out of my present income, the rest to be supplemented by additional funds from my account. I've written Condon about this, adding that in case my account can't afford it, now would be the time to deduct from <u>your</u> monthly check the $250 (or is it $300) that was meant for New Canaan expenses. I know without your saying, as you have said as much before many times, that you will understand and gladly accept this possible alteration. I think, in view of gift taxes, now the house is sold, it probably ought to be made anyhow. Well, we'll see.

I'm sorry my letters seem so involved with this; I mean, I'm sorry there isn't more you can share with other people—I know that <u>you</u> want to hear about what's most important to me. But really, there is nothing else, at the moment, to write about. My life is absolutely empty, except for these hours; they are the only hours, I mean, that I "come alive." So that, while I wish I could write letters directed also to Miss Annie and Bill and Betty—for they are in my thoughts, of course—I simply can't at the moment. I've told everybody I'm going to tell—except for Freddy: that is, the Becks, Tony Harwood, Bill Meredith, Irma, and the family. Doris wrote me a lovely letter, as did Daddy and Mer; I don't think you need send me hers to you. Her headaches, I'm sure, go far beyond her worries about Daddy, though these may precipitate them at times. I've never thought of her, in the past five or six years, as happy; and should be overjoyed to see her so. But it's a rare thing. I'm glad that I don't expect to be happy, myself, as a result of analysis; only to be able to meet what comes my way, and turn outward those energies now consumed in defensiveness and fear of myself.

Much love,
Jimmy

Frank Huckins (1886–1951), Jacksonville friend of Helen Plummer's, known for crafting PT boats for the Navy during the Second World War.
Condon Lawrence Condon (1899–1973), Merrill's lawyer.
Mer Merrill's sister-in-law Mary Merrill.

To Hellen Ingram Plummer   WUSTL
                                          8 August 1952
                                          Rome, Italy

Dear Mama,

How long it's been I can't remember, since my last letter. Not much happens, I have stayed put in Rome and seen any number of people, including the Morris' and Bulpitts, and now Ben Brower and his wife, who are here for two weeks or so; a great pleasure to see them. Also, I am "sitting up" now, all through with the couch—so that the end is in sight, though probably not for another 6 or 8 weeks. My doctor is going to the seaside for ten days, during what corresponds to Bank Holiday, the last part of August, and I thought I would go to Greece with Robert Isaacson (who is back in Rome, as of a month or so) for that time. I really saw none of it before, and it seems a pity to miss it. We plan to sail from Brindisi on the 18th, arriving in Piraeus at dawn on the 20th; we would have four days in Athens, two days in Delphi, and a few days probably on Delos or Mykonos, one of the islands, depending on inter-island boat-schedules; I'll be back in Rome by the first or second of September. You can write me c/o the American Express in Athens up to Aug 25 or 26. I shall provide myself with relevant pills before leaving . . . People say the climate is much better than Rome at this time of year; well, I have no choice as to season.

Thank you for sending the photographs, also the ones of you and Bill and the house; the former I return along with Daddy's letter to you which I had mislaid.

And happy, happy birthday. It's reached the point now where no special occasion can make me wish to be back more sharply than I do on perfectly ordinary days. You know I would be with you if I could, and that you will be very much with me here, in my mind, on the 14th. What it must be hard for you to realize is the extent to which, and the way in which, you <u>have</u>, all this year, been in my thoughts, not as a mere cordial image, but ever sharpening into a focus I wouldn't have imagined possible. It is true that I feel more understanding of people in general, and that this understanding is indeed a matter of <u>feeling</u>, wonderfully free from judgments of any sort; this is particularly true of you and Daddy. I have the sense of knowing you absolutely as you are; this will have come, I suppose, through knowing myself—but it is not only in relation to myself that I feel it. The relation is of the first vividness, as of two buildings in a landscape—but I feel that I also know you, your strengths and weaknesses alike. The knowledge trembles on the edge of words, but defies time; it is simply <u>there</u>, and considering the twin gratifications of understanding and of being understood—the only time I broke into tears during my treatments was at the moment of his deepest perception of me; not that it was a painful thing, or even a surprising thing, but that he <u>saw</u> it and knew that it was the crucial thing—considering these, there is no gift I would rather offer you than this, my sense of knowing you. Only now does the absolute truth of the words break on me, about loving one's neighbor as oneself. If one doesn't love oneself, one can love nothing and nobody. Everything starts from that, and it isn't to be confused with vanity, or even self-respect. It is simply the seeing of one's life, the unhoped-for good and the trivial and the irremediable bad, and being able to say of the past that is all right, that it can't be helped, that there is nothing to be made of it but the best. Once that vision is reached—and I reach it only at moments, one <u>can</u> only reach such things at moments, but they make all the difference—it opens up and extends to all of the people who have been important to me, who are after all the only ones to bring up the question of loving; and once again, it's all right, nothing's to be made of it but the best. I know you have feared, as I have myself, what my treatments might have produced along these lines—that I might have been left with a sense of bitterness towards the people and circumstances that have made me what I am. That has come at times, but I think it is gone forever now. The difference is simply in seeing; the world and other people have become so much realer for me, there isn't room for narrowness in my view of them; I don't feel like blaming them any more than I want their flattery—all this has become superfluous, and it's all right, it's all right.

Perhaps I overstep my capacities a little; so much of this has come this evening, in the course of writing this letter; and it pleases me so to see what is coming out of me that it's maybe put a bit too positively and too well to be, in itself, my actual state of mind in the long run; but that's no matter, it's true enough.

Just now, I feel that something is missing in this letter, and I know what it is. I want to be writing to you and Daddy together. Would it seem a curious request, my asking you to send it on to him? It's so much for you both, and for nobody else; and, after all, I am the child you made and raised between you, and I love you both very much—

Jimmy

Ben Brower and his wife Reuben and Helen Brower. Brower (1908–75), professor at Amherst and later Harvard, a literary critic who advocated the practice of "slow reading," was the advisor for Merrill's undergraduate thesis on Proust.
Robert Isaacson (1927–98), an American studying Italian painting in Rome who was first Fredericks's and then Merrill's lover. On his return to the United States, he became an art dealer in New York, and eventually an influential collector of nineteenth-century academic French painting.

To Kimon Friar   WUSTL
                                              6 November 1952
                                              London, England

Dear Kimon,

Mercy me. I don't know what to say. My teeth were chattering after
reading your letter. The whole business terrifies me, and of course
tremendously pleases me as well. But I don't know what to say. This at
least is what I shall do: write Shapiro to express pleasure and interest,
and a desire to know what would be expected of me. I imagine I can
write him a decent letter, but, between ourselves, what keeps com-
ing up before me is that in my own eyes I am a fraud and a fool and
only under the falsest of false pretenses could anybody ever dream
of offering me such a thing. When I think it over nothing comes to
my mind but a stream of sad half-truths gleaned from my hours on
the couch. I'm filled with somewhat the same dismay one might feel
upon having struck one's enemy and being in return kissed by him. I
mean that the dear good gullible world, if only in the person of Karl
Shapiro, has been taken in by me; has been led to suppose much that
simply doesn't at the moment ring true to my own ears—that I am in
any way competent to judge, to be of service, even to be deeply <u>inter-
ested</u>. That must be one of the prime torments of the smiling villain,
to have worthy motives attributed to him. Dear Kimon, I know very
well what I'm saying and how pointless it is; and I'm sensible enough
not to let it color my judgment in this matter. My judgment is, as far
as I can foresee, that I would like to accept the position, depend-
ing on what my duties would be; that I would neither be particularly
good nor particularly bad as Advisory Editor, but that in time the
magazine and I might do a little bit for one another.

I take these other considerations into account. By the time I
would begin this work there will, I trust, have been changes. I shall
feel more assurance, perhaps even know enough of myself to set
forth my opinions, make coherent use of them, without, that is, the
sheer embarrassment of doing so which may or may not have elicited
my first paragraph. Also, for the time of my analysis, I cannot really
expect to get much of my own work done. This state of affairs may
change within the month, but I can't count on it and it's perhaps best

to have something else to turn to, to remind me that I'm, along with everything else, a person involved with literature. So.

I should have written you Saturday when your letter came, to convey some of the pleasure I felt, and particularly at having it come from <u>you</u>, the proposal—before it became all complicated by these fears and reflections. Also the prize, of which I hadn't heard; that pleases me too, so I guess I'm not as jaded as I might be.

Oh my oh my, the weight of the world. Had a letter from Mr Gauld saying how charming they think you are, both of you.

Wayne asks a favor of you: there is, or used to be, on 35th St, towards 2nd ave, on the same side of the street as 231, a small cleaning and pressing establishment. He left there, last spring, a navy blue suit, and wonders if you would be good enough to redeem it for him, before they give up and sell it. Probably it is under his name, Kerwood; but might be under mine. He will reimburse you, and greatly appreciate your trouble. He also wants me to remind you of his parents' address in Washington, 3037 Dumbarton Ave, NW; in case you and Mina go there, and hopes you will have a chance to tell them how well he looked in September. About the car: you may take it out of storage, as I said, and ask Tony Meyer to pay the storage bill. I don't however think I can ask Meyer to pay for the parking lot in New York; that is a monthly affair, and under the circumstances I think he would feel it strange. For <u>him</u>, I don't care; but it might easily be heard of by my father or brother-in-law, I mean, and <u>they</u> would think it very strange indeed. If you are agreeable, it occurs to me to give you and Mina, as a birthday-Christmas gift, the six-months cost of the parking lot; not a very glamorous present, but it depends what use you make of it! Let me know . . .

What ship did you put my bedding on? I can't understand what has kept it from arriving by now; in five days I must give up my sheets, borrowed from via Gregoriana, and it would be absurd <u>both</u> to buy and have sent such things. Do write me the name of the ship and when it sailed from NY. Perhaps you <u>didn't</u> put them on a ship (you appeared not to have read my letter too carefully)—in which case there's a <u>chance</u> they will arrive before Christmas . . .

My mother received the apology, and is happy to have it. She arrives in Rome Nov. 29.

Oooooohhhhhh dear. You ask me to write more fully about myself and Claude. I simply can't; and I'm certain you understand that. We are, yes, living apart. I am lonely and bored, and don't see many people, but I guess things are going well. Claude moves in a few days into a big room, bath and kitchen in the house right next to the Keats house. I've not seen it, but it sounds very nice.

Love to both of you, and, somewhat in advance, a warm kiss for your birthday.

Ever,
Jimmy

The whole business The poet Karl Shapiro, editor of *Poetry* (1950–55), offered Merrill a job as an advisory editor for the magazine.
Also the prize Merrill won the Harriet Monroe Prize from *Poetry* magazine.
the Keats house The house, near the Spanish Steps, where Keats died, now a museum.
both of you Friar and Mina Diamantopoulos, who had married, lived in Merrill's New York apartment while he remained in Rome.

To Marilyn Lavin
LAVIN
8 December 1952
Aboard R.M.S. Queen Elizabeth

Dear Marilyn—

I am here [X *drawn from boat image on letterhead to this place in text*]— listening to an organ concert, but apart from that calm + relieved and still a bit shocked, if I may say so, by the loveliness of your letter. Not that it was so unexpected (though it <u>was</u>)—or that one couldn't have looked for such a letter from you (for one <u>could</u>); but I have spent these last weeks in such a rush, seeing new faces + buying old things, + never for an instant managing to face what I was doing, masking it in trivial excitements, when really it is as you say a grave + curious fact, an action of the sort that stands in relation to our other actions as a branch to a leaf. Your letter, more than any receding shore, leaves me in an air of sweetness, a kind of astonished calm, for no reason that I could name unless it is that the very words you use—"the very air we exhaled + left there"—"golden days"—"no possibility of loss" are words that might have figured, + perhaps did, in the poems I wrote when I was eighteen, at the time which was in itself a kind of Golden Age, the time we lived before caring about caution, one's breast on a thorn, and <u>all</u> lived in the imagination, there being no other visible road. These were not, to be sure, poems composed for publication. Their recollection is very beautiful to me, and enhanced by the growing sense that I must reassume what is left, older, less golden, of that sensibility. It struck me in London, seeing the Pieros + hearing the *Magic Flute*, all in one day. These things, it seemed to me, <u>had</u> the quality I wanted—that extraordinary honesty, putting away question of means, or technique, entirely out of mind. One could have made them oneself, granted genius. Nothing was hidden. Time had made the finished landscape show through the angel's wing—and the air of something a bit gaudy, a bit unconcerned + simple, appeared, infinitely touching. *Don Giovanni* is the Cellini cup, next to the *Magic Flute*, which is a shape of glass, pure, of varying thicknesses with tiny bubbles.

Hubbell saw me off at Waterloo Station. I loved London, I felt at home, comprehended. There was a severe fog, we had to walk everywhere, peering into it. It was very beautiful. The rooms weren't as cold, or the food as poor, as we've all been led to expect.

Well, I had only to say what perhaps I've said. I'll communicate from N.Y.

Love
Jimmy.

Marilyn Lavin Marilyn Aronberg (b. 1925) befriended Merrill while doing research for her PhD in art history in Italy. She married the art historian Irving Lavin (b. 1927). Both Lavins became distinguished scholars of Italian art. She is the model for Jane in *The Seraglio*.
the Pieros Masterpieces by Piero della Francesca, in the National Gallery, London, include *The Baptism of Christ*, *The Nativity*, and *Saint Michael*.
Cellini cup An elaborately decorated gold and enamel cup believed to be made by Benvenuto Cellini, later identified as a forgery; also called the Rospigliosi Cup.
a severe fog Air pollution, aggravated by cold weather, produced a health emergency in London in December 1952. Between 4,000 and 6,000 deaths were later attributed to the event.

To Doris Magowan   AMHERST
                                              12 January 1953
                                           St. Thomas, Barbados

Dear Doris,

Daddy has such trouble using his eyes that he has asked me to write to you, as I had planned myself to do in any event, to give you the news. I think his sight is improving, but it seems that after three or four minutes of reading or writing, what he's looking at tends to blur. However, there's a bridge game scheduled for Wednesday, so it isn't as bad as it sounds. As to how he is otherwise, it's never easy to say. I think he looks very well; I'd never imagine that two and a half years have passed since my last glimpse of him; in conversation he is as charming and quick as ever, if not moreso; he is furthermore blessed with two delightful nurses, and of the few people he sees regularly, nearly all of them seem to him to give him considerable pleasure. The exception is perhaps Mrs C, for whom his feelings have somewhat diminished—and it's just that, the diminishing, the sense that he may be withdrawing, neglecting, offending, that makes him uncomfortable. I've seen the Coes twice, once for lunch with Daddy and for lunch alone yesterday. Lady Saint, on the other hand, I've seen every day since my arrival, and I like her enormously; I think she's a very unusual woman who has a genuine liking and respect for Daddy. As I told you I had my doubts as to whether [or] not I would like her, but I do with all my heart; she is lovely with him and has been very kind to me. I fancy she feels the lack of widespread charm and intelligence, which seems to be a characteristic of most island life, so that if she is his oasis, he is certainly hers. We had a very nice dinner with the Saints last night, further ornamented by two elderly women, Lady Hudson and Miss Ibbertson, the former quite crippled but "wonderful," as they say, in spite of it; the latter a welfare worker, very imposing and very witty. Tonight a dinner at Canefield: the Coes, two unattached young women, an American from the Consulate (?) here and her niece, and Mr and Mrs Wolff (she is a distant cousin of Freddy Buechner, whom I've known somewhat and very much liked for years; she is here with her new husband and had seen my name in the paper).

It all sounds very active, I suppose, but we're both taking things very easy. Daddy usually sleeps after breakfast, and always in the afternoon; he goes upstairs by 10:30 at the latest. This house is so beautiful and homelike, as you know—I can't imagine a nicer place for him to be,

I loved seeing you and Bobby and the boys, however briefly. How nice it will be once again to live in the same city with you! We must arrange a viewing of the apartment as soon as I return. Your Christmas presents are so lovely—I long to set them out among my treasures when I get back, the leaf-shaped dish (I <u>won't</u> call it an ash-tray) on my Chinese table, the wonderful inkwell down in the study, and the crystal figure I don't know where, but in some place of special prominence; I love them all. None of my family but you would I trust to choose such things for me.

I think Daddy will want to add a postscript to this. Much much love to all of you. You looked so <u>well</u>, I thought, even after the holidays; are you really sure that Europe does you good? You and Bobby both seemed so much more cheerful and relaxed than in Rome. I know I feel it for myself, that foreign parts make me nervous in a number of ways. Well, who knows. Again love,

Jimmy

Dearest Darling Doris:

Do not worry about my eyes. I had a slight stroke, but it did not cripple me and Dr. Bayley says no damage was done. Canefield is lovelier than ever—more so, perhaps, because Jimmy is here. We both wish that the Magoogles were with us. All love to you and yours,

Daddy

Mrs C Lilian Coe.
Lady Saint Lady Constance Saint, model for Lady Constance Good in *The Seraglio* (1957).
Canefield Charles Merrill's home in Barbados, a plantation house on the highest point of the island.

To Claude Fredericks

GETTY
[March 1953]
New York, NY

Dear Claude,

Your two letters are here, and I want to write you in a way I've writ-
ten nobody in so long, about a strange feeling I have, almost a strange
experience. There are so many other things to say, which at least I
can say briefly. (I will keep the crates for you; only one is huge. The
reading went very well, all <u>my</u> friends said I was the best, and I really
enjoyed it after it got going. Today—horror—I have to meet Oscar
Williams for lunch at something called The Excellent Restaurant on
5th Ave between 42 and 43. I had a letter from Detre, he arrives in
NY on May 14th, and has given as a temporary address the building
where the Fords live which, as you may recall, is flanked by a half-
dozen Hungarian restaurants, reading rooms, whatnot.) There.

I don't know quite how to describe this thing, but I feel it's very
important in a number of ways. I want to write some poems about it;
here is a draft of one of them, which might be the last in the group:

> Hans there are moments when the whole mind
> Resolves into a pair of brimming eyes, or lips
> Parted to drink from the deep spring of your death
> A freshness they do not yet need to understand.
> These are the moments, if ever, an angel steps
> Into the mind, as kings into the dress
> Of some poor goatherd for their acts of charity.
> There are moments when speech is but a mouth pressed
> Lightly and humbly against the angel's hand.

I suppose it is no new experience, for I have mourned him in one
way or another ever since he died; yet it seems to me I am feeling it
in a different way, and the feeling is so pure and so illuminating. It
began on my return from Atlanta when I found waiting for me a new
edition of his book, greatly enlarged, with a letter from his father say-
ing that whereas a book of verse in Holland usually was issued in an
edition of 500 copies, Hans' book (this new one) had already sold

1500 out of the edition of 2000. I was reading my mail and my grand-mother was watching television and I began crying and couldn't stop and threw myself crying into her arms, poor sweet surprised old lady. What is strange is that really it hasn't left me, I haven't lived it down. One can say, to be sure, many things: that if I had ever gone to bed with him I wouldn't feel this way; or wouldn't hold on to the feel-ing were it not for the words and images that calls from me. And yet these are the devil's excuses, I think. He is so alive for me, <u>in</u> me, I cannot distinguish his presence in my heart from a positive virtue, almost a physical characteristic that I have assumed. I dreamed the other night I was walking with a woman who had known him, and whose own son had died. She asked me about him and I said, Didn't you know, he died also. Then I said, Now I will show you the house we built together; and turning down the road came to a kind of cot-tage in the forest. I showed her my bedroom, with a view of trees and mountains, and then his bedroom lined with books mostly sealed up with corrugated paper, no windows, and a large bed in the center of the room, surrounded by a black balustrade. I told my dream to Robert when I woke. He said that in dreaming of another's death one is really dreaming of one's own and that I, as he has often before told me, was in love with death. Why am I writing all this to you? It puzzles me and I feel such a sadness and such a happiness. There is a sense whereby his death <u>is</u> my life. Do you remember the Apollinaire poem?

> Car il y a-t-il rien qui vous élève
> Comme d'avoir aimé un mort ou une morte
> On devient si pur qu'on en arrive
> Dans les glaciers de la mémoire
> A se confondre avec le souvenir
> On est fortifié pour la vie
> Et l'on n'a plus besoin de personne

It must be wrong to write in this way; I can imagine your reac-tion as ambivalent as my own feeling. I suppose I really need Detre now; it echoes so in so many directions, and I am reluctant to speak much to Robert about it. Well it isn't more than I can bear; indeed

I rejoice to bear it, but I am bewildered. I feel—well. Ought that to be strange? Enough, enough. I listen to *Die Schöne Müllerin* day and night.

Wire me if you can know in advance what day you'll arrive, and I'll have a dinner cooking for you. Otherwise I'll simply wait.

Thank you for trying to reach me on March 4; I had to meet my great-aunt at Penn Station, then have lunch with her and my grandmother and it took HOURS.

Love,
Jimmy

Oscar Williams Pen name of Oscar Kaplan (1900–64), an American poet and the editor of a popular anthology, *A Little Treasury of Modern Poetry, English and American* (1947).
Hans there are moments "A Dedication," final poem in Merrill's *The Country of a Thousand Years of Peace* (1959).
a new edition of his book Lodeizen's *Het innerlijk behang* was republished with additional poems in 1952.
Robert Robert Isaacson.
the Apollinaire poem The lines in the conclusion of "La Maison des morts" in *Alcools* (1913): Because nothing lifts you up / Like having loved a dead man or woman / Each becomes so pure in arriving there / In the glaciers of memory / To be confused with recollection / One is fortified for life / And has no more need of anyone.
Die Schöne Müllerin (The Beautiful Miller's Daughter), a song cycle by Franz Schubert.

To David Jackson   POSTCARD | WUSTL
Tuesday, 10 June 1953
[New York, NY]

Old Dave! Such a hot day. I wish I <u>had</u> met an iceberg, like the nice man did. When are you coming back??? I've planned a little evening.

J.

David Jackson See Biographies.
met an iceberg The front pictures a young man and a young woman in old-fashioned dress, gazing intently at each other. Above the couple is the caption: "I MET AN ICEBERG IN" Merrill wrote "Fire Island!" He and Jackson had spent a day at the beach there. This is the first piece of correspondence between them.

To David Jackson

WUSTL
[June 1953]
Southampton, NY

Dear Uncle David:

How shall I begin to describe the many mishaps and Adventures that befell me since Parting with you this afternoon?! Well, first I got a ride from three boys—only about 2 miles, but they told me I had beter get a good ride before dark Fell, or I wd. be out of luck. Then a Navy man picked me up (oh <u>no</u>, before that an old man wanted me to get into his car, but I saw the 1/2 empty wisky bottle on the seat next to him and remembered what you had said about Old Men and, as he wasnt going very far anyhow, I thanked him politely and said I would try to get a beter ride). Then the navy Man took me to Mystic Acres or some such place and then the two boys who were out "crusing" took me to Moriches and then a nice man in a big car full of his Children and Religious literature took me to Westhampton. By then it was nearly dark. I was tired and Hungary. So there I was at a place [called] Harry's Diner between Westhampton and Quogue ("the Palm Beach of Long Island") and I telephoned for a taxy which brought me home about 9:45. Daddy met me at the door. [*In the margin next to an ink stain*: excuse spot] The buxum nurses all smiling and Leroy made me a tall cold drink of something, he said it was Skotch. And now I have eaten and gone to my room. Daddy and I had a good lagh over what to call his new house. I suggested Dunwedden and he had to lagh. The sea is very loud out the window. It is cold too and I am sorry you arent here with me. We could keep each other warm and happy. I didn't get mutch of a chance to tell you how I did enjoy the weekend with you dear Unc. David. I love you very mutch and hope you recipprocate. I will [ink stain] oh dear another spot—see you Wednesday at 10th Str. Until then keep well take care of your Burn and believe me ever yr. affectu [crossed out] loving nefew

Jamie

Sun. P.M. (11:45 I said I wd go right to sleep but wanted to send you a Line.)

Morning now: I have slept 10 hours, the day is fine, mangoes are promised me. I love you David. These have been strange and wonderful days. It is nearly Wednesday, or so it seems. I love you!

Dear Uncle David Merrill assumes a boy's voice and writes with a childlike looping script. In the postscript, "Morning now . . . ," his adult hand and voice return.
Mystic Acres Like Moriches, Westhampton, and Quogue, Mystic is a town on the south shore of Long Island.
Dunweddin The name refers to Charles Merrill's third and final divorce and pokes fun at his admiration for the British aristocracy and their stately homes.

To David Jackson
WUSTL
[June 1953]
Southampton, NY

Dream. Big house.

No; before then an enchanting area of N.Y. looking like Paris, Venice, all places at once. Going up in an elevator. Vaguely sexual events taking place in the elevator.

[Then I woke + phoned Suzel. She is coming. Ring lost.]

Big house. I am at a strange age. Very young but given responsibility. With me—or to me rather—comes a friend from whom I've been separated. We embrace under the surveillance of a woman who disappears. We play delightedly together. We run upstairs (after talking about sex) to inspect each other's genitals. Impossible to remember now who had the larger penis of the two <u>visible</u> children—I mean I don't know which was myself—one of them was all admiration, the other a trifle condescending.

Enter the mother suddenly. Racing for shelter. I hide in a closet.

One knows that she loves the friend. That all this would be all right <u>if</u> we were wearing pyjamas. But we aren't. I am in pants. I am trying to conceal 5 neckties—two of them identical—which also give me away.

I am grown up almost by now. We express antagonism. I am wearing evening clothes, all but the tail coat. The scene rises in tension. She begs me not to do something—perhaps simply <u>leave</u>—I beg her not to do something. She finally threatens—<u>if</u> you leave I will break this—a crystal compote whose base she puts at me soon filled with water—whose top she puts at another to prevent me.

At last she smashes it. I in great anger cry that does it! + mean to destroy something of hers. Then a <u>great</u> tenderness. Weeping we embrace. I say I can't help what I must do—she says I know I know. Off I go.

[signature missing]

To David Jackson

WUSTL
[Fall 1953]
[St. Louis, MO]

Dear friend:

Two good pages done today, and now I must upstairs, having seen little enough of anybody. It <u>is</u>, after all, a great pleasure to be here. What I hate is simply traveling, usually when I arrive there's a minimum of tension; one simply, for a while, basks in the thought of the traveling being at an end. But I miss you, I keep thinking you could so easily be here; not perhaps in any practical way, but in my imagination, since you are <u>there</u>, you could be here as well, effortlessly. N'est-ce pas que la machine a ecrire de ma niece est admirable? No, I cannot write the letter now, I have worked four hours, and I shall put it off until my mind is clearer.

12:45 now, my teeth brushed and head swimming. A really <u>nice</u> evening with two couples from the school including a young man named John Hunt who had been in my class at Lawrenceville (and whom, for purely euphonic reasons, everybody used to call Mike). He has written a novel, has an agent in NY, and an interested reader at Harcourt, the same old story; but very, unlike most of the classmates I can call to mind, pleasant and <u>truthful</u>. Roast beef, wine, ice-cream, cognac. I feel so much "from the East," a bit simpering and false, but <u>that</u>, out here, doesn't seem too much to matter. It <u>does</u> matter though, to me. There are times, as now, when I <u>do</u> so see myself as weird, difficult, arbitrary, something of the crotchety bachelor—see myself so without, I mean, rejoicing in the vista—and on the other hand seeing <u>you</u> as—without meaning in any sense to complain; rather, indeed, to wonder and hope in time to emulate—easy and fine an Example to live <u>with</u>, being (I fancy) reasonable and thoughtful and inspiring in the very respects that I am <u>not</u>. . . . And seeing this much, I can't but feel that I must, to you, appear to be asking prodigious things, straining your patience, so much <u>more</u> than your patience. Is it possible to explain now one of the things that is behind my saying this? I doubt that it is possible, or even perhaps desirable, but having said this much I can't <u>not</u> say it, that on finding your letter, crumpled and unfinished, to Sewelly, and thinking somehow it was a forgotten or unread letter from Freddy to me (because we both know a Debby who says, or might say, Hi!) I looked blankly at it, trying to remember, and came upon the words "moral and emotional pot" and their context—and realized then who had written them and in respect to what—Well, what I mean is probably something like what I tried one night to say to you in Southampton, that I <u>do</u> understand the strain, that I <u>know</u> I can't be "everything" to you, that indeed I should brood if that were so; but, beyond all this, my dear David,—and can you understand how very much I feel for you at this precise moment?—(I don't mean to keep putting exclamations, it's just the way this machine works)—beyond all this, that I, for myself, don't want you to feel you must <u>hide</u> the strain from me, conceal a sense of lost bearings, bewilderment, even perhaps shame. A voice in me sounds now saying that it is a cleverness in me, that I am striking just the note that will leave you all the more defenseless. But another voice, less of a reflex than the first, can only repeat what I've said. And this furthermore: that <u>whatever</u> relation we may in time find ourselves in, together, will be more beautiful and real to me; that perhaps what is between us now is no more than some marvelous baroque foreground, past which the essential relation, that in which <u>you</u> will not be called on to feel tension and uncertainty, and <u>I</u> will not be called on to write such words as these, will in time be discerned. All I'm saying may be that cheapest of consolations, after all, that "we shall always at least be friends"; but I've said it often enough and dishonestly enough in the past to know that I mean it as I've never meant it before, absolutely and joy-fully without for a moment wishing to hurry past any of the (as they may appear then) intermediate stages.

Morning now, toothache, headache, long coffeehour with Mary, the birds twittering, the day bright and chill. I have reread last night's page and begin wondering what it will mean to you, once past the annoyance you must feel at my having, as it now appears, pried. But I have pride as well, and what comes to me now to ask you is: mightn't it somehow be possible, and what would it involve? for us to keep what we have without its being such a pot, as you put it? It isn't so for me, which accounts for my pride . . . but for you I believe the question isn't hastily to be answered, if at all. Oh why must the mails be asked to bear such weights? I'm not in any sense dismayed or depressed, you mustn't read this thinking I am or was; I feel so full of love and so happy in the knowledge of what I feel, of what you are, of what we are and its being, I trust, strong and flexible enough, a joy forever . . .

Jamie

N'est-ce pas . . . admirable Isn't my niece's, i.e., Catherine Merrill's, typewriter admirable? Merrill was visiting his brother, Charles, and his family in St. Louis, where Charles had founded the Thomas Jefferson School.
John Hunt John Clinton Hunt (b. 1925), on the faculty of the Thomas Jefferson School, later worked for the Congress for Cultural Freedom, and became a publisher in England.
Sewelly Doris Sewell (1925–2012), a graphic artist, met David Jackson when they were students at UCLA. They married in 1947, and never divorced. Sewelly moved to New York City, then Mystic, Connecticut, and remained close friends with Jackson and Merrill throughout their lives.

To David Jackson

WUSTL
[Fall 1953]
[Ponte Vedra, Florida]

David, David,

The wind has changed, the sun is out and in it I walked a mile or so on the wide white empty beach, where little hills of cream-colored foam are clustered and reflected and fly away at a kick, picking up shells, only the beautiful ruined ones, pocked and polished, that give away any number of formal secrets; the water is warm but treacherous, a man drowned yesterday, so I did little but wet myself in the shallows—great arms of water, my grandmother calls them sea-pussies, are apt to reach in and spirit one away. All this before lunch, and then your letter came, just as we were sitting down to our artichokes and mangoes, and it stayed unread throughout that and a bit of movie-making afterwards, until I could take it down to the water to read. It made me very happy—and yet I was dismayed that my own letter, the one from St Louis, should have weighed so heavily upon you. I hadn't felt, while writing it, that I was asking for reassurances. I wanted to say that—no matter how special the circumstances that led to your letter to Sewelly—I could understand how you felt at that moment; wanted particularly to confess to you that I <u>had</u> come upon your expression of uncertainty, and to tell you, perhaps foolishly, that it is something you needn't <u>not</u> share with me, since even before that I had tried to show you that I could imagine it to be there . . . But I think you see all of this; what you might see imperfectly, judging from your letter today, is what I meant about always "being friends." I didn't say that out of pride, or because I was hurt; I meant a kind of friendship that could only pragmatically (if that's the word) be distinguished from loving . . . Is it worth the risk of <u>more</u> ambiguity, to seek to explain it now? Yes, I suppose it is, yes. I mean, <u>does</u> it go without saying that most likely we haven't yet reached the point in our lives (if indeed we ever do) when we shall be fairly sure of what we want or expect from the world and the people about us? Each of us is so aware of the Difficulties—there is an easier way of saying what I meant. I meant that I could never believe, with Claude or Robert, that the relationship, if ever altered, would turn into a friendship. They meant very much to me, but they meant one thing only, and I called it love. You mean so many things to me, every day with you has a different shape, this is all far beyond my power of suggestion; I think of some great warm creature, amphibious surely, that, losing some part of itself in an encounter, would promptly, witlessly, inevitably grow it back. I meant to say that we possess such resources—! that I can't imagine anything <u>truly</u> harming us, destroying the <u>essential</u> charm, the secret of the relation, however it may be <u>expressed</u>. It could even, I meant to say, be expressed in a friendship—which (as all devout writers are given to adding) God forbid. But still—Is it clearer? Should

I not have said any of it? You see, I don't <u>mean</u> this to be a weight on you, and I don't conceive of it as one on me. Rather, things keep happening, between us, to be sure; but also, wonderfully, within each of us privately, so that writing you as I did, and as I do now, is not so much a call for response, as the record of a kind of dance already accomplished inside of me, a dance of which something from you, some gesture, some memory, if not simply that deep consciousness I spoke of the other day, is the only source. It ought to come to you lightly, and would, I think, but that we are far, there's a distortion in distance, an exaggeration implicit in <u>letters</u>, so much wrenched onto a little space. Enough of THAT.

Marjorie came yesterday afternoon, a hurricane lily in her hand. We went to a screaming bore of a party, came back, endured television until ten; then I drove her to St Augustine and met Christopher, her lover, a small young man in need of a haircut with "intense" eyes, rather pleasant, <u>very</u> young I felt, and oh, hopelessly one of those earnest people who just <u>won't</u> make a go of it. I saw his drawings and a few of his poems . . . and shall spend the day with them Friday. Ah if you were here! The beach is so beautiful, the loveliest barnacles, white and mauve, like Meissen, not a soul in sight, all vanishing into a white haze. Dinner tonight with Lalla and Charlie and Rosalie, dear good <u>loyal</u> dull old friends. Ah me.

J.

Meissen Fine porcelain, named for the German city in which it was produced.

To David Jackson

Oh my dear David,

Talking of the moments in which not even Schumann speaks to us, I have just spoken with the British West Indian Airlines and learned that my flight to San Juan has been calmly cancelled. When? How? Why? All this I shall never learn, and tomorrow morning I must hie myself to Bridgetown, to see what arrangements can be made. I refuse to be delayed—if I have any choice in the matter; I'd much rather leave a day early. Possibly the solution is to fly to Trinidad and take from there a direct plane to New York—but I don't know how often a week these flights go; well . . . I shall know, if not all, some of this tomorrow. Oh it's part of the total horror of being in primitive countries. I am persuaded they keep on doing these things in order to <u>stay</u> primitive, which, to be sure, from their point of view, is just about all they have to hang on by, but, oh, oh, oh, it's so hopeless, Mister Johnson or whoever saying: Ah but, Sah, if your plane from San Juan doesn't leave till six p.m., then you can take our morning flight on the 10th. No, I reply, you haven't understood, I must be in <u>New York</u> on the morning of the 10th. I must leave San Juan on the 9th. There had been the same kind of ghastly mix-up last year about perfectly explicit reservations, so that it's all evidently nothing more than the ordinary circumstance under which one visits the islands.

Today I read *The Heat of the Day*, liking it very much, but thinking (it now seems) the ending odd. Tonight we are going with the Saints to see a Rattigan play in town. Yesterday the ex-consul to Paraguay and his wife were brought unexpectedly to call by the American consul here. The day before, equally unexpectedly, the former Governor-general and Lady Savage (the names they think up, in the higher circles . . . !) had looked in on a junket up from British Guiana. One shows the house, one drinks a bit of rum, and wonders, Is it really I who am doing these idiotic things? My father has talked of very little but "deals" he "swung" in the 20's, in the 30's, and in the immediate present. These are very long stories, and many of them I realize too I have heard before—the McCrory Deal, the Kresge Deal, the Safeway Deal, each, as it were, larded with scandal which at least is preferable to the financial aspects I never manage to understand. Did you know that Mrs Kresge (once a tart named Doris Mercer) revealed to her husband in their last fierce quarrel that she had been keeping a beautiful Cuban girl for years, and that, all considered, she loved her rather more than she loved him? Well, <u>I</u> didn't. As against this, Mrs K had, in her husband's words to Daddy, "the prettiest pussy he'd ever seen." I wonder if there's any connection . . . ?

Sat in the sun nearly three hours this morning, reading and writing a letter to Umberto which I'd owed for months. I'm pleasantly burned; and rather thirsty; and a bit nervous and bored; and angry with the Airline. I'll wait until I've gone to the office tomorrow before I go on with this. Oh, if you were here I wouldn't care when I left, but you're not, and I do.

Tuesday: Well! It's all for the best, as it so often is. I leave here <u>Sunday</u> night, the 7th, sleep in Trinidad, and take a plane the following morning which gets me in New York around 5 in the afternoon, PAA flight 204. I doubt that I'll get into <u>town</u> much before 6:30, as there will be customs to go through at the airport, and I'm already beginning to worry if it wasn't foolish not to have brought my passport. I have a driver's license and people seem to think that will get me in. I left behind my vaccination certificate, so I'll have to have <u>that</u> done here, Friday, always a bore, why didn't I <u>think</u>? I <u>did</u> think, I remember saying to myself, that I used to think it was chic to travel with passport, and now it seemed chicer yet to travel without one. Oh dear. But there I shall be, some 30 hours ahead of time, and hoping you will not have too pressing an engagement the evening of the 8th. Daddy is quite saddened by the change of plans; yet there's no other way to get to NY before Wed. night, too late for Scarlatti. Besides I promised a friend I would not be delayed. I suddenly feel like writing a page of fiction, how strange, what ought I to do? make a stab? Very well.

Which I have now, an hour later, written—a page only this size, but around it the possibility of something more—perhaps even a little book, about Daddy and all these women. The Harem it might be called . . . something, at least, to think about for the summer's work in Stonington. It's really curious, how <u>long</u> it takes for ideas to reach the stage of even the first clumsy attempt at expression. This would in a way be the book I have been urged to write for years, by my mother, by Dotty Stafford <u>last</u> summer—and now for the first time it seems plausible and interesting.

Two yellow-breasted birds are outside my window. It doesn't seem right as a play, but if I write it then I'll have done one of everything, and I'll have spread myself too thin. Well. I wonder if you mightn't yourself be working this afternoon. I feel so near to you. I close my eyes and there, effortlessly, is your face, with all its expressiveness, looking happy, or serious, or tired. Probably you are talking to somebody at this moment—or else I should be able to summon only <u>one</u> expression. I wonder who you are talking to, Tuesday at 5:30 NY time?

I realize I must get this off to you, so you will know when to expect me. I shall, as planned, come directly to your place. If I'm able I'll phone you from the airport. Should you not answer, I'll be in a pretty pickle with no keys to anything. To be on the safe side, I'll send you a cable from Trinidad Sunday night, so that—unless you are in Stonington! good heavens, how complicated it is—I'd best send you a cable today or tomorrow. Well, I shall. So this can wait a bit, and now I'll go up to Daddy and weigh myself and Get Material.

Late at night. I've gotten it, too, in such quantities . . . a long charming talk with Daddy, that I can't begin to describe or even, alas, write down. Here, at any rate, is a list of topics I may ask you to let me refer to, once I'm in New York:

a) Dottie Stafford and the Reason Barbara was Fired.
b) The Weekend at the Donaks Hotel over Dee-Dee's Dead Body, or The Twenty-Page Letter.
c) Winifred Brown, her Life and Times: How They Met; on the Dock at Sheepshead Bay; her Similarity to Guitou in Respect to Technique.
d) The Fourteen-Year Old Girl Next Door, and how All That Nonsense was Looked Askance on by the Older Group.

. . . The curious feeling I have is that of being excessively alive and human. I have the sense of understanding more and more and more, as if each moment marked the reaching of a boundary, and the following moment the crossing of it . . .

Wit and Wisdom, stand by my Side, now and evermore!

Strange . . . strange . . . We went to call on Mrs Coe, now in extreme disrepute. She talked about the Green Flash, something one sees only in the Caribbean or the Indian Ocean, a phenomenon of sunset; and the Big Deal was discussed . . . all against the most exquisite sea Background I've ever experienced—long delicate pine-needles against a grey-and-lemon sky; six o'clock; a few inches of beach now and then traversed by a black dog or a black woman with a cloth about her head; the smooth opalescent water with, some hundred yards out, thirteen sailboats, their masts at thirteen different angles, quietly rocking; all very luminous and bland, despite talk of the soot from the molasses factory. Mr Coe is relieved. Mrs Coe was dressed in a red towel. When we left Daddy remembered something she had said, and said, "That's the kind of needle they give spinal injections with."

You see, I'm rather drunk—but how curious it is—everything means something immediate and important; the effect is that of an excruciatingly detailed needlepoint. Oh yes:

e) Mrs Telephone Shine; sister-in-law of Mrs Popeye Shine. Please remember all this, and know that I love you with all my heart. I do. I do.

> Now and ever. . . . .
> Jamie

Mister Johnson The eponymous protagonist of Joyce Cary's novel (1939) about a young Nigerian man who finds himself at odds with British colonialists.
The Heat of the Day Elizabeth Bowen's novel (1949).
the Saints Lady Constance Saint and her husband, a British businessman.
a Rattigan play Terence Rattigan (1911–77), British playwright.
Umberto Umberto Morra. See Biographies.
perhaps even a little book This "little book" turned into *The Seraglio* (1957).
Dotty Stafford Dorothy Stafford, one of Merrill's father's lovers; Natalie Bigelow in *The Seraglio*.
Guitou Guitou Knoop (1909–85), Dutch sculptor influenced by Charles Despiau and Constantin Brancusi whom Merrill met in Italy and who figures as Xenia in *The Seraglio*.
the Green Flash A meteorological phenomenon, varieties of which occur in many parts of the world, at a clear horizon, often over an ocean, at sunset or sunrise.

To Kimon Friar

WUSTL
11 August 1954
Stonington, CT

Dear Kimon,

A hurried note. David and I are back from 2 weeks with Claude, and find your letter with the translation. On the basis of two brief readings, my own feeling is that the poem would be more accessible and entertaining if put into prose. The verse, though very well done, I think, borrows from imagery a kind of predictable stateliness which, in so long a work, would give out increasingly a numbing effect. This will be hard enough to avoid in prose. I say it blithely enough; but the poem really <u>doesn't</u> move me, though if it were not a contemporary poem I daresay it <u>would</u>. Yet even here I wonder. I am not so moved by Homer himself, but that I need to bear in mind, for pleasure in reading him, that it is a breath from a world some 3000 years old. It seems to me that Kazantzakis is working in a context disarmingly absent. A ship without a sea. And that, no matter how superior in language and vision he may be to novelists who treat of Egyptian or Early Christian societies, I get the same sense, heretical though it be, of an irrelevance, even a glibness, a falling-back upon situations already accepted as significant, epithets, nobilities . . . Of course his advantage lies precisely in being able to take these things for granted; while the torture of a writer with a wholly contemporary subject is that most of his pains go into the sheer <u>establishment</u> of a signifi-cance upon what would otherwise be thought barren ground. With all that behind one, what brilliant things <u>can't</u> one project? Perhaps I am too American, though; Odysseus means too little to me. Even <u>he</u>, no doubt, struggles to be, but in some golden classic air that has long since been seen as cordial to his struggle: the historical becomes too close to the heavenly, and one isn't interested in what people <u>do</u> in heaven; it's enough that they're <u>there</u>. Well, myth-making . . . ? you would say. Yet even there, isn't the Odyssey (Homer's) rich enough as it stands. To what end remodel the fine old structure in the taste of today? There is a flavor of up-to-date psychology, or <u>consciousness</u> of its emphasis nowadays, that sits like a television aerial on the palace roof. Wouldn't it be better, if that's what one <u>wants</u>, to move into a modern house and leave the palace to posterity?

Well, none of this is what you've <u>asked</u> to hear, but I think I've, though briefly, replied to your question, at the outset. All is well with me, Claude is printing a booklet of my poems, which I'll send.

David sends his best. As ever,
Jimmy

the translation Friar's translation of Greek writer Nikos Kazantzakis's *The Odyssey: A Modern Sequel* (1938; trans. 1958), which Friar dedicated to Merrill.
a booklet Merrill's chapbook *Short Stories* (1954).

To Claude Fredericks

Dear dear Claude,

Pink from the beach, and pinker yet with pleasure, to have rowed back over the weary waste of water and found the finished book! We have gaped and gawked over it an hour now and I am all admiration and delight. I think the cover paper is <u>right</u>, the label beautifully placed, the <u>shape</u> that the cover lends so generous! and within, the really extraordinary juggling of centimeters by which you've managed to <u>shape</u> the title-page into something even more handsome than it had been. I see nothing whatsoever to sigh over, except rapturously; the whole book seems to fit the poems so well, to bear them out, here and there to sustain them actually—where they are weak through some irrelevance or inattention to detail, one can positively feel <u>your</u> attention in the completeness of their <u>cadre</u>; I'm put in mind of such things as the frames Seurat decorated for his paintings . . . What I most like, I think, is an air of—how to express it?—well, something austere and non-committal, one might even call it a dead-pan or poker-face look about the book, a kind of genteel understatement which <u>really</u> makes the poems show to their best advantage; they have never, before, in reading, seemed funnier or more vivid—the way one tends to listen to an unemphatic voice or (supply your own dozen immodest analogies) . . . Certainly this has never happened before, seeing things in print; the excitement had always been that they <u>were</u> in print, just that. The Knopf book looks more and more dismal and overfurnished. My feeling is much closer to that of seeing the oneact play performed, with all the enhancement of production, working <u>for</u> one's language, giving it tone and gesture, even the wrong tone. There are those, evidently, who will feel this to be the wrong tone. Bernie was here yesterday and took his habitual high-handed view of proof you had sent earlier, complaining of this and that with reference to some vague "knowledge" of the subject. I feel, as I say, strongly that the tone is right; but even if it weren't it would still <u>be</u> tone, a harmony, a production (almost in the theatrical sense) which the Knopf book simply is not. Well, I'm ever so happy about it. May I write you again and again on the subject? And thank you now and ever, for <u>your</u> work and <u>your</u> inspiration and <u>your</u> sweetness, of which the book speaks to <u>me</u>, this last; let it speak to others of the rest [*in the margin:* principally, I mean].

These have been lazy gossipy days; Bernie left last night; Lewis Freedman leaves tonight; tomorrow we visit Kay and Naya and Freddy etc in Pine Orchard, this side, a bit, of New Haven. Others loom. Guitou is very well, dieting and working; we had a more or less successful talk about the trouble—inconclusive, except that to have spoken made an end of <u>not</u> having spoken. We've seen a lot of George Copeland who is more and more divine, and we grow fonder and fonder of Marianna, did you meet her? in the little shop across the way. She said she would take 3 or 5 copies of the book to sell there.

Have you been working, along with the printing? I hope so. On the poems at all? on the play? or just on the Major Work? David is about half-way through re-working and -typing *Amy;* it gets better and better, I think. <u>He</u> likes the book so much and feels you have given <u>him</u> something beautiful . . . Well, for now, to work. I dropped my watch in the shallows yesterday, then put it in the oven and forgot about it; Bernie took the poor baked thing to NY with him—I keep suspecting that it's later than I think. Give Jimmy my best, I'm sure he has done a lot to help you with the book, beside the admirable cutting of pages; are you both well and happy?

Love and love,
James

The lovely <u>sewing</u>, I just noticed, fitted to the print!

the finished book *Short Stories* (1954).
The Knopf book *First Poems* (1951).
Bernie Bernard V. Winebaum (1923–89), sometime poet; later followed Merrill to Athens; subject to mania.
Kay and Naya Frederick Buechner's mother, Katherine Kuhn Buechner, and his grandmother.
talk about the trouble Guitou Knoop had an affair with Charles Merrill while commissioned to create his bust. When they quarreled, Merrill took Knoop's side.
George Copeland (1882–1971), a pianist who had studied with Debussy and toured with the Isadora Duncan Dancers; Merrill's neighbor and friend in Stonington.

the Major Work Fredericks's voluminous diary, now at the Getty Research Center, Los Angeles.
Amy Working title of a novel by Jackson.
Jimmy Fredericks's partner.

To Claude Fredericks

GETTY
3 October 1954
[Stonington, CT]

Dear Claude,

Mrs Alfred Knopf is an altogether charming person. You will like her. She spoke so admiringly, yet so simply, of your work. We must get together this winter.

The luncheon was held on a very hot day, in a rented diningroom (4 East 60). Among those present were 3 Knopfs (pere, fils et Blanche), 3 Knopf Editors (but not Harry), and only two Knopf poets, unless I missed somebody.

The guests to whom I was not introduced included Conrad Aiken, W R Rogers, Irita van Doren, Lionel Trilling, Harvey Breit and five or six unimportant looking people—I wish I knew for sure.

Those I met can be taken up in turn. Mr Stevens himself has a face that bothers me—as being far too florid, salmon-colored, against a green shirt, gaudy tie and, apparently, his only suit—the one that appears in all the late photographs. But he was very civil, said he had just written you a note about the book, but "this isn't the time to go into that." It had been decided by one and all that nothing but small talk would be allowed. Between him and a groaning buffet of hors d'oeuvres, in a black tricorne, stood Miss Moore, but I had first an interesting passage with Louise Bogan who remembered meeting me at Bard and immediately (unconsciously) initiated precisely the conversation we had had there, five years ago. What does one do when the lyric gift departs? How evanescent is the lyric gift! If one's own small talent is a lyric one—or rather (with a smile of peaceful acceptance) <u>has</u> been a lyric one—one can do one of two things: Nothing or (as she herself does) sit at one's desk writing Imitation Poems. "I'm not a story teller—oh I've written stories because I've learned the <u>tricks</u>—yes, I wrote a novel, once," on and on. She is obsessed with the topic; and the five minutes with her explained with almost frightening simplicity the state of mind behind her review of my book—doesn't it seem so to you? There was Auden. As soon as he stood up to talk to someone I slipped into his seat and introduced myself to Marianne Moore. "Oh hello there, I'm glad to meet you, I've always liked your work" and then, as I was leaving she said so again, "in fact, a couple of times I've been about to sit down and write you a letter," which just destroyed me. Chas Rolo and Delmore S and Carlo all appeared, separately, after which Mrs K, hard upon a whispered talk with Stevens, said would I sit at their table? (a moment before Alfred had been in earshot: Where will he sit? Blanche: You take him. Alfred: No, you take him. Blanche: All right, I'll take him.) So we all sat down, I between a charming man named Norman Pearson—whose name everyone I've asked knows, but nothing about him beyond what <u>I</u> know, that he's hunchbacked, and a friend of the Sitwells, had been staying with Stevens, very close to Auden, etc—and someone to whom I was never introduced and whom I only identified 40 minutes later as Barzun. Miss Moore and Stevens and Blanche were the others. Before long Alfred had come sniffing about in his chalkblue suit. "Ça marche," Blanche told him on a surprised note, "ça marche!" And it did. M/M began talking about her friends in prisons, the letters she had written on their behalf; from this to a subscription to the *Breeder's Gazette*—the *Police Gazette?* wondered Mr Pearson, who had just finished defining innocence as a sort of aftermath of guilt—no, the <u>Breeder's</u>; she had begun to help a boy through college, and since then renewed it many times. How much there was to learn from it: all about Black Angus and Hampshire Pigs—the Pig, a noble animal (we were eating Roast Beef). Mr Stevens alone was offered a second helping; he looked at it disagreeably. Take it away, I don't want it. Oh but you must, said Blanche, it's like a second piece of birthday cake. No, I couldn't eat it; besides, I'm used to eating roast beef with English mustard. Looks of horror exchanged between Blanche and Waiter. Have we any English Mustard? We'd have to send downstairs for it. Stevens: Don't bother, forget it! Blanche: No, it's your birthday; fetch the mustard, here give him that thick piece. And he was served it, and the mustard came and he began to smile secretly with Joy. The talk turned to music. Pearson remembered Violet Gordon Woodhouse. Miss Moore had not read Kirkpatrick's Scarlatti book, but wanted to (Pearson had asked her earlier if she had seen "Ezra's" Chinese translations; she hadn't but was very eager to)—then politely asked Stevens if <u>he</u> had. Why should I read about Scarlatti? he asked. She laughed and threw up her hands as if to say: Is it possible that <u>anybody</u> <u>anywhere</u> could not passionately desire to read <u>everything</u>? Barzun and Blanche talked under their breaths about Colette. Raspberry ice came and went. Copy 1 (of 2500) was brought out and everyone had to sign it for Mr Stevens. A cupcake with a candle burning was put down before him. We all rose and sang Happy Birthday to You (dear-Mr-Stevens) and then he got up and said, as I found out, truthfully, that he was the world's worst public speaker . . . (long pause) . . . that the thing about growing old was not that one lost one's ability to do what one did as well, sometimes better than ever before, but that one lost the will to do it, one grew lazy, one didn't care. Auden listened attentively. Stevens said he had written 12 poems this summer, and thought that was pretty good for anybody. (I thought so too.) Mr Knopf, he said, and himself had always had a very happy association. He had simply sent the manuscripts to Mr K and Mr K had printed them; that's how poetry ought to be published. But he wanted to go on record as thanking Carl van Vechten who first showed his work to Mr K. He's thanking <u>you</u>, hissed Irita van Doren in Carl's ear. Carl shook himself and looked up—what? <u>Thanking you</u>. To Stevens: Say it again, louder, won't you? Stevens: You say it, you're nearer. Then reconsidering: I was just saying, Carl, that you had been the first to show my work to Mr K. One might say you were the <u>father</u> of this party. Carl positively blushed and grinned, muttering Thank you, Wallace (he alone called Stevens that) and a moment later confessed, when Stevens asked him, that he hadn't heard another word of the whole little speech. Can <u>you</u> think of something I haven't said? Stevens asked Auden. No, laughed Auden a bit too jovially. So he sat down and the party broke up. I left almost at once, nearly prostrate from the heat and all. Weinstock spoke warmly of the book and how beautiful he thought it; he had, in fact sent me a little note, scarce worth forwarding to you. It seems odd that I've not heard from Harry about it; did you know they were going to Europe in March for 6 weeks—Elizabeth a bit longer. I talked to her, that afternoon, from Robert's, on the phone. Robert seems very well; thinks his analyst, now, a very dangerous woman. He seems a bit more like the "old" Robert. Forgive this zany letter, I fear it is too long-winded and will not amuse you as it might have. The rest is lost to the world, though; <u>they</u>'d never bother to recall what happened.

One tiny touch more: Marianne Moore spoke of a boy for whom she used to save stamps—then broke off, turning to Stevens—"but, <u>never</u> the elephant stamps <u>you</u> sent me! I'd never part with those!" Well, I just adored her. <u>Did</u> you send her a book? Because, if you haven't, I'd send her one of mine—if you'll send me her address, and don't mind.

Marilyn and Irving left not long ago, after bringing the car back. They had the full treatment at Guitou's last night (Stuart Preston was there; <u>he</u> was dazzled by the book—I told him it would be on sale at Miss Steloff's, not feeling that I really needed to give him one)— both M and I hated my head, but violently, though they seemed to get on well enough with G herself. Elie needed of course only to know that they were art-historians to attack them and all they stood for; he got the worst of it, I'm glad to say. I feel myself a bit angry with G, freshly so; the Lavins seemed to think Doris was quite justified in complaining that she had received a marble "copy" and I am really sick to death of hearing G defend herself and attack the Magowans. I tell her as forcibly as I can that I want to hear no more of it, but it doesn't seem to help. Oh God! She thought <u>your</u> letter a puzzling "artificial, neurotic" one—I suppose we can blame it all on change of life or perhaps Dr Tenney. Her horoscopist, Ostertag, has announced a period of unrelieved disaster from last week until May of 1956—for <u>her</u>, bien sur. Enough, enough! When are you coming? Love from us both to the both of you.

Jimmy

The luncheon Alfred A. Knopf hosted a luncheon at the Harmonie Club in New York in honor of Wallace Stevens's seventy-fifth birthday and Knopf's publication of Stevens's *Collected Poems* (1954).
Conrad Aiken (1889–1973), American poet.
W R Rogers William Robert Rodgers (1909–69), Irish poet.
Irita Van Doren (1891–1966), book editor of the *New York Herald Tribune*.
Lionel Trilling (1905–75), American literary critic.
Harvey Breit (1909–68), poet and editor of *The New York Times Book Review*.
Chas Rolo and Delmore S and Carlo Charles Rolo (1916–82), literary editor at *The*

Atlantic; Delmore Schwartz (1913–66), poet; Carl Van Vechten (1880–1964), writer, photographer, and patron of the Harlem Renaissance.
Norman Pearson (1909–75), professor of American literature at Yale; intelligence officer for the OSS during World War II.
the Sitwells Edith (1887–1964), Osbert (1892–1969), and Sacheverell (1897–1988).
Barzun Jacques Barzun (1905–2012), French historian and essayist.
Violet Gordon Woodhouse (1872–1948), British harpsichord and clavichord player.
Scarlatti book *Domenico Scarlatti* (1953) by Ralph Kirkpatrick (1911–84).
"Ezra's" Chinese translations Pound's *Cathay* (1915).
Weinstock spoke warmly of Merrill's *Short Stories.*
Robert Robert Isaacson.
Stuart Preston (1915–2005), art critic for *The New York Times.*
Miss Stelloff's The Gotham Book Mart, owned by Frances Steloff.
M and I hated my head A portrait bust of Merrill by Knoop .

To Marianne Moore

ROSENBACH
16 October 1954
Stonington, CT

Dear Miss Moore—

I hope I do not presume too much, in sending you this. But the poems themselves would probably have a different ring, if I hadn't read and marveled at your own. And the very book owes something, I think, to your Egoist Press *Poems* which for many years has seemed to me the most elegant of its kind. It was a real pleasure to meet you at Mrs. Knopf's luncheon.

Sincerely,
James Merrill

sending you this A copy of *Short Stories* (1954).
Egoist Press Poems Moore's *Poems* (1921), published without her knowledge by the British writer Bryher (1894–1983) and the American poet H. D. (1886–1961).

To Hellen Ingram Plummer   WUSTL
13 January 1955
Stonington, CT

Dear Mama,

I return from Stonington tomorrow, after some not altogether satis-
factory days here; I'm too restless, I think, to be even this far from
the city where so much is happening. I did do a few essential revi-
sions, mostly in Act I, and I guess the calm of the country was neces-
sary for that much work. Telephone conferences daily announce that
the 1st rehearsal went well, that the sketches for sets and costumes
are finished and beautiful, that yet another enthusiast has backed us
to the tune of $75.00 (!) etc etc. I met Wm. Sheidy the afternoon you
left—a good-looking, good-natured, not-too-tall and not particularly
distinguished person who read, however, really extraordinarily well,
considering he wasn't even familiar with the entire script. The actor
who was to play the father etc. backed out, and that's just as well as
he wasn't old enough in appearance. Herbert talks now of a late Feb.
opening, because the intervening play is rumored to be hopelessly
bad, but we can't tell till it opens on the 23rd I think. I just lie awake
nights thinking about it all.

I really enjoyed being with you this Christmas. When you ask if
writing my novel has helped me, I would say that anything helps if
it breaks ground for the kind of talks we had. As I said, so much has
gone unexpressed for so long, good and bad; perhaps only relatively
violent means can be taken to repair. I do think, or at least hope, that
whatever hurt you sustained is the kind of hurt that heals.

And I love my candlesticks.

As a backer you will undoubtedly receive 2 seats for opening night.
If you rent a limousine I'm certain Mis A can make it there and back,
and the theatre is surely adequately heated. If, when we learn the
opening date, you find that Bill is able to come too, it will be a simple
matter to get an extra ticket. By and large, I'm not going to ask for
many free seats, or if I do, I'll pay for them myself; but on the first
2 nights 250 tickets have to be given away—to critics, police, fire
dept, etc etc; it's really disgraceful. As soon as the releases come out
about opening, in NY papers, that is, you at last have full sanction
to get the play mentioned in Jax. and Atlanta papers; there's always

a chance somebody from down there will be going to NY and would want to take in the show. Of course, if the reviews are at all good, an article <u>after</u> the opening might be more to the point.

Much love to all,
Jimmy

revisions, mostly in Act I Merrill's play *The Immortal Husband* (1955), which was about to be performed off-Broadway in New York.
Wm. Sheidy William Sheidy played Tithonus in *The Immortal Husband*.
Herbert Herbert Machiz (1919–76), the play's director, partner of John Bernard Myers (1920–87), American art dealer, partner in the Tibor de Nagy Gallery, promoter of the New York school poets. See note on Herbert Machiz for letter of 13 January 1955.
Jax. Jacksonville.

To Claude Fredericks

Dear Claude,

How nice to have your letter on this flawless day. <u>We</u> bought a phonograph too—not a beautiful one, but better than that crazy brown bobbin of yore. We also bought a (beautiful) plant stand for the tower room, it is covered with plants and, peeping betwixt leaves, here and there an objet. We also bought a wonderful new mattress, and sleep like angels. What else,—oh yes, we have bought the building itself! At least we go today to sign papers. Two weeks ago, strolling out at dusk, thinking nothing bad, we saw a for sale sign tacked by our door—a four-masted schooner (4 Sail, get it?) with the agent's name. Panic ensued. We tried to get hold of old Hoxie and found out all kinds of alarming things—that he is clearing out of Conn, that he is mixed up with a scheming widowwoman, goes off weekends to Vermont (local papers please copy) with her. They wanted $16,000 for it which seemed sort of unfair, considering that a generous fraction of that price would be our own improvements. And then the agent said that no leases are respected unless registered in the town hall—ours isn't. Eh bien! yesterday we heard that our offer has been accepted: we take over a $6000 mortgage and pay $5000. My word, we ought perhaps to have offered less . . . Anyhow we have great plans, to turn the attic into a gorgeous studio room with lots of glass and big terraces high above everything, black + white linoleum squares on the floor. We are inquiring about for a frugal architect-contractor. And then <u>paint</u> the bldg. And <u>fix</u> the basement. In short, have something splendid to come home to. We're terribly pleased about it. There is an income of about $1000 from the little shops below. The taxes are next to nothing. Tralalalalalalala.

I'm very glad of your decision about the book. It's certainly not for me to say, without reading it, how much work it needs, but novels <u>do</u> need lots of work and one can't rush through the myriad tiny corrections of the surface. I think you'll be much much prouder of it and yourself at the end of another draft. It has once or twice occurred to me that it wouldn't hurt me to do the same—but I just cannot. Yesterday I got stuck on a page and wrote it three times; how wildly difficult to make any change, particularly to clarify! I'm past the midway point as of yesterday, though. That rewritten page may just have been home-stretch nerves. I've had my own spells of horrid depression: how little gets said, how many words to say it, how the faces get warped beneath the verbal mildew . . . if mildew warps . . . ! Oh my, to spend the rest of one's days writing quatrains!

Later. Bayard has rented his house for the summer. To Truman. Capote. He hasn't hit town yet, but when he does . . . We have, of course, Bernie to thank for recommending Stonington. Doesn't that make you want to visit even more?

We're sorry not to have made contact May 19 in NY—not even to have phoned Dolly. Our days, both of them, were very packed—as yours sounded, prospectively,—so that it would only have been to say hello. (Hello <u>now</u>). And now to work.

Hugs to both. Make date for visit. D. will add.

Ever,

J.

Hoxie Stanley Jerome Hoxie (1895–1981), American painter. Merrill bought 107 Water Street from him.
Bayard Bayard Osborn (1922–2012), American sculptor, boyfriend of Knoop.
Truman. Capote (1924–84), Capote lived in Stonington during the summer of 1955.

Merrill adds the last name facetiously to distinguish him from former President Harry S Truman.

To Hellen Ingram Plummer

WUSTL

July 1955
[Stonington, CT]

Dear Mama,

Your letter is just here, and it's <u>wonderful</u> to think you may be able to move Mis' Annie away by the 25th. I'll of course plan to come in Sunday, as you suggest.

I think I've understood more deeply than you may know what you've been going through. It's been almost impossible for me to show you this—perhaps because the whole situation is so unutterably sad. The sadness seems to be that of the very <u>heart</u> of life, somehow, I don't know how else to say it. I think of you over and over moving about that apartment, of the confusion you must feel now and then of not knowing whether it's your mother or your child you're caring for . . . but when we get so very closely involved with another life, as you are now with Mis' Annie's, these things <u>are</u> confused. Just so, you have, I think, felt yourself horribly to blame for all the suffering, in a way you can scarcely admit to yourself, and why is it that an impulse that meant so well could have backfired so disastrously? That's what I mean about the heart of life; life does this, at least in my experience it does. I remember that summer of 1947 when Gert gave me a long talk about you, how your "change" worried her, but you no longer cared about clothes, etc, and had I noticed it? Of course I had noticed it; I felt, in fact, that I had <u>caused</u> it, but could scarcely admit that to myself. What I know now is that it takes two to bring about these crises. As far as Mis' A's eye goes, <u>deep</u> <u>inside</u> us, where our consciences lie, we know that the doctors' role in the situation means <u>nothing</u>; subjectively, the disaster has been created by the people who matter emotionally—herself, yourself, myself. That is why you continue to reproach yourself, even though your reason assures you that such reproach, or its degree, is unreasonable. <u>Do</u> try to see <u>all</u> of it: to see that along with Mis' A's tenacity (of which we spoke in the spring) there is will towards failure and relinquishment—a will expressed, however trivially, by that very little high quavering voice we joke about. There is in her something fatalistic which you and I have both inherited, I think: an air of shaking the head, of knowing better, of feeling that things which may turn out, later, most successfully, are somehow foredoomed to fail. It sounds like a silly paradox, but I've felt it so often, and think you have, too: that along with our fierce wish to be independent, to do things on our own terms, there comes a hopeless, almost disgraceful, longing to lie back, to let other people for once take care of us, to let ourselves be guided absolutely by the judgement of others. I have worn myself out, now and then, through these two conflicting wishes. I wonder if at last Mis A hasn't let herself give in, not altogether, but enough to accomplish a transition she needed to make, between relative independence and, now, relative dependence on others. Only an "accident" could have permitted her to do this, because she has such a moral [sic] horror of it . . . What I mean is, we have no choice as to the circumstances of such transitions; they are nearly always violent—think of the circumstances that set <u>us</u> apart from each other; and yet they are the real raw material of our souls and we <u>cannot</u> repudiate them. When you write that nothing around you is real, it is the shock of the violent nature of one's inner life that makes you put it this way. I don't know, I think each of us is terribly knowing as far as his own hidden needs are concerned; even when some external disaster takes place—within a matter of hours, like the forming of a pearl, one begins to change it into the event most appropriate to his inner life; in that respect, the mind is a most marvelous thing. Think of all the people who live their lives without blaming themselves for what happens around them! And think how often you, on the other hand, have felt responsible! It doesn't mean that you <u>are</u> responsible, any more than it means that the others aren't. But you keep wooing the <u>experience</u> of responsibility, and your need of it is so deep that it seems to you you have absolutely no alternative . . .

All I'm saying, I guess, is that this sense of floating in space, of being a bobbing cork in an ocean, is very much as it should be. One can go years and years without being caught up in a situation that permits such sharp insights into everything that's at stake. Remember that you have chosen to be conscious of things that may have hurt you, and at your very best I think you ought rightly to be proud of that. I am proud of you for it; I believe we should <u>see</u> as much as we possibly can. That hasn't been Mis A's way, she has never wanted that. And when you consider how much more you see and understand than (for instance) Aunt Mil, and with that difference in mind, how one feels a little pang of pity, a sense of being stronger and more capable—that pang is multiplied a millionfold when it's your own mother who elicits it. Well, you have been wonderful, and are. Get what you need from these dreadful weeks; and don't forget that, as I said, <u>she</u> may be getting something she has wanted for a long time, without daring to admit it.

> Much much love,
> Jimmy

what you've been going through Merrill's mother took her mother, Mis' Annie, to New York to get her cataracts removed; complications after the operation led to the removal of Mis' Annie's left eye.
Gert Gert Behanna (1903–95), Hellen Plummer's friend; author and spiritualist.
circumstances that set <u>us</u> apart His mother's discovery of Merrill's relationship with Friar.

To Hellen Ingram Plummer

WUSTL
2 September 1955
Stonington, CT

Dear Mama,

I guess I'm all "coked up" today—did about 4 pages and 3 yesterday, of a chapter describing life in Barbados, which I think ought to come off very well. I have already written the chap. ahead of this—taking place in Xenia's studio; it will be followed by a second Barbados (or Jamaica) chapter, and no more than 5 after that, some 80 pages I fancy. I've also been at work on some poems, one from long ago which had never satisfied me; and a new one.

I've been having a series of very strange experiences which have in a matter of 10 days made a profound change in my life. It comes from some 8 or 9 evenings, in which for several hours I have been at the Ouija board with David. We have talked to a single spirit—a Jew named Ephraim who lived at the time of Christ, became attached to Tiberius' court, and was later executed by him after the court moved to Capri. He has described in considerable detail his own life on earth and the afterlife, as well. The latter, as far as I can say now, is set up in the following way:

As in Dante, there are nine Stages through which the souls progress. Ephraim is at Stage 6, having worked himself there from Stage 3, where he went upon his death. (Everybody in Christ's generation moved automatically to stage 3, when He died.) What determines one's promotion from Stage to Stage is the behavior and life of one's Representative on earth—the soul that goes through incarnation after incarnation until at last it is sufficiently refined to reach Stage 1. When such a soul does reach Stage one, his "Patron" moves to a higher stage. Certain souls go through as many as 750 incarnations. They are often those who recurrently die as infants, or who begin as animals. Ephraim's present representative was reborn the day following the night we contacted him (otherwise, I suspect we would not have been able to make contact), somewhere in England. Of this soul, E. said: "He was first a dumb, deaf, mad boy dead at 16. He has been my link for centuries. He is of a weak, if not animal mentality, which does return to earth and never achieves sufficient wisdom to be allowed our stage, usually dying early and violently." Upon my inquiry, he said that Horton G. was another one of these, that he is now about to be born a third time since his death. In a split second, E. can answer these questions by referring to the person's "Patron." Mine is a man named Ford, out of the 18th Century. Yours is "Maria-Antoinette of Portugal"—whoever she was. Daddy's was a Hindu mystic. (E. says there is one Deity, of which God, Allah, Jehovah, Brahma are the various names, depending on whoever was His prophet.) He does not know what happens on Stage 9. It is his hope that the body is resurrected. I inquired about Wallace Stevens, who as you know recently died. He had been raised at once to Stage 6, because of strong intervention from Plato. I then was allowed to speak to him. He remembered meeting me and quoted me a line from one of my poems. We had little to say. "We are embarrassed," he said, "like guests who have met too recently at one party and find each other again at another party." There is intervention for me as well, I gather, from Hans—who is at Stage 1. I have had messages from him. His representative is a boy named Manuel in South America who "cuts coffee, that is when he is not cutting himself and others."

Well, if you think I am mad, do so. For myself, I believe it <u>utterly</u>, and that is an experience I have never had before in my life. In fact I had never believed in an afterlife at all—and of course, now that I do, everything on earth seems so much more glorious and worth living for. I can feel all kinds of hatred and fear draining out of my mind—a great energy, a will not to waste myself: in short, the state of mind I have kept waiting to achieve through analysis. I am most curious to hear what Detre can say about it. I am seeing him Tuesday, en route to NY (he is now with the Yale Dept of Psychiatry), and will tell him what I can. My intuition is that I have no further need of him, but we shall see. What happens from now on is, of course, the test of everything. I cannot calculate how much I must have suffered in my mind from the fear of absolute annihilation. Now it seems all kinds of exalted utterance, whether scripture or poetry, point to truth.

What I think Gert has not understood is—well, whatever is shown by the way in which she treats <u>everybody</u> as if they were all on the point of zooming up to Stage 9 directly, and there were no intermediate points along the way.

I will tell you more as the conversations progress. I take it you know how the Ouija works, the teacup inverted over a board on which the alphabet is written—the handle points out letter after letter, often so rapidly one can hardly write it down with one's free hand. (Two people must each place a hand on the cup.) I asked E. about mediums—he said: "They are like old rattling chariots. They take you to me, but fatigue you on the way." If the two people who are attuned to a certain spirit sit at right angles holding mirrors before them, the spirit can see them and himself, at the same time. This, he says, made Versailles such a marvelous place for psychic experience, and indeed the most famous records of our time that deal with these phenomena are the testimonies of two ladies at Versailles who lost themselves in a crowd of people, wandering through the gardens—people dressed in the style of 200 years ago, and the gardens looking as they did then.

I am so glad to have your news about Mis' Annie. Give her all my love. When is she coming North? Before you go to Calif? Will you go to San Francisco—it sounds like such fun. If she arrives in NY on a weekend, I can arrange to be there. I still, however, do not know whether I shall have all day Saturday or all day Monday free.

I'll be in S'hampton 2 nights, then back here; heading up to Amherst on the 14th. I may spend the next 3 nights at Claude's, but I'll surely be in residence as of the 18th.

All my love,
Jimmy

Xenia's studio Xenia, based on Knoop, in *The Seraglio* (1957).
Ephraim The familiar spirit communicating with Merrill and Jackson on the Ouija board. In AD 36, Ephraim was murdered by Emperor Tiberius's guards.
life on earth and the afterlife As Ephraim presents things at this juncture, there are two levels of existence, this world and the other. Embodied souls in this world are "representatives" of their "patrons," souls in the other world, whose status depends in part on the behavior of those representatives. The soul of the representative on Earth goes through successive incarnations until it is sufficiently refined to reach the other world, at which point it becomes a patron itself and enters one of nine otherworldly Stages, usually Stage 1 (but Stage 3 in E's case, for the reason explained), while its own patron is promoted.
Horton G. Horton Grant (1925–44), Merrill's freshman roommate at Amherst, who died in a car crash while a student.
two ladies at Versailles In August 1901, Anne Moberly and Eleanor Jourdain visited the garden at Versailles and claimed to have encountered people in eighteenth-century attire. Moberly and Jourdain pseudonymously published *An Adventure* (1911), detailing their experiences.

To Hellen Ingram Plummer

WUSTL
15 September 1955
Pawlet, VT

Dear Mama,

I am writing this from Pawlet (Claude's) where I arrived yesterday and shall stay until Saturday a.m.—so that I've spent only one night in the house. It was cleaner than when I'd last seen it. There was nothing I could do about my classes—as no students will be there before Monday; so I have had to choose at random 4 or 5 names to fill up the writing course, not all the applicants having submitted samples of their work. Stopping to see the Summers' in Storrs, Conn, where Joe teaches, and they have just bought an old red farmhouse—I saw all three children and all five kittens which I found so delightful that I let myself be persuaded to take one along—a little white, gray and tan mite of a thing with big blue eyes. I have named her Maisie and she is, of course, with me here. [Drawing of a cat]

I was very happy to have your last letter about Ephraim. As I had feared, Detre didn't take too bright a view of it—he said that the voice comes from my own soul, that I ought to be able to feel it as my own intuition of these things, rather than to take it as the utterance of some exterior authority. I don't know <u>what</u> I think about <u>that</u>. He has been right so often that I don't like to ignore his advice—which is, not to converse with E. any more—but on the other hand . . . well, I'm not too depressed.

To answer your questions: the soul is reborn over and over again until it is judged worthy of admittance to a Stage, usually the first. When it moves to a Stage, its Patron also moves up one Stage; the Patron acquires then a new representative on earth, many times to be reborn; and his former representative, now at Stage 1, becomes a Patron on his own.

Sometimes a soul goes through as many as 700 incarnations. Some souls do begin as animals—"Have you not known cats, dogs, pigs— that is, people who retain these animal traits?" I think E. is exaggerating when he says that his representative "never" makes progress, or will "never" reach his stage. This just means that it will take many more incarnations.

Yes, E. is the Patron of the soul recently reborn in England. The Patron cannot help his representative, only be "on hand" in case of any threat to its life. Once we were talking to him and he was called away; the child was ill with a fever, and E. had to be on hand to receive the soul in case the child died. He would then go in search of a woman 6–7 months pregnant, place the soul into the body of her child. Sometimes there is no soul for these infants—and this explains the babies who are stillborn.

Though the Patron does not help, the souls are helped by other spirits who intervene—in Stevens' case, Plato; in mine, Hans; in David's, his grandfather. The intervention is helpful proportionate to the importance of the stage from which it comes.

Well, that may not be very clear. I do have certain doubts, of the kind you have about Meriel Milam; it certainly shouldn't, the Board, be used for specific instructions as to how to Live. She ought to remember that these voices are essentially human—hence fallible, prejudiced, even as we. Very often they do not recall the past accurately, and are unable to predict the future except in very abstract ways. To be <u>guided</u> by it is surely dangerous. What it has given me is simply proof of a world I had not hitherto believed in—like the proof of the existence of God. Upon such proofs one must build one's own systems, or go to priests or philosophers for guidance. Yeats quotes an ancient utterance attributed to Orpheus: "Do not open the gates of Pluto, for within is a people of dreams."

My next letter will be about Amherst. Much love to Mis' Annie; I'll keep her birthday present for the 8th—I'll be down that afternoon. My soph. class meets Tues, Thurs and Sat—so I can't make it before. I do have Mondays free, though. Is Bill with you now? Give him my best and love to all,

Jimmy

the Summers' Joseph Summers was teaching at the University of Connecticut.
Meriel Milam (1898–1995), friend of Bill Plummer in Jacksonville, Florida.
Yeats quotes See W. B. Yeats in *The Dreaming of the Bones* (1919) and his essay "Swedenborg, Mediums, and the Desolate Places" (1914).

To Robin Magowan   WUSTL
                                                   13 February 1956
                                                     Amherst, MA

Dear Robin,

I've been thinking while you were here and since you left, of things that your way of hastily agreeing to the disagreeable might have kept from full expression in talk; and so I write.

When we last spoke about the chances of your going into analysis, I recall that it seemed to both of us something to do in the future, say, five years hence. The point is, I wonder if you mightn't be ready for it now. Your self-knowledge has vastly increased over the past year; so, I suspect also, has your confusion on many scores. You <u>can</u>, of course, wait as long as you choose, but I must say, considering the year you've planned, your notion of being at Harvard to "make your-self more intelligent," I can think of no more fruitful way of using that time or achieving that end, whether it means relinquishing 6 weeks in Europe or not.

I <u>don't</u> want to be didactic, or take a tone; if I do so, it is perhaps only in proportion to my sense of your having come to Amherst looking for some clarification of a problem, and of your having left talking of a kind of "cure." The one thing I want to get through to you has to do with this notion of being <u>helped</u> by people we're involved with, who are significant to us, whether relatives or friends or who-ever we sleep with. It simply doesn't happen; those aren't the people we get helped by. The involvement keeps it from happening. If you assume, as I did at 19 and even at 24, that a satisfactory, steady sex-life would be the answer to every emotional problem, the chances are you will run the risk of hurting a lot of people and getting your-self into a deeper rut—nothing more. The point of the analyst, I need only remind you, is that he infinitely absorbs your fantasies and <u>isn't</u> hurt; that he isn't hurt means that you are not—in a curious way a habit is broken . . . I'm not very good at describing all this, it's still too close to me. Perhaps you'll take my word.

A great advantage you have, which I did not, is that you love talk-ing about yourself. (I love talking about myself <u>now</u>; that is one of the rewards in my case.) You would not find it difficult to communicate. Naturally you are full of snobbery and whatnot about the powers and the insights of the analyst. He expects that. Other people don't; I, for instance, wonder how much more you think I have understood about things, than I actually have. One reason to do it now would be that you are rapidly getting in command of a jargon which, the more you perfect it, will make the problems it masks harder to get at. Last and (in some ways) least, any psychosomatic symptom of the kind you described to me, however short-lived, is a healthy sign that the victim is ripe.

I hope you will not dismiss all this as impossible. Perhaps, if you get to S.F. this spring, you could talk it over with your parents. If that doesn't appeal to you, I would be willing to write them, for what little it might be worth. If you would like me to inquire of my own Dr. the name of a Dr in Boston or Cambridge you might go see, I would be glad to do that. One unfortunate thing is that this business

<u>does</u> interfere with our lives; it changes our plans, controls our move-
ments. When Dr Simeons in Rome suggested that Doris' headaches
might be helped by 3 months of such therapy, she couldn't find the
time to give to it, understandably. The way you're situated now, my
impression is that you have literally nothing better to do.

I may not even send this letter. If I do, and it irritates you, I won't
be surprised or put off by that. My real argument is: you are so know-
ing, how can you resist knowing more?

Thank you for coming to Amherst and reading the novel. Did I tell
you that I'm planning to dedicate it "to my nephews and nieces"? In
your case that will be more than a phrase; you've made me feel really
encouraged, even at times a Prophet.

David sends greetings.

Yours ever,
Jimmy

To Hellen Ingram Plummer

WUSTL
13 May 1956
Pawlet, VT

Dear Mama and Mis' Annie,

A big sign on the road to N'hampton told me that Mother's day is
today! Oh dear. Remember all those cryptic telegrams during the war
years? Well, here is a letter, late, but with lots of love.

I'm up in Pawlet with Claude for the weekend, and have spent all
day typing, revising as I go, six pages. Already I'm through more than
a quarter of the book, but it is hard going. The Fords were in Amherst
last weekend and Harry said it would be very smart (as I well knew)
to submit the book as long as possible before I leave the country, as it
takes a month or so for the people who count to make up their minds,
and then there might be changes they'd want. I'm resolved, if there
are too many changes asked for, simply to try another publisher—
unless something really pertinent is suggested. I'm doing now every-
thing that seems needful to <u>me</u>.

It is lovely here, very warm, wild pear branches in the house forced into bloom. I had a heavy week. Wed. p.m. Marianne Moore arrived in Northampton; I met her train and stayed talking with her for an hour or so. The following day she came to my writing class and talked about student work—which she'd been studying all morning; then that evening, before her reading at the college, came to an early dinner at my house, with two couples on the faculty—roast beef, potatoes, peas, crème brulée—an elderly Poet's menu as I'd discovered last fall the day I had two dinners in honor of Frost (one at the Pres's house, one at Mrs Whicher's) with exactly that meal. She—M.M.—is pure enchantment, delighted everybody; lectured in a chalky faded blue ankle length dress with lace round the neck (Claude said she wore it at a reading at Harvard in 1942)—her manner is all generosity and modesty and simplicity, and of course she is one of the half dozen poets of the century (I said so in introducing her).

Thursday reading period begins. I'm going to Stonington for 2 days, then to NY for 2 nights—Sun and Mon; will have dinner with Guitou, and hope to see *Waiting for Godot*. Tuesday back to Amherst. Wed. I have a big beer and spaghetti party for my writing class and a few others. Boom Boom will drive up with me, and Robin says he's coming over with his girl—no, he's coming <u>this</u> week. Saturday another big party (just liquor) for faculty friends—that's the 26th, and from then on I expect I'll be mostly in Stonington. I will go back for commencement—Rosie and I plan to tour beerparties the night before; but after the 26th start writing me on Water St (107).

Sorry this is so rushed. My tail aches, and my back for that matter after all the typing. Now for a drink. Maisie joins in love to you both and Bill. (I took care of that paper and mailed it Tuesday to the power—?—Co.)

> Ever,
> Jimmy

Mrs Whicher's Harriet Fox Whicher (1890–1966), English professor at Mount Holyoke College, and wife of George Frisbie Whicher (1889–1954), English professor at Amherst.
Rosie Rosemary Sprague.
Maisie Merrill's cat.

To Hellen Ingram Plummer

WUSTL
6 July 1956
[Stonington, CT]

Dear Mama,

I haven't time for a long letter—people are coming and I must shave and fix the place up. I wanted to say that the box came and that I appreciate your sending it. I spent about an hour looking through the things, reading some, leaving others for a rainier day. My first reaction was to be glad all of that was cleaned out of your keeping; it isn't a collection to be reminded of—and while you might never have looked at it yourself, you couldn't but have felt burdened, knowing it was still on your hands. My second reaction—should I blush to admit it?—was regret that it should be, in many ways, so incomplete a record. On one hand, those exhaustive files of witless telegrams; on the other, less than a dozen letters—excluding those more or less "publicly" composed—that bear the lineaments of what I imagine was the real situation. Even those letters—CEM's for instance—seem, if only retrospectively, woefully adept, as if he were forever saying, "What can best be <u>said</u>? I shall set about feeling <u>that</u>." I find this most interesting, from the point of view of my description of him in the novel—that even then he should have been such a showman. Gert's letter, too, is fascinating. To hear her talk about her life, you'd think she had undergone a tremendous change—and yet, her letter to CEM reads as if it had been written <u>after</u> her conversion. She even speaks of "praying" for him. We change, I guess, so much less than we think! I notice he had a lot to say about your "shell"—which made me realize that you, perhaps, have felt that my own sense of remoteness in you has been instilled in me by him. This isn't so; I had been interested to know, or to learn, that Daddy and I both felt it—but I can't, again, say much for the <u>way</u> in which he feels it, so tremendously oversimplified, as if click! on went the mask—as if, even, it ever was anything as cut-and-dried as a "mask" or "shell." I do not feel it that way myself. I have never doubted that you suffered severely, and I haven't needed <u>your</u> example to show me that one adopts a putting-off attitude as a defense against what is known to give pain. It may be that your incapacity to cope with me in 1946 was nothing but a long-range effect of that disaster 10 years before; when we suspend feeling we get out of practise, how well I know that. <u>He</u> of course has never had that trouble; he is a virtuoso, a Paderewski.

One must war constantly against vulgar alternatives. Good <u>or</u> bad, mask <u>or</u> face, right <u>or</u> wrong. I have never had the slightest doubt that you were a good and faithful wife to him—I mean, I don't need the servants' statements to convince me. The really painful thing, of course, is your bewilderment when you had to learn that your goodness didn't get the response it merited—increased love and esteem. The dangerous word is perhaps "merit"—yet what other word does one use? We are taught all our early lives that to behave well insures our getting what we have our hearts set on, it's too unfair that, out in the world, things are differently arranged. One thing I am grateful for, over the last ten years, with their silences and subterfuges, is that whenever anything goes wrong between me and another person, my first reaction is to assume the fault is mine—I don't know how often I will keep on feeling that, but it's a reflex. It's one I see coming and going in your letters, those in this collection, and the struggle to admit it without self-consciousness . . . Well, these are random thoughts. It is a day later now, still raining. Gert's visit was very pleasant. We did the Ouija board for her, and Sewelly came up with a great shaggy dog named Chancellor who rushed adoringly from guest to guest while Maisie crouched in a jealous rage under chairs. I heard by the way from Ephraim that Betty's child will be a boy named William born on Sept 14—it came up because Hans L. was looking for a mother for his "charge" and I suggested her. Keep it to yourself and see what happens. I didn't go to S.H. as Daddy went to Boston to the hospital where he still is. Gert and I phoned him—he sounded dreadful, drugged perhaps. I have perhaps 3 more days work on the book, then 10 days in which to think and make sure I haven't done something stupid somewhere, and I'll take it in to NY. Miss Francis says she has my ticket to Jax. on the "West Coast Champion"—does she mean "East"? on the 7th. Pete F. and Pam are coming up on the weekend after next.

Much love to All.
Jimmy

the box Letters and news clippings relating to Merrill's parents' divorce.
to cope with me in 1946 When Merrill's mother discovered his affair with Friar.
Paderewski Ignacy Jan Paderewski (1860–1941), Polish pianist and statesman.
Betty's child Betty Plummer Potts was pregnant.
S.H. Southampton, Charles Merrill's home on Long Island.
Boston to the hospital Charles Merrill was being treated for heart disease in Boston.
Pete F. C. Peter Forcey.

To Claude Fredericks

GETTY
24 September 1956
[American President Lines Cruise]

Oh <u>Claude</u>,

How <u>could</u> you? All that saw us through the sailing was that beautifully typed envelope with all its parentheses. Keeping it in view we choked down our champagne and our tears, kissed everybody goodbye, enduring those endless minutes of paper streamers, Hawaiian band, faces smiling upward—Liam and Robert arrived too late, with a monster dahlia—then, once under the Golden Gate, raced back, tore it open and found (ugh) in vain (as it seemed) against the dreariness of <u>them</u>, full of obscure, one might say <u>reflected</u> squalors, as if you had been powerless against some long complaining scrawl they had sent you. Well, it left us glum; the kick quite went out of the champagne. Worst of all was imagining the rich letter <u>they</u> were reading, full of news and happiness—at the end of which they could but sink back, all wild surmise, muttering between their teeth, "Fancy! He never writes this kind of letter to us!"—producing the first flush of annoyance in their feelings toward you. Enough—but <u>do</u> get our letter back. Theirs is enclosed . . . We have just had the first of 2 fire drills and D. is in the cabin working. The cabin is small. The sea is calm and the purest sapphire. Our first acquaintance is an Oak Park (Ill) dentist, 82 years young, with bad knees; his maiden daughter is with Brownell Tours, and conducting a group of nice middle-aged people around the world. She is a heavy, disagreeable looking woman, which comes as something of a relief in the midst of so many animated faces. It may be too early to tell but I'll risk saying there is

Nobody on board. The service makes you sit straight up quivering with rage. David reveals himself as a match for Tony Harwood when it comes to complaints. But today is his birthday.

San Francisco was lovely. We liked Liam and Robert more than ever before. They gave me a reception after my reading, then drove us to their just finished house (5 years old but rebuilt completely) in Belvedere. An exquisite place. It had been designed originally by the Dean of some local school of Architecture. He kept conveying via 3rd persons troubled inquiries: What are they doing to my house? The reply went back: Refining it. It is now very fine indeed, mostly Japanese, set among pine and eucalyptus, 200 feet above milk-green waters. Much latticework and thin wooden bandings against white. A great kitchen once photographed by *House Beautiful* was the first thing to be ripped out. The reading itself was pleasant in spite of many qualms. There is (as you may know from Eberhart in the *Times* 2 Sundays ago) quite a wild little group of Zen-Hipster poets, most of them West Coast converts and therefore much more ardent. Ruth Witt who manages the Center kept murmuring before, "I hope there's no trouble . . ." There wasn't; they came up to me in the intermission with cries of: "What's the matter? Why don't you scream? That's what people out here want! Embarrass yourself! Talk about cock! We'll do anything if you just <u>scream</u>"—one of them was a tiny monkey with hair in his eyes, name of Gregory Corso. Bunny Lang found him on the NY East Side, took him to Cambridge and "was kind" to him; one of them, Allen Ginsberg, said he'd met me at John Hohnsbeen's. They made more of a show at the reception, taking off their shoes, reading <u>their</u> works in squeaky faint voices, piling slices of turkey high on bread, calling Shelley the "greatest poet of all time." What else? One of them went up to the German maid and said, "I sympathize with you!" The maid, startled, said, "Oh my, you don't need to do that!" "Well I do," said the poet, "whether you want me to or not."

Terrible music is coming out of the loudspeaker, talk and songs and news. Two little Japanese are playing chess. I can't go on. Love to you and Jimmy, thank you for your wire and Send Us Our Letter!

Jamey

Liam and Robert Liam O'Gallagher (1917–2007), avant-garde painter, sound artist, and spiritualist, and Robert Rheem, his partner and collaborator. Fredericks had

sent a letter to them to deliver to Merrill and Jackson, and another letter to them, and mixed up the envelopes.
Eberhart in the *Times* Richard Eberhart's assessment of the San Francisco poets appeared in "West Coast Rhythms" in *The New York Times Book Review* on September 2, 1956.
the Center San Francisco State University Poetry Center, founded by Ruth Witt in 1954.
Gregory Corso (1930–2001), American poet, partner of Allen Ginsberg.
Bunny Lang V. R. Lang (1924–56), poet, playwright, and a founder of the Poets' Theatre in Cambridge, MA.
John Hohnsbeen's Hohnsbeen (1926–2007) worked in New York galleries before becoming a friend and secretary to Peggy Guggenheim, whose art collection in Venice he helped to curate.

To Claude Fredericks

GETTY
1 October 1956
Tokyo, Japan

Dearest Friend,

Your longest and kindest letter makes today, though of the grayest, nonetheless brightest and best. We are a tiny bit hung over from an evening of pubcrawling in Shinjuku-ku (is your map outspread on your knees?) with Guitou's friend Meredith Weatherby. He is an odd, not wholly appealing person; one feels . . . oh I don't know what. Anyhow, we walked through the red light district, a little stage set, a hundred pretty girls in Western dress, in a hundred clean, artful doorways, as if only waiting for Gene Kelly to come and turn it all into a vast dance number. To my American eye, which connects any pleasing bit of building or decoration with paying through the (American) nose for the right to be tasteful, an uncanny air of prosperity hovered over the scene. And yet one knows the people are poor; even more, now that prostitution is being abolished (they have been given a year in which to find new jobs) these particular people are probably desperate. But how the eye is sustained! We then wandered through a glowing labyrinth of booths and shops, stopping to sit at a scrubbed board, perhaps edged with copper, to drink sake and eat tiny slices of squid, a long toothpick of chicken remnant alternating with a bit of scallion and grilled over charcoal—or <u>not</u> to eat tiny dead fish, silver, staring—and make contact with the other customers. David lost his heart to a young and virtuous student, I mine to a young and drunken postman. It would be wrong to say that English is spoken. Yesterday—wandering without MW—we realized his immense helpfulness; he had, it seemed, taken us so deeply into the city (we've spent both evenings with him) that, once on our own, we found ourselves floundering, trying to regain the depths, constantly cast back upon simple looking, like a beach—but what a beach! with balloons trailing neon characters, with the Nara sculptures, 2 dozen of them, in the museum, with 2 young people all rouged and powdered, pirouetting in the street to their own music, drum, bell, flute—the opening of yet another arcade where a kind of vertical pinball game is played; this has swept the country, the people play it in a daze, like the slot machines in Reno. Before we left the last tiny bar two lady musicians, a singer and samisen player, regaled us; one song was light in spirit, a dialogue of which a few mild phrases from the instrumentalist (contralto) were answered by a vivacious chattering tune from her companion; another song, very sad, the lament of Townsend Harris's Japanese concubine, who had to lose, among other things, Face, in order to keep that distinguished foreigner in the country. Oh, we've done so much! The first evening we dined at MW's, bathed at the luxurious Tokyo Onsen, along with a crowd of youths in Egyptian costume, the extras from *Aida* (an Italian opera troupe has come to town; completely sold out); then saw a geisha do a striptease in a workers bar. Why we've even seen the 5 candidates from Tokyo for Mr Nippon of 1956 being selected (out of 21) at a bodybuilding club. Before the results were announced, a well-known sculptor addressed the group, with tips on posing and an exhortation to back up their efforts with a philosophy. I could go on for another page. And shall.

But not about Japan. Your words about the *Seraglio*, so warm and so extensive, touch me more than I can say. I feel you have completely <u>felt</u> the book and that is the fairest tribute it could receive. I do understand your feelings about the second half; to a slight degree I share them—those sections contain elements that were clearly not in the original scheme of the book; I trusted the accidental inspirations, in fact I can't remember what alternatives presented themselves, if any. The real difficulty, I daresay, is one you have seen working in my poems: that of trying to <u>present</u> emptiness, in this case Francis's own, as something beautiful, rich, a goal, however frightening. Two things are meant to happen in the last chapters; F's conviction that he is, in your words, the agent of all the transformations, and, glimpsed through that, the sense that he cannot be, that the castration was his final gesture as a real person, a gesture whose magic slowly but surely exhausts itself and leaves him stranded. This may be too close to the way things happen in life for full expression in a book; I don't know. As with Tithonus, I have to take the rap for a hero who gives up his raison d'etre, and this has to be faced along with whatever his situation gives off of beauty and virtue. Lily, in this sense, is more of a counterweight than a parallel; their acts are similar, but hers will permit others and his will not. I'm writing now at this length in part because I <u>haven't</u> written my father and know that I must do this at once. I guess I can't imagine that he will read the book. And what can I say except: DO read it! Oh, Guitou! And oh that Dr Tenney!

We're so delighted that Ivan liked your book. That is, isn't it, the first and worst hurdle? Perhaps by now you are having lunch (or rather a nightcap, since noon here is midnight there) with a clutch of editors. Oh I do pray that they will say, sweetly and sanely: Yes we will publish it; we trust you to make the slight cuts you have in mind; here is a largish cheque; please at once provide us with an 8x10 glossy photograph of yourself, good and gifted Mr Fredericks! I think you needn't worry about the accusation of murder. No such murder was ever committed (or was it?)—so that you'd really have an argument on the side of Fiction rather than anything libellous. As for Aunts, one cannot but trust them to be ample, amiable, auntlike—the other way, madness lies . . .

We both miss you so much and send love love love. I think we'll stay in Tokyo through the 12, and may return for a visit in Nov. Embraces to you and Jimmy, ever,

Jamey

Yes, I have reached within the last 20 pages of completing the revision of AMY; no, I have infinite amounts of work to do on the NEW NOVEL (is that a title?). But Tokyo—no, the personalitylessness of everything visual and human, here (that's it)—reduces one to some monster, JM's monster in Iceberg, perhaps; bringing out all those irrelevant footnotes in place of thinking, experiences every hour are covered with asterisks—one couldn't feel more humble, less able, more enchanted. Someone named Tom Hiam is here, he appeared in the form of a small white note slipped under the door, just now, as I watched. Several of these have been slipped under the door, like invitations to leave our typing and writing and try again. We will discover a sure way of mystically forcing Harcourt's hand, a midnite shrine, an offering.

Love, David

Meredith Weatherby (1915–97), American expatriate in Japan, publisher, translator of Yukio Mishima (1925–70).
Townsend Harris (1804–78), the first American consul general to travel to Japan.
As with Tithonus Merrill is comparing Francis, his surrogate in *The Seraglio* (1957), to the main character in his play *The Immortal Husband* (1955).
their acts are similar In *The Seraglio*, Lily, niece of Francis, cuts an oil portrait of her mother with a knife. Later in the novel Francis castrates himself with a razor.
JM's monster in Iceberg Merrill's's poem "The Octopus" in *The Country of a Thousand Years of Peace* (1959).

To Hellen Ingram Plummer   WUSTL
                                                          23 October 1956
                                                          Kyoto, Japan

Dear Mama,

Two letters from you yesterday and one from Charles brought me the first news I have had since Doris's cable on the 8th . . . I guess it hadn't been very real to me until then. When I'd received your cable, and talked to Doris, Bob and Charles—from that time until yesterday, the days seemed to pass without very much conscious awareness of what had happened. Then your letters; when I read about the burial, and your wedding ring, I understood at last, and the tears I had been waiting for came. I'm so glad you were there in Palm Beach; I feel that you <u>did</u> represent me there and that every gesture you made was the absolutely right one. My tears are, still, I guess, partly for myself, that I wasn't there; but partly too for the terrible way in which death smooths out all the anxieties and confusion to reveal the feelings one hadn't really been aware of feeling, they were so choked by pointless fears and awkwardnesses. In one stroke it is as though the <u>beautiful</u> surface of that whole world (which in my book appears so riddled with pain) had turned towards me, a mild sweet surface, the way the faces of the dead are said to look young and peaceful. I ask myself now: what is life, that it should withhold such peacefulness until the end?

What a nice letter Bill wrote me! I will try to write him before long; till then, please tell him how I appreciate it. I hadn't known that Daddy was buried in his uniform; that is indeed, as he says, a touching insight.

What news here? We went last weekend to the Shinto shrine at Ise, just about the most sacred place in Japan. Extremely beautiful, great forests, and very simple buildings of natural cedar wood, some protruding roof-beams tipped with polished brass. The shrine is ceremonially torn down, razed, every 20 or 30 years, then rebuilt in exactly the same form in an adjacent lot, with new materials. So that, while the shape of the building is ancient, they are perpetually in perfect condition. Shinto is of course the state religion and the atmosphere of the shrine is not so sweet and human as it is at many Buddhist temples with their mossy gardens and thatched roofs, the stain of old red lacquer barely visible on the wooden columns, 300 to 1000 years old. Last night, late, we went with a student-interpreter to a "fire festival" some 30 minutes outside Kyoto, on a hill. Great bonfires, torches, processions of rather drunken boys carrying big shrines on their shoulders. We were home by 3, choosing to miss the dawn climax. Saturday we are going to Miyajima, a temple built out into the water, 40 miles from Hiroshima. If you saw the color movie *Gate of Hell* there was a scene of priests at Miyajima.

Autumn is beginning; the air is soft, cool, drizzly often; the miniature leaves of the maples are turning here and there. I have never seen such natural beauty anywhere; the landscape seems to combine what is most prized in England (moss, thatch, etc) with the best of tropical flora (bamboo, vines [*in the margin:* rice fields everywhere, + tea bushes]) and waterfalls, wonderful rocks, nevertheless very clean—nothing one ever needs to hack a path through.

The bath is about to be announced; then dinner and early to bed. Much love to Mis' Annie and Bill. Letters usually take 5–7 days—

yours took long only because we missed 3 days of mail, being away Fri and Sat. David sends greetings to the 3 of you.

> With ever so much love,
> Jimmy

it hadn't been very real His father's death. Hellen Plummer placed her wedding ring from their marriage in the flowers on his coffin.
Gate of Hell (1953), directed by Teinosuke Kinugasa.

To Frederick Buechner

WHEATON
30 October 1956
Kyoto, Japan

Dear Freddy,

David has gone through the rain (it rains ALL the time) to the Tourist Bureau to pick up 4 days' mail; I must make haste, before new letters touch off new crises, to write this one to you. Yours came as a delight and a comfort. I'm glad now, at last, that I didn't go home; it took longer, this way, for me to understand (feel) what had happened, and it was very strange, having nothing to <u>do</u>, no vigil, no wake, but as the letters began to reach me—and particularly one from Mama in which she told of leaving her wedding ring among the flowers on the coffin—the whole business became real to me, moreso perhaps than if I had got there after 45 hours in a plane. Then Ephraim described him, looking about 32, in a green suit, surrounded by pretty women, and I had to smile.

We returned last night from a 3 day trip, partly through the Inland Sea, to see the shrine at Miyajima, built out onto the water, or onto the mud as it happened, for we saw it only at low tide in a dusky drizzle. Great bronze lions held their own, but the Shinto fondness for vermilion and white—so wisely avoided at Ise—suggested rather some lakeside amusement park. It is a puzzling religion, as you may know, in which everything is holy, but as it were automatically so, unlike Buddhism where it seems to be one's own reverence that reaches for a perception of divinity in all things. The Shinto shrines are full of booths, tended by temporary vestals in white robes and bright red trousers with the self-possession of starlets. At Miyajima, a live white horse lives (very well) on the food-offerings of the pilgrims, but in a tiny hut. We met an awfully nice American girl poking around there, Helen Hawks from Greenfield, Mass. She had fled there from Hiroshima which she couldn't bear. We went there, nevertheless, the next day and spent 3 hours between trains poking around. To the surprise of both of us, Helen was right; it is one of the most painful experiences imaginable. Oh, some of it is built up, a big shopping section, a few buildings that either stood up under the Bomb or were purposely designed in the style of 1910 to look as if they had. But the rest—! mud streets, great empty purposeless lots full of rubble and strange stunted trees, trunks like toothpicks. There is no interest, anywhere in Japan, in keeping up a Western Garden—why should there be? Judging from the samples we've seen of Western cooking, W. rooms, W. anything—a matter of oils, chipped plaster, fringe, chambers of horrors all . . . Anyhow, in the middle of the wilderness rise up 3 modern cement buildings, the New Hiroshima Hotel, the Peace Museum, and a special museum with a poorly-named "Grill Room" upstairs. The Peace museum is given over to displays related to the Bomb, from scientific charts and diagrams all the way to the end of a child's thumb, with nail, brown, dry, cooked, which dropped off during the five days before the little boy finally died. This is displayed with a photograph of him in school uniform, a sickly-delicate face, great big eyes, even the picture somewhat faded. Melted rock, flattened bottles, scorched clothing, photographs of horrible burns, a shot of Truman at the telephone—and beyond the plate glass, that filthy flat field with a man on crutches picking through a garbage pail. Well . . . I had never for a moment, before this, felt, what my brother would call, the national burden of guilt; but there we couldn't meet people's eyes. It is a great tourist spot; busloads of Japanese come, gape, "realize the mistake of their militarism" as the brochures say. There is an "Atomic Souvenir Shop" selling postcards of the horrors and chunks of rubble . . .

A letter came from Harry enclosing a sample page from my book, a real thrill; it <u>looks</u> like a novel. Back in Tokyo, the morning of the 7th, I'll find the galleys waiting for me. It will be strange to read it now. When you write again, tell me more about yours, if you can—even things like your musings over the particular page in progress; I am so curious about it, anything you say would make it clearer. Perhaps, by now, it's finished?

A long letter (read once sketchily) from Charles has come, with David, now. He speaks of Geo. Todd in East Harlem, with whom you have worked, I gather. Chas. is interested in helping that project, and wants to corner as much of the "Protestant Activity" money in Daddy's will as he can, to support it. I have heard only indirectly about the will, so don't know what this wd amount to.

Well, old friend, I'm being made nervous by these small segments of paper. We are sitting in our cold salon, 9 x 9, closed in by paper, straw and wood, and some plaster colored (possibly made of) dung. Around us lie the evidences of spent money—dolls, knives, lacquer, used film, a bottle of rum; no pearls yet, and only one pair of binoculars. Quilted kimonos are being delivered later on, and at least part of the afternoon will be passed hunting for hardware for Stonington. This doesn't, I fear, give any sense of the charms of Japan. They exist; but are largely addressed to the eye. Nobody speaks more than, at best, passable English. Even high mountain places reek of urine. Really we are beginning to look forward to Hong Kong, but a night at the Mt Koya monastery (in Toynbee's tracks) may clear the air. Love to you and Judy. Send snapshots of apartment.

As ever,
Jimmy

Harry Harry Ford.
tell me more about yours Buechner's novel, *The Return of Ansel Gibbs* (1958).
Geo. Todd Merrill's brother Charles supported Rev. George Todd (1925–2019), who led an urban ministry at East Harlem Protestant Parish.
Toynbee Arnold Toynbee (1889–1975), British historian and philosopher of history.

To Hellen Ingram Plummer   WUSTL
1 November 1956
Kyoto, Japan

Dear Mama,

Back in <u>warm</u> Kyoto after a bitter-cold 24 hours atop a holy Buddhist mountain, Koya <u>by name</u>—the most beautiful place we've seen yet. There are 120 temples, of which perhaps half take in guests in return for an offering. We went with the young priest of the temple we "talked our way" into (postcard Sewelly read to you); were given two beautiful rooms on a garden, a magnificent vegetarian dinner, some 9 courses; rose at 6 to participate in the morning service, a matter of kneeling in the cold incense-filled air while the priests chanted and made weird sound effects with bells, woodblocks and their own voices. There followed 6 hours of sightseeing, during which we encountered the celebrated Professor Toynbee and his party ("noble interpreters and noble priest, I think," as our friend said) more than once, a tall, ethereal man smiling, with a wife rather like Jessie MacIntosh.

Now, finding your letter, I gather you didn't get mine sent to the Sulgrave (you had written you weren't sure where you'd stay, but would call there in any case). I mailed it Oct 9 or 10, I believe. In it I suggested a different Kyoto address, but it doesn't much matter now. I may have marked it HOLD, so send them a card to forward it.

About the book. I honestly don't see what Daddy's death does to change it. This may be because I feel I've made a very true and lovable portrait of him. It seems to me, if I recall correctly, the only objection to his characterization that you made was that I showed him as old and sick—which might, I agree, conceivably have offended him. Now that he is gone I'm more than ever glad to have made a kind of memorial that will offset some of the obvious garlands anybody could contrive. As for Doris and Bob, I feel that to "prepare" them is first of all an acknowledgement of guilt. In S.F. I did have a talk with Bob saying (apropos of Doris's letter to you in which she called Keenan's book "complimentary") I hoped she wouldn't be dismayed by my own picture of CEM, which corresponded to the man <u>I</u> knew, etc, and he said yes, he hoped the same. I think, furthermore, that Robin has talked to them about the book—not at my request by any means—but Daddy said, last summer, that he believed Doris was apprehensive. I feel that any word from me, of preparation, would only increase that apprehension; and that the more her fears are aroused, the less chance there is of her giving the book any kind of fair reading. I wrote Daddy from Tokyo, a letter he will never read, asking him please, if he could, to read the typed copy I sent him all the way through; that it was a book in which the characters <u>are</u> shown in different lights, etc . . . I suspect that far less damage will be done by the book than by the glib reader (Cora J. or a TIME reviewer) who simplifies the motives behind it. I can appreciate your difficulty when people ask you what it's about; I go mute myself. The kind of person who asks that question will not take the only sensible answer—it deals with the problem of finding a way to live in a high-powered world (something like that). A plausible answer might be: it's about old age, or: the difference between 2 generations. If I were you, though, I'd say in most cases that it is largely based on life in Southampton; that you haven't been in on the goings-on and so aren't sure how much is true and how much made-up—your statement is helped by the clearly fictitious marriage to Lady G., among other things.

This way, by showing a minimum of embarrassment, you manage to undercut any excessive reaction <u>after</u> your friends have read the book. (This is what Guitou said she was going to do; she hadn't been much pleased with the character of Xenia, but after the first surprise she resolved to take the line of being amused and delighted by the portrait, which clearly had all kinds of fictional touches, etc.) If she had said, an awful book has been written all about me, the people who read it would say, Yes, yes, it is awful. It's the same problem as with Doris: one finds what one expects to find.

The changes I have made—well, I took out the story about Bob and Buster; I did not name Francis's act as a castration, so that the squeamish reader may take it as a suicide attempt, if he must; I had the Cheeks devoured by sharks at the end. Oh, there are countless small changes I couldn't begin to list.

Morning. More headlines about Egypt—don't worry, we will proceed warily.

2 days ago I received from Harry Ford a sample page of the book; it looked fine. It will be 320 pages long and sell for 3.95.

Yes, I'd like to know more about Daddy's will: even the major part of it is vague to me. I had a sad letter from Con, sounding terribly bereft. Poor Charlie P. I will write Lalla at once; I gather you won't be going to that funeral—or didn't go, I should say. I know you'll miss him, so will I.

That's all for now. Much love to everyone.

Jimmy

Keenan's book Unpublished biography of Charles E. Merrill, commissioned by him.
Cora J. Cora Jaeckel (1891–1969), Southampton socialite.
headlines about Egypt In late October, Israel invaded the Sinai Peninsula. Britain and France joined the conflict, intending to regain control of the Suez Canal from Egypt, and failed. Egypt was on Merrill and Jackson's itinerary.
sad letter from Con Lady Constance Saint.

To Irma Brandeis   WUSTL
                                                         6 November 1956
                                                              Kyoto, Japan

Dear Irmchem,

But I don't <u>keep</u> a journal, not after the first week or so; letters have got to bear all the burden. I've been on the point of writing one to you ever since yours reached me in Kyoto with a great bundle of tidings, wires, obituaries, which I've not yet done acknowledging. I would, probably, have sat down to it (cross-legged on tatami) sooner if I hadn't felt strangely, even unjustly, scolded by you for my improper choice of words in an earlier letter, and I really couldn't think (nor can I yet) how to reply to that. I've had absolutely no experience with death (this I suppose <u>is</u> the reply) and what I meant then and still mean now is that it takes, at this distance, a long time to understand what has happened; a process of pains and visions one by one over the last weeks, adding up to what might have been an instantaneous awareness had I been at home. From that point of view the letters, yours especially, helped more than their writers can have known. I was having dreadful backaches myself (the tatami have cured them) so I can sympathize with your incapacity to go to the church; bless you for wanting to; I wish I might have been there through all of it. The galley-proof reached me 2 days ago. I read it a bit dully; uncertain whether my loss of interest is due to my no longer being able to alter the book, or to knowing that he is dead. In a letter from my nephew at Harvard, received today: "Before he lapsed into the coma, he called my mother and Charles over, said he had a long story which he wanted them to hear. There was a pause while they waited and then he said that he felt so tired, but would tell it to them later."

Japan, in any event, would be a lonely place. We have found it extraordinary from every visual standpoint; the Kabuki, the gardens, the simplest rooms. But the language barrier is monstrous and so is the barrier of manners; one can endure just so long feeling barbarous. I don't in the least blame them, and it isn't of course a strain for them—they sink back into their splendidly contrived formulas as into those scalding baths, while the Westerner (in either situation) either screams with pain or, mercifully, faints. Kyoto of course is where all this reaches fever pitch, and we have been most grateful for Joe C's friend Eidmann who, while practising the amenities on all 8 cylinders, is amusing and articulate about them. With him we have seen puppet-shows, jugglers, even, last night, accompanying his secretary to his weekly acupuncture treatment—a number of 2-inch needles delicately inserted near the spine. When they touch the nerve a faint electric shock is felt, nothing else; and on the next day, soreness. But 6 months ago he could scarcely walk and is now lifting not only huge crates but Eidmann himself, who looks heavy. We've taken lovely trips, to Ise, to Miyajima, to Koyasan—where who should materialize but Arnold Toynbee, saintly, white-haired, in a crowd of sages. The papers had written about him, in an early, characteristic interview: "His magnanimity was evident to all who met him. Never once did he display his true feelings." Italics mine. We return to Tokyo tonight for a final week, I'm not sure why, before retracing our tracks to Kobe and sailing for H.K. Egypt looks out of the question, so we may take a bit longer to reach India—Singapore?

Bali?—and fly direct to Istanbul from Bombay or Delhi. Much love to Polly and Muffin. David greets.

Ever and ever your
Jamie

I had a long letter from Ted W. about helping finance some books of poetry. I will write him when I can—it sounds offhand like something for the Foundation!

Joe C's friend Eidmann Phillip Karl Eidmann (1924–97), an American ordained as a Buddhist cleric, was an authority on the arts of the tea ceremony and flower arrangement, and a friend of Joseph Campbell (1904–87), the American scholar of comparative mythology and religion.
Ted W. Theodore Weiss (1916–2003), poet and editor of the *Quarterly Review of Literature*, who had invited Merrill to teach at Bard in 1948.
the Foundation Merrill had recently formed the Ingram Merrill Foundation, his personal foundation for supporting the arts. Brandeis was on the small advisory board.

To Claude Fredericks   GETTY
                                    24 December 1956
                                    Bangkok, Thailand

Dear Claude,

A week ago I had a wire from Knopf; the proofs, mailed in HK, have not reached them; my head falls on my arms with a long groan whenever I think of this. It is my fault furthermore for idiotically not registering them; evidently my mother's letters have had their effect—I don't <u>want</u> the book published, might that be it? Ughghghgahaga-hahhaha . . .

Only 3 more days in Bangkok. Last Wednesday we went on an excursion in a group of—somebody called them culture-vultures; mostly wives of people stationed here in one capacity or another. They have been studying Siamese art with a Prince Diskul, curator of the museum, to whom we had had an introduction from John Goodwin. The Prince is in his late twenties, pas joli, and is said to be the only authority who really knows his stuff. I wonder. Hashing the day over with an enchanting couple, the Hofers from Cambridge (he is head of Houghton Library) a few doubts were expressed. And what's more, Mr Hofer declared—we were all having drinks on our veranda— what's more, not that it has any bearing on the case, the Prince is known to be a notorious pervert. Oh really! said I, rolling my eyes; and then of course 5 minutes later the Prince walked in (invited) with a très joli friend. The H's were instantly on their feet. Well, the excursion took us to Ayudhya, the capital from 1350–1767. In two "barges" we glided from Wat to Prang to Stupa. An elephant trap is being restored, at great expense, and buddhas regilded, roofed over, all in rather questionable taste by the Prime Minister who is a notorious fool in cultural matters. These edifices are wonderfully strange; the prangs really resemble nothing so much as buildings in Buck Rogers; others were very Berman, tall crumbling affairs, much bared brick, the squeak of bats inside, flowers and shrubs all over. There is a tree hereabouts called the cheese tree (fromagier) which dotes on wats and bade fair to swallow up all of Angkor Thom, great round pale green roots 30 feet long, lounge and coil, or lock and loll (as American music is called in the Orient)—to the point that they were mistaken, by the first western visitors to Angkor for monstrous serpents in the glooms. The high point of our excursion, well there were two, but the first was to find myself in an itsy-bitsy boat, a mere dried peapod, leaning precariously against the knees of an American woman, while the Prince Himself paddled us down a country klong. I was just thinking, how far I had travelled in how many directions since, oh, Jacksonville, when suddenly I moved my head to avoid being hit by the dock and over we went, the three of us, into the warm green water. The Prince's eyes narrowed, thinking possibly: why must these Americans <u>force</u> their democracy on us? In another boat, D. was fracturing himself laughing. Then, later, five minutes truly rich and strange in the high priest's residence at an old temple; up some wobbling board steps into a 2nd story room, scarcely floored, with very thick walls covered with the remains of, it appears, the only examples of the late Ayudhya fresco style; we took in a reclining Buddha under palms . . . but the room itself was incredible! An old priest swathed in gamboge (real gamboge from Cambodge!) squatting in front of a small bleachers full of images; elsewhere, a tall carved palanquin; a pallet whose white sheet and pillow-slip had been stained all yellow from priestly robes;

a younger priest stood by; the wall glowed yellow from the simple reflection of him—everywhere, this orange gloom; then out, down the springing stair. Fifty years ago, I wonder how many people here ever felt firm surfaces beneath them, with any regularity. It must have always been a matter of moving along boardwalks of varying flexibility like a xylophone, entering little barques so tiny you could feel a fish nuzzle them; the charcoal vendor boat in ash gray, and she in black with a lampshade hat; the butcher's boat is red; the houses along the canals offer themselves to the eye, there is nothing but what one sees. We went with Rollie McK's husband's friend, Chew, to his house 15 km away. After a mile of boardwalks, we were there. "The big fat lady is my mother," he explained; big and fat she was, toothless, and waddled off to cook for us. They live on stilts, in perhaps 5 rooms; off the living room is a desk with a shrine and, 20 feet higher up, a hive of bees, shimmering, coming + going through a hole in the roof; the LR is all dark wood with 2 cabinets of ornaments, a photograph of Chew as a scout and another as a 7-day priest, with head shaved, at the age of 7. Innumerable pictures of stars. Rory Calhoun, stripped to the waist, driving a nail into something; Jimmy Dean on the grandfather clock. Chew thinks he is JD (indeed, a slight likeness can be found) and has his name writ large on his shirttails and inside the trousers a sister was ironing. He wants to go to Hollywood. After lunch we put on sarongs and had a dip in the klong with him and his friend Suripong. He gave us his photograph with this inscription: To James and David my best American friend. I hope you will not remember me. I love you forever. . . . . To Ceylon at Dawn Saturday; we shall stay there through Xmas, then Madras for a week; Bombay + environs, flying to Istanbul (I think) Jan 15. We begin to long to settle down. We love your letters, and you. Hug Jimmy for us and kiss Tenth St.

J.

Have you been to see Callas? Why don't you phone the Met. Opera Club + ask Mr Simmons (or Mr Fream), using my name, to see if he can get you seats as I'm sure it's difficult otherwise. Do this far ahead—he will know before the papers announce it.

HK Hong Kong.
the museum On the grounds of the Varadis Palace.

the Hofers Philip Hofer (1898–1984), founder of the Department of Printing and Graphic Arts at Harvard's Houghton Library.
Ayudhya The Ayudhya (Ayutthaya) kingdom in Siam (now Thailand), 1350–1767.
prangs Corncob-shaped spires characteristic of ancient Khmer architecture.
very Berman Eugene Berman (1899–1972), Russian-born neoromantic painter noted for the dreamlike sets he designed for the Metropolitan Opera.
the cheese tree (fromagier) *Ceiba pentandra*, commonly known as *fromager* in French and kapok tree in English, which has huge buttress roots.
wats Buddhist temples.
Angkor Thom Walled Khmer city made of laterite, occupying some six square miles, enclosing monuments and artwork and surrounded by a wide moat, founded late twelfth century.
klong Canal.
The Prince's eyes See "The Beaten Path" in Merrill's *Collected Prose* (2004), first published in *Semi-Colon* (1957), edited by John Bernard Myers.
little barques Compare Merrill's poem "The Current" in *Nights and Days* (1966).
Rollie McK's Rollie McKenna (1918–2003), American photographer, best known for her portraits of poets and writers; Stonington resident.

To Robin Magowan

WUSTL
26 December 1956
Colombo, Ceylon

Dear Robin,

Your letter, with clipping, was waiting at Cook's today, a most agreeable surprise—the mail in Ceylon has been <u>awful</u>, what there's been of it, mostly very long letters in sentences of 200 words from Condon's office about the setting up of "my" foundation. He is really an admirably thorough man but I do feel, as a guide up-country put it, weather-eaten after reading a 4 page reply to a casual query. I also received, in Bangkok, your letter sent to HK, but by then (not having heard) I'd begun to wonder when you were leaving for Europe; I remembered something about a six-week holiday . . . ? Of course I still don't know <u>where</u> in Kitzbuhl or Munich you can be addressed and I hope that circumstance will be considered should my silence at Christmastime ever come up, regretfully, over the coffee and cognac. I sent your father and brothers some handkerchiefs from Hong Kong, airmail to SF; your gift is being shipped in a crate with some other things I bought in Bangkok, it is a smallish oldish head of Buddha in bronze, rather battered; you'll get it before school opens next year I suppose. Bangkok is far and away the best place, a land of heart's desire, but I have just turned out 4000 words on it, and Japan, for *Semi-Colon* and don't really feel up to any more travel notes.

I'd be very pleased to have some poems in *Audience*. Let the editor choose what he wants; he will certainly know how to make the proper acknowledgement to the previous publishers. For a while I thought the *Seraglio* wouldn't get out at all. This is the stupid thing I did. Worn down (or again weather-eaten) by my mother's trepidation about the book (mother-eaten?) and by the guilts arising like fumes from her letters, from the whole distant apprehension of the Death, when I got to Hong Kong I casually stuffed the corrected proofs into a manila envelope and sent them off to NY by air freight, unregistered, uninsured—all the while perfectly aware of the sheer necessity that they be dispatched first class, etc etc. So that of course 12 days later, in Bangkok, on the sickest morning of my whole life—at death's door after a far from successful experience with opium the previous evening, of which I can recall little beyond the fierce desire for Visions, drawing at the pipe till smoke came out of my toes, and my cracked, dehydrated, toneless voice complaining, Nothing's happened yet . . . —on that morning, sure enough, came the cable from Knopf—no proofs received. Far too embarrassed to admit my secret motive, which I do only to you and David, I sent off a note, scarcely able to hold the pen, all bluff and bewilderment, begging to be cabled should they be received. In the meanwhile people said there had been a cargo of mail from HK to LA 9/10 destroyed by an elephant gone amok miles over the Pacific. Well you can imagine the three weeks before their letter reached me saying they <u>had</u> arrived, 2 days after the cable. Only then did I decide that yes, I <u>did</u> want the book published, after all. I'm almost chipper about it now. We returned to the opium den, by the by, and I very cautiously took a wisp or two of smoke into my mouth, well, five pipes in all, but nothing happened except that back at the hotel I found that I could do 15 push-ups without the least effort; 7–10 is my usual breaking point. David the rascal had waking dreams all night, no help at all as I lay groaning and retching.

We are off to India in the morning; we shall stay 5–6 days in Madras, then Bombay (trip to Ajanta) and possibly Delhi + environs or Benares, flying to Istanbul at midnight on the 14th. It is a ludicrously short time but we are both sort of eager to get to Munich and spend a month in one place for a change, and to be out of the mysterious east, for all its glories. You see what it has done to my sentence structure.

I've been reading my 1st Dickens novel, *Bleak House.* I suppose Betty is or has read it with Craig? I heard him read a paper on it last spring. He is quite a novelist. Then *Back to Methuselah;* I'm thankful I wrote my play before reading it; it's full of a wild humor and, unless these old eyes deceive me, poetry. I hope I'll be able to read Charles' plays in Paris. One marvelously good book was put into my hands in Tokyo—Henri Michaux's *A Barbarian in Asia.* I do not know the French title, it was published there in 1933, and by New Directions in 1949, said to be out of print. With the lightest touches he draws the noblest conclusions—in a preface to the American edition—to wit, his advice to the world: Create Civilizations!—like the prologue to *Les Mamelles de Tiresias:* Faites des enfants! Every page is a joy to read and the style, even in English, contagious, as you will see if you compare my own travel notes with it.

The really frightful thing about traveling is the way you cannot shake slight acquaintances; we have said goodbye 4 times now, for-ever, to some jokers named Blatchley from SF. This doesn't stop them from walking into the lobby an hour ago. And a brusque, fat, mournful, opinionated Negress from Nagoya (in education) who kept us company for 8 hours in the airport at Angkor Wat—who but she would telephone at 7 on Christmas morning?

Enough for now. Don't dream too much, there are waking adventures to be had. If it's any comfort I found it next to impossible to write during the first 6 or 8 months. But then—! Just make sure you have enough paper on hand. David sends greetings to you and Betty. Anch'io.

As ever,
Jimmy

my mother's trepidation *The Seraglio* contains sometimes unflattering portraits of his parents and other relatives.
Betty Elizabeth Rudd, Robin's girlfriend, whom he would marry. As a Radcliffe student, she took a course at Harvard with G. Armour Craig, a former teacher of Merrill's at Amherst.
Back to Methuselah Subtitled *"A Metabiological Pentateuch"* (1921), a series of five plays by George Bernard Shaw.

Les Mamelles de Tiresias Francis Poulenc composed his comic opera *Les Mamelles de Tirésias* in 1945, an adaptation of Apollinaire's surrealist play of 1917 that ends with the plea "Dear audience, make babies!"

To Claude Fredericks

GETTY
15 January 1957
Jaipur, India

Dear Claude—

Que de fois (as the French, of whom in India I have begun to think differently, say) que de fois we have relived that Round Table Discussion in Stonington, you and Grace at swords' points, and wondered, even right on the spot, which of you was closer to the truth. It is chilly in Jaipur. I write on the porch of a disagreeable hotel to which we have been obliged to slink back, after haughtily departing for the Station, with all our baggage, only to discover the train for Delhi— which under any circumstances takes 8 hours to travel 200 miles—is 2 hours late already; our venom then turned onto the Tourist Bureau Guide, for not having inquired beforehand, since Indian trains are notorious etc etc. The poor man, all pitted from pox, shook his head acquiescently, leaving us with the uneasy sense we've had before, of there being no resistance here, not even passive; one makes a gesture and it reverberates on and on until it is spent—or the gesturer himself is. Well we are back at the hotel and D. is in the sun, and the 4 ancient turbaned porters at the station whom we at first grandly refused to pay saying it was for the Tourist Bureau to do that etc, until we learned that they wanted only a penny apiece—again no resistance, somehow—those 4 <u>have</u> their pennies and we are thinking about lunch, chilled and spent, with no prospect of Delhi until 10:30 tonight. The only reason we are taking the train is because J. Laughlin said, don't miss that great experience; this is not the first time his advice has puzzled us. It is, willynilly, far more exciting—India—than Ceylon; and Rajputana is positively thrilling after Bombay. Nobody had prepared us for the red sandstone, seen first at the Fort in Agra; an indescribable color, flecked with ochre or streaked with buff, like vin rose to the eye, crepe de chine to the fingertip, brilliantly carved and at times, though not at all times, brilliantly painted. Through an embrasure, across a plain, perhaps a riverbed in the shade of discolored marble inlaid with trees and bales of hay the same gray-green and ochre of the discolored marble terrace, the dear old Taj Mahal endured our first suspicious gaze, and this time <u>we</u> did not resist. For all the thunderheads and rain in which we visited it, it is lovely; a bit maddening too—imagine carved marble panels of big realistic flowers asway or adroop; these panels are set on either side the center door, and are perfectly symmetrical. Horrors! A tulip on one side bends to the right; on the other side, to the left. Really, I nearly lost my breakfast. Now, after lunch: we went, I guess, to Ajanta and crawled about in the killing heat. One really glorious thing is the Kailash temple at Ellora, a great complex monolith whose parent rock is 100 feet high, 200 feet wide, probably 300 feet deep. Talk about no resistance—! it's as if some vast Shaping Spirit had plunged both arms up past the elbows into its medium, which happens to be rock but could as easily have been mud or dung; I can't think when I've had such a feeling of sheer <u>creation</u>. It is the same Shaping Spirit that in Japan can be thought of as working with matches, tweezers, glue—the timbers already aged as Warner says to get the devils out of them, while in India the devils are simply kneaded into the rock—to build the Nara temples, at exactly the same moment in history. Hmm. What else have we seen? Jaipur, all painted rose, full of camels + peacocks + gems; a palace of the '90's here with rooms full of glorious miniatures and some dreadful-grand-luxe-Aga-Khan-type furniture, indoor fountains, monumental hookahs, howdahs, purdahs; a game room over whose door WELCOME is spelled out by knives and scissors . . . The deserted cities (soi disant) of Amber and Fatehpur Sikri, the one all plaster inlaid with mirrors or pastel vase-shaped niches, the other all red sandstone . . . People? Yes we have met people almost bewilderingly charming and alert, these <u>all</u> thanks to Laughlin. Two hours in Bombay at a Mrs Jayakar's house; she writes, runs a handicraft center, does a hundred other things; she sits on the floor in a sapphire sari, serves orange juice, has mammoth eyes, 2 inches long each, and entertains a Swiss photographer who has spent 4 years in India as follows:—Swiss: I am just back from R—. Mrs J: Oh, I adore R—! my favorite place! Swiss: What you've been there? Mrs J: Of course, isn't it heavenly? Swiss: Excuse me, but when were you there? Recently I suppose? Mrs J: Not at all! 3 or 4 years back, was my first visit. Swiss: But I thought <u>nobody</u> had been there before 1954. Mrs J: Oh but you see <u>I</u> was the <u>first</u> person to go there. <u>I</u>'d heard these rumors about it in the villages, so I tracked it down after months of work. <u>I</u> sent the archeology dept. there—they'd never have found it by themselves. Let me give you this little monograph I've written on the subject. Swiss (in a Secret Rage): How kind of you! Thank you very much!

Ah me, we shall be in Istanbul in six days, flying the night of the 15th straight from Delhi. We'll stay perhaps 10 days, then shove on to Vienna (c/o Amer. Embassy) and Munich. What bliss to settle down for a whole month dressing up + party-going. I suppose there is no prospect of your coming to Europe? Would you, do you think, if the book got accepted? David had a rejection from Day Lewis which, though reluctant on L's part, was nevertheless a horrid disappointment, after their having been enthusiastic enough to ask for revisions. Do, if you are able, urge Jean, if she needs urging, to sell it instantly in NY! After all, she <u>said</u> she could. No news about the *Seraglio* except that the proofs did arrive; if you see Harry ever, pump him and let me know—oh, anything, everything; I know nothing now.

We had a wonderful talk with Ephraim. He says the air over India "howls" with spirits; he's hugely enjoying the whole trip, isn't that nice? Then I finished reading *Bleak House*, loving it—the Blyth book having put me onto Dickens. This letter is getting gabby and dull, I'll end it with love.

Jamie

J. Laughlin James Laughlin (1914–97), founder of the publisher New Directions.
Warner Langdon Warner (1881–1955), a Harvard professor, an authority on East Asian art, who taught Fredericks as an undergraduate.
dressing up For Fasching, or Carnival.
Day Lewis Cecil Day-Lewis (1904–72), Anglo-Irish poet, editor at Chatto & Windus.
Jean Jean Detre, literary agent, wife of Dr. Thomas Detre.
Blyth book R. H. Blyth, *Zen in English Literature and Oriental Classics* (1942).

To Donald Richie

WUSTL
21 January 1957
Istanbul, Turkey

Dear D.

Apart from being one of our favorite writers, you are one of our very finest readers. Bless you for writing about the novel so pleasingly; the crowsfeet your silence caused are all smoothed away [*in the margin:* I have read neither *Dracula* nor *Adam Bede* (only *Madame Bovary*) so perhaps a fine point or two has passed me by . . .]. Today's post brought two detailed descriptions of T. C. in a prospect of flowers; the other from our friend in Bangkok who fears he was found wanting for being tonguetied with admiration, his letter trailed off into an account of a drunken evening he indulged in, to get over the strain of luncheon with the Travelers. I am so glad the cable bore fruit and we have thought enviously of you, no less enviously of him. (A Turk met last night at "the" bar, called the Green Cock, said that he had certain knowledge of Truman's being in Paris right now. Can it be?)

Oh Istanbul! The sun came out today after 4—one can't call them <u>days</u>, of fog, sleet, bitter cold. On numb feet we tramped about peering at mosaics through steamy glasses and trying out the <u>wrong</u> bains turcs, where under great beehive domes old men get scrubbed by youths with gloves of steel-wool, and upstairs are small <u>glassed-in</u> (fools!) cubicles where you bundle up and drink tea. (3 hours later) BUT we have just returned from a much more plausible place where a giant de trente ans, splendidly proportioned, took us into a little marble cubicle and gave every inch of our bodies a good soaping; anything we could do for him in return was little enough.

It <u>is</u> bliss to be back in Europe. Perhaps this is <u>the</u> city after all, as I long ago suspected. David was sick this morning so I took off with camera and recklessly thin shoes to look about, and soon was in a state of considerable excitement. Wherever I looked, something quite painfully beautiful was to be seen: glass in an ash-heap, a little ring of painted boats outside the sea-wall, a tombstone topped with a stone turban, a pigeon—nothing, that is, remarkable in itself; until I suddenly realized what it was: the light of Europe, which exists nowhere else, that high, sad, eloquent painter's light, mightn't it even be responsible for the materialism of Western culture, for shedding such a magic over things? The things themselves have a good deal of charm, of course. A muezzin called me to the former church of St Serge + St Bacchus (!) also known as Little Hagia Sophia, an octagon set in an irregular square topped by a dome and all quite complicated by Muslim accessories. Ten oldsters bowed + swayed. In Ste. Sophie, looking far, far down from the Exonarthex (ahem) suddenly a gorgeous silvery roulade broke from one of the ant-like tourists. Eleanor Steber, no less, on a tour that will eventually land her in Japan. Attached to her turned out to be a NY acquaintance named Keene Curtis; he has your names, I don't know how nice he is, really, but he can dish if not cook.

Then there are the jools in the Sultan's palace, or, you might say, Seraglio. Thrones studded with poils + diminds, and, what tickled us, a great big crystal box, size of a livingroom aquarium, half-filled, casually, with largish cabochon emeralds; an effect of bon-bons (Oh go on Fatima, have another, I've got more than I know what to do with). Still, it is Europe, with cobbles, peaked rooves, roofs?, white-faced students with raw red hands and often auburn hair. Delicatessens! No cows lounging in city intersections. Scandalous bus service. For reasons of no importance (largely a matter of my brother's plans) we are flying to Rome on Wednesday the 23rd, and will spend 2 weeks there before darting up to Munich for our Month. American Express in Rome, Piazza di Spagna, is for letters. We thought we'd have a proper stool analysis, too—though India had a <u>most</u> unexpected effect on us, if you know what I mean. Well of course Freud would say we resented all the beggars + couldn't bear to part with any of our wealth.

We're glad all the (both the) HK parcels reached you. Yours (yours + Tex's) are the nicest letters we get. Keep 'em coming. I will say no more about Mr Yamamoto; you ought to know my thoughts on <u>that</u> disagreeable subject. Here is D. Hugs to Terui, Tani and (this time) Truman,

Love you both.

J.

[*Postscript by David Jackson:*] Oh my, how we adore you both! I hope you get T.C. as Jon ought—he's such a dream. JM got me out of a deep

feverish couch to go round to this bath, this afternoon: when I <u>think</u>
of the number of baths we've taken, since leaving S.F. (No, <u>in</u> S.F.),
my skin burns. Thank god our attendant, today, got too interested in
making us right at home he left off the serious sand papering. Tonight
we fly off to the Green.

Donald Richie See Biographies.
T. C. in a prospect of flowers Truman Capote's summer in Stonington. Allusion to
Andrew Marvell's poem "A Picture of Little T. C. in a Prospect of Flowers."
Eleanor Steber (1914–90), American soprano.
Keene Curtis (1923–2002), American character actor who managed Steber's world
tour.
Tex's Tex was the nickname of Meredith Weatherby, who was born in Waco.

To Marilyn and Irving Lavin

WUSTL
2 February 1957
Munich, Germany

Dear M + I,

A little letter about why we are not liking Vienna—is that the way
to spend part of one's last afternoon here, with the sun out and the
suitcases already yearning for the Schlafwagen back to Munich? Yes,
why not? Here are some reasons: 1. The Vermeer is not on display. 2.
Your letter, when we called at Am. Emb., was not there. 3. We heard
a very bad *Don Carlos* and are missing *Die Wilshutz* in Munich. 4. I'm
not sure how much we're getting on with C+M. They seem, I don't
know, remote, perhaps unhappy, pompous, disinterested. C. has a
new novel, far better than any previous one I'd read, but he talks, in
and out of it, so much about duty + dignity, that I begin to feel it is <u>I</u>
who am remote, perhaps unhappy, etc.—remote from the great world
of Right Feeling in which he moves so easily. Munich on the other
hand has been enormous fun. We both have invested—hold on to
your chairs—in contact lenses which I now wear all the time without
any distress; these, along with a big black cape I couldn't pass up, are
producing marked personality changes. Don't even try to meet our
boat, you'll never recognize us! There must be some good to say of
Vienna . . . perhaps that lovely Titian of the Nymph + Shepherd? the

Lotto youth? the 3 Philosophers? Durer's Bunny + Violets? A Barocci, too, lingers agreeably in the memory . . . We loved Schönbrunn and the Prunksaal, a church or 2, and have *Elektra* ahead tonight before the train. But oh we will be glad to get back: we'll look for Pott stuff and will make a move towards Prof. H. Who knows, maybe a copy of the Novel will be there waiting. I rather like the jacket too, in fact I liked it right from the start, having understood that the Ingres wasn't going to be used at all. I had also understood no picture was to be used, and am still a bit uncertain; it seems to me just one more aid to identifying me with my hero, but that is perhaps purely subjective. As you can imagine I'm most eager for your impressions of the book, and hope they will not be too hard to disengage from other impressions that come from knowing too many circumstances. Hardly anyone has been able to read it objectively, to the point where I no longer expect such a reading and perhaps secretly never wanted one in the first place. Chas. reports that my sister flatly doesn't intend to read it, a solution which in my vanity I had never envisaged; will this allow her, I wonder, to think the best or the worst? And have I written about Rome? seeing all those faces unchanged, Bomarzo, the new stucchi in the Museo delle Terme, the gorgeous <u>tiny</u> mosaic we acquired, dated Napoli 1818, of the *Trionfo dell'Aurora*? Well, I leave you to guess at it. Send the articles and a recording of the lectures!

Love,

J.

Die Wilshutz Der Wildschütz (1842), German comic opera by Albert Lortzing.
C+M Charles and Mary Merrill. Charles was with his family in Graz, Austria, where he was on a Fulbright fellowship.
Schönbrunn The palace in Vienna that was the summer residence of the Habsburgs.
Prunksaal State Hall in the Austrian National Library in Vienna.
the Ingres Merrill wanted to reproduce Ingres's *Le Bain turc* (1862) on the cover of *The Seraglio* (1957). A negative black-and-white photo of the painting was eventually used.
Bomarzo Hilltop village near Viterbo with a rich Etruscan history, famous now for its Monster Park.
Aurora The goddess of dawn is a character in *The Immortal Husband* (1955).
recording Irving Lavin delivered the Charles T. Mathews Lectures at Columbia in 1957 on the subject of Italian art.

To Hellen Ingram Plummer

WUSTL
26 February 1957
Munich, Germany

Dear Mama,

I have your letter about the book and am glad you can write so honestly about it. Surely we are beyond the stage where one is silenced by the fear of giving offense, even though there may be more important things at stake. It is very sweet of you to feel that, if I am satisfied, much of your distress will be relieved. And I trust you to believe me when I say that I am satisfied, more than I had ever expected to be, by seeing the book in print, and by the contents of the book. As I have just written to Guitou (who, however, had scarcely begun a careful reading when she wrote) I may have had to slight or distort certain individual truths for the sake of my overall composition, but it seems to me that the book, seen as a whole, is very strong, not just as "writing," but as a vision of life, of a life if you will, glimpsed and expressed. I went on to say that the coldness of the vision might be either the quality of my sensibility at present, or a primarily esthetic matter: a kind of "academic" palette, showing that I am not yet able to handle warmer colors (which, translated back into literary terms might mean the expression of deeper affections, a dispensing with irony and paradox; letting oneself go where love is concerned etc.)—I truly cannot say. But as for the picture itself, and your saying I have chosen a subject unworthy, I do not even need, in order to disagree with you, to resort to the painter's tenet that all subjects are potentially worthy, oysters or the Last Judgment; the subject—it strikes me still—is wonderfully charged with suggestion and human meaning, the interpenetration of different social and personal assumptions; I really don't see how I could have done more, and reading it, I have felt over + over how easily I could have done less. The great novelist (I am still reading Dickens) of course has a vision so wide that every individual or object it embraces is permitted to be itself, and is lovingly seen, good + evil alike, like flowers + weeds beneath the eye of heaven; this needn't even be at the expense of intensity—Dostoevsky is an example, but with him I wonder how much pleasure his characters would have given to their prototypes or, indeed, did; Turgenev was deeply wounded by his "portrait" in *The Possessed*. I drop these names only to remind you + myself that I <u>can</u> judge what more could have been done with the subject in a master's hands. And one final point—which is, alas, unanswerable: what other subject, at this early stage, have I at my fingertips? what world comparable in complexity + richness to the formed world I have watched since infancy—a world, moreover, that lends itself to a number of most valuable literary traditions—the comedy of manners, the novel of the young man's "education sentimentale"; impossible to overestimate the value of working in a tradition; I read last year a serious novel about human problems on the Texas plains, which feel utterly flat because the only books heretofore written about that scene have been either picaresque novels or frankly juvenile adventure tales. To recognize a group of people, certain places, ways of feeling + acting, as a "world" may be the first step in writing about it: there is none other I have thus far so keenly recognized + strongly responded to . . . I mean, for me, what could the subject be but very big?

Your other point about the purge—I don't know. The book has given me, I feel these days, vast assurance in many ways; where Daddy + the Magowans are concerned I cannot tell whether a change of feeling comes from the writing or from Daddy's death, probably both; where you are concerned I think you have seen how not the writing so much as the fact of the book's having been written + being the book it is has led us into a much more open relationship simply, perhaps, a relationship, there having been precious little before. Probably the act of writing about something does not free us from our fears + bitternesses—otherwise wouldn't we all be tapping away at diaries and long searching letters?—but it does set a lot in motion.

I would be curious to know your impression at the end, of which you mysteriously speak. Perhaps you will feel able to write it to me before long.

Now: we leave Munich on the 7th. Write c/o Amer. Express, 5 Marktgasse Basle, Switzerland; we shall leave there probably on the 14th. Then we head vaguely up the Rhine—Colmar, Köln, into Holland. The next address I can think of is Amer. Express, Amsterdam, where we shall definitely be on, and perhaps before, March 29. Mark letters HOLD.

Vienna—? not too much of an impression, sad, shabby, fine music + pastries which seemed to enhance the sadness. Nice times with C + M. His new book is the best I've read to date.

The contact lenses are wonderful. I wear them all day long without discomfort of any kind. David joins in love to all of you.

Ever,
Jimmy

To Gerrish Thurber   WUSTL
                                                16 April 1957
                                              [London, England]

Dear Gerrish,

A hasty note to thank you for yours (not, I mean, that <u>it</u> was hasty) (rather that London, sunlit, awaits) and to say that a date has been fixed for my Return—May 29, on the New Amsterdam. What joy! There will be 101 things to attend to, chiefly regarding the Stonington house—and perhaps my 10th reunion at Amherst—but there will also be time to get back to work, a work whose meaning I have all but forgotten these months. Projects: polish up new book of poems and (maybe) start a 2nd novel. Your feelings about the book correspond quite exactly to intermittent feelings of my own, which are (still) in flux; it was written in something of a trance, there was the illusion that everything in it <u>had to be</u> (not altogether dispelled, that illusion) and [only] when all the work was done did I begin to perceive Consequences. I realize all too well that the link between Consequences and Motives is all too real—but I feel now that, with the book, I have reached the end of a long dark period that could not otherwise have been reached but by writing as I have, not only the novel, but a number of rather hard and cold poems. My mother has been quite fine on the whole; I'm sure, however, that she would welcome anything you would care to write her on the subject.

Perhaps you + Mary could stop in Stonington if the summer takes you anywhere in New England. It would be good to see you there. Otherwise, Stone Cottage. Greetings to you both, + Edw.

as ever,
Jim

a 2nd novel Merrill had already begun drafting a novel that would become *The (Diblos) Notebook* (1963).
the book *The Seraglio* (1957).
Stone Cottage The Thurbers' home on the Lawrenceville School campus.

To Kimon Friar

WUSTL
5 December 1958
[Stonington, CT]

Dear Kimon,

What to say? Do you want to extract from me the confession that I am not "deeply moved" to do anything? It is an embarrassing one to make, but your love of Opposites requires it of me, asks me to choose between being "deeply moved" and going to hear you out of "duty". Kimon, these phrases caricature my feelings and belittle what I have come to consider the nature of feeling itself. I have already made an analogous comment in terms of the language of your introduction to the *Odyssey*. It is a use of words at key moments that leaves me "deeply moved" by skepticism, distrust both of my own motives and of yours. It is a language for politicians, not for those who are already disposed to be attentive.

I knew perfectly well that you wished me to attend your reading. My error clearly was in not wanting to say I would come until I was absolutely certain that I would be able to; I knew that I <u>had</u> to be in NY once copies of my poems were available, and, while they had been promised by the first days of December, there's always a slip, and I freely admit that if they had not been ready by the 8th I would not have come in; it is a wearing trip to make twice in a week's time and it isn't as if you hadn't given us a reading all to ourselves in

November. Well, you will see me there, not deeply moved to attend perhaps, but not out of duty either.

I do want to say this: that you make it very hard for me to praise and encourage you. I should like to do so, I am full of admiration as I read the *Odyssey*, I am truly glad for the reception it is getting, and I would be touched by the dedication under any circumstances. But it is hard to express these things, for me, in the face of your own phenomenal efforts to push the book, to have it praised by friends, by strangers. I understand that you are doing it in part for your dead friend, its author. But I can't escape feeling snobbish about the public, and particularly cynical towards the middlemen, publishers and reviewers, and it seems to me that praise and blame, on their level, is a worthless coin flipped in the air, and the outcome forgotten in a year. Bowra is a different matter, but isn't the point that to get his letter you exerted yourself precisely in your translation, while with these others . . . ! I mean I personally do not feel that the artist can afford to involve himself in these transactions; I trust you will have the courage to disinvolve yourself. My praise is here waiting to be uttered until I have finished reading the poem, by which time perhaps the crowd-noises from Times Square will no longer be on your radio.

Yours, as ever,
Jimmy

Odyssey Friar's translation of Kazantzakis's *The Odyssey: A Modern Sequel* (1958).
my poems *The Country of a Thousand Years of Peace* (1959).
Bowra C. M. Bowra (1898–1971), English classicist, specializing in ancient Greek poetry.

To Claude Fredericks

15 January 1959
[New York, NY]

Dear Claude,

Your good and kind letter of this morning made and keeps me happy; thank you so much and so much. We are finishing up packing, the book-box is abulge, and there is really little left to do but dine at the Fords (how one's stomach heaves at the foretaste of <u>more</u> whiskey after last night's do at John + Herbert's) and sail, all simply, at noon.

I <u>am</u> glad you like the book. But you must stop brooding, or begin to brood in a different way, over my reply of years ago to your question about the play. It is a reply I would still make, to any such question; and particularly to someone whose understanding I value as much as yours. There has never been anything I cared to express more, than I cared for the act of expressing it. (This sentence, clumsy and ambiguous, may be considered an exception.) No, I do mean that; it may be yet one more of my defenses, but even with the novel, all that hot subject matter, the thrill was always to be writing prose. Put that way, you may say, oh, of course—do you? am I so very silly?

And you must not feel that I am not your friend. I do know what you are talking about. The time since our return from Santa Fe has been, for me, very aimlessly and frustratingly spent. Whenever I am in a situation where I feel I <u>ought</u> to be working, and cannot or do not, those are the times when I am not fit for human contact. As you can see, these are difficulties I do not learn to cope with except perhaps by escape—this last week, for instance, back from Atlanta, with nothing to do but wait for tomorrow, has been ever so happy: we went to a rehearsal of *Don Giovanni* and ate in small, foreign restaurants and heard Gielgud read and saw the *Play of Daniel*, and it's as if we were already far, far away from this year's burst pipes in Stonington (yes, they burst again this year). Also, I am taking vitamins and they seem to be giving me more energy. But Claude, I can't help it; so much of the time life <u>does</u> seem hard, friendships hard, the use of one's senses hard—to the point where I cannot resist shirking all of it, quite as if there were never to be an end of opportunity to redeem myself. Surely <u>that</u> is the evil side of Ephraim. Where you are involved personally in these feelings is hard to say for certain. Are we not perhaps like the Fox and the Crane who do not function perfectly in each other's houses? I love Pawlet as you know but its rhythms are not mine. And I love your coming to S'ton and wish only I knew how to make having guests <u>easier</u>. I wonder if the reason you said, on leaving Santa Fe, that you had never felt so close to us, wasn't that you spent so much time away from the house, whole meals, whole nights, so that your every appearance had the glamor of an unexpected, scarcely deserved treat . . . Well this is not the time to enlarge upon it; I mean, I couldn't. And, as you say, it is all most likely a side-effect of the other difficulties.

So write us (c/o Spindler, 2 Giselastr. Munich, till 1 March) and tell us that you are coming to Greece in June. The Lavins, it now seems, aren't.

D. joins in fondest farewells to you and Hal

as ever,

J.

John + Herbert's Myers and Machiz.
Play of Daniel Medieval liturgical drama performed by the New York Pro Musica, an early-music ensemble led by Noah Greenberg and supported by the Ingram Merrill Foundation.
vitamins Merrill regularly took shots of B_{12} and other vitamins.
the Fox and the Crane One of Aesop's fables.

To Hellen Ingram Plummer   WUSTL
[March 1959]
Burgos, Spain

Dear Mama, Mis' Annie + Bill,

Greetings from Spain! The road was so good yesterday that we pushed on through Bayonne (stopping to see a pretty Basque museum) and the border where as usual we were taken for Germans, and on to San Sebastian for the night: a resort out of season, dead, cold, milky green waves breaking against parapets. I think we were the only guests in the "luxury" hotel. We managed to wait until 10 pm to dine in a very pleasant restaurant where David had some sort of white fish in a sauce of peas, asparagus, clams + garlic, and I had a deviled crab almost as good as Mis' A's, but with pimento and (ugh!) garlic added. We drove today through really magnificent country, very high and rocky (the Pyrenees in fact) and raining most of the way as it does all winter long in this part of Spain; but not a miserable rain, a rain in gusts out of flying clouds like black pearls, or even white ones, parting here and there in the huge sky to show clear patches, each one a different blue—white blue, lemon blue, blue blue—depending on distance or the Lord knows what. The country is very severe and graceful, cubist fields and shaven hillsides; fruit trees blossoming like puffs of smoke; donkeys; aqueducts. We checked in at our hotel here in Burgos and ran off to the Cathedral. For miles it had alternately been stormy black and sunny, like playing She-Loves-Me with a daisy, but the sun was out at last and for good, and traveled through blue stained glass to rest upon a coiling gold column, and filled the octagonal dome with clarity (the dome, as David said, is what the trompe-l'oeil church decorators have been copying forever, existing here at last in 3 dimensions). The church is built on a steep slope, allowing one to walk almost at roof-level on one side. It is heavily encrusted with statues, saw-tooth ornament on the edge of spires; reliefs—coats of arms, lions posing with sun-bursts, or angels quarreling over them. I am not sure that the total effect is very "spiritual" but it would be nice to live nearby such a thing.

The past week has been such a jumble of things I'm not at all sure I can recapture them. The birthday was very pleasant; Charlotte Arner and I had a joint cake and 4 or 6 people looked in during the afternoon including David's friends the Wildis whom I'd met 2 years ago; he teaches at the Univ., Eng. Lit. and said he gave an hour's talk on my novel after reading it. Then a night in Besancon, 2 in Dijon (good meals, a pretty town, and an unforgettably bad performance of *Manon*); the next day, the great church at Vézelay, and the greater but less beautiful one at Bourges, where we spent the night; we spent the next night on the road in a nameless town in a vile hotel—the bad taste of the French passes understanding—where the local rugby team was having a banquet, not that this was unusual, seeing that wherever we ate, noon or night, there was invariably a ceremonious gathering of some description, the county clerk and his minions, conceivably, or the Friends of Urban Beautification—; then a night in Toulouse, after lunch in Albi, and with that an end to France for the time being.

I'm awfully sorry to hear about Mary Hurt; give her my love. Perhaps she is better by now. I <u>wondered</u> why Mrs von Karajan opened the Vienna Ball. Hope Mary Ann got the Danish things. Oh, I have done a stupid thing; the girl's name + address from Paris, who was to be in Spain, is deep in a suitcase we just can't open till Lisbon—I should have sent her a note right off in Munich, but didn't and, well, now I'm afraid she will have left Paris; I'll try all the same when I lay hands on the letter. Thank you again for your birthday letter; and all of you for the cards; and the ladies for those two fat checks which have been put in the bank. I haven't seen a thing I wanted so far except a pair of painted butterflies made out of shells that cost $4, but I suspect that Portugal and Madrid will have something lying in wait for me. If the worst comes to the worst, I'll be having some shirts and slacks made, and will <u>think</u> about an overcoat.

Did I explain about Alison Bishop? She was a faculty wife at Amherst—they are now in California—when I taught there; a very good unpublished writer. Bunny Lang, a friend of hers, David's and mine, also long ago of Tony H, died two or three years ago of leukemia, aged 32; she was a charmer and a very clever girl, wrote poems and plays, lived in Boston, a real character; had been married about a year when she died. Alison wrote this memoir—some 30,000 words—which is really beautifully and gaily done; the *New Yorker* nearly took it, but there is no other chance for it that I can see so D. and I are having a small edition (300 copies) printed in Munich. It will be ready when we pass through in August. Judy M's cousins the Stadelmayers recommended a publisher and I think it will be very handsome. Tony H. by the way is in NY at Hampshire House; his mother is very ill, has had 2 or 3 strokes; and <u>he</u> sounds sicker and wearier than ever. A little note? It is darkish now—none of these places are lighted; I'm actually writing this in the john, with the machine on the throne and me on a stool before it; it seems a bit brighter than the other room where D. is napping anyhow. <u>Hours</u> before dinner. The Pernod in Spain is 136 proof. What to do? Love to the whole household, the Residential District, and Yourselves.

Ever,
Jimmy

Charlotte Arner (1926–2011), wife of Robert L. Arner (1922–2002). Born in Berlin, she emigrated after Kristallnacht and became an artist, translator, and archivist. **Robert Arner,** who had been Merrill's student at Bard, was a painter who became head of the art department, the Masters School, Dobbs Ferry, NY. Merrill owned some of Arner's small geometric paintings.
Mrs von Karajan Eliette von Karajan (b. 1931), wife of the renowned Austrian conductor and later founder of the Eliette and Herbert von Karajan Institute in Salzburg.
Alison Bishop Alison Lurie (b. 1926), American novelist, married to literary scholar Jonathan Bishop, befriended David Jackson and Merrill during the year they spent in Amherst. Merrill arranged and paid for private publication of Lurie's *V. R. Lang, A Memoir* (1959).
Judy M Judith Merck (b. 1933), wife of Frederick Buechner.
Tony H. Tony Harwood.

To Mary Lou Aswell   WUSTL
                                                2 May 1959
                                                Florence, Italy

Oh Dear One,

We are <u>not</u> home, and will not be for months and months. Your letter found us in Barcelona, just before sailing on the Venezuela—a little one night crossing during which we spent far too much time with Cesare Siepi—for Italy. Now we are in Florence for about a week, headed for Ravenna and Venice, and two months in Greece. Home in late August for the height of the Stonington season. I am, we are, so sorry to hear about your father, and terribly disappointed that we cannot see you, keep you near us for many days, even take you to Connecticut College as often as you want to go. Do give our love to Mary, and to the crowd there. We particularly know Bill Meredith, the John Hollanders, and the James Brodericks; also dear Bob Palmer who does things in the library. You should give them all greetings from us.

Drat, drat, drat. I knew this trip was going to be much too long. Spain sort of took it out of us, though the presence of Little T. and Big C. in Madrid did much to put it back in. Such a peculiar pair, Beaton all bored and British—should he have a suit of wine red or of midnight blue velvet made? Truman terribly funny—buying capes and bullfighters' shoes and eating caviar to a ruinous degree; he showed us at some length the beauty treatment he must go through 3 times a day in order not to change for the rest [of] his life; it costs him $200 a month, some Dr Laslo in NY "handles" Garbo and Cary Grant and Mrs H Williams etc, and apparently he will never change except to get more and more heavenly. They had to go to Seville for the Feria, in Arturo Lopez' plane, along with a Maharanee (or Marihuana, as a friend's mother used to say); it sounded awful, we were glad we did not go, all that drinking on horseback and being sung at by gypsy women. As Jane Bowles said in Tangier, a propos her Spanish nurse, a quite pretty but temperamental creature, "Can you imagine anything worse than living at close quarters to a passionate Spanish woman with whom one is not in love?" Jane, by the way, was divine; still not well, but quite spry and funny; we saw lots of her and she spoke so warmly of you. She took us to see her former house in the Casbah and to a restaurant with real dancing boys (all wrapped up in colored stuffs doing grinds and bumps with a tea tray on the head) and was the only thing there—Jane I mean—who made us want to go back ever again. We loved Barcelona and Salamanca, Granada a bit less, and the landscape more than anything. Really it is so noble and civilized and grand, with marvelous skies, granite upthrusts, tonsured hilltops, olives and oranges and corktrees and tiny cubist villages, tan or white, depending on whether it is north or south. And then the Prado. You and Agnes ought to give it a try before you settle in England, though of course if you get very English indeed you will be spending your winters in Portugal whence it is easy to get to anywhere in Spain.

David is out doing a watercolor of S. Maria Novella, but will add a scribble. Our address through May: c/o American Exp, Venice; from June through July, ditto, Athens. Much love to all the dear creatures in Santa Fe, from Augie all the way down to Jinx's newest litter. But most of all to you and Aggie.

Ever,
Jimmy

oh, he's too clever! But I send warm hugs + kisses and a sob that we'll miss you, and do give that delightful Mary a hug and say we'll see <u>her</u> in Sept. xxxxx David

Mary Louise Aswell (1902–84), fiction editor at *Harper's* who published Capote and Eudora Welty (see note to letter of 15 January 1962).
Cesare Siepi (1923–2010), Italian basso, especially known for the role of Don Giovanni.
James Brodericks Broderick was a professor of English at Connecticut College.
Bob Palmer Connecticut College librarian, partner of the painter Tom Ingle, also Merrill's friend.
Agnes Agnes Sims (1910–90), Aswell's longtime partner, an artist and petroglyph expert who designed their residence on Canyon Road in Santa Fe.
Jinx Jinx Junkin, locally famous character with a colorful theatrical background, founder of a children's theater in town, designated a "Santa Fe Living Treasure" in 2000.

To John and Anne Hollander   YALE
23–24 May 1959
Venice, Italy

Dear John, Dear Anne, Dear Martha,

We keep meaning to bring back from the outside world a few leaves of prettier paper than this, but it's more easily said than done, and meanwhile there is an open window giving onto animated and (even when closed) noisy throngs, by which to sit and start a letter. Bravi to all three of you! We have toasted the third one's appearance in gin, rum, and the wines of the country, and if a small, appropriate gift should appear from Venice—something like her Very Own Ashtray—you may know it is from us.

The first person we saw in Venice, as we lifted our heads from the map and were about to ask directions to the Piazza, was Chester Kallman. The encounter led in a matter of seven strides, to Mr Ansen himself, slumped in a state at a café table. We have seen him relentlessly since then. Sometimes he is wearing a bright red double-breasted suit, sometimes a white one. After midnight he is often sound asleep in Ciro's where nothing wakes him, not even sharp prods from an umbrella. There is apt to be a half consumed creme de menthe + soda in front of him. It <u>has</u> happened twice, so I feel I can generalize. He is working on a dialogue about the Beat Generation with Peggy Guggenheim's daughter's lover, a British situationalist painter. His pockets are full of poems which he reads in a loud voice, waving one hand and bursting into laughter. "Fried shoes . . ." he had to disapprove of, but reluctantly I thought. We rather adore him.

Let's see, what else. David has started a sketchbook which already has 4 or 5 completely professional watercolors, and I have started nothing at all. We keep saying that maybe in Greece . . . For the first time ever, we have begun collecting and using letters to people. Oh, nothing much, a countess here, a countess there, but it has already gotten us to I Tatti, and may to Maser.—I'm sorry, this window is too much; you wouldn't believe the kind of people going in and out of the Luxembourg consulate right across a little canal. Is there something they're not telling us? So: until tomorrow.

A sunny day at the Lido. I don't think the sand is quite so bad as you make it out, at least not until the movie stars begin to scamper about in it, but it can't touch Watch Hill.

Look, do let us know your plans as soon as you have any. We're foolishly hoping you will still be there when we get back around August 28. Or is there a chance of your staying on another year? One can't really ask for a handier institution, handier to Stonington I mean, than C.C., but if you must go elsewhere couldn't you make it New York or Boston where other people would see you now and then? The Lavins are going to Vassar with little Amelia, thereby adding Vassar to our list of plausible places. Think it over.

There is clearly a lot more to relate, Jane Bowles in Africa, Truman and Cecil in Madrid, etc—not to mention our Piero d. F. tour (yes, I'd say that between us we'd seen them all by now)—but it must wait until we can fill it out with slides and gestures.

Remember us to your colleagues.

Yours,
Jimmy

It is so satisfying to have a "Martha" in our circle of friends because J.M. + I play a duet called "Martha Martha, how I love you," by a '20s composer named Joe Macarthy. And don't think you won't hear it!

Love,

David

<u>NO</u> the song is "Thelma, Thelma," but to the tune of "Martha, Martha," J.

John Hollander See Biographies.

Dear Martha The Hollanders' first child, Martha, was born on March 24, 1959.

Chester Kallman (1921–75), American poet, translator, and librettist who collaborated with his lover W. H. Auden on opera libretti.

Ansen Alan Ansen (1922–2006), close friend of some of the Beat writers and secretary for Auden.

British situationist painter Ralph Rumney (1934–2002), English painter, founder with Guy Debord and others of the Situationist International group, married to the artist Pegeen Guggenheim, daughter of Peggy Guggenheim.

"Fried shoes . . ." In response to a taunt by Gregory Corso—"No square poet would ever begin a poem with 'Fried Shoes'"—Hollander wrote "Two for Gregory," both beginning with the phrase, the second incorporating it in a refrain in a villanelle.

I Tatti Villa I Tatti, home in Florence of the connoisseur and collector of Italian art Bernard Berenson (1865–1959), whose estate became the Harvard Center for Italian Renaissance Studies, a "lay monastery."

Maser Villa di Maser, or Villa Barbaro, in the Veneto region of Northern Italy, was designed by Andrea Palladio (1508–80).

so bad as you make it out Hollander's poem "Late August on the Lido," set in Venice, ends by alluding to Jaques's "seven ages of man speech" in *As You Like It:* "the wind, increasing, / Sands teeth, sands eyes, sands taste, sands everything."

C.C. Hollander taught in the English department at Connecticut College in New London.

Jane Bowles (1917–73), American novelist and playwright, living in Tangier. She had suffered a serious stroke (see Merrill to Mary Lou Aswell, 2 May 1959). Wife of author and composer Paul Bowles (1910–99).

Truman and Cecil Capote and Cecil Beaton (1904–80), English fashion and portrait photographer.

To Elizabeth Bishop

3 November 1959
Stonington, CT

Dear Elizabeth,

I was so happy to have your letter today, though terribly depressed to think you didn't get my book. Only yesterday a friend was here for the weekend and let fall that she hadn't got her copy until late April when they had all presumably been mailed out before Christmas. My vexation is complicated by the fact that everyone I knew at Knopf (barring the eminences grises) left during the summer with Young Alfred to start their own house, so that I truly don't know whom to complain to and, not knowing, shall not be able to do it very effectively. Meanwhile I have a spare copy here and it will go off to you at once.

The Memoir we sent was written by John Peale Bishop's daughter in law who was a faculty wife at Amherst when I taught there. I guess we did know a lot of the people involved but Alison writes very well and I wonder if she isn't herself the most interesting figure in those pages.

Oh yes we are back and don't plan going away for at least ten months. How good it will be to see you and Lota! We are hoping that this time you will be able to squeeze in some days in Stonington. It is lovely in the winter with the little harbor glittering off to the west, and peaceful if you have any work to do or even letters to write. David is going to have a party on New Year's Eve—put that on your calendar.

We saw a lot of literary people at Wesleyan yesterday, a reception for the publication of 4 books of poems by Simpson, Wright, Plutzik and Barbara Howes, none of whom were present which didn't seem to bother anybody. Holly Stevens asked me if it was true I had communicated with her father on the ouija board and from that point on I felt rather awkward and defensive. We saw the Wilburs' house and heard all about the son et lumière text that he is writing for Philadelphia's summer festival, then drove drunkenly back to a Rock Hudson and Doris Day movie in New London. Strange. We feel very out of touch after the trip, for instance we've seen no poems by you for, oh, nearly a year, but at least we are back at work with some stored-up vigor. Greece was specially exciting in every way—monuments, plays at Epidauros, delicious food in small quantities that left us looking like Giacomettis. Did you ever get a postcard from Volubilis? We went there <u>entirely</u> because of "2000 Illustrations."

We can't offhand think of a sublet for you but will ask around and keep our ears to the grindstone. Please don't change your minds. And remember, you can talk Portuguese in Stonington.

Love to you both from David and
Jimmy

Elizabeth Bishop See Biographies.
my book *The Country of a Thousand Years of Peace* (1959).
their own house Alfred A. Knopf Jr., with Knopf colleagues, including Harry Ford, left his parents' firm to found Atheneum Books, which became Merrill's publisher.
The Memoir Lurie's *V. R. Lang.* Lurie's husband, Jonathan Peale Bishop (1927–2010), was the son of the American poet John Peale Bishop (1892–1944).
Lota Lota de Macedo Soares (1910–67), Bishop's partner.
Simpson, Wright, Plutzik and Barbara Howes Louis Simpson's *A Dream of Governors: Poems* (1959); James Wright's *Saint Judas* (1959); Hyam Plutzik's *Apples from Shinar* (1959); and Barbara Howes's *Light and Dark: Poems* (1959), all Wesleyan University Press books.
Holly Stevens (1924–92), daughter of Wallace Stevens. Shortly after his death, Merrill contacted Stevens on the Ouija board and related the conversation to Holly.
Wilburs' house The poet Richard Wilbur (1921–2017), a professor of English at Wesleyan University, lived with his wife, Charlee, and daughter, Ellen, in Portland, CT.
Rock Hudson and Doris Day movie *Pillow Talk* (1959).
"2000 Illustrations" Bishop's poem "Over 2,000 Illustrations and a Complete Concordance" mentions Volubilis, the ruins of an ancient Roman city in Morocco.

To Claude Fredericks

GETTY
24 January 1960
Stonington, CT

Dear Claude—

Your candles really look too pretty of a sunny afternoon against the red walls. When are you coming back, if ever? No doubt you are wise to have an apartment, though one can see it as the final capitulation to the Reality–Principle. I am in bed with a fever + flu, 3 days now, and not coherent.

Irmgard is singing Schubert. David is fetching the repaired vacuum cleaner in Westerly. The days are getting longer.

Mary Lou + Agnes should be here before long. The Foundation gave A. a grant and they are going to Europe. Bernie came for a whole week. I didn't snap at him once. That weekend Howard Moss came, and we all sat around working on examples of the new art form I have invented: setting Proust to the "River Kwai March." Here is my original stanza, the cornerstone of the whole glittering structure:

Swann's Way, a book by Marcel Proust,
Tells how the hero took to roost
Racy
Odette de Crécy
Who to his friends could not be introduced.

And here is a later, more subjective example (by BVW):

Françoise, don't make me go to bed!
I'd rather play with girls instead.
Later
I'll have a waiter,
But only after my grandmother's dead.

Many more await your leisure.

We talked to the Lavins last night. Really somebody up there hates them. Their car was broken into + robbed. I got them tickets to *Fidelio* (they had never been to the Met) and it was changed to *Faust*. Our newest passion is Leonie Resanek in *The Flying Dutchman*, all fire + modesty + sort of softly shingled hair—terribly Norwegian I suppose. Such lovely music too. Have you read Kenneth Koch's epic, *KO* (Grove Press)? or *Jealousy* (Robbe-Grillet)? I don't know why I ask, but both impressed me. Also a book I think you would like, that I'm partway into—*Life against Death* by Norman Brown. Lines of verse dropped from me like beads of sweat after the 1st chapter.

Saturday is Sewelly's birthday. She + Bernie are coming up. She +

Maude have "split" + she has had an unhappy time recently with a little woman named De.

But please write + please come back. I'll be in Atlanta a week beginning either Feb 22 or Mar 12. Otherwise our time is yours + our house too. Love to you + Hal.

Ever.
Jamie

About Montale: Irma is very interested in collaborating on trans. + selection, but thinks it might be a better project for summer '61, so that T. Weiss can get his Montale issue out without haste.

Irmgard Irmgard Seefried (1919–88), German soprano.
Howard Moss (1922–87), American poet, poetry editor of *The New Yorker* for thirty-nine years; author of the critical study *The Magic Lantern of Marcel Proust* (1962).
"River Kwai March" The "Colonel Bogey March," composed during World War I by a British army bandmaster, became a popular tune during World War II (with variations in the lyrics such as "Hitler has only got one ball") and was whistled in the film *The Bridge on the River Kwai* (1957), directed by David Lean.
BVW Bernie Winebaum.
Leonie Resanek Leonie Rysanek (1926–98), Austrian soprano.
Montale Italian poet Eugenio Montale (1896–1981).
T. Weiss Theodore Weiss's *Quarterly Review of Literature*, vol. 11, no. 4 (1962), was a special issue on Montale guest-edited by Irma Brandeis.

To Hellen Ingram Plummer   WUSTL
                                                        20 March 1960
                                                        [Stonington, CT]

Dear Mama,

A beautiful sunny Sunday—on the surface. We have been caught up in the strong, soupy vortex of Hilda's life. She came up the stairs Friday after midnight, weeping and bleeding. Her husband (twice her age) had "heard talk about her" at the Holy Ghost Club on Main St (for Portuguese drinking men) and had beaten her up. The talk just may be true. The other man is the mysterious stone-deaf English inventor (also twice her age) who bought Bayard Osborn's house and who had come to see David to ask, as it were, for Hilda's hand, saying "there's something in her nature, primitive don't you know, that appeals to me . . ." Well, we thought we had had it all patched up last fall, but now this is the End. The beauty of life in a small town is that everyone has a little part to play and can be watched playing it by the others: the lawyer, the old lady and her son who run the newspaper store, the proprietress of the inn into which Hilda has moved, the priest she will not see, and, prominently, ourselves. There is also a loathsome high-school junior "chum" of Hilda's who tracked her down to our house where she spent most of yesterday and gave her a priggish bawling out at the top of her lungs: "Listen to me, you're married to a <u>man</u>, he's your husband, he gotta right to beat you, you promised to honor and obey, why that guy's so crazy in love with you it ain't funny, and what do you do? I suppose you think you can——everyone in town!" The Englishman meanwhile saying in his pursy little deaf voice, "Hilda I don't understand why you're listening to this brat." I had gone to fetch him at his house (he doesn't of course hear the phone) in pure self-defense, to give her another ear (even deaf) to pour her sad tale into. I also performed a small errand at the store (she had left home without money or Modess) and answered the phone at 7:30 in the morning when the police sergeant (whom we had at once notified of her refuge in our guest apt.) called to say her sister in Martha's Vineyard was trying to reach her by telephone. During the few moments we've had to ourselves (she is finishing lunch downstairs now) (while David calls the lawyer) we return to one another like the characters in Ivy Compton-Burnett who remark, "It is a scene from real life. Have we ever witnessed one before?"

In New York we had gone to the Modern Museum to watch a so-called "self-destroying work of art" by a Swiss madman—a huge affair of wheels and pulleys and pianos and rolls of paper being mechanically painted on—going up in flames and finally, I suppose, collapsing, though we had left by then having waited 70 minutes for it to begin. But poor Hilda's performance more than makes up for what we missed.

Otherwise things are fine. I feel the effect of the thyroid and the iron and am bursting with vigor. Can you believe that Dr H's bill was only $132? Slight change in April plans: we go to NY on the 25th, I leave on the 27th spending that night en route, the next with the

DeMotts in Amherst, <u>then</u> Mt Holyoke and back to Amherst Saturday, and to Stonington either Sunday or Monday, May 1 or 2. David's parents arrive April 28 in NY and we'll all meet here on the 2nd for, oh, probably 5 or 6 days. Please return Freddy's letter.

> Much love to all,
> Jimmy

Hilda Merrill and Jackson's house cleaner.
Swiss madman Jean Tinguely (1925–91), whose autodestructive assembly *Homage to New York* (1960) burned to the ground, as designed, in the sculpture garden of the Museum of Modern Art.
the DeMotts Benjamin DeMott (1924–2005) and his wife, Margaret. DeMott, an Amherst English professor, was a cultural critic and novelist.

To John and Anne Hollander

WUSTL
14 November 1961
Munich, Germany

Dear John, dear Anne,

Well now we are back from Berlin. I flew, David took the train; when we met in Munich we agreed that it had been worth the trip, if only for the ART. The city itself, or call it the life, struck us as flimsy without being febrile enough to capture the imagination. I daresay in summer it is autre chose. But my, that museum! The Bellini *Christ*, too pre-Raphaelite for words. And the Rembrandt *Rape of Proserpina* which could have been done by Moreau if not Max Ernst. And those Amberger portraits. And a strange snake-throne with figures holding rifles, <u>all</u> made out of small red, white + blue beads, from Africa. Nefertite looks out of place, they should have let Hearst buy her. There were pretty things in the East zone too, the best Tanagra lady I've ever seen; and a good *Figaros Hochzeit* instead of the *Frau ohne Schatten* which was probably never meant to be performed anyhow. <u>Your</u> opera sounds terribly exciting; I mean terribly. I have met some of those theater people. You only meet with them once a week? Just wait till they lock you into a small hotel suite full of smoke and Them, and a Strong Man leans sneering against the door fingering something made of metal, and says, OK, Hollander, create. But you are just doing lyrics? It won't be durchkomponiert like the *Golden Apple*? That may save you from the Ulcer and the Couch.

We are off in a few days: Brindisi to Egypt (Nov 29—Dec 14); then Athens (Dec 16—Jan 10—American Express); Brindisi again; Sicily; Rome for a week around Jan 20; and the Leonardo from Naples Jan 29. Dr Park has never let me know whether they want me or not, but we'll be ready to come home in any case.

Alan is already in Athens, it seems. Venice is under six feet of water, and we are perhaps fools to think of looking in on it, but we shall, if only long enough to take Haydn to the bindery—if there is still one unsubmerged. I wrote him (Alan) what I thought about cuts—I do think some of *The Old Religion,* like the poem to Gordon Sager, could be replaced by new work; in fact all the new poems I've seen are so fine and so strong, it would be a pity not to put them before the public. As for the masque, though I said nothing about it to him, I should think it belonged in a small private pamphlet. It will tip the scales of the book in a very odd way. Yet it is the way Alan tips his own scales and he must be allowed to do as he pleases, don't you think?

About the photographs: have you been in touch with Sandra Roome who took them? I don't know whether your budget includes a fee for photographers, but she ought to be paid something and if Yale can't do it, I will. Perhaps you could call her when you are in NY. Her address: 37 West 10. If her name isn't in the book, look for her husband Fred Segal. She will probably want the proofs returned.

We didn't see Gregory in Berlin, but we met a poet. Scene: Elli's Bier-Bar, miles from everywhere, full of the oldest transvestites I've ever seen, and a few bespectacled clerks. One figure stood out. A lean + hungry young man dressed classically in black leather, boots, keys, etc. David spoke to him in halting German, the intended ironies dissolving under pressure: what do Keys mean in Germany? Reply incomprehensible. Later the figure speaks to us. Are we Americans? He is from California, though British by birth. And of course when all is said and done it is Thom Gunn en vacance. He had lunch with us the next day—changing his leather pants for Levis in honor of the occasion. We took him to see the tanantuals (I'll leave that, I mean tarantulas though) and pythons and crocodiles, then parted amicably in the gathering dusk.

Was Bruges an immense success? One gets good pressed caviar in Brussels. David's favorite thing is here in Munich: the right panel of a triptych, a St George in whose breastplate the virgin and child (center panel) are reflected. Memling of course. And if you're looking for smut, there's a certain Rubens a few rooms away. . . .

> Love to Baby Martha + to you both
> Jimmy

Did you ever meet the Morses in Stonington? We are traveling with Robert M's book, *The Two Persephones* (Creative Age—1942)—2 long poems, very much worth reading, the 2nd in particular. If you have a moment . . .

Amberger portraits Portraits by Christoph Amberger (1505–62) in the Gemälde-galerie, Berlin.
Nefertite The bust of Nefertiti (1345 BC), wife of the Egyptian pharaoh Akhenaten.
Hearst William Randolph Hearst (1863–1951), American newspaper magnate, politician, and collector of antiquities.
Your opera John Hollander wrote the text for Milton Babbitt's electronic serial composition *Philomel* (1964).
durchkomponiert "Through-composed" music, uninterrupted by recitative or spoken dialogue in opera and in musical theater like *The Golden Apple* or without repetition of musical arrangement between stanzas in art song.
Golden Apple The Golden Apple was an off-Broadway musical (1954), based on Homer, with music by Jerome Moross and lyrics by John Latouche.
Alan . . . the masque Alan Ansen's chapbook *The Old Religion* (1959), published by Tibor de Nagy Gallery, sponsored by Merrill, was incorporated in Ansen's *Disorderly Houses: A Book of Poems* (1961), published in the Wesleyan University Press poetry series. *Disorderly Houses* included a verse masque, "The Return from Greece," dedicated to Merrill, Jackson, and Peggy Guggenheim, which was performed in the garden of Guggenheim's palazzo in Venice on August 3, 1959.
Gordon Sager American writer who contributed to *The New Yorker*. A friend of Paul and Jane Bowles, he published a novel in part about them, *Run, Sheep, Run* (1950).
Sandra Roome . . . Fred Segal Fred and Sandra Segal are the dedicatees of "The Lawn Fete of Homunculus Artifex" in *Water Street* (1962).
Gregory Corso.
Thom Gunn (1929–2004), English poet, living in San Francisco.
pythons and crocodiles At the Berlin Zoo.

To Alice B. Toklas

TEXAS
18 December 1961
[Athens, Greece]

Alice dear—

I read about your pictures in *The New Yorker* and was appalled. What an ugly thing to do, and what an ugly way to do it. My heart aches for you—whether you can <u>see</u> them or not isn't the point. I think of them as <u>watching</u> <u>over</u> you.

Today the so-called *Artists + Writers Cookbook* reached me with your charming introduction. I am so flattered that you mentioned me.

How and where are you? Where do you plan to be in early March? David and I sail for Paris March 3 (my 36th birthday) + will spend the 8th + 9th + maybe 10th in that city. I don't imagine you will be there, but what joy if you were. We are then driving through Jugoslavia to Greece, so may not get to Rome at all.

David's story was taken by the O. Henry Award People.

I developed hepatitis in June and am only now again in excellent health.

Let us hear from you. We think + speak of you constantly and love you with all our hearts.

Yours,
Jamie

I read about your pictures Gertrude Stein's will gave her modern painting collection to Toklas, her partner, for "her use for life" before being transferred to Stein's family heirs. While Toklas was away from Paris to treat her arthritis, Stein's brother's second wife seized the art. Janet Flanner wrote about the episode in her "Letter from Paris" in *The New Yorker,* December 5, 1961.

Artists + Writers Cookbook Toklas's book (1961) featured recipes by figures such as Marcel Duchamp, Marianne Moore, and Man Ray. Merrill's shrimp *à l'orange* made it in.

David's story Jackson's story "The English Gardens," published in *Partisan Review* (March–April 1961), was chosen by Richard Poirier as one of twenty winners of the O. Henry Award for Short Fiction for 1962.

To Daryl Hine

WUSTL
[Winter, 1962]
[Stonington, CT]

Pet,

One tries so hard to be serious and not waste time, but at 5 this morning I flung back the covers in the hot grip of such an amusing idea—something absolutely made for Raoul. Let me at least describe it to you, in the hopes that I shan't have to write it myself. You can, or we can, or perhaps a precis will suffice. It will be a sort of parody of the *Hérodiade*. Time: Present. Scene: The inside of a trailer in Fort Lauderdale. Herodias sits before her open jewel box while Salome scrambles about dressing for a date. Herodias is an old Follies Queen. Ziegfeld saw her and instantly starred her in a series of immensely successful tableaux with costumes copied from Gustave Moreau, etc. She was given Mallarmé to read, to get into the spirit of the thing.

As she rambles on, the familiar mystique of jewels and chevelures and whatnot is developed, as in Mallarmé, as symbols of rare + valuable states of feeling, ideas, icy spiritual heights which her mere presence on the stage came to express. She loved the horror of being a virgin. She was respected by the Lions (and the Elks) when she danced for them. Finally Salome is ready—a toilette de beatnik, no make up, not even a bracelet. Herodias shakes her head—what are these young people coming to? Salome expounds <u>her</u> theory: there is no ornament but thought and emotion. A fact drained by lust or pulsing with shame [*in the margin:* or breathless over a page by Sartre] gets considerably more attention nowadays than one set off by diamonds. The mother is alarmed by this speech. "Who are you going out with tonight, dear?" "Oh, just John, as usual." "Is he a nice boy? Is he Jewish?" "No, he's from down here. He's a Baptist." John appears. He <u>is</u> a Baptist, refuses a drink, doesn't smoke, suggests Bingo at the church. Salome pouts, she wants to go dancing. As they leave, John turns to Herodias: "Ma'am, Ah'm so crazy bout yo daughter, Ah'm like to lose mah haid." Alone, Herodias, by now completely decked with glass and zircons [*in the margin:* hair white + streaming], closes the shutters. . . .

A rough sketch, but do admit it has possibilities!

No news since my last letter. Except for this enclosure, which pray return. My brother's oldest son, Bruce, 14, comes tomorrow for four days. We are putting all the Olympia press books where he can find them.

Love to you + John,

J.

Daryl Hine See Biographies.
Hérodiade Dramatic poem by Mallarmé, on which Paul Hindemith and Martha Graham based their ballet of the same name (1944), which Merrill probably has in mind.
Olympia press books Paris press known for publishing scandalous books in its Traveller's Companion series, including *Lolita* and *Fanny Hill*.

To Eudora Welty

MISSISSIPPI
15 January 1962
Stonington, CT

Dear Eudora Welty,

Thank you, thank you for your lovely essay on Henry Green. David Jackson and I both read it with the greatest pleasure. How wonderful of you not to quote! He is one of those writers (Wallace Stevens might be another) one should either read in quantity or let the work recompose in the mind—as you invite us to do. I can't help wishing, though, that <u>he</u> would quote <u>you</u>. That somehow your paragraph on the shape of *Party Going* might be stealthily introduced in a future edition of that book.

David + I saw Mary Lou all too briefly over the holidays, before catching our first colds of the year. We sail in March for 4 months abroad. It would be exhilarating to return on July 4 and hear that your book is finished.

With all best wishes.

Sincerely,
Jimmy Merrill

Eudora Welty (1909–2001), American short story writer and novelist.
your lovely essay "Henry Green: A Novelist of the Imagination," *Texas Quarterly* (Autumn 1961).

To Alice B. Toklas TEXAS
27 March 1962
Thessaloniki, Greece

Dear Alice,

Forgive me for taking so long to say how lovely it was to see you, even briefly, and how we appreciated your sharing our little hour with Grace Stone. David and I were delighted to find you looking and acting so well. I wish only that we could have seen you a second time.

Jugoslavia was <u>dreadful</u>. Mountain snows, uncleared roads—when there were roads—rain, the smell of coal smoke everywhere. We met one charming man, an art critic named Markuš, but the weather was too much. We bolted, leaving everything unseen, and are now drinking up the sun, and the resinated wine, of Salonika. What a difference.

Tomorrow we go on to Athens where we shall be until mid-June (at the above address) if there is anything we can do for you.

With much love as always from
David and
Jamie

To Daryl Hine WUSTL
21 April 1962
Athens, Greece

Poor angel!

It is too dreadful, what you write. I wonder if you hadn't better see another doctor. I wish I knew of a good one in New York. I suppose DP <u>is</u> good and that one had best leave ill enough alone. One can, however, do more than take vitamin pills. One can take vitamin shots; they are much stronger and their effect is longer lasting. Ask DP about this. I wonder if what your intérieur hasn't always needed is, along with fireplace and winding stair, a few hypodermics cozily sterilizing themselves over a hard blue flame. Very suggestive for the eunuch book. Such a good idea, that. Will you "deal" with Christine Jorgenson? The Test-tube Eunuch, you might call that chapter, and proceed to disparage the whole affair.

This last week has been very shaking. On returning from a picnic with Peter Mayne and Eddie Gaythorne-Hardy I found I could not move the right side of my face. Well, of course, Alison Bishop has been that way all her life, but it gave me a turn, let me tell you. The lower eyelid sagged, people had to look the other way when I laughed or ate. A doctor came and ran pins up and down my palms and foot-soles and pronounced the word Psyxis (freezing). Since then I have gone to the hospital every morning for x-ray and diathermy, and every afternoon received a distinguished gentleman from the corner drugstore, he wears a black armband yet, who gives me one shot in the rump and another in the vein of my golden arm. Another doctor, called in by David and Tony Parigory who feared I was getting too much medication, prescribed cortisone along with everything else. Anyhow, I am much better now, I can close that eye and curl that lip, and my smile, once again, drives men mad [*in the margin:* I'm superstitious. Be a dear + don't bruit this about until I can assure you it has utterly gone]. I suspect that we have here the materials of a poem: the crack in the mirror of the soul, if that is what the face is, but I think the setting ought to be Istanbul—where by the way we aren't going because my mother fell and broke her kneecap (is our house doomed?) and will have to put off her trip either entirely or for two months.

In the midst of all this Umberto Morra arrived from Rome. I wasn't able to do very much for him as I was confined to quarters. We did throw a rather huge party, 14 for dinner, with specimens of the Fair in the persons of 3 aging Alexandrines, one of whom, very drunk, turned her little painted face and orange bangs onto Umberto (gaunt, bald, lame, impeccably formal) and chirped out of a clear blue sky, "Ah, you're so sexy—yum, yum, yum!" One instantly disqualified her for the Golden Apple. Umberto left yesterday, at which point my face began to mend. I have toyed, fustily, with the Psychological Interpretation. His being here was going to <u>cramp my style</u>, and so it did, in one way if not another.

The Exploits continue unabated. Athens is changing—more and more people are doing it for fun instead of for money; sign of a stable economy and corruption from outside. There is even a genuine Queer Bar such as you find in every other city in the world, complete with striped walls + overpriced drinks. It is too dreadful for words.

My nephew + his wife blew in from Istanbul and Persia yesterday. Thus far they have not had a glimpse of our untidy coulisses. We keep telling ourselves that they are grown up and should be able to take whatever, or whoever, comes. On verra.

<u>Please</u> keep us posted. Let John write a line if you are too weak. Take care of yourself. We <u>worry</u>. Let me say to you what I say now and then to a Greek youth— θέλεις νά τρελλαίνομαι*;—and promise to be perfectly well soon.

> Love from D to you and John and from James

*Do you want me to go crazy?

DP Merrill's Dr. Park.
Christine Jorgenson Jorgensen (1926–89) was an American transgender woman whose gender-reassignment surgery in the 1950s stirred international attention.
Peter Mayne English travel writer (1908–79).
Eddie Gaythorne-Hardy The Honorable (Ralph) Edward Gathorne-Hardy (1901–78), one of the "Bright Young Things" of the 1920s English tabloids, major figure in Martin Green's *Children of the Sun* (1976), and source of an anecdote attributed to A. H. Clarendon (an invention of Merrill's) in section Q of "The Book of Ephraim" (1976).
the materials of a poem See "The Thousand and Second Night" in *Nights and Days* (1966). The ailment is Bell's palsy.
the Golden Apple The apple of discord, which led to the Trojan War after it was tossed into the feast of the gods, was inscribed "to the most beautiful."
My nephew + his wife Robin and Betty Magowan.

To Louise Fitzhugh

FITZHUGH
29 May 1962
Athens, Greece

Dear Louise,

No, I wish we were, but we're not—buying a house on an island, that is. We've never exactly been in the vanguard, you know, and probably in 2 years—or whenever things have begun to cost the Earth here—we shall make that imprudent move.

I wouldn't worry about the length of your play. It seems to the point to break that mould of the 2-hour drama which is as oppressive as the eight foot ceiling. One remembers things that are uncommonly shaped. To think that in your delicate + graceful frame there throbs the soul of a Strindberg is most exhilarating.

We've had a lot of sun + sea +, now that I think of it, sex. It is a very strange place. Time flows like water. One does not read or write very much. My mother did not come (broken knee) but Mrs. Stone did, and is here, full of complaints, requirements and "plain, dull charm."

David sails back June 18. I fly on the 24th, will go straight to Atlanta, then straight to Stonington to get the house in shape before he disembarks. We'll make a sign shortly thereafter.

Love to you + Alixe from us both,

as ever,
Jimmy

Alixe Alixe Grodin (1922–2018), casting director, Fitzhugh's partner.

To Kimon Friar

WUSTL
4 July 1962
Stonington, CT

Dear Kimon,

The wiser response would no doubt be silence, for you to interpret as you choose. But there are certain things I prefer not to leave unsaid, if only for the sake of my own self-awareness. (I mean, I am not counting on your faith or interest.)

Your letter eats to the bone. It is so much what I thought you would say; thus, in a sense, it must be what I hoped you would say. It confirms in me a respect for you which you imagine I do not have. You are managing to be yourself; it's what we're all trying to do.

I am now past the age you were when we met. When you went to Greece in 1946 you asked me to be faithful to you, adding that you, of course, would have "experiences" but that I must know they would mean very little. How must I have known that, I wonder—now that I <u>do</u> know? Perhaps you would have liked me to find these things out by hearsay, and perhaps you would have been right. Alas, I have always been tempted by the lives of others. The truest perception in your letter is the phrase "as though you were trying to show that you too can have many successes, etc." For me, these "successes" are a novelty of much the same quality as Hollywood was for you. I would like to protest—as you did with respect to Hollywood—that just because I have taken them up, it does not follow that they will take me over.

It makes me smile to think how I lectured you about your intimacy with rich and corrupt people, and how you now lecture me about sex—as if in both cases one had trespassed on the other's terrain.

For better or worse, Greece is the stage on which my strangest experiences have been made. I did not need, on my first visit, to behave in the way you complain of, in order to be affected deeply, physically, as psychologically now. I have never left that country without feeling that my fate was there. If that means I come back "for the wrong reasons", well and good. I cannot ask you to see these reasons any more sympathetically than you do my—pleasures? experiments? ordeals?

Neither can I thank you for having discussed all this with Gordon in front of a perfect stranger, but then I've erred in this direction myself, where you are concerned.

I suppose your view of our own relations is as accurate as any one-sided view can be. It is true that I have never shown deep interest in your translations. On the other hand, I feel I have always responded warmly to your <u>own</u> poems, and with enthusiasm whenever you have spoken of doing your own work for a change: the set of Elegies, the novels you want to write. Nothing would make me—or you, goodness knows!—happier than for you to set about <u>this</u> work, even if it means forgetting Homer and Kazantzakis. You, on your side, have repeatedly spoken of how shy you are of saying anything to me about my work, feeling that I don't want to hear anything from you about it. In a sense, again, this is so; it embarrasses me for <u>anybody</u> to speak to me about my work; it is too private, perhaps, it means too much to me. (Feeling as I do about mine, you will understand that you have often struck me as vaunting your own achievements in a way that makes me, and I suspect others, blush for you.) Still, your perception of my indifference to your responses as a reader permits you, I have fancied more than once, to forego those responses. You liked my poems best when their substance was closest to our shared experience. Now that they are less "yours" it is only natural that you find them less arresting.

As people, we are, as you say, very far apart indeed. Where you find me affected and querulous, I find you narcissistic and pompous. It is always as though you were the first person to have felt anything. This trait may be what draws young people to you—they are after all under the same illusion. It may also be what divides them from you after a bit.

I think of Mina's silence during your anguish over the cottage on her property—how well I understand it. I think of your glee when Arthur Gregor fell out of his chaste resolve into the arms of somebody he met at your house. I quite see that it pains you not to break with me exclusively on your own terms.

Like Greece, you are part of my fate, whether or not we ever meet again. Your letter does bring relief, for which I can only thank you.

Jimmy

Your letter Friar had spoken loosely about Merrill's sexual promiscuity in front of Grace Stone, who was visiting in Athens. After Merrill complained about his indiscretion, Friar told Merrill he no longer wished "to see or know him."
Gordon Gordon Sager.
Mina's silence When she separated from Friar, and denied him future access to the cottage on her property on Poros.
Arthur Gregor (1923–2013), Austrian-born American poet.

To Tony Parigory WUSTL
18 September 1962
Stonington, CT

Why dear—

It is too sad, and—as you say—too Greek. One wishes for Cavafy to make a little epigraph out of it. We are both deeply shaken both by the awfulness <u>and</u> the rightness of it. Last night in Isabel Morse's bedroom—she with her broken hip, Grace with her lame knee—both of them old and clever and not meaning to die for a long time if they have anything to say about it (and they do, it appears)—I could hardly bear to look at them. The news had taken nearly 12 hours to be felt, and suddenly there it was, and no one's presence but yours would have helped. Yet, as Grace said,—she could afford to say it—there are worse things than dying young and quickly.

Today your second letter came to our aid as did Planchette, toujours consolatrice. Breaking a long silence we inquired of our enchanting familiar (Ephraim, a Greek slave + lover of Caligula!) for Taki, who was instantly summoned. E's mother came from Larissa, and E. volunteered a comparison between Taki and the centaurs of old, whose mental powers were often not very strong. "How he chatters!" said E. "Taki mon-polylogoū!" said I, and the reply was: "Sika!" He was in high spirits, thrilled to "be" in America for a bit, wanted to know what truck-drivers' wages are here, in case he is reborn in this country. Ephraim began to rehearse a long history of early, clumsy deaths (a pattern familiar to us through our talks with him) and probably more to come, but thought him a charming fellow, while Taki thought E. a big Sika. He worried about the letters, said that you should send them to the Frenchwoman to give to a friend of his, also named Adonis, who could go to Germany in T.'s place. And he sent you much love, said he missed <u>everything</u>, and hoped we had photographs of him. Ah, one amusing moment: he "saw" the Tsarouchis—"A greek sailor, ah of course, la Mimi had him—haha; you are just the same + now I start again + we will be too much different in our age . . . Ha ha. I think I will recognize you + run holding my pants on."—it is foolish to carry on like this, I mean telling you such things, but they do mean something to us even if someone else would call them blasphemous.

Dear, charming, dumbbell. Why is it always the sweetest who are stolen away? How I wish you were with us, so that we could console one another—lacking that, thank you again + again for the gentleness of your letters, and the lightness and understanding with which you have broken the dreadful news.

Well.

Have you by now settled down with the blond George? You do have an uncanny knack of leaving your readers <u>wild</u> for the next installment. Let us have it soon. With snapshots! And in my next letter there will be (I foresee) several curious things to relate.

With a heart full of love for you.

Jimmy

Tony—It was like Taki, I do believe. But it is very small comfort even so. I <u>wonder</u> if Germany would have preserved him or been a kind of washing out of his fine colors. I will miss him, too. I sometimes feel his friendship—with no talk really possible but only every exertion being made to show warmth and responsiveness—is one most delightful, or anyway restful. Well bless him!

Ah, your letters have turned us toward the mailbox again. Expectations charm our days, again. And, lo, they've produced—as JM hints above—all kinds of mortal and local mysteries. Next letter the full American-Indian chauffeur. The <u>Unsigned Letter</u>, etc. We had never realized these searching, sinister aspects of Creepyville ever before.

It is not Greece; but it is every bit that made England neuroticness so justifiably FAMOUS! Ho ho.

Love,
David

Tony Parigory See Biographies.
Planchette The Ouija board (by way of the usual pointing device), cast here as a female domestic.
Taki A truck driver killed when he napped in the shade of a truck and was run over, an accident that was the source of a passage in section 2 of "The Thousand and Second Night" (*Nights and Days*, 1966); to be distinguished from Christos Alevras, Merrill's friend in the 1970s, also known as Taki.
"Taki mon-polylogoū!" "Taki, my polyglot" in a mixture of French and Greek.
"Sika!" "Figs" in Greek, a vulgar term for flamboyant homosexual men.
the Tsarouchis Painting by Yannis Tsarouchis (1910–89), a major Greek modernist known in particular for his homoerotic subjects. Friar introduced Merrill to Tsa-

rouchis and his work in 1950. Over the years Merrill bought a number of his small prints and paintings.

American-Indian chauffeur A Stonington acquaintance of Merrill's and Jackson's who was arrested for sex with a minor. As Merrill explained in a letter to Hine (March 26, 1963), the man was put "in jail on $15 grand bail, accused of things the local police couldn't even tell Billy Boatwright, among them, it appears, 'sodomy' (ah! que che cosa quella?)."

Creepyville Truman Capote's nickname for Stonington.

To Daryl Hine and Samuel Todes

WUSTL
26 September 1962
[Stonington, CT]

Dear Ones,

I've looked up Flycatcher (a member or the Tyrannidae family) and thought about <u>that</u> for a bit. How little we know ourselves! How little we know our friends! Surely Bernie is the sloth, not you, do sloths have those fever-bright eyes?

Teleny and *The Artist's Dilemma* are quite safe, in one sense, and we shall bring them in next month. It simply slipped the mind last time. What fun last time was, what a lovely dinner you gave us, how nice to see Virgil and to meet Anne. When you name your pretty house I will see about letter-paper with your telephone number next to an engraved "Princesse" phone on one side, and an engraved ferryboat on the other.

I don't really feel like letters these days, but I wanted to reassure you about the books—after reassuring myself first that they were here. Thank you, too, for writing about mine. What you say comes like a sip of wine, or honey, after the plates of roughage served up by, say, my mother + the Stone Women, in the goodness of their hearts.

Isabel has been loaned 5 or 6 jigsaw puzzles that belonged to Paul Leake's mother, ca. 1915. They are head + shoulders above any puzzle I have ever worked, both in subject and execution. The subjects thus far: "A Masque"—a Pierrot + Pierette rapt in each other beside a fountain (or stove) while ill-drawn amoretti pull back curtains and shoot darts; "A Farewell"—two stenographers atop a palisade waving at a battleship on the brilliant sea beneath; "The Sure Shield"—a Pekingese, proud and beady-eyed (Robert called his own eyes, the other night, "these venerable beads") between the paws of an immense bulldog, alone on the shore of a wintry sea. The colors: pale oranges, pinks, vast stretches of grays + browns, some sick greens. The pieces fit together most devilishly, in the weirdest strata—suddenly 5 inches of straight line which one took to be border will fit dos à dos with another straight line, thus bisecting half the picture; all colors are cut along their outlines—never a clue to interlocking masses; four scimitar shapes will fit one against the other. Well, my dear, the total effect is of a freedom, an audacity, that keeps us crying out with surprise— quite like the first people to know Haydn's keyboard music.

I've never read *Sylvie + Bruno.* . . .

Let me leave you with some lines I have put together about Hagia Sophia, plucked from something that sprawls:

> . . . The apse
> Militantly dislocated
> Still wears those dark green epaulettes
> On which (at least for the visitor who forgets
> His Arabic) a wild script of gold whips
> Has scribbled glowering, dated
> Slogans—"God is my grief!" or "Byzantine,
> Go home!"
> Above me, the great dome, etc. etc.

Love from David. Love from
James

Samuel Todes Hine's partner. See Hine in Biographies.
those fever-bright eyes Merrill is probably thinking of the lemur, known for its eyeshine or reflective eyes, rather than the sloth.
Teleny *Teleny, or the Reverse of the Medal* (1893), homoerotic pornographic novel possibly by several hands, though often attributed to Oscar Wilde.
The Artist's Dilemma (1947), short book by New Zealander James Boswell (1906–71), painter and writer.
Virgil . . . Anne The Burnetts.
Isabel Isabel Morse.
Pierette Pierrette is the partner of Pierrot, the stock character in commedia dell'arte.

Sylvie + Bruno (1889), the first volume of Lewis Carroll's last novel published during his lifetime, completed by *Sylvie and Bruno Concluded* (1893).
. . . **The apse** Draft lines from Merrill's poem "The Thousand and Second Night" referring to Hagia Sophia, the great mosque in Istanbul (from *Nights and Days*, 1966).

To Frederick Buechner

WHEATON
[Fall 1962]
[Stonington, CT]

Oh dear, dear Freddy,

I shouldn't reply to your letter; why should the oldest and best of friends gratuitously have the fires of his own unrest fanned; but, Lord, I am terrified as you are, the big Explosion seems nearer every year, perhaps even every week, if one thinks of the way wars are meant to begin "once the harvest is in" . . . I have been reading all winter, off and on, an extraordinary and difficult book called *Life against Death* by a Classics professor at Wesleyan. It begins with a long précis of Freud, of all people—something nowhere else supplied as far as I know; and proceeds with some historical observations that point to such things as the invention of "modern" time-sense, its connection with the economy, the connection of <u>that</u> with excrement, the connection of excrement (by way of the Viennese doctor's law of Repression) with the sublimest reaches of human thought, etc, etc. It seems we, the world that is, is bent on destroying itself, unless—and here Prof. Brown begins to wonder about the resurrection of the body, the body that in infancy was wholly an instrument of pleasure and knowledge, but that inexorably over the years channels that pleasure into one or two organs, and that knowledge into intimations of immortality scarcely borne out by the fear and estrangement we accumulate like debts. When you write that you "miss" me, and when I think how I "miss" you, I wonder if we are not both alluding to a time of life in which we had not yet begun to miss our own bodies (though even then they were no longer ours). Well, I don't know, but it does seem as though one's body and one's planet were, at this moment, in the same boat and on the same schedule. It is a situation that positively

<u>extorts</u> an act of faith from one, [and] that act is the very one I most want not to perform—because [i]t would mean to me now that there is no other hope, none. [And] as I said, I miss you too.

The next day. I think I know what the soul is. In childhood it is not to be distinguished from the body; that is why children are always being <u>watched</u> with joy. In our maturity, the soul can be identified with <u>the</u> <u>body</u> <u>we</u> <u>no</u> <u>longer</u> <u>have</u>, the body of childhood that instructed us in pleasure and wisdom which we now call "spiritual" because they are so clearly not within our physical capacities. (Thus it may be said without irony that the debauchee is "searching for his soul"—he is trying to recapture the infinite sensuous receptivity of the little child.) (The Earth, likewise, has become the mature body on which we inflict a wealth of gross sensation—poisons, explosions— partly hoping that it will prove itself still young, partly in guilty rage at the steady exhaustion of its resources, all too analogous to our own. Are we not reassured, if briefly, by news of a Volcano in eruption? It means there is life in the old girl yet!)

[The rest of the letter is missing.]

Life against Death Life Against Death: The Psychoanalytic Meaning of History (1959) by Norman O. Brown.
what the soul is In "The Thousand and Second Night" (*Nights and Days*, 1966) Merrill attributes a version of the following speculation to his Alexandrian friend Germaine Nahman. See note to letter to Tony Parigory of 4 February 1973.

To Robert and Charlotte Arner   POSTCARD | WUSTL
[January 1963]
[Stonington, CT]

The days are growing longer
And March the 3rd is near.
James won't enjoy his birthday
Without Carlotta here.
Some come in early afternoon,
And spend the night—spend two!

There're beds in which the little ones
Can mach' die Augen zu,
And what with food + wine + song
We shall make whoopee all night long.

D + J

Robert and Charlotte Arner See Merrill's letter to his mother, March 1959. The poem, written in Merrill's hand, is decorated with the sketch of a banner, with "1926" to the left of the poem and "1963" to the right.
postcard A plain card, address on front, message on back.

To Robin Magowan

WUSTL
1 February 1963
[Stonington, CT]

Dear Robin,

I'm very grateful for your letter about that long poem. It will help me make a few small changes when the time comes; and permits me (far more important) to consider and, finally, reject the major change you suggest—that of beginning with carnivals—thus, I mean, in a round-about way, confirming the structure as it stands. Now I can say, with some relief, that I <u>like</u> the diary-entry-type unfolding of it; that, if the tone of III is suddenly stronger, it is useful right there as a shot in the arm; that the poem as a whole couldn't support what would in effect be a monstrously long flashback; usw. The ill-starred motorist is half-Taki and half every America-smitten Greek. I don't think I could change the accident back to being run over in his sleep—it would mean giving up the "headlong emigration out of life" which may be my favorite line in the whole thing. I'm seeing what I can do about the lines that end III; you do put your finger deep into my little bag of tricks, and that point is very well taken; whatever happens, it will serve to prevent too much more of the same in the future. You are quite right too about the Piaf-preamble to the postcards, but so far no way around it occurs to me. I did hope, I did try, to cling less to artifice—in vain; my muse <u>will</u> pluck her eyebrows despite my prayers.

Nothing much of interest on this coast. Well, Irma Brandeis sponsored the NY premiere of *Le Sorelle B.* before a glittering and rapt public of perhaps 20, including a Dante scholar who teaches at Julliard, the Chiaromontes, etc. It was an immense success. I had gone to Schirmer's that morning and spent the afternoon learning a few more songs. The night before, the Hollanders gave a big party to say goodbye to their 70 most intimate + distinguished friends; not a trace of John Simon, but Merwin, Simpson, Warren, [*in the margin:* Auden + Kallman who have asked us to dinner in 10 days to hear a tape of *Elegy for Young Lovers*,] and a fascinating couple whose names I forget because they <u>were</u> the Lavins: both art-historians, fresh from Rome, put on a nice act together, it was uncanny. Anne finished her painting of Tithonus + Aurora for us—the problem now is where to hang it. If only (between ourselves) she painted well. The night before that was the opening of *Milk Train* which I must say I loathed from beginning to end, a vague, wilful, charmless play. The trouble with Wms. I used to think was that one knew all too well what he was writing about; in this case I can't believe that I knew at all. Perhaps if Grace had played it instead of that ghastly frump, all brittle vulgarity, it would have been a little better. Afterwards Herbert gave much too nice a party for about 150, took over a restaurant, drinks, dinner, the works; lots of famous people; around 12 a messenger entered breathless to report that Walter Kerr on TV had given it a dreadful panning; and inside of 20 minutes two-thirds of the guests had simply got up and left. We sat with the Gruens + wish we hadn't.

Daryl Hine is coming for the weekend tomorrow with Virgil Burnett who illustrated D's little book on Poland—which I'll send you when its last borrower returns it. Virgil and his wife—not that we know them very well but they inspire confidence—may just live here this summer while we're away. She is a prof. of Greek at Chicago; the story goes that, tired of being considered a pretty, featherbrained girl and being asked "Oh, you're working on Euripides? what are you <u>doing</u> with him?" she replied one day: "I have proven him to be a Renaissance forgery."

While at Amherst, by the way, I asked De Mott what had happened in the last year or so to ruin his relations with the entire rest of the English Dept, and lo! it turned out to have been all because of Roger Sale. Ben didn't think he deserved promotion, thought in fact that he was being used as a "gunman" by the senior dept. members like Baird + Craig, and said so to their faces, and the rubble still hasn't been cleared away.

Time to go to Westerly for vitamin shots. Our love to you and Betty.

Jimmy

that long poem Merrill's "The Thousand and Second Night" in *Nights and Days* (1966).
NY premiere of *Le Sorelle B. Le Sorelle Brontë,* performed by The Little Players, the puppet theater of Frank Peschka and Gordon (Bill) Murdock, and written by Bernard de Zogheb (1924–99), Alexandrian librettist, writer, and artist.
the Chiaromontes Nicola Chiaromonte (1905–72), Italian socialist and man of letters, and his wife, Miriam, both friends of Mary McCarthy (1912–89), American fiction writer and critic.
Schirmer's G. Schirmer, Inc., publisher and seller of classical music.
John Simon (1925–2019), American film and theater critic.
Elegy for Young Lovers Three-act opera (1961) by Hans Werner Henze, for which Auden and Kallman wrote the English libretto.
Anne Anne Hollander.
Tithonus + Aurora Characters in Merrill's *The Immortal Husband* (1955).
Milk Train Tennessee Williams's play *The Milk Train Doesn't Stop Here Anymore* (1962), premiered at the Morosco Theater, directed by Herbert Machiz, with music by Paul Bowles, starring Hermione Baddeley ("the ghastly frump") in a role based on Tallulah Bankhead.
Walter Kerr (1913–96), prominent American theater critic.
the Gruens John Gruen (1926–2016), American art, music, and dance critic, photographer, and composer, and his wife, Jane Wilson (1924–2015), American painter.
D's little book Hine's *Polish Subtitles: Impressions from a Journey* (1962).
Roger Sale (1932–2017), literary critic and professor of literature at the University of Washington.
Baird + Craig Theodore Baird and G. Armour Craig.

To Daryl Hine

WUSTL
28 June 1963
Athens, Greece

Ma Soeur—

Ta pauvre Sophie n'a pas le courage de te ranconter dans sa propre langue ce qui lui est arrivé après ce qu'elle à mis à la poste cette carte funeste et menteuse d'hier. D'accord il faut le dire que ta soeur à été follement distraite pendant ces jours. Elle était avec sa mère et deux autres dames une âgée de 70 ans, l'autre de 17—celle-ci sera en 10 années une lesbienne charmante, mais à present elle n'est qu'un Garçon préadolescent. Bien. Comme je te l'ai dit je n'ai réussi à trouver ni le Hamam "L'Etoile" ni le bar "Le Coq Vert." L'ennui m'a poussée jusqu'au parc ou il y avait un tas de types tels qu'on trouve dans les parcs. Idiote que je suis, je suis entré dans un taxi avec un beau jeune homme, petit moustache, sourire éclatant, et assez bien vêtu (vêtu, comme j'allais voir, en criminal réussi). Il avait refusé de m'accompagner à l'hotel, et m'invita "chez lui." Je n'avais sur moi que 30 lires ($3) et encore 20 dans ma poche secrete—qu'avais je à perdre? Après 12 kilometres, ample distance pour faire refléchir à ta folle Sophie, on arriva—on renvoya le taxi. [*in the margin*: il m'avait fait voir qu'il avait beaucoup d'argent—d'autres victimes sans di] C'était minuit. On était sur une colline sans maisons, sans sentiers, entre la demi-lune et une vue ravissante du Bosphore. Il me dit—en turc, il savait exactement deux mots de français et deux d'anglais—Donne ta montre, et je te rendrai quelque chose à moi—en produisant un article de manicure des plus communs. J'ai ri (haha) et refusé. Alors il m'a demandé des dollars. Je lui ai donné ma porte-feuille—il a pris 20 lire en me laissant 10 "pour le taxi"—"C'est un monsieur," me disais-je même alors. Puis j'ai fait mon "devoir" et nous avons fumé un cigarette après laquelle au lieu de m'escorter jusqu'au taxi hypothétique il m'a pris sauvagement par la jacquette en redemandent ma montre. Il était sérieux! Pour la première fois je n'étais plus ivre de la lune et du saké que j'avais bu—et j'avais une peur affreuse. Je lui ai donné ma montre. Je me rappelle maintenant qu'il m'a offrit à ce moment une seconde fois sa manicure, et que je l'ai refusée avec un geste sublime. "Le taxi! Le taxi!," criais-je alors. Il m'a indiqué les lumières duprés du Bosphore. "Donne moi encore un peu d'argent, 10 lires ne suffiront pas," dis-je en trés belle pantomime. Pour réponse j'ai en un coup de poing au mâchoire* et un coup de pied dans le dos—moi qu'on n'a jamais battre de la vie, qu'on a toujours embrassée, dorlotée, enfin que sais-je? Avec ça nous nous sommes séparés. Après 10 minutes j'ai trouvé un village, une foule sortant du cinéma, tout le monde étourdi par le chien de Chrétien sorti des enfers pour tout qu'ils en savaient—et un taxi qui m'a ramené à l'hôtel où sont commencés les vrais horreurs: les fantaisies de ce qui m'avrait <u>pu</u> arriver au lieu de cette petite aventure—qui tout de même me laisse glacée et blême lorsque j'y pense. Tu riras, mais à deux heures du matin, ta soeur était à genoux, toute nue, pour remercier le bon dieu—en français, la parole me manque encore en anglais—de lui avoir sauvée la vie.

En plus, David, qui dêvait arriver ce matin, n'était pas là quand Tony est allé à sa rencontre. Ou serait-il? Pris comme ôtage par les Croates? <u>Pas</u> <u>un</u> <u>mot</u> depuis Southampton. Allume donc une vingtaine de bougies comme la folle que tu es—ne raconte à personne l'honteuse expérience de ta soeur—moins Sophie que Justine, je crains—et écris-moi vite-vite. Nous partons pour Samos le 4 juillet et espérons trouver une caïque pour Rhodes sans rentrer à Athènes.

Je t'embrasse. John aussi.

Justine (sinon Juliette!)

*Ce qui me rappèle l'histoire de Tony sur Jean Dessès qui voulait toujours paraître jeune, jusqu'au jour où son jeune amant grec l'a legerement gifle dans un moment d'impatience—et l'autre c'est recule en disant d'une voix calme et triste: "Tu a leve la main contre un vieux monsieur."

Sophie The name probably comes from *Les Malheurs de Sophie* (1858), the well-known children's book by the Comtesse de Ségur, as **Justine** alludes to *Justine, ou Les Malheurs de la Vertu* (1791) by the Marquis de Sade.
Jean Dessès (1904–70) Greek-French fashion designer.

My Sister—

Your poor Sophie lacks the courage to tell you in her own tongue what happened to her after she mailed that dreadful, deceitful card yesterday. I must tell you that your sister has been crazily distracted these past days. She has been with her mother and two ladies, one aged seventy and the other seventeen—the latter will be a charming lesbian in ten years, but right now is only a pre-adolescent boy. Well. As I told you I found neither the bath "The Star" nor "The Green Cock." Boredom drove me to the park where there were a bunch of guys that you find in parks. Idiot that I am, I got into a taxi with a handsome young man, small mustache, bright smile, and well-enough dressed (dressed, I came to realize, for criminal success). He had refused to accompany me to the hotel, and invited me to "his place." I didn't have more than 30 lires ($30) and 20 more in my secret pocket—what did I have to lose? After 12 kilometers, ample distance to reflect on Sophie's folly, we arrived—to send the taxi away. [*in the margin*: he had let me see that he had a lot of money—from other victims no doubt] It was midnight. We were on a hill without houses, without paths, under a half moon and with a ravishing view of the Bosphorus. He said to me—in Turkish, he knew exactly two words of French and two of English—Give me your watch, and I'll give you something of mine, producing a cheap manicuring implement. I laughed (ha-ha) and refused. Then he demanded dollars. I gave him my wallet—he took 20 lires and left me 10 "for the taxi"—"He's a gentleman," I told myself even then. Next I did my "duty" and we smoked a cigarette after which, instead of escorting me to the hypothetical taxi, he grabbed me savagely by the jacket and demanded my watch. He was serious! For the first time I wasn't drunk from the moon and the sake that I had had—and I had a frightful fear. I gave him my watch. Now I recall that he had offered me just then a second time the manicure [implement], and that I refused with a grand gesture. "The taxi! The taxi!" I cried out. He motioned toward the lights along the Bosphorus. "Give me a little more money, 10 lires isn't sufficient," I said with a very fine pantomime. In response I got a fist to the jaw and a kick in the back. I have never been beaten in my life, always held, pampered, after all what do I know? With that we separated. After 10 minutes I found a village, a crowd coming out of a movie theater, everyone stunned by this Christian dog from hell for all they knew—and a taxi took me back to the hotel where the real horrors began: the fantasies about what *could* have happened instead of that little adventure— which all the same leaves me ice-cold and pale when I think of it. You laugh, but at two o'clock in the morning, your sister knelt, altogether naked, to thank the good God—in French, I still lack the words in English—for having saved my life.

Moreover, David, who was due to arrive this morning, was not there when Tony went to meet him. Ah where could he be? Taken hostage by the Croats? *Not a word* since Southampton. Light twenty candles like the fool you are—don't tell anyone about the shameful experience of your sister—less Sophie than Justine, I fear—and write to me quick-quick. We leave for Samos on July 4th and hope to find a caique for Rhodes without going back to Athens.

A hug to you. John too.

Justine (if not Juliette)

*Which reminds me of Tony's story about Jean Dessès, who always wanted to look young, until the day his young Greek lover slapped him lightly in a moment of impatience—and he flinched and said in a voice calm and sad: "You have raised your hand against an aging gentleman."

To Mary McCarthy

VASSAR
15 October 1963
Stonington, CT

Dear Mary,

We've been home about 2 weeks—well, I arrived a bit earlier, by plane—and would have written long before this to thank you for *The Group* had it not been for David. When I met him at the pier (this in itself takes some doing nowadays; one has to have at least, as I did, the identity card of a customs broker—I was Bernard N. Brady) I found a wraith. He'd been in bed, with fever, living on liquids, for five days. It's nothing grave, a "low-grade infection" according to our good doctor in Westerly, but he's still supine and will be, I imagine, for about another week. So our return hasn't been the ecstatic thing we imagined it would be, back in Athens. It has given us lots of time for reading, at least, and your book was doubly welcome. We both liked it immensely. It is so beautifully done, so funny, so sad. The girls seem to be plotted on a slow clear spiral. I think what I liked most was the very "lifelike" passage of time; one scarcely notices it, it is so wedded to incident, and the girls, or the incidents that illuminate them, come to resemble a neo-Hogarthian Progress from the first stage to the last. With this book I feel, not without a tinge of nostalgia, that you've produced something stranger and unwieldier than its gemlike forerunners; or that, to change the image, you've dispensed with the diving-bell—which might account for a stronger allegiance to surfaces than I can remember in other books. It seems, I mean, a splendid warning to anyone who would want to type you. We've been reading the *Theatre Chronicles* and *The Oasis* and feel rather like hooked addicts. All we need now is you and Jim downstairs.

The YMHA announces you on November 10. Will you be in New York much before, or after? We're going West around the 13th—David to Los Angeles, I and a friend from Athens to Chicago, Seattle, and San Francisco where David expects to meet us—and not returning East much before the 7th or 8th of December. I do hope we see you though. If you're not completely taken up, it might be simpler for you to make a sign. Or how about something like a long lunch on the 12th or 13th?

The invalid has asked to scrawl a few lines.

> Love to you both,
> as ever,
> Jimmy

Dear Mary—

Hand and head are pretty weak; but your novel has been the most satisfactory experience I've had in years of reading. I am a fool for Polly's father, but then Pokey charms me, utterly. And then it all combines and I go on remembering, and looking up again, chapter after chapter. And I envy and admire you. And send thanks, with love,

> David

The Group (1963), McCarthy's novel, a roman à clef whose characters were modeled on members of her class at Vassar.
Theatre Chronicles and *The Oasis* Respectively, a 1963 collection of McCarthy's theater reviews from 1937 to 1962 and her second novel (1949).
Jim James R. West (1915–99), American career diplomat, McCarthy's fourth husband.
The YMHA The Poetry Center at the 92nd Street YMHA.

To Elizabeth Bishop   VASSAR
                                    14 December 1963
                                    Stonington, CT

Dear Elizabeth,

Thank you for your beautiful card (os noivos) and your letter which
arrived today. David and I have been back about 5 days from Califor-
nia. Our resolve had been to write no Christmas cards, to send none
in fact—which means only that we are twice as busy writing Christ-
mas <u>letters</u>.

Please don't worry, I haven't been ill! Well, I did have a touch of
Bell's palsy, as I believe it's called—the facial paralysis—but that
was the Spring before last, in Athens where it is called "psyxix" yes,
psyxix (a freezing) and everyone you know has an uncle or a cousin
who has had it. I look back fondly on those days. They told me not
to go out, so that the salon was always full of well-wishers, drinking
beer + orangeade, and playing cards. Around 5 p.m., at the height
of the rout, a well-dressed elderly man, wearing a mourning band,
would arrive from the pharmacy to give me an injection (we retired
to the dining-alcove but within earshot of the merriment). It was fun
somehow.

I've been reading your translations in the current *Poetry*—they're
wonderful poems—but was especially happy to see, in the contribu-
tors' notes, that a new book of your own will be out next year. How
I look forward to it! How everybody does! I spent a night with the
Summerses (they look forward to it, or will when they know) in St
Louis last month. They're all in fine form except perhaps Joe who
is on either 8 or 16 committees and has no time to give his courses.
U.T. by comparison seems immensely composed, if not Luini at least
Berthe Morisot in porcelain. As for Hazel, she must be seen to be
believed.

David and Howard and I talk twice a year about Brazil. I suppose
we might turn up one of these days or decades. It's very naive of me
(and you have written a beautiful refutation of this position—a poem
about styles of birdcages, if memory serves) but only recently I've
begun to feel that the imagination takes better care of things than
the senses do, like glass-front shelves one doesn't have to dust the

insides of. But then Brazil can't be all that fragile, can it? I'm afraid it will still be Greece for a few more years. Will you + Lota come to the States next year? Please let us know if you do. We'll be in Stonington at least until mid-October. Merry Christmas to you both.

As ever,
Jimmy

(os noivos) The newlyweds (Portuguese), in reference to the postcard's image.
a new book *Questions of Travel* (1965).
if not Luini at least Berthe Morisot Bernardino Luini (c. 1482–1532), Italian painter; Berthe Morisot (1841–95), French painter. Merrill is alluding to "Luini in porcelain!," the first line in Ezra Pound's "Medallion," the final poem in his sequence "Mauberley (1920)" at the end of his *Hugh Selwyn Mauberley*.
Hazel The Summers' young daughter.
David and Howard David Kalstone (see Biographies) and Howard Moss.
a poem about styles of birdcages See Bishop's poem "Questions of Travel": "Never to have studied history in / the weak calligraphy of songbirds' cages."

To Robin and Betty Magowan

WUSTL
17 October 1964
Athens, Greece

Dear Robin + Betty,

Your letters—for all the time it has taken to say so—made us feel very welcome indeed. How I wish you were here. The weather is lovely beyond words. Yesterday, no 3 days ago, I decided to explore the grounds; crossed the street and climbed, in a very few moments, the bald white crest of Lykabettos, where there are all kinds of things to see, near and far, including masses of tiny wild cyclamen + autumn crocuses quivering up from every crevice, and a large flattened "crater" invisible from below, in which a solitary figure had changed into a green sweatshirt + shorts in order to practice football against a rugged team of cliffs. The house looked distinguished enough from up there. From close it is even handsomer—the door + shutters grey-blue against the unchanged flaking-pastry walls; and from inside it is a dream of comfort + joy. The salon in particular is all we could have wished with the brass rods gleaming and the lengths of denim lengthening (to the point where the lining had to be removed!). Above the fireplace which is of cream colored brick hangs a grim little piece of Americana—a tiny white child staring at a broken birdbath in back of a cream-colored brick church and next to a faded red brick store in whose window a wee sign announces: "Hugh Baby Hop—Bo Diddley Nite" (courtesy Stonington Art Gallery). We have bougainvillea in a pot on the balcony, also a very weird dark purple plant with leaves like brushstrokes which Maria gave us in Sounion the other day when we went with her + Nelly for a picnic + even a swim. Maisie lounges on the cozy-corner, trying to make up her mind whether to starve or eat minced lamb-heart. Kyria Kleo cleans + cooks + turns pink + shaky with laughter at everything we do or say. Tomorrow, no Monday, is our official housewarming—no Americans invited except Joe Glasco who is sortabilissimo now that he doesn't drink; other guests include Tsarouchis, Bernard de Zogheb, Maria's lovely niece Nina + her husband the architect who made the fireplace; Maziki has gone to Paris so we get the credit for asking him without the bore of having him. And Tuesday, praying that the weather hold, we set out for 8 days in the Peloponnesos, to all those places we haven't been, like Pylos, Bassae, Mistra, Monemvasia, and Kalamata where a reunion with D's foster children has been planned. We haven't <u>done</u> anything of course. David added a pastel view of Hymettos from the living room to his sketchbook. I read my galleys again + again. There's perhaps a shade too much hide-+-seek in the book; I kept wondering if I mightn't be the only one to see all the fine points—but that's how I usually feel about poems so I guess what I'm saying is that I'm very pleased with it. Oh, and today we paid for our piano—an upright Gaveau some 25 years old in excellent condition owned, oddly enough, by our former landlady, "Tin Baby" (as she was called by tired women asking for her over the phone we shared) on Ploutarchou. You may even have been sitting below when a stray note drifted through the ceiling.

I love the pictures of Felix, and the impression that comes through of your paintings, Betty; and the way Robin's book is taking shape. If only a publisher will <u>see</u> that it makes sense, that it isn't just a miscellany of what you've done to date. I'm not absolutely convinced myself that in the last analysis the Persian piece will fit among the poems. The question to ask is, perhaps, do we want, along with so much compression, the built-in respite of a prose passage? The answer can only be an arbitrary yes or no. I'm eager to see it all in one piece, though. (The Persian pages came back here from *Encounter* by the way—c/o Tony whose name, also by the way, is spelled Parigory— with a note from the S S man suggesting *Holiday;* I've readdressed it to you.)

I told you I believe that I saw Stephen in London; have had since a clever chatty letter from him. He <u>is</u> remarkably poised, ze dois dire. But now I must stop. I'm still hung over from Tony's self-inflicted birthday party last night; and within an hour or two we'll have to start drinking again. He sends love, so does David, so does

Jimmy

Lykabettos The highest point in Athens; Merrill lived across the street from the south side of the wild mountain park.
The house Merrill bought the house at Athinaion Efivon 44 in 1964.
Sounion Maria Mitsotaki had a house on Cape Sounion.
Nelly Helene Liambey, longtime friend of Maria Mitsotaki and Tony Parigory.
Kyria Kleo Merrill's housekeeper; see his poem "Days of 1964."
Nina + her husband Nina and Dimitri Koutsoudakis.
Maziki Mezeiki, partner in Parigory's antiques shop.
D's foster children Jackson applied through "Foster Parents' Plan, Inc., Greece": he was assigned to brothers Dimitrious and Elias Alexandropoulos.
my galleys For *The (Diblos) Notebook* (1965).
Felix The Magowans' son.
S S man English poet Stephen Spender (1909–95), founder and editor of *Encounter.*
Stephen Robin's brother, Stephen Magowan.

To Daryl Hine

WUSTL
17 November 1964
Athens, Greece

Kalè,

David is upstairs with a commando named Niko, out of bed with whom I have just reeled, taking photographs to document an organ all but unprecedented in the experience of yours truly. Now that I've calmed myself by playing very much en sourdine some 3-part Inventions, I find my thoughts winging, like a Pompeian phallus, in your long-neglected direction. We have delighted in Lady Sara, it is ever so deft. (Had you thought to put a question-mark after "Her rivals" in the last stanza? It would make the yawn more "condescending.")

It is a mild bright afternoon. There <u>are</u> deciduous trees here, since you ask. We watched leaves fall—where? when?—not too long ago, anyhow. And I have found a shop that sells Chantilly by the gram (cream, not lace, pet). Chester's example has helped me make a beginning in the kitchen. Oh, nothing to match <u>him</u>—serving dinner to 12 the evening of the day he moved into a new apartment—but a Chicken Marengo one day, a chocolate soufflé the next. Considering that I'll never master the formula for turning Celsius into Fahrenheit, I'm quite proud of the results. And the boys "eat it up". I've met absolutely <u>the</u> nicest one in all these years of shopping about. His name is Strato Mouflouzelis, 22, has another 8 months to do in the Air Force where he repairs vehicles. He knows hundreds of weird Greek jokes involving degenerate priests, morons, elephants, "sisters"; he is always in a good humor—never once has stared moodily off into space while exhaling through closed lips; he is nifty in bed and, if appearances can be believed, more than a little devoted to One; why he even helps clear the table—and he knows no English, gioia! Well, let me just slip a tiny snapshot in with this page. He spends about 3 nights a week here, with or without his friend Aleko who is something of a lump (prettier than S. but quite without his sparkle) and D. has been very good trying to turn him into the silken purse you would think he was at first glance. Ah—how much easier if you were <u>here</u> + could get it all firsthand. All, all, all.

I don't want to go into Chester's life, but here is a wee illustration. He phoned today (he's giving a party this evening so that John Lehmann can meet some youths) to say that an elaborate summons had been delivered to his absent landlady, a long-stemmed blonde about 40 named Zina Rachevsky; he turned it over to his beloved evzone Kosta who turned pale and said "Chester, du musst ein anderer Wohnung <u>heute</u> finden." She had been charged with running a brothel. Neighbors had reported <u>men</u> of all sorts climbing her stairs and often staying overnight, and surely no evzone could risk being seen in such a notorious building. So—a new baisodrome must be found which another huge dinnerparty will no doubt inaugurate. Tu vois le genre?

These last weeks I've been simmering over an exchange with Tony

Harwood. He has just discovered Isak Dinesen and written a long, fantastically pompous essay, mentioning her perhaps twice, about the profound meanings of history, the "élite de la pensée," the wrong track that everything has been on since the French Revolution. I made the mistake of telling him very gently how it struck me, and have been bombarded by letters containing phrases like "levels all of which are significant if not the Ultimate except for those who Know" and "I suggest you meditate upon the Third Eye"—I who have never knowingly meditated in my life! He is on a slow boat to China right now, so I have another month to distill a rebuttal as brief and transparent as a drop of prussic acid. In his best moments the dear man is awfully good. I had drinks with some friends of his in London who were describing his ghastly, minutiae-crammed life there—or rather quoting his description of it. "Every morning we take the Rolls to Fortnum's or Harrod's." "And what do you buy?" asked Ursula. "Ah," said T. with a magnificent smile, "a little something that will have to be taken back in the afternoon."

Give our love to V + A. We've owed them a letter for so long, and I'm afraid this one isn't especially to be shared. We think of you in your lair of gold (eyes ashine with that glare of old) and send you endless hugs + kisses.

J.

Kalè Abbreviation of *kalimera,* good day, hello.
Lady Sara See Hine's poem "Lady Sara Bunbury Sacrificing to the Graces by Reynolds" in his collection *Minutes* (1968). Hine didn't include the suggested question mark in the last stanza.
Chester's example Chester Kallman was a near neighbor in Athens.
John Lehmann (1907–87), English poet and man of letters.
"Chester, du" "Chester, you must find another place to live *today!*" (in ungrammatical German).
meditate upon the Third Eye See Merrill's poem "Mandala" in *Braving the Elements* (1972).
V + A The Burnetts.

To David Kalstone   WUSTL
                                                    2 January 1965
                                                    Athens, Greece

Cher Enfant,

The house is filling up with lovers (it's a Saturday), all taking baths,
telling jokes, smearing their mugs with our last drops of Floris Bath
Essence under the impression that it is cologne. They're so child-
ishly eager to find favor that I don't doubt one or two will, but not
until I've at least begun a letter to you. My reigning favorite is still
the boy I met my first night in Athens this year: Strato. He has quite
rejuvenated me, by which I mean, I guess, that I'm tranquil + happy
enough with him not to mind my age. Also, his are the best jokes.
Would you like to hear one? Man has two parrots + takes them to the
parrot-doctor in hopes of discovering which is male, which female.
Rien de plus simple. The doctor perches them side by side and tells
the first one to say co. Co. To the second: Say co. Co. To the first: say
co-co. Co-co. To the second: say co-co. Co-co. To the first: Say co-
co-co. Co-co-co. To the second: ay co-co-co. Ah lay off, you stupid
jerk, you've made my balls dizzy. This bird, says the doctor smugly, is
the male.

   You can't imagine how painlessly the holidays have passed. A
few rich meals at home, a few in other houses. A pinch of last min-
ute shopping occasionally impeded by the presence, in some of the
larger stores, by as many as 6 or 8 people ahead of one. A tree. A fire.
A turkey shaped like a destroyer, for once, instead of a landing-craft.
Chester Kallman's angoisses providing a daily counterpoint. His
evzone is getting demobbed today. This will occasion another round
of parties. Wystan is flying down for 3 days + we are trying to line up
the most German looking boys for him to go down on—will people
do that for us when we're old + wrinkled + famous? What else, let me
see, well, the Carissimo, the café-confiserie where everyone used to
sit, has been redecorated. Now there are no tables inside downstairs,
one must go up to a ghastly balcony + be quite invisible, so that it's
completely impossible. All over town one runs into the dispossessed
regulars buzzing like hornets whose nest has been destroyed. Some
of them, like Tony and the Black Maria, have been known to sit in our

<u>house</u> until 2 in the morning, having no other place to go. A pretty pass. Oh, and an American zombie we know has a cello + I've found myself playing duets with him—Bach, Boccherini, you name it. We stay together, and each is too rapt by his own sound effects to notice the other's mistakes. But <u>who</u> are the sadists who fill in the figured bass for Vivaldi + Pergolesi? Impossible chords, and in such rapid succession. I fear I have but a two-track mind.

Your account of life in Cambridge leaves to be desired only the effect of your Sonnets course on impressionable youth. Surely there was <u>some</u> note-passing, stammers + blushes, sudden vibrant hushes as you made your "points." And by now Richard + Kenneth are no longer one flesh? No more bubbles, only dirty water in the bath? We've had our own little sadness. Poor Maisie. The vet thinks she may have a tumor (there was blood in her urine) but there's no time to recover from an operation before she flies home with me. Will she last? If it doesn't quite make an opera—Die Haushaltgötterdämmerung—it does pluck a string or two deep in the breast.

We'll talk on the phone in a few weeks [*in the margin*: Will be back in S'ton on 28th probably], d'ac? Meanwhile, much love + happy new year from us both.

J

David Kalstone See Biographies.
life in Cambridge Kalstone was a junior professor of English at Harvard.
Die Haushaltgötterdämmerung The Household Twilight of the Gods, an allusion to the title of Wagner's opera.

To Donald and Mary Richie

WUSTL
17–18 January 1965
[Athens, Greece]

Dear Donald + Mary,

David left last night by train, not quite in the low spirits of yesteryear, since a friend named George with very long soccer-playing legs was sharing his minute compartment as far as Salonika (he then took the next plane back to Athens and phoned at noon to say that that part of the trip had gone off painlessly). My friend (his legs are rather short but he's the first person I've felt as I do about, in years) and I saw the train off, as did Chester Kallman and a few giddy friends of his. D. will now be jogging slowly through Jugoslavia. Ahead of him lie Paris, a soirée chez Mary McCarthy, a new VW to pick up, and the *United States* to the country of the same name—unless the threatened dock strike keeps him indefinitely removed from the Eager Young Minds of Conn. College for Women. I have, what? eight days before flying with Maisie in my lap. The poor creature hasn't been well. Blood in her urine, perhaps a tumor, but no time to have an operation before her flight. The symptoms have been stopped at least.

I'm writing, therefore, principally to say that we'll be in S'ton from Jan 28th on—I'll be in NY for 2–3 days before that—and that we want one or both of you to come and stay for as long as you can bear it. In David's suitcase is your last letter, so I can't refer to the dates you mentioned. My dim + perhaps incorrect impression is that Donald is going to Germany round about now, then to Greece (?), and will be passing through NY—but when, when, WHEN?—and that Mary is going to America in March or April. Please be specific if you can, + we'll transfer the dates to the Master Calendar. We want so much to see you both and, as they say, "get to know the little woman"; it is the one thing—since clearly we aren't going to get tickets for the Callas *Tosca*—we have to look forward to in the months ahead.

These months have been perhaps the happiest + easiest we've ever spent here. Space makes such a difference. In this house we can actually get out of each other's way. I've cooked in at least 4 nights a week. My friend, whose name is Strato, has gained 3 kilos. Oh, he is so nice! Very simple, never bored, a mine of silly jokes, and he likes me too. Me! About 3 weeks ago he arrived unexpectedly at the house and caught me red-handed. The scene that followed was so wrenching, and the reconciliation so exquisite, that I have turned into a one-man dog, much to Tony's amusement. How I hated those ghastly strolls through the gardens.

Today I got two sets of sewn sheets of my book. If I can face the postoffice I will mail one to you before I leave. We were dazzled, by the way, by your prolific output. You will, won't you, bring all these manuscripts to Stonington? Yes, now it is morning and I have wrapped the book only to remember that I forgot to write anything in it. Well, you'll have a bound one, too. It comes out on March 23.

It is a lovely sunny day. A week ago exactly I was driving to Kolonaki and saw a familiar figure trudging up into the pines of Lykabettos on her bad legs—Kyria Kleo who cleans for us. I honked + honked + finally she looked around. She is fat and sixty with the face of a Palmyra sculpture done in horsehair + guttapercha, but that day she was wearing a tight sky-blue sweater + had painted + powdered herself within an inch of her life, or mine. Was she off to a rendezvous? to sell herself? Was she "just lucky, I guess" like the "Smith" girl in the brothel? The memory absolutely <u>haunts</u> me. And with that I leave you. Write, and soon, when we are to expect you. Tony sends lots of love.

Me too!

J.

George George Lazaretos, an engineer in the Greek navy, Jackson's lover.
Conn. College Jackson was hired to teach a fiction-writing class at Connecticut College, substituting for William Meredith.
my book *The (Diblos) Notebook* (1965).
your prolific output Richie was an authority on Japanese cinema.
Kolonaki A square near his house on Athinaion Efivon.
The memory . . . haunts me It became a source for his poem "Days of 1964" in *Nights and Days* (1966).

To Strato Mouflouzelis   WUSTL
                                                22 January 1965
                                                   [In flight]

Dearly beloved Strato,

It's 20 to 7 (Athens time) and I'm writing you 10,000 meters above the sea. I'm waiting for the third meal in eight hours! We'll land in New York exactly at midnight (18:00 there).

I thought I would die when I left you. Please, forgive me. I didn't want to cry in front of you. Now, even though I will miss you terribly and I would give five years of my life just to hug you, I'm well. The moment of saying goodbye has passed and all I think about is the beautiful time we had together and the beautiful time that lies ahead for us. And the wonderful person you are.

We stopped in Paris. Big surprise. I phoned a lady friend of ours and found out that David was there. "Come, Jimmy, take another airplane out, tonight at 11!" and perhaps I could have. But I know Maisie and we would get into a nasty quarrel if we didn't return home right away. With this letter—which I will post immediately upon landing in New York—you will know that I arrived very well. Know also that I love you: with all my heart. I will write to you again on the 28th, when we get to the village.

> I kiss you, my love, now and forever.
> Jimáki

nasty quarrel Merrill uses here a beautiful colloquial Greek idiom which literally translates as "we would become of two villages," meaning loosely that we would end up bitter rivals in a fight. [Translator's note]

To Mary McCarthy

Dear Mary,

Thank you now and ever for your letter, for taking the time to read and to write, both, at such thoughtful length. You see the book so clearly (so much more than I—the author's prerogative being never to understand entirely what he has done, or so I had thought before reading, yesterday, that extraordinary letter to your Danish translator; today I am embarrassed to have thought so) that I can only blink and wish I'd shown it to you last summer. You are particularly right, I suspect, about the ending belonging to the notebook rather than to "life." But as I had never, over many attempts to rework it, been able to see for myself what was wrong, I deserve no better than the puzzled pang with which, on each rereading, I've been left by those final pages.

Your image of the modern bank is marvelous + shattering. Only the most naive or the most corrupt <u>set</u> <u>out</u> to create something fashionable, but hundreds of others end up, to their dismay, having done so. The "serious" motive behind my using these techniques had been to try, almost literally, to catch the eye, to put prongs on the page in the form of those deletions and broken sequences. In poetry, which usually I don't have to strain to read with care, tricks of format madden me. With prose, though, where, despite any amount of interest, my eyes tend to roll like marbles all over a page, I'd felt the need to try imposing a certain slowed tempo upon a reader. Before the book was done, I had seen the folly of this hope, but by then I was stuck with a whole family of smartly-dressed devices that had gathered as it were for the christening (or the funeral!) of the original infant. Now, when I look at the result, what holds me is not at all its trompe-l'oeil aspect, rather a few mysterious (to me) and unintended strands of imagery which no one else will or should get caught in.

Forgive me for rattling on, but I know no better way to show you how gratefully I take your letter. From what you say at the end, I gather you don't mind my sending it on to Harry Ford who will no doubt let you know what he decides to quote from it.

I'm still regretting not having brought Maisie to dinner last Monday. Had I known ahead of time that we should stop in Paris I'd have tried to arrange it. As it was, my lifelong resistance to doing things on the spur of the moment once again came to the fore and once again deprived me of some delicious hours.

Eleanor drove me up here Thursday. (She sends love and wonders, did you ever receive an ice-cream freezer she sent last Fall?) Grace, who did <u>not</u> crack her pelvis after all, but merely insulted her spine, is back in N.Y., hobbling from party to party. Stonington is icy, empty, depressing beyond words. Come back and save us all!

Love to you and Jim, and to the children.

Yours ever,
Jimmy

your letter Merrill to Vassilis Vassilikos on February 5, 1965: "Mary McCarthy wrote a letter about my book"—*The (Diblos) Notebook*—"comparing it to a modern bank—

all the workings exposed behind plate glass so that people will think ah, how honest! and implying that she wasn't to be that easily deceived. It doesn't bother me. One can never trust the praise of the famous." Merrill had asked McCarthy for a blurb.

To Louise Fitzhugh

FITZHUGH
11 February [1965]
Stonington, CT

Dear Louise,

I just tried to call the number you gave David (he wrote down RE73140 at any rate) only to find you unknown to the young woman (nice voice—call her up!) who answered. I'd been trying the old number night after night for <u>days</u> before you called. Your book is so good—so <u>serious</u>, as well as being funny; full of truth + understanding. I could find no fault with it (I don't mean that I tried very hard). I wish it hadn't been sitting here all fall. One wants to respond at once when something is that fine. Is it a big success? Do you get letters from real-life schoolchildren? Governesses? Vegetables? Wonderful YOU.

Oh we are so depressed. Athens, Athens . . . ! I can see expatriation descending upon us like a fine film of marble dust.

David is over his impetigo now + the girls at Conn. College are eating out of his hand. He has almost twice the number he'd been led to expect. He has already used the word "homosexual" in class. <u>I</u> never dared, I just stammered + twitched.

We'll be in N.Y. only briefly on the 27th, but for about 8 days beginning March 19. Perhaps a whole evening <u>then</u>?

Much much love +
C·O·N·G·R·A·T·U·L·A·T·I·O·N·S,
Your old flame,
J.

your book *Harriet the Spy* (1964).

To Strato Mouflouzelis

WUSTL
[February 1965]
[Stonington, CT]

Strato, my huge love

I received your letter with so much joy, you won't believe it. Ten days had passed with no news from you, and I was starting to fear for who knows what—did you get sick? getting loved elsewhere? or, you're in jail for twenty days, not five? (You're turning into quite a tramp!) It doesn't matter, my love. You might get old, a forty-year old soldier, and my love for you will never change.

A friend of ours (a teacher from Boston) is here with us for two days. I can tell him something about you, show him your photographs, play our records—the bed, the alarm—which I don't dare play alone, or even with David, for fear that I will faint from nostalgia. Last night I made a beautiful dessert, Eleanor was with us, we drank many wines, and when I went to sleep, I was surprised not to find you already in my bed. But, later, I found you in my dreams.

I'm always thinking of you, my love. I read your letters, I look at your photographs, and I try to understand why my life has given me such happiness. I've written a poem for you (69 verses!) which I will place at the end of my new book of poems. This way you will understand how close [*the page is folded here, making the rest of the sentence illegible*]

Did you go to the dentist? What did he say? And your hair?—did you cut it? And the shoes? Don't go back to jail!

Well, my love, I have no more news. I kiss you with all my heart.

yours,
Jimáki

a poem for you (69 verses!) "Days of 1964" in *Nights and Days* (1966), and it is 74 lines long. It might have been 69 lines at the time Merrill wrote this letter, or as the exclamation point perhaps indicates, the number 69 might be erotically suggestive—or both.

back to jail The references here are about soldiers getting jail time for infractions such as letting their hair grow or not being properly in uniform. [Translator's note]

To Strato Mouflouzelis

WUSTL
7 June 1965
Stonington, CT

Strato, my love

Today, I feel really well because I received your letter. I'm joyful to hear your news and that your trouble with your gums has passed. Next time this happens you know you should go to the dentist immediately, OK?

Don't get angry when I tell you such things. You understand how much I need your letters. So very much. I want to hear how you are, if you're thinking of me, your news, etc. In my letters, I ask you about your release from the army, if you received the cigarettes, and you don't answer. And I lose one day after another imagining the worst. Imagine what I become when you don't write me for 30 days! Nervous, white-haired . . . Do I truly deserve this?

So, I love you and wait. Only 58 days left now. It's difficult for me to be patient. In my fantasies, I fly. Without an airplane, just in your arms.

My mother is here with me. She is tired and has lost her sense of taste. It's a pity, because as usual I make miracles in the kitchen. Tomorrow, we'll go together to New York, and 3 days later David will return from his trip.

What else? I finished my new book—only poems—and the day after tomorrow I will pick it up from the publisher. The final poem is something I wrote for you back in February. It also describes Mrs. Kleo in Lycabetos with her face all made up. Remember?

Both Maisie and I send you sweet kisses. Goodbye, my great love.

Jimáki

The final poem Again "Days of 1964" (*Nights and Days*, 1966).
all made up There is a strange word here in reference to makeup, which does not exist in Greek: *kosmetikoméno*, "cosmeticized." [Translator's note]

To Robin Magowan

WUSTL
12 October 1965
Athens, Greece

Dear Robin,

Vassili, Mimi, Strato + I were on the boat from Hydra yesterday when it clouded up; we sat in the increasingly jammed lounge, rainwhipped + brainwashed from four solid hours of xerí, and watched, or rather didn't watch, the summer end. Back at the house, David + George were sitting staring into space. Night had fallen, yet they were unable to contemplate so much as a Votrys and soda following an evening they've still not succeeded in telling me about except that it ended at a cabaret in Piraeus with a stripper named Miss Lydia. Your letter was here, along with many kilos of other mail. Tony Meyer must be stopped. Imagine paying $3.90 to airmail me a copy of some poems by George Oppen. There have been 2 postal strikes, 6 days all told, and a resulting delay of about a fortnight for (informed sources say) some 50 million letters, most of them ours.

Thasos was an immense success. We whittled the whole trip down to 9 days, and spent five of them there in a dream of trees and bees and crystal waters—well, a little vignette is enclosed. I keep changing what the radio plays each time I type it out. We got along very well. Mimi especially grows on one. In a society of four pregnant cousins, it took a certain amount of style to carry off her childlessness. She even managed to declare (truthfully?) in front of Vassili's fine old walnut-stained grandmother, in a salon full of fierce photographs and a delicate bit of embroidery ("This too will pass" among garlands on a black ground), that Vassili was sterile—in English, to be sure! V's grandmother shares the house with an ancient contemporary named Maria. 60 years ago, on her wedding night, Maria tied herself up to the neck in a linen sack. Seven nights of this and the husband left—left her a respectable, married virgin who now smokes and enjoys off-color language. After Thasos we drove to Xanthi for a night, bought lots of blue-and-yellow Turkish "eyes" to ward off the Evil one, then spent a night in Salonika where we saw, at the opening of the film festival, the perfectly frightful movie made last summer in Molyvos. You wouldn't want to miss it, although I didn't see your faces in the crowd. But we left before it was over. It is called *The Fate of an Innocent,* and made Molyvos look, if anything, worse than it does in reality.

Your letter, now. Do I understand it? I think so. I would not have called the mood you were in "self-destructive"; but then neither would I have called it "courageous." These two qualities, though, don't really exclude one another, do they? Life kills us all, in the long run, and what you are presently doing is deciding, now that the Toccata has been played, at what tempo you mean to take the Fugue. I guess the psychiatrists are a good idea; they will protect you from one another, and the rest of your loved ones from both of you, until a door opens somewhere.

It's another day. Sun. Bernie's for drinks yesterday. He had the first copies of his book. Did you know there was a poem dedicated to Felix in it? Leafing through the pages, it came over me like a wave of nausea—the excellence that print confers on what I know are by + large trivial poems hardly worth writing except as therapy. Yet there they were, printed therefore distinguished, and I found myself positively admiring them as a result. There will be no eluding a copy of your own.

I'm off to Kolonaki.

And back. The rhythm of a <u>bad</u> day has begun, so I'll simply seal this and send it off. Write me all and when you can. You both know how concerned I feel. David joins in love.

Jimmy

xerí Greek card game.
George Oppen American poet and political activist (1908–84), who returned to publishing poetry in the 1960s after a three-decade hiatus; his collection *This in Which* appeared in 1965.
Thasos Merrill, Jackson, and Mimi and Vassilis Vassilikos (called Vassili by his friends) visited the island of Thasos, Vassili's birthplace, in the northern Aegean, and celebrated Jackson's birthday there. See Merrill's poem "16.ix.65" in *The Fire Screen* (1969).
The Fate of an Innocent Greek film (1965), directed by Grigoris Grigoriou.
both of you Robin and Betty's marriage was coming apart. See Merrill's poem "Ouzo for Robin" in *The Fire Screen* (1969).
his book Winebaum printed his poems privately in Athens.

To Laurence Scott   WUSTL
                                              17 November 1965
                                                Athens, Greece

Dear Miss Moore,

When a letter from you comes out of the blue, it's a red-letter day
indeed. I feel doubly remiss about letting you hear from me, but there
has been so little news of the kind I can entrust to the mails. Were we
but alone together, or with Laurence S. as a discreeeet "third," I could
do my bit towards keeping vos jours en feu. I say "keeping" because
L.S. has clearly spared you nothing of his shall I say activities. His
unclad friends in Michigan. He has, I dare say, shown me (why me?)
photographs of this sort, but their details, at this distance, elude me.
It's not the side of his character that most appeals to one, don't you
agree? Such an obsession, in one so gifted, can only distress his real
friends. I mention him in my prayers every Sunday, here at the Amer-
ican Church, and mean to do so even more frequently when Lent
rolls around. The rector, a Dr. Truffle, had given me some tips on the
line to take with Laurence when I see him—alas, too briefly—next
month. We shall see what fruit is borne thereby. I have yet to enjoy a
full account of his vertigo in Stonington. David Kalstone—now he is
the soul of tact—has kept the veil closely drawn upon that visit.

   I do hope a copy of your bar-room poem comes to light. All the
friends who have seen the stanzas about the "drag queen" out West
consider it among your most inspired short pieces. For me, it takes
its place beside Mr Auden's "The Blow Job" in my imaginary Under-
ground Anthology. You are a person of much wider sympathies than
perhaps even you yourself realize.

   Dear Mona Van Duyn! But was the moose male or female?

   Forgive me if I end this letter abruptly. The sun has set, and only
Greek is spoken (or written) in this house after dark.

                              Ever your iron-digesting ostrich fan,
                              J.

Dear Laurence,

Miss M. is bound to be back on Cumberland St. by now, so I've sent
my letter there. This carbon is merely that you not feel I'm doing

anything "behind your back." Looking forward to Dec. 14. Tell David K. (whose letter came today) to do what he thinks best. Not a large crowd, or if so, only for a maximum of 100 minutes. Σε Φιλώ όπως πάντα.

Τζάημς

Laurence Scott Laurence Herbert Scott (1933–2005), teacher at Harvard and later MIT, polyglot and maker of broadsides of poems for poet-friends including Merrill (his "Violent Pastoral" in *Nights and Days*) and Marianne Moore.
Dear Miss Moore As if Scott were Marianne Moore.
Mr Auden's "The Blow Job" A pornographic poem by Auden, "The Platonic Blow (A Day for a Lay)," written probably in 1948 and circulated underground for years before a pirated version appeared in 1965 in *Fuck You: A Magazine of the Arts*, a mimeographed publication printed on construction paper.
Mona Van Duyn (1921–2004), American poet, who, with her husband, the fiction writer Jarvis Thurston, became good friends with Merrill. Merrill began donating his papers to Special Collections at Washington University St. Louis, in 1964, at Van Duyn's invitation.
the moose The reference is to a frightening experience Van Duyn describes in "West Branch Ponds, Kokadjo, Maine" in her collection *Merciful Disguises* (1973).
iron-digesting ostrich fan Merrill has in mind Moore's poem "He 'Digesteth Harde Yron,'" whose title quotes John Lyly's *Euphues*.
Not a large crowd Scott and Kalstone had invited Merrill to read at Lowell House, Harvard.
Σε Φιλώ όπως πάντα "Your friend always." Merrill then signs his name "James" in Greek transliteration.

To Robin Magowan   WUSTL
                                                       5 March 1966
                                                       Isfahan, Iran

Dear Robin,

8:00. The morning after one of the most beautiful days of my life—life perhaps does begin at 40 after all, though a birthday in Persia would hardly be counted, would it. Luckily I shan't have to describe anything to you. Outside of a little walk yesterday I've seen nothing of Isfahan but the inside of a house belonging to the friend of a friend of a friend of a friend. This man is named Yahya Bachtiyar. If I understand correctly, he has his own <u>tribe</u>. He is probably 45 and so charming that even if this place were a mud village full of flies and amoebas it would have been worth the trip. He is rather in the style of a darker and more active Robert Morse. We were taken to one of his houses straight from the airport. After breakfast he was insisting we stay at the other (the other half of we is Donald Richie) and I rather wish we hadn't opted for the hotel as it is a very pretty big house right next to Our Embassy. As we were sitting down to lunch he remembered that he was expected at two other places, so he called one of them up and said he had guests but would they please send some of their lunch over to him? By now we are back in the first house in a room full of braziers and cushions, chests of drawers, a rug portrait of Yahya's father and an enormous rose tree (les roses d'Isfahan) which is gigglingly revealed to be false. There is also a gaunt clown of a major domo named Hussein who smokes his pipe or two of opium in front of one and then acts out his deception of a whole roomful of people, some of them European, whom he made to believe that he was an old village woman having a baby, refusing the doctor, and at an hour's end producing, from under his chaboor, a swaddled & squirming dog. Outside is a yard full of sheep, goats, chickens, and Bachtiyari tribesmen who wait—mostly wait, it seems, though once in a while one of them comes into the room looking dazed with a bottle he has forgotten how to open. A steady flow of other guests. I had given Yahya a copy of *Nights & Days* and he had found time to read "A Carpet Not Bought"—an obvious choice, seeing that he runs a carpet business. Perhaps you remember, or even <u>have</u>, Bachtiyari carpets—tans, browns, blacks, whites, grays, of a bit rougher workmanship than the others. After a walk we were back again. This time the room was full: an English engineer with his wife and mother in law who had all driven from Malaya, then 5 or 6 cousins of Yahya's, one of whom, in those splendid black pyjamas I mean to buy today, eked out English enough to say that he had a daughter in Fresno. His wife was concentrating mainly on the opium pipe, as did we all, right down to the mother in law of the Englishman, by the evening's end—all except our host who "used to be an addict" as he said with a faraway smile. There was a bit of drumming and song. Food; drinks; tea. One <u>could</u> <u>not</u> leave. It was my first and perhaps only glimpse of that life—diluted & citified in this instance if you like—of tents and herds and hospitality so effortless, indeed such an obvious tonic to its dispenser, that one had no recourse but to sit back and glow. I left Athens 5 days ago, and will be back in another 3. Donald is on his way to Tokyo. David, as usual, wouldn't fly. I had to get away, and couldn't write before. I was drowning, or burning, or being buried alive, or whatever one does when something one lives for has come to an end. I can only hope that I've behaved well, that it's not more than half my fault. There is no resentment at least; the whole experience has given me back to life. I fear I gave Strato very little by comparison.

Back now from our tour. Oh the beauty! And in the bazaar, since David asked for a rug, I found a small length of azure foam rubber printed with pilgrims to Mecca.

How is everything? David Kalstone wrote how much he'd enjoyed seeing you (and regretted missing Betty). Let me hear. And much love to you both. Send more pages & poems.

Ever,
Jimmy

Yahya Bachtiyar For a richer version of the visit, see Merrill's poem "Chimes for Yahya" in *Divine Comedies* (1976).
(les roses d'Isfahan) Reference to the Fauré song, in which the singer prays for the return of a young lover.
chaboor Chador, cloak worn by Muslim women.
something one lives for Merrill and Strato's relationship, which in fact continued somewhat longer (see letter of 14 July 1966).

To Louise Fitzhugh

FITZHUGH
14 July 1966
[Athens, Greece]

Dear dear dear Louise,

I've been meaning to write <u>you</u> for ever so long, since receiving <u>your</u> book (and being pleased by a review of it in the *New Yorker*)—but letters haven't been easy to write, these months, in any direction. I loved the book, by the way, and never guessed who was writing the anonymous letters. Will Harriet enroll at Bard in the next installment, and turn into a fast-drinking party-girl, a hot-tomato sandwich? Your gift for characterization is so rich, somehow the people are all the more real (realer than "real" people) for being squarely based upon types.

It is my dream to write that kind of tale, in which one has hardly ever to explain the characters, only to present them.

But even with us whom you know and are so good as to love, I fear a certain amount of explanation is due. Or can I simply set a scene. Upstairs the radio is blaring away, balcony doors open; midday. David jitters to and fro, wondering whether he will accompany his friend George to Crete on tonight's boat—all cabins are booked, they'd have to slump till dawn in the lounge. George, uncommunicative as ever, sits playing cards with my friend, Strato, who decided (as he does more often than I like to think) not to go to work today, but to shed, as he can, considerable light and charm and usefulness (yesterday he plastered wallplugs, today he repaired a bed) upon the house. Our lives are not our own, which must, as I think about it, have been exactly what we wanted after all those placid, fruitful years under the tin dome at Stonington. George is a petty officer in the Navy. His parents sold him to the state at the age of 14, and he has still some years to go. Strato is now a civilian and has even gone so far as to acquire a passport. It looks as if he will be coming back with me, on a tourist visa, in October. Terrifying prospect! He is so nice and so good and so . . . unimaginative, it's left to me to imagine what on earth he will do in Stonington, and all I can think is to try and get him work at the garage. You, as one of a handful of friends I can trust to be nice to him (not that it will be easy, he speaks no English), are high on my list of People To See—as you would be in your own right, anyhow.

Now it is after lunch. David is packing. George has gone to see his sister. Strato is sleeping. Into the Scotch cooler go: wine, tomatoes, bread, salami, peanutbutter. George is embarrassed to eat in the ship's dining room because of his bitten fingernails. Embarrassment! I have virtually exhausted my capacity for it, but it remains <u>the</u> ominous Mediterranean bugaboo. To wear the right clothes, to be seen constantly (and falsely) as the master of one's fate. It only took to describe the Italian character. Small wonder the surfaces matter so.

Hubbell + Bobby Isaacson have been through on a cruise. I went to Persia in March and Rome in April (where I saw Elsie) and can't face going anywhere else. Let the islands rot!

Yes I know Fred and Sandra were divorced, but nothing else. I'm awfully sorry about it. Please give Sandra my love. My nephew's getting divorced too. Something very strange seems to be happening to nearly everybody. Are you really all right? I hope your stepmother lasts the summer. It is very sad when Banal Types get seriously ill, they have so few defenses or resources. Look at Paula Strasberg.

Our love to Connie—what happened to her play? Hope it's running like trout.

Hugs + kisses always,
Jimmy

<u>your</u> **book** *Harriet the Spy.*
Fred and Sandra Fred and Sandra Roome Segal.
Connie Constance Ford, with whom Fitzhugh lived for a couple of years, a steadily featured Hollywood actor, who from 1967 to 1992 was the resolutely enthusiastic mother in the NBC soap opera *Another World.*

To Alison Lurie

WUSTL
25 July 1966
Athens, Greece

Darling girl,

Your letter arrived minutes ago, and I have just time to tap out a page or part of one before Bernie arrives bringing money (owed), tomatoes (requested) and gossip (obligatory), and spoils everything thereby.

Congratulations on the finished book. We are (I am already and David will be when he gets in from Crete this afternoon or tomorrow) madly eager to see it in typescript or print or whatever. In order to be proud of the dedication we do not need to put you to the trouble of mailing a copy to Greece. Nor can we flatter ourselves that you have put us into your pages a second time. But if you have a spare copy and a bulging wallet, send it on. The next paragraph will describe some of the uncertainties attending our return.

I shall definitely be coming back in early October. Supporting me in the illusion that I shall be doing it of my own free will is my young man's acceptance of an invitation to accompany me. The prospect is scary. Will he get a visa? What will he do? Who will be nice to him? One has heard too much from the Stone Ladies about "those ridiculous middleaged Americans we knew in Tasco" with their "demon lovers" to expect mercy from that quarter. Your John is probably too mature by now—Strato is very simple—but if he is learning <u>modern</u> Greek perhaps he will feel like doing The Village + the Empire State Bldg. some weekend, with conversation, always at the beginner's level, thrown in. David's young man is a more complex person, and more complicated circumstantially. His parents sold him to the State at the age of 13, and he has at least one more year, perhaps 5, before he can get out of the Navy. Only now, after 11 months of stringpulling, is he being transferred from Crete to Athens. David wonders if he will be able to tear himself away so soon after getting what he wanted. His parents, D's, are agitating, though. They write plaintive letters: will they ever see him again? And I think it would do him a world of good to get away if only for a couple of months. He has been nowhere all year. Even <u>I</u> have been to Rome and Isfahan.

It has been a year full of ups and downs. Have we put too many eggs into those (may I say) baskets? I've managed to do some work, these last months. The strain on David has been greater. He keeps wryly quoting "The Guided Tour"—do I expect him to have more than one idea a day? But everybody's life seems to have taken on one or two strange dimensions. My nephew Robin is getting a divorce. Marilyn is going to a shrink. Claude wrote, ecstatic, from a monastery in Tokyo. Tony Harwood has taken to "massive doses of champagne"—which turns out to mean a half bottle in the course of a long evening, but still. Jonathan's step seems relatively harmless and sedate. Me, I believe life begins at 40.

BW-hour is drawing nigh. I'll leave this unsealed on the chance that David can add some little touch of his own.

> Love. Lots of it.
> Jimmy

Dear Pal, well, he's laid it on the line, above—we'll see . . . What a cool refreshing thought to think we'll soon be reading YOU. How even MORE refreshing would be you, in person, looking around and advising us on our Greek scenery. You'll soon be getting my story, some parts of it you may like. I go on painting houses and will personally show you those, with love and anticipation.

> David

the finished book *Imaginary Friends* (1967), a novel satirizing spiritualism, dedicated to Merrill and Jackson.
a second time Lurie's novel *Love and Friendship* (1962) included characters based on Merrill and Jackson.
Your John Lurie's son.
my young man's acceptance Merrill hoped to bring Strato to the United States.
David's young man George Lazaretos.
His parents, D's George and Mary Jackson in Sun City, California.
Jonathan's step Lurie's husband Jonathan Bishop.
BW-hour Visit from Bernie Winebaum.

To Robert Isaacson

MORGAN LIBRARY
17 August 1966
Athens, Greece

Roberto mou,

Your enchanting screed came this noon. I do the unheard-of and reply at once, with repellent legibility. Well, not at once really—I'm back from lunch (sic) with Vassili & Mimi and 2 hours of feeding him ideas for a scenario he is unwillingly at work on, all about a new drug that comes in lipstick form and must be kissed off the mouth of the person to one's right. Now the alarm clock rings (in my home movie) and it is time for Strato to wake up from his nap. How his feet smell today! My heart is sore & I am full of fears—his visa was quite summarily refused when we went to the Embassy. He has, they said, "no adequate incentive to return to Greece"—meaning that they expect him to vanish into the American landscape the minute he sets foot there, and cause all kinds of fuss & paperwork. My—up to now—infallibly resourceful lawyer has been wired to pull what strings he can, but still, io tremo. Of course it doesn't matter to S. at all; or that at least is the face he puts on it. But I simply don't dare contemplate ten months without him, and even though I'd go to NY in October it would be with the thought—<u>almost</u> as distasteful—of putting in another winter here. Well, we shall, as they say, see. David meanwhile has been in Crete, it seems forever; due back tomorrow. Desperation has driven me to spend, oh, 3 or even 4 evenings with Bernie—out at "his" tavern where his goldenhaired friend waits table and does the danse du ventre. He did not censure <u>my</u> behavior, our last evening all together. Maybe he is afraid of me? <u>I</u> would be, in his shoes.

The Haydn sonata is Vol 4 (Peters) No 36.

Your welcome back to New York sounds like all one could have wished. Be calm, be thoughtful & wise & loyal. The Scout Troop one joins in second adolescence is very like its earlier counterpart, except that we have no superiors to show us about knots and fire-lighting. The (qualified) rapture continues to be, for me, that my life, now, depends on something beyond my control. The Other must not be allowed to suspect as much; it will tempt him to misbehave. I trust you to see through this tone all the way to the troubled crystal depths.

Letter from Hubbell—very "hurt," still, by your weariness with his repertoire. Don't say I wrote you so.

No other news. I read (or had I when you were here?) Bill Weaver's translation of the Gadda novel. It is a charming, thrilling book, and I wish Bernie would return it. I didn't know Frank O'Hara very well either, but had counted on his being around for another 30 years. Emblematic deaths (like Rilke and the roses) are no comfort to the victim. That's all. Back to my solitaire—S. is taking his sister to the movies. I wish you were still here, but New York will be soon. You will be the only one there who Understands.

> Love till then,
> Jimmy

repellent legibility The letter is typewritten.
Bill Weaver's translation William Weaver (1923–2013) translated Italian author Carlo Emilio Gadda's (1893–1973) *Quer pasticciaccio brutto de via Merulana* into English as *That Awful Mess on Via Merulana*.
Frank O'Hara American poet (1926–66), died after being struck by a jeep on Fire Island.
Rilke and the roses Rilke died from leukemia, but his death was supposedly when he pricked himself while gathering roses.

To Louise Fitzhugh   FITZHUGH
                                                    23 September 1966
                                                      [Athens, Greece]

Dear Louise,

I meant to write long ago but nothing has been clear. It used to be, you could ask me where I'd be in six months, in a year, and I'd be able to say, and it would be true what's more. Now it's all uncertainty. "We" didn't give Strato a visa. No special reason. Insufficient cause to return to Greece. Immigrant rather than tourist Image. Perhaps they smelled out my role in the whole business. Anyhow, we've tried everything and it's not working. I feel so sorry for him (he has been doing stupid + dangerous work on a temporary basis, thinking he'd be leaving soon) and for myself (who out of pure vanity had wanted him to see me in my habitat). If I weren't a writer, if I couldn't, that is, <u>use</u> the frustration somehow, I think I'd be in a really awful state. As it is, it's bad enough. I'm still coming back, only for 2 months—which is plenty of time, he's such a weathervane, for S. to do something silly.

Enfin. This is really just to say that I'll get to NY on Oct 16 and shall be in town for 8 days. My mother will be there and I'll be in the usual tizzy of return, but I really hope we can see each other. You'll just be getting back yourselves, so you'll have your own tizzy to cope with . . .

All those surfers, and people dying. I remember years ago, with Claude Fredericks in Rome, getting one of my mother's letters—they become more frequent with the years—in which she reports the death of <u>three</u> dear old friends within something like ten days. I read the passage aloud to Claude, and guess what he said. "Snap. Crackle. Pop." In a way, I wonder that you don't want to get out of America. Why don't you come here? Life is still very inexpensive and you and Connie wouldn't be threatened by what has undone so many nice American girls <u>and</u> boys: The Greek Male.

That will do for now. I leave here the 11th and stop in London. Want anything from Carnaby St?

                                        Love always,
                                        J.

Snap. Crackle. Pop. Gnome-like characters on the Rice Krispies box.
Carnaby St Fashion central in London in the 1960s.

To Strato Mouflouzelis

WUSTL
25 January 1967
[Athens, Greece]

My Strato,

This letter is like your phone call yesterday. Not that I'm embarrassed to say something to you face to face. But so as not to forget all the other things I want to say. Read it SLOW, with attention, with love. And twice.

I'm not angry. I don't have a serious complaint. Of course, you somewhat struck at my pride. How many times have I said that Yiorgos hides everything from David, while you tell me most of what goes on in your life. Now, don't you say again that you're different from other Greeks. You all look alike, like ten million lentils. Is it my fault—again? I'll know by your behavior from now on.

On the one hand, I've become cynical. Our past, which once was a garden, I now see as arid, bitter. Thankfully, I don't have the courage to revise past things in the light you threw at me yesterday. Besides, our future seems worse. You never gave me and you will never give me, not only our life together, but even the time, the 6 months together that I so longed for! "Be patient," you told me. No!

You got caught, my dear boy, in the tender trap. How are you going to live?—with a home, with a baby? Do your own people have anything you expect to get? (Yet, I do want to hear everything you can tell me about the affair. Who is she? How did it happen? Etc. You may think I have guessed it all—but how can I know? You will do me the honor to tell me the truth. I believe I'm worth it.) So, how are you going to live? Who is going to pay for the house, the baby? Me?

I'm speaking to you harshly, I know. And yet . . . And yet . . .

Deep in my heart, I love you, Strato. I've loved you from the first month, and I will love you until death and beyond. It doesn't matter that you behaved like a jerk, like a sly little girl—you also behaved like a man. The love I have for you makes me ashamed to ask you for things, to seek out bargains. It's possible I will change—aren't I a man too? And as you said, "if I didn't love you, would I come back?" If I didn't really love you, I doubt that I would want to see you. And even the way things are now, there is no other person that means more to me. My home is yours, as is my heart. I want to help you as I can, however much I can.

Here is something I wrote almost two years ago. For me, somehow, it tells of all the other things. [text of letter ends here]

pride In Greek, *philotimo*, the term for the famously multifaceted Greek virtue.
SLOW Capitalized in English.
like ten million lentils Merrill's notebook draft of this letter makes it clear that he intends the equivalent of "like peas in a pod."
Here is something Presumably a poem, probably on a separate page, but not included.

To Donald Richie

WUSTL
28 February 1967
Athens, Greece

Dearest and most Distant,

Bless you for your letter. Of course you Know Too Much, but only time will take care of <u>that</u>. Many developments since. I have met Her. She understood the score soon after the second encounter (recognized various household backgrounds of pix Strato had shown her) and in the first relief of finding it not to be Another Woman, professed not to mind. But she does mind of course, is terribly unsure of him, and has, he tells me and I believe, far too ready a tongue. One consequence of her former job—always to have something light or not so light ready to say when spoken to. And whenever a record starts on the juke-box she lights up and hums and snaps her fingers, a bar-girl to the marrow. She is not, however, for all that he swears she is clever, a deep-dyed villanous slut. As for cleverness—we who judge from the cleverness of 40 can only be touched by the innocent animal slyness of the young. He has behaved, considering all things— such as her nagging, my entirely commendable placidity <u>and</u> generosity, his lack of work, his cock—he has behaved damned well. Oh is he dumb, though, and short-sighted, and is he ever tied up in the situation. But he is (to me) kind and patient and open, and I need nothing else to behave in exactly the same way. He's fat as l'Homme Michelin, everything I don't find attractive, except that—let's face it—I just plain love everything about him, the narrowness, the inflexibility, the pride, even the folly, even the fat. As I say, he is my Child. Late last night, when the phone rang—D. and Geo. and I were sitting quietly together—and Harry Ford in NY told me I'd won the Nat'l Book Award, I could only think: Let me give it back, let me have Strato instead. And to be sure have him I shall (the perpetual lesson of Proust) but, like that prize which would <u>really</u> have meant something to me 5 years ago, too late to be thrilled by the miracle. Well. This means at least that I leave towards some kind of fanfare. I spent all day today alternately coughing my lungs out and writing a stilted, mean-spirited acceptance speech which must be in their (?) hands on the 3rd. The 3rd, you will recall, is my 41st birthday. I am having Strato and Vaso (that's her name) and his brother Kosta and David + George to dinner here—chicken breasts and champagne—but apparently she plans to be sick. Saturday, my last night, S. has promised to send her to her sister's to sleep and stay the night here. Poor love, his life will be hell for days afterwards. Things as they were a year ago keep coming back to me, all suffused by your firmness in the face of despair and kindness and inventiveness and—all the things you are. I cannot for the life of me imagine what they will be like a year from now. <u>If</u> he gets his visa I honestly believe he will want at least a breather in America. If he doesn't, I have promised him—granted he would like to get away—to go with him anywhere in the world for 3 months or so; madness, I know, but where will you be in July?

David is sailing on the Q. Eliz., either on the 15th from Piraeus or the 18th from Naples (he's hoping Geo. will get 10 days leave for them to spend in Italy together). After Easter and until the 20th of May or so, I can be reached c/o Dept of English, U of Wisconsin, Madison. Or they will forward from Stonington.

Would you be a perfect Saint and make some kind of sign to a girl I know who is to be in Japan March 2–13; till the 5th at the Okura in Tokyo; thereafter at the Miyako in Kyoto. She is the daughter of my mother's closest friends in Atlanta—Miss Bert (Bertha) Broyles. I actually like her very much; she's quiet and sort of offbeat and good company. I don't think I've ever met the girl she's traveling with. Even a phone call—explaining the rush I'm in, and that I'll write her about Greece later on—would be kind of you beyond words. I leave you now. A cretan lyra player is about to ring the bell. Bowed to tears, as usual.

Love always from us both,
Jimmy

Her Strato's girlfriend, Vaso, who was pregnant with their child. They had been lovers for more than a year before Merrill became aware of the fact.
l'Homme Michelin The jolly iconic figure's torso, arms, and legs comprise stacked white tires.
Nat'l Book Award Merrill won for *Nights and Days* (1966).
lesson of Proust See Merrill's poem "Days of 1971" in *Braving the Elements* (1972): "Proust's law (are you listening?) is twofold: / (a) What least thing our self-love longs for most / Others instinctively withhold; / (b) Only when time has slain desire / Is his wish granted to a smiling ghost / Neither harmed nor warmed, now, by the fire."
c/o Dept of English, U of Wisconsin Merrill had been invited to teach a poetry workshop for spring semester 1967.
us both Merrill and Jackson.

To Robin Magowan   WUSTL
                                                 14 April 1967
                                                 Madison, WI

Dear Robin,

I guess I didn't come through with that letter last weekend, but yours was here when I returned from Chicago, so it all evens out somehow. I saw *La Grande Jatte* and I saw David. The former seemed finally very unmoving, the latter was full of beans—whole ounces heavier than he was 35 days previous to our reunion. It seems quite certain that he will come up to SF, possibly however with his parents in two, two, no: TOW, so no need to alert or alarm Doris just yet. Or maybe one should. I adore them but they are peu sortable.

My social security number is 007 (seriously)-28–9935. As far as parties + people, do with me what you will. I hope I will see Stephen Orgel in not too vast a crush. Likewise Betty.

It seems impossible to read for pleasure anything later than Byron. This morning's joy was *Beppo* which I had only known about. Imagine my pleasure in coming upon this brief character-like sketch of <u>me</u>:

His heart was one of those which most enamor us,
Wax to receive and marble to retain.
He was a lover of the good old school,
Who still become more constant as they cool.

But I have had to put your book aside so as not to dirty it in the qualitative trash-heap of the New which daily gets poured into my lap. It makes everything seem so awful. I can't say, though, that I'm not still fascinated by having to deal with it. I wish someone would do an essay on the language of the naively literary. Where does it come from? It's not quite greeting-card jargon, not quite drawn from the breasts of both Testaments, not quite ("branches ominously clutching") Gothic translated into movies and back again—and yet it is an exact and unmistakable idiom, inexhaustibly nourishing (I know, I used to write in it myself), and one which disappears almost without a trace as soon as the young person wises up. Now that I'm deep in second adolescence, feeling all the things I felt from 14 to 20, it occurs to me that a life's work may very well be the construction of a bridge back, if not to that language, at least to what one was trying to express in it. This has, I hope you understand, the potential importance of Freud's theory of dreams . . .

I can't even read my own work, which only a few months ago used to be a curious solace. We have spent 2 hours in class on the first 2 poems in *Questions of Travel*, however, and She is entirely spatterproof.

I gave one of your copies to Daryl Hine. I thought you would probably want to inscribe one for David, so I merely showed it to him. They are both ready to find it as good as it is beautiful. Enough for now.

Love,
Jimmy

La Grande Jatte *Sunday Afternoon on the Island of La Grande Jatte* (1886) by Georges Seurat and owned by the Art Institute of Chicago.
Stephen Orgel (b. 1933), a scholar of Renaissance English literature.
Beppo A long poem by Lord Byron.
Wax to receive and marble to retain This line stuck with Merrill. He called it up in connection with his Greek epigraph for "Strato in Plaster" (in English "breast of marble, heart of potato"), and quoted it to describe his own character on numerous occasions.

your book *Voyages* (1967), a book of poems.
daily gets poured into my lap Student poems from his workshop at the University of Wisconsin.

To David Kalstone

WUSTL
19 April 1967
Madison, WI

David dear,

Your funny funny letter is just here and gives me the only warm happy feeling I've had for weeks—I exclude the sensation of the day's first drink; one learns into what that can transform itself by 11:00 p.m. "Peter's beatnik mother and grandmother" is too heavenly; I thought of phoning Rome. It's funny also because Mrs Streeter is (was?) one of the really snappy old ladies in town. I've made smalltalk with her a dozen times, well a half dozen, and she is pure charm, possibly through her understanding that I couldn't have cared less about pushing it further. I don't think I ever knew Colin. There were some boys with floppy blond hair but they were named Palmer.

There have been such horrors, I can't go into them. Except very briefly. Strato's baby was born. A boy. He has not taken steps to cure himself of the souvenir I left him with. Now his darling brother seems to have developed the same thing. They are both in despair and, naturally, need, yet there seems to be no way of reaching them. Tony can't. George can't—as a letter this morning made clear. Isn't it awful? I saw David 10 days ago in Chicago. He looks much better than he did in Athens: several ounces heavier, and in rather good spirits. He went to the doctor and found that a mysterious lump at the base of his spine (which had been worrying him terribly for months) turned out to be merely a slow-blooming abscess, nasty enough in itself, but we are all Relieved.

I've given 5 classes now. The last one was dreadful. But there have been two good ones on Elizabeth Bishop and there will be a lively one today, I trust, when I take the phonograph and assign them a singable translation of "Ich grolle nicht"; <u>then</u> I mean to unveil some A. D. Hope prefaced by remarks about what I suddenly discovered, looking at it for the first time in years a few days ago, must all along have been my absolutely favorite poem in the whole wide world, Fitzgerald's *Rubaiyat*. I wish I knew more about it—how it got done, what the original must be like, who Fitzgerald was for that matter, did he do anything else? I have forgotten how to "use" a library, if I ever knew, so do not consider these rhetorical questions. Tonight I give a reading here, tomorrow I give one in Milwaukee and tape a TV interview the following morning. Next weekend I'll leave for Chicago after conferences Thursday and have 3 days of repose before returning for one class and flinging myself out to Frisco. I wrote Robin that I hoped to see Stephen in not too large a crowd while I was there.

Daryl telephoned last night. He fell off his bike after a cocktail party. No breaks or stitches but a cut on his eyebrow and bruises and a gravel-pitted palm. His job came through at Chicago, so he has moved to the ground floor apartment of the same house, where there is room enough for Sam who will be at Northwestern the 2nd semester of the coming year. Seems awfully far ahead to "know." They have what is probably a very sensible viewpoint—though it's too sensible if you ask me; I'm the "world well lost" type—which consists in neither one giving up anything for the other, career-wise and I suspect in other departments as well.

I keep having crushes on various students, but they all turn out to be married or (as I instantly imagine if I so much as glimpse them walking to class with a girl) straight as ramrods. Friday I'm going to a girl student's for dinner; it's come to that; but she is gentle + intelligent + terrifyingly unspoiled—doesn't even drink, I'm to bring my own, she said, if I can't live without it. I go to the movies all the time, and there was a concert where they played *Pierrot Lunaire* twice. English, then German. I suppose I must call the Taylors, why don't I do that now? I did. No answer. So I called Harry Ford in NY, thus talking to the first eye-witness to convince me that Bernie W. did indeed get back to America.

If there is more news it eludes me. Oh, the ladies will indeed be back in early June, and Alan Ansen (abhorred by Eleanor) is planning a 4-day visit shortly thereafter. Promising . . .

sempre il tuo amoroso

J.

the souvenir A sexually transmitted disease.
"Ich grolle nicht" A song in Robert Schumann's song cycle *Dichterliebe,* words by Heinrich Heine.
at Chicago Hine took a job teaching at the University of Chicago, where he had earned his PhD in comparative literature.
Sam Samuel Todes.
"world well lost" John Dryden's *All for Love, or, the World Well Lost* (1677).
a girl student's Judith Moffett.
Pierrot Lunaire Arnold Schoenberg's 1912 setting of a German translation of Albert Giraud's cycle of poems.
the Taylors Peter Taylor (1917–94), American short-story writer, and his wife, Eleanor Ross Taylor (1920–2011), American poet.

To Donald Richie

WUSTL
9 May 1967
Madison, WI

Donald dear,

A few lines from Anxiousness-on-a-Monument. Two or 3 letters daily arrive from Mimi—occasionally one from Vassili—and, even allowing for the well-known liberal paranoia, things do sound very grim in Greece. They, as luck would have it, are in Rome. The extreme left party wanted V. to run for deputy in the no longer forthcoming elections. He, unwilling to say either yes or no, dawdled in Paris and Sweden, and was finally on his way back when the coup occurred. Now they are preparing themselves for indefinite exile. His name was right at the top of the list of intellectuals to be arrested. Who knows, maybe I shall not be able to get back in, since he has translated me! From Tony comes a very different tale, positively euphoric (even allowing for a natural wish not to vex the censor): high time a firm line was taken, people "in all walks of life" are overjoyed, everyone eagerly buying antiques, investing inside the country, etc. I find all that hard to believe.

Letters from Strato have reached me (all about needing money, not having found work yet, the child to take care of—a boy it was, born the last days of March) but from George, nothing since an Easter card to me; the letter he said he had sent to David that same day never arrived. We met, D and I, in San Francisco last weekend for long bouts of handwringing, but came to no conclusions. From one point of view we want and expect to go back in mid-July, but part of me remains numb and reluctant as it was even before the coup. I keep feeling S. is lost to me, that it's all too recent to bear going back and risking falling once again into that daily pain of waiting for him, not seeing him, or, when I do, seeing principally how deeply involved he is in a life in which I have no part. Vassili is probably right in saying that the civil war, like my unhappiness over S, is itself too recent for the people to contemplate more bloodshed—though bloodshed (at least those fatfaced colonels hanging by their heels) would be the only conceivable cure. Bloodshed would simplify things. <u>Then</u>, for all that I am too old and not as famous as Byron to be following in his footsteps, at least I could go over in the Red Cross—or would I? Certainly it's a recurring fantasy. Silence still surrounds S's visa. If only they would say yes or no, then it could be up to him + there would not be this, for me, ghastly sense of waiting, waiting, waiting, for something I know in my bones will never now come to pass. Japan is still in the back of my mind as a possibility sometime during the summer, but then so is simply not stirring from Stonington. Which do I need more—peace or distraction? One thing I know, I <u>don't</u> need heartaches.

The "teaching" here (what else to call it?) has been a distraction of sorts. But I'm not used to spending evenings alone, particularly in one room with a closet in which the Murphy bed stands on its head until I am so dazed with drink that I can only pull it out and fall face-down across it. All the agreeable students are simply too busy to carouse with me. Well. I'm settling for a string of dreary dinners with faculty, and the whole thing will be over in 17 days. I'll drive back to NY, spend a week there with my mother, and join D. [*in the margin:* he is still out in California visiting his parents in their geriatric ghetto. Hopes to break away early next week] in S'ton by the 3rd or 4th of June. 6 weeks of blissful village life is (are) the minimum I will settle for. And as you've gathered from the above, beyond July 15 is anybody's guess.

I've gotten myself too upset writing this letter to go on with it. Forgive me, my dear. I long for you and love you.

Jimmy

the coup On April 21, 1967, right-wing Greek army officers known as "the Colonels" took over the country. Thousands of their political opponents were arrested, imprisoned under brutal conditions, tortured, or exiled. Vassilikos, as a prominent leftist, escaped arrest by chance, being abroad at the time of the coup.

he has translated me With Merrill's help, Vassilikos translated ten poems into Greek and published them in 1965 as Οι Χιλιεσ η Δευτερη Νυχτα και Αλλα Ποιματα (*The Thousand and Second Night and Other Poems*). These poems have since appeared as the first section of Ο Μαωροσ Κυκνοσ: Χρονικα Ερωτα και Απολειασι (*The Black Swan: Chronicles of Love and Loss*. Athens: Gravity Editions, 2015), translations by Vassilikos and George Chaldezos.

To Strato Mouflouzelis

WUSTL
17 May 1967
[Madison, WI]

Strato, my love

Yet another lonely day. This evening I went to the movies, I drank two–three glasses, and now I sit in my horrible room in order to write you. To tell you what? This one thing only:

I love you. Never in my life will I have another dream but this one: to have you with me, to find a way somehow to make a life together. I'm not saying forever, if you don't want it so, but enough time so we can see how it is, how it goes—you understand? I think of you one hour—five hours—every day and I go mad not knowing what's happening with you, what's on your mind. What's happening to me I know well. I'm getting old. My hair is turning white. But what do I care? You tell me to wait—and I wait. Until when, to what end? You tell me. Tell me also if it's worth the wait. I know nothing, other than that I love you and I want you with me.

Please do me a favor and phone Tony—maybe he's heard something from the embassy.

Now, to sleep. I kiss you a hundred times.

J

My hair is turning white Merrill was forty-one years old. People who knew him at the time saw no white hairs.
Tony Tony Parigory.

To Mimi and Vassili Vassilikos

9 June 1967
[Stonington, CT]

Dear Mimi + Vassili—

Well, <u>that</u> was certainly a charming little war. Clever, brief, and to the point. Such an example to its older brothers, don't you think? We just heard on the radio that all through "the holy quarters of Jerusalem" a cry is being raised: Pharoah has fallen!—which gives one a dazzling glimpse back almost to the dawn of history as well as into the tenacious follies of the human heart. Other lessons can be learned—though nothing one didn't know before—from Nasser's resignation and even more from the agony of the people he betrayed. I mean, I think again (as if I'd thought of anything else for the last year) of that in us which chooses betrayal, puts a wreath on its head, sits at its feet taking notes and never learning. Virtually <u>nobody</u> on earth wants a wise ruler—either for his country or for his heart. Beckett is right. Plato is wrong.

Eleanor arrived yesterday and came to dinner in a yellow, see-through dress. Full of news about you. Grace gets in late this afternoon. We shall all be at the Boatwrights' for dinner. The town has never looked prettier. The revelation for David has been the new luncheon shoppe with little round orange tables, bric-a-brac for sale, creamy soups fresh from the blender—now he need never go hungry again, or want for company during the daylight hours.

I understand now about Laourdas—though someday I must sit down and try to understand the CIA. The only helpful image that comes to me is of your plant, Vassili, thriving in every crevice of that building, choking the pipes, mistaken for cables, the malignant luxury of it all . . . Anyhow, imagining Greece, life there now, is not fun—despite the Japanese theory that five is the perfect number of people for a cozy party (even their cups and dishes come in sets of five). I guess we are going back. David may be sailing late this month; I have to read in Boston July 11, and could fly soon thereafter. S's last letter said Vaso was going away for 3 or 4 months—her father isn't well, and the thought was to get some katharó aera mazí tou. I can't make out how he feels—he simply says that apart from there being no work available under the present government everything else is fine! Apparently Melina has made some extraordinarily effective TV appearances, speaking out in tears against the colonels. If I have any time in NY I'll try to see the show and say a word to her backstage. I don't think I want to spend more than 2 or 3 months in Greece (D. says he feels the same); I need profoundly to be here and do some work. On my way home in the fall I would try to stop in Paris, or wherever you are, and tell you what I've seen.

Do you remember Bernard de Zogheb? He might be someone you could have coffee and gossip with, Mimi. Send him a note, if you feel inclined: 91 rue de la Pompe.

Everything in me wants not to go back to Greece now. But I must. I think of it as my last trip for a long time, and one that my spirit will spend quietly + mournfully (whatever giggles and twitches and cries of rage escape my flesh) taking leave of Strato, of Greece, of the final moments of my youth. Do I sound too pompous, too like Kimon? He was never, alas, 100% wrong . . .

I'm surprised to hear that all of Vassili's books haven't been banned. Maybe those people haven't read the last section of *The Photographs*. Or *The Angel*. How soon will the Gallimard books appear?

This isn't really a letter, but I wanted to make a sign. Perhaps by now you'll be settled in that horrible city, and able to make some sense out of life. Tack to the wall this photograph a newspaper photographer took in Wisconsin.

Love,
Jimmy

I want to add Hellos! And say you must not think I'm not with you. I get less political every minute—and being for anything less than friendship seems a terrible waste of human energy in a century of such lies and folly. Stay well. We all belong to the one world.

Love,
David

---

charming little war The so-called Six-Day War, in which the Israeli military overwhelmed Egyptian, Jordanian, and Syrian forces and took control of the Gaza Strip, the Golan Heights, East Jerusalem, and the West Bank.

Beckett is right. See Merrill's poem "Matinées" in *The Fire Screen* (1969): "We love the good, said Plato? He was wrong. / We love as well the wicked and the weak."
Laourdas Vasileios Laourdas (1912–71), classical scholar, friend of Nikos Kazantzakis.
katharó aera mazí tou Uncertain. Merrill probably means that fresh air will be good for Vaso's father.
Melina Melina Mercouri (1920–94), Greek actor, friend of Vassilikos. At the time of the coup, she was on Broadway in *Illya Darling*, Jules Dassin's adaptation of his film *Never on Sunday* (1960), in which she also starred. She became a leader of the opposition to the Colonels' rule. The street on which Merrill and Jackson lived in Athens has been renamed Boulevard Melina Mercouri in her honor.
The Angel The third in Vassilikos's trilogy of novellas, translated into English and published by Knopf as *The Plant, The Well, The Angel* (1964).
Gallimard books Éditions Gallimard, Paris, published French translations of Vassilikos's *The Plant, The Well, The Angel* (1967) and *Z* (1967).
that horrible city Paris.

To Judith Moffett

NYPL
15 June 1967
Stonington, CT

Dear Judy,

I was happy to hear from you—such a long letter, too; fits + starts are all I can manage these days, and now that we have a start of 2 lines perhaps the fit can be dispensed with. Contact lenses—you never told me, did you? How brave to wear them right off on a camping trip. Mine were (are) German and I got used to them within 2 or 3 days, though for a year or so they tended to flutter forth from the eye whenever it was suddenly caught by anything. This can be costly; you might consider insuring yours—foolhardy companies do exist that will cover your first several losses. You'll probably find in Sweden an agent for the German lensmakers (Söhnges) which are still the best as well as the cheapest. Do you find you are tilting your head backwards these days?

Stonington, I must say, is bliss. The daylong sunny haze, the harbor dotted with little sailboats blackened by the glare and all the nicer for there being no question of ever setting foot in one of them. The Stone Women (Grace + Eleanor, mother + daughter) are back from Italy and we have resumed our 4-times-a-week cooking and bridge duels. They have a garden full of lilac, laburnum, black, white, and yellow tulips, Chinese peonies a foot in diameter, and the first, slightly smaller, mosquitos. I still do not know about Greece, but it seems likely I'll go around the 14th of July.

I'm glad you liked the *Seraglio*. I like it too, there's more to hang on to. It's no rarity in this house—there are still at least half of the hundred remaindered copies I bought for only pennies apiece—and I'm sending you one. In mint condition (for what that might be worth to Mr Pollak some of whose rare books looked rather badly cared for).

In New York I had tea with Marianne Moore—a glass of cold water, that is, and some endless, nicely-phrased ramblings-on, mostly (as with my grandmother at that age) bearing on her self-sufficiency of which she is understandably proud. Once a week she allows the elevator man to do a spot of cooking for her. She keeps her hats in a bottom drawer, like pancakes.

No other news. Did you enjoy at all that little chamber war in the Middle East? I thought it had "concentration and gusto"—two of the 3 things Miss Moore looks for in poetry (the third is humility)—and could well serve as an example to other wars in the present + future—but I can see, from here, that I'm not amusing you. Besides, the page is already 2/3 gone.

> Yours,
> James

There was once a parody of Milne in *The New Yorker*, having to do with the H.J. revival. It began:

> James James
> Matthiessen Matthiessen
> Fadiman Rahv Dupee
> Took great
> Care of their author
> In essay and anthologee . . .

Judith Moffett See Biographies.
Mr Pollak Felix Pollak (1909–87), poet and curator of rare books at the University of Wisconsin.
"concentration and gusto" See Marianne Moore's lecture "Humility, Concentration, and Gusto" (1949).
Milne A.A. Milne (1882–1956), English author best known for his children's books.

See his poem beginning "James James / Morrison Morrison / Weatherby George Dupree . . ." in his book *When We Were Very Young* (1924).
H.J. revival Henry James rose to new prominence in the postwar period in the US; his books were rereleased, occasioning numerous critical studies.
Matthiessen Fadiman Rahv Dupee F. O. Matthiessen (1902–50), American literature scholar; Clifton Fadiman (1904–99), intellectual and author, popular radio and TV personality; Philip Rahv (1908–73), editor of *Partisan Review;* F. W. Dupee (1904–79), literary critic.

To Mimi and Vassili Vassilikos

WUSTL
25 July 1967
Stonington, CT

Mimi dear,

You were next on the list, and I do feel guilty to have gone so long without writing. Let me see, shall I present you with some excuses? Well, around the time of my last letter, I hurt my back—bent over to pick something up and was absolutely paralyzed with pain. That lasted about a week, in the course of which David sailed for Greece. The next thing to strike was a mysterious diarrhea which lasted about 2 weeks (and may return—I'm taking my last medicine today) and brought with it a really dreadful case of piles. That week I was in New York, and out on Long Island for the weekend with my former Bard student, Louise Fitzhugh and her new girlfriend, a monumental, humorless mezzo-soprano. Luckily they have a little plane service from East Hampton to New London, a charming 20 minute flight for only $32—just me and the pilot—on the single sunny day we have had out of the last 25. And by the next afternoon I was meekly obeying the doctor. Meanwhile (possibly even the cause of these last troubles) letters and telephone calls from David had been bringing home to me that at last everything between me and S. seems to be over. I haven't heard from him now since June 19. David saw him, and Vaso, and the baby. S. of course isn't working, but fatter than ever and not thinking of the morrow—very grasshopper. But I am turning against him. It is the last thing I ever imagined I would do, and I wouldn't be doing it if he had played the game according to the rules—that is, if he had done one-third of the very little I asked of him; if he had answered the questions in my letters; if the very tone of his letters had not been cold and hasty and as if he were writing to somebody he hated who was, however, still useful, but <u>only</u> useful. I cannot bear writing this to you. I had wanted him as a friend for life, but he has not the faintest conception of "putting" anything into a friendship, and suddenly the strain of doing it all by myself is too much—or I think it is too much. I'm not "over" the experience by any means. I still spend hours a day having imaginary conversations with him, answering in imagination <u>any</u> kind of letter he might write, indulging in fantasies of the extremest coldness and sarcasm, then suddenly remembering that he has no more wits than a puppy. Vaso I think is beginning to be a perceptible influence—some of her old profession is rubbing off on him. I found a terrifying portrait of a person like S. in Santayana's *The Last Puritan*—books like that, "great" books, burn us like radium, with their decisiveness, their terrible understanding of what happens. One should be very careful when one reads them, at what time in one's life. And still, there is a tiny voice exclaiming: "But that is all myth! Life doesn't <u>need</u> to follow these patterns!" Just now a hasty letter from David. S. wants to come to America, that's the latest. Not that he has his visa, not (probably) that he will get it, living as he does under <u>Vaso's</u> surname somewhere in the Votanikó area. Do I want him? I don't think I do! I don't think I can <u>bear</u> any more of it! It's like a question of somehow saving my life. Ah, saving it for <u>what</u>? I can decide nothing, nothing, nothing. I am certainly not going to Greece now; possibly after Labor Day, on a 3 week excursion, not before.

What did I want to tell you or ask you? Tony writes that the "foreign boycott" is hurting business—I wonder how much he sees by way of connection between the boycott + the regime. And does anyone know where Theodorakis is? Can it be he is still hiding in Greece? has he been captured + imprisoned? has he family there who would suffer if he made a sign from abroad?

Stonington social life continues. Grace + Eleanor. Bridge games. Discussions of Viet Nam (only here, in a town like this, would there be pros and cons to discuss). As I thought to say, brilliantly, last night: Here, the Tedium is the Message. I am writing a bit—not writing so much as polishing things hastily flung on paper a year ago. I must leave you now and go meet a train.

> Love, <u>lots</u> of it, to you + Vassili.
> Jimmy

grasshopper See Aesop's grasshopper-and-ant fable, on which Merrill draws near the end of "The Summer People."
her old profession Merrill earlier referred to her as a "bar girl."
Theodorakis Mikis Theodorakis (b. 1925), Greek composer and songwriter, imprisoned by the Colonels.
Tedium is the Message "The medium is the message," Marshall McLuhan's catchphrase from *Understanding Media: The Extensions of Man* (1964).

To Mimi and Vassili Vassilikos

WUSTL
31 July 1967
Stonington, CT

Mimi dear,

I received your long and charming letter the other day. Last night Grace + Eleanor were over for an omelet and I read it aloud to them. It really made an impression. By the end, not two sentences could go by without their exclaiming, "But that's very sweet! But she writes a charming letter!"—I of course was correcting your grammar as I went along (you have begun to use "as" after a comparative when you should use "than"!, etc) and <u>they</u> imagined I was skipping various things I didn't want them to hear, but it went off very well.

Oh dear, I put some Greek records on the phonograph a few weeks ago and had to go into the bathroom + cry.

I just read a very interesting book called *The Flight of Icarus* by Kevin Andrews. Somebody says he lives in Athens. All about wandering through the Pelopponesos in 1947–50 and talking to people about the civil war.

You say that Greece will never again be the same because its youth will have lost confidence in it. Well, yes and no. <u>Don't</u> make this mistake made by all the idle people in the world. You hear the complaint wherever café society is to be found: Such-and-such a place is spoiled, one can no longer go there, it used to be <u>heaven</u> before this-or-that happened. What this usually means is that the speaker has been ruined and can no longer go anywhere with anything approaching youthful enthusiasm. A large part of what you mean is that <u>you</u> will never be young in Greece again, that your <u>real</u> youth is over. I myself don't worry that profoundly about Greece—there is after all an adult generation or two right now with no direct experience of the Occupation. They jump with joy at the sight of a German tourist. If you want to be really subtle of course I agree with you. Even these silly eyes of mine can make out ever so faintly the legacy of the civil war in <u>this</u> country, or the effect on the British + French of the two World Wars in which so many genuinely promising people died.

I am flying down to Long Island in a few hours for two days with my sister. In mid-August I'll go to Boston for my brother's birthday, and the next day Grace + Eleanor will pick me up and we shall drive to Castine, 4 hours up the Maine coast, for the weekend with Mary McCarthy! She and Eleanor have just discovered (thanks to the badly done "inside" book about Mary) that they shared a young man—a perfectly ordinary goodlooking bum who danced well and resembled Fred McMurry BUT who died under most mysterious circumstances in Mexico the month Trotsky arrived there. So we are all kicking the dust of Stonington from our satin slippers and I must say are behaving like children on the eve of a delicious treat.

David <u>phoned</u> you in Paris? Was that wise of him to do? I'm thinking of the house being watched, George being trailed, things like that. His letters sound rattled. Life must be quite boring on the surface if not au fond. He sent a picture of Vaso + the baby—V. tansfigured and radiant with motherhood, the bitch, and a chubby, almost audibly laughing infant Strato in her arms. Insofar as there is any decision to make, I haven't made one. I'm not well. I wish I still believed in psychosomatic illnesses, mine would be so easily explained. Meanwhile I stick to a vile bland diet and do not drink and know that as soon as I stop the medicine the cramps + trots will begin again.

I sent Harry a card asking him to mail you 5 *Nights + Days* and 1 *Water Street*. I will send from here two copies of the translations and a paperback *Diblos*.

I am working a bit. Mostly fussing with a medium-length (60 line) poem called "To My Greek" which I began last spring. You will think it is about Strato, and you will not be wrong, but it is ostensibly addressed to my imperfect command of the language. Then I am trying to write something about what going to the opera meant to me as a child: the destruction of what Henry James would have called the Moral Sense—through watching all those characters love and betray and kill and renounce and catch TB merely, as it now and then seemed, in order to have something beautiful to sing on the subject.

What are these crazy clothes you're buying? Are they very mod and mini? Think, Mimi! You're FREE of Thalia now! Free of her bizarre notions of the stylish! You're in Paris—la shrimp can be forgotten! Reflect before you choose, is all. . . .

Speaking of clothes, Levi's now make the most extraordinary varieties of trouser, cut like jeans, but of wild materials—paisley, camouflage cloth, white corduroy with yellow-and-blue houndstooth check printed on it, and (my favorite) charcoal gray with a splendid, rather widely spaced white stripe. All at Katz's in New London. If you tell me Vassili's waist in inches and trouser length I may find him something. After all you're in France now, I keep forgetting, where packages can arrive swiftly and without fuss.

I perhaps had more to say but forget. Don't go to Cuba, your passport will be taken away. My niece's was 4 years ago and they still haven't given it back to her.

A hug to Vassili and a kiss to you—
J.

The Flight of Icarus By Kevin Andres, describing his travels in Greece.
Fred McMurry Fred MacMurray (1908–91), American actor.
the house being watched State surveillance of Athinaion Efivon 44.
"To My Greek" In *The Fire Screen* (1969).
what going to the opera meant The sonnet sequence "Matinées," also published in *The Fire Screen*.
My niece Catherine Merrill (b. 1943), ceramicist, activist, writer. She was part of a group who went to Cuba in 1964 to protest the travel ban and, at the expense of the Cuban government, to experience the country's culture. As they had anticipated, the American government confiscated their passports on their return.

To Judith Moffett

NYPL
6 September 1967
[Stonington, CT]

Dear Judy,

Some, as it was, last words from the unprecedentedly sunlit terrace. Marilyn Horne (a mezzo, Rossini specialist, and my latest vice) is pouring forth from her namesake of plenty. In two days I must pack up and hie me to Athens. Not that I'm well or anything, but I'll simply take the amoebas and the 100's of pills they thrive on, with me. A month will be about as long as I can stay, as I want to stay in Paris to see Vassilikos on my way back, and I mean to reach N.Y. by Oct. 23 to have some days with my mother there + spare myself thereby a visit to Atlanta.

The summer has been so dismal, you can't imagine. A single bright spot was a weekend up in Maine—where we stayed (my beloved 80 year old Grace + her daughter Eleanor) (and I) with Mary McCarthy. The Lowells have a summer house there. We were shown Nautilus Is. and the Union Soldier, saw a seal but no skunks, + had all in all such a good time that people here got a bit tired of hearing about it. Finally on the 4th day after our return, the wittiest man I know buried the topic once + for all by the inspired words of "Hail Grace, full of Mary"—so now we're back where we were.

Another morning, the same terrace and sun. Today's opera is *William Tell*. I'm glad I stopped writing yesterday, because I feel cheerfuller today, and in between came your letter. How nice that you like Lund. I suppose Sweden is technically "Europe" even though none of our best people have written about it, Twain or James or (smile) Hemingway, thus leaving you with no choice but merely to live there, coping with the language and the refrigerator just as one does at home. What was to be expected, of course, is the upset of balance vis-à-vis Joe. Is anything more bewildering, especially if one is the more conscious + dependable of the two, than this finding oneself less involved? 1000 voices, from Plato to the Beatles, tell us that love is fleeting—no matter: there's always the same outrage, or shame, or "innocent" wonder when it happens inside us. His (Joe's) sudden moral rearmament is very much part of the pattern. We begin to imitate those whom we feel slipping beyond our reach. It's in these winds that my own weathervane has been gyrating, at velocities ranging from amusement to despair, for the last year or so, and I've had to conclude that nothing can be trusted, there's no telling what to do, or being told—time will tell, garrulous as ever, what it is one <u>has</u> done, but only after the fact.

About your poetry—your having nothing to say equal to your ability to say it—that seems to me a most natural state of affairs, and should be the case with any self-respecting poet during the first ten years of his career. How many poems are ruined by precisely that inflated urgency of a Message—at its worst, all greasy with sincerity; at its best, made impenetrable with avant-garde rhetoric (Rimbaud?). Just write a lot and let what happens happen. Am I meant to <u>ask</u> to see that sestina, by the way? Oh and tell me, too, about my "mannerisms" that put you off—one's often so unconscious of things like that.

I won't promise an intelligible letter (or any letter) from Greece, but would welcome one from you at: Athinaion Efivon 44 / Athens 601. Count on its taking a week to reach me even by air. A wonderful dragonfly has made his appearance: in a sheath of scarlet felt, with orange whiskers and a black dot at the end of each wing. Now he has attached himself to a plainly dressed lady for an unbroken minute of lovemaking aloft. Their wings are audible, and glitter. Goodbye.

Yours,
James

amoebas Merrill had amoebic dysentery.
The Lowells Robert Lowell and his wife, Elizabeth Hardwick.
a seal but no skunks Merrill has in mind respectively Lowell's poems "Soft Wood" (*For the Union Dead*, 1964) and "Skunk Hour" (*Life Studies*, 1959).
the wittiest man Robert Morse.
Joe Moffett's boyfriend at the University of Wisconsin.

To Judith Moffett   NYPL
                                                           23 September 1967
                                                              Athens, Greece

Dear one,

(Smack!) Trust me. Your letter and sestina found me on an otherwise
unaccountably Good Day, although David has a grippe, thunder-
heads are piling up, and sixteen people are coming for drinks. Mme.
Kleo, hair dyed maroon, is moaning and making her delicious little
meatballs in the kitchen. Also stewing an octopus that had been lying,
dried hard as scrap metal, in the bottom of the dridge. Fridge. I've
been here only ten days, it seems forever. Acquaintance—friends—
people (who are they really?) drop in unexpectedly for a cognac and
game of cards or backgammon. The telephone, in constant use, is
nevertheless all but buried in a glistening web of prevarication. All
so familiar, all so strange. "The only reason you're going back," said
Eleanor with a smile of terrible experience, "is to have one of those
disastrous conversations designed to convince somebody who will
have no idea what you're talking about of the comparative fineness
of your behavior." And indeed an occasion arose for this conversa-
tion, and will again, but it passed (perhaps thanks to her) in a blaze
of smalltalk.

I like the sestina, you know—is that horrid of me? Mr Pollak as
a grapefruit is pure joy. The last sentence strikes me as obscure.
What "sound" do (or did—past tense) you mean? As far as its per-
sonal content goes, even without your warning I would have read it
very much—it asks to be read so, with its careful departure from a
time + scene—as an incidental page in a longer story; though what
anyone else would think is, well, anyone's business. Talk all you like
about ethics, what I trust more in you is the "wanting," the "tena-
ciousness," the conviction that people cannot separate without tear-
ing something—whether it is the tearing of tissue paper or a kind of
feline tearing of flesh. You must not simplify and say that you sent
me the sestina and that my reaction was to accuse you of savagery.
I'm not, anyhow, accusing—only admiring. And going a step further
to add that whatever one intensely wants is never given at the time
or in the form one wants it (Proust's Law) and that this will be a great

source of vitality in whatever you do, like writing poems. Emily's formal feeling after pain. There is one moment in one poem of hers that might illustrate it. Whether it does or not, I find it immensely touching—at the end of "The gentian weaves its fringes": (quoting from memory) "Sister, swallow, seraph / Let me fly with thee" and then—call it arch, I don't care: "In the name of the bee / And of the butterfly / And of the breeze, Amen"—something at the opposite pole from her idiosyncrasy, her piquant phrases, as if language itself were kneeling briefly in submission. Of course, too, if my Psyche "is" anyone except her author, she is Emily—the New England old maid par excellence. But I would not want to use E's mannerisms to excuse my own. I suppose what I feel about them* has to do with liking language, written or spoken, that doesn't pretend to be anything but an approximation, or representation if you prefer, of the unspeakable reality. The writer who feels that he can really express, dig out, the whole of his subject with words + rhythms is a perfectly respectable phenomenon but at my best (or worst, even) I can't shake the suspicion that I know better than to—hours have passed—how to end the sentence—better than to . . . be so . . . naive? Hence my love of the cliché, the worn-out phrase with or without a twist (In the name of the bee)—used side by side with the ne'er-so-well-expressed ones (there goes the ribbon—frayed, threadbare) to show that their intrinsic value is the same. One has only to push the argument a step further (which I shall not do) to get the kind of objet trouvé poem that made a little splash in a recent Sunday *Times*—baggage checks, gossip columns, advertisements for Preparation H all broken up into lines and rediscovered for pop purposes. Anyhow, the practise behind notions like this is conceivably a thread in the fabric I weave. I dare say it comes to me from Henry James who does it relentlessly + sublimely. [*Handwritten in the margin*: Inte sant? or ετσι δεν ειναι;]

I'm feeling alright, on 8 pills a day. I have amoebic dysentery—not for the first time. Vassilikos is the young Greek novelist. 3 novellas came out in the U.S. in '64. But he is very left wing & was away, luckily, when the coup took place. Now there's a kind of Free Greece in Paris. Everything is quiet here, and pleasant enough, except that lots of people are out of work. Goodbye for now. Yours,

James

Dear One . . . Trust me In her letter to him, Moffett had remarked on the "archness" in some of his poems and had cited the narrator's address to his senses in his poem "From the Cupola" in *Nights and Days* (1966) beginning *"Dear ones* I say bending to kiss their faces / *trust me."*
Talk all you like about ethics Moffett had given Merrill a copy of her college essay on ethics, "The Vigilance That Must Never Falter."
(Proust's Law) See Merrill to Donald Richie, 28 February 1967.
Emily's formal feeling Dickinson's poem "After great pain, a formal feeling comes—"
(quoting from memory) Merrill misremembers these lines: "Summer, sister, seraph, / Let us go with thee!"; the last three lines he quotes from Dickinson are correct.
my Psyche Merrill's poem "From the Cupola" in *Nights and Days* is addressed to Psyche.
Inte sant "Isn't that right?" in Swedish (a phrase Merrill got from Moffett), followed by the Greek equivalent (the semicolon being the Greek question mark). Moffett was in Lund, Sweden, on a Fulbright.

To David Kalstone

WUSTL
4 October 1967
Athens, Greece

Dearest Old Bunny,

We have had some bad news. I was in Crete the last 4 days (visiting someone you may remember as The Monkey, a small brown soldier-athlete with great fringed green eyes—about whom I wrote that ballad-like poem) and came back early this morning, David having telephoned to say that his brother had, as it seems, simply not woken up the previous day. Two years his senior—leaving wife, daughter, granddaughter, and of course D's parents, most of whom now expect him to drop the mask of amiable eccentricity and damn well take a plane to Los Angeles. And he can't, he simply can't. He's in the saddest state, as you can imagine. There is no sailing till the 15th, a Greek boat that reaches NY only a day later than the *United States* which leaves Le Havre on the 28th, so he'll take the latter which gives him the extra 10 days here he wants in order to have some time with George, find him a little flat, etc. It's not that we haven't been foreseeing, these last many years, the spell when everybody is going to die, mothers + fathers + stepfathers, the spell at whose end we shall ourselves have become oldsters, aged like drink in the oak of assumed responsibility, but who would have thought it would begin with someone nearly our own age? My plans, I guess, remain unaltered: Paris on the 15th, NY on the 22nd.

Perhaps I can still tell you about Crete. I must say I had <u>one</u> of the times of my life. Kosta met me In A Taxi at the airport (Herakleion) one evening at 8 and brought me "home"—that is to a room the size of my study, all whitewash and mosquitoes + plastic curtains + photographs of incensed-looking male relatives. A mother, spectacled + dumpy in black, a brother + sister-in-law, a brother-in-law, 2 nine-year old nephews who kissed my hand—the merest cross-section of a gigantic family—received me, inquired after my trip, my mother, my sister Monica (whom K., it is widely known in Crete, is going to marry next year) and watched him + me eat the first of several unforgettable and all too describable meals. (Potatoes, potatoes. "Do you like okra" the mother was to say another time; or, "Do you like an omelet?" And, hearing that I did, would come forth with <u>pounds</u> of potatoes mixed with a very few filaments of the precious vegetable or perfumed with a single egg.) Afterwards we went on his motorcycle to his shop—a little room with a big table where he makes "jewelry," or repairs a broken key, or takes a blowtorch to a handful of gold and copper dust which becomes, 15 minutes later, a tiny ingot cooled at once in a cup of water; where also, late at night, there would be just enough room to do something passionate standing up. I slept at the brother's house all but one night when I didn't sleep at all. The next midday we went, by motorcycle, to his village 10 miles up in the hills, where a half-brother owns a cafe (and most of the surrounding vineyards). We must have spent 10 hours, drinking, playing backgammon, eating rabbit + chicken after chicken pounced on and carried screaming to slaughter, talked endless politics (it's so <u>easy</u> in the demotic!), and came back the next day to gather an herb with a fine authoritative smell, a specific for amoebas. I have made the decoction and shall start the cure tomorrow. Then suddenly we were on the motorcycle driving 62 kilometers, after dark, in bitter cold, to a panegyri in a far village. A room packed with people, a pair of musicians (guitar and lyra—like a child's fiddle), K. in the jacket of his insane mustard-gold suit with black crosshatching dancing marvelously as the evening went on + more + more black fringed handkerchiefs were bound round more and more blackbrowed heads. That was when I thought of writing you, suddenly the way he danced made sense, his being always happy not to steal the show; one saw exactly how he fitted in. A note scrawled on the spot reads: "K, the viola in the family quintet: unobtrusive resonance. S, the 1st violin. G, the mournful cello. And 2 second fiddles—D and I." But by 2 a.m. something had gone wrong. 50 furious young men had leapt upon him, you've never seen such a brawl. Then came perhaps five minutes of passionate talk, largely genealogical I gathered, and they were all fast friends again. Mercifully a truck was headed back to town. The motorcycle was fitted in back among little cases of drygoods, the driver and his partner sat in the two seats. K + I somehow squeezed between them. K. sang cheerily for the first few miles, then passed out cold. The brakes gave out, we had to proceed at a snail's pace, I still ache from holding him in position. We were home a bit after 6. With tyrannical cries he roused the mother + the two nephews curled like twin foetuses. "Virgin! What happened to your eye?" "Silence! Make the beds and get out. We are going to sleep here. You (to a nephew) take this key, open the shop at 8. No more words! Out!" And sleep we did, while the room filled up with sun and the voices of a steady stream of neighbors dropping in to ask who, what, how, why, where and when. Only after that did the mother confess that she had grown to love me like her own child. Monica is taking on a formidable reality. She is slightly plumper and coarser than I, I'll know soon whether she is younger or older, when I send her photograph from America. I'm taking her a knitted doily and lots of raisins, which she never stops eating. Although she's my own sister I suspect she is heartless + fickle and doesn't take the engagement very seriously; it's I (wax to receive + marble to retain) who'll remain the friend of the family, soberly shaking my head over her follies. She's a creature of Antonioni's, that's it, a heartless, unreflecting somnambulist, eyes glazed, a raisin lifted to those expressionless lips. It may even have all been <u>seen</u>, in a flash, by the little uniformed figure standing, with nothing to do + nowhere to go, outside a movie in Omonia Square. Don't laugh—or I'll slap a blonde wig on <u>you</u> and march you off to Bachrach. Bye now.

Love,

J.

someone you may remember Kostas or Kosta Tympakianakis, whom Merrill met through Tony Paregory, and about whom Merrill wrote the "ballad-like" eponymous poem in *The Fire Screen* (1969).
my sister Monica Merrill and Kostas made up a cover story to account for their closeness.
his brother Jackson's older brother, George Jackson Jr., died suddenly of a heart attack.
he simply can't Jackson was afraid of flying and therefore traveled only by train or boat.
panegyri Greek "gathering" or celebration.
Antonioni's Michelangelo Antonioni (1912–2007), Italian film director and writer. Merrill had recently seen his *Blow-Up* (1966).
Bachrach Historic men's fashion chain.

To Marianne Moore

ROSENBACH
11 November 1967
Stonington, CT

Dear Miss Moore,

A word of greeting on your birthday. How glad we all are that you were born. Please arrange to stay as long as possible.

Yours ever,
James Merrill

To Mimi and Vassili Vassilikos

WUSTL
1 December 1967
Stonington, CT

Mimi dear,

I'd have written today anyhow, even if your long letter (with its charming invitation to complain) had not come in the mail. Nothing to complain <u>about</u>, that's my single complaint of the moment. I don't even mind the idea of going to New York tomorrow, to Charlottesville the next day (one could, I suppose, complain that the name hasn't been changed to Mimiville, or Mimi<u>burg</u>—more expressive somehow). I'll see Monticello, cradle of Jeffersonian Democracy, and the beautiful campus of the University. Long-legged students who have grown up on horseback will sit at my feet drinking juleps. Thence to Princeton where Mike K. has arranged dinner-parties and receptions—not, I trust, his usual kind at which the really interesting guests are denied access to the Poet. Mary is having tests in the hospital but will be there for my second evening. I may begin complaining, ever so faintly, the next day when I go to New York and try to accomplish Christmas shopping. That won't be fun. I thought I'd go to Korvette's and get David a tiny TV set, on the chance of its making Stonington a more beguiling place for him. But he'll just take it off to Greece, I know—well, I'll have tried. My cold ostensibly ended last Sunday afternoon, but Pernod-colored mucus keeps pouring out of my eyes, nose, ears, and throat. I have planned to say with a grin, in the event of having to blow my nose on the lecture platform: Ah, if it were only this easy to blow the mind.

I have been reading that big book on *La Resistance Grecque* by Kedros. It is absolutely fascinating and appalling, but I had to smile because so much of the time I feel the way you feel reading Nancy Mitford. Just as for you her father's Fascism strips away the charm + humor of her narrative, so, time + again, I stop in the middle of a sentence by Kedros and exclaim, as it were, "But he's simply a Communist! All these wonderful people courageous + brave were acting the way they did because they were something <u>else</u> than merely 'human' Greek men + women." Indeed, he makes very plain that most of the Greek population behaved selfishly and badly until the EAM "educated" them—i.e. Shot them for stealing another peasant's chicken. It is very complicated, this topic, and the feelings it arouses. If I admit that Nancy M's characters do + say the absurdly charming things they do <u>because</u> they are Fascists, the day instantly seems darker and colder. The point I'm trying to make probably has something to do with the degree of self-awareness. We all hate the person who acts on principle—who is, say, generous <u>because</u> Jesus tells him so. There is a world of difference between the action of two young men who took down the Nazi flag from the Acropolis and one of them's account of the exploit written years later for a partisan newspaper. What is impressive in Kedros's book is to see how the Communists made it possible for perfectly uneducated, unpolitical people to behave heroically—something they would otherwise have been unable to do except wastefully, unavailingly. Sabotaging the occupation, killing Germans, blowing up bridges—these were things any one of them might have privately dreamed of doing. Where I begin to feel uneasy is to see how these immediately imagineable aims were linked to something as sophisticated as post-war political reform, no matter how admirably set forth in terms of free elections and what not. The connection strikes me as too intellectual a one to have accurately mirrored the desires of most of the people involved, except of course for the leaders. But, as you know, I am an anarchist. There's a sorry sense, too, in which all military organization makes it possible for a simple individual to fight (or fall) gloriously. No doubt there were far fewer brave Germans than brave Greeks, but there must have been some and they may even have believed, especially when the time came for them to defend their own land, that they were doing the right thing.

Sylvia Plath doesn't grab me all that much—she's too easy to read; you never need to understand more than the images + emotions. And she's so EARNEST. Just keep on reading me, dear. David will be back in 2 weeks, well before Xmas. I can barely keep my chin above the floods of correspondence in Greek—mostly back + forth to Crete, where I must not only write my letter to Kosta and his mother, but Monica's letters as well. Her memory of the Greek language is disintegrating fast, she can barely spell and her handwriting is so awful that most of the time, now, she simply lets me send a few affectionate messages. Quite right she is, too. One doesn't want one's sister exchanging letters with a man she hasn't married yet!

Stratos too—I write one kind of letter to him at his house where Vaso and the baby and the dog will read it; another kind I send c/o Tony's shop. It's a full life.

I had not heard the results of the trial; please keep me posted should you hear anything more specific from or about Dora.

How silly I feel, writing at such length about that Greek book. But I've never formed any ideas and they flock, the right ones with the wrong ones, to my corn-filled hands like pigeons. Why shouldn't one after all apply to politics the disciplines so familiar in art? Americans who believe in the seduction of glossy images, corruption from within—the Russians committed to exterior organization, an imposed format . . . Who knows (are you ready for the day's final cliché?) if the truth may not fall somewhere between? Baby Doll! I'm going to start a newspaper!

Je te laisse maintenant, ma très-chère môme. Embrasse ton mari et ne m'oublies pas. Où en est-on dans la traduction anglaise de *Z*?

Love forevaire,

J.

Mike K. Edmund Keeley (b. 1928), American poet and translator of modern Greek poetry, and his wife, Mary (1926–2012).
EAM The Greek National Liberation Front, during World War II, formed by a coalition of leftist leaders.
La Resistance Grecque (1966), Greek author André Kedros's (1917–99) account of the 1940–44 Greek Resistance.
Nancy M's Nancy Mitford (1904–73), witty, aristocratic English novelist and biographer, considered an authority on manners and breeding.
Monica's letters See note to letter to David Kalstone of 4 October 1967.
Je te laisse I leave you now, my dearest child. Kiss your husband and do not forget me. Where are we on the English translation of *Z*?

To Judith Moffett   NYPL
29–31 December 1967
Stonington, CT

Judy dear,

Such pretty ties—the only ties, what's more, that I got for Christmas; others were taken in by something superficially <u>bookish</u> about me, though somebody gave me a Tarot pack and a tin for baking madeleines (very dry, the first batch). It took no nerve whatever to put on the one with red + blue in it for my Xmas cooking effort at which it was admired by seven pairs of eyes. Sweden, I said negligently. The other I shall save for *Rosenkrantz + Guildenstern Are Dead*, next week in NY, as being a vaguely Scandinavian occasion. You shouldn't, of course, but thank you, thank you, twice. The holidays are passing quietly enough. I decided against some parties in the city, last night and tonight, and shall venture out to a staid New Year's Eve here in the village—all grown-ups who will have to make an effort (slight compared to my own) to keep animated until midnight. I'm glad you got to Stockholm and into a real family (I assume it was real) instead of singing Silent Night with the other Americans.

Another day. I'm halfway through a long-cherished project: reading *Anna Karenina* in French, not entirely, I hope, out of snobbery. Constance Garnett's English was perfectly good the first time around but, trying to reread that version, I bogged down; it seemed so thin. With a foreign language one takes on faith all the richness + finesse clearly lacking in the English version, and is so busy making sure of a mechanical understanding that this all but takes the place of an allusive one. One tiny + marvelous exception. When Kitty refuses Levin she says in French merely "C'est impossible" which <u>cannot</u> have the stagy period charm of Garnett's "It cannot be." The tone of the latter couldn't be more perfect with its echo of a 2nd rate play, the faint falseness perfectly true to Kitty herself who without knowing it all the time is saying something conventional she doesn't mean. How beautifully all that fits with the second proposal where neither risks using words at all but only their first letters writ in water (wine?) on a table top. I'm startled, too, by how much I've changed since reading it long ago. Then, I couldn't race through the Kitty-Levin chapters fast enough in order to get back to Fascinating Anna and Vronsky; now it's almost the other way around. The book must be virtually truer than life. And so concise! Nothing that doesn't connect + reveal. Apart from *AK*, I'm using my idleness very badly, worse than usual, that is. One shortish poem in the manner of somebody I don't recognize or specially like, and a pile of illegible snippets unrelated to themselves or anything else. Oh my, time to cook again. The Stone Women (Grace + Eleanor) are coming for roast lamb, kasha, oranges, and bridge. You see how little news there is. The weather has been unseasonably warm. . . . . . .

And so here it is New Year's Eve. After the party broke up I pushed on in *Anna K* and found that Kitty + Levin write in chalk on a slate like good children. So much for memory. It is a gray lifeless lightless day, itself written in chalk on slate. You I fancy see no daylight at all, this time of year. Grace got all misty-eyes over Roman Christmases and the shepherds who used to ride their horses into town (they still come in Chevrolets) and stride about in fleece coats, swaddled legs, with bagpipes. What with a massive transportation strike in NY, picture me following in their footsteps the day after tomorrow.

Happy New Year!
Jimmy

To Strato Mouflouzelis   WUSTL
30 January 1968
[Stonington, CT]

Dear Strato,

Let me write a last letter as well. I've written it 4 times; if you read it twice, then we're even.

You're truly crazy. I'm writing you in a state of suffering and you respond with rage. I didn't call you a liar, nor a bum. I told you politely that you don't need this much money just for the child's therapy. (And you become all spite.) What do you care if I believe you or not? Didn't I do everything you have asked me so far—and more? In fact, I did believe you once and you deceived me, and you got caught and ruined your future.

If you want, you can burn the papers from the embassy. They wrote to me, so I know what they will say to you. Your visa application has lapsed on account of the long delay since the inquiry began. I'm not surprised at the delay, since you never told them under which name they should look for you, since you stubbornly refused to even look at the papers. In order to make such a thing happen you need to be aggressive, a quality you lack. So, this story too has ended. We'll sleep more peacefully now that we no longer dream.

You say that now I'm loved by others. If it's so, then good for them. I deserve friendship, I deserve love—and you know this. I loved you and I still love you. I go to sleep and wake up with your name on my lips. I belong to you, bones and soul—and you know this. But you still prefer to be angry rather than give me the signs of love I regularly give you. This time I can't handle it, I give up. You won the game. And you lost your friend.

It was true when I said that I would help you whenever you needed it. But I said that before returning to Greece in September, before I saw that of the five weeks I stayed you only found five hours to spend with me. You will laugh, but I too have a bit of honor, Strato, and my honor suffered for your lack of interest, not even in some companionship, not making love even once, in all this time.

Whatever. Sorry that I dared complain. I remember and bless every moment we spent together. I kiss your mouth, your eyes, your face. May your child live long. And now you are forever relieved of

Jimmy

I've written it 4 times The sentence is written over another one that has been erased. [Translator's note]
{And you become all spite.} Crossed-out, but visible. [Translator's note]
honor This word, like "pride," translates *philotimo*. [Translator's note]

To David Jackson   WUSTL
                                                        7 April 1968
                                                      Stonington, CT

Davidako mou,

Sunday early afternoon. I'm going later to a poetry reading at the college (no one I've heard of) followed by supper at Wm's. Last night, a lovely roast chicken at Eleanor's. When I got back from Bun + NY (Bunny!) there was a ghastly letter from Grace full of scorn for the ballad, hatred of me, "you realize this is the end. . . . how can one have orange hair unless it's dyed. . . . you have certainly treated your beloved Morses abominably. . . . I will never trust you again and, sadder yet, never trust anybody else"—a marvelous document of which I believe next to nothing in spite of all the evidence. Luckily there was a lovely note from that attractive Peggy Yntema (we met her + her husband at E's) who is now a senior editor at the *Atlantic* (I had left the poem with Billy, thinking they might want it) who, without saying yes or no, said she adored it and thought it was as if Watteau had set out to paint a Primitive. Speaking of the *Atlantic*, I read over your story this morning and you know what? I like it <u>very</u> much. You've done some excellent work on it. Maybe it's partly that I miss you, but it now seems both plausible and gripping. I had one idea, tell me what you think: to put a brief paragraph at the very beginning, reading, perhaps: "More often than we think, in countries of whatever size, public upheavals shed light upon an individual dilemma. Let me tell you a story." Then let your first paragraph follow from that. This seems to underline the future importance of the "military takeover" you refer to in your opening sentence. It also (simply through the "me") becomes a strangely final + efficient removal of any remaining confusion between the author and Margaret. If you agree, send it back to me, written in your own words, and I will type out a new first page before trying to send it somewhere else. Billy still hasn't returned it; he's been in NY. He'll probably bring it with him when he comes to E. on Easter weekend. DK and Mary R are coming here.

Peter T came by yesterday afternoon for a reconciliation—though neither of us discussed the past. His wife is pregnant again—it's already a month or so overdue. Apparently the 2nd child was not born until <u>48</u> weeks after the doctor said she was pregnant ¡¡ a whole year's gestation. Somebody is writing a book about her.

A notice came from your bank, $1316.35 has been deposited, that should make you feel better. What makes me feel better is to be tipping the scales at 134.

I telephoned Claude this morning. As we might have known, another love affair (with "a very difficult person") has kept him incommunicado. He was on his way to hear Freddy preach. He may come down here for a weekend before long—precious few of those left free, what with one thing + another.

Mary wrote from Paris that she'd written you—they expect to get to Athens around 25 April. What on earth is G. thinking of, not moving into Chester's with you? Tell him he must answer to me if he doesn't. If he ever says that again about T. being the only friend who never propositioned him, ask him if by any chance he (G) propositioned T. first. That should get a rise. Strato's call. There's only one thing I want to know, which you can find out if brother K. comes by some day: my final letter to S. I sent it c/o Tony, Tony said he would forward it to Kosta to give to S.—did this in fact happen? I don't want S. pretending he never received it. I'll write K. c/o you from now on—probably enclose his letter in yours. It would be too confusing to have him coming for mail to the house while C + M are there.

I talked to Bernie, wished him godspeed. And last night had the oddest dream about him. He had died. Part of his body (like a thigh), partially embalmed was brought to us in a deep cardboard box, swarming somehow with corruption and life. Putting one's head in the box <u>with</u> the remains, however, one heard his voice distinctly announcing where he was—a kind of celestial suburb made up of 2 Latin names, where he did not know anybody but where everyone was very kind, the sun was shining, and people were (this is the only drawback) so prosperous that there was very little traffic in flesh. Could those Latin names be Ath. Efivon??? Time to shave and get dolled up.

Love you.
Jamie

Wm's William Meredith.
Bun David Kalstone.
the ballad Merrill's poem "The Summer People" in *The Fire Screen* (1969). It included humorously disparaging portraits of Grace Stone and Eleanor Perenyi.
Billy Billy Boatwright.
DK and Mary R David Kalstone and Mary Richie.
Freddy Buechner, ordained as a Presbyterian minister, lived across the valley from Claude Fredericks in Pawlet, VT.
Mary Mary McCarthy.
G. George Lazaretos.
T. Christos Alevras, or Taki. In the same paragraph "Kosta" is Strato's brother, and "Tony" is Tony Parigory.
C + M Charles and Mary Merrill. They were visiting Athens, and Merrill had promised them use of the house, requiring Jackson to relocate while they were there.

To David McIntosh

WUSTL
20–25 April 1968
Stonington, CT

My dear.

It is Wednesday. Tomorrow you are off, and will no longer be what
I think of, inaccurately, as within reach—for of course I can't reach
you, or would somehow intrude + perhaps displease you if I were to
try. Life has arranged, as it doesn't always do, some bizarre consola-
tions which can be felt, with shut eyes, to proceed obscurely from
you. Charlotte, for one, whose nature is clear, unmuddied, sparkling
like spring water in a child's cupped hands. She has had one of those
<u>successful</u> Catholic upbringings that keep her pure + unrebellious,
knowing everything without having had to learn it from experi-
ence. Her family are all theatre people in London (she has brothers
with names like Simon + Sebastian) so that she has seen it all as if
from a plush loge, a bit musty + threadbare, through big round eyes
unaware of how deeply they are discriminating. And then the cat. It
came upstairs yesterday afternoon and will not leave. She's gray with
paler markings, throat + belly of finest eggshell, and bluegreen eyes
that shade outward to lemon. Her purr is an ecstatic whimper and
she loves to be held and slept with. She also has unnatural prehensile
thumbs, prefers lobster to tongue, and already poses an emotional
problem quite out of proportion to her size or the length of our
affair—

These aren't, you know, the things I want to be saying to you. Only
a week ago you were on your way to me. I said we "knew" what that
evening held in store, but truly I didn't know, didn't know at all. I
miss you beyond words. Perhaps this evening at the Reeves' there
will be talk of your coming back East in the fall. But if you don't, and
if you wanted me near you for a little while, I—well, you "know" or
should if you have read this far, know what I would do. David. Oh
dear, it <u>is</u> Wednesday and the shrink is coming from New Haven to
drink from <u>these</u> old cupped hands. Enough, I love you, David.

Thursday now, and you are on your way in all this wind + sun, the
good Saint round your neck. I feel at peace for you, after last night's
storm, and for myself. These evenings here have all been floated on

music, things unheard for years, some of them, ending at full flood
with the Lehmann-Schumann *Rosenkavalier* + (by utter seeming inad-
vertence) that Schubert song with the clarinet we had heard a week
before, to the very hour. It woke something in Charlotte, she had to
stop sketching and hide her eyes, and I had to stop being sketched
and hide mine, perhaps the 1st week of a separation is the most pain-
ful after all, for today we have been merry, she has painted a new chair
an odd + excellent blackish yellow, there was shad at the fish market,
and the world in short has steadied itself. Let me end this letter on
that note. With 1 or 2 perhaps superfluous reassurances. These aren't
things I'm used to saying or feeling, and I believe (though one under-
stands about the cup + the lip, and the mirages that both love and its
absence give rise to) that I mean them with all my heart. I'm not spe-
cially a fan of the Italians, but there are nice things in their language.
When they mean to say "I love you" they say in fact, "I wish you well."
Ti voglio bene. Bless you now + always.

James

How times change! Gosh,
Thirty years ago
Nobody I know
Knew David McIntosh.

David McIntosh See Biographies.
Charlotte Charlotte Hafley (b. 1938), a British artist in Atlanta; married to Bruce
Hafley (1920–2011), a portrait painter who later painted Merrill.
the Reeves' F. D. Reeve (1928–2013), poet, critic, Russian translator, and professor
at Wesleyan University, and his wife, Helen Schmidinger.
the shrink Dr. Albert Rothenberg (b. 1930), a psychiatrist at Yale, visited Merrill
regularly for several years at Merrill's apartment in Stonington to discuss his dreams
and the composition process of his poems. His work with Merrill was the basis for
an anonymous case study in Rothenberg's *The Emerging Goddess: The Creative Process
in Art, Science, and Other Fields* (1979).
Lehmann-Schumann *Rosenkavalier* A 1933 abridged recording of Richard Strauss's
Der Rosenkavalier (1910), in which Lotte Lehmann sang the Marschallin and Elisa-
beth Schumann sang Sophie.

To Donald Richie   WUSTL
                                                           29 April 1968
                                                          Stonington, CT

Dear Donald—

No no, I'd better avail myself of the machine because I may have lots
+ lots to say. Oh how strange life is! I've gone + done it again—fallen
in love (I must have been right about 2nd adolescence) and this time
it is with somebody "real" all the way down the line to his being even
a painter, and Intense as well as handsome. Is there such a thing as
a real painter, though? Actually, he is not real at all, I know him so
little + he is so quiet + goodlooking. He is in fact shrouded in mystery,
a mystery that is not helped by his being at this very moment in a
car going through Ohio en route to New, then Old Mexico where I
am going to follow him either next month or early in June (delaying
Greece some 10 days) so as not to start my embroidery on a virtually
nonexistent canvas. For the first time this is something I feel I cannot
tell DJ. He is so hectic + unhappy in Greece, and we do after all know
all about the cup + the lip, do we not. The painter is also named David
(McIntosh) and his father is a cowboy in Wyoming. DM is 30 today.
I saw him last at a huge blacktie dinner in Middletown Conn (where
smiles of sickly but hurtable intent were being beamed at him by Ste-
phen Spender, in fact I had to leave them on the street together, but
that's all right too, I am practically an Older Man myself)—a dinner
for which I was dressed 3 hours in advance, as for one's first prom. Oh
silly—all these complications, tequila here I come!

   A letter from Tex today—I see a copy has been sent to you. My sil-
liness goes so far as to wish he would simply use the blurb I sent, into
whose phrasing a certain degree of care was put, rather than reword
it, fill its disconnected (by him) phrases with dots, all for the sake
of—I gather from his letter—making it a trifle ampler. That can be
done by a larger type-face, placement on the page, all those things he
must know about. I don't want to sound fussy in a note to him. But
I thought you might mention it to him, as if it were your own idea,
and suggest that he print it as it stands. Whatever else they want to
say can be put outside the quotation marks. I know you'll think I'm

right, even though it makes little or no difference, but we "crafts-men" must stand together against the editorial neurosis.

An angelically sweet + pretty English girl has been staying here— left this noon after 8 days. She is married to an Atlanta painter. We adored each other on sight so what did she do but leave him with the 2 babies and come to stay? After the first 2 days in which there was some innocent confusion (she is a pure convent girl without so much as premarital experimentation with her husband, let alone any other man in her life before or since) as to the course our affection might take, we had a lovely, lovely time. When I got back from Middletown (she had been to Boston that day) at 2:30 a.m. she woke up—"Jimmy! Tell me <u>all</u>! Did you <u>see</u> your friend? Were you able to <u>talk</u>?"—and I pretended to tell her all about it. So sweet. The whole town was madly impressed—Eleanor, the Lesbian faction, even the grocer who cannot speak of her without a funny sort of aw-shucks blush. Now she is going to make her husband rent a house here for a year. Life . . . it never ends, does it?

I leave you now, my dear. I'll let you know what happens. You let <u>me</u> know, too, will you? About yourself, about everything?

> Love always,
> [*no signature*]

Tex Meredith Weatherby.
the blurb Merrill's blurb for Richie's *Companions of the Holiday*, published in 1968 by Walker/Weatherhill, Weatherby's publishing company.

To David McIntosh

WUSTL
20 May 1968
New Brunswick, NJ

Dear David—

I am in New Brunswick at David K.'s (he is at a faculty meeting and has just called to say he'll be delayed). Masses of green outside. This morning early—we had gone for the night to our beloved Morses in Bedford Hills—after one of those by now quite involuntary half-waking colloquies with you, I went out into their garden, sunny, windless, glittering with moisture: the lilacs only slightly rusted, the pink dogwood in its glory, tulips frosty with dew, and the great Chinese peonies easily a foot in diameter, their petals a dazzling crinkled white—and all of these, like those flowers that talk in the 1st song of the *Dichterliebe*, speaking to me of you; as everything does, these days. The air was full of seeds downspinning, fluttering petals, & my heart like still water. I began thinking once again of your pictures, and I thought I understood why I was drawn to them. Can I explain it, I wonder? It has to do with your choice (or so it strikes me) of images that allow, as it were, at the center of the canvas some live & energetic emptiness—felt not as a lack but as a virtue—like a spirit rightly unidentifiable within its sensual perimeter: your wave, your dustcloud, your blank blue sky that already has partly dissolved the window it is seen through—as in a line of Stevens, "Eye without lid, mind without any dream" or like a mirror not at the moment being looked into; the Subject treated as the final absence of a subject. I do not know how near or far I am to your own feeling, but I believe that this is a crucial stage in the evolution of any serious artist—and I began to remember poems I wrote 10 or 12 years ago, and to see them as occasions for an intense play of language on a level at which the "subject" is, strictly speaking, immaterial. I felt I had understood something extraordinarily intimate about you, and wanted to tell you so, even at the risk of phrasing it carelessly. I think that even what Mr Canaday said about fashions is essential to what you are doing, as it is to me. At this "stage" I speak of, it seems that one must use techniques that are no longer popular or explosive, in the interest of a secrecy by which one masters oneself before there can be any real desire to master one's audience. Your willow half-lost in the elements—it is precisely with that kind of reticence that the things one knows begin to enter what one does . . .

I have never wanted to speak of these things to anyone. Perhaps I could not do so to another writer—they would get a bit grimy with particulars. What I could learn from you, though (oops, here's David back, now he's gone downstairs with his houseplants) seems endlessly rich & real. What you might learn from me I can't imagine— I'm something of a waterbug, skating upon the depths—but love does learn & love does teach, and love supplies even the most ordinary person with a wizard's hat & wand, and these lessons are not found in books.

Bye now.

1st song of the *Dichterliebe* "Im wunderschönen Monat Mai" (In the wonderfully beautiful month of May). See Merrill to David Kalstone, 19 April 1967.
a line of Stevens From "It Must Change," section II in *Notes Toward a Supreme Fiction* (1942).
Mr Canaday John Canaday (1907–85), American art critic, appreciative of the Old Masters and critical of contemporary movements, especially abstract expressionism.

To David McIntosh

POSTCARD | WUSTL
6 August 1968
Athens, Greece

woof!
    grrrrr. . . .
    bow-wow?

To David McIntosh

WUSTL
12 August 1968
Athens, Greece

Dearest of Davids,

I cannot tell you how much it meant—on our return yesterday from Zakynthos (an Adriatic island whose pretty Venetian harbor, leveled 15 years ago by an earthquake, has been rebuilt in poured concrete)— to see, out of the corner of an eye, your handwriting among the letters on the table. A quiet + ever so slightly dizzying happiness came over me. I brought in the bags + towels, read a letter from David K (who is pretty dear himself, having gone all the way to Southampton + back to see a play of mine in summer stock) and one from Eleanor, took a bath, made coffee, and lay down with your envelopes beside me. I feared them, I trusted them, I even—finally—opened them.

About your solitariness, of course, I had known, and understood, and applauded. I could feel you gently smiling at all my little ruses to get you to say what you had already said so well by saying nothing. As you've seen, I went so far as not to write myself, which was difficult + sad for me, and no doubt childish as well. But my motive, insofar as it was pure, had been simply to <u>let</u> <u>you</u> <u>be</u>; not to be (myself) in the ranks of those who are forever plucking your solitude by the sleeve; not to resemble that ghastly Eye in Tolkien, roving every crevice of the landscape for the small stouthearted Ring-Bearer whose stillness, dappled by foliage or trembling with the heatwaves that rise from the riverbed, might otherwise have been less than absolute. But I knew that you couldn't think that of me—you simply couldn't!—and therefore knew that something else had happened. You were in a coma, or in a prison cell, or on a white yacht under a black flag, and much too far from shore for my toy opera glasses to read the labels on those ceaselessly popping bottles—no: I knew that something had happened to upset you, and now that your letter confirms it, and tells me that it has passed, I'm doing my best not to imagine what form it took, + to be happy with you in the knowledge that you are where you want to be, and at work after so long. David, your letters bring me more than I could have dreamed to ask. I'm so touched that my letters please you, that the days in Kelly keep their magic for you as well; touched by everything you've cared to tell me about your work and state of mind. Your silence had been precious enough, even in those moments when my own selfishness chose to be pained by it (and, full of scorn for exotic verse-forms, nevertheless wrote a haiku on the subject: No coffin without / Nails. These you drive into mine / At least are golden.)—but your words are bread + air. As for the photographs—oh my.

I've been at work too, though a slump usually comes when I finish something. Our Kelly poem has undergone a number of changes— notably the reduction to a dependant clause of that rather smug + vulgar passage about the love that dares not speak its name—and I like it far more than I did. You'll read it while I look at the Painting you've done. Then I finished a set of 8 "entertaining" sonnets, begun a year ago for David K, about opera-going. Now suddenly my time here is short. Although Bayreuth fell through, I'm going to Vienna on the 15th to spend 5 days with Chester Kallman + Auden. The former will give me enough to eat + drink so that for once (I trust) I'm not turned to stone by the latter's brilliant + unanswerable discourse. I saw Chester first 20 years ago, white + gold + willowy across a theatre lobby. "That person," said Meredith, "has the most untenable position in all Fairyland." Now he is puffy, bleary, sagging + humped over, a Jewish Mother inside and out. I mean I dote on him, though once in a while I wish he would say something I didn't understand.

On my return I'll have to see Kosta once again. We've talked on the phone, the last conversation left him in tears. I am ashamed to tell you the kind of lie I permitted him to fabricate—or maybe I did tell you: that he was engaged to my nonexistent sister Monica, who at once stepped fullgrown, as from an Antonioni film, into the minds of all concerned, blonde, blowsy, expressionless, heels calloused by the straps of her patent-leather pumps, a gum-chewing Embassy secretary who would marry K. as soon as her divorce came through. It seemed so funny at the time—that was the phase in whose utter misery I could see no qualitative difference whatever between fantasy + truth. Galloping Pirandellosis. Anyhow, we agreed that she must die. That very minute she collided with a truck, the steering-wheel pierced her spleen, and six days afterwards she expired with his name on her lips. Kosta at least did not have to dissimulate his chagrin, only its cause; but I would have liked to spare his mother the tears that in the goodness of her heart she has been shedding ever since. A kinder + truer solution would have been to turn Monica into a bitch, involve her with a Lower East Side gigolo, and let poor Sophia be indignant rather than unwittingly blasphemous, lighting candles for the soul of a defunct joke. But the milk's spilt, the last lie of my life—I hope!—told + swallowed. It leaves a nasty aftertaste. There's some dull comfort in the reflection that family life here is a tissue of just such daydreams + distortions + withheld essentials. One hates to lend oneself to it, is all. <u>No</u>. It's not at all. It's a matter of good vs. bad faith, and I ought to have known better. Life's not long enough for all there is to learn.

I'm glad you like the music. There's a record of the Mahler in the house, and I stumble through the *Winterreise* accompaniments on the piano every week or so—extraordinary how telling those stark little tunes are. Athens is emptying, the nephews have flown away, Philip Johnson came + went, Mme Kleo is going (along with 250,000 pious others) to celebrate the Assumption on Tinos. How she does it we'll never know. She can't read, she doesn't know where anything is. Last year David wrote the address in Piraeus on a scrap of paper to show the taxi-driver. When she arrived at the boat she forced her way through the crush to a ticket counter crying "Mr David told me to come here"—and to our total astonishment it worked: thousands were being turned away, but she was waved up the gangplank. She expects the same thing will happen this year, and who knows? maybe it will.

Enough for now. My arms around you, my cheek against yours. October.

James

a play of mine *The Immortal Husband* (1955).
Eye in Tolkien The eye of Sauron, the omniscient villain in J. R. R. Tolkien's *The Lord of the Rings* (1954).
days in Kelly Merrill and McIntosh met in Kelly, Wyoming, in June.
a haiku Merrill published the poem under the title "A Silence" in *The Yellow Pages* (1971).
Our Kelly poem "In Nine Sleep Valley," a poem with nine sections, representing the nine days of the Kelly trip.
smug + vulgar passage A draft section cut from the poem, in which Merrill talked about McIntosh and himself putting aside sexual desire for each other.
8 "entertaining" sonnets "Matinées," dedicated to David Kalstone, in *The Fire Screen* (1969).
Pirandellosis Luigi Pirandello's *Six Characters in Search of an Author* (1921) attacked the theatrical "fourth wall" with its boundary between the illusory and the real.
Philip Johnson (1906–2005), American architect.
Assumption on Tinos The feast of the Assumption on August 15, an important holiday in Greece, marked by a pilgrimage to the island of Tinos to see an Icon of the Virgin Mary.

To David McIntosh

WUSTL
21 August 1968
Athens, Greece

David my dear—

You've been ill and I wasn't there to make broths for you. Such a miserable business—mumps—and painful + dangerous too. Can one catch it from prairie dogs? Did you receive a delegation of infected children? No, but you must be very careful. Is there a doctor within reach, + are you doing what he says? I had the same thing my first week at college, only it went (as they say) "downstairs". One testicle swelled up to about 7 times its normal size, then shrank. And shrank, and shrank. To something the size + texture of a half-cooked black-eyed pea. So take care, won't you? And send 2 lines, a card, anything to let me know if you are well. I'll be worrying. Surely by now the worst is over. But I worry.

The letter that greeted me returning from Vienna last night was colored (I fancied) by your having been ill. My dear, you have not hurt me or failed me in any way. Hush! The very thought! I wouldn't dream of wanting you to be "red smoke + lava", or of seeing you as "mist + snow." You are first of all God's child, my beloved DMc, human in flesh + spirit, and as such could fail me only by conscious bad faith. Metaphorically you are (as an old song put it) my sunshine, a cool spring sun if you like, a sun with ice in its veins, but one by which I might hope to see + read + bud + wither till the end of my days. Still, you have put your finger on something—that "vein of tension" in these letters + in the poem, and which you also felt in Kelly. It exists, but needn't, I think, alarm you. It has to do with my knowing how little time is given us (was or will be given us), with my fear of being too dull or too complex or too old, or of revealing, through shyness, too much or too little of myself; all of which is no doubt present in letters, and apt to recur in October. It may be (he said with a rueful smile) <u>the</u> difference between Love + Friendship. I can only hope that I am perfectly housebroken in this respect, + that you will draw when-ever necessary—as more than once in the cabin—that firm + gentle line. The subject would be of no interest, a small squiggly piece in my puzzle, if it didn't interlock with the act of writing. For language by nature deals directly + dramatically with times and places remote from what's at hand, with the layers that underlie whatever one finds oneself doing—as if those tensions you speak of literally became tenses, pasts + futures, on the page. To me at least it is rather less mysterious than the transformation of experience—past, present, or future—into the eternal Present of a painting. Those are the secrets <u>you</u> know, secrets which in their turn profoundly interlock with a peculiar piece in your own puzzle, whose shape I would not change for all the world. The line, for instance, that upsets you most in our poem—about fearing that you will tell me something—is perhaps the most direct <u>and</u> the most artificial of them all. The feeling it grew out of came + went, as feelings will, leaving just the words to vibrate by themselves—as words will. That poem, I mean, is not written <u>to</u> you, David, in the sense that this letter is. Though it addressed you, don't forget that pronouns like You or I or We are also deep in the nature of language, and help bring it to life. It is <u>for</u> you—it couldn't have been written without what you showed me by way of landscape and happiness and, yes, tension. Don't take it too personally: as a gift, if you will; as a message, no. Now if you are alarmed that others may see it in print and draw conclusions, that's another matter, and I should entirely respect your instinct here. In that sense the poem <u>is</u> yours. When you read it (revised) in October you will tell me if I am to rumple it like the 2nd bed in Kelly, with new + misleading clues, or put it in a drawer for 50 years. I would do so with a light heart.

Yesterday morning I saw the great Vermeer—under restoration when we were in Vienna 10 years ago. Within a quarter hour it took its place among the wonders of the world. When I was little my mother used to say that there was an animal heaven where pets went after death. Lawns for dogs to romp on, canary forests, pools full of guppies—it seemed plausible + consoling at the time. Vermeer makes you believe in a heaven for things + textures—cracked leather, brass, paper, silk, + yarn. You couldn't choose (and luckily don't have to) between the woman's hand + the black wooden spindle just below it. The two chairs are enough to send you to your knees, they've been so used, so seen, so utterly sanctified. I felt like singing with joy when I saw, in the upper right hand corner, barely visible, the lightly painted tangle of untrimmed threads: the back of the tapestry! as if to say, in the softest of voices, that no miracle is separable from its humble accidents, its seamy side. The genius of Vermeer (or is it the genius of any painter?) struck me as a highly personal selection of the exact point in distance at which the surface no longer "represents" but disappears into sheer brushwork + color; at which one no longer "reads" the young woman's glistening lip—only those 3 little moons of clearest pink spaced across its brownish rose; a step forward, a step back, and the device becomes one with the illusion. The way Vermeer does it, though, makes even wonderful Pieter de Hooch seem naïf and wonderful Franz Hals seem showy by comparison. It can't just be a moment in history—it's all too much a labor of love. The painting within the painting makes that clear, I felt. The artist has only arrived at his model's crown of leaves, the topmost of her allegorical attributes—all bestowed upon her by a mixture of convention, caprice, + necessity. The real test (I thought at first) would come presently, in the rendering of the human element, in what he would make of <u>her</u> (always supposing that he loves her); but of course the point is that he will take no more + no less pains with her face than he has taken with her crown or will take with her book + her horn. It's all one for his purposes, just as he himself, for Vermeer's, is one with her + the arras + the shadow on the floor + the chair's brass studs. That is a mask lying face-up on the table. And a map of Holland—the "real" world?—rippling + cracking on the wall. I wished for you then + there. I wish for you now + here.

I'm in Athens another 2 weeks—until, oh, the 5th or 6th of September. Please let me know how you are.

> Ti voglio bene—
> James

The line From "In Nine Sleep Valley," section 5, in *Braving the Elements* (1972): "the fear / That you will tell me what I live to hear."
the great Vermeer *The Artist in His Studio* by Johannes Vermeer in the Kunsthistorisches Museum in Vienna

To David McIntosh

WUSTL
6 September 1968
Stonington, CT

David—

A few bare lines to say that I got back in spite of pile-ups + traffic patterns, not much the worse for wear. The house looks rather dingy, mirrors dusty, an old glacier in the deep freeze quite unperceived by dear myopic David K—but a joy nonetheless to find so many things in place (the votive glass, the rocks from Kelly!) and sink down among them. I went to the Stone Women last night, and go to the Morses this evening to have my <u>other</u> ear filled with—no: the Morses don't revile their loved ones, and the Ladies are too old to take a leaf from that book. DK comes back for a few days tomorrow. So far we've only talked on the phone. Outdoors is dingier yet—warm, overcast. I wonder if I recognize faces on the street . . .

Are you well? I hope so. Those ten sedentary days should be up by now, + you with them, up and about. I wish I could call you, but I can't—and as you say, one doesn't get the electricity by telephone.

Reading Dickens kept me quiet during the days before leaving, and on the plane. A genius in the medium of stiff paper, like those penny theatres one can still buy in London + put together with scissors + paste at home. He will present a character (like Mrs Lammle in *Our Mutual Friend*) in utter flatness at first. She is the Mature Young Lady with powdered shoulders at the Veneerings' first dinner. Then she marries an equally flat character, and it emerges that they are both fortune-hunters under the mutually false impression of having made a good match. This leads them quickly to anger + bitterness + (2 pages later) the resolve to work in unison for their own fortune—a second, purely conventional identity set, however, at a perceptible angle to the first. A third wing is applied much later in the book when Mrs L pleads with a virtual stranger to frustrate a plot in which she + her husband are accomplices—and suddenly, it's done! That woman's spirit stands up by itself, in depth, entirely artificial + entirely convincing, realer than life. Surrounding it all, like the darkened auditorium, is an extraordinary pessimism regarding human nature—in those last novels at least, where even the figures most beloved of their author move like marionettes in settings that are deeper + moodier + more "humanized" than themselves. What are people thinking when they give him to their children to read!

I suppose I must go out now + take part in a series (finite, luckily) of double-takes. Eventually I'll go to NY for a day or so, and to my brother in Boston, but in principle I'm here until Oct 5 or 6 when I would go to NY for some days with my mother before driving out to St Louis. That's if you want me with you in October. My stint in St L begins on the 27th. Count backwards from that day and tell me when it would suit you for me to come; or if the last week of Nov is better. I see I am free as of the 23rd. Please be indulgent of my fatal addiction to plan-making.

Ever your
James

My stint in St L Merrill was the Fannie Hurst Visiting Poet at Washington University in St. Louis for three weeks in fall 1968.

To Stephen Yenser   YALE
18 October 1968
Stonington, CT

Dear Stephen,

Boris Gudonov is dying to the saddest sounds, made keener + sadder I suspect by a 4th drink here at my side. I'm afraid, though, that unless I send you a few lines now the thread will snap. So here goes *Ariadne auf Naxos* as background for a brief bulletin.

The return from Greece, effectuated a good 6 weeks ago, seems barely to have occurred. Long spells of staring out the window, or at a half-typed page, withdrawal of time-sense—as if space + time <u>were</u> linked like the physicists say they are. The weather is partly at fault: one flawless day after another, the leaves have all turned red or yellow but none has fallen, no wind blows, you feel that only a declaration of war will set things right. Of course where you are Season doesn't exist, but surely you remember how things are meant to be—sun, then rain, then cold + snow, am I wrong? Walking in my sleep I managed to put a new book together, actually got it out of the house and into the arms of Atheneum. This is always a depressing moment, but more than ever in the present instance because I truly don't <u>like</u> the poems, most of them; it's as if someone else had written them and left them like changelings on the desk. What one does in such a case is anyone's guess. A stronger nature would put them on the fire, but I am weak + publish. And now in only 42 hours I must load the car with all the old Madison equipment—phonograph + turtlenecks—and drive out to St Louis for a month's "residence." They give me a house, at least, and I don't have <u>any</u> courses—all I can think to do is give parties. It ends before Thanksgiving, at which point it looks like I'll fly to Santa Fe à la recherche de last June's Happiness. If only someone had told me at an impressionable age: NEVER live in the future!—but it's too late to change and, besides, those big empty rooms are irresistible + the view breathtaking.

Do you really know Old English? Does it help? Our local wit (Andrew in the ballad) produced a little map he had drawn between meals the other day, made up of such topographical features as Robber Barrens, Widow's Peak, Loch Smith, Chicago Copse, Bouche Bay, Pratt Falls, Slow Burn, Mosquito Bight—and of course Grendel's Dam; it was all I could do to recognize the allusion. Without having read a line, I've come to think of the author of *Beowulf* as a notch or two below whoever decorated the caves at Lascaux; wasn't he, I mean, one of those who simply <u>missed</u> <u>the</u> <u>point</u> by being, through no fault of his, utterly provincial? while that painter ten (or 50?) thousand years earlier had lived without reference to any point missable. I see I had better stop. And wait for "piquancy." Now finish that dissertation. Is Lorna painting—decorating the cave? I miss you both.

Yours ever,
James

Stephen Yenser See Biographies.
Boris Gudonov Title character, misspelled, in Mussorgsky's opera *Boris Godunov* (1873).
where you are Los Angeles.
a new book *The Fire Screen* (1969).
Our local wit Robert Morse.
that dissertation Yenser's dissertation was revised and published as *Circle to Circle: The Poetry of Robert Lowell* (1975).
Lorna Lorna Roberts, Yenser's wife, a painter.

To Judith Moffett

Dear Judy,

With everyone writing by return mail, the old planet spins like a
head. I have a very sore throat + flickers of fever down my spine +
arms, but such moments (like you with your codeine) bring their own
clarity. In today's I perceive, not without dismay, and not for the first
time either, that I must be a deeply insensitive person. It truly had
not occurred to me that you had suffered a "collapse" of anything
except your ability to go on in that particular job. And while you are
good enough to thank me for the "restful, commonsensical" tone of
my letter, it is a slight mortification to know that one has acted like
an octogenarian from whom Catastrophe elicits, at most, a regret-
ful clicking of the tongue. (Before the mail came my New Mexico
friend had telephoned. He is in Chicago having tests—an eye infec-
tion that will not clear up. Can you imagine a biopsy on the eyeball,
with stitches + everything? I couldn't, evidently. All I could talk about
were the dinner parties I would have to excuse myself from in order
to go see him, unless he's able to come down here—isn't that awful?)
Luckily most people with <u>real</u> <u>feelings</u> would put this down to wis-
dom of a sort: not to fan the fire by accepting the sufferer's own view
of his plight. And there may just be a grain of truth here. I couldn't
possibly leap to Lionel's conclusion. Group therapy is bound to be . . .
what? interesting? helpful? But these are qualities it shares with life
itself. And in the latter one is a degree or so freer to choose one's own
group. This of course isn't the last word on g.t. The grain of truth is
outweighed by whole <u>ounces</u> of evidence to the contrary. Still, no one
can ever be sure that, in the 2 years or however much time one gives
to therapy, Living on one's own, without recourse to those artifices,
would not produce the same results. You are an uncommon + highly-
strung person. Life has spun you round + round and left you (as in a
game of "statues" holding what would be for many of us an unten-
able position. Naturally the idea of <u>changing</u> appalls. When I was
closeted in misery a couple of years ago, the worst part almost was
that crack of light under the door. I <u>did</u> <u>not</u> <u>like</u> the person I should

become once I was out of the closet. To be in a group of people bent on modifying their own positions might reconcile you more easily to how the self survives these modifications. What I've mainly been alert to in your last 2 letters is that note of wanting to be among people who will "let" you love them. This is a dream that you + I share, from time to time, and it is a . . . wrong dream. One wrongs oneself, one wrongs whoever one loves, one wrongs whoever is ready to love you in <u>his</u> way. No accident, I think, that this onesided loving finds its finest flowering in mysticism where Jesus or Gautama are luminously present whenever we want them (which is all the time)—but human objects are less pliant, less forgiving, less tickled by <u>being</u> loved; they know that loving is the indispensible condition, and if they sniff out that all you want to do is love + not let them love back, well, they have mixed feelings. I'm talking mainly about myself here—the Great Lover in person—so if this old shoe doesn't fit just give it away with all the clothes you're leaving behind.

You don't have to answer it either.

It looks like I'm not going to New Mexico. My friend will be back there before long, but will have to be staying with friends within reach of a clinic for some time. So I may get East in time for the ritual Thanksgiving with Robert + Isabel—except that Robert is in the hospital with hepatitis; well, East, in any case.

Just take tranquilizers for a day or so before you fly, + keep remembering how BORING it is going to be.

Love,
Jimmy

my New Mexico friend David McIntosh.
Lionel's conclusion Moffett had written a friend about a breakdown she was having, and he wrote back that "the only reasonable thing to do" was to begin group therapy immediately.

To David McIntosh

My dear—

There is not much to tell since this morning except that it is now evening, I've had a drink or two, and my ears are filled with music. In NY I bought a really extravagant phonograph—it took up, along with the Xmas champagne, the entire car—and discovered about an hour ago that I could (and had!) put most of its parts together with sinister ease. The sound is ravishing, too ravishing. The speakers may have to face <u>into</u> corners like children who have been vulgar + noisy . . . was it a wise step? As for the 18 year old, the delinquent, the resident machine with its single tubercular speaker, the rest is silence. Its farewell performance was of *The Magic Flute*, an appropriately ancient + scratchy recording. Little Martha Hollander whom I'd taken last Saturday with her mother to *Simon Boccanegra* had shown what <u>she</u> thought of Verdi's middle period by going to the piano before her coat was even off, at home, and picking out one of the bird-catcher's childlike songs. I knew right then I'd have to hear the whole wonderful thing, though I've never dared see it since the performances in Salzburg, summer of 1950, done in the baroque Riding Academy against a rock wall—the mountain itself—carved with niches—and these on occasion filled by the Queen of the Night's torchbearing ladies. On the stage, plinths, garlands, sunbursts. The audience, looking very elegant + international, sat under a tent where also a bird or two might flutter through on the off-chance of being caught by Papageno. Furtwängler conducted, and I heard Irmgard Seefried for the first time. It was the summer when the Korean war appeared a most ominous affair. One's mother's letters dripped with atrocity rumors—what the Chinese would do to us tourists when they overran Western Europe later in the fall—and to please therefore arrange to have some money in Lisbon in order to get home before the world was blown up—so that you can imagine the effect of Sarastro grave + smiling stepping up to us to sing his music of peace and friendship, those disciplines of humanity at once warm + rigorous, against which the comic characters and even the ignorant evil ones could shine with a flowerlike beauty of their own . . . How pompous I am: "never dared to see it since then"—when I would go to see it in the Stonington High School!—that divinely anonymous music, quite beyond personality, that music <u>about</u> the power of music to undo evil. In the little Mozart museum were simple wooden chairs, so fragile, whose weight could they have borne? And bare white walls, and a late portrait of Wolfgang, unfinished, in strong snuff colors, eyes huge + charged with some kind of pain, on the threshold of immortality.

Now I am listening to *Lulu* in full 12-dimensional sound. Luckily it is a score I scarcely know, so much of its awfulness is over my head . . . I talked a while ago to David J whose ship has left Nassau + will reach NY by early Thursday morning. Thank goodness he doesn't need to be met because the car won't be ready in time.

Morning, bright + windless. I feel that we've been talking all night in my sleep; frightened + worried, both of us, but together, too. The flute in the flames, the flute in the flood. There is a treatise to be written about the harmful distortions of seeing whatever happens as Symbol or Allegory. And another in reply, to prove that there is no comfort in events, only in their interpretation. Big thoughts at 8 a.m. Back to deciding whether <u>the</u> or <u>a</u> is best in a line about a tablecloth.

James

the Korean war The war began on June 25, 1950.
Sarastro High Priest of the Sun (a bass) in Mozart's *The Magic Flute*, to whose concluding aria Merrill alludes.
Lulu Opera by Alban Berg (1885–1935), left incomplete at his death; its first two recordings in stereo appeared in 1968.

To Stephen Yenser YALE
17 December 1968
Stonington, CT

Dear Stephen,

Your letter finds me here, if anything does. Actually it beat me by about a week. Meanwhile I've had to go back to NYC for some days + drove up "for good" only yesterday—the car breaking down <u>in</u> the carport to be repaired at some distant date because the garage man's father has just been decapitated in a turnpike collision, and, well . . . On all sides the cells of Christmas are horribly multiplying, nothing diminishes except the cast of characters. We'll be five at table this year and there are moments when it seems like four too many.

On the very good chance that I didn't write you from St Louis, let me report (even if redundantly) that it's very nice there. I was given a typical St L house, which is to say enormous, all dark wood + stained glass from an era when it must have been a lost art. But room after room!—some I never found time to sit down in. Far cry from that dismal place in Madison. And the dining out, never a free evening. It has aged me dreadfully. The students were dear good souls, none of them excessively bright, or maybe <u>those</u> stayed out of contagion's reach. The high point was perhaps an hour spent visiting a class that had been prepared by reading 6 or 8 poems (mine, but who could have told?) asked me questions. Not, Why did you use that word? but What is your Position? or Does the poet have a Role in Society? By the time this last one came I was so rattled that I heard a loud voice from somewhere inside say: Yes he does; it is NOT TO PARTICIPATE—and the stunned silence that staircase wit told me I could have filled with images of Henry James on his park bench in Jacksonville, Fla. resounded instead with crowing cocks + clocks striking the end of civilization as we know it. Probably did 'em good. Dickey is there this month—different noises. It may all be too close to Kansas to amuse you + Lorna (when she is good + sick from Durrell's sticky liqueurs, have her try *The Towers of Trebizond* by Rose Macaulay at 80—the driest champagne) but I thoroughly enjoyed it. None of the grad. students had that hunted, overworked look you recognized them by in Madison. Santa Fe boiled down to six beautiful + harrowing days. The friend I visited has slowly, in spite of all that medicine can do, been losing the sight of an eye over the last months—being a painter it matters dreadfully. The house was a 4-room Pullman car of adobe. Swans lived in the pond below, or on it, mornings when it had frozen; and there were peacocks traipsing about through a kind of brush called chamiso with dry pale gold flowers. To have brought home stones in June and feathers in December—the poem all but writes itself . . . Ah yes, Mary Ellen wrote, but those people aren't in my ken. I hope you'll send those "slight offbeat things" in your next letter, even if music comes to seem the only art. In St Louis I saw the Olivier *Othello* + spent the next week drowning my impression of it in Verdi's which is a masterpiece of equal magnitude with considerably more cohesion + verve. I am listening to it right now. It is beautiful (and painful) <u>beyond</u> <u>words</u>. Bon. Merry X etc to you both.

As ever,
James

Henry James . . . Jacksonville, Fla. See the pages involving that city in James's *The American Scene*, his book of impressions of the United States after his return to his native country.
Dickey American poet James Dickey (1923–97).
too close to Kansas Yenser was born in Kansas and earned his BA from the University of Wichita.
Durrell's sticky liqueurs Lawrence Durrell's tetralogy of novels, The *Alexandria Quartet* (1957–60).
the poem "Under Libra: Weights and Measures" in *Braving the Elements* (1972).
a 4-room Pullman car In "Florida," the last chapter of *The American Scene* (1907), James moves from a view from the park bench to that framed by "the great moving proscenium of the Pullman."
Mary Ellen Yenser's friend Mary Ellen Stagg Capek.

To David McIntosh

WUSTL
14 January 1969
Stonington, CT

My dear—

Today began in that state of complete emptiness following a festive evening—as if the last glass had been drained + left to dry precariously upside down on morning's sunny ledge. I must say it <u>was</u> a nice evening. Just the Reeves + Eleanor + us. I made chicken along the lines of that Chinese duck—first simmered in a soy broth with ginger + garlic + Five Precious Spices, then cooled, dried, coated with a mixture of cornstarch + ground walnuts, and deepfried to a color + a succulence indescribable, served on a bed of chopped lettuce. And Chinese broccoli in a glaze of oyster sauce. One hates to gloat but my, it was good. Franklin + Helen were in marvelous form, funny + quick + ablaze with health. It brought out the best in Eleanor, who purred + arched her back + never once showed her claws—so that suddenly it was a quarter past one and we were all still at table drinking the nth round of raspberry liqueur on the rocks with K. 271 in the background. I couldn't imagine, when I woke up, doing anything all day but sit in sunny silence—yet here it is now, 4:30, I've been working ever since lunch and think that I have somehow solved the poem that has come out of the time in Nambé. It's still a bit tenuous (on one hand) and clever (on the other) but the hardest part is over. The psychiatrist who has resumed his weekly visits is the only person who has seen anything of it—yellow pages scrawled with lines in pencil or different color inks—and I was glad I'd showed it to him if only because he [asked] a question so obvious I never thought to ask it of myself: "What other associations do you have with stones + feathers?"—and it was as if one strand of an intricate, airy web had been twitched, I remembered my mother's account of how I'd been terrified as a very little child by her room full of floating feathers (a pillow had come apart); and then a dream in which a number of large + beautiful stones belonging to my father had been turned into pens (penna, the Latin word for feather) which I should one day be able to write with; and even a little dream I dreamed in Nambé, that I was on a visit to a man + wife whom I dearly loved—and just as the interrelation of those mere 3 details is beyond words, so is the reassurance that even in a poem like this which I'm trying to keep "pure"—without personality or incident—my whole self is present, like it or not.

Tonight we're by ourselves, thank goodness. I must have ten letters to write—and no heart for writing them but (hours later) I have ground out 4 or 5, awkwardly, like somebody enrolled in a crash course at Berlitz, who cannot speak his own language at the day's end. You, I mean, are the language that immerses me; the others, except at their literal level, say so little by comparison—no, I exaggerate, or the 4th highball does, and I must try not to. A lifelong lesson. What talks + gives vs. what listens + receives. What am I remembering? A walk at night as an undergraduate with my Dutch friend Hans. It was cold, we had no coats, my teeth were chattering. He wanted me to put on his scarf but I refused—if any scarves were to be offered I would offer them, if any caring was to be done I would do it. The wrongness of that moment's refusal has never left me. At the oddest times it comes back and undoes me no less than it sets me right somehow. Now to the post office. Bear with me, David.

> And bless you always—
> James

K. 271 Mozart's Piano Concerto no. 9 in E-flat Major. Merrill imitates the structure of the rondo he describes in the last section of his poem "The Will" (*Divine Comedies*, 1976) and refers to it several times in these letters.
The psychiatrist Albert Rothenberg.
by ourselves Merrill and Jackson.

To David McIntosh

WUSTL
26–27 January 1969
Stonington, CT

David—

We are just now back from New York, properly stuffed with culture + people. Movies, museums, the opera, lunches, a dinner party of 42 for Peggy Guggenheim on Staten Island last night to wind it all up. Our gravest mistake was the sculpture show at the Whitney. People are mad, there can be no other explanation. No, there was one nice thing, a big plexiglass prism shaped like a W laid on its side, about 3 x 4 feet. Looking through it, you could see everything but yourself, beyond, behind, to the side, all slightly distorted and outlined, each person or object, with a rainbow aura; it wasn't a work of art so much as an elegant piece of criticism, which is more than the surrounding shit deserved. We were too depressed afterwards even to go see *Yellow Submarine*. But the next day we saw a heavenly Fairfield Porter show at John Myers' gallery. And then of course *Rosenkavalier*— better than one could have dreamed from start (that orgasm of the French horn throbbing among strings) to finish (a smile through tears as the little blackamoor dances offstage). Christa Ludwig's Octavian was of a perfection—she <u>was</u> an adolescent nobleman, all beautiful manners, impetuous poise, moments of shyness that gave way to the most chilling egoism. She will sing the Marschallin later in the season, which of course is <u>the</u> role; the words alone undo you, but together with the music + Rysanek's unexpectedly marvelous interpretation—well, we were all blowing our noses by the end of Act I. "I've got to find the ladies' room," said Grace through her teeth. DJ (thinking of her glaucoma): To put drops in your eyes? Grace: No, my dear—just the reverse. I can't find my libretto here to copy out for you what Hofmannsthal has her say about time to Octavian, but it ends with more or less these words: ". . . it flows in mirrors, flows between you and me. Oh Quinquin, there are times when I hear it flowing, when I get up in the middle of the night and stop the clocks, one after one (this above 2 unison notes from the harps, gently striking the hour in her head). And yet we must not be afraid of it; for time also is a creation of the Father who has created all of us." Isn't that beautiful? And to have an opera in which heights like these rise up out of a world of farce + filth, snobbery, opportunism, cheap waltzes + practical jokes!—one leaves the theatre the way I imagine one leaves the confessional, at peace with one's follies, forgiving + forgiven. Distrustful, too, of too great a concentration of Pure Beauty in anything; mindful of the preciousness of what is base, dull, wasteful, dissonant, if the heart is going to be mirrored with any degree of accuracy; remembering finally that some people despise this opera, its characters no less than its music, as Irma does, and said so at length over her tabasco snails. I'm sorry, as usual I've had too many impressions these last days to clarify even a single one of them in a letter. Better to take a long hot bath + hope to reach you by telephone later on.

Monday. I must plunge back into the cauldron tomorrow afternoon, so shall try to work as much as I'm able today. Bless you, my dear.

Always—

J.

John Myers See letter to Hellen Plummer of 13 January 1955, note on Myers's partner Herbert Machiz.
Christa Ludwig (b. 1928), German mezzo-soprano.
the Marschallin The Marschallin (a married princess in her thirties) and the teenage nobleman Octavian (a trouser role) are in bed together at the beginning of the opera.

To David McIntosh   WUSTL
                                                     5 February 1969
                                                     Stonington, CT

David—

We go to New York again tomorrow for more opera, another *Rosen-kavalier* Saturday afternoon, + Bernard's little puppet opera the night before. I don't know which I'm looking most forward to. Bernard himself arrived last Wednesday at 6, by Icelandic airways, with perhaps $80 in his pocket plus "some Kennedy half-dollars that I'd been given as tips"—he has an all but menial job with a travel agency meeting people's trains in five languages. In Alexandria of course he is still the Count de Zogheb—whatever that means, very little now, I'm afraid. His father was a great ladies' man, his mother knows Victor Hugo by heart, and he, with his Levantine face dimpled + creased like a bride's first muffin, eyes tiny as currants, has only this extraordinary talent of setting kitchen Italian to popular tunes which are then shaped into an irresistible little drama. The one the puppeteers are doing is called *Vacanze a Parigi* (Holiday in Paris) and was written in 48 hours to commemorate his first meeting with DJ + me, when we had sailed to Paris with Grace 10 years ago and taken him, that first night, to dine at Prunier's. DJ insisted, after dinner, that we all go and admire the belle epoque decorations in the ladies' room where we fell into talk with the very distinguished attendant who told us that <u>her</u> decor was widely preferred to that of the ladies' room at Maxim's—and suddenly there, ready-made, was the cast of Bernard's opera: due studenti americani senza aucun experienza; Mme Lavabo, una grande principessa slava; il maître d'hôtel; una grossa putana (Grace?); and una levantina isterica (himself?) . . .

I knew I oughtn't to have sent you that poem. It wasn't finished, I've done all sorts of things to it, like transferring the essentially very private image of your inflamed eye to a new section in which the old man, Angel, is sitting in a truck after a paralyzing stroke, half quick, half dead. He is very real to me, in a way that entirely made-up people often are, and the texture of the whole is correspondingly less ethereal. I sent a copy to Richard Howard yesterday. He is not only terribly bright as a reader but a most accomplished flatterer, and he has just called to say everything I want to hear. And DJ has had a letter from George, which should by rights make him happy but doesn't because he no longer reads the words, only what's between the lines.

These have been wonderful days for me. They began with talking to you last Thursday morning, + I stay full of happiness + hope for you + myself. I feel that you will be able to start working at last, and that the absorption + fulfillment will make you entirely well. If my picture is on its way, so much the better—you'll have to paint a new one for company! I'll give a party for it when it arrives. Ah—Rollie has had trouble with her back. I've not seen her but she talked to David. She has a new doctor in NY who refused to examine her until she had lain in bed for 2 weeks. They are up today; she + Evie Cole have gone to town together—Rollie, I gather, feeling much better thanks to her rest. There. That's all.

Bless you—
James

the cast of Bernard's opera Murdock and Peschka's Little Players.
that poem "Under Libra: Weights and Measures" in *Braving the Elements* (1972).
Evie Cole (1927–2015), a real-estate agent and longtime Stonington resident.

To A. F. Lodeizen

LITERATUURMUSEUM
10 March 1969
[Stonington, CT]

Dear Mr Lodeizen,

It is a great pleasure to hear from you after such a long time. I too have thought often of you and Mrs. Lodeizen, and am embarrassed not to have kept in touch. It is hard to use (without sounding pompous) the demands of a literary life as an excuse for no longer sending so much as a Christmas greeting—but I fear my shameful silence has already spoken for itself.

Yes, I am still living in Stonington. I also have a house in Greece, where I go now + then for some months at a time, but the house here will always be what I come back to. After nearly ten years in which I'd not heard from Ray, I ran into him the summer before last. He came for a weekend, and we talked endlessly about Amherst days and (of course) Hans. His address is 400 East 56th St., New York City, and his memory is in far better condition than my own! I think you might also write to Oscar Schotte who, when I saw him last at Amherst last June, spoke wonderfully and at length about Hans as a student. Probably you know his address; if not, Amherst College would be sure to reach him.

My own recollections of Hans—! I have been trying to make some order out of them, since receiving your letter two days ago. He had not been long at Amherst when we met. Professor Brower had mentioned him to me, and I knocked one late afternoon at his door. He had a room in Valentine Hall. He was shortly to move to a dormitory (which he hated, as it was full of undergraduates all noisier + younger than himself). Eventually, as you know, he lived at Mrs Miner's, but by then I had left Amherst. My impression of what he was remains far more vivid than my recollection of anything he did or said. I had never met a person of such luminous charm, culture, gentleness and intelligence. The notion that somebody could love + understand science as well as music + poetry struck me as of a dazzling novelty—and indeed, if Hans had not been such delightful company, he would have intimidated us all by what he knew and what he [sic] would imagine of his feelings. One day he began talking about Nietzsche. He quoted the last lines of "Die Sonne sinkt . . ." where the self vanishes, a little silver fish, into the dark waters. This led to Nietzsche's ideas—of which I knew nothing, but which seemed to fill Hans with an odd, dangerous relish. "But that is all very frightening," I remember saying at one point. "Yes," he agreed, "it frightens me terribly too"—and his smile + dancing eyes showed what an <u>amusing</u> thing it was to be frightened by an idea. There was the same look on his face an evening in New York when we stood through the last performance of Sartre's *Huis Clos*. "Dreadful! Terrible!" he kept repeating, as much shaken by the dreadfulness as delighted to have recognized and survived it. He valued above all the kind of lightness + gaiety that goes beyond terror. I can hear him quoting Rimbaud—"J'ai tendu . . . des chaînes d'or d'étoile à étoile, et je danse."—or see his face at a performance of Mozart's *Entführung* in New York; such moments gave me my first human glimpse of a nature that reaches <u>through</u> suffering +

drama towards innocence and serenity. Some friends and I gave him an enormous costume party only a few weeks before I left Amherst. The theme was "Paris", and Hans came as Apollinaire with a blood-soaked bandage round his head—

But I see I am carried away by your letter; and that you mean to reply to Mr Berger's specific questions. This I shall of course be glad to do—and you are free to show him this letter if you wish.

I should like to send you and Mrs Lodeizen two of my recent books—a novel about Greece, and a collection of poems which was given the National Book Award (something very grand over here) in 1967. I'll try to mail them in the next few days. This brings warmest greetings to you both. I hope that we may see each other before too many more years go by.

Sincerely yours,

Jim

Ray Ray Daum, Lodeizen's roommate at Amherst.
Oscar Schotte (1895–1988), biology professor at Amherst.
"Die Sonne sinkt . . ." "The Sun Sinks," one of Nietzsche's "Dionysian-Dithyramb" poems in *Thus Spoke Zarathustra*.
Huis Clos No Exit, play by Sartre.
"J'ai tendu" From Rimbaud's poem "Phrases" in *Illuminations:* "I have stretched . . . chains of gold from star to star, and I dance."
Entführung Mozart's opera *Die Entführung aus dem Serail* (*The Abduction from the Seraglio*).
Mr Berger's Peter Berger, coeditor with H. Pierre Dubois of a collection of Lodeizen's poetry and prose (1969).

To John Hollander

29 April 1969
[Stonington, CT]

FAN LETTER

xxxxxxxxx

xxxxxxxxxxxxxxxxxxxxxxxxxxxxxxxxxxxxxxxxx
xxxxxxxxxxxxxxxxxxxxxxxxxxxxxxxxxxxxxxx

XXXXXXXXXXXXXXXXXXXXXXXXXXXXXXXXXXXXXXXXXX
XXXXXXXXXXXXXXXXXXXXXXXXXXXXXXXXXXXXXXXXXXXX
XXXXXXXXXXXXXXXXXXXX
XXXXXXXXXXXXXXXXXXXXXXXXXXXXXXXXXXXXXXXXXX
XXXXXXXXXXXXXXXXXXXXXXXXXXXXXXXXXXXXXXXXXXXXXX
XXXXXXXXXXXXXXXXXXXXXXXXXXXXXXXXXXXXXXXXXXXXXX
XXXXXXXXXXXXXXXXXXXXXXXXXXXXXXXXXXXXXXXXX
XXXXXXXXXXXXXXXXXXXXXXXXXXXXXXXXXXXXXXXXXXXXXX
XXXXXXXXXXXXXXXXXXXXXXXXXXXXXXXXXXXXXXXXXX
XXXXXXXX
XXXXXXXXXXXXXXXXXXXXXXXXXXXXXXXXXXXXXXXX

XXXXXXXXXX
XXXXX

Dear John—

I doubt that I can take time away from turning your so-long-awaited
pages to fulfil this rough schema, no, in fact it's out of the question.
The book is a marvel of invention + beauty, and I don't see how anyone
could have lived even one more week without it and all the exquisitely
playful reflections (upon what gets done, and how) that it gives rise to.
Why, the very shape of shapelessness becomes ideal. Perhaps you're
familiar with the philosopher who knows how to arrive at that point,
but I am not. For me he's you, nobody else. Teased out of thought,
I can always turn back to the dedication, and swell with pleasure at
the sight of it + recalling the terms in which you announced it to me
last year. It is one sumptuous gift. Hope to see you soon, though not
at *Prince Igor*. Love to Anne + those no longer quite so tiny or blonde
daughters. And countless thanks + compliments.

Yours ever,
Jimmy

The book Hollander's *Types of Shape* (1969) consists of shape-poems in which the
typed letters of the poem make forms that represent, for instance, "Swan and
Shadow." Merrill's mock "Fan letter" consisting of x's imitates Hollander's visual
templates for the poems. Hollander dedicated the book to Merrill.
Teased out of thought Merrill alludes to Keats's "Ode on a Grecian Urn": "Thou,
silent form, dost tease us out of thought / As doth eternity: Cold Pastoral!"

To Stephen Yenser   YALE
                                                26 May 1969
                                             [Stonington, CT]

Dear Stephen,

A lovely late afternoon, powdery gold above still blue water. I've watered the geraniums, the pot of basil + the pot of pot, and poured a still untasted glass of, I'm afraid, champagne. Nothing to celebrate, beyond the changed weather and the prospect of an evening without company. There have been 2 old people in the house, David Jackson's parents—dear, doddering, au fond terrifying, with minds like milkweed that will neither settle anywhere nor, when they do, be shaken loose until hours have passed of dreamlike fixation upon, say, the star's name whose daughter studied piano in 1938 and indeed played in the annual recital held in the lobby of . . . An embassy, at any rate, from the great vacant heartland that has shaped us all. They will be back tomorrow. Meanwhile, tiny exhilarating bubbles rise + rise. Atlanta seems far away, and though I've never heard of Doraville or the Druid Hills it's perfectly possible to believe in them.

A single cultural event, this past month: Elizabeth Bishop's reading at the Guggenheim Museum. Your Mr Lowell introduced her to a full house that included Marianne Moore (in the clutches of a uniformed, Faustina-like nurse), myself (in a tie given to me by Mrs Lowell) and a lot of never-to-be-accounted-for young people. After talking for some time about "their generation" (and adding to the big, obvious names that of Weldon Kees) RL praised EB's "famous eye", good heart, etc, made a few magic passes + there she was. Her very first words dispelled any anxiety: "The Famous Eye will now disappear behind glasses!"—we were wax in her hands after that. She reads without variation of cadence or volume or pitch, but somehow it's perfectly all right. Also, she read "Cirque d'Hiver."

I know so well what you mean—time passing, those flickers of panic. One solution is surely a change of scene. What we need at such times are not Deep Insights, for these are simply not available in foreign parts—unless on the black market where they are not only outrageously expensive but so adulterated as to cause acute nausea within a few hours of ingestion. What is available is a sharpened attention to surfaces, speculation as to manners, and all that, which to be sure we <u>ought</u> to be capable of at home—the anthropologist's monocle screwed into place—but aren't. I wonder mainly about Italy. I was so lonely + unhappy there, for reasons that had, or so I thought at the time, nothing to do with the place. Or did they? That national spirit is so smoothed + rounded, like a pebble, by the waves of enchanted tourists that have been breaking on its shores these last 5 centuries. It is like a vast floating graduate school. I made only one Italian friend in 2 years. The others were pleasantly competitive dilettante Americans, high on Mannerism or Etruscan Places or whatever. One missed the imagined astringency of France. Now, Greece—But this is all beside the point, isn't it? But since the point is just what you expect to do with your life, isn't it also out of the question to face the issue directly? not watch the pot, having first placed yourself not too far from the likeliest brazier . . . ? I do think your instinct is right to the extent that it will spare you having to face Americans in class. As for <u>teaching</u> them America—teaching them Lowell, teaching them me—well, the mind boggles. You do have Hölderlin's *Gesetz* to remember. Here is Hofmannsthal's, concerning Time: Auch sie ist ein Geschöpf des Vaters, der uns alle erschaffen hat. Or: Nothing if not amenable.

In Santa Fe last month I appear to have rented—though nothing has been signed—a 3 room cottage 18 miles from town, August through October. Why not take the train back from Chicago and stop off? In any case I would plan to spend a week or 10 days in California as soon as my lease is up, which would mean LA around Oct 31 for at least 3 days, then on to Frisco. (A recent guest here has been, to the mild consternation of the elder Jacksons: the director of Studio Watts, whom I'd rather like to see in habitat.) If "They"—your people I mean—invite me to read, I won't say no; but that would scarcely be the motive for passing through. It is dark by now. Enough.

Yours as ever,
James

Doraville . . . Druid Hills Communities in the Atlanta, Georgia, area, where Yenser's mother grew up.
Your Mr Lowell Referring to Yenser's work on Robert Lowell.
Faustina-like See Elizabeth Bishop's poem "Faustina; or, Rock Roses."

Mrs Lowell Elizabeth Hardwick.

Weldon Kees (1915–?55), American poet who disappeared after abandoning his car near the Golden Gate Bridge.

Hölderlin's *Gesetz* Yenser had mentioned the fragment beginning "Reif sind, in Feuer getaucht" which includes the claim that "ein Gesetz ist / Daß alles hineingeht" (it's a law / That everything goes in).

Auch sie ist From *Der Rosenkavalier:* "It too is a creature of the Father who created us all."

Nothing if not amenable Elizabeth Bishop's "The Shampoo": "Time is / nothing if not amenable."

director of Studio Watts The Studio Watts Workshop, founded in 1964, provided workshop space for local artists in the Watts neighborhood of Los Angeles; its director was James Woods (1935–2006).

your people At UCLA, where Merrill did read and where Yenser was an assistant professor.

To David Jackson

10 June 1969
Stonington, CT

David dear,

DK and I got here shortly after midnight last night. I have a strange mild cold, touches of fever to match, nothing serious, simple exhaustion merely. Too tired to talk to any of the people I saw in NY—a little party Saturday: Harry + Kathleen, Donald + Mary, Hollanders, <u>Bernie</u>, Tony of course. Too tired certainly to talk to my mother, or to Tony, or to Richard Howard at lunch Sunday. But all expressed regret that you'd left without being seen. Too tired particularly to see Meredith + Rollins for a drink this afternoon, which isn't stopping them from coming. The weather is heavenly at last, a radiant hour in the sun before lunch, reading a revision of an old long poem of Chester's (he says a friend may be driving down with the pouf + pillows in July) and Mailer's *Armies of the Night*. How strange I'd never read anything by him: he's absolutely marvelous; it's how Henry James would write if he lived in this decade—long flexible floats of rhetoric decked with <u>all</u> that is salient in the parade. My mother tried very hard to reach yours on the afternoon of the 5th but the operator at the International Hotel for one reason or another made it impossible; and Mary didn't call her; so we did what we could to bring the old people together.

Mine will be 70 in August, she confessed over her 3rd drink last night, but I was pleased not to tell even you! Eleanor is unwell also—same thing as I've got, by the sound of it. We telephoned Helen W, HIP, Tony + I, yesterday afternoon—DK had brought her letter in—and it sounds very grim. But Will D—a veritable Eisenhower—is being kept alive, plays cribbage, takes a drink, cannot speak, and will in due time be returning home from the hospital. We went to the ballet in town, also to *Promises, Promises!* (snappy + tuneless) and 2 movies—the old Lola Montez and the new Isadora which you must see in Athens: V Redgrave's uncanny performance. Tony's new refrain comes from the Russian episode where young blond doomed Essenin, the poet lover, bursts in on her with his one English sentence: Ve—vill—make—luff—like—TIGERS! You might tell Maria, so that she can welcome him back with these very words. There's a letter from her here, to both T + me, which I'll open when I call him later.

I was so depressed to see you go. We must by now be used to the way our time together passes, without any of the essentials being said, foremost among which is that I love you dearly + wish I knew better how to show it; but it seemed uncommonly painful, this year's separation—perhaps because the remaining years seem, as never before, numbered . . . Oh, we've always felt that the years of our youth were; but now it's the years of our age that are, the years of our lives, + that is a bit more disquieting, no? More + more I feel (you don't, I think, and perhaps your salvation lies in the other direction) that one can't, one positively mustn't, live for others—enough, no sermons. No news either, beyond this smattering. My love to everyone there: George (I do hope he can be with you from the start), Taki, Kleo, Maria, Nelly. This is just to welcome you. A better letter will go off in a few days. Oh, Sandy Holland called, sounding as if she might well turn up in Greece by August; she's going to write. Not a peep out of Joe. A nice note from Jim Woods—not worth forwarding. On the train back to NY, going through Harlem above ground, black youths threw stones at his coach window . . . I hope your trip wasn't too awful, that you got your car from Naples to Athens + that you mailed me a letter from Italy.

Love always,
Jamie

Harry . . . Tony Harry and Kathleen Ford; Donald and Mary Richie; John and Anne Hollander; Bernie Winebaum; Tony Parigory.
Meredith + Rollins William Meredith and Rollin C. Williams (1922–2012), a psychiatric social worker and the first African-American hired as a professor at the University of Connecticut.
Promises, Promises! 1968 musical.
Lola Montez The historical romance *Lola Montès* (1955) directed by Max Ophüls.
Redgrave's uncanny performance Vanessa Redgrave's performance as Isadora Duncan in Karel Reisz's biopic *Isadora* (1968) which won her the Best Actress award at Cannes.
Essenin The "poet lover" Sergei Esenin (or Yesenin) (1895–1925), eighteen years younger than Duncan.
Maria Maria Mitsotaki.
Sandy Holland Novelist Cecelia Holland (b. 1943).
Joe Joe Bruno, Stonington friend of Merrill's and Jackson's.

To David Jackson

WUSTL
29 July 1969
[Stonington, CT]

David Dear—

The summer's back is broken. We've survived the Gold + Fizdale visit as well as the function described on the back of this page. Judy Moffett left this morning after the dull evening I felt obliged to give her. Laurence Scott called off the lunch he was driving down for today— one could hardly hear him for the thunder + lightning + torrents of rain; it has been cold + misty for days + days, which made his excuse (an infection proceeding from sunburn) sufficiently piquant. There have been bridge games + various rowdy evenings. John Myers spent an entire week, sleeping at Anne's gallery by night, + sitting about our various houses by day, using up lemons + vodka. DK's party didn't include him—and was in fact a triumph of convivial gastronomy (caviar, tongue tonnato, tabouli, and a wonderful spongey orange + lemon cake which DK baked for himself and Elaine expertly iced); Rollie came without Pat and was in tears, she had such a good time; the Morses, or rather Robt + Daniel + Regan appeared after dinner; and only at 1:30, in fact, interrupting our performance of Le Sorelle B for Bobby + Arthur, did John enter drunkenly for 5 minutes (we held him to that) to say that "Mr Gorgeous," an anonymous pickup from the

Harbor View, was waiting for him on the corner. The Wimpfs had had that evening a cocktail dansant to which we didn't go—but 400 others did! Only a few more ordeals—dinner at the Hallowells, the Barnards, the Morses, a final evening here (G + E refusing to cook any more, though they "owe")—and I can escape to NY. Wednesday Aug 6 I fly to New Mexico, and shall be staying 3–4 days with Bob + Tom (717 Camino del Monte Sol, Santa Fe) before moving into my house—where, I must admit, visits will be promptly forthcoming: Charlotte on one hand, Jim Woods + his friend on the other; but it is bound to be quieter than here. The reading, Pati's + mine, went off wonderfully well. She sat crosslegged on cushions + was enchanting behind large spectacles; I leaned against the stage + read better than I ever have before, though John said I rolled my eyes too much. Just our crowd was there—Wimpfs, Boats, Irene, Mrs Lenroot, a few children, Peggy O and her black boy—80 or 90 altogether. John Brinnin, etc. Don't panic, but Al Merrill (New London) called for your address—a couple he knows are headed there, but they don't want to see you, just to get some pointers on where to dine + what to see. Man + wife. More serious, but not till fall, may be Inger McCabe; she + Bob seem to be planning some months apart.

I've read all of Jonathan's 648 pages, and mailed him a letter only a few hours before he phoned, worried about not hearing; how rarely things turn out so fortuitously. After no word since a postcard June 26, and not a peep out of <u>me</u>, DMc phoned yesterday sounding very eager, offering to meet my plane, concerned about my health, would I stay with <u>him</u> for a bit, etc . . . You would have been in constant chuckles during all these occasions. Grace is especially herself. Invited to DK's birthday: "Nobody ever gave <u>me</u> a birthday party. I hope you don't expect a present. No one ever gives <u>me</u> a birthday present . . ." but finally she wrapped up 2 little persian enamel slipper-ashtrays that have been knocking about the house for years, while I confirmed her presence at our table last January 9 and was <u>almost</u> able to remember what we gave her: a bottle of creme de m. no doubt. She has lost the GZS memorial lighter already—at Muriel Spark's. Talked to Claude; he is alone again after some strange + violent terminal scenes—by now they shouldn't be all <u>that</u> strange. Bill had gone to call with yet another black friend. "I don't want to go anywhere," he told C, "that I can't take Albert (Alfred?)." Albert is a

fashion designer. Poor Rollin calls all the time—ignorance is not bliss
in his case, although our Joe did go up for a few hours one evening
during which both agree that Nothing Happened. Wasn't a great
Love Affair going to begin for you on June 24? Why are you being
so secretive about it? Don't you know you can tell me <u>anything</u>? You
won't hear from me until I'm out west unless something very excit-
ing happens. Don't forget the address: Rancho Ancon / PO Box 2291
/ Santa Fe NM 87501. I love you. WRITE.

Jamie

Gold + Fizdale Arthur Gold (1917–90) and Robert Fizdale (1920–95), duo pianists
and authors.
the Wimpfs Louise Wimpfheimer (1923–2002), founder of the Stonington Players,
a community theater group, and her husband, Jacques (1918–2000).
the Hallowells Frank and Priscilla Hallowell, Stonington residents.
the Barnards Stonington residents Diana Barnard and her husband, J. Lawrence
Barnard, the author of a memoir entitled *Gently Down the Stream* (1976).
Pati's and mine Pati Hill (1921–2014), Stonington resident, model, novelist, artist
who used an IBM copier to create images of household objects.
Al Merrill No relation to the poet.
Inger McCabe . . . Bob American photographer, socialite, and entrepreneur Inger
Abrahamsen McCabe (b. 1933) and her husband Robert Karr McCabe (1929–2016).
Jonathan's 648 pages Jonathan Bishop's manuscript of *Something Else*, published by
Braziller in 1972.
Muriel Spark (1918–2006), Scottish writer, author of *The Prime of Miss Jean Brodie*
(1961) and other works.
our Joe Joe Bruno.

To David Jackson

WUSTL
21 August 1969
Nambé, NM

David dear,

All is well, the better for receiving your fine long letter that followed
the jaunt to Corfu. How I envy you Ioannina. For no reason at all—
unless the memory of some Lears + of hard-to-please Maria's having
liked it—it is my Dream City in Greece, what Parma or Venice were
to Proust. Let's do it together one of these days. I hope, too, that you
had some delicious Adventures. . . . ?

Our trip to Hopi country took only 3 days, less, but somehow 800 miles got put on the car—not a few of them merely going back and forth between the motel and the "second" or "third" mesa, as they are known, in small filthy villages on the tops of which the various dances took place. The 3rd member of our party was a school friend of DMcs, Tom Bissinger, who is turning into a very successful stage director—things at Lincoln Center, his own theatre this year in Philadelphia, etc. He is very mod, granny glasses, mop of black curls, says "Wow!" when even slightly impressed or amused; straight, or as straight as one can be dans ce genre, a French mistress off in the East somewhere; to make it all clearer, the spit + image of Walter Goldfrank. We ate relentlessly out of doors, rain, shine, starlight, sunsets, lightning, smoking joints to make it all grander than it already was. Luckily we didn't have to sleep outdoors, but our motel room was a Marx Bros cabin, me in the bed, Tom + David in sleeping bags on the floor—the waste! On our way home we saw, by design, the very beautiful canyon de Chelly—small, stylish, all extraordinary arabesques of red rock, with, far below, little green corn plantations + one or two jewel-like cliff-dwellings plastered white under huge tawny thunderheads of stone. We also saw, by accident, having gotten lost several times, and dangerously close to no more gas, the Chaco canyon, 30 miles over a dirt road from any direction, where there is a 1000 year old apartment house which held, oh, 800 people, 5 stories high in places, and all done in the most delicate masonry imaginable, very thick walls but no stone thicker than an inch and somehow altogether darkly shining. It was after 7 by then and we didn't get home until after 12:30—exhausted, but having managed to keep our tempers nonetheless. The Hopi dances themselves aren't easy to give an account of. They chant + stamp rhythmically about in single file, form rows, pair off, I don't know. The Antelope Men carry seed rattles, the Snake Men have turtle rattles attached to their right calves. They are kilted and stained and feathered, all very strange + savage—but set, still, in a plaza one-quarter the size of Kolonaki, if that, and jammed with onlookers, most whites, the vacant young + vacant old alike, sitting on the ground, in shade, in sun, or (as we did) on the roofs of houses, legs dangling, while the broiling sun shone, or rain fell out of nowhere, quite wet + chilling, or fell from clouds. You felt somehow: how <u>could</u> their hearts be in it? And yet, to see at dawn runners converging on the mesa from a certain sacred spring some miles off in the desert; and to see an 8 year old Snake Man dancing with a coiling rattlesnake in his mouth, held like a kitten by the scruff of the neck—these aren't the sights of every day. Some 60 snakes must have come into play. Each pair of dancers would pause at a mysterious little hut covered with poplar branches (the Underworld, said the book) and emerge with a snake in his mouth: first boll snakes, then racers, finally the rattlers. The snakes would then be let run free in the dancing place, slither, coil, dart in panic for the crowd (ooh! eek!) only to be plucked by hand or charmed back by the stroke of an eagle feather. A row of women in red + white blankets kept lightly pelting them with white meal. When the dance ended an hour later all the snakes were gathered up and at a signal thrown into a circle of meal where they tangled for a beautiful moment before being deftly plucked up again and carried off, by runners, to the six points of the compass where they would give good news of mankind to the dark forces under the earth. Then it was over, and the village elders (shirts, pants, beads, headbands) began saying things like: That's all, folks, clear out now, that's all.

The day after we got back, Paul Merrill arrived by bus from Gallup—he'd been trekking about in a group all summer. I just took him to the airport this morning. He slept in his sleeping bag on my porch, and seemed to have a nice enough (dull enough) time these 4 days. We went to the opera—*The Devils of Loudun* by that young Pole—splendid theatre plus sound effects; and last night to *Che* at a drive-in with DMc—surely the worst film ever, ever, ever made, without a memorable image, a vestige of sympathy for anybody, undiluted, weary opportunism—don't miss it! Then one day Paul + I found the very lovely waterfalls in the Nambe pueblo. We had them to ourselves, ate lunch, after which I stayed below with my book + Paul went exploring with his copy of *Playboy*. Finally I climbed to the upper falls—a marvelous salon of rock + rushing water + sunlight— and found him (and perhaps managed to be looking somewhere else by the time he saw me) with his little shorts around his knees and his page open, no doubt, to a double-spread Playmate. He + DMc got on very well together—as for that matter DMc + I seem to be getting on. I remain deeply charmed. His face seems older (he has a moustache) and now and then a long downward line appears in his cheek, and my heart melts. He goes to Denver for a few days next week—his mother is entering the hospital there, for tests. By then Cahrloot—who's that? <u>Charlotte</u>—will have arrived from Atlanta for 8 days; and hard upon her heels come Robin + Michela for 2 or 3 days—and then perhaps the coast is clear. I wrote Jim Woods that there truly wasn't space for him + a friend, but that I'd be happy to put them up in a motel if they still wanted to come: no answer so far.

Yesterday Paul + I spent mostly in town: a sandwich at Bob + Tom's, the Folk Art museum, some shopping. In a fine little shop full of good jewelry, kachinas, fetishes, etc, I was waited on (buying a turquoise parrot for the ladies) by a sort of cheery, chirpy <u>hag</u>, wrinkled with rotting teeth and sparse drab cropped hair. When I wrote a check she asked if I weren't staying with Mary Lou. Why no, I said, but Mary Lou's a great friend. "I know," said the vision. "You don't remember me—Jinx Junkin." Of course she hadn't known <u>me</u> either until she saw my name on the check. Such rencontres should be avoided whenever possible!

Atlanta news sounds very grim. Bill back in the hospital—glucose—tests—frantic with nerves. I truly don't see how he can last more than another month or two, and am already selfishly vexed at the thought of having to leave here if only for a few days. That's what I'd do, it now seems, should he be snuffed out during my stay here; then perhaps skip Frisco and go for 2 or 3 weeks in November. Agh. Touch wood. I will try to phone Geo + Mary after 5 o'clock—and now leave space for the results. Love to Tony + thank him for his letter; perhaps he will feel that this letter is partly for him, because it is, + I'll write him one of his own in the next days. Love to George + Taki + Kleo. And to you, dear one. I have a phone by the way: (505) 455 7565—but, like all phones out thisaways it's out of order more often than not.

Je t'embrasse.
Jamie

Ioannina Alternate spelling of Yannina. See the poem of that name in *Divine Comedies* (1976).
Lears Edward Lear (1812–88), British artist and poet, known for nonsense verse and limericks, produced beautiful landscape watercolors and views of ancient ruins on his visits to Greece.
Hopi country Home of the Hopi and Tewa people in northeastern Arizona.

Walter Goldfrank (1940–2017), a sociologist, Merrill's niece Catherine Merrill's first husband, active in Students for a Democratic Society (SDS).
said the book *Dancing Gods: Indian Ceremonials of New Mexico and Arizona* (1931) by Erna Fergusson.
Paul Merrill Merrill's teenage nephew, son of Charles and Mary Merrill.
The Devils of Loudun Opera (1969) by Krzysztof Penderecki (1933–2020), based on John Whiting's dramatization of Aldous Huxley's novel *The Devils of Loudun* (1952).
Che Biopic (1969) about Argentine revolutionary Ernesto (Che) Guevara (1928–67), directed by Richard Fleischer.
Charlotte Charlotte Hafley.
Robin + Michela Robin Magowan and his girlfriend Micaela di Leonardo visited from Berkeley.
Bob + Tom's Bob Palmer and Tom Ingle.
Atlanta news From Hellen and Bill Plummer.
Geo + Mary Jackson's parents.

To Eleanor Perenyi and Grace Stone

YALE
3 September 1969
Nambé NM

Dear Ladies,

I've just put Charlotte on a bus to Prescott, Ariz. The bus station itself, or rather the crowd that got on her bus, deserves a word before I go any further. Wasn't there a play called *Bus Stop*, in fact? If so it couldn't have had a more interesting cross-section. Three teenage French girls being propositioned in sign-language by three drunk Indians. Now and then the toughest of the girls would step back and take a flash photo of the scene—to prove back home that le folklore is alive + well + living in New Mexico. A long suffering British couple. "You can tell she's British," said Ch., "just look at those ankles." A tall pasty Spanish boy with a book in the *Power of Positive Thinking Series* entitled *ENTHUSIASM IS THE SECRET*. And then of course Charlotte herself with her Papier d'arches sketchpad and Hermès bag. She begged the French girls to let her sit with them, and they were all jabbering gaily as the bus left [*in the margin*: while the Indians bided their time in back]. Driving home I turned on the radio. First news in over 3 weeks. Ho Chi Minh? Bishop Pike? A bomb in Colorado? How far away it all seems. Haven't people learned <u>yet</u>? Your letter, dear Grace, reached me today, both delighting me + shaming me for not having sent more than a postcard (which you h-h-haven't answered, p-p-p-pets—as our friend loves to say) in this whole month I've been away. It stirred many ripples of homesickness I must say. Dot + Lillian! Pati in the sky with diamonds! Shouldn't we start a local "woman of the year" award and give it to Anne for simple ingenuity? There is nothing on that scale to report from here—or rather there is, but what I hear of it is as limited as my acquaintance. Before moving out to the valley I was taken to swim at a sumptuous pool shaped like a belly-dancer, mountains + clouds everywhere. It was owned by a drôle de menage: a most dignified Englishwoman, once married to some Hollywood producer, whitehaired + chatty; and her friend a hulking overgrown child of around 59, an ex-Olympic swimming champion from Hawaii, who had also been married but only for two traumatic weeks, long, long ago. Something about her (and her marriage) came to light in a story told me on the way home from their pool. The Englishwoman had taken Cecily to see *Hair*, and during the nude scene Cecily turned in utter confusion to ask in a very loud whisper: "But where are the erections?" Vivamus, mea Lesbia! Mostly though I am out here, 20 miles from the City Different (they call it that), under my portal beyond which all the flowers, fields, horses, mountains have yet to cloy. No, no riding for me yet, though Charlotte + the 11 year old daughter of the main house went out yesterday for nearly 3 hours and boy, were those parents frantic long before the girls got home in ecstasy. There have been lots of picnics, by sun and moon, to hillsides and some lovely falls only a few miles away. I'm getting to feel quite at home out-of-doors. You should see me scramble up the slippery rock-face at the falls, with a lunch-filled satchel in my teeth. David M is just a mile away—well, these days he is in Denver (mother in hospital there)—and painting all day; we usually have dinner together, prefaced twice, during Charlotte's visit, by a punting party on his pond—C. at the oar wearing a boater, and a bottle of bubbly in the stern; while the dog does an accomplished dog-paddle without ever seeming to tire, in our wake. I've been working a good deal, and reading *The Possessed* (so <u>funny</u> in places) and listening to the Schnabel Beethoven sonatas for the first time in 20 years. This is the first real change of scene I've had (discounting those teaching stints) since I can't think when, since the days, I suppose, when Greece was still an Eleusinian mystery, and I'm really loving it. DK will have told you there is a Cottage Organ on my premises? Everything I play sounds so awful, I keep leaving fingers on keys or taking them off too soon, but how it strengthens the hands and feet! That winds up the immediate news. David sounds happy <u>enough</u> in Greece. He's been taking long drives: Corfu, Ioannina. His birthday is Sept 16 if you want to send a card. Meanwhile much much love to you both (and to the Morses). Write!!!

Jimmy

Bus Stop Play (1955) by William Inge (1913–73), the basis for the film starring Marilyn Monroe (1956).
Ho Chi Minh . . . A bomb in Colorado? Ho Chi Minh (1890–1969), a revolutionary leader and president of the Democratic Republic of Vietnam, died of heart failure on September 2. James Pike (1913–69), a progressive Episcopal bishop, died on or near September 2; he had been lost in the desert in Israel while researching a book on the historical Jesus. The US Atomic Energy Commission was planning a nuclear test, intended to release natural gas, in Rulison, Colorado; the devastating explosion took place on September 10.
our friend Bernie Winebaum.
Dot + Lillian! Dorothy Parker and her literary executor Lillian Hellman.
Pati Pati Hill.
Anne Anne Fuller, married to the architect Charles Fuller, bought the Baptist church near 107 Water Street, and converted the building into an art gallery showing work by artists associated with the Betty Parsons Gallery in New York.
Vivamus, mea Lesbia! Ode by Catullus, "Let us live, my Lesbia!"
Schnabel Beethoven sonatas The complete Beethoven piano sonatas as recorded during the 1930s by Austrian pianist Artur Schnabel (1882–1951).
Cottage Organ A small reed organ.

To David Jackson

WUSTL
9 September 1969
Nambé, NM

David dear,

Your very welcome letter was here yesterday morning just as Robin + I started off, in a drizzle, for Taos. Michela stayed in bed. She has a sleep problem as well as others, like insufficient cartilege in her knees, and chronic vaginitis—all of which she serenely alludes to (during her waking hours of course). I quite liked her. She seems grown up, rather aglow, eager to fill her mind, in love. The vegetar-

ian side is a bit of a drag, but she handles it well. She is afraid of the
dark, of snakes and insects, had never seen lightning in her life until
Paris, and again here. Our picnic with DMc at the foot of an extraor-
dinary thing called the Black Mesa was not a success. <u>He</u> reminded
her of an old boyfriend, <u>I</u> reminded her of Robin; she felt "trapped
in an echo chamber," stopped talking, and in fact never said another
word all evening, not even goodbye to David who she would not be
seeing again. Still, I enjoyed their being here. They watched birds.
Everything was "Wow!" or "Neat!" just as if World War II had never
taken place. What were we fighting for, I now wonder . . . ? I was
sleeping those nights at DMc's, and enjoyed nightcaps + breakfasts
alone with him. Enjoyed? Oh it is all so hard to explain. There was
a <u>terrible</u>—terrible precisely because of her gentleness—showdown
with Charlotte. Never mention this. I had been stupid enough to
assume that she had gotten over her crush; but no. Finally came tears
+ some mild London version of hysterics. She would leave, she would
go in a taxi, she knew not where (she was leaving anyhow by bus for
Arizona that evening). What she couldn't understand was why her
suffering left me so cold—indeed paralyzed—why I couldn't put my
arms around her + commiserate. The poor thing. Poor things both
of us. And she was so ashamed afterwards, fearful (quite rightly!)
that I would TELL, that I would never see her again. I really wanted
never to. I couldn't breathe. I caught cold at once + am still a little
feverish, after 5 days. Kalá. I spoke of it in the most general terms
to DMc, who then made us another drink and said he couldn't <u>not</u>
tell me—but someone else has come into his life, very recently. They
have only met twice. It is a Polish refugee, age 30, who had come here
displaying jewels—can that be right—but who is also a pianist with
a law degree. "He isn't beautiful but he makes life wherever he is."
He lives in Montreal. There are all sorts of barriers—papers perhaps,
a disabused wariness on both sides—but D is clearly very intrigued,
and <u>I</u> am reasonable enough to see that this is a far more plausible
thing for him than whatever I could offer, what with my age, and a
life already studded with ties + commitments. It hurt, but I was glad
to know. It was something I had been waiting to know. I spent an
all but sleepless night, and got up in the lovely morning, went out,
down to his pond from the far side of which, across the smooth dull
green water, the great swan came gliding, wings ajar, followed by his

mate. <u>That</u> made me cry a little, but they waited it out gravely, clear-
ing their throats now + then for attention, until I got up and fed them
from the pail of corn a few yards away. Everything seems easier now.
It embarrasses me less to show him my own feelings, and he is full of
the same warmth + concern that Charlotte so keenly found wanting
in me. I have a feeling that Mr X will pay a visit before I have left—D.
having asked if I would be "willing to meet him" should he do so. He
had actually thought I might say no!—but I explained that one sim-
ply doesn't refuse experience. Charlotte will be back probably in a
week. Ariz. is full of British tourists. She's alone in a huge stucco +
gingerbread house with 78 rpm recordings of Verdi. The caretaker,
the last time we talked, had just killed a rattler "long as a skipping-
rope and fat as a rat."

And this was meant to be your birthday letter! Forgive me for all
this, about which you can do so little, except tuck it away in your
head. Harry F telephoned. My book won't be ready until later this
month, too late for you to have a copy on the 16th and to discover by
leafing its pages that it is, for better or worse, your very own. Why
shouldn't it be? You've lived through what lies behind each + every
one of those poems—the ballad, Strato, all of it—there are times, as
you must understand, when I can't bear how much you know, how
much of my weakness + silliness you've seen, and you have even had
to live through my lashing out at you as a consequence. Here any-
how is your noncommittal dedication in proof—and with it a world
of love and gratitude.

Jamie

the Black Mesa Sacred land in San Ildefonso Pueblo, near Santa Fe. See "The Black
Mesa" in *Braving the Elements* (1972).
Kalá Okay, or very well.
My book *The Fire Screen* (1969).

To Tony Parigory
WUSTL
19 September 1969
Nambé, NM

Darling Tony,

Your letter of today lashes me into action—action I've positively stripped for, sexe à peine cachée in the beautiful hot dry powdery sunlight among the birds + bugs. It is all so amusing, what comes to me from Greece, from David himself and now from you. People are having fun at last, it would seem, not just the sex marathon, but conversations, bridge parties. Be careful, my dear, lest you find yourself at a concert one of these days! Ah, maybe we've all arrived, with flying colours, at the Finish Line of that exhausting erotic race. Shall we agree that David won it—since he still in one way or another has George? You can place 2nd, and I have come limping in last—but it doesn't matter one bit. These last 10 days have been more curious than I can describe; and they leave me "happy" (since you ask) for the first time since this situation began, and in the most unexpected way. What happened is that DMc met, in Denver, a mysterious person his own age, and decided within 2 days that he had really, for once, fallen in love. Being reticent he wasn't very helpful—and I as a result was about as frantic as I get, any more—and only last weekend when I was asked over for a drink to meet ze lovair did the skies begin to clear. He turns out to be a Count Esterhazy (mère Radziwill) born in Poland, a musicologist, worked for Dior in Paris, all his life very lonely and unloved. Now he is going about the U.S. with exhibits of minerals + gems from South America, knows nobody—you can imogene what a windfall somebody like DMc is in his sad + pointless life. The more I listen (and there is now a lot of listening to do) the more I am glad to be out of it, out of love; and the more, naturally, I shine as a sympathetic understanding friend. A divine gaiety seizes me—and sadness too, because it is all too plainly the way he felt about me—when I hear DMc describe Andrew's lovemaking as "disastrous," something that must be gotten over + thrust out of the mind. Nevertheless they are putting their tiny heads together (and their even tinier pocketbooks) and trying to imagine a shared life—and already the prospect alarms D more than he can say; though <u>say</u> is what he does + does + does. I am very glad I didn't pack up + bolt, as I was tempted to do before sounding the depth of el rivál (and he is deep, earnest, emotional, qu'en sais-je, his hands were trembling with fear when he met me, and has a temper, mauvaise augure, and, I save this for the last, makes all his own clothes on a sewing-machine, even the great bell trousers to conceal his knock-knees). I hope you believe how innocent my malice is au fond. It is. And I'm having the time of my life. You may share this with David but, please, with no one else— knowing as you do how paths will cross in this world. A. has gone back to Denver, clouds shroud his future—will he quit his job? or suffer a removal to Montreal? Meanwhile I read + write + play Scarlatti on the little upright organ—the only one I have touched, apart from my own, for six whole weeks—and cook, and count my blessings.

I hope to arrive in Greece as shortly after Dec 15 as possible, perhaps even before, if I should decide to skip Paris until the trip home, and only stop off in Rome for a few days to see Umberto. When I leave here (end of October) I plan 8 days in California, and I must certainly spend a short while in Atlanta where things are of a grimness! much as I don't let myself feel guilty about not holding the maternal hand more frequently than I do. Ah, you will also be interested in a letter I had from the Cretan Monkey asking for a loan of 120,000 drachmas; and in my reply, enclosing his monthly $50, which told him, with many apologies, that I didn't have it, and was in fact so strapped that I doubted I'd be able to come to Greece this winter. But you know that I'm coming, and I hope to find 6 of those low-cut undershirts dyed in rainbow colors for me to wear in the evening with long mod bead necklaces + gray flannel slacks. Robin + Michela were here for a visit—I quite took to her in every way, even her vegetarian habits. I think of you every day, too, and love you dearly. I kiss madame's hand, and that little modest rosebud between your so reduced fesses. Write again.

xxxxx
Jimmy

sexe à peine cachée Sex barely concealed.
George George Lazaretos.
Count Esterhazy (mère Radziwill) The Esterhazy family is Hungarian nobility; the Radziwill family is Polish nobility.

imogene A play on "Imogen," the heroine of Shakespeare's *Cymbeline*, and "imag-ine."
the Cretan Monkey Kostas Tympakianakis.

To Richard Howard

Dear Richard—

Your letter came an hour ago and I've been pulsating with excite-ment ever since, and with eagerness to write you at once (but the electrician was here, bells rang in <u>this</u> house when the news came, let me tell you; and some preliminary steaming of veg had to be com-pleted for tonight—Chester + Alan are coming to dinner; how not to tell them? though I shan't and besides C probably has heard from the big Wystan Hugh). I couldn't be more delighted for you and your Subjects—pray number me among them. A glimmer had reached me in November, from Big WH himself and <u>his</u> delight in the vol-ume. And now that Big Jim + Monstrous Phyllis have concurred, what is there but to join hands and dance round the rose? I did tell David J who (you will understand) took it sulkily at first—he wanted me to win, bless his Heart—but I've explained that Jim + WH have already outdone themselves on my behalf; repeated to him certain shaky feelings of mine as to the quality of my recent product; and even intimated a positive sense of relief of being spared, pour une fois, the ticklish laurel. (Pres. Cole of Amherst, introducing a read-ing: "The winkles that you see on Mr Fwost's bwow are not due to old age or wowwy, but the weight of the weath.") On you, my dear, it will look better than any Paris hat, and it is too vexing to be shut in this chilly dripping room in the faery land forlorn, gushing onto onion-skin instead of at you over champagne. The French, I daresay, know how to write a far more appropriate letter on such occasions—you may even receive a few samples if the news ever registers behind the Structuralist Curtain—but from me you'll have to make do with what you're already used to, the old affection, the old admiration, and of course my pride in knowing them to be mutual.

Nothing new here except a phonograph needle and every day's broken glass or saucer. My Taki comes most days to repair something or other very clumsily, play a few games of rummy, and so forth—then goes back to the Piraeus where his 2 year old daughter has already [learned] to say "Kiss me please" (in English) to her doll, such excitement has the prospective removal to Stonington awakened in that unthinkable household. He will not be Villiers' kind of valet who could live for me (much as he swears he wants to) and I'm afraid he can't count high enough to be much use as Leporello. You'll see for yourself soon enough. I must leave you. Tonight's dinner keeps nagging—dozens of things undone—and I'd meant only to register this rapture while it's still warm (not that it will cool—!). Meanwhile D. has climbed the stair ostensibly to repot a mammoth in full dotage, but really to beg that his love + congratulations be added to mine. Hugs + kisses to you both.

More later.
James

the news Howard won the Pulitzer Prize for poetry for his *Untitled Subjects* (1969).
Big Jim + Monstrous Phyllis James Dickey and Phyllis McGinley (1905–78), American writer of children's books and light verse, were judges for the Pulitzer that year.
he wanted me to win For *The Fire Screen.*
Pres. Cole Charles Woolsey Cole (1906–78), president of Amherst 1946–60.
the faery land forlorn Merrill alludes to Keats's "Ode to a Nightingale."
My Taki Christos Alevras.
Villiers' kind of valet Auguste de Villiers de l'Isle-Adam (1838–89), who wrote in his play *Axël:* "Vivre? les serviteurs feront cela pour nous" (Living? Our servants will do that for us).
Leporello The Don's servant in Mozart's *Don Giovanni,* who keeps meticulous count of his master's many conquests.

To Robin Magowan   WUSTL
                                              23 January 1970
                                              Athens, Greece

Dear Robin,

A cold snap here, causing the singing workmen 2 doors down to keep
their golden throats shut; but the sun is out. I went to that shoe store
today + was received like a madman—sandals in winter! So that's that.
The EVGA places don't even stock ice-cream, though it is meant to
keep nicely under refrigeration. One day I may just visit the Acropo-
lis + see about a photograph of your ephebe.

    Classical music. I've been listening mostly to the 19th cent. these
years. Dvorak + Schumann. Nothing more beautiful than at least
the 1st 2 movements of the former's Piano Quintet (Op 81?), or than
the latter's songs (*Dichterliebe*), piano works (*Davidsbundlertänze* for
instance) and the slow movement of the 2nd Symphony. Pour com-
mencer. Back into the dark ages, there is Nadia Boulanger's album
(now on LP) of Monteverdi *Madrigals*. You probably know the *Bran-
denburg Concertos*—who doesn't?—but what about the Handel *Concerti
Grossi?* There are 12. One of the last—11th or 12th—has a movement
designated, I believe, andante staccato, which opens vistas. The *Six
Concerts en Sextuor* of Rameau are ravishing—try + get the recording
with the smallest string ensemble—as is his keyboard music. Scar-
latti you know about. And the 4 great Mozart operas, his late piano
concertos <u>and</u> an early one (K.271) nicely recorded with Ashkenazy
playing—this has the glorious rondo which lapses with hallucinating
effect into a minuet before finally coming to its senses; there's also
the String Quintet in G Minor. Haydn's piano sonatas are bread +
wine—Glenn Gould has recorded the great one in E Flat Major, and
one of the Richter albums includes a late one in C Major. Gould also
does Beethoven's Opus 111, more music to live by, as are the last Quar-
tets, Op 131 in particular. Here we are back in the 19th century—that
was painless, no?—and I want to make sure, before saying goodnight,
that Berlioz' *Romeo + Juliette* gets through to you; I think the best
recording is with the Boston Symphony under Munch (?)—anyhow
Rosalind Elias is one of the singers. Make me stop. You would like
the sound of Mozart's *Serenade for 13 Wind Instruments*—or is the

title alone enough. In the same vein, there's a Mendelssohn octet, I believe, and the Schubert quartet for flute, guitar, etc.

No urgent news here. George has left for untold months in Crete + Kos—a swart shape lifted from the bust of Pallas, which leaves D accordingly more cheerful. (Not for nothing did David K. describe Strato + George as L'Allegro + Il Penseroso.) Taki scrambles all over Athens collecting papers for his visa. Nothing, it seems, will prevent him getting it unless his physical exam does. He passed blood from 3 critical apertures the other day, but his "doctor" said it was just a cold.

Otherwise all is quiet in the Ivory Crypt. Freddy Buechner's new novel came, which I liked better than anything in ages—by him; I wonder if you would, though. *The Entrance to Porlock*—Porlock being the name of a horse still legible over a stall "where the drama is" in an old barn turned into a bookshop. The general boredom here remains unspeakable, though oddly enough I don't mind it at all—I work + work—and the others seem not to notice it. 4 o'clock; time for my snooze. Life <u>did</u> begin at 40, it sometime seems . . .

Love to you both,
Jimmy

EVGA places Greek outlets for dairy products made by EVGA, S. A.
your ephebe Sculpture in the National Museum.
Ashkenazy Vladimir Ashkenazy (b. 1937), Russian-born pianist and conductor.
Richter Sviatoslav Richter (1915–97), Russian pianist.
Munch Charles Munch (1891–1968), music director of the Boston Symphony Orchestra 1949–62.
bust of Pallas The ominous allusion is to Poe's poem "The Raven."
L'Allegro + Il Penseroso Paired poems by John Milton, "L'Allegro" (The Happy Man) and "Il Penseroso" (The Serious Man).
Ivory Crypt Nickname for Merrill's Athens study, a whitewashed laundry room on the roof of the house, which Merrill adopted at his nephew's urging.

To Judith Moffett   NYPL
                                                    9–11 February 1970
                                                       [Athens, Greece]

Judy dear,

Here I sit in the sun with your paper beside me, amused + a trifle shaken by so much that you've put together. Is this the kind of coherence one had hoped to make? Maybe so. Better far than no coherence whatever. I see that you've not been able to dot all your eyes and cross all your tease under the circumstances—still, I read it with breathless interest and quite fail to understand how Dr Leonard could have been so lukewarm. May I now enlarge upon a point at which my own obscurity seems to have resisted your searching gaze? In "A Fever" the dialogue isn't with a "predecessor" or "ex-girl" but with an effigy, if you will—to be specific a Raggedy Ann doll (shoe-button eyes, candy heart) who somehow takes on, experiences, expiates a good deal of philandering on "my" part. Her lips are effaced by kisses bestowed elsewhere. Cf. Byron's "the soul outwears the breast." There now comes to mind the first poem of Yeats' that really absorbed me, at 17—a short earlyish one beginning "A doll in the dollmaker's house" (I think) and describing the dolls' anger + disgust on finding a baby under their eyes. The dollmaker + his wife console each other (and placate the dolls?) by admitting "it was an accident." It's a long road, but a strangely direct one, from that poem to the last stanza of "Sailing to Byzantium" + the triumph of artifacts. Hardly stated at all in "A Fever" is a revery of consuming the mask, using it up—even though the paints are renewed as often as they are kissed away; yet on the doll's face they aren't renewed; and somehow when she is entirely destroyed life will have ended—heavens, what a nasty thought! A line of Wilbur's now: "Fate would be fated, dreams desire to sleep" . . . Too many associations for a brilliant spring day, but they keep coming, if only to prove that you drilled in the right place! I leave here in 30 days—did I tell you?—and stop only briefly in Paris before resuming Life in S'ton. Hope the new apt. is working out. More later.

                                        Love,
                                        Jimmy

I didn't mail this because something was nagging in my head and now it is a trifle clearer. Prompted by your overlooking of Benji's sleeping-mask. (Remember, none of this was "conscious" at the time.) The parallel scene is I think when Lily misses the Pope's ring + kisses his bare hand. As a result she is "pardoned" by the Pope and forgiven by her mother, and allowed to sell her ring in the shop where F. bought it—a shop of images + effigies, notably the box of phalloi from statuary, what one might call without stretching a point too far, genital masks . . . stripped from monumental or divine figures + rejected by F (just as he tears up the "infant Hercules" photo, with snake, at the end). Lily is always able to distinguish between mask + body, able to reach beyond the mask, whether with a knife or a kiss. Hundreds of strange (to me) filaments connect mask + jewel + money + sleep (indifference/peace in your terms) until we have Dora in *(Diblos)* asleep at the theatre "muffled in gold"—but here I leave you, appalled at the number of times I've filled my plate at this buffet of yours, and by the number of dirty dishes herewith stacked for your contemplation.

Bye now—

J.

your paper Moffett was writing about Merrill's work in her PhD program at the University of Pennsylvania.
Byron's "the soul . . ." From "So We'll Go No More a Roving," though the line is actually "And the soul wears out the breast."
"A doll in the dollmaker's house" "The Dolls," W. B. Yeats's poem in *Responsibilities* (1914).
"Sailing to Byzantium" Yeats's poem in *The Tower* (1928).
A line of Wilbur's From Richard Wilbur's poem "Merlin Enthralled" in *Things of This World* (1956).
Benji's sleeping-mask Benjamin Tanning, character in *The Seraglio* (1956) based on Charles Merrill.

To David Kalstone   WUSTL
                                                                  10 February 1970
                                                                    Athens, Greece

Dearest + Best,

Downstairs, more excavations to accommodate the monstrous new electric meter necessitated by our ruinous Xmas kitchen. They have made a hole in the wall large enough to accommodate Bobby F's torso. The head can be sent floating + singing down the Hudson River. Of course he is ill at ease. Who can bear rejection even when it's tit for tat? Strato can't. He turned up last week in a cast from bicep to wrist—from too much malakía? I inquired with finesse, using a popular word which means both stupidity and masturbation. He drank his coffee while the household—Taki with paintbrush, Kleo with mop, DJ with hangover—ebbed + flowed around us. But when he mentioned that he'd be back in Athens Saturday to have the cast removed, I set about arranging to be alone all afternoon + evening. He called, he came over. He is living in Oropos, 30 miles away, with his leman + child—3 years old next month. "I've behaved very badly," his speech began, "but what could I do? One of you had to be hurt"—and at least he never banged my head against the wall as he continues to do quite regularly to her. "Hush, hush, my dear," said I. He: "Nobody ever treated me as handsomely as you did. Even at home I could wait an hour before anyone spoke to me, while in this house I was always welcome, always made to feel I belonged." His elbow looked crooked, there was a pustule smack in the middle of his absurd razor-thin moustache (which always means, a moustache like that, Cherchez la femme), his body (for we were in bed by then) older, colder, softer, more <u>used</u> and not so much modest or immodest (we were both of course impotent—it had been 3 years) as merely <u>there</u>, at last, in my arms. "She understands, I've been able to explain what you were in my life. I want to move back to Athens. I'll be free to spend nights here again, a weekend, whatever, if you want me. You're leaving in March—must you? Is it because you have work, or—" The time comes to tell him about Taki, and what is odd is only how small a difference it seems to make to either of us. "You'll come back next year? Will he come with you? No? Ah . . ." (Meanwhile his youngest brother is married and in <u>Chicago</u>.) Well. I have no notion what's in store. He is changed in many ways. One feels (one is writing a poem), deep in that beautiful goldenskinned arm that all these years has kept pounding as if for proof the crummy end of the world's table, the splintering bone working its way to the surface: something broken in him, L'Allegro laughing still but not as happily. But whatever happens next, <u>nothing</u> can spoil for me the sense that he remembers and that memory <u>matters</u>, as it does to me. DJ is too punchdrunk from his own life, and Tony too aghast already (like Eleanor) over the Taki situation, for either of them to lift an eyebrow more than a millimeter further. I doubt that I'll see him more than once or twice before I leave, but this, I insist, is beside the point. There is still a self in each of us that is the other's own—Basta.

My dear, do what you think best about coming to Stonington. After your trip to Florida, by all means. I'll plan to come in for *Manon*, but you might want to come up for a couple of days before—like April 2?—and again of course for Easter. Easter will be difficult for Taki—it's their big holiday—and I know E. won't want him at her egg-roll (we've put it to her that he's <u>merely</u> a handy-man; how long will she believe that, if in fact she believes it at all?) The Greek Easter is the previous week, but it's the eggs + bonnets that make life worthwhile, <u>as</u> <u>we</u> <u>know</u>. I do hope your prostate has cleared up once + for all. If HB were a better doctor, wouldn't he arrange for the therapy he so blithely prescribes? Ask him.

Love undying,

J.

Bobby F's torso Robert Fizdale, with whom Kalstone had been involved.
Strato can't Merrill wrote "Strato in Plaster," in *Braving the Elements* (1972), in response to their reunion.

To Stephen Yenser   YALE
                                                    22 February 1970
                                                      Athens, Greece

Dear Stephen,

It is a brilliant noon after a night of quite unprecedented nonsense.
David Jackson's ex-student (now the famous historical novelist)
Cecelia Holland is in town—all boots + suede fringe + grannyglasses,
but only really happy when she knows where her next joint is com-
ing from. Well, people get what they ask for in this house, and the
upshot was a spell of euphoric roving through Plaka's confetti-filled
streets until 3 a.m. when we all fell asleep in our Arab gear + our cork
moustaches. It seems sometimes that I remember what it was like to
<u>live</u> this way, but I could just as easily be thinking of a book read or a
movie seen—foreign, with misleading subtitles. Out of a movie surely
was that woman, at the last tavern, dancing on a tabletop, skirt up to
her waist, and in a pirate hat . . . Anyhow, I've done my duty by Car-
nival; spent, last week, a morning on the Acropolis. Nothing remains
now but to leave.—Just as <u>you</u> begin contemplating a summer here.
It's probably the best season for a first visit. Athens is far too hot +
dusty to retain you for more than the few days necessary for "doing"
it; and then you are free to escape into Greece itself, to the islands,
to the Peloponnese. Avoid Rhodes, Hydra, Mykonos (for longer than
you need to visit Delos). Order now, study in advance the simple ele-
ments of pronunciation, and carry with you everywhere Donald C
Swanson's *Vocabulary of Modern Spoken Greek* (U. of Minnesota). Plan
to be somewhere very remote in mid-August when Athenian trip-
pers explode all over the map—Aug 15 is the Virgin's day. Paros is a
most agreeable island; Crete can be wonderful; southern towns on
the mainland, like Gytheion, Monembasia, Pylos, Methoni, may be
somewhat crowded, but not by the Club Méditerranée. A willingness
to cope with the language even at the simplest level will keep you
from the clutches of those dreadful old gaffers, one to each tiniest
hamlet, who have spent 40 years in Pittsburgh or Detroit. The fat
they chew is very rancid indeed.

   Wonderful Milanov. There's the story of Toscanini striding back-
stage after a performance, confronting her with hands atremble

inches from her ample + still panting person. "If only," he growled, "those were brrrrains!" Her recording of *Trovatore* is beyond praise. I so agree with you about symphonic music, and hope that you will brave the Beethoven quartets before long. The famous Op. 131 makes total sense without your having to know anything about music, it's so ravishing in texture. Much easier than Bartók, to my fin-de-siècle ears.

I was (as always) very glad to have your impressions of the last poem. At first I couldn't imagine what you meant about the 10th Elegy in "Days of 1964" until I remembered the former's last phrase, "when happiness falls"—by which time I'd already finished the poem you'll find overleaf, where, it only now strikes me, a personification of happiness has literally fallen + hurt himself. It's not, I know, what you were "asking" of me; still, that much of it I suspect I owe to you, for better or worse. The epigraph is a phrase you hear now + then, which might be rendered "breast of marble, heart of mush (potato)" or by my favorite line in Byron, "Wax to receive and marble to retain." One morning last week (while the house shuddered beneath some mural excavation to accommodate a new electric meter) I spent reading that selection of Montale (bilingual, printed in Edinburgh)—what magic, what conviction! if only, once again, to these fin-de-siècle ears . . .

Keep well, and don't despair. I'm hoping to see those "longer" poems, and perhaps their author, before you leave for a better world in the summer. Love to Lorna.

Yours ever,
James

Milanov Zinka Milanov (1906–89), Croatian-born opera singer who enjoyed a lengthy career at the Metropolitan Opera.
the last poem "Days of 1964" in *Nights and Days* (1966).
the poem you'll find overleaf "Strato in Plaster" in *Braving the Elements* (1972).
that selection of Montale Eugenio Montale, *Selected Poems*, edited by G. Singh (1965).

To Tony Parigory

WUSTL
23 June 1970
Stonington, CT

Tony darling—

FINALLY I have some clear days ahead, and yours is the first letter to get written. The three weeks since your last reached me have been very full, as you will see. On June 5 I went to NY, met my mother and drove her up here on the 7th for eight full days. One day too long, I realized (and told her so!) when on the last morning I heard her expressing her disapproval, to David K in the kitchen, of my putting my "good" silver in the dishwasher and "whole" grapefruit rinds into the Dispos-all. We left the house in good spirits, though, with lots of bridge and little parties behind us, and returned to NY by way of New Canaan where we used to live, and where we lunched with 6 widows. That evening I dined, went to a Jap film, then played cards with Donald and his little Jap friend—then even went per sudare in a new bagnio on East 45, rather San Francisco in <u>ton</u>; returning to 72nd St late I found to my utter horror that David McIntosh had arrived <u>that</u> evening and waited for me at the airport for an hour before coming into town and taking a room in the only hotel that had one, genre *Midnight Cowboy*, right on Times Square. <u>I</u> had forgotten!! and expected him only the next day, which had been the original plan. In any case, we met for lunch chez maman, then drove up to Stonington where we spent 5 nights—always with David K or somebody as a chaperone. We played with the Ouija board, and drank champagne, and smoked pot, and took a picnic, and gave a luncheon on the terrace in the mist. One night after <u>eating</u> some Marijuana-laced hamburgers we slept like 2 babies together, and everything was easy + serene. Sunday we drove to the Morses (whose grandchild has just been born: Samuel Bedford Morse, in the Westerly Hospital) and Monday came to town, as DMc had a doctor's appointment. In the car he said, Must you stay at your mother's tonight? I said no, I'll tell her we're dining + sleeping in New Jersey at friends of yours. That way we can be together our last evening. We went to the *Satyricon*, and ate some cold cuts at 950 1st Ave, and drank yet one more bottle of champagne; and I went to bed in the front room when much to my

surprise there he was in bed with me urging me—me!—to remove my
undies per fare l'amore. Isn't life strange, the way one gets what one
longs for again + again as soon as one no longer cares? But of course I
do care; he is very dear to me, and I'm still dreaming (as he is) of our
being together in Greece for several months next year. Don't upset
our DJ by mentioning this now—he + I will talk it over when the time
comes. Besides, there's no reason why DMc would want to stay very
much in Athens. He is much likelier to settle on an island where I
could go now + then to visit him. Well, he flew out West yesterday
evening. I dined with Daryl and his friend Sam, and drove up here
today. Presently I shall telephone Grace who is safely back, with an
eye to darting over for an hour of cuddles.

And now—off to Peru + Brazil! Everyone says the mail is most unre-
liable in Brazil; that the postoffice workers steal letters with foreign
stamps. If you write perhaps it would be safer to get an aerogramma
form at Omonia—the girl will tell you the right value for South Amer-
ica. I'm getting slowly excited at the prospect, and only wish—no, I
don't even mind the thought of travelling en famille.

How are you? I hope your pains have diminished, I don't like the
sound of that "numbness" in your arm. How is Madame's arm? Not
being twisted, I trust, by Nelly's megalo moutro chauffeur? Waves
of intense apprehension keep breaking sur ces rives at the thought
of Bernie's arrival on the half-shell. His friend Lynn knocked at our
door yesterday morning, wondering If and When. She is by now just
under one meter in height, but perfectly formed, with little fingers
+ eyelashes just like a newborn child. As long as Bernie doesn't step
on her, there will certainly be room for them both in this apartment.

Are you still planning to come in October? You'd better be.

Much much love always—
Jimmy

72nd St 164 E. 72nd Street.
Midnight Cowboy American film (1969) directed by John Schlesinger.
Satyricon Fellini Satyricon (1969), written and directed by Federico Fellini, based on
the *Satyricon* by Petronius.
Madame's arm Maria Mitsotaki's.
Nelly's megalo moutro chauffeur "Big mug chauffeur."

To David Kalstone

WUSTL
14 July 1970
La Paz, Bolivia

Caro,

First words from Bolivia where your letter made for enchantment undiluted by any other—any other letter (Elizabeth? are you there?) and any other enchantment. We shuddered across Lake Titicaca in a hydrofoil boat, too bumpy + awful, how can they put such things across on the public?—stopping, however, at a ravishing island "of the Sun" where water came cascading down a long flight of stairs—"the waters of life" so I drank of them, as I have so often in so many parts of the world, one of these days we'll see if it has helped or not—and little, little girls in those wonderful Peruvian skirts, bellshaped, of burnt orange or dark hot pink wool looked through my binoculars at the snowcapped "Royal Range" and then sold me an Inca bobbin for two pennies. We then took a bus through a poorer countryside than I've seen anywhere except in Persia—mud + thatch + scrub—and 2 hours later sighted La Paz in a deep basin, ripe for pollution, where I sit now, windows open, sun pouring in at eyelevel looking down into a shabby (but perfectly gorgeous by La Paz standards) square with a statue of Isabel La Catolica + a Chinese restaurant where we mean to eat lunch. The best thing that has happened since leaving Machu P. was a 10 hour train ride from Cuzco to the Lake. We sat in the buffet car with a delightful German woman whose husband is with Unicef in Rio—she was on everyone's wave-length, which is saying a great deal if you think of Chas <u>and</u> Mary <u>and</u> me. We traversed the "altiplano" or massif central which goes up to nearly 4200 meters—grazing land, streams, high peaks, villages, never a dull moment, broken by little feasts of broth or chocolate or white wine. All around us on the train—like some inept novelist's "party scene"—were the ghastly bit players encountered constantly these last 10 days, the mother + daughter from Wisc.—the mother who actually <u>cried</u> at Machu P. but not because of Beauty or anything, but because none of the hip youngsters spoke to her when she entered the lounge with Norma, both in their ponchos, pair of exquisite sisters, eh, Padre? They were mistaken for Mary's <u>daughters</u> in fact, by some bottom-drawer Germans re-encountered at the Lake. Then there is the young woman, hatchet-faced, mini-skirted, with hair in unwashed ringlets held to her temple by a pink plastic buckle-barrette. <u>She</u> is from Frisco and her name is Faye. Yes, Faye. She doesn't think much of anything. Friends told her to take the trip. She works with retarded children, and oh the <u>backward</u> looks she got when she appealed to our party: should she buy this poncho, did it look well on her? Tonight we have parades to look forward to, and tomorrow is a holiday . . .

Oh my dear, <u>don't</u> brood about that "lack of generosity." In any nature less divinely good than yours it would have passed unnoticed. Deep down, perhaps, we are all of us ungenerous and bitter as well—if we can judge by those Dialogues of Reproach that play out, if only in mournful whispers, the moment the needle lifts from our favorite *Fidelio*. <u>I</u> think your trouble—and it is a real one [*in the margin:* save it has been our own trouble more]—is that you see yourself on the verge of getting your wish, of getting that for which you were ready to sell your soul as a much younger person: a place in the world of letters, your name in the Sunday *Times*, lunches, nay, <u>summers</u> with all us enchanted, articulate chickens who wear our success so lightly and <u>never</u> <u>suffer</u> for a moment on any score. And at the same time you are obliged to consider that, as Ted Gorey said of his ballerinas, your life is pretty much what it always was—the same drudgeries + dissatisfactions, heightened even, it may be, by the sensed passage of time. This is (as we know from books if not from experience) what everybody feels, if they feel at all [*in the margin:* cf a terrifying entry in WHA's *Commonplace Book* under "Hosts"]. This and one other thing. Which is that nothing helps except to do one's work and to love as much as one can, wherever one can. You are afraid of this. You hate the thought of being <u>used</u>—get over doing so as quickly as possible, that's all I can say. Be as ridiculous as you like in other people's eyes; you'll no longer be ridiculous in your own. If it allows you anything, the place you are making for yourself in this fairly artificial world of ours, it will allow you that. So get up from that bed + fly to Rio. ("Oh Motherrrr . . . ")

No word from DMc—I don't really expect any until Ouro Preto. I've written. I hope he wants the apt. below, but if he doesn't that's all right too. I told him I'd accompany him per antre e lande inospite if he wished, if Mexico doesn't seem right for the present. That's all I can do—offer, I mean, those two things.

No lineaments ici bas, but lots of love.

J.

Elizabeth? Elizabeth Bishop.
Ted Gorey Edward Gorey (1925–2000), American artist and writer; like Kalstone, a frequent attendee of New York City Ballet.
a terrifying entry "The men and women who make the best boon companions seem to have given up hope of doing something else. . . . Your ambitious man is self-ish. . . . But the heartbroken people—if I may use the word in a mild benevolent sense—the people whose wills are subdued to fate, give us consideration, recognition and welcome" (from Auden's *A Certain World*, 1970).
the apt. below One of two second-floor apartments on 107 Water Street that Merrill rented out.
per antre e lande inospite "Per antri e lande inospite" (through caves and desolate moors), from Elvira's aria in Act I of Verdi's *Ernani,* as she imagines what she would endure to be with her lover.
No lineaments ici bas See William Blake's poem in *Songs and Ballads:* "In a wife I would desire / What in whores is always found / The lineaments of Gratified desire."

To David McIntosh

WUSTL
24 July 1970
Ouro Preto, Brazil

David dear,

I am sitting in an empty sandbox—no, now the Siamese cat Suzuki has jumped in beside me—near a woodpile, a wheelbarrow, a wall draped with laundry. More to the point: I am sitting in sunlight, after five days of freezing drizzle spent huddled by the fire or making quick excursions to admire (in E's phrase) the "mildew's ignorant map" on the wall of this or that church before repairing to drink a sugar-cane brandy cocktail in some disreputable little shop like an amateur stage-set for *Rain*. Why, this very paper is beginning to turn crisp. The typewriter roller wrung moisture from it yesterday.

Your two letters from the hospital finally reached me 2 days ago, and I was greatly relieved to have word, even if the word is none too cheering. At least the hospital sounds luxurious in its grisly way, but

I'm not convinced, I still think you'd rather be sharing this sandbox with me + the cat.

If you can't read this letter, just put it away till Autumn. There'll be nothing urgent in it.

Elizabeth met my plane in Belo Horizonte and took me straight-away to a children's party which, at 9 p.m., hadn't quite broken up. The cake was a soccer field, complete with players + goals, 2 feet long and covered with green coconut grass. The next day we drove here, some 50 miles, to find the town shrouded in mist + rain and filled with dejected young people wrapped in their pension's bedclothes—wet blankets, all of them. July is the annual Arts Festival—movies, lectures, concerts, classes—and it confers upon the place, in spite of the weather, this faint glitter + flush of unreality, like a degree or two of fever; while boites + boutiques have positively sprouted in the damp, like mushrooms. Ouro Preto is an 18th century, non-Tuscan Hill Town: stone, whitewash, colorful windows + doors, cobbles, towers—it reminds me of an Australian village, the baroque is so un-pompous, so amiable. (Behind one of the hills, a kilometer away as the crow flies but so hidden that only a stationary cloud betrays it, lies a whole inferno of Industry—an enormous aluminum mine where everybody works—plus a little "paradis artificiel" of Housing: bungalows, lawns, a tennis court. One feels that to drive through is not entirely legal, as if a camouflaged site had been inadvertently penetrated.) There are churches all over, some tastefully restored, like Santa Efigenia whose altar, in a deep recess, looks like a many-tiered, petrified wedding cake topped by a doll under a roof of faded chalk-blue boards through which needles of daylight creak; some not restored, like San Francisco where I've heard 2 evening concerts—a church designed by the much-loved local genius, a mulatto hunch-back named Aleijandinho; some not even open, like Santa Ana on a distant hill, simple as a Greek chapel, whitewashed trimmed with blue, the "baroque" elements reduced to two mere wartlike growths at either corner of the facade.

Elizabeth's house dates from 1715. There are 7 or 8 spacious, irreg-ular white rooms with painted ceilings, or rush ceilings. The lower garden with its avocado + guava trees terminates in an untended banana plantation fast becoming jungle. Near the woodburning stove in the living-room is a big wooden figurehead from an Amazon barge: white lion or cat-face, but with horns, blue eyes and long yellow, human hair—if it is not Luandinha herself, it is probably Carson McCullers. Two artists, male + female, are also staying in the house. We converse in what passes for French, but they are out from early morning until . . . early morning. An 18 year old maid named Eva and a sporadic beggar-child named Adam complete the picture.

Elizabeth herself is a wonder. I feel infinitely close to her for a dozen reasons. The talk is easy + funny + intimate, and all the more 'binding' for not being bookish—binding in the sense, of course, of gleaming calfskin lettered in gold. There was one <u>bad</u> evening, which I will tell <u>you</u> about, and no one else. When I returned from the post-office with your letters—I'd not been away more than 20 minutes—E was sitting in an odd mood listening to Brazilian popular songs. On the floor beside her were suddenly books of poems by Lowell + Marianne Moore, as if for comfort—the 2 poets she most loves. It took me a while to make out that she was drunk—how? when? We talked for hours. Something I'd written from Athens last winter had led her to conclude that the person I loved in Greece had died. I did my best to explain about Strato, but can't be sure how much she took in. She was in tears by then, weeping for her own dead friend Lota, whose house was always in order, who never touched a doorknob as a girl, whose very <u>soles</u> were polished, and who may or may not have killed herself, staying with E in New York, 3 years ago. Elizabeth has written nothing since that time, and the horror is that a young American girl living with her as secretary + friend has gone all but mad herself and been sent back to Seattle whence she writes long terrible letters every day, which leave E shattered. She couldn't stop weeping, telling, apologizing—it was heartbreaking to see the author of those beautiful serene poems in such depths of suffering + shame. "I think you love me," she said once, "so I can talk to you like this, can't I?" It had been something like six months since she had spoken English, since whenever Roxanne left. José Alberto, the painter, turned up around midnight and was concerned to find her in tears. "Don't be upset," the wonderful woman told him in Portuguese—"I'm crying in English!" Oh my dear, the world is a sad sad place. Between E's broken heart and your corroded cornea, I feel even more helpless than usual . . .

As for the apartment in Stonington, I'll leave it unrented at least until I'm back + have spoken with you. David J has written; he returns around Oct 1 but plans to leave almost at once for California, as far as I can make out.

Now I go down to the post office, and to buy beef + cucumbers for tomorrow's long-awaited curry dinner, with Pappadums from Stonington!

I fancy that I'll arrive in New York Sunday morning August 2, and will stay that night at 950 First Ave, and somehow get up to S'ton the next day. I am happy to feel that I can count on seeing you "in the East" then or whenever. Bless you, dear David.

> With love always,
> James

the **"mildew's ignorant map"** Quoted from Bishop's "Song for the Rainy Season."
Rain Short story by W. Somerset Maugham, adapted for the theater and multiple films.
from the hospital McIntosh suffered from recurring eye infections.
Aleijandinho "The Little Cripple," born Antônio Francisco Lisboa (1738–1814), architect and sculptor in colonial Brazil.
a big wooden figurehead A *carranca,* or gargoyle-like head, from a riverboat, intended to protect the transport from evil.
Lota Lota de Macedo Soares committed suicide in 1967.
a young American girl Roxanne Cumming, whom Bishop met while teaching in Seattle in 1966.
José Alberto Last name Nemer. Bishop's houseguest, an artist.

To Elizabeth Bishop

VASSAR
9 August 1970
Stonington, CT

Dear Elizabeth,

It's 5 a.m. of a Sunday morning and I wake up suddenly feeling, for the first time since getting home, that I know who I am; and wake, as it were, with your name on my lips. I wanted to write days ago, as soon as the first flurry had died down, but instead took to my bed— literally; it's been 3 days now of unshaven stupefaction, imagined symptoms, seeing nobody except dear good David Kalstone who like a more resourceful Cordelia <u>cooks</u> and is silent . . . But as of today I'll take the former burden off him, and even look forward to chatting a bit. Yesterday the *Partisan Review* came to the house, with his review of you printed beneath a title not of his contrivance ("All Eye"); plus an odd, shallow, gushy piece on Lowell, Jarrell, Warren, Sexton, etc. by G. S. Fraser who says in effect what fun it is for an Englishman starved by the reticence + rationing of London, to gorge himself on this gooey calorie-packed American stuff. Then there's a piece on smut by that gorgeous Italian girl (Gaia Servadio) who nearly went, I forget both why and why not, to Hanoi with Mary. Well, you'll see soon enough.

Rollie is very happy with her clay figure. I dined there shortly before the Collapse, on an enormous striped bass stuffed + roasted over coals. We sat outside, the sky filled up with stars, the water lapped, and little lighted boats kept passing; you would have liked it. The toy stove also weathered the trip, with not a bean or rice-grain missing. It is installed now in the dining-room, with a bronze Japanese cricket for company. My own gifts were less well received. Grace + Eleanor at first thought the 4 pretty agate dishes were casters, and nobody (except Isabel Morse) sees the point or the beauty of those strange little bride's biscuit geodes (if that's what they are) that never puffed but just turned black + sparkle-dusted, not much bigger than a quarter. (G + E had, I think, expected large aquamarines. As Brock Arms warned us, the dazzling white beryl is no longer being mined or cut. We can, Robert Morse deduced in an undertone, <u>rule</u> <u>out</u> <u>the</u> <u>beryl</u>.) And that's the news.

I keep on missing you, and imagining that I'm still there. In my distraction I've forgotten to have the books by Hine + Howard sent to you, but will write a note today. And you yourself will be here soon, I hope. One imagines you turning over the keys (and Eva?) to Mr Ramos before long, then being measured for that Chicago pants suit, then boarding the plane. Any single step sounds so easy, but what endurance it takes to execute that long pas seul of removal to a new place. Please, please, please let me know if I can do anything at this end to ease matters. Call people about apartments in Boston, weed out student work, meet your plane—which I could easily do. (I'll have to go to Santa Fe in late August to keep a friend company in a cross-country drive, but there is no fixed date so far; it could be before or after you arrive.)

Meanwhile I trust you're well, and that things out in Seattle are easing up. Abraços to the Nemer family, to Eva, Lili, Suzuki—the whole crowd.

With love always—
Jim

Partisan Review Spring 1970.
Gaia Servadio (b. 1938), Italian writer in several genres, now resident in England.
Hanoi with Mary Mary McCarthy, who opposed United States intervention in Vietnam, visited North Vietnam several times during the war. She published *Vietnam* in 1967 and *Hanoi* in 1968.
Rollie McKenna was a friend of Bishop's, had visited her in Brazil and made photo portraits of her there.
the toy stove Bishop's gift to Merrill, it is indeed a "toy" or miniature tin stove made by a Brazilian craftsman, replete with pots filled with "beans" and "rice-grain" on the burners. Bishop's watercolor of it is reproduced on the cover of *Exchanging Hats,* a book of Bishop's paintings edited by William Benton (1996).
removal to a new place Bishop moved from Brazil to the United States in order to substitute for Robert Lowell at Harvard in 1970–71. Although she never had a continuing position at Harvard, she taught courses there for several years.

To Elizabeth Bishop

VASSAR
29 August 1970
Stonington, CT

<u>Dear</u> Elizabeth—(don't be alarmed, it's only me),

Your long wonderful letter is here today; and I fling some words onto the page hastily, otherwise you will have left for BH and Frisco . . . I'm so happy to have word (a postcard would have sufficed, seeing how pressed you must be); and to know that you're all right; and that the bad spell is over. You must never never never say that you aren't sensible. Actually I think we are both enormously sane; you even more than I, at least at the present writing. These last weeks things have happened which leave me feeling that I've begun to juggle my life instead of holding it, however clumsily, in both hands;

always some spinning object in the air which <u>must</u> be beyond me if I'm to manage at all. And I dream of getting AWAY; then I think of you there in your house, with Eva + the laundress, and whom I never saw. I don't know—these inklings of what life has to be; Randall J was so good at expressing them [*in the margin*: and questioning them, both.]

. . . I'm writing too quickly to <u>say</u> anything, forgive me. David Kalstone + I have been having (to us) fascinating conversations about your work. He thinks he is going to do an essay on Pastoral (his field) and "At the Fishhouses"; and all at once we were talking about this knowledge from the sea; the seal's curiosity making the singer sing— each learning from the other; the dredge in "The Bight" rummaging below the surface . . . DK's point had to do with the reversal from the classical pastoral in which the poet addresses himself to a world; now, so often, the world is asking, touchingly or otherwise, to be seen (Stevens' sparrow who says "Bethou me . . ."). Everything flows in 2 directions, Heraclitus might want to say if he were still alive; or as you put it, "up the long ramp descending into the water . . ." In Boston the other day I squeezed my way through 8 rooms of Andrew Wyeth who is, I suppose, the first major American in the arts since Frost. The public was fan-tast-tic: pure mass hypnosis; everyone suddenly knew more [about] art + the world than ever in life before. Boys of 9, freckled + 50 lbs overweight were talking about Thoreau. Old ladies slow on their feet + feeling the heat were saying, "Look at those red-rimmed eyes in that picture. Can't you tell how hard that woman's life has been?" As with those Frost audiences towards the end, you felt that the people had complacently come to show themselves to the work, rather than vice versa; and, while the experience wasn't wholly agreeable, it seemed to be of a piece with this two-way flow. (I bought Simone Weil's *Gravity + Grace* that day; opened it to <u>such</u> an astonishing paragraph that I've not dared to look in it since.) I'd been up in Hancock NH (4 miles north of Peterborough) with my friend David McIntosh, a painter from Santa Fe who has taken a vacant apartment downstairs for the rest of the year. His health is very bad; he's lost the sight of one eye, and even the best hospitals in the country are stumped. Rollie + he are great friends, too. In Hancock my brother has a big piece of wilderness, barns, ponds, beavers + cranes. Perhaps 2 cars a day pass by. David did watercolors,

I sharpened a pencil or two; we'd meet for lunch by the pond and swim with a pair of black retrievers who were so smitten by the end of the afternoon that they lay in front of the house after our return, howling in the most heartbroken way. Beautiful wildflowers, berries, deadly nightshade, etc. I hope you've received Hine + Howard. I've spoken to Bill Meredith about your reading at Conn College. He is technically director of that program, but will be in Pittsburgh all this semester. Now that I've heard for sure that you're coming I'll speak to him (next week) and set up a date some Fall weekend (they usually have their readings on Sunday afternoons)—a date which you can surely change if you like. He said they could pay $250—not bad for the stir. [*in the margin*: Offhand I can't answer your questions about Logue, etc. And wouldn't know whom to ask—a weekend, with all the experts in their cabins, far from the telephone . . .]

Please call from Boston as soon as you're there. I must go to NY Sept 29 for 3 or 4 days (David Jackson and my mother are returning, separately, from Europe on the 30th); but will [be] back here by Oct 3. Perhaps the following weekend you'd like to come down? Oct 9???

Oh—no, the *New Yorker* has never reviewed any of my vols of poems since Louise B did a really withering paragraph on *First Poems*. A phrase from it stuck in my mind; everything, she said, "smelt of the lamp"—which I finally "did something with" in my Eros + Psyche poem from *Nights + Days;* so I guess I'm more grateful to her than not. I'd be entirely thrilled to have <u>you</u> mention me; but what most pleased me in all your letter was when you said that reading me had made you feel like writing. More to the point, then, to put off the review indefinitely; a poem written in its place would do us <u>all</u> much more good.

Yes I'd heard about Cal; but no details; only that, for some odd reason, Elizabeth + Mary are far away in Castine with their heads together—WHY? I've been given a xerox of the (unrevised) proofs of the new Berryman book—loaned it rather by Frank Reeve whom JB is prone to telephoning late at night. It is a new phase, very uneven, at first glance now dull, now upsetting, with the unexpected flashes one expects. He refers once or twice to your loss of Lota ("Miss Bishop's friend has died") and, in a brief survey of those of whom he is proud to be a contemporary, he mentions you as writing "a mean lyric" (quoted from memory, but, I think, accurately). Which last may swell your autumn enrollment . . . ?

I've got to stop! You'll lose patience. Besides, tonight is a great party in the defrocked Baptist church next door; and one wants to lie down beforehand. Bobby + Arthur sent love over the phone. So do I. Please congratulate José Alberto on his prize. I remember his purple trousers. And dear Linda, my love to her. The batida cartoon has us all giggling. Of course I'll return to Belo H.—with his family-size bottles of meat-tenderizer, enough for a whole decade of armadillos . . . Do I remember why you are suing Lilli? Give <u>her</u> my best, and Donald Ramos, and Eva. And the cat.

> Until very soon, mucho, no, muinto (muito?) amore—
> Jim

BH Belo Horizonte, Brazil.
Eva Bishop's cook and housekeeper.
Randall J Randall Jarrell.
Gravity + Grace Brief and fragmentary writings by Simone Weil (1909–43), French philosopher, mystic, and political activist.
Hancock NH Charles and Mary Merrill had a house and woodland property there.
my Eros and Psyche poem See the lines near the end of "From the Cupola" in *Nights and Days* (1966): "The lamp I smell in every other line. // Do you smell mine?"
Cal Robert Lowell's nickname. Lowell had been hospitalized during a manic episode in London.
Elizabeth + Mary Elizabeth Hardwick and Mary McCarthy.
proofs of the new Berryman book *Love & Fame* (1970).
batida cartoon The cartoon is missing, but Bishop had enclosed it in her letter to him of August 4, 1970. When Merrill was in Brazil, they had gone to a bar that specialized in batidas, the national drink based on cachaça. Shortly after Merrill had left, the police raided it and, Bishop writes, "[t]his cartoon appeared in the paper next day—batida means 'beaten,' and a police roundup is called a batida too." See her *One Art: Letters,* edited by Robert Giroux (1994).
Lilli Lilli de Correia de Araújo, Bishop's neighbor.
Donald Ramos (b. 1942), professor of history at Cleveland State University, who was writing a social history of Ouro Preto and whose family had rented Bishop's house there.

To David Jackson   WUSTL
                                        29 August 1970
                                        Stonington, CT

David dear—

Your letter found me back from Hancock (where we stayed a few extra days; until Wednesday). I've read it over lots. I don't think it's selfish. I think it is full of the best of you. Intelligence, maturity, what you will. I don't want to "answer" it; being together will, let's hope, take care of the answer. (One peripheral point, though, I might as well clear up. Of course you were offended by my reassurances about not losing out on DMc's rent. I would never have dreamed of mentioning that if it hadn't been so much part of your argument against having Taki + Vaso living downstairs. You said you counted on the income from the house; as indeed you should count on it, having so little from other sources. So don't be embarrassed to do so, and I won't be embarrassed to let it figure in the Situation.) Anyhow, I'm glad you phoned, and glad at the prospect of seeing you and of your being here. I continue to long to see the novel. Eleanor got very excited over it when I told her. She said (she'd had a few drinks): Of course what D needs is editorial guidance. Naturally he won't take any suggestions from you—not that your editorial sense in prose is particularly developed, Jimmy mou—but I wonder if I couldn't be of help. *Pigeon Vole* began so marvelously. I could have shown him how to maintain it at that level, etc etc. Pay no attention except to her love for you; a generally felt feeling, by the way. Robert is always saying (often too audibly for poor DK's total comfort? I suspect) that nobody will ever take your place. As for DMc, he doesn't especially move in that world, or anyone's. Apart from me, Rollie is his good friend here. The ladies clearly feel that his presence complicates things, and they would rather be cool + remote than have to set another place (literally or figuratively) at their table. He doesn't have the strength to socialize. It is terrible to see how much weaker he has grown in less than a year—and with tears in my eyes I put arms around you: please, please try to understand + help; don't think of him as an intruder or a threat. Who can say if we'll get to Europe at all? It helps him to make plans; he can't answer for his state of health, what it may be by then. In any case he doesn't like the idea of Athens; a cottage by the sea or up in the hills is more likely. In your letter you say that you still think of S'ton as your house, too. Of course it is, although for years now you've been saying exactly the opposite: that you feel it is no longer yours, that I have taken it over, filled it with my friends, etc. You have also said that you feel the Athens house to be yours: the one place where you take responsibility, make the decisions, etc. That makes sense to me, more + more. I told you, after the DeMotts' stay, or was it Chas + M's, that it would never never happen again, that kind of really pointless dispossession; it is your house, it is our house too, but mainly yours, and I have no project to undermine your use of it. If DMc + I come in March, I doubt that he would spend more than a week with us (a cot in the piano room?) before either finding an apt. or little hotel or a place outside Athens. These are things he has said; and not for your sake but out of his own need for privacy + independence . . .

Later: it is such a beautiful day, sunny + (for once) cool, I've let the breeze blow away whatever remained, if anything, to be said. A lovely letter came from Eliz B. It sounds as if she'd gotten a grip on herself and would definitely be coming to take over Lowell's Harvard classes in mid-September. Won't it be fun to have her down for an Oct weekend? Tonight the Potters are having a cocktail which we'll skip in order to gather strength for G + E's pointless dinner before a huge party at the church given jointly by Inger McCabe and Pati. Whole town invited, everybody on Elaine's P.O. route. Robert wants to "turn on" beforehand. John Myers is here, staying with Dan + Ick. We dined there the other night, first glimpse of the Stones since Aug 15 when we all got mad at each other. (DMc is going to the dance with Rollie and has not or won't be part of the rest of it.) Anne told John (though how can we know, with her dulcet voice + his deafness) that my Greek family had returned to Athens. Maybe so. I haven't seen them since yesterday a.m. when I took Taki for his drivers test. Some crony of Joe's had said Shit, all he needs is to know the signs— I'll examine him myself. As it happened T didn't take the test at all. A cool officer began by asking him, "Ever been arrested?" Big smile from Taki—"Yes! Yes!" T was then asked to sign his name which he cannot do; only print it. I quickly interposed (thus saving T $5 and the black mark of a failed test against him) and we've made a later appointment by which time he imagines he can learn enough to answer the extremely tiresome + difficult questions at the back of the manual. Joey is getting married—to "Toni"; I had it from his own mouth this noon outside of Mr Saddow's. Our invitation is in the mail. And you thought you were getting away from that sort of nonsense? Edith Camp just called to ask DK + me to dine there tonight with Marian Anderson. "There's no one I can ask," she said; "I'm not ashamed of having my friends meet <u>her</u>, I'm ashamed to have her meet them!" Alas. Peter T. has (he <u>says</u>) a malignant tumor on his upper thigh, which won't be cut out for another few weeks. He has also broken a couple of toes. Geo. Copeland is now in a Princeton rest home—with <u>his</u> tumor (hip, following a fall) which is also malignant, having cobalt treatments daily. Horst came to lunch (with an old Lawrenceville Latin teacher, Floyd Harwood, who must be 88— how I hope <u>I</u> meet a gerontophile like Horst when I'm that age) and told it all.

Tony's account of Mika's rape had DK + me gasping for breath. But I am sorry to hear about la Dame etc and hope Maria isn't permanently dampened by the news. DK + I had the Boats for dinner + cards, just us 4, last night; very agreeable. I'm sorry to blurt out so much news, but it seems so long since I've written you about all these happenings on the surface. DM + I saw the huge Wyeth show in Boston museum. Un-be-liev-a-ble. Crowds of people on a weekday afternoon. The great vacant Amer. public. "This painting reminds me of Thoreau," opines a fat freckled 9 year old boy. Or (from an old permanent-waved wash-dress woman): "Look at those red eyelids. Can't you tell how hard she's worked in her life?" A curious paradox, swing of the pendulum, one feels with all "greatly loved American artists" (cf. Frost's last readings)—that the public complacently comes to <u>show</u> <u>itself</u> to the work, rather than vice versa. Hang on. Be brave. See you very soon.

LOVE—
Jamie

---

the novel Jackson did not finish it.
Jimmy mou My Jimmy.
Pigeon Vole (1966), subtitled *A Short History,* privately printed in Athens in a run of three hundred copies.

the Potters Mélisande (b. 1945) and Dan Potter (b. 1946), whose puppets, which performed locally, were known as the Mystic Paper Beasts.
Pati Pati Hill.
Anne told John The Hollanders.
Joey Joe Bruno.
Edith Camp Bridge-playing friend and resident of Watch Hill, Rhode Island, whose children, Margo and John, were friends of Merrill's in Athens.
Marian Anderson American contralto (1897–1993).
Horst Horst Frolich, a much younger German whom Copeland met in Barcelona in the mid-1930s and was Copeland's secretary and partner for thirty years thereafter, committed suicide in 1972.
the Boats Billy Boatwright and her family were Stonington residents.

To Louise Fitzhugh

FITZHUGH
[Fall 1970]
[Athens, Greece]

Louise dear,

We rather live for the postman, ourselves, so you can imagine with what joy we found your long newsy letter. It's not every day one hears only good news from a dear friend, but this time you have set a flawless example to the writing public: Mr Fitch, the new book, glimpses of domestic bliss . . . Personally I think the giving up of a civilizing glass of wine is going a shade too far. However. It was always all or nothing with Madcap You.

Rain again today, after a week of such glorious sunshine that we sat in it, noon after noon, turning honey tints. Life is very quiet. I clomp up the skyblue iron spiral stair every morning with my pot of kindness, switch on an electric heater (which only last week set fire to Vol. I of the *Shorter OED*) and sit, ostensibly working, until noon. Then it's time to go downtown with a shopping bag, pockets full of play money. Often as not I stop in the basement kitchen of an eye clinic near Tony's shop, where an old peasant woman (after first immersing her needle in a kettle of broth for sterilization) gives me a vitamin shot. There follows a recuperative coffee with Tony himself. His old cockroach of a partner, for lack of anything else to say, asks one of 3 set questions about English grammar. (On Xmas eve he quite outdid himself. Someone had brought 2 very scruffy US sailors to Alan Ansen's eggnog party. Suddenly old Mezekis was heard to ask them "I suppose you boys are starved for women?" Appalled silence. "Agh, my American idiom has grown so rusty—should I have said <u>hungry for girls</u>?" The boys looked at their watches + left without further ado; there had been shipboard lectures, no doubt, to warn them of pro-curers ashore.) Then I buy a chicken or perhaps the leg of a lamb so small that it could hardly have gamboled a month before slaughter—and back home again until the following day. In fact it's all very dull, but I don't mind and nobody else appears to notice. Yesterday when I returned, David told me that my fatal Strato had telephoned—first time in 18 months—+ my heart began to throb + flood like a sinking ship. Still, I don't think I'm in any real danger—not from him. The people one falls in love with over 40, as you say. Circumstance has fur-nished me with Taki whom we've known for some 5 years and who—although (because) he is now married with a child and has lost most of his looks—will be with me (family to follow) when I come home in March, to Make a Life in Stonington. He is goodnatured, pas du tout sortable, devoted to One—but thank goodness for the family which will occupy a good deal of his leisure; I've never wanted the Villiers de l'Isle Adam kind of valet "qui vivra por nous". A Leporello would be nice, but I doubt that T. can count high enough for that particular role. Anyhow, when you + Lois come to Stonington, you'll hear how convincingly I shout things in Greek up + down flights of stairs. The little girl (2) can already say "Kizz me plis" to her doll—which oddly enough is virtually her father's only phrase in his new language.

I'm relieved that Mr Fitch is working out. Condon himself isn't well, and must save his strength to fry only the very biggest fish when swimming, I suspect, in Government waters. They must be gnashing their teeth in Memphis—don't they all dress like Mr Coffee Nerves down there anyhow? The new book sounds too fascinating. Why do you make the title a question? It reminds me of that marvelous say-ing of Valéry (known only to me in English—from a late '30's *Readers Digest* of all things)—The future isn't what it used to be. Thank you for letting me know how that evening came out—nothing would have surprised me <u>except</u> a romance between Alixe + Miss Westport.

David sends love to you. I send love to you both. Will make sign when I'm back. xxx

Jimmy

old Mezekis Tony Parigory's business partner.
Lois Lois Morehead (1931–2009), Louise's partner at the time and her literary
executor.
the title a question The question mark was originally at the end of the young-adult
novel published as *Bang Bang You're Dead*, which Fitzhugh wrote with Sandra Scop-
pettone and illustrated.

To Stephen Yenser   YALE
                                                        16 November 1970
                                                          Stonington, CT

Dear Stephen,

More than halfway through my short circuit, I touch home base
and find your letter. Sounds as if you'd turned up trumps with Mrs
Forbes + Co—if only a little slam in clubs, say, rather than the major
suit of an entirely Gallic contract which, however preferable, might
in the long run leave you "down" some decisive number of Interna-
tional Match Points. It's uncanny the way those wonderful withered
British primroses (for I so imagine her) are found growing in every
Mediterranean cranny, to the point where the gaudy melon-flower
becomes the positive rarity. Nothing to do but smile + swallow the
brew of local experience through the overfine mesh of one's common
tongue; at the very least your stomachs won't be turned, and you can
always make forays in search of the spicier stuff.

I may be having a reaction to a flu shot. Or to this rainy evening
alone with *Les Troyens* playing. It's after all 4 a.m. in Athens, and I've
barely been back ten days. To someone's asking why I went, I heard
myself reply, "Why, Sir, to take the rugs to the cleaners"—and I guess
I'll just leave it at that. No, I'm glad I did go, even if one particular
rug never again flies as high or as fast as it did when it was dirty.

This little tour is an eye-opener. Should one confront one's audi-
ence, ever? They change a lot from place to place. Much appreciative
laughter and no questions asked at Yale; stunned silence at Housa-
tonic Community College followed by everyone's wanting to know
"how it's done"—without reference to anything as far out as craft
or even feeling. "You say you work in the early morning, Mr M. Is
that a good time to work? If I changed my schedule around, would

I have a better chance of getting published?" Then they are hurt + incredulous if you don't like Rod McKuen. You tell them the God's truth—that a mass audience means nothing, that collaboration with the media should be punishable by death—and they look at you as if you were a scorpion they had found in their panty-hose. Our nation is very sick.

So your star was a star<u>fish</u> in that little poem? I might have known. I'd even seen a Cousteau film of clams on the lam 10,000 leagues under the sea. It is terribly depressing to be so slow-witted. Or so literal.

Elizabeth B. cheered me up on the phone yesterday. Somebody once asked her after a reading: "Do your ideas just come to your or do you make them up?" Her Harvard classes (says the grapevine) are a great success. Unlike Lowell who gave a course in his own problems, she has the students writing sestinas and parodies, and they've taken to it like ducks. What are you teaching, by the way, in those 4 hours a week? Le Grand Gatsby? La Lettre Ecarlate? Do you have to do it in French? Do they understand? Do they care? Are you their first American? When I met Yves Bonnefoy last March (he had been teaching in some provincial university) he said that all of the really extreme, anarchistic students were reading nothing but Mallarmé—thrilling if true. Is it like that where you are? Is Adelaide Mrs F's ward? Or is it too soon for them to have told you the whole truth? I'm looking forward—as you see—to April. Don't be alarmed if I appear with a carload of Greeks. Please explain "rooki" and "mazout." Work well and keep well, both of you.

Ever yours,
James

Mrs Forbes + Co Patricia Forbes, who lived with two half-jackal hounds and a parrot, owned the old farmhouse in Jurançon, France, in which the Yensers rented a flat.
little tour The Connecticut State Poetry Circuit annually supported a poet's reading tour at local colleges and libraries.
Rod McKuen Popular American poet and singer-songwriter (1933–2015).
Cousteau Jacques Cousteau (1910–97), French conservationist, photographer, and marine explorer.
do it in French Yenser was teaching in France on a Fulbright fellowship.
Yves Bonnefoy French poet (1923–2016).
Adelaide Forbes's parrot.

"**rooki**" A collapsible canvas camping chair once used by British officers in India, where Forbes and her husband had served.
"**mazout**" Low-quality fuel oil used in room heaters in the French provinces.

To Stephen Yenser

YALE
[December 1970]
Stonington, CT

Dear Stephen,

A crick in my back is cutting off the happy flow of thought, but let me start a letter all the same on the chance of its reaching you in time to keep a Xmas wish from sounding like staircase wit. I got back here yesterday afternoon just under the line. By dark a great snowfall (our 2nd) had begun, which turned to torrents of rain during the night, and the house seems sulkier than usual after such a brief absence. I slept, though, in Miss Bishop's sheets (having given her the Best Bed) and this morning found a gray cosmetic pencil of hers, not in the sheets, with which, one finer day, to write something beautiful. I'd brought her back last week after a packed reading at Yale. When she finished a man asked her to read "Under the Window" "as a birthday present." Oh, was it his birthday? No, he said, but it was Emily Dickinson's. A pause; after which she wondered, just audibly, whether she approved of the cause; then, declining to read that particular poem, searched through her pages for something appropriate. What did she find but "The Prodigal"? (ED's "little tippler" aspect?) The man thanked her in a stunned voice, the reading was over; but it took us a long time finally to make our minds up to go home. She makes the most adorable household pet, sitting about all day over gallons of coffee, telling stories. One I liked was about an afternoon of drink and theological talk with the Lowells + Wm Alfred. Lowell went off to the john but Mrs L hung on to the thread, or perhaps snapped it, as follows: "Oh dear, I know just how it'll be. There'll be this Day of Judgment and God'll say, I gave you My commandments and you didn't keep them—and oh Bill, it'll all be so <u>boring</u>!"

I keep by me your commentary upon the "Yam," for the day when I can bring myself to look at that poem again—if the day ever comes.

It was written mainly for the eyes of an awfully nice shrink who visits me once a week from New Haven. I get to air my problems and he gets (he <u>says</u>) insights into the creative process. Sensational subject matter in this case left us both—as I fear it did you—with some figurative attack of the piles. It's just possible that there are still things that can't be written about. The yam itself, if memory serves, is Polynesian, and comes from Jos Campbell's account of a people who worshipped it—or worshipped, rather, only the yam grown from seeds which had already been eaten and excreted. I hope you're not reading this just before lunch. Anyhow, I'm back in a phase of aiming for ease + lucidity—with nothing to show for it so far. What's most impressed me, these last months, was the O'Keeffe show at the Whitney, of all things. I wonder how you + Lorna feel about her. A few of the paintings ought perhaps never to have been done in the first place, but even those somehow contributed to an oeuvre—like Miss Bishop's—beyond technique. It was marvelous, I mean, to see how the mere competence of the painting kept one at a distance: one couldn't look closely at the surface, the painting obliged you to receive it as a total vision whose means were all discretion and the barest unbrushed adequacy—welcome as cold spring water. How vulgar many things are by comparison.

Dark has fallen. Time to think of tomorrow's dessert. Oh these dreadful holidays. No, I haven't read Jaccottet <u>or</u> Marcuse. If nobody ever wrote another book, do you imagine it would be possible to catch up? Is there an opera house at Pau? Wouldn't it be nice to hear a really bad production of something like *Thaïs*? Failing that, we can make do with Bernard de Zogheb's *Phaedra*—his latest + greatest libretto. I'll bring a copy in April. Write me about the Grande Nuitée Dansante at Year's End—there always <u>is</u> one in places like that. Don't overdo.

Love to you both,
James

took us a long time Merrill alludes to the last line of Bishop's poem "The Prodigal."
gallons of coffee Merrill quotes a phrase from Bishop's "A Miracle for Breakfast."
Mrs L Elizabeth Hardwick.
Wm Alfred William Alfred (1922–99), playwright and Harvard English professor.
"Yam" In *Braving the Elements* (1972).
Jos Campbell's account See *The Masks of God: Primitive Mythology* (1959).

O'Keeffe Georgia O'Keeffe (1887–1986) was the subject of a career retrospective at the Whitney in the fall of 1970.
Jaccottet Philippe Jaccottet (b. 1925), French poet.
Marcuse Herbert Marcuse (1898–1979), German-American philosopher.
Thaïs Opera (1894) by Jules Massenet.

To David Kalstone

WUSTL
2 May 1971
[Athens, Greece]

Caro,

Impossible to give you, by now, more than a few scattered impressions of the last weeks. I used DJ's typewriter once only, that last day of relative calm at the St Simon; it's been the roller-coaster ever since. From Paris we drove to La Rochelle, where indeed there is that pretty harbor scene—the rest, alas, is New Rochelle. Thence to a hillside, half farm, half woodland, above Pau, with view of the Pyrenees whenever the skies cleared. Stephen had the top floor of a comfy old house with many British-in-India accoutrements including his landlady, the "P. Forbes" whose name appears on the titlepage of dictionaries published by Chi Sa Chi in England. We stayed five days. S.Y. is quite adorable, had ordered many local specialties, pre-fab quiches + brandades de morue + boules de neige. He and Strato got on particularly well—S was exactly the kind of boy SY had gone to highschool with in Kansas. Hundreds of jokes told + translated to unflagging appreciation. SY is gaunt + grinning with long straight hair, a kind of wax taper face with something of Peter Perenyi's sly glint and something of Dorsey B's velvet-eyed earnestness. Who knows what kept me from making a declaration right on the spot? Meanwhile poor S got more + more constipated, literally I mean. As soon as his bowels moved we tore off eastward, seeing neither Toulouse nor Les Baux (but stopping at St Bertrand de Comminges and the Cimitière Marin instead); spent one night outside of Nice, another on Lago di Garda; finally reached Venice. Sunny, clean, warm, exhilarating—S liked it to no end—que dis-je? the weather changed, a sirocco blew, I went with him to the Scuola S Rocco and by myself to Madonna dell'Orto, bought an expensive sport shirt in that new puce-plum color which is absolute uniform throughout Italy for man, woman + beast; then subsided into card-games in the hotel room. Hours of that. Telephone calls, to Grace + Bill Weaver, finally revealed that Umberto would be expecting us on Sunday—a week ago today. Back onto the autostrada. The car, by the way, is a d,r,e,a,m. Purring along at 105 mph through Tuscany, quite smug about all those beautiful things one wasn't ever going to see again. But we were in Arezzo too early even for lunch, so I broke my rule and spent a while in S. Francesco. At Umberto's there was a little house party—he was leaving for Turin (casa di cura cum research for a month) on Tuesday morning, and had two guests: a Count d'Entrève whom I'd met with U. in Athens years ago, a historian, had taught at Yale, silver-haired, unwrinkled, very mild + British; and a Baroness Ricciardi, née von Platen, according to U. a most distinguished psychiatrist. But (S. wanted to know) who were all those other people, men + women old + young, children toddling about— were they renting part of the house? I explained about family retainers without any tactless reference to my own (HF). Everyone very sweet to him. 3 or 4 times an hour someone would bethink himself of a classical word which S then found the prompt demotic equivalent for. After dinner chairs were set up in the kitchen while the servants stood, shushing their issue, during the news on TV. S. had a marvelous attic bedroom, I had U's own "summer" bedroom—he not having yet moved out of the small, lowceilinged "winter" one. I really took a long look at the house. It is too extraordinary—every room is painted, the bedrooms with pale wall-papery stripes; a striped Arab tent in a little library; sunlit rustic boards in U's bedroom antechamber. Old immaculate white slipcovers on every bit of furniture in "my" room, which also boasted 2 fat white marble columns + a greenish pier-glass that made it all look like a submerged quarry. In the stairwell is a sedan chair battered with use. Except for one not-so-gay 90's salon, nothing has been changed since, oh, 1830. Books + mags on every surface, or else photographs of faded people in crowns. Heaven. U. was in good spirits and asked after you, not by name of course. (But we have a new name for you, or rather S. does. Confused in his own way by so many Davids, he began enumerating them: David the Tall, David Jackson, David Klaxon . . . So start blowing your own horn, my dear.) Grace next. I'd called to have her reserve a room at the N'ale. "You're with that Greek, aren't you? Don't you want two rooms?" No thank you, one will do. "And you're only staying one night? Oh it's too tiresome, I thought we could have some <u>fun</u>, I'd give a party . . . Yes, I see. Under the <u>circumstances</u> . . ." But there was a hotel strike, no room at the N (and no Spartaco either), so a note informed us that we'd been put in the Milano across the square. I went to the desk. Yes they had a reservation: two single rooms! The réception couldn't imagine why I broke out laughing at that point. We got our double, and reported to G on the stroke of 7. What? S couldn't speak English? How about French? Italian? She threw up her hands, blew him a perfunctory kiss, and paid no more attention to him that evening, or next day at lunch, or the 2nd bonus evening when she took us out with 2 friends of Mary's + Carmen's, the Du Viviers, who live in London. (Mrs Du V used to live in Princeton, knows Freddy, Meredith, everyone; I don't see their becoming des nôtres however.) That first evening we went on to Gore's for a drink with his stepmother, her lover, Rat (Howard Austin) and Rat II (a toy terrier), Eli Wallach + Anne Jackson. But enough. We reached Brindisi at noon Wednesday and were on that night's ferry. Athens by 11 pm on Thursday, delay due to part of a mountain having fallen onto the Patras–Corinth road, and 100's of cars shunted about by ancient ferries to a village on the far side of the disaster. A Belgian tourist who begged a ride from us provided a mouvement de gaité. He was staying in Athens with—but perhaps I had heard of the great poet Cavafy? Yes? Well he was staying with <u>him</u>. I drew him out with fascination before breaking the news that C. had been dead these many years. "But I've seen his books in French + English translation! All my friends say, C'est un monument!" My dear young man, you have been deceived. He didn't speak for hours after that.

Here it's much as it always was. DJ had arrived to find Geo. in hospital—fainted in a bar, vomiting blood, etc. He's back on his ship now, but may be arriving this evening. Chester is away, but the overflow from his apartment (practically next door) keeps up a provocative parade under our windows. Tony slender, depressed about health + money. Bernie <u>utterly</u> MAD. Castles in the air, apt buildings he plans to put up (You don't need c-c-c-capital, pet, these things nowadays are all done on p-p-paper)—architects + contractors follow him about mesmerized. What do Greeks with their tribal madness know about our fancy private manias? Luckily he is leaving Wednesday on some free Swissair inaugural flight to Zurich + Boston. Not entirely luckily, as he won't be on hand to help out with the senior Jacksons who arrive on the 12th with <u>three</u> cronies for nearly a month. D has made lots of arrangements. My motto is Scarlett's—Ah'll think about that tomorrow.

Your letter c/o SY was a delight. Please let there be another on the way instantly. Love to S.O.

Tender, lingering kisses from D +

J.

DMc had an awful car accident—not his fault, nor was he hurt except for a whiplash neck; teenagers rammed him from behind in the left turn lane where he was waiting. He says poor Mary Lou is beside herself. Duncan's shrink told her she might as well expect D (if he's still alive) to kill himself once his money runs out. Truman C has got an FBI friend on the job. As Mrs Lowder said, "I'd be crying now if I weren't writing letters." It is too awful. Have you heard anything else?

St Simon Left Bank Paris hotel.
the roller-coaster The road trip is the basis of the sonnet sequence "Days of 1971" in *Braving the Elements* (1972).
Chi Sa Chi Who Knows Who, Merrill says flippantly. In fact the relevant dictionary is *Harrap's Concise French and English Dictionary* (1969), which Patricia Forbes (among others) edited.
Peter Perenyi Eleanor Perenyi's son.
Cimitière Marin Cemetery by the French Mediterranean on Mont Saint-Clair, originally named Saint-Charles but renamed after Valéry wrote his famous poem "Cimitière Marin" and was buried there.
Scuola S Rocco Grande Scuola di San Rocco in Venice, which features paintings by Tintoretto.
Madonna dell'Orto Church in Venice with art by Tintoretto and others.
S. Francesco The Basilica of San Francesco in Arezzo features the frescoes of *The Legend of the True Cross* by Piero della Francesca.
casa di cura Health center.
Count d'Entrève Alessandro Passerin d'Entrèves (1902–85), Italian philosopher and historian with a PhD from Oxford.
Baroness Ricciardi Alice Ricciardi von Platen (1910–2008), German psychiatrist and author of *The Killing of the Mentally Ill* (1948), the first documented account of mass killing of the ill and the disabled by the Nazis.
my own (HF) Merrill referred to Christos Alevras and his family as "the Holy Family."
the N'ale Hotel Nazionale.
David the Tall David McIntosh.

Mary's + Carmen's Mary McCarthy and her friend Carmen Angleton (1921–2001), sister of James Jesus Angleton, chief of CIA Counterintelligence. Carmen lived in Rome.

Gore Gore Vidal.

Howard Austin Howard Austen (1929–2003), Vidal's companion. Their dog Rat was a gift from Paul and Joanne Newman.

Eli Wallach + Anne Jackson American actors (1915–2014 and 1925–2016), a married couple.

Belgian tourist Merrill's polished account of his encounter with this passenger appears in his essay on Cavafy, "Unreal Citizen," reprinted in his *Collected Prose* (2004).

Duncan Edward Duncan Aswell (1936–88), Mary Lou Aswell's son, who had disappeared, but would resurface having renamed himself David Cutler.

Mrs Lowder Kate Croy's meddlesome aunt in Henry James's *The Wings of the Dove*.

To Daryl Hine

WUSTL
[Summer 1971]
Athens, Greece

Mon gros bébé,

Your letter is here today with its ravishing enclosure. The former being less than legible, I make haste to commend the latter's lovely clarity. Transparent monument to youth indeed. The water as waiter must be a late touch—I love it. So would Marcel if he were more than a Wave nowadays. Perhaps he is. A case in point: we drove from Patras to Athens, 9 days ago, with a complacent young Belgian hitch-hiker. He said he had no money, and would be staying with a Greek friend. (Quite.) As it dawned slowly upon him that One was not without culture, he wondered if I had ever heard of the poet Cavafy. I had? Well (very pleased with himself) it was with ce monsieur that he would be stopping in Athens. Fascinated, I drew him out. <u>The</u> Cavafy? Oh yes, known throughout the world. He had been shown many volumes of verse in Greek, in French + English translation. All his Belgian friends knew the name, of course, and pronounced him "un monument." Ils ont raison, said I, puisque Cavafy est mort en 1935. He didn't believe me, though I must say he remained strangely silent for the rest of the drive. Who could that charlatan be? Who but a Belgian would have believed him? Who but a Greek would have lied so preposterously?

But there must be some way to "stay with Proust" when one is next in Paris, don't you think?

I decipher your disinvolvement with The Good Gay Poets with mixed feelings. It could have been such a marvelous coffee-table book—photos, don't you know, taken from beefcake magazines and labeled with all our names. But it would <u>kill</u> my mother, and she has been, poor soul, forbearance itself these last years.

Strato + I had on the whole a pleasant 3 weeks between Paris + Greece. He is terribly overweight, with a gastric complaint, and wasn't really at his best—especially in circles that included, on occasion, Umberto and Grace. (We spent 2 nights in Rome just to see the latter.) But there were five lovely days outside of Pau where we stayed with Stephen Yenser, whose dear little wife had just moved to a hotel in a neighboring village, no doubt to Find Herself. Stephen coped heroically, rôtis and brandades were brought in from local shops, ready for heating. He was Strato's most appreciative audience since the Early Me; he's gone to highschool in Kansas with hundreds of boys just like S., same good humor, same simple-minded jokes. He approved your new format, and remains very set up by those poems accepted.

Here in Athens, bright sun, cool wind, lovairs to burn. I feel like a hotel-child in a field of daisies—how can new crops of those flower-faces come up year after year without one's <u>doing</u> anything beyond the occasional tweaked petal? Chester, who has moved Right Next Door, is of course in Austria, but may be back by the time you get here. August is when everybody should go to an island, and does, I'm afraid; if you want to leave Athens you'll have to risk 5th rate accommodations, or none at all. Live dangerously, "it's a mistake not to."

The copies of the April issue arrived safely, with check. Thank you again. Things look so much better in print. No news really. I'm at work every morning at the top of the house. D. sends love. Mine to you + Sam—a <u>what</u> with revisionist tendencies, did he call you?

xxxx

J.

Wave The Marcel wave, a hairstyle popular especially in the 1920s and 1930s, having nothing to do with Proust outside Merrill's sentence.

the April issue Of *Poetry*, which Hine edited. It contained seven poems by Merrill: "Another April," "Seaside Doorway, Summer Dawn," "Banks of a Stream Where Creatures Bathe," "The Black Mesa," "Komboloi," "Desert Motel with Frog Amulet," and "Flèche d'Or."

To Mary Lou Aswell

WUSTL
2 June 1971
Athens, Greece

Dear Mary Lou,

Buckets of rain are pouring down! You can't imagine—but of course you can. There is probably a full New Mexican flash flood, red with the mud of Lycabettos, for the one inevitable car to get stuck in, across the street. David took his party of Senior Citizens to Crete 2 days ago, which means I am here alone and blissfully so. Even my nephew Robin, who just arrived from Africa full of memories of beautiful and infectious Masai women, has gone off to Myconos. Tony will come around later for whiskey and ravioli. If you + Agi were here, I'd light a fire, and we could all watch the European Cup soccer match on TV. The Greeks expect to beat the Dutch (doesn't "beat the Dutch" mean something?) and who knows, if they play dirty enough, maybe they will. The Jacksons and their friends—5 people whose ages total 407—have been a terrible strain. David is extraordinary. Not simply that he is on hand all day long, biting the bullet, hugging the bear, driving them to waterfront lunches, whipping them up marble slopes; but he <u>relates</u> to them as well, snarls back at his father, gouges old Mr Neiswender's share of expenses out of his mummy-tight fist, turns on the hideous little rouged widow who wants (don't ask why) George Jackson for herself, telling her to stop asking stupid questions, stop complaining, stop thinking she's so cute. Well, it's a lesson in Confrontation. Quite beyond me, I'm afraid. The day they leave, June 9, we more or less expect Elizabeth to arrive, which will be a change, if not the Utter Dead Calm a doctor would order.

Last week I read *Bleak House* for the third time. My! Do you remember when Esther is delirious and sees against black space a starry, fiery necklace "of which I was one of the beads"? It sent me striding about the room (I was alone in the house, fortunately) delivering a lecture, out loud, about the ancestry of "type characters"—back through the commedia dell'arte, through the Roman and Greek gods, to those earliest fictions by which priests rationalized the movement of heavenly bodies; ending up with a suggestion that the Intelligence Dante attributes to the celestial spheres was somehow akin to that "fashionable intelligence" which, in the book, observes Lady Dedlock's comings + goings. It was a marvelous hour, I got it all out of my system, and haven't had a thought in my head since!

For successful hard-boiling, your eggs must be several days old. Preferably a week.

My dear, I don't want to "answer" your letter. I couldn't. But I've read it again + again, and it touches me in so many ways. You are constantly in our thoughts, your name is on our lips, our lips are on your brow. As for more material help, I won't mention it again; you know that you need only say the word.

Did you like *War + Peace*? Eleanor + Charlotte + David K + I saw it in New York—a bit unsubtle, but wildly beautiful in places. The way the camera swooped through the battles, and waltzed through the balls. I thought Pierre could have had a touch more Charm, but Eleanor said that was the whole point.

Love to Agi, and to David (don't feel you're imposing on him; he needs you, too).

Bless you, darling—
Jimmy

Elizabeth Bishop.
Esther . . . fiery necklace See chapter 35 of Dickens's *Bleak House*.
the Intelligence Dante attributes See *Paradiso,* cantos 28–29.
War + Peace Sergei Bondarchuk's film adaptation (1966–67) of Tolstoy's novel.

To Mary Lou Aswell
WUSTL
17 June 1971
Athens, Greece

Darling,

We are so relieved, quite euphoric indeed. It's just what one needed to hear, no more, no less.

Maybe this is euphoria talking, but I am curiously impressed by what I read between your lines. Everybody has fantasies of doing exactly what Duncan did: snapping fingers + taking off, cutting all the ties and, in the bargain, taking on a brand new identity. It is the <u>very</u> uncommon person who is strong enough (or unhappy enough) to act the fantasy out.

Naturally nobody can be in on the secret. He hasn't spent years listening to English Dept. gossip for nothing; he knows that everybody discusses everyone, even after being sworn to secrecy. It's dreadful what he did to <u>you</u>, these months, but I guess there was no other way.

Now, as you say, he is strong enough to make a sign. I've had some experience of Double Lives myself—though not as drastic as Duncan's. To the outsider the double life often represents a form of escape; but to the person who lives it, it is a form of growth. Year after year I re-entered a world, here in Greece, a routine, a way of feeling + acting, whose beauty was precisely its lack of connection with anything in Stonington or New York. (Someone else could have lived that Greek life in New York, but not me.) What I want to say is that over the years, to my surprise, to my sadness <u>and</u> my delight, the gap between my two lives has narrowed. One can barely detect the crack, one wonders if there ever was one, or what all the fuss was about. There is no such thing as a double life. There's one life that takes new aspects and is enriched. I believe that this will be Duncan's experience. Let him give away his books, let him even imagine he is giving away all that he has learned from them; that isn't so easily forgotten, and it will give a fineness, a glow, to the very dish he may be washing as you read these words. Books will have taught him, if nothing else, that life is shaped (what are those ghastly Marxian terms—? Antithesis? Synthesis?). It seems to me that he has rejected his past ties and achievements only to be the more deeply affected by them (unforeseen by him!) in the long run. He'll be all right, that's the carol, the carillon, for today. You'll meanwhile be patient. And I will end this early-morning letter.

A thousand hugs + kisses + blessing from us both to you and wonderful Agi without whom you'd be, by now, I tremble to think what!

Jimmy

Double Lives Merrill discusses with sympathy the kind of undertaking Aswell's son ventured upon in his interview with David Kalstone, republished in the *Collected Prose* (2004). See also his poem "Yánnina" in *Divine Comedies* (1976).

To David McIntosh

David dear,

Here's your postcard on the heels of your letter that begins with a mockingbird and ends with faces in the supermarket. It makes your days somehow very vivid—would that ours were a little less so. Sunday noon I was inaugurating a marvelous French gadget for slicing cucumbers, and before I knew it a 5 carat ruby was missing from a finger I need to trill with at the piano. The blood! the tears! Worst of all, finding the missing piece—by then drained to the gray of a tooth—resting quietly still on the block. David ran out for bandages and everything got under control except for whatever in me kept uttering, at quarter hour intervals like some gruesome clock, moans of horror + nausea. Two days later, it's all back in perspective, only a healthy throb now + then from under the changed dressing. I blame it on John Myers, that night's unwanted dinner guest. Lots of other dear ones are in town, leaving soon thank goodness. Robin is the only one I'm really happy to see. We ended up by ourselves last night in a public place, obliviously opening our hearts as if we'd met that very week instead of when I was eleven and he was not quite one. He leaves in 4 days, by which time Stephen Yenser will have arrived.

Earlier last night we'd heard Donald Richie lecture on experimen-
tal films, with two pretty weird illustrations, one by Brakhage that
moves at the speed of a card-shark shuffling, "cosmic" images inter-
spersed with peek-a-boo genitalia and somebody chopping down a
tree. Tonight he is showing some films by Maya Deren which I've not
seen since she died—since before she died. She was too "cosmic" her-
self to be a close friend, in fact she used rather to scare me with her
beautiful white-skinned, rather negroid face, and body out of Hindu
erotic sculpture, her voodoo + sacred cats, passion for Mozart; but
Ephraim thought she was first-class, and still does, and I loved her in
my way, as well. We had the first heatwave last week—perfectly awful.
One felt pressed, weak as a flower, between heavy yellow pages. Stra-
to's been around. We found some jobs for him to do—fixing a hole in
the roof, helping DJ with the pots, getting the dent he put in the car
mended! I used always to resist the notion of employing him; love
shouldn't be on that footing. Yet it's a footing that lets him feel that
he's giving something, and we never fail to embrace very gently +
chastely when he takes his leave. So I suppose I don't have a lover any
more than you do, because I simply can't use that word in connection
with a certain nutty Manoli who spends most of his time breaking
the heart of a fat, strait-laced German girl. They have each learned
the same 100 words of the other's language. We ran into them in
Plaka the other night, they fell upon us like a pair of strangers who'd
been shipwrecked together—"Tell her that I—" "Tell him that he—"
Greek + German bubbling up from his boredom and her outraged
incredulity. One gets just as tired of Mediterranean machismo as of
Teutonic masochism. Meanwhile the (nine) sonnets have been deliv-
ered, like that lady in Canberra's litter of underweight babies; there
may even be a tenth on the cutting-room floor. And other poems
started—anything to avoid that novel!

It's very encouraging to think of you off drugs, and able to keep
working by + large. I'm sorry the painting didn't turn out well, but
don't those failures always lead to something stronger in their devi-
ous way? When the land is yours you'll take a deep breath, I know,
and your card makes it sound like any day now. Won't you send me
a rough sketch of the Site? Ah, here is DJ with bad news. Sewelly's
mother's had a stroke, brain damage, etc; and S had just moved into

<u>her</u> dream house, happy as could be. I hope this letter hasn't worn you out!

Love always—
James

Brakhage Stan Brakhage (1933–2003), experimental filmmaker, beneficiary of an Ingram Merrill grant.
Manoli Manos Karastefanis, Merrill's young Greek friend, the subject of an eponymous poem in *Divine Comedies* (1976).
the (nine) sonnets "Days of 1971," a ten-sonnet sequence in *Braving the Elements* (1972).

To Richard Howard

HOWARD
22 July 1971
Athens, Greece

Richard dear,

Most gratifying to have the sonnet, which is just as amusing as I remember it. It's certainly not in <u>my</u> Pleiade Racine (acquired in 1949) but no doubt they keep issuing NEW IMPROVED editions à l'américaine. The 2nd sonnet, I'm afraid, doesn't turn me on at all, beyond the notion of those same rhymes put to a contrary purpose. Quote or allude to it in your own note if you must, but <u>please</u> don't let it appear as a "preference" of mine.

There is a note from Mona, 2 flights down, saying in effect: "Richard told me over the phone that you haven't had time to read my poems—I shouldn't have thought they needed much time, etc". Was that tactful? Luckily I had written her about them before the reproach was even penned. They invite me to spend (and cast) another spell out there sometime in the coming year—only 18 days, in an apt. rather than the diaper-haunted RC house, and for the same princely sum. Has she asked you? Shall we plan to "overlap" again? Let's!

I've been to an island (Paros) these last days with 3 adorable Americans named—and BVW tells me what it means in Yiddish—Yenser. Stephen was a student at Wisconsin; Strato + I stayed with him outside Pau in April. He + his brother Kelly + KY's wife Pamela have rented Bernie's second apartment for the summer. They all write, of course, and Stephen, at least, is the closest thing I've ever had to a disciple. All too Platonic, but pleasant. On Paros I began reading *Walden* for the 1st time, with rapture, and under the growing conviction that it must be attributed to Proust for whom the mere dropping of the final e from a famous Square in Paris was enough to let him imagine a never-never place in the wilds of "Concord" where "Henry" lives out a thousand and one fantasies of our nature-loving shut-in. A tour-de-force of worldliness turned inside-out, shades of Chateaubriand, parodies of the late Tolstoi—who but Proust could have written this poignant, hilarious book? The description alone gives it away. Surely I'm right. Tell me I am. Then we took donkeys to a nunnery, thermoses to a beach, and finally a pitching little boat to Mykonos where there were no rooms and I couldn't find either of my gay nephews—yes, yes, two by now—although we sat till nearly 3 in the boite they frequent; fun was fun. Now back in Athens we await Tom Victor, the Colonel, an elderly black friend of R Morse (organist in a Harlem church), Daryl + Sam, John Myers' return from his cruise, John Brinnin, the Burnetts in October. How wise of you to stay in empty New York. Another summer I'll simply arrange to be packed in ice at one of those clinics. Still, the hours at the desk accumulate—would you like to read ten sonnets? All right, here they are [*in the margin*: Pass them on to Harry sooner or later. Ta.]

What about Japan? When will you be going and for how long? Our love to you + Sandy,

James

the sonnet For his anthology *Preferences* (1974), Richard Howard asked fifty-one poets to pair a poem from the past with a poem of their own. Merrill's choices were his "Matinées" and, surprisingly, the first of three sonnets contre Racine's *Phèdre* by the duc de Nevers and the duchesse de Bouillon.
Mona Mona Van Duyn.
the diaper-haunted RC house Residence for visiting poets who occupied the Fanny Hurst Chair at Washington University.
BVW Bernie Winebaum.
in Yiddish "Yentser" means "fornicator."
Kelly Jon Kelly Yenser (b. 1945), Stephen's brother, author of the volume of poems *The News as Usual* (2019).
Tom Victor (1938–89), American photographer, noted for his portraits of authors, including photos in Howard's *Preferences*.

the Colonel James Boatwright (1934–88), English professor at Washington and Lee University and editor of the literary magazine *Shenandoah*.
Sam Samuel Todes.
ten sonnets Merrill's "Days of 1971," also in *Braving the Elements*.
Sandy Sanford Friedman (1928–2010), American novelist.

To David McIntosh   WUSTL

2 August 1971
Athens, Greece

David dear,

These last weeks have found me so little incommunicado—within everyone's reach, it would seem—that I'm afraid I've been excessively incommunicante, as far as letters go. Yours about Oliver's wedding, with photographs of your estate, came long ago; and today your card from the Albuquerque airport—which made me wish that I were sitting in some air-cooled corner of it, even listening to those cowboys complain about Jews. I would like about an hour in which to rid myself of worldly attachments, and then to have you + Who come dancing into view, to drive me off into the hills I feel older than. As never before (or so it seems) a whole segment of my life strikes me as over + done with, like so many summer clothes crammed, dirty or clean, into a suitcase I need my full weight to shut. Having done so I turn unseeing eyes here + there. The pines of Lycabettos might as well be the Albuquerque airport's check-room, a place to <u>leave</u> all that life for someone else to imagine it is worth stealing. We were out late last night (DJ, my nephew Stephen, Stephen Yenser and I) at the discothèque where Bernie does his solitary therapeutic dancing. He drains his glass, rises like someone being summoned to a dentist's chair, and begins to hop up and down, revolving counterclockwise with a look of despair on his face, but withdrawn, as if pretending that the floor underfoot were simply a floor and not, as it is, a bed of coals. One could hardly bear to watch. And yet the spectacle told as much truth, or more, as my nephew's dazzling chorus-boy gyrations, or my own immobility. What am I saying? That "man delights me not"? The old faces certainly don't. Evenings with Tony or Chester are like sitting through a movie for the 20th time. Of the new faces only the young Yensers' have any appeal—they are quick + alert and profoundly <u>decent</u>. I remember your use of that word last fall. You came back from Kolonaki after talking to your friend George in Patras; and said wonderingly, "He was so decent on the phone." It puzzled me; I thought, of all the words to use! But today it seems to sum up everything one most needs + values. You will divine that I am half in love with Stephen Y.—which is, in turn, only half true; the main thing is that he's my first "disciple," it's that that <u>really</u> touches me; it's not his fault or mine that he likes girls and has a face like candlelight. Nearly 2 months have passed since Strato last made a sign. Perhaps I ought to have let him solve his own problems; instead I gave him some more money, money which I can see us <u>both</u> interpreting as a final gesture—of decency? of indecency? Who can say. It has freed him from his worries for a bit, and freed me of him forever. I needn't explain to you how little one enjoys that kind of freedom, but it's in that suitcase full of summer clothes, and maybe I can wear it another year. You must be feeling by now that you opened, instead of my envelope, Pandora's box. Forgive me, and try to forget it before you write again! Last week Margo Camp gave a party in her enchanting house, full of Pavlo's paintings. The next day he was inducted into the Army and she went into a clinic for a scary operation. Her mother + sister flew from Watch Hill. And three days later we went to her bedside with some champagne. The cyst on her ovary had not been malignant. Pavlo was there, his beard + flowing locks shorn—quite unrecognizable; but he'd wangled a year's deferment, and they were besides themselves with happiness; only Margo couldn't laugh, it hurt too much. With her hair in a ribbon and big black circles under her eyes, she looked like a 12 year old drug addict. Voilà.

My love always—
James

Who On the origin of the name of McIntosh's dog, see "Ginger Beef" (a poem Merrill held back from publication for years) in *The Inner Room* (1988).
"man delights me not" *Hamlet*, II.2.
Pavlo Margo Camp's boyfriend, who painted a double portrait of Merrill and Jackson in their house at Athinaion Efivon 44.

To David Kalstone   WUSTL
                                                      7 September 1971
                                                       Athens, Greece

Caro—

Before your letter arrives, here is one to "cross" it. Rain in Athens.
Chill drops down one's neck as one mounts the spiral stair. Every-
one has left, except of course Bernie where we are going for a drink
later—how fin de saison can you get? Today's events also include my
injection of 10cc of novocaine into that ghastly wart on my sole
(sometimes it makes them go away for good) and putting the next-
to-finishing touches on an excessively rhymed ballady sort of thing,
some 300 lines, which I've been at off + on all summer. It's a kidnap-
ping fantasy in which a child so fiendish that none of my <u>friends</u> will
recognize him has his way with both Bonnie + Clyde (or Jean and
Floyd, in this case). What was the Lindbergh baby's year? '33? '34?
I thought I'd call it "Days of 1934"—the last two lines go: "It's past
belief, past disbelief . . . / Well. Those were the days." No one's going
to be wild about it. Even if I am at the moment, I can tell that that
will wear off all too soon.

Stephen and I drove to Igoumenitsa last week—where he should
have taken the ferry to Otranto, but in fact had to take <u>my</u> ferry
to Corfu because <u>his</u> had decided to leave from there that day. We
stopped a night in Yannina which over the years has become for me
what Parma was for Proust. Nor was I disappointed. An enchanting
town on a lake, with a fine high-up kastro, mosques, minarets—you
know it from the Lear views; it hasn't changed that much. A little fair
was underway—lots of booths, ferris-wheel, a "jungle" from which
tape-recorded roars + screams kept wafting through the night, even a
Karaghiozi (the Greek shadow-puppets) in the biggest outdoor café.
A little boat takes you across to a not-much-larger island, genre Tor-
cello, with monasteries, frescos, crayfish and eel restaurants, and the
house where Ali Pasha was murdered. He is the big name there—he
and the 2 Greek women in his life: Frosíni who spurned him (lurid
postcards depict "Kyria Frosíni's Drown"—he had her drowned) and
Vassiliki who didn't. The town was in Turkish hands until 1913, and
you can still see old men asleep in tall grass on the verge of waking

up and hearing that 60 years have passed like a dream. S. has 3 poems in the August *Poetry*, by the way; see if you like them. Thank goodness it's all inexorably Platonic—the friendship, if not the verse; I've grown far too susceptible for a lover.

Back in Athens, we saw Tom Victor two evenings, and not Daryl + Sam who returned very late one night and left very early for St Petersburg or whatever it's now called. Daryl got up every morning early and wrote a sonnet—si la vieillesse pouvait—with the result that he now has what seems to be an enchanting sequence called "Tablets" with lots of lacunae in brackets (representing the dull bits he couldn't be bothered to fill in) and ending with the line "An analgesic comprimé of song." Now, as I say, they've all vanished. I don't even think the Burnetts are coming. Furthermore I've stopped taking all those gut pills and feel ominously well. The last time I stopped was in Alan Helms' cottage, with Tony, where I had a frightful Attack; but I'm hoping that was mere coincidence. Now DJ + I are about to pose for a double portrait (3/4 life-size, standing, with the sea in back) by Margo Camp's lover, Pavlo, who is just 20. A birthday present for D—Sept 16, if you wish to do good for evil and send him a card? When is Grace's operation? I'm still uncertain about the exact date, but I ought to be <u>home</u> by Oct 20, pottering about in the old kimono. Ti lascio. Write us everything. Have classes begun? Can you <u>bear</u> them?

Love to you + yours—

J.

"Days of 1934" In fact the ballad came to be called "Days of 1935," and the kidnapping occurred in 1932.
Yannina Merrill wrote the poem "Yánnina" (*Divine Comedies*, 1976) about this visit.
Lear views Watercolors by the British poet and painter Edward Lear.
si la vieillesse pouvait Allusion to French saying "Si jeunesse savait, si vieillesse pouvait": If youth knew, if age could.
Alan Helms Writer, dance critic, and professor of English at the University of Massachusetts Boston.

To Robin Magowan   WUSTL
                                              10 September 1971
                                                Athens, Greece

Dear Robin,

The summer's last swallow (swallower, rather) departed about a week ago. We have been sitting in a stupor ever since, enjoying the cool + the quiet. Having a double portrait done as well, by Margo Camp's Pavlo. It shows us 3/4 life-size, standing in a doorway with our backs to a sunlit sea. After 2 sessions we look exactly like the Duke + Duchess of Windsor—should we stop posing while we're ahead? Bernie says Stephen is back. He saw him in a bank collecting great wads of $$ and drachmas, and gave a small cocktail party that evening so that we could see S. but S. didn't turn up. B. also finished the Indian which was installed in the restaurant (but invisibly, in a rear corner of the balcony). <u>Nonetheless</u> "an American collector" has bought it and is having it shipped to 79th St. I drove with Stephen Yenser in his Renault demi-cheval to Corfu where he caught the ferry to Italy. We spent the night in Yannina which has been my dream these many years. I wasn't disappointed—it is pure bliss, 40-year old bliss at that. The Kastro, minarets, the lake, Karaghiozi, squalor + delapidation plus all the verve that comes from having a lot of <u>recent</u> mythology. Ali Pasha is everywhere, and the 2 women in his life—one who refused him (there's a postcard of her being tossed, bound hand + foot, into the lake) and one who didn't (she gets an oil painting of Ali, white-bearded by then, asleep in her lap). I think a poem is underway; there are symptoms. Another excursion took Daryl + Sam + SY + me to Ramnous where there is a temple of Nemesis. Indeed. David had to come and tow the car back to town (50 km) because a bump had split open whatever holds the transmission oil. Then just last Wednesday we drove with Tony, Maria + Nelly, to scout for property off the new Corinth–Epidauros road. Stopping to ask directions we watched (and D at the wheel was powerless to evade) a truck back into us, crumpling our hindquarters like Kleenex. Paros was a success, at least—unchanged really, because the 200-odd American kids spent all day + night at their chamber-music and expressionist dance classes, and never went to the beach or anywhere that we could tell, unless the one local discotheque where now + then a soulful girl would dip + pirouette her way through somebody else's zeimbekiko. Our rooms overlooked the cinema, and we could fall asleep early, watching a fringe of little dangling legs against the window's starry oblong. Through it all I've been working—and have just about finished a perhaps ill-advised ballad (300 lines) about my early kidnapping fantasies. What madness to come here in the summer. Now is the heavenly time, and now is when I must think of getting home—in about 5 weeks probably.

Your letter. I quibble only with one point. From the vantage of my years, I'm afraid the bloom of youth + beauty can still be detected on faces well past 30; so there's no escaping that. And there's no cure for these piercing differences in age, as you are learning all too painfully. You're getting older, while M. if anything is getting younger, more at home with her impulses and needs. No wonder you can't bear to watch, let alone participate. One has read books + seen films in which it dawns on Flighty X. that Loyal Old Y. has been the answer all along; but I've never heard of it happening in life. Or at least the books end there, and life doesn't. It's not yet seven, and already too dark to see this page. Love from David. You're one swallow we wish were still here. Love always,

Jimmy

Stephen Stephen Magowan.
zeimbekiko Improvised Greek folk dance usually performed by one man.

To Stephen Yenser   YALE
15 November 1971
St. Louis, MO

Dear Stephen,

This machine, help! Nothing moves except for an arcane little metal module encrusted with ugly type. It keeps humming to itself, and is easily the most perceptible object in these 2 rooms; moreso even than the fourposter still warm from the newlywed Hechts or

Carolyn Kizer's vulgar paper flowers. What will my own decorative contribution be? To hide the latter under the former? Outside an odd asphalt balcony runs round the building with no apparent access except through windows. I took Proust & a pillow out into the misty noon sun. The trees are bare & browny-gold. Later I took a walk under them. Oaks predominate. The other tenants appear to be Orientals which must mean—mustn't it?—physicists or economists. The hallways are full of tricycles. There must have been more God-fearing people in the 1920s than we realize, to have built so many dismal little brick houses—yet the effect is funny & charming, thanks to the oaks perhaps, or the golden weather in which they don't for a moment look about to be demolished. I was so happy to find your letter in the mailbox. Hours passed before I could read it—Mona & Jarvis took me home for a scandalously early cocktail hour followed by the consumption of a great slab of meat which, all during it, had been lolling on its pyre like the late Aga Khan. Mona says she's "all right" but these judgments are relative. After I'd praised Tom Victor's photographs of her, I let fall that he'd taken an ingenious one of Diane Wakowski (just her face reflected in a motorcycle mirror at the heart of a busy street scene) and you'd have thought a snake had come down the chimney. "If SHE'S in that anthology I'm withdrawing from it. Richard hates my poems anyhow. Otherwise he'd have put me in *Alone With America*. He just pretends to like them because you do. I've been publishing for years without ever being in any anthology—haven't I earned the right not to be in this one?" It seems to me we discussed it at some length, but the conversation was never at any point between two consenting adults. I see that my path, these next weeks, crosses vast shimmering quicksands . . .

Now about that reading. I'm all for it. $200 should keep us in caviar & champagne for several evenings thereafter; and I wouldn't LET anyone but you introduce me. You have only, now, to let me know "when classes are in session" (or when they aren't, if that's easier) so that I can plan. I have a reading near Washington Feb 21, and thought of heading West after it, but my goals, as usual, are multiple—Frisco, LA, Santa Fe—and their order can easily be shifted.

OMELETTE SOUFFLEE (for 4): Six eggs. Combine with the yolks 4 tblsp. granulated sugar, 1 1/2 tblsp. flour, pinch of salt (unless you use salted butter later on), 1 teasp. vanilla, an the zest of an orange and a lemon. Melt 1/2 stick butter (or less) in an iron or enamel skillet while beating the egg whites stiff. Fold yolk mixture into these, and the whole kaboodle into the bubbling butter. Cook for about 3 minutes over medium flame, then transfer for another 3 minutes to your broiler until nicely brown. Dust heavily with confectioner's sugar shaken through a sieve. If you feel it has browned too quickly under the broiler, let it stand a couple of minutes in the heated oven before adorning with sugar & serving.

I turn out to have misremembered Eliz B's address; make sure you have it right: 60 Brattle St, Cambridge Mass. Did you see her Crusoe poem in the Nov 6 New Yker?

In your letter you strike, not for the 1st time, a wondering note (Why, James, should I be given a part of you?) and it occurs to me, not for the 1st time either, that I should try to say something about my feelings lest you feel in any serious way teased or confused by what, on the other hand, you surely sense—since you sense everything. Indeed I've grown to love you very dearly, and more freshly than—well, than S or T. (If you doubt that one can love more than one person at a time, reread *The Tale of Genji*.) The thought of you makes me smile; when something happens it's you I want to tell; I trust you utterly, and try for your sake, if I try at all, to be better than I am. What is more, & wonderfully so, I know, with or without your telling me, that these are things you feel in your way for me. Anything further to be desired, at my age gets shrugged off as a technicality. Not that I haven't imagine a life shared with you. Despite our so differently scheduled & appointed trains de vie (you still facing the onrushing scenery, I with my back to the engine, watching it dwindle away) I find myself believing that we're made for each other, that there is a destination for us alone, one which the baggage of things past, following by slow freight, would take months or years to catch up with. One never knows; one simply imagines—and my trust in you is such that the one thing I can't imagine is that any of this will alarm or dismay you. And if you're afraid that I shall now go on to tell you why I feel as I do, rest easy. A gentleman in Chamfort gets no further than, "Ce que j'aime en vous—" whereupon his lady claps her hands to her ears: "Ah, Monsieur, si vous le savez je suis perdue!"

Well, that is a shadow-play of mine. The one we saw in Yannina was called Karaghiozi.

> Yours ever,
> James

This machine An IBM Selectric typewriter.
that anthology Richard Howard's *Preferences*.
Alone with America (1969), Richard Howard's collection of critical essays on contemporary American poets.
her Crusoe poem "Crusoe in England" in *Geography III* (1976).
Chamfort Nicolas Chamfort (1741–94), French writer known for his aphorisms. See Merrill's "Selections from Chamfort" in *Semi-Colon* (1955) and *Collected Prose* (2004).
"Ce que j'aime en vous" The whole exchange: "What I love about you—" "Ah, monsieur, if you know I am lost!"

To Stephen Yenser

YALE
22/25 November 1971
St. Louis, MO

Dear Stephen,

The Fanny Hurst Chair, which it turns out I am occupying, is situated to the right of one's nightly hostess. You can't imagine the amount of dining-out; with nothing to dine out on, since no effort is spared to keep me from participating in campus life. Well, Donald Finkel was in hospital, so I "took" one class of his; and I gave a reading (after which there was a very small reception for top brass—would you have thought St Louis had a British Consul? well, he was there—in a remote sanctum of the library); and this afternoon I am to see my first undergraduate, Peggy Pryzent by name, whose poem about people sharing an umbrella contains the line "but the shorter one gets wet and sees the world." The weather has turned nasty, cold & wet; I wouldn't mind sharing a short person's umbrella. Chicago was quiet. Daryl has finished "Tablets" his poem about the Greek trip. Actually the new title is LINEAR A—some 200 lines of games with brackets. We sat down with a blue pencil, and removed over half of them in three hours, plus rewriting lines & rearranging stanzas. It was as if he had no conviction of his own, or saw what he'd written as scarcely more valuable than the product of some after-

dinner bout rime. (It has begun to snow.) Daryl has, however, been plagued with headaches which disappeared on his giving up coffee & tea, and taking for relaxation, in an old phrase of Alan A's "a drop of sobering beer." How's your head, by the way? Couldn't coffee be what made it ache? Remember Mr Coffee Nerves in the old Postum ads? Sam slept through most of my visit, or pored over accounts of the Middle East Crisis. The house they bought was once a club-house attached to a golf course, with appropriately thick golden-green wall-to-wall carpeting throughout. There's a hospital next door, and, a few blocks East, great lakefront estates, like a sort of Northern Palm Beach off-season, no signs of life anywhere . . . Here in the mail is a letter from Kelly. He's coming to fetch me on the 30th for an Appearance at Milliken and, much more to the point, a glimpse of himself & Pamela. Trains chug out of the little Athens station, and look where they lead.

Thanksgiving day. I have just looked again at Tom V's photograph of you and yes, you are angry. If it's because of what I wrote last week, what can I say? That I'd been thinking your 21-jewel mechanism made you shockproof as well? Think, in that case, of me as the grand-father clock from whose brow, for the first time in years, a cuckoo popped forth. The wonder is that the bird should still be in place; and if I was the first to be surprised, then you should be the first to smile. A line in your letter had touched me so: ". . . not that I could love you any more, I'd say, except that I don't know that I believe that . . ." And my instant thought was, But that's how I feel about Stephen, and I've never told him so, except in *so many* words. Isn't it self-evident that no one ever means the same thing by love? Don't bonds between people vary genetically like any other kind of off-spring? Don't we care only as we can? And doesn't, on the other hand, the fiction that results from feeling assume, far more than it modi-fies, the contours of who elicits the feeling? What I've come to feel for you—what's given me a delight so novel that only you, perhaps, could have expected me <u>not</u> to strike the cuckoo note at one stage or another—stems from your having reconciled me in 100 ways (as no one else, by the way, has) to being precisely Older. I mean, if the sun-set years bring a face—a heart, a spirit—like yours to look into, why then RB's Rabbi was right, and the whole question of whom one does or doesn't sleep with sinks into an even deeper slumber on cushions beside the point. (That you might not believe this easily at your age doesn't prevent it from being so at mine.) So: if you've been worried or cross this last week, you simply must not be. It means everything, it means nothing.

> Yours ever,
> James

Dear Stephen . . . Merrill enjoyed taking the italics function on his new Selectric out for a spin.
Donald Finkel (1929–2008), American poet on the faculty of Washington University in St. Louis.
bout rime *Bout rimé,* rhyming game.
Alan A Alan Ansen.
Pamela Pamela Yenser, Kelly's wife.
the fiction that results from feeling A phrase from Wallace Stevens's long poem *Notes Toward a Supreme Fiction,* "It Must Give Pleasure," section X.
RB's Rabbi See Robert Browning's poem "Rabbi Ben Ezra" (1864).

To Stephen Yenser

YALE
22 December 1971
Stonington, CT

Dear Stephen,

A misty morning at 7:30—the mist almost a relief after days of fantastic clarity (if only weatherwise), every brick, every blade distinct + rinsed in it. Quickly a schedule discovers itself. Before noon, trot over to the Morses for an hour at the piano with Robert (Bach and Fauré yesterday, Weber the day before). Then back to sit in the sun, or in the dentist's chair. At five, over to Grace's who, especially with one eye still in stitches, can absorb more attention than a lung can tar. I am reading a slim, deadpan, autobiographical work by Lord Berners aloud to her. It is he who had a piano built into the back seat of his Rolls Royce, and was driven, playing it, through brutalized French villages, wearing a white mask. Only painful shyness explains behavior like that. Downstairs, the Holy Family spread food before me, as indeed does everyone. Taki is progressively Americanized; a vandal has drawn black crayon sideburns + moustache all over his simple brown face. Vaso is fat and beginning to speak English. The dreadful child, Georgía, has become a model of deportment thanks,

I truly believe, to the clout Doc Winthrop gave her last spring when she told him in Greek (she is 4) to go fuck himself. In short, all is well, and I am thinking how I can get away fast. Richard Howard's once-in-a-lifetime move from his old apartment to a new one is being delayed. Later this morning I may telephone St Louis to see if they'd like me to take his stint, which begins in mid-November, instead of February. In which case I'd leave here in 8 days, to give me time in New York, a week in Atlanta, etc, before reporting.

The trip home was something. Motor trouble kept us in Athens 7 hours. They herded us into busses and gave us lunch at the unspeakably horrid Asteria Beach Hotel. The daughter + son-in-law of a Stonington friend were on the plane; that didn't help. When we finally took off, already prostrate with fatigue (I'd been up since 5), I found myself sitting next to a maniac. Tall, doughy man about my age, wearing 2 pairs of glasses, one extremely dark, who instantly produced a sheaf of papers and began to scribble in a sick chicken-track hand. I glimpsed words like Struggle and Fate, and once a whole phrase— "the raisin loses its point." Soon he put the papers back into a small battered aluminum valise. That's a handy suitcase, I said. (We had already spoken when he sat down; he, not knowing when planes generally left for NY, had arrived at the airport by bus, just in time to get on ours. That made me furious. You should have phoned at least, I said. But then I wouldn't have made the plane, he pointed out; I've travelled a good deal, he added, this is how things work out for me most of the time.) His aluminum case was originally made to hold rollerskates, he now said; he'd bought it in Monastiraki. (How did Bernie miss it?) Then he began talking about literature and Great Ideas. We talked for 2 hours. It was like the Zoo story. I wanted to kill him. Nietzsche. Kazantzakis. Kimon Friar (whose lectures he had heard). Start at the top of the mountain, go beyond the furthest extremes of human consciousness. Risk exposing your soul to the cosmos like a raisin to the sun (aha!). I suggested he might learn something from Rilke, the modesty of whose early work seemed particularly appealing. He wrote down the name. Then I addressed to a closed door a little speech about how the Great Ideas, far from being the achievement of men of genius (or look what happens when they are—Nietzsche + Hitler, Einstein + Hiroshima), are the work of thousands of anonymous generations, and take the form of those brain-coral reefs, slow myths + taboos, which keep the shark from the shallows our children swim in, and now if you don't mind I have taken a pill and must try to get some sleep—no, I'm afraid this last is esprit d'escalier. One tried to be gentle to the nutty, and besides one didn't want to wake up with one's throat cut. I got to David Kalstone's at 2 a.m. where a bottle of champagne was waiting. I know <u>you</u> can stay up for much longer than 27 hours, but for me it was a record I'm still celebrating.

Robert Morse is going through my poems; he doesn't approve of the very obscure ones, but it's too late to do anything about <u>that</u>. The only title that comes to me with many recommendations (*Green Rooms* is another possibility, cf. the so-described emerald my mother gives me in a poem you may recall) is *Braving the Elements*—which in turn chiefly refers to the end of "Dreams About Clothes." I don't like titles that applaud the author's seriousness or whatever, titles like *Necessities of Life* or even, forgive me, *Responsibilities*; but with *B. the E.* it would seem that the cliché does its habitual blessed work of mitigation, what do you think?

Time to make a number of phone calls. The mist is now fog, a white, wet blanket. I wish you were here.

Yours ever,
James

Lord Berners Gerald Tyrwhitt, Lord Berners (1883–1950), author of one of Merrill's favorite memoirs, *First Childhood* (1934).
Monastiraki Athens flea market.
the Zoo story *The Zoo Story* (1959), a play by Edward Albee (1928–2016), whom Merrill knew at Lawrenceville.
The only title For his next book of poems, which was indeed *Braving the Elements* (1972).
a poem you may recall "The Emerald," part 2 of "Up and Down" in *Braving the Elements*.
Responsibilities Title of a book of poems by Yeats.

To Stephen Yenser   YALE
19 January 1972
[Stonington, CT]

Dear Stephen,

Bon. Reading on the 2nd, seminar on the 1st. <u>Three hours!</u> I'd thought only encounter groups met for such a long time. Luckily David, who watches talk shows every night, is here to train me in the techniques of chatty discontinuity. And since <u>you</u> won't be present you'll hardly be able to credit the accounts, from those who are, of glibness + irrelevance in high places. Finally, it will all be on your head—which is how I suspect you secretly like things to be. You might even, by way of a happy outcome, have to leave California for good. I'll do what I can.

I've written this Prof. Yoch at Oklahoma requesting a simple yes or no. If yes, I should get to you on the 25th. If no, I'm thinking of spending my week in Santa Fe before rather than after California, and I'd arrive in that case on the 28th or 29th. By next Monday all may be clear.

A party consisting of "almost no one" sounds terribly stylish, in fact ideal. But you mustn't feel that Mumms is mother's milk to me (or conversely that mother's milk was Mumms) in any part of the country that produces Almaden's Folly, the delicious Blanc de Blancs, or indeed our smooth American blended whiskies. Better to save your money for bridge debts in Stonington.

<u>That</u> gave you a scare, didn't it? Relax, nobody needs to know that you play the game. I am simply going to overlook your "maybe" (which you may, of course, cling blindly to up to the very point of settling in across the hall) and count on your coming. My advantage, I suppose, is that I <u>see</u> you here; which isn't quite the same thing as merely wanting you. As for those dissatisfactions with yourself which you uphold the better to hesitate, don't I know them by now, and have they ever dampened me? Come huddled in your own wet blanket; we have plenty of lovely warm dry ones. Indeed the only excuse <u>I</u> would accept for your not coming would be that you were immensely happy somewhere else—or expected to be. I really mean that, you know; about happiness if not about excuses which au fond it's always

best to accept, no matter how flimsy. So—drôle de conclusion—either be happy or come to Stonington!

Yes, yes, Berryman . . . Not to have been surprised says something about the authenticity of those most appalling poems; still, one had trusted to the very end in the strength + balance of his mind. Beyond the very end, I suppose: I don't myself see suicide as an unbalanced action—jumping off a bridge certainly isn't, not compared to years, day in, day out, spent drinking himself to the jumping-off point. As usual it's all one. (Did you see the *Times'* obituary? I'll enclose it.) I had met him twice, with 20 years between meetings. Once at Princeton ca. 1944 when a friend took me + my trembling sheaf of typescript to his office. Then in New London after a reading of early *Dream Songs* plus "Roosters" + "Visits to St Elizabeths" (2 poems which, according to him, <u>really</u> put men in their place). We sat across from each other at dinner. He could hardly speak. Somebody made a remark that identified me. It brought him very much to life—"What! You're JM? God! I'll never forget those poems you brought me long ago. I really <u>envied</u> you! That <u>typewriter</u>!—" They'd been typed on a very fancy electric machine my father gave me, and dear JB had never forgotten how beautiful they looked. I thought I told you that story in Athens.

Enough for now.

Yours ever,
James

Prof. Yoch James Yoch (1938–2018), professor of English at the University of Oklahoma, where he originated the Contemporary Authors series.
Berryman John Berryman (1914–72), whom Merrill met in the 1940s and admired, committed suicide in Minneapolis on January 7, 1972.
2 poems Both by Elizabeth Bishop.

To Stephen Yenser

YALE
20 April 1972
Stonington, CT

Dear Stephen,

So exciting—I've just come back from my first Meditation Lecture, and must tell somebody. It was given in the Westerly Library. Our crazy local abstract painter told me about it, because his son is now very high on the Maharishi's list; in fact he was there, the father, telling me what to expect in terms that nearly had me back in the car before it began. All at once out came a pale green blackboard and a girl named Susan with a generous layer of baby-fat, pre-Raphaelite hair + jaw, and our own time's miniskirt, boots, and hesitant delivery. She drew bubbles and arrows on the board, and said a number of things that would have made me smile if there'd been anyone to smile at or with but which, as it was, there seemed no point whatever in not believing. Susan is going to be my Instructor or Initiator, and on Saturday, instead of listening to <u>Don Carlo</u> by Verdi and writing you a letter, I shall be in Westerly carrying 6 to 12 freshly cut flowers, 3 pieces of "sweet fruit" (no lemons please, and no segments), a <u>new</u> white handkerchief, and $75, in exchange for which I will receive my personalized mantra which just by thinking of it reduces the oxygen in one's bloodstream to a level far below that of the deepest sleep, plus a treasurehouse of fringe benefits to be enjoyed throughout + beyond one's allotted span. I can hardly wait, and already want all my dear ones to get into the act. (The number you call in LA, which is of course Vatican City for the whole movement, is 478–1569. Don't pretend this hasn't priority over anything else in your life.) Driving back I remembered a letter my oldest and weirdest friend ("Mandala's" T.) showed me from a saintly man he knew who lived behind a tailor's shop in New Delhi, instructing him always to carry a sapphire + a small piece of iron in a clean silk handkerchief, and on Fridays without fail to feed some white bread to a black dog. We could have gone together last month if we'd only known—pity. Death Valley with a difference. How I expect to bloom!

Letter from Elizabeth, who will be there when I read at Harvard May 9. The munificence you conjured up on my behalf from UCLA turns out to be contagious; they're giving me $500. And I've had to turn down—since I'll be in Greece in October—twice that from the Library of Congress where I was invited to appear with a Ms. Sexton, whoever that is. EB has written 3 poems, her first in two years—only one is a Phi Beta Kappa poem which probably doesn't count.

What else? David K. comes up Saturday. I hope there's time to see him!—the ceremonies in Westerly continue through Sunday, Monday and Tuesday. Forgive me, it's all I can think of, that and the look on your face as you try to decide whether I'm serious or not, or will be once closeted with Susan muttering Sanskrit in her white robe. Thank goodness I don't have to decide; every cell in my body, each with its arms flailing in Shiva's own dance, decided for me hours ago. You'll admit it's better than Billy Graham . . . One thing Susan said was that It makes us more aware of other people's natures + needs; so that, while retracting no part of the other day's letter, I may not have to burden you with too frequent rephrasings of it in weeks (or years) to come. Om.

Yours ever,
James

Meditation Lecture Lecture about the spiritual movement Transcendental Meditation.
Maharishi Maharishi Mahesh Yogi (1918–2008), Indian guru, founder of the Transcendental Meditation movement.
"Mandala's" T. Merrill's poem "Mandala," in *Braving the Elements* (1972), begins with an epigraph: "'I advise you to meditate on the Third Eye.'—Letter from T." "T." is Tony Harwood. See Merrill to Daryl Hine, 17 November 1964.
Ms. Sexton Anne Sexton (1928–74), who had won the Pulitzer Prize in Poetry for *Live or Die* in 1967.
a Phi Beta Kappa poem "The Moose."

To Stephen Yenser YALE

14 May 1972

[Stonington, CT]

Dear Stephen,

I thought I was tired this evening. We were 9 at table last night: a massive roast, with Yorkshire pudding, and too many wines. Tom Victor had come for the weekend (he left a few hours ago) and spent every moment that I wasn't cooking or meditating discussing a miserably unhappy love-affair, his, which may or may not have come to an end. My Enlightenment having reached the intensity of a magnesium flare, everything I said made absolute dazzling sense; or so he gave me to feel by the time he left full of, I fear, all too perishable confidence. However. It's raining tonight, chill + peaceful after so many days of people. Vermont was beautiful—one day of sun before it turned wet; but full of wildflowers, yellow violets + Dutchman's Britches growing along Claude's stream. I mostly sat reading the 450 single-space pages of his journal for 1967 (which he now thinks of trying to publish as a unit). It is so intimate as to be, finally, impersonal. Every anxiety attack, every philosophical flight, every lustful fantasy gets more space than one could ever have dreamed it deserved. Will he or won't he come back to earth?—the suspense is considerable, strangely enough; then, sure enough, real figures appear; I even appear, preoccupied, bored, distant, just as I must have been that summer; and music sounds, and meals get cooked; and presently it is another radiant morning of contemplating the *Diamond Sutra* or the *Iliad*, or given over to ironing shirts. We might drive up there in July, if you liked; it's beautiful country, and the nearest house seems miles away. Claude + Yoshitsune (a Golden Retriever) drove to Boston when I did, through driving rain which, people there kept assuring me, was more than enough to prevent all but some 40 wet faces from materializing when I got up to read. Never mind: Elizabeth was there, and gave drinks to half the crowd afterwards. Before we left the hall a mysterious young man asked if we could possibly talk the next day. More of him later. The evening ended, after dinner in an agreeably sleazy Greek restaurant, drinking ginger beer + cognac. The next morning I'd arranged to go to a friend's apartment to look at some pictures. In the room, wavering through marijuana fumes, some other people were distinguishable—a boy with a ragged orange beard, a rather spectacular black man of about 40 dressed in purple velvet trousers, red windbreaker, a jaunty beret. It was into his hands that the pictures had "fallen." Weird, primitive, carefully painted idealizations of Motherhood or Education; nunlike girls sitting under portraits of Alexander Graham Bell; or pink-faced children with axes in their hands; astronautical fantasies; the planet Venus as a green-lipped starlet. Where the artist was nobody knew; some local insane asylum seemed a good guess. "I've had some life," said the black man, sitting down to talk, with a fresh joint; "I've killed a man, spent 20 years in prison. All I <u>really</u> know how to do is fuck. Yeah, I've traveled, been to Arkansas, California—" "I just got back from India," said the orange beard. "You wouldn't believe some things I've done," the black man went on. "Man, I used to deliver ice in this neighborhood, and one evening this man said to me, Want to come in for a while? What for? I asked him. Well, says his wife, I've cooked some beans. Beans! Man, those two were fart-smellers! I sat down and ate beans, then they had me lie down and told me I'd get 25 cents a fart. Put their heads right under the covers. I must have made ten dollars and fifty cents that night." I said goodbye round about then, and went to Elizabeth's for lunch—a simple Brazilian meal of rice and . . . black beans. She gave me copies of 2 ravishing new poems, the first in what must be years. You'll see them. I almost didn't tear myself away, but did, and met my mysterious stranger, as we'd agreed, in a record shop. We walked to Longfellow's garden—he had, in fact, something of Edith <u>and</u> Allegra from "The Children's Hour" about him, long blond hair, aquamarine eyes. Larry by name. He told me at some length about his 4 years of yoga, during which he's never been ill, has overcome all fleshly desires, and lives (even while teaching Greek—he's a Junior Fellow at Harvard) in a kind of perpetual ecstacy. "I've learned to direct energy to different parts of my body. I can even transfer energy to friends far away. That's what one likes about the whole business—it's so immensely practical." I told him in turn about my 10 days of TM, and he said "Yes. That's why I spoke to you. I never wanted to talk to any of the other poets. But I could tell that you were full of happiness." (So it showed! That <u>did</u> rather please me.) When we parted at the subway he reached into his wallet and produced—

not his address, which would have been vulgar, but a heart! a small heart of shiny red paper. That evening I peeled the backing from it + stuck it in the notebook you gave me. The whole day, I mean, was a miniature Divine Comedy—the morning's Inferno, Elizabeth's lunch by way of the truly <u>human</u> element, and finally that hour in Eternity. It wouldn't have happened that way a month ago.

I mustn't tell you how happy I've been. It might imply too much about whatever I'd been before. Also, you may have the sneaking suspicion that happiness isn't altogether "right" for <u>you</u>. And yet everything I could possibly want seems to be here, within me. (You are within me, shaking your head, skeptical or at least bemused.) Poems seem to hang within reach, slowly ripening. No more nervous shaking-down of sour green apples; they'll wait + grow delicious. If something else gets felt, a sadness, a solitude, it's more like the sweat on a piece of chilled sweet fruit. It's a feeling I've known before only from the relatively few minutes (perhaps an hour's worth in any given year) of absolute absorption in work; or from those other times, familiar surely to my best reader, when the wheel, so to speak, is taken. It's "love" I'm "in" now, I suppose—but love that for once doesn't depend on another person; that "fallible god" of Borges. It's not really love for myself, even, except as the vehicle for the angelic chauffeur. There—I've gone + overstated it, deliberately: you mustn't take it too seriously, neither must I. Goodness: 11:30. About happiness, though. Hearing about someone else's, now + then a twinge of resistance to it, or resentment of it, can arise. Don't resist. Call that number. If not absolutely delighted by the results, don't forget, one can always leave off the practice and start agonizing just as efficiently as before. Night-night.

Yours ever,
James

Claude's stream On Fredericks's property in Pawlet, Vermont.
the *Diamond Sutra* Sacred text in Mahayana Buddhism and the world's oldest printed book.
mysterious young man Identified in the following letter as Larry Christie.
"The Children's Hour" Henry Wadsworth Longfellow's poem (1860) pictures "laughing Allegra / And Edith with golden hair."
"fallible god" of Borges "To fall in love is to create a religion that has a fallible god": in Jorge Luis Borges, "The Meeting in a Dream" (*Other Inquisitions*, 1964).

To Elizabeth Bishop

Dear Elizabeth,

Before I can catch my breath to write <u>you</u>, here is your letter—mortifying but lovely on this cold wet morning. Can you imagine how it vexed me to get up and leave in the middle of all the nice things you were telling me? A very strange hour followed. I met Larry Christie and we walked to that long garden in front of Longfellow's house, and sat down on a cement curb behind the monument. There was something of Alice, Edith + Allegra—all three—about him: long blond hair and sparkling eyes. He told me about his four years of yoga; how he had conquered all of his desires and learned to transfer energy not only from one part of his body to another, but to other people in far places—fascinating. Here on earth, he's a Junior Fellow, teaching Greek. I told him about my ten days of Transcendental Meditation. It was like a conversation in Elysium—where else, indeed, could one have gone after your delicious lunch?

I really adore the new poems you gave me. How can you <u>not</u> write at least once a month, for all our sakes? This afternoon I'll take them around to read to Grace + Eleanor. Strange, in retrospect, what Octavio said—I don't see the bitterness of that line, "the little that we get for free"; or if it's there, so deep within acceptance + serenity (the goose in all of us being perhaps what feels such things) that it doesn't count as bitterness at all. What <u>you</u> feel, the way you feel these things, is precious beyond words to me.

As for Claire Coe in "Tehuantepec," she is the imaginary star of an imaginary movie. And you're right, rivière is a necklace—as a witty Frenchman said, "la seule au monde qui descend vers sa source . . ."

Well. I'll picture you in your black gown, dear sorceress, receiving the Order of the Golden Broom. But perhaps there'll be a glimpse of you before you fly to Brazil (when?). Bless you again for the cocktail party, lunch, poems.

With love always,
Jimmy

Octavio Bishop's friend Octavio Paz (1914–98), distinguished Mexican poet and diplomat.
"the little that we get for free" Line in Bishop's "Poem."
Claire Coe in "Tehuantepec" See Merrill's poem "Days of 1935" in *Braving the Elements* (1972).
"la seule au monde . . ." Merrill puns on *rivière,* "river," but also a style of necklace, which he says is "the only one in the world that descends to the source."
the Order of the Golden Broom On June 13 Bishop read "The Moose" at the Harvard-Radcliffe Phi Beta Kappa ceremony.

To David McIntosh

WUSTL
27 July 1972
Stonington, CT

David dear,

I have a feeling that if I start a letter this bright late afternoon you will telephone as soon as it is dark where you are. Whether you do or not, the very notion cheers me. We've had bright blowy coolish weather ever since the heat broke last Sunday night at one o'clock: thunder, lightning, horizontal rain that blew practically into my bed from the dining-room window, then rattled against the panes like gravel flung by an angry lover locked out among a hundred popping flashbulbs. I've spent the days indoors, mostly, working a bit. Another essay has been proposed to me—by the *NY Review*—about a French poet (Francis Ponge, still living at 70) whose work I love too dearly to refuse to write about him. But how hard it is! Critical prose is a technique like any other, and my fingers have never learned the stops of that flute. Sentences come to me, like "Beauty is the marriage of fashion (habit? style?) to bone structure," but how do you fit <u>that</u> into an article? The night I returned from NY, last Saturday, Rollie had 18 souls to dinner—a table set in the garden. John Brinnin + Bill Read, the Hardings, Ginny + Rick and a rather enchanting friend of theirs named Silly (Lucille) who looked like an elongated Disney chipmunk in drag. She had "received knowledge" from the 15 year old Guru Maharashi (?) several months ago, and couldn't <u>wait</u> to tell about it. There wasn't much to tell, but she was fun to look at. Later, on the other side of the house, the moon had risen, nearly full, extin-

guishing most of the stars Stephen and I had had identified for us
the previous week at the little planetarium in Mystic. (One constel-
lation, which the girl lecturer called the Ice Cream Cone, might have
melted away with the heat.) Freer sat on the wall, making sounds
with his new flute, or quoting me some song lyrics he'd written—no
talent there, I'm afraid. Rollie had left your slides at the studio, and
these days she's in NY, but I'll get them from her. A neglected post-
card—I mean it sounded neglected—came from the Reeves, wanting
to see me, wanting to see you. So I lied when I called, said we'd tried
to phone them (they had sailed to Nantucket sometime in June, any-
how). Now they're driving to California in August, and sounded very
eager to look in on you en route. I didn't really think you'd mind that.
At any rate they have your cabin's address and your parents' phone,
and it would be easy enough to invent some days' absence among the
mountaintops if you preferred your solitude. Your solitude! I am still
reading the letter you wrote 3 weeks ago. It's the most moving one
you've ever written me, I think. To picture you in that landscape,
with those thoughts. Until I knew you I'd spent so little of my life in
a landscape (a coastline is quite a different matter), and indeed never
knew anybody who loved nature the way you do. Except through
reading: Wordsworth, Coleridge, Goethe. (Shall we read *Faust*
together some day? if I can find a not-too-painful translation . . .)
This whole self within you, that draws so much strength from Earth,
has still about it, to my eyes, something of a dream come true, some-
thing read about and believed in (because the words were so thrill-
ing) but never encountered. Oh, I'd met peasants, men who knew
Earth, whose lives were so bound to it that nothing less mattered—
except money; and if I squint I can make out a glimmering of that all
but prehistoric earth-man, stubborn, sad, knowing what he knows;
but so transfigured in your nature, like a rustic dance reorchestrated
for angelic instruments—are you laughing? Don't! There is no love
without fiction. And besides, don't we know each other well enough
to improvise a bit, now and then, on the old sweet song? Without
worrying too much about it, I wonder if I've ever been able, or shall
ever be, to show you things as real and beautiful as you've shown me.
And then I think that somehow I must have done so, or you would
not write me the letter you wrote.

You'll receive my book in a few more weeks. Two-thirds of the poems in it (I've just counted) were written with you in my mind, in my heart—for better or worse! I had thought for a long time to dedicate the book to you; then came that spell I hope we never need to talk about, which ended this year, of feeling shy, distrustful—who knows now! The book, in any case, is dedicated to my mother. I'm glad: it pleases her so immensely, and conveys something of my own rediscovered (after so many years) love for her. You'll find your name twice, though—once in the acrostic poem which nobody has ever noticed <u>was</u> an acrostic, and in the dedication of "Under Libra," a poem obscure enough to discourage the curiosity-seekers. I'm as pleased with it as anything I've done, and I couldn't have done it, not a word of it, without you. Let that stand for the rest.

Now for a drink. And chicken livers.

Love,
James

Another essay It became "Object Lessons," in *The New York Review of Books*, November 30, 1972, gathered in Merrill's *Collected Prose* (2004).
Bill Read Brinnin's partner (d. 1978).
Guru Maharashi (?) Guru Maharaj Ji, né Prem Rawat (b. 1957), controversial son of the founder of the Divine Light Mission.
my book *Braving the Elements* (1972).
the acrostic poem "Flèche d'Or" is in fact a double acrostic, with the first letters of the even-numbered lines spelling one half of it and those of the odd-numbered lines the other half.

To Elizabeth Bishop

VASSAR
9 August 1972
Stonington, CT

Dear Elizabeth,

How oddly things happen. I was on the point of writing you a couple of weeks ago, writing you in Ouro Preto—when I heard that your "Moose" had appeared. Appeared and disappeared. Nobody in Stonington had seen or saved that issue. Isabel Morse remembered the cover with a shudder; but wrote to Bedford Hills for it—where it would seem to have been thrown out. Meanwhile one received a sense that le tout New-York had gotten the poem by heart. Last week I went to the dentist, who always has his office filled with *New Yorker* magazines; but he had taken his copy home. He lives with nice James Baird who's written books on Melville + Stevens (separately). Yesterday Baird telephoned that he was mailing me a xerox of the poem, and today—along with your postcard—here it is. I've only read it twice, it seems to me a perfect triumph, it will go with me all the places I'm going (Southampton after lunch, Greece next Wednesday) and my single regret is that waiting for it kept me from writing earlier, not that a letter to Brazil would have reached you. I'm sorry too about your asthma, and hope that Scandinavia + Russia will stop it cold. Oh I can't <u>not</u> let some impressions come through, of your poem, which in the last 40 minutes since the mail came has been working in me like a wonderful pill. That male bus, with all the seed of histories under its hot hood; and that great homely harmless she-moose—that is, isn't it? the "point" of their confrontation? It could hardly be more magical, or more mild, or more deep . . .

Another quarter in which I inquired for the magazine (but theirs go to Paris) was on a visit to Mary in Castine. Grace + I drove to Boston and flew to Bangor for 2 nights—fun but exhausting. The 2nd night, after a 5 hour picnic-swim-drive-visit-to-the-"Blackhouse," which got us back in time to change + go to a cocktail party, everyone was so tired after dinner, no question of <u>more</u> Good Talk, that Mary bravely read aloud, for nearly 2 hours, a story by Adalbert Stifter about children lost on a mountaintop—after which it was late enough to go to bed. She was so happy to hear how well you were, though of course at the time you weren't.

My summer has been a bit frantic, nothing to show for it either. Greece looms through the mist like a haven. I want to stay 6 months, come back in February, then perhaps return to Athens fairly promptly, like late May, for another 6 months; and see how much of this novel I want to write gets written.

David Kalstone has been in Venice all summer, turning 40, and meeting Pound. Not entirely silent: he turned, once, to their mutual friend, and asked, cutting an eye at DK, "What's <u>he</u> up to?" I just finished reading *The Pound Era* (Kenner) which you've surely seen, and feel very exalted by it by + large. DK's coming to Greece for a week at the end of August. David + I will meet him in Corfu and drive to Athens by way of Yannina and Delphi. If only you and Alice were coming too!

Forgive this jumbled page—and please, when you get it, send a note to Athens (Athinaion Efivon 44) saying how you are and how the trip was.

With love always,
Jimmy

James Baird Author of *Ishmael: A Study of the Symbolic Mode in Primitivism* (1956), in part on Melville, and *The Dome and the Rock: Structure in the Poetry of Wallace Stevens* (1968) on Stevens.
"Blackhouse" The Black House is a museum on the Woodlawn estate in Ellsworth, Maine.
Adalbert Stifter Austrian writer (1805–68); the work in question is his *Bergkristall* (Rock Crystal, 1845).
The Pound Era (1971), monumental study of literary modernism by Hugh Kenner, one of the few literary critical studies Merrill extolled.
Alice Alice Methfessel (1943–2009), Bishop's partner and literary executor.

To Hellen Ingram Plummer

EMORY
30 September 1972
Athens, Greece

Dearest Mama,

The weather keeps changing. Two days ago was a scorcher. Last night we lit the fire and sat home in sweaters and furlined slippers ($1.35 a pair) providentially ordered in Delphi last month. Today they came to clean + light the furnace. And the living-room is being repainted; white paint scraped off the ceiling lies everywhere. D. has gone to bed with a pillow over his head.

Your note about the review is here today. Lots of people have written about it. No, I hadn't seen it beforehand, nor have I ever met Mrs Vendler. She was pointed out to me leaving the auditorium where I read at Harvard last spring—a rather hefty person, 35ish. David K. says her books are good. I'd known her only through other reviews in the *NY Times*. I quite understand what gives you pause in the review, and how you must feel at the thought of "other people" reading it.

I'm very touched by the gentleness with which you mention it. It has taught us both a hard lesson over so many years now. I've thought more and more of late: How can it be that something so crucial, for better or worse, to my life, can't be aired between us except in the most oblique fashion? Its principal, and not least oblique, "airing" is of course in my work. Anyone who reads me with the slightest intelligence knows pretty much what my life has been and is. One doesn't outgrow a sense of shame by silently nursing it. And as long as one isn't going to change one's ways, it's precisely the shame that must be <u>lived</u> <u>down</u>, as I think I have managed to do, for my own peace of mind if not yours, over the last 25 years. Happily those years have also seen a marked change in social attitudes + conventions. It cannot be <u>merely</u> because I'm who I am that people are so nice to me. I mean both strangers and a world as "conventional" as Atlanta or even Anniston where I increasingly feel that I can be myself, without having to hide <u>or</u> to emphasize what this involves. The subject <u>is</u> so important to my work, and in it, that I didn't feel HV was encroaching, but simply mentioning a fact for which there was plenty of textual evidence. I was in fact impressed by her own easy acceptance—not even resorting to phrases like "not for everybody" or "limited appeal"—and felt that in her own mild-mannered way she had made a private decision analogous to that of the court (was it the Supreme one?) when it ruled that homosexuals could hold government jobs. I also believe that this general relaxing of attitude is reflected in your own. It can't be <u>merely</u> because you have fretted and suffered and blamed yourself and been snapped at by me for your pains, that you can minimize the issue to the scale of your letter. It cost you something to do so, I know my dear; what I feel, and hope I am right in feeling, is that it cost you far less than it would have done in the past. Enough.

Love always,
Jimmy

the review Of *Braving the Elements*, in *The New York Times Book Review*, 24 September 1972, by Helen Vendler (b. 1933), American literary critic and Harvard professor. **that of the court** Merrill probably refers to the 1969 case of *Norton v. Macy*, in which the Washington DC Court of Appeals decided that federal employees could not be summarily dismissed for homosexual conduct, and that a "rational nexus" between homosexuality and employee incompetence must be shown to justify dismissal.

To Claude Fredericks GETTY
3 October 1972
Athens, Greece

Dear Claude,

These days, while work is being done on the house, seem like the best time to send you an early birthday greeting—but what has gone wrong with the typewriter? ah, I see. We've had the salóni repainted by Manoli, with whom I find myself en menage after some 3 years of casual gettings-together. David mixed the colors, striving for tobacco brown (shades of 35th St?) and came up with the most extraordinary bilious ocher which however has miraculously dried to a rich clay-gray, too smart for words. Today my study ceiling is the target; it has been falling down; and now for a while, it won't. These weeks have been quiet but . . . hectic too. I've worked a lot but not well. Partly my growing distaste for writing prose must be at the root. It is what the gutting of fish is to the arrangement of the sashimi plate—raw material in either case, but what a difference between the slime + stink and those overlapping transparencies. And time seems to pass so quickly—over 6 weeks already! What couldn't one get done in 6 weeks 20 years ago. Did you see my beautiful big puff in the Sunday *Times*? It made my flesh crawl with pleasure for a whole day. My poor mother gagged at "12 letters of the alphabet"—which I figured must mean the phrase "with his lover"—but mothers mellow with the years, as you know, and I felt she had simply given in to an involuntary reflex. Pushing my luck perhaps, I even wrote to say so! (Manoli is sitting behind me reading the paper and singing a song about Lorca, "Why, why, did they kill the cheerful poet in Granada?")

How are you, dear friend? I left you on the threshold of much new, or resumed, experience—classes, Tim nearby once again . . . Shall I read all about it in your journal next spring in Pawlet, or will you provide me meanwhile with an abridgement? Maybe you don't agree with me that getting things done grows harder + harder as time speeds up; but I do so hope that you will make the 3 or 4 all but impossible decisions necessary to preparing a volume of the journal, make them if need be with eyes tight shut; or don't make them at all but indicate what they are in the letter with which you send the copy out; and

<u>send</u> it out. What can you lose? And the gain is conceivably immense. Shall I authorize you to include my disease of that year, would that help? Oh dear, well . . . refléchissons-y.

David lived through a birthday last month, his fiftieth. Celebrations went on all week, lunch at Sounion, dinners at home, an L-shaped cake, and more one-noon, one-afternoon, and one-night stands than the poor dear could cope with. Photographs keep being developed at which he stares in applied fascination: "Look at those wrinkles! those pouches! that double chin! Is that ME?" And of course it isn't, we never tire of assuring him. I'm not exactly a walking advertisement for TM, but I wish he'd try it. There's a center in Nea Smyrni, quite near though as yet unvisited—think of being given a Greek mantra. It is dark, a dense purple-blue, and only 6:30. Yeats + the *Cantos* keep me company up here. The Kenner book worked like cataract surgery on me, I can begin to read Pound at last—still loathing the mannerisms but no longer blind to the extraordinary beauties + rightness of feeling. Knowing that you love him gives me further courage. I also read a lot more Ponge (in order to write a short lopsided piece for the *NYReview*) and admire <u>him</u> more + more. He has a programmatic side too, dullish reflections + pronouncements; but as he disarmingly says, if he'd thought anyone would simply read him and understand, he would never have bothered with the critico-philosophical context. My dear. Many happy years.

> Love always,
> James

To David Kalstone

WUSTL
6 October 1972
Athens, Greece

Vita mine,

(This is a complicated pun. You are known by Greek members of the household here as David II, or David Beta—pronounced Vita, so you see? Not so complicated after all. "Who are we going to send this photograph to? To David B?" asks Manoli, by then bent double with laughter. We'll see if he straightens up by this evening when I tell him I've done just that.)

A cold snap has made us turn on the furnace. Luckily M. had finished repainting my study "after the fire" (the water-pik that burned up last year) <u>and</u> the salon. You should have seen DJ mixing colors. Finally we had to settle—there was so much of it!—for a bilious yellow which has however dried to the most beautiful clay gray or olive drab imaginable. Tutti quanti very pleased. Letters keep pouring in about what John Myers, in his, calls "Helen Venable's review." My mother made a brave try, but couldn't help admitting that her delight had been overshadowed by "12 little letters of the alphabet"—which I've figured must mean the phrase "with his lover." I'd been so particularly pleased by HV's cool acknowledgement of so much hot subject matter that I forthwith wrote Mrs P the first frank letter in over 20 years, saying how times have changed, and what do her enthusiastic friends think those poems are <u>about</u> anyhow? <u>Terribly</u> affectionate in tone, you understand. It remains for me to thank <u>you</u> properly for your hand in it all. Even if you didn't pick HV, you must have had everything to do with the dimensions of the review, and its prominence, even perhaps the felicitous selection of the Geode extract. It is so far + away my finest hour vis à vis the media, that I keep repairing to it again + again, quite as if the two intervening Book Selections hadn't made it ancient history, gilt o'erdusted. Another letter was from Bobby Fizz, even though I'd forgotten to send them a copy of the book. (My Greek copies haven't come. Would you be an angel and phone? Her name is Ruth Yanovich, at Ath—HF's assistant—and ask her to check on if and when the 10 copies they were sending me here got mailed. This way, they'll probably arrive tomorrow. They were the 10 complimentary copies I had coming to me.)

Finally we've written a long newsy to the Ladies—your account made us take pity on them. How sad, how dismal it sounded. Here, on the other hand, Chester has arrived wearing a Charlie Chan moustache (Kaiser Wilhelm, says Alan) which mercifully veils that huge nude MOUTH (100's of satisfied users). Maria spent a day in court, on the banc des accusés what's more; she crossed her legs comfortably, then saw her lawyer frantically signalling to uncross them: RESPECT! Preposterous people swore they owned some property belonging to her.

"I was offered 500,000 drachmas not to testify," testified one young man. "And you didn't take it?" marveled the judge, shortly before ruling in Mme's favor. Bernie is (perhaps) leaving on Tuesday—very, very low in his mind. I meanwhile grow fonder + fonder of Manoli; is this wise? At my age! D keeps cynically adding up all the <u>other</u> people I'm in love with, or loved by, and when I make some feeble allusion to his one-noon or one-night stands, says he would rather run a bordello than a seraglio. Tell me where <u>you</u> stand with Ed. I get a sense that he's causing you more pain than pleasure once again. Remember that everyone is <u>more</u> <u>or</u> <u>less</u> selfish, and think if he's not distinctly less than most. And write about your tests. Who does Granny love? You, dear one, you.

J.

"after the fire" Title of a poem in *Braving the Elements* (1972).
"Helen Venable's review" John Myers was likely punning on the name of Violet Venable in Tennessee Williams's play *Suddenly Last Summer* (1957).
the Geode extract Quote from section 8 of "In Nine Sleep Valley," also in *Braving the Elements*.
gilt o'erdusted From *Troilus and Cressida*, III.3.
Ath—HF's assistant Atheneum, Harry Ford's assistant.
the Ladies Eleanor Perenyi and Grace Stone.
Alan Alan Ansen.
banc des accusés Defendants' dock.
Ed Edmund White (b. 1940), American novelist and memoirist, writer on gay love.

To Richard Howard

POSTCARD | HOWARD
10 October 1972
Athens, Greece

Dear Richard—

I am too blissfully busy writing a poem FOR YOU (if it turns out well, or perhaps even if it doesn't) to write the pages you deserve. You are our fastest link with the real world, bless your heart. The poem is already longish + involves a jigsaw puzzle, a Rilke translation of Valéry, "and much, much more." Chester is here with lots of Charlie Chan facial hair that makes him look less vulnerable—so deceptive. His 3rd or 4th Kosta is behaving abominably; he + Alan sip their cocktails pretending ladylike unconcern, but <u>we</u> must hear all about it morning, noon, + night. That is the only "Futility" of any distinction I have come across. And a cock ring! Rush me a <u>dozen</u>.

> Love to you + Sandy.
> James

Richard Howard See Biographies.
postcard On the front, reproduction of a painting of Ali Pasha in the arms of Kyra Vassiliki, historical characters discussed in Merrill's poem "Yánnina" in *Divine Comedies* (1976).
a poem "Lost in Translation" in *Divine Comedies* (1976).

To David McIntosh

WUSTL
12 October 1972
Athens, Greece

David dear,

This afternoon I've written one of a series of letters that should eventually result in a new Will—which leaves me feeling almost as extinct as the dodo. But then came a lovely meditation, which seemed to be organized about a single musical interval, the minor third, or some three-dimensional version thereof, so that faces appeared, and walks were taken, within it; and I feel rather cheerier.

Your account of Tom is too painful. It seems important to keep in some sort of touch with him right now, but words all but fail me when I sit down to write, and the result is a far gloomier message than any <u>he</u> would send. Poor man. Selling the Old Lyme house is bound to be a frightful strain; if they can survive that, they'll probably be attending pueblo dances in 1990. I like the sound of your Jungian—his name is particularly promising. Not that I've ever read any Swedenborg, but isn't he full of ghostly moonlit cavalcades and talking angels? Henry James says so somewhere; his father was a great believer in S.

If he takes you as a patient, you must be prepared to commit yourself very much to him—otherwise there is no point. I mean, don't "decide" after 5 or 6 sessions that you want out. Unless of course he has reached the same decision. I may be mistaken, but it often strikes me that you are somewhat naïve about words + terms. Terms like "guide" + "inner self", etc., have their counterparts in the Freudian vocabulary (don't ask me what they are!). Indiscreet probings, such as you felt endangered you at Bethesda, raise questions of mere manners; the truths they were reaching for were nonetheless essential for the doctor to know. Language itself is only one of many languages, don't forget that. Along with preparing yourself for some bad times, remember how free you are, should the occasion arise, to call him a clumsy fool to his face. It is part of his business to know better than to take it personally. And it will bring you closer together in the long run.

I wish I could see your "Father"! From what you say, a slide might look too much like a smear. I've been quite blissfully at work on a longish, loose poem, another shaft sent down into childhood, at whose bottom, or near it, a glorious jigsaw puzzle is being put together by me and my French nurse. A quote I wanted to check even sent me yesterday to the local German Institute, where such a nice, kind, helpful librarian has promised to find someone in the German colony who might have the book, that I felt all at once what I've missed by no longer going to Munich (we used to go every year). But of course all that niceness soon enough wears thin, like any mannerism . . .

Here it is nearly seven, dark, time to shave. I miss you very much.

Blessings + love—
James

"Father" A painting by McIntosh.
a longish, loose poem "Lost in Translation" in *Divine Comedies* (1976).
A quote From Rilke's translation of Valéry's poem "Palme."

To Elizabeth Bishop VASSAR
20 October 1972
Athens, Greece

Dear Elizabeth,

So good to hear from you, and know that you are safely home. Your northernmost postcard didn't show Louis-Philippe but a reindeer posing with a red-and-white "Lappgirl" (as in "Lappdog" do you suppose?), and was greatly admired by us who have never seen the like. I'm appalled that a copy of my book didn't reach you. Your name headed a very small list of Prominent Persons, and I'm sure I indicated the Cambridge rather than the Brazilian address. I wrote Harry Ford yesterday to send another. Now that Helen Vendler's Sunday *Times* review has Told All, I'm receiving some curious fan mail. I hope I'm not turning into a Gay culture-hero. (Without the beard, how could I?)

I haven't the heart to correct your delusions about me—my "faultless discipline" and my "wide (and possibly rich) international acquaintance." My list-making is like that of a friend's mother—all efficiency, but then she would mislay the list (along with her glasses, her purse, etc) and have to improvise at the shop. When her son ventured to remark on the futility of it all, she gave him her lovely nearsighted smile and said, "But I'd be lost without something to look for!" Still, I am at work, somewhat. Not on the novel (prose is all uphill) but a poem about an old jigsaw-puzzle and a Rilke version of Valéry. So far the title is my favorite bit—"Lost in Translation." Maybe I'll have to dedicate it to Richard Howard.

Our tiny little world, here in Athens, presently spins around poor Chester Kallman whose (rather suicidal I fear) soap-opera—he thinks it's Grand—goes on day + night 10 doors away. But Rollie arrives next week, staying in a little hotel I'd forgotten about, practically a private home run by a Greek-American lady—a common salon (a salon in common, that is), drinks on the honor system, etc. I hope she'll enjoy it. And as soon as she leaves, our friend Tony + I are flying to Istanbul for 5 days. He's never been, although a branch of his family spent centuries in Trebizond; and the Turks hanged his great-grandfather at the age of 98. My only preparation for this trip is to go through a book someone has surely sent you (if not, let me know)— the *Penguin Book of Mediterranean FISH*. Each fish is nicely sketched, and identified in at least 5 languages (including Turkish). I was sorry to learn about a region in Italy where they eat porpoises. "Porpoises" brings me back to Chester, who is big around as one (though the face is plutôt walrus); I read him "The Moose" the other night. A Greek friend of his, when I'd finished, said, "Why did you go to sleep?" Chester: What do you mean? I didn't go to sleep! The Greek: But look at you, you're rubbing your eyes. Chester (proudly): If you must know, I've just heard an extremely beautiful poem, and I'm <u>crying</u>.

More later. I miss you. Love from us both to you + Alice.

xoxox

Jimmy

David K. remembered a poem of yours about a desktop-battlefield (?). If you have a xerox, won't you send it to me?

safely home Bishop and Alice Methfessel had been in Scandinavia.
Louis-Philippe Louis-Philippe (1773–1850), king of France 1830–48.
the beard Merrill had grown a beard for a while.
a poem of yours "12 O'Clock News" appeared in *Geography III*.

To David Kalstone

WUSTL

14 October 1972

Athens, Greece

Caro,

Your letter here yesterday. The week in Calif. sounds very à propos. I can't think how I misread your signals about Ed. Excuse it, please. And please send me JA on Ponge along with you on Schuyler when those appear. And finally—the first of several ridiculous requests. I've looked high and low for my little rhyming dictionary. It is GONE. And it did so facilitate things. Like having an adding machine instead of doing long tedious sums on foolscap. Could you send me one by air. The one I miss wasn't very grand or very good; I think it would fit into an ordinary long envelope—vest pocket styling; the sort of thing sold at the <u>counter</u> of book-and-novelty shops. I think I got it at Doubleday's in fact.

Too frustrating about Rod McKuen. Whose idea was that? And what's wrong with having us share an issue, like *Ariadne auf Naxos* (him Ariadne, me Zerbinetta)? More subscriptions cancelled! Everyone on the whole seems to have liked HV. DMc thought she was too wordy, but agreed about contour + content. Dr Rothenberg (!) thought she was superficial, but <u>I</u> say thank goodness she hadn't been given access to the abysses HE knew so well. HV herself wrote a charming letter in reply to a note from me. She's been worried how I might feel—all that privacy invaded. Not knowing her, I have refrained from quoting that little poem I love so: "A friend of mine (well not a friend) . . ." which ends "I rather think he wants it known." My mother is in clover, thanks to the Honest Letter I wrote her. A dear, if histrionic page came from her yesterday: "The evil was in <u>me</u>, not you—the evil of Intolerance and Pride, etc etc." Some of her friends, however, whom she knows perfectly well have seen it, are not mentioning the review. Carol Longone (my old piano teacher) wrote her saying she was saving the review "because it seems to be about J's new book." The Reeves sent a spare copy. We leave them around. The boys goggle.

I'm working on a longish poem for which I need (I think) to see Rilke's translation of Valéry. The myth of Alan's *Gesammelte Werke*— he's boasted of the acquisition more than once—was exploded when we discovered that so many new poems had been found that the new edition of the *GW* has elbowed out all translations. I've been to the German Institute where they have only archaeological books; but a nice young man promised to ask about in the local German colony. Since I thought I'd dedicate the poem to Richard, I'm shy of asking him [*in the margin:* I'm not really. I'm not at all! Why don't you ask him <u>for</u> me? I've already mentioned the poem on a p.c. written when I still thought A.A. had the text]. If you, however, see an old *GW* on shelves anywhere, would you transcribe the last 4 stanzas of "Palme"? It's a dreadful bore. This letter is <u>all</u> requests. (And when you are in SF I want a metal inhaler for poppers; they sell them in the gay bars— along with poppers!) But where else can I turn?

Which doctor is refusing you the barium test? On what grounds? Sue him. Tony + Manoli + I are planning 5 days in Istanbul as soon as Rollie leaves. The weather has broken here. It's wet a day, bright a day, blowing hot + cold.

Love to Tom V. Love to You.

J.

Crystal Lithium (1972), titled "A Poetry of Nouns and Adjectives," appeared in *The New York Times* on 5 November 1972. John Ashbery admired Ponge's poetry but did not publish on it.

share an issue An article on McKuen appeared in the same issue of *The Saturday Review* as Kalstone's interview with Merrill focused on his poem "Yánnina."

A friend of mine On the basis of a 1950s entry in a Merrill notebook, Chad Bennett (*Word of Mouth: Gossip and American Poetry*, 2018) has identified the poem Merrill cites as "Publicity" by Daniel George Bunting (1890-1967), who published it under the pseudonym Daniel George in *Alphabetical Order: A Gallimaufry* (1949).

Alan's *Gesammelte Werke* Alan Ansen claimed that he had Rilke's collected works in German, but it couldn't be found.

To David McIntosh

WUSTL
13 November 1972
Athens, Greece

My dear David,

Back from Istanbul yesterday evening—after 3 days (perhaps my card said) without water in the hotel. Somehow it never occurred to us to move to another one, or even to go to one of 100 more or less louche hammams (for which I'd have made a naughty bee-line 15 years ago)—just kept pouring on cologne which came off black on the towels, and going out for another rapturous walk in the autumnal light. The squalor is live and entirely without self-pity (a book says there are no suicides among the Turks); the grandeurs are grand and wholly of the Past—yet so recent, some of them (after all, the last Sultan wasn't ousted until 1922), as to set virtually visible ghosts strolling through them in turbans and lice-infested silks, hung with great pale 10th-rate emeralds like sucked candies. Surely Arabic calligraphy, which decorates so many surfaces (painted, carved, glazed), is one of the most beautiful inventions of the human mind—a sort of macramé, if that's how it's spelt, whose medium is Meaning: pure Meaning to us who can't read it, refined of every sediment of sense. We ate delicious fresh fish, huge deep-fried mussels, washed down with delicious wines or orange-juice; took a boat up the Golden Horn; were practically raped by an eleven year old belly-dancer; bought glass rings that break when you look at them, and a leather jacket for Manoli in the bazar. The Hippies had renamed a street "Utopia"; some of them kept monkeys on leashes—and others, no doubt, monkeys on their backs . . . Still, it is good to be home again; and to find your letter, even though it is not a very happy one. You shouldn't feel apologetic about your state of mind. It is to be expected, and those who care for you, if <u>you</u> care in turn to share it with them, can only respond with sympathy and respect to what you tell and what you hold back, both. I'm greatly touched by the degree to which you reach out to me in your trouble, need my love for you, want us to be together. It is something we must talk about in the Spring, by which time you will have a far clearer sense of what is essential to you, and I will know more about my own commitments. <u>My</u> trouble of the last few years has been this living of multiple lives + affections. I say so (to set you a good example) <u>almost</u> without apology, and surely without the faintest trace of reproach. I'm only human, and when it became clear to me for the second time that we were asking the impossible of each other, it seemed kinder to both of us for me to look in other quarters. Not for that same "impossible." Perhaps the strangest thing that my experience has taught me is how profoundly feeling is colored by its object. The love I have for you is unique and irreplaceable—as all loves are. (Perhaps being a Pisces makes me over-suggestible?) The other side of this paradox has to do with recurring patterns of the sort we both know. "Don't turn from me now, like everybody else," you wrote at one juncture or another—showing what your experience of patterns has been. I turned and . . . didn't turn. As you know. You know all that I'm saying, there's no need for me to repeat it, except perhaps to dramatize the ambivalence I live with. It worries me less and less. It becomes the very stuff of my art. I would fear that it might scare off another person—that it <u>has</u> scared off someone like Stephen, and become a source of pain to DJ; yet it hasn't escaped me that you seem positively reassured by it. Am I making sense? You like and trust me more now than in the days when I asked no better than to put my whole life in your hands. <u>That</u> asking (whose recurrence we shouldn't be beyond fearing) made it all too difficult for you, in ways that you will now be coming to understand. And this is where I'm leaving you tonight, my dear: <u>in</u> those ways, <u>in</u> that growing knowledge of your nature. Bless you always.

Love,
James

To J. D. McClatchy

Dear Sandy,

Back from a few beautifully lighted days in Istanbul, I couldn't be more entertained by your young lady's travel notes. Just the sort of thing one wants to save from the flaming lava of Life. Her tiny mind. The thud of those Carnival bouquets. The hours spent selecting stereoscopic views. She attains something resembling consciousness at Sorrento, do you remember—"Every point on which the eye fell was a picture. . . . realized a poet's or a painter's dream of a visionary Italy." But then she catches another cold and retires early. As you suggest, the Jamesian flower could hardly have blossomed without lots of this sort of mulch. Putting it together, stereoptically, with the crowds of absolutely uniform young foreigners camped around Syntagma in their sheepskins, one gets a glimmer of hope: all that will be made sense of someday in a beautiful book.

I hadn't been to The City for 9 years. Aside from some refurbishing of monuments, and the Hilton + environs, it seemed less cosmopolitan than before. The Greek population had vanished, don't ask me where. The Turks were all happily fishing from the bridges, from little boats. We ate fresh sardines, mackerel, bluefish, and the famous turbot which looks like a sole round as a gong, belly covered with nasty russet warts I must keep looking to make sure haven't broken out on mine. This was served in a gloomy old hangar (which can't be what it looks like from the outside, the rectory of the Armenian church next door) run by 5 Russian ladies—marcelled hair, cigarettes, awful French, all pushing 70—at least one of whom had been a mistress of Kemal's. Peter Mayne, who ought to know, says that in that very room, during an all-night carouse, the great man's wolfhounds ate a belly-dancer.

Your letter, it might amuse you to know, was one of six (an unprecedented number from where I sit) addressed to me on Election Day. Never having voted is beginning to bear fruit. Who won, by the way? Funny too, I'd just been reading Valéry's "Faust"—rather a Czerny exercise for him, don't you think? Enough, I must go down the street to Chester Kallman's to confer about our joint Thanksgiving effort. "If for nothing else," said David Jackson, "we'll be thankful not to be any of the other people at that table."

> All best,
> James

J. D. McClatchy See Biographies.
your young lady's travel notes McClatchy wrote Merrill a fan letter after *Braving the Elements* was published, initiating a correspondence. In a used-book store McClatchy found the memoirs of a young American woman's first impressions of Europe, from the nineteenth century, and he sent it to Merrill as a gift.
The City In Byzantine times, because of its importance, Istanbul was called simply the Polis (City), and the term remains common today among Greeks and Armenians.
a gloomy old hangar The name of the restaurant was Rejans and has been smartly refurbished and renamed 1924 Istanbul.
Kemal Mustafa Kemal Atatürk (1881–1938), founder and first president of the Republic of Turkey.
Who won Richard Nixon won the American presidential election in 1972 in spite of spreading knowledge of the Watergate burglary.
Valéry's "Faust" *Mon Faust*, an unfinished dramatic piece, was one of Valéry's last works.
Czerny exercises Carl Czerny (1791–1857), an Austrian composer, wrote rigorous studies aimed at perfecting the technique of the beginning piano player.

To Rachel Hadas

RUTGERS
26 November 1972
Athens, Greece

Dear Rachel,

My cold has run its course, and I can pay some mind to your poem, which I like without quite trusting my judgment. It has a willful, contradictory charm, which I am partly won by, and partly not—to the degree that you may have used it to save you from taking any further pains. Nothing I can really put my finger on; yet it seems to me, for instance, that the last 2 stanzas are so distinctly better than anything else, the rhyming subtler, the early doggerel done away with (much as its echo lends to the change of your tune); illustrating incidentally "your" altering obsession which begins in the pages of Romantzo and ends with a classical love-death. All this seems to me very good, I mean. Something as careless, as <u>bored</u>, as the rhyme of "went" in stanza 2; as self-indulgent + sleazy as the middle rhymes in stanza 6; as those sudden "self-dramatizing" pentameter lines in 4—these all make for interesting overtones. The flexing sinews of the village—an odd notion which remains odd. Either it is phrased too artificially at the outset, or—or something; but it doesn't come through except as a conceit. Probably I'd have no trouble with it in stanza six if I didn't feel I was being sent back to the opening exclamation. Try something more matter-of-fact in your first line. The Greek song is charming (I may not hear it until you sing it for me, though) and I see here + there what you've learned from its lightness. I also see that I've contradicted myself in the above—starting out to find fault and ending by finding none. I wish there were more of that in the world.

Chester got stagefright last night and at the last minute couldn't cook the wondrous raw goodies Alan came laden with. Horrible Kosta joins C's table every noon at Apostos—one sees where that is leading. As for E F Benson, it was David + I who had Chester read him in the first place. He's no Jane Austen; still, a solid delight whether or not one is experienced in village life. You won't like him until you're over 35.

I left my passport at the Ambelokypous P.O. yesterday—just forgot about it and the package I'd produced it in order to claim. Hadn't I better go down there right now? 9 per cent of 337 is exactly 30.33.

Love to you + Stavros.
Jimmy

Rachel Hadas (b. 1948) American poet and translator.
Apostos Or Apostolis, a venerable ouzo bar and hangout for artists and writers.
E F Benson English writer (1867–1940), among whose many books are the *Mapp and Lucia* series, set in the fictional coastal village of Tilling, of which Merrill and his Stonington village circle were enamored.
Stavros Stavros Kondylis, Rachel Hadas's husband.

To Elizabeth Bishop   VASSAR
                                              30 November 1972
                                                Athens, Greece

Dear Elizabeth,

A letter from the YMHA last week said they wanted to put us on
the same program next spring. I do hope you've said yes! We needn't
<u>read</u> the whole time, you know. A ping-pong table could be borrowed
from some recreational wing of the Establishment, or a samba rou-
tine worked up, with spangly blouses + purple lights. Once long ago
David and I were in the audience, looking up at the gold-lettered
names under the moulding: SHAKESPEARE, DANTE, GO—but the
balcony cut off the remainder of what turned out to be the great Ger-
man's name, but only after DJ had guessed GOD. Think what a nice
party John Myers will give for us afterwards. (You've already been
there once this season, but who's counting?)

Here in Athens, after months of very odd weather, we're enjoy-
ing a lovely bright chill spell. 21 Shopping Days till Xmas, warns the
English-language paper—and indeed in another two weeks one may
walk into a shop and find as many customers as salespeople. [*In the
margin:* This causes <u>terrible</u> confusion.] Most Greeks simply settle
for Marrons glacés and mistletoe (huge, incredibly heavy bunches of
it—how do the oaks stand it?) and disappear into their houses where
they play cards all night long until Epiphany. Whatever luck you have
in those days will stick throughout the new year. (Have you <u>really</u>
anything better to do than fly over for the holidays?) We'll probably
join forces with Chester Kallman, as we did on T'giving. David has
spent long, largely thankless hours helping him—I can't say "redec-
orate" because there had been no original decor; but now the walls
are painted, the floors waxed, the pictures hung, and poor Chester
has fallen prey to the fussiest house-pride, is forever emptying ash-
trays, stopping exuberant friends from dancing ("You're scuffing the
floor") and what not. A dinner at St Marks' Place last January had put
the bee in DJ's bonnet. Won't you miss New York? he asked Auden,
whose fond gaze thereupon took in cracked picture-glass, disem-
bowelled sofa, piles of sooty papers everywhere, the kitchen's arras
of roaches shimmering faintly in the light of a Geo. Price bulb. "Of

course I will," he said, "especially now that Chester and I have really fixed the place up . . ."—as indeed, to do them justice, they <u>had</u>, ten years earlier.

How I love the array on <u>your</u> worktable. It's simply uncanny what you do with tone in that poem—the newscaster's idiom grows into the saddest, truest analogue of that strange, remote "involvement" even I have felt, those few nights I've ever been sober + lovely enough to work late. That snow-covered peak—"White is their color, and behold my head!" <u>This</u> may be the saddest poem you've ever written.

(Chester quoted, by the way, a line from a review by Nigel Dennis: "Mr Alvarez appears to feel that Auden should be burnt. But who can hold a candle to him?")

That "assenting groan" is something I know, too, though from where I couldn't say. I practise it daily to spring on you when next we meet. Oh!—Yes: Mrs Sprague, a faculty wife at Amherst, used it. Still does—she came to cocktails at Mary's in Castine last August; the groan had seldom been more affirmative than in that elegant setting.

What plans have you? I'll be home around Feb 10th, but soon after shall have to go South + West for 5 or 6 weeks. If you're in Cambridge, I'd try to arrange a day there before setting out. Merry X, etc, to you and Alice from us both.

With love always,
Jimmy

YMHA The Poetry Center at the YMHA in New York.
St. Marks' Place St. Marks Place, the street where Auden lived in Manhattan's East Village.
Geo. Price bulb A reference to the bare lightbulbs that *New Yorker* cartoonist George Price (1901–95), who signed his cartoons "Geo. Price," sometimes depicted in his cartoons.
that poem "12 O'Clock News." Merrill interprets the poem, which she had been at work on for many years, as referring to the American "involvement" in Vietnam.
"White is their color, and behold my head!" Merrill is reminded of "The Forerunners," by George Herbert, one of his and Bishop's favorite poets.
Nigel Dennis (1912–89), English writer, whose *Cards of Identity* (1955) was praised by Auden and admired by Merrill.
Mr Alvarez Al ("A.") Alvarez (1929–2019), English poet and literary critic.
"assenting groan" See Bishop's "The Moose": "'Yes . . .' that peculiar / affirmative. 'Yes . . .' / A sharp, indrawn breath, / half groan, half acceptance . . ."
Mrs Sprague Mary Ann Sprague.

To Judith Moffett   NYPL
                                                              23 December 1972
                                                              [Athens, Greece]

Dear Judy,

Here is your sad (and beautiful) little carol, and your "brown" let-
ter. We've hung up our mistletoe and turned, as it were, the other
cheek. A mean bullet-shaped turkey hangs in the cold kitchen, I've
made a cornbread stuffing, and Mrs Walton sent round some of her
very own mincemeat for our Pie—not that we Scrooges <u>like</u> mince
pie. At our table will be Tony (animation courtesy of Preludin) and
Eddy (who once knew Lytton Strachey, and now is old + toeless) and
Manos (young + monolingual, but still "real"), and night will fall upon
us every one . . .

   At the risk of maddening you, may I say that I'm not sure what you
mean by <u>knowing</u> <u>people</u>? I'll admit that the characters drawn from
life in my novels are less convincing than the few who are invented
(like Arthur Orson and the N's) but that could be due precisely to
their being drawn from life, and to my squeamishness about what
I fancied I could or could not tell. I don't say that this is so, but it
might be; even <u>I</u> have scruples. As for knowing people, I would say
that it is a matter of habit + hazard. One can live years in a place with-
out ever having visited certain neighborhoods. Perhaps I am wrong
in assuming that it comes as naturally to others as it does to myself,
to "favor" this or that aspect of my nature, depending on whom I'm
with, or writing to, or writing for. The <u>truth</u> we reach with respect to
others (or to our own selves) strikes me as arrived at through some
triumph of simplification; or a series of these in recollection. You
are talking, I suspect, about something else: the truth (am I right?)
implicit in the last line of your carol, or in what Cordelia might call
the human <u>bond</u>. How I wish my faith in it were stronger! One seems
to see more of it here than in America, indeed that's one reason I
like living here: glimpses of what children + parents can be to each
other, the highpowered teamwork of my grocer + his wife. But I also
know exactly the degree to which an outsider may presume upon this
bond, and the knowledge carries with it the single practical recom-
mendation: Watch Your Manners. Just as thought without language

is quicksand, so is truth without style. You, of course, are concerned with style without truth—which I admit to having practised in my day, being only human, or with only this corrasable bond at hand. I'm realer in my poems than my prose? If so, it's because my style is more geared to poetry. To be specific, though, when I reread *The Seraglio*, only a few of the characters fail to convince me: Jane, Enid, and perhaps Lily. The others may well be "two-dimensional" but they do not break their bond with the action; call them therefore comic if you like (you don't, but I might)—there could still be truth in them. Naturally I am the last person to judge. What <u>you</u> mightn't be prepared to believe is that some people have spent all their waking hours applying those 7 coats of shellac, that it wasn't just my style but theirs. Ah well. Tell me how much of this makes sense, if any of it does. As for Dr R's piece, let's wait until I've seen it. You might trip + fall into too deep an archaeological trench ever to reemerge.

Snodgrass + his wife looked us up last week, which made for a very pleasant evening. He talked about early instruments and the *Niebelungenlied* in a voice not unlike an early American instrument, reedy + nicely pitched. Enough for 1972. Since I haven't heard from Hoffman, I still expect to see you on April 12.

Love,
Jimmy

Preludin Brand name for phenmetrazine, a stimulant similar to amphetamine, used formerly for suppressing the appetite, now commercially banned in the United States.
Eddy Edward Gathorne-Hardy, who had had gout.
Lytton Strachey (1880–1932), English writer, founding member of the Bloomsbury group.
Arthur Orson and the N's Characters in Merrill's novel *The (Diblos) Notebook* (1965).
what Cordelia might call the human _bond_ In *King Lear* (I.1) Cordelia tells the king that "I love your majesty / According to my bond; nor more nor less."
Dr R's piece Albert Rothenberg's case study based on his work with Merrill.
Snodgrass + his wife American poet William De Witt ("W.D.") Snodgrass (1926–2009) and his third wife, Camille Rykowski.
Niebelungenlied The Nibelungunlied (c. 1200), epic poem in Middle High German based on oral tradition dubbed "the German *Iliad*" in the eighteenth century.
Hoffman Daniel Hoffman (1923–2013), American poet, professor of English at the University of Pennsylvania, Moffett's dissertation director and then her friend, who had invited Merrill to read when the latter came to read at Penn State Behrend, where Moffett was teaching.

To Stephen Yenser

Dear Stephen,

Your package, announced by a slip from the P.O. 2 days ago, is in my hands this morn. I am so glad to have it—your letter, Marilyn's book (I'll quickly dispose of the copy her publisher sent, without inscription) the coincidence in whose choice pleases me more, believe me, than it must frustrate you, so stop tearing your hair right now; and of course the magical little Thoth. He is surely the oldest object I've ever held in the palm of my hand—how beautiful his glaze is, like something sugared for a Pharoah's teaparty—I cherish him. He weighs my heart + finds it lighter + livelier for your own place in it.

My dear, of course I'll be at your wedding (so long as I'm not expected to dance at it). I'd felt that was in the air, if only through your reticence on the subject. Reading your page, a big tear came to each eye, one of happiness, one of—I hardly know what by now. Surely it is the right thing for you both, + therefore for me as well. Where I'm concerned you have been entirely "responsible"—unless indeed we are so alike, you + I, that my own selfishness + susceptibility has now + then been echoed in you. But no. Each of us knows well enough what both he + the other are humanly capable of, we've honored the strong + the weak side of the medal—+ I'll never be anything but proud + grateful for the love you give me + the love you accept from me. I am sure that I shall love Mary "for herself" as the years bring us together, + not merely for the happiness she means in your life. Whichever date you decide on will suit me. After reading in Phoenix (March 7–8) I shall spend 12–14 days with DMc in Santa Fe, + could be in LA by the 22nd. Our excursion might be a shade inappropriate just then, don't you think? I mean, you can't <u>want</u> the Bombas to call you <u>irresponsible</u>, at least for another year or so. If it seems that I'll be at all underfoot I can dart up to Frisco before or after the wedding (depending on its date) + <u>could</u> give a reading April 2 or thereabouts, if it doesn't mean too much fuss for you; could fly East a day or so later.

Sorry about this letter. I've fallen into a tradition initiated last year, of ending each year in bed. This time it's my own stupid fault. A B12 needle must have strayed into a nerve in my hip. Yesterday's dr. is sending me to another man this afternoon when we'll decide whether the resulting lump is apt to dissolve of itself or need what the Godfather might call "persuasion." Tiresome.

The author of the pamphlet you received painted his own moon + sun. The seal is Jap, + says "Ja-mu-su" (no question of "Merrill" with all those r's + l's); it means Young Village.

Bonne Année—my love to Mary—bless you for your gifts, for everything.

> Yours ever,
> James

Marilyn's book Marilyn Aronberg Lavin's *Piero della Francesca: The Flagellation* (1972) examines a painting that figures in *The (Diblos) Notebook* (1965).
the magical little Thoth Small ancient statuette of the Egyptian deity, who served as scribe of the gods and weigher of human hearts in the afterlife.
your wedding Yenser and Mary Bomba were to be married in March 1973.
the Godfather The eponymous figure, a Mafia boss, in Francis Ford Coppola's film *The Godfather* (1972), based on the novel by Mario Puzo.
the pamphlet Merrill's poem "The Thousand and Second Night" was published in a limited edition (1963) in which he hand-colored the images he specifies.

To J. D. McClatchy

YALE

13 January 1973
[Athens, Greece]

Dear Sandy,

Sorry not to have thanked you before this for your Christmas letter and poem, and those beautifully selected clippings. Miss Moore, years ago, once said from the very platform on which I'd introduced her: "Now Mr Merrill tells me that he doesn't read the newspapers. That's hard for me to understand. Just last week I learned from the *NY Times* that our State Department is donating all those egret feathers confiscated by the U.S. Customs during the '20's to the Kingdom of Nepal, where they're <u>needed</u>. How would you find out about something like that if you didn't read the papers?"

I hope you had a good time in Sea Island. I've never been there but my mother lives in Atlanta, and her friends all go. (Are you "Southern"?) Myself, I went right to bed after coping with the turkey carcass, and stayed there until New Year's Eve. Nothing really wrong, just an annual tradition begun last year.

Isn't the Zeffirelli *Otello* <u>something</u>? The Credo Iago ends with his foot on a <u>book</u>? Anne Hollander had tears in her eyes merely because, under her fancy brocade dress, Desdemona for once was wearing "the right shift." Athens can't compete, although tomorrow we do get *Macbeth* with Paschalis, and have had all week the new Bunuel film, amusing + intelligent despite some evident local cuts. Time's running out. I fly to Paris on the 31st, thence to Boston and S'ton by way of the 7th or so until the end of February when I must go South + West for 5 weeks. If you'd like to come for an afternoon or evening, just say so. With so little time before I leave again, I don't expect to get seriously down to work.

The doorbell is about to ring: a photographer from the *Boston Globe*, can that <u>be</u>? Bonne Année.

> Yours,
> James

Zeffirelli Otello Franco Zeffirelli (1923–2019), Italian stage and film director and designer, staged Verdi's *Otello* at the Metropolitan Opera in 1972.
Anne Hollander She was the author of *Seeing Through Clothes* (1978), about the relationship between the human body and costume from the Greeks through the Renaissance in Western culture.
Macbeth with Paschalis Verdi's opera with Greek baritone Kostas Paskalis (1929–2007) in the title role.
Bunuel Luis Buñuel's *The Discreet Charm of the Bourgeoisie* (1972).

To Tony Parigory

WUSTL
4 February 1973
Paris, France

Tony dear—

There is a glaze of sorrow over <u>everything</u>, since talking to David on Friday. You must feel it more than anyone else + I'm so terribly sorry not to be in Athens these weeks—precisely the weeks in which you must learn to live with the truth about our beloved M. How blind we have all managed to be!—but it is a blessed blindness I suppose, for her as well as for us. By the same token, it now appears that the Greek doctors have not been wholly idiotic or exagérés in their handling of the case (inexcusable though it was not to have made her stop smoking years ago)—and there is accordingly hope that they can give her years of apparent comfort + vitality, in which we can all continue to drink deep of one another. What else can one say? Just my arms about you + a gros baiser.

I'm being very quiet in Paris—hours in bed with a book every afternoon. Lunches with Germaine, The Princess Nina (Tony is <u>once</u> <u>again</u> in NY at his father's deathbed). We took Mary McC to the Grand Véfour last night, + Mimi was 1/2 hour on the phone this morning raving about how "casually" MMc was dressed—"I'd <u>seen</u> that dress before, those same heavy white stockings. These shoes, worn by her at 5 in the afternoon. How dare she wear them in the evening, making <u>me</u> look ridiculous." Very hard not to say, "Mimi, <u>Mary</u> didn't make you look ridiculous" but the memory of a mammoth figure in shapeless wool to her ankles and a brown velvet jacket <u>painted</u> with red + yellow leaves, ugly beyond your wildest dreams, kept me from contradicting her. MMc of course looked divinely elegant in a charcoal + white tailleur with a blazing diamond clip on one shoulder. Speaking of diamonds I summoned all my courage + stumbled into several Place Vendôme jewellers looking for a gift for my mother. Germaine had said "why a jewel—why not un joli objet?" But I thought No: the joli objet would be <u>mine</u> in another 10 years or so, and I am the only person left on earth who would give a gem to the poor woman—so I took a deep breath and found at Chaumet a <u>bee</u> (for Bollingen?) with diamonds on its body and two wings of pinky-mauve opal slightly netted over with gold, which is all I can do not to wear myself stuck in my new pale-blue Charvet tie.

The V's rushed me off to see *Le Dernier Tango* which we all more or less disliked, though the girl is very charming + the photography ravishing + the tango competition towards the end wildly funny + graceful. The "frontal nudity" promised by *Time* consists only of lot of MOYNI-muff + a glimpse of Mr B's jockey shorts. And the sex is immensely unconvincing—he might as well be a fat evzone who can't bother to undress. Mary went to see it as soon as her husband left for Japan, + she agreed . . .

Germaine in very good form—much gossip about Jackie, etc. She getting lots of fucking + being very careful not to fall in love ever again. How well one understands—I was 43 myself once!

Will you conduct a little inquiry for me—really for Princess Nina? Now that she has all the Conan-Doyle rights, she + her divine Chinese secretary are very concerned about being paid for foreign translations etc, + have received no answer from one Greek publisher they know to have put out an edition of at least one book. She wants simply the name of a reliable lawyer in Athens who could advise her about Greek copyright laws and, if necessary, help her bring suit against the violators thereof. Vitsentsatos isn't the right man, I suspect, but perhaps Nelly could inquire of one or another of <u>her</u> literary friends, or if Mme. takes a turn for the better she could ask Prevelekis. Don't worry if it's too difficult—I could also write Mike Keeley who might come up with a name; somehow none of it strikes me as being of any ultimate interest or urgency.

Tomorrow—Boston. Only one more meal in France, Thank God! How does anyone live past 30 on this diet? La pauvre Mimi, I forced her to cook a dinner at home to avoid the distraction (just <u>once</u>) of public settings—Lipp & Coupole & Vietnamese cubby-holes. She made a <u>very good</u> baked fish, + bought excellent pâté de volaille + cheese on the Rue de Seine. She is nervous + melancholy, always breaking into tears over the cold tone of a letter from her sister—but then she is cut off from everything except Vassili. Luckily he still loves her. <u>Why</u>, I don't imagine.

I talked to Henri on the phone—but le M's possessiveness kept me from having to see him. No one has written him about his house. I suggested he telephone the builder; it had never occurred to him!

Look for a Penguin book by J. R. Ackerley, "We think the world of you"—full of oddness + situations you will recognize. Enough for now. A thousand kisses.

Be strong, with love always.
Jimmy

beloved M Maria Mitsotaki had been diagnosed with terminal cancer.
Germaine Germaine Nahman, wife of Jean ("Johnnie") Nahman, socialites Merrill met in Alexandria in 1959.
The Princess Nina Princess Nina Mdivani (1901–87), of "the marrying Mdivanis," the Georgian noble family, who married Tony Harwood after her second husband, Denis Conan Doyle, the famous author's son, had died. She prevailed in the complex lawsuit—which pitted the heirs against one another for ownership of the literary estate—only to squander, with Harwood, the profit.
bee (for Bollingen?) Merrill won the Bollingen Prize in Poetry for *Braving the Elements* (1972) and used the prize money for this purchase at the luxury jewelry boutique. An unusual editorial in *The New York Times* had objected to the awarding of the prize, one of the premier prizes in American poetry, to Merrill on the grounds that it represented narrowly academic taste and elite northeastern provincialism.
the V's Vassilis and Mimi Vassilikos.
Le Dernier Tango Last Tango in Paris (1972), Italian-French film directed by Bernardo Bertolucci, starring Marlon Brando and Maria Schneider.
MOYNI-muff The first term, in transliterated Greek, means "pussy," as does the second in American vernacular.
Jackie Jacqueline Bouvier Kennedy Onassis.
Nelly Nelly Liambey.
Mme. Maria Mitsotaki.
Mike Keeley Edmund Keeley (b. 1928), writer and translator of twentieth-century Greek poets, Princeton professor.
Henri Charles Henri Ford (1908–2002), American writer, artist, editor, and experimental filmmaker.
le M Manos.
J. R. Ackerley English writer and editor (1896–1967), whose one novel, *We Think the World of You* (1960), concerned a gay man and a German shepherd named Evie.

To Tony Parigory

WUSTL
16 March 1973
[Nambé, NM]

Tony dear—

After 2 minutes "in town" with DJ I've moved back out into the valley, where DMc has a pretty 2-room house surrounded by his landlady's 100 acres with their 75 peacocks, Arab steeds + what not. Everyone sends you much love, and in fact <u>nearly</u> everyone plans to pass through Athens. Mary Lou + Agnes will be there for 12 hours on May 13 (a cruise) + hope that they can see you for lunch or dinner, if you aren't in America. Then, from Stonington, May 21 or 22, you will have Rose York—but DJ will be back in time to cope with her;

<u>and</u> on April 28–30, at the GB, Frank + Priscilla Hallowell—whom I seem to recall you especially liking. Jot it all down in the Stonington calendar!

I've been bad about letters, but it's hard away from a real desk (can't you find me a traveling desk du 18<u>eme</u>?) Also I keep falling prey to the strangest depressions—they'd begun last December, + are perhaps connected with not working, but perhaps there is something wrong physically too, like Pernicious Anaemia (Agnes' suggestion). One will have to have some tests. The news about Mme. is very cheering. Give her a pinch + a kiss de ma part.

One stupid thing I did, for instance: I was carrying a canvas tote-bag containing some manuscripts, a package of pastry from Vaso to my mother, and Stephen Y's wedding present: that stone ibis (old + valuable) that used to sit brooding in the upstairs room in S'ton. I <u>left</u> the bag in a taxi from airport to my mother's house + despite a great number of efforts to get it back it is evidently gone forever. How careless? How deliberate? There is no saying.

Robin met me in Phoenix (Ariz.) where I stayed 3 nights with his brother Peter + family. He flies today to Nepal with his (according to Peter) horrible new girlfriend—who says she's 26 but looks 40: very "masculine"!—where they will trek into the mountains, 19,000 feet high. DJ keeps brooding about Stephen + Carl, has decided it is they who will finally "ruin" Athens for him. He seemed most cheer-ful + calm, although once again Mme. Guitou was a passenger on his ship.

Letters pour in from Manoli—9 kilos, unbelievable! I wish I knew when I would embrace that silhouette again. DMc + I keep making half-hearted plans for a summer dentro la bruyèra, but something tells me it will not come to pass, or be compressed into 3 weeks before coming to Greece (in July?).

I wonder if we shouldn't make a tentative reservation for Mrs Plummer + whichever friend travels with her. She <u>may</u> be coming the last week of September. Could you see if 2 singles + a bath can be had at the GB for 10 days beginning, say, Sept 24; then for a 2nd spell from Oct 9–15? We can always cancel when the time comes. Her lat-est coup was to close the car door on her toes (shades of lo sai chi) + fracture one of them. If GB is full, some other downtown hotel?

I assume Maria Stamati has no rooms with private bath—but if she does, that would be a possibility too. She's in the catálogo under her own name. Thank you dear one again for your birthday cable, + for the letter which reached me yesterday. The 188-person luncheon in Atlanta was of a madness. I knew perhaps 30 by name, another 30 by sight—but the rest! Still, as I've often observed, time passes v. quickly when one is the center of attention.

Lent + Connor also send love. Everytime I see them, they tell me (+ I always forget) how happily they remember paréa with Yanni (Chester's) in the spring of 1965. Let's try never to tell Chester about that! We dined with them + I <u>think</u> disappointed them—<u>can</u> they have expected one of our old late 1950's orgies? Quelles folles! The clipping about Mouflouzelis amused me no end. And Panagisti—married? or just engaged? Either way. Love to him.

And love to you, dear heart.
J.

the GB Hotel Grande Bretagne on Syntagma Square in Athens.
Vaso Christos Alevras's wife, then living with him and their daughters, including the infant Ourania, Merrill's goddaughter, on the second floor at 107 Water Street and not to be confused with Strato's wife.
Stephen Y's wedding present For the loss of this bag in Macon, Georgia, see JM's poem "The Will."
Stephen + Carl Stephen Magowan and his lover.
Mme. Guitou Guitou Knoop.
dentro la bruyèra Obscure phrase.
lo sai chi You know who.
catálogo Telephone book.
the 188-person luncheon in Atlanta Hosted by Merrill's mother at the select Driving Club.
paréa "Party," "fellowship," "group" in Greek (here "partying").
Mouflouzelis Strato's last name.

To J. D. McClatchy
POSTCARD | YALE
4 June 1973
[Stonington, CT]

ON THE ROAD
　Homeward bound just now I took
　An exit labeled SANDY HOOK,
　So called your number while the tank
　Filled up. Back came my quarter, clank.
　It is so frequently one's fate
　To take the Hook & miss the Bait.
　Pisces

postcard A plain card, with address on front and message on back.
Pisces Merrill's astrological sign.

To Rosemary Sprague
AMHERST
16 June 1973
[Stonington, CT]

Dear Rosie,

There is now this fantastic new machine in the house—which you will get to use if you come down. You can change it to roman type as well as italic! So good to see you, and thank you for the much needed company & steak & wine. I did not have the courage to tell you something I've gone & done, but it can't go much longer unconfessed. Last summer my brother-in-law gave me a talk about my Will, with the result that I made a new one. Then, during my winter Depression, I kept thinking, What a pity not to just go ahead & die; at least my dear ones will be a shade better off than they were. As you see, I didn't follow that argument to one of its logical conclusions. But it had others. In short, for a few friends whose lives don't seem exactly beds of roses (among them yourself) I wanted to set up some really tiny monthly benefit that would correspond to what they'd be getting if I were indeed dead & gone. The only person I have (or shall) mentioned it to is my mother, and it is she who said firmly "Don't tell them in advance, just go ahead and DO it." It is now for your conscience to struggle with, because, beginning July 1st, the office in NYC will be sending you $150 each month. I think I know you well enough to imagine how cross this will make you, but I very much hope you will try to understand how pleased I should be if you bit the bullet & swallowed the pill. You can, after all, give it away if it doesn't seem right to spend it on yourself—though of course I'd rather you did the latter. And if you feel awkward about telling your parents, then don't—as I say, aside from Mrs P, this will remain our perfectly innocent secret. Please don't mortify me by taking it the wrong way—by not taking it, that is. Well, enough of that, people are coming to dinner.

> With love always,
> Jim

new machine His Selectric typewriter.
my brother-in-law Robert Magowan.

To Rosemary Sprague

AMHERST

19 July 1973

[Athens, Greece]

Dear Rosie,

We are having the most monstrous heatwave. I don't dare translate the thermometer readings into Fahrenheit, but suspect that if it were <u>body</u> temperature our brains would have burned out like the motor of my little electric fan in the middle of last night—causing sheer dank heat to wake me. You can bet I was out early this morning to buy a new one—only to have the clerks in the first 4 electrical supply shops appear puzzled by my request: Electric fan, who would ever want such a thing? No, we don't carry them. (The fan I bought appears to be a <u>winter</u> fan, nicely heating the air it circulates. Maybe <u>it</u> will burn out tonight.) Which is to say, among other things, that I lack the strength + wit to write last month's letter all over again. It said what I meant. The questions your letter raises are subtle ones, but I can't really feel that they apply. I mean, we already see so sadly little of each other, it would be unthinkable to see even less. What I am most apt to do—unless you keep reminding me—is to blank out entirely where the money is concerned, forget that you are receiving it, and to keep thinking of you as I always have, do, and shall. Where money is concerned, it's the ONLY thing to do; it takes one a long time to get the knack, but I've managed. We have both learned, haven't we, from our reading, the kind of comic phosphorescence engendered by characters who do otherwise? Or if not comic, then wicked. As for your keeping it secret, I make no stipulation. I'd fancied that you might breathe more freely—even, who knows? vis à vis your parents—if it weren't known. But should you want to tell them, go ahead. I suppose things like this always do get around, and whoever wants to misunderstand in the present case will just have to be reborn as a one-eyed counterfeiter.

Aside from the heat, nothing much to tell. Venice was gorgeous, but smelled, and cost the earth. David K and I rented a car for 3 days, paid a visit to my now elderly friend Umberto near Arezzo; and returned via one of the handsomest small towns in the world—Urbino—where the great Piero della Francesca *Flagellation,* some 400 square inches of magic, can be seen. Ah, but in Athens meanwhile, David J has done a mural in the house—one whole wall representing a column-framed, poppy-spattered downward slope to an unspoilable (unless it peels off) private cove. Thank goodness we can now give up looking for the real thing; I trust that is the message of the painting. 7 p.m.—time for a dip in a cold tub (not painted but drawn).

Love always,
James

Umberto Umberto Morra. See Biographies.

To J. D. McClatchy

21 July 1973
[Athens, Greece]

Dear Sandy,

I'm afraid I shall have to upstage you where heat waves are concerned. A girl we ran into last night, who digs at the Agora, said it had been III degrees in the shade there yesterday. And in the sun? Well, her thermometer stopped at 122, she said, and when the mercury reached that point she applied a cold compress. Not dry heat either, pollution sees to that. We keep the tub filled for periodic immersion; which came in handy yesterday afternoon, l'heure de l'arrosage, when everybody's water was turned off for 12 hours without warning. A plumbago can look almost as reproachful as a cat.

You've had a bad time. I'm sorry. I had one last Christmas, the first in ten years, and didn't really pull out of it until April—this is not to upstage you, just to show you that I understand. What is the cure? Work—as the unhappy girls in Chekhov keep telling us? Easier said than done. In retrospect I think (and from what I've seen of you it might well be the case) that these are growing pains. Certainly they have everything to do with a sense that the life one has arranged to live is intolerable, that a skin must be shed, that something more is in motion than the manic-depressive pendulum so familiar to others. Others, indeed, become suspiciously two-dimensional during these spells, and this is a kind of hell for sociable types like you and me; one resents having to spare them; or resents even more, if one turns to them for help, the way one's black mood seems positively to settle their stomachs, like Fernet-Branca. But if the point is to change, to be changed—how else can this happen except by learning to recognize, among 1000s of objects, which few have secret meanings for you; and to trust them, they being the only ones that can't, to the degree that their value lies within you, betray the trust. By objects I mean people, mainly, as in that passage in one of the Oz books when Dorothy finds herself in a palace crammed with bibelots only seven of which are the enchanted King and his family (these turn out to be the seven purple objects, as you may recall). Something like that, in any case. As for trusting me, of course you can; but you will have to trust yourself even more.

Since getting here—only 8 days ago—I've kept busy trying to do a bit more with "Urania." David Kalstone thought it was condescending toward the Greeks, and my nephew Robin said it was cruel. (Not his kind of perception—I suspect it belongs to his latest companion, a girl from San Francisco whom I quite liked, actually, though she is overweight and going bald. They were in Venice, and are now in a cave on Santorini.) Still, a helpful reaction; things mustn't always go without saying—things in a poem, I mean—and I've set about blending in a non-euphoric visit below stairs to the parents feeling anxious and homesick. Your remarks help in another way; we all need encouragement and praise!

Three o'clock—l'heure du cottage cheese (unavailable here, but easily made). If it helps to write me about your troubles, don't let shyness hold you back. (In fact, remembering Nancy Mitford's Cedric—is that his name?—and his first appearance at the Montdors'—perhaps you'd do well never to mention shyness again.) And if you'd rather I didn't comment, another time, upon what you tell me, I should understand that very well.

Bless you, my dear—
James

the Agora The ancient marketplace, a major excavation site in Athens.
"Urania" Merrill's poem "Verse for Urania" in *Divine Comedies* (1976), concerning his goddaughter Ourania and her family (here "the Greeks").
Nancy Mitford's Cedric Cedric Hampton, a character in Mitford's novel *Love in a Cold Climate* (1949).

To David McIntosh

WUSTL
17 August 1973
[Athens, Greece]

Dear David—

I am a bad, bad correspondent this season, for which there is neither any real excuse nor any unspeakable reason. Then I look at the calendar and see that I've only been here 34 days. It seems like 3 months. I've been working so well that my sense of time becomes non-sense. Goodness, what a difference it makes. My fingers are blistered from touching wood. I found I had a number of things half-done—a poem about Persia that got frostbitten last December; the poem about the lost ibis I was still too close to to make any headway last spring at Nambé. It's no gushing oil-well by any means, just a steady almost idle flow that I can cope with, not being Rilke at Muzot. I hope something of the sort is happening to you. Your state of mind sounded very fruitful after all the pain of Wyoming. You understand, I think, how lucky you have been to make so much peace with your mother and father before they are lost to you. Mendings do take place after death, but one is always a bit ashamed of them, like badly patched clothing, next to the seamless raiment two living people can weave when they must, out of past tatters. That's as bad as some of Maharishi's metaphors. (And the 15 year old guru with his face full of pie? And his assailant practically killed? How absurd the world is, and how evil.)

Our poor Maria. Pressure on her from all sides to take another course of "rays." A slow haemorrhage has begun, somewhere below the waist—which means? Means, for all visible purposes, that she simply carries a more commodious bag with her when she goes out. Yesterday, for the first time, she told Tony that she was frightened. Frightened specifically of the rays, which are extremely debilitating, frightened no doubt that it is all graver than she has dared admit. (These rays, I think I wrote you, won't do any good, according to her doctor; just make the end less painful.) Can you imagine what she is like in company? Merry, macabre, mild, made-up. So often, in other people's trouble, I've felt a kind of taboo, an instinct to avoid them, like those animals that shun the one who is hurt or sick. With her one feels not a trace of that. 2 nights ago was her name-day. She asked to come here for spaghetti (her favorite food now, you should see her clean up, gaunt as she is, a huge plateful) and a cake I ordered (without the courage to have the conventional "Many Years" inscribed on it—just a circumference of <u>Marias</u>). Tony was there, and Bernie, and Kitty whom you didn't meet—and the fun we all had . . . ! Elizabeth B's favorite phrase in all her poems, "Cheerful but awful," gives something of the atmosphere, but leaves out the sweetness, the silliness, the appalling sadness. You had better write me about Tom + Bob, while we're on this subject. I've not brought myself to write them yet; but know that I must.

Manoli came + went. I saw him about 15 times in 20 days—which would be far too much under normal circumstances, but we got on quite well. He made Braunschweig come alive in all its dismalness, but I did not offer to press the magic button and relocate him in Athens. By this time next year he thinks he'll have made enough to come back and think about a karate school. DJ is having horrible headaches. A teaspoon of wine, or nothing whatever, will bring them on. X-rays show what may be a polyp or cyst in the sinus, but the dr. wants new x-rays after a month before deciding about an operation. Enough. Love to ML + A (that may have been the burden of my rose stain)—and to you.

Ever,
James

a poem about Persia "Chimes for Yahya," included in *Divine Comedies* (1976).
the poem about the lost ibis "The Will," also in *Divine Comedies*.
Muzot At the invitation of Werner Rineheart in 1921, Rilke lived at the Château de Muzot, where in February he finished the *Duino Elegies* and composed the *Sonnets to Orpheus*.
the 15 year old guru Guru Maharaj Ji was hit in the face in August 1973 by a shaving-cream pie wielded by a politically radical journalist, Pat Halley, who was later assaulted by the guru's sympathizers.
"Cheerful but awful" The last line of Bishop's "The Bight," inscribed on her gravestone, is "awful but cheerful."
Tom + Bob The painter Tom Ingle and Robert Palmer, a librarian at Connecticut College, were friends of Merrill's from Connecticut who lived in Nambé.

To J. D. McClatchy

Dear Sandy,

Sunday, a day for letters. The one David is writing downstairs begins, "After many a summer sighs the douane." It is as <u>long</u> a summer as I can remember. One day after another of cool meltemi (ghastly for the people who charter yachts, heavenly for us). We don't even go to the beach, partly because D is having miserable headaches which sun aggravates, partly because I'm content to stay in my study. Evenings are quiet too, wine no longer seems to agree with anyone, and restaurants are so absurdly crowded. The iron gates of life have seldom seen such traffic, to judge from the confused rumor that reaches us here in the shade of the pearly ones. The real absurdity, you will say (and I'll agree, it's all still so novel), is to feel in one's bones how utterly a boundary has been crossed. Here one is in Later Life, and it's perfectly pleasant really, not for a moment that garden of cactus and sour grapes I'd always assumed it <u>must</u> be. Oh dear, this sort of thing is probably just what you mean by my being "recessed" into myself—at least I can't imagine what else you mean. But it's odd. I mean, the times of greatest recession into the self have always been, for me, times of helpless suffering, such as you're going through; when there's no escape from the self. Perhaps any circumstance, any frame of mind, content, pain, trust, distrust, is a niche that limits visibility—for both the occupant and the onlooker?

I read your last letter, in any case, with pangs of recognition. There's no special comfort, is there? in being understood at times like these. One is so mortified by one's predicament, and at the same moment so curiously proud of its ramifications. You won't be ready yet to <u>like</u> the fact of belonging to a very large group who've all had—allowing for particular differences—the same general experience. Later on, when your sense of humor and proportion returns, that fact ought rather to please you: to have so shared in the—or at least <u>a</u>—human condition. Write me as much or as little about it as you see fit. As you say, the particulars should probably be saved for the couch. Don't waste time feeling superior to your doctor. You are no doubt cleverer and more presentable than he is, but (with any luck) he knows his business, and the shoes he is making for you will last and last. Also, don't be too hard on yourself if your work suffers, if your thesis moulders or your poetry congeals—because right now your task is the other matter.

The other evening we made an exception and went next door to meet Alan Ansen's houseguest, a Mr Burroughs—sallow, nondescript party who talked of nothing but drugs and sex-crimes, just like my mother's Atlanta friends. Alan seems to have been very helpful in putting together the ms. of a book this man wrote ("The Nude Meal"?), indeed still <u>had</u> the ms. which Mr B came all the way to Athens to repossess in order to sell it—n'importe quoi being marketable nowadays. Luckily dear old Eddy Gathorne-Hardy was there. He told a story about a chair he'd had recaned at great trouble + expense, then thought a bit and said, "I wish somebody would recane <u>me</u>!"

That will be all for now.

With love,
James

"**After many a summer**" Spoonerized parody of the famous phrase in Tennyson's "Tithonus" (1860), "After many a summer dies the swan" (also taken as a title for a novel by Aldous Huxley).
The iron gates of life A phrase from Andrew Marvell's "To His Coy Mistress."
Mr Burroughs William S. Burroughs (1914–97), American writer, whose novel *Naked Lunch* (1959) represents his friend and collaborator Alan Ansen as the character A. J. Merrill is being disingenuous.

To Judith Moffett   NYPL
                                                    26 October 1973
                                                    Athens, Greece

Dear Judy,

At first it seemed wiser not to tell you the consequences of our struggle to gain possession of your beautiful + useful gift; but such laughter shook the household as the curtain descended, that I can't resist. You, be assured, are not to blame—except perhaps for scrupulously addressing the parcel to us both, which meant we both had to go to the P.O., with passports, lest, in the matter of a joint gift, one deceive the other—as of course any Greek would naturally do. A twenty minute wait, while DJ fumed and the postlady cross-questioned a poor young man who was trying to get six packages from the National Cash Register Co; then it was our turn—the usual forms, receipt for the pittance of duty, etc—and presently we were back in the car deciding that after all it <u>had</u> been worth the fuss many times over. Other errands. A coffee in Kolonaki. Finally, back at the house, asking nothing better than a nap <u>then</u> a thermos of freshly-made espresso, D discovers that his passport is missing. Nowhere to be found. I remind him soothingly that I left mine at the P.O. once last year, and that the girl had put it safely in her purse to await my reappearance. But <u>his</u> girl is off duty when he drives there; so back to Kolonaki, retracing his steps, piteously inquiring—all in vain. We begin constructing dungeons in the air. The cleaning-woman comes, full of <u>her</u> troubles (mother ill + gaga, history repeating itself) so that the gloom thickens as the day wanes—when suddenly comes a cry from her: "Mr David, your passport!" She has explored the clogged toilet's depths and removed the dripping obstacle: indeed, the pass-port. Instant merriment. D comes forth with a towel to start blot-ting. "No," begs Photiní, "let me rinse it off, it <u>smells</u>!" "Let it be," says J; "so does the government that issued it"—and by today it has dried nicely and all the official stamps are still legible. So we have also a notably lighthearted hour to thank you for. (Are you wondering how it got <u>there</u>? So are we.)

Other news? Maria is in hospital after being found unconscious—a minor embolism which hasn't paralyzed her, but left her weaker yet, and compulsively talking. Chester Kallman recited the last poem Auden wrote:

He still loves life, but
oh oh oh how he wishes
the Lord would take him.

No more rain since you left: bright + cold, we've turned on the heat. I'm leaving now on the 6th instead of the 8th, stopping 2 days in Frankfurt to see a friend.

So things are winding up quickly. I don't think D has any intention of getting a face-lift (a clinic, knives, stitches? out of the question) but he may have to have a nasty sinus operation. The headaches have come back with a vengeance. Even though the very last passer-through has departed. We both enjoyed <u>your</u> visit very much. As for the \$\$\$, I'll either write these days or phone when I'm home; you'll have the 1st installment by Dec. 1 and, as we agreed, never remind me of it thereafter. More next month.

Love,
Jimmy

your beautiful + useful gift In her memoir, *Unlikely Friends* (2019), Moffett calls it "a sleek insulated carafe" meant to be "a Swedish improvement on a tea cosy."

To J. D. McClatchy

YALE
20 December 1973
Stonington, CT

Dear Sandy,

It pleased me to no end to have your letter. I've read it upside-down and held it to the light, parts of it being too well-written to make perfect sense—not that that matters, as you know. What, at this stage, does matter? Pure dull good will, attentiveness, one eye for possibilities, another eye for impossibilities—what always mattered in short. You have all that where I'm concerned, I think, and I hope that I can keep whatever exposures of my own you care to look through unclouded for that purpose. My other immediate concern are these tropical fish in the next room. They keep dying—even while I watch (since I watch them constantly, and see them long after my eyes are shut)—and being replaced faithfully. By Xmas morning, when the Holy Family takes them downstairs, I'll be both vastly relieved and drained of gallons of emotion—emotion that includes some tiny darting catfish-masked hatred of the kind we all feel for whatever sickens under our care; though that is the least of the emotions. Dinner party here last night: my brother + his wife, the Reeves, Grace + Eleanor +

E's son Peter (the young Baron). My brother is unused to gatherings whose target is pleasure. He kept retreating behind the bookcase and only began to enjoy the party at breakfast when it was safely past. The great holiday snare is tightening. This is my last free evening till January 8—or would have been had I refused an impromptu supper for "young people" chez ces dames—when I'll phone. Bless you, my dear. Take things easily, and watch out in Chicago. I have read that it's full of gangsters.

Love,
James

these tropical fish A Christmas gift for the Alevras daughters, which Merrill cared for in advance of the holiday. See his poem "Think Tank" in *Late Settings* (1985). **the Holy Family** The Alevras family.

To Robin Magowan   WUSTL
                                                          25 January 1974
                                                          [Stonington, CT]

Dear Robin,

Let's hope you haven't been counting the weeks, the months; at least not as remorsefully as I've been doing. This year took me 3 or 4 times longer than ever before to feel myself settled. Impossible to do ANYTHING until just about two weeks ago—anything that is but go to Atlanta, go to the dentist, go to the opera, stop smoking, read V. Woolf; and not work, not write letters, not read with the least attentiveness the many pages you and others are still, I fear, hoping for some word about. Well, you do have a choice, you don't have to forgive me, but make an effort, please. (And let me know if the *NYRB* is reaching you; I wrote as soon as your letter came.)

Maria died—a great light gone out of the world. These last few months her sufferings were even worse; constantly on morphine; dry eyes fixed on the doctor—her devoted and sinfully stupid cousin—whenever he appeared, asking him "Póso akóma?" None of us, not even Nelly, saw her after September; though Tony went hardly anywhere, stayed at home Sundays, just on the chance there might be news, or a phone-call from herself feeling like a chat. It can't have been entirely the illness that carried her off. I remember a letter she wrote T. to S'ton in 1969: "I have such an envie de mourir that everyone mistakes it for a joie de vivre." The light air in which one says such things can be lethal.

And in New York after Christmas I went to the hospital to see—indeed to meet—Dr Cotsias. What your impressions were I can't recall. I sort of half fell in love with him. If one could imagine a Greek Larry Condon . . . ? who was also literary? We talked for over an hour in a dreamlike shipboard-acquaintance intimacy. Well. As Bob Grimes said in November after meeting Donald Richie for the first time—stammering + blinking with enthusiasm—"I just li-<u>like</u> D. R. I'd like to buy up all his c-common stock!" (which makes me think: Our favorite stammerer BVW is either in Western Europe—watch out—or in a flight pattern above Boston airport.)

A lot of seemingly wasted time has, however, led me to some conclusions about the Ephraim book. I can only write it in verse. The prose is entirely dead, while the "numbers" can be induced to flow + sparkle. It may run to, oh, 1500, 2000 lines, a regular little Divine Comedy. E. himself will be furious—he wants to reach a Larger Public. Well, he can always see that I leave it in a taxi. (The drafts from which I had typed the pages of the lost novel were left behind, in a file containing several unfinished poems, in a Frankfurt hotel room last November; and not found, when I wrote to ask. You see?) I hope it takes me a long, long time.

May I keep your xeroxed pages a while longer? I haven't felt like reading anything <u>new</u>; but when I do, it will be to them I turn first. Let me have your news. Here I'm not freezing thanks to a snug almost weightless undergarment called I think Ski-Skins. You probably knew about it all along. It has changed my life.

Love to you + Kate—always,
Jimmy

"**Póso akóma?**" How much more?
Dr. Cotsias George Cotzias (1918–77), Greek-American physician and scientist who helped to create L-dopa, the standard treatment for Parkinson's disease, to whom Merrill was introduced by his sister, Doris. Contacted posthumously via

Ouija board, he became an important character in *The Changing Light at Sandover* (1982).

Bob Grimes A friend of David Jackson's whom he had met as a student at UCLA.

BVW Bernard V. Winebaum.

Ephraim book Merrill's poem *The Book of Ephraim* began as a novel.

E. himself The Ouija board's spirit was so integral to the poet's life by now that he was regarded as a friend, and in letters was often referred to as such, often using just his initial.

To Stephen Yenser   YALE

25 January 1974
[Stonington, CT]

Dear Stephen,

I'm sorry to have let so much time go by (it <u>has</u> gone by, or are you too busy to notice?)—in fact I'm trying to remember when it was we talked. If I'm not mistaken you'll not have heard that Maria died. David phoned the evening of the 14th, just after the funeral (they're so civilized, the Greeks; the dead are buried within 24 hours). Years ago, Tony had been forbidden to go to her funeral; so he didn't; D + Nelly went round afterwards and took him to the grave. I wonder if that was the same year she wrote him to Stonington: My envie de mourir is so great that everyone else mistakes it for a joie de vivre. Well, a great light has gone out of our lives.

Now Claude has come + gone. We spoke of David Rodes and to my shame I can recall little of the conversation, unless it was something to the effect that DR would surely want to know something long before the Bennington committee met—as they will not until late March or early April. I should have written it down, or forced him to write you then + there. It was a happy ten days. He couldn't of course lift anything heavier than a teacup or an eyebrow, but just the sound of his typewriter drumming on the other side of my study wall kept me serene, even somewhat at work; while now once again the spectre of Solitude extends its bony fingers, out comes the tattered Patience, I fall asleep only to dream that I am smoking Gitane after Gitane (in waking no such matter—YET) . . . I suspect that I have arrived at some final decision regarding "The Book of Ephraim." A dozen other decisions involving structure, the question of the direct vs. indirect discourse, etc etc etc etc, are still pending. But it seems that it must be done as a kind of poem (with transcripts as interludes? or paraphrased?); and having decided <u>that</u>, it is at least in theory possible to sketch a few lines every day or so. It <u>could</u> be perfectly awful, or it could be the *Divine Comedy*—the result will as usual lie somewhere between. I have at present no idea how long it will take, how long it will <u>be</u>. What I can't imagine, either, is showing it to anybody until it is much further along. Ephraim will be furious. This isn't at all what he had in mind—too <u>arty</u>. Still, one does what one can. And it can always be lost in a taxi.

Last night (sleepless despite codeine; the dentist had excised one root of that tiresome molar in the afternoon) I finished *The Voyage Out* which I'd not read since 1944. I almost believe it is her masterpiece—the richness, the freshness, the wonderfully classical yet utterly arbitrary progression from first to last. The later books appear by contrast sadly mannered, trapped in their method; here, in this one, everything can be expressed; and it breaks your heart in the bargain.

I told DJ I'd fly to Athens for 6 weeks at the very end of April. He plans to come here for much of the summer; no fixed dates for him, naturally, up to now. We'll see. Love to Mary.

Yours ever,
James

David Rodes Yenser's friend and colleague at UCLA, who had applied for a position at Bennington College, where Fredericks taught classes.
Patience European name for the card game Solitaire.
Gitane French brand of cigarette.
The Voyage Out Virginia Woolf's much-revised first novel.

To John Ashbery

Dear John,

Yesterday afternoon I rolled up all my strength and sourness into one ball, called La Hornick, and withdrew from that April reading at the Museum. Her original letter had said nothing about reading in company. When the grapevine bore the luscious fact that we—you + I—would be sharing the occasion I began positively to look forward to it: a chance to see you and (who knows) maybe hear "Parmegianino" which as yet remains an impression of deep beauty barely skimmed (by me). But when a letter came saying we would be <u>three</u>—well, in that direction lay vaudeville, I began to think, and of how much I could get done at home rather than hanging about NY for two days for the sake of a quick "turn" on 53rd St. She is no doubt mad as a Hornick—I couldn't care less. But I certainly don't want you, whom I love + admire, to misunderstand.

As ever,
Jimmy

John Ashbery The American poet (1927–2017) was a friend of Merrill's from the mid-1950s onward.
rolled up . . . into one ball See Andrew Marvell, "To His Coy Mistress": "Let us roll all our strength and all / Our sweetness into one ball."
La Hornick Lita Rothbard Hornick (1927–2000), patron of the avant-garde arts, publisher of Kulchur Press, who arranged the reading at the Museum of Modern Art.
"Parmegianino" Ashbery's poem "Self-Portrait in a Convex Mirror" (published in his book of that title, 1975), which responds to Francesco Parmigianino's painting of the same name (c. 1524). Merrill had read the poem in David Kalstone's typed copy; it appeared in *Poetry* magazine in August 1974.
we would be <u>three</u> Ron Padgett (b. 1942), American poet, translator, and editor, had also been invited to read his poetry.

To David Jackson   WUSTL
                                                      16 February 1974
                                                      [Stonington, CT]

Dearest D—

I miss you <u>so</u>. Your long letter (yes I read it all, read it twice) came yesterday, and today a Valentine. But you still aren't well; and the house is full of paint-fumes. There are 100 things to say; but mainly that I love you very much. It is hard to think what the future will bring; and just as hard to think what the past has brought. A weariness between us, a coldness—which I think may both have been forms of a subtle distrust: a doubt as to whether either of us really had the other's good at heart. Maybe it's age, but I don't imagine I shall ever again try to imagine a life lived with anyone but you— together or apart—and so, yes, if you want me, I'm your Valentine for another 20 years at least.

Is it wrong to say to a sick friend?—I feel so marvelously well these days. Yesterday I spent in a kind of salutary RAGE. *The Yellow Pages* arrived (an advance copy) and they had left out a note saying the edition was limited—something I'd particularly asked for lest the book be taken as more public than I mean it to be. Well, they'll glue in a sticker—they said. Otherwise you can't imagine how charming the edition is. Then came a letter from a Ms Hornick, whose invitation to read at the Mod. Museum in April I had accepted with pleasure. It even pleased me to hear through the grapevine that J. Ashbery was going to read with me. But yesterday's letter said we would be THREE (Ron Padgett) and the whole idea began to smack of vaudeville, and I thought of what I might get done up here rather than hanging about NY for 2 days; so I called her and withdrew—then stalked off to the Boats still trembling with vexation (mad as a Hornick? mad as a hairnet?—what IS the idiom) and unbent at dinner so far as to drink two small glasses of wine. Which did not keep me from scolding Grace at the bridge table. (Yes, I'm afraid I'm on the wagon as well—since last Sunday; where will it end? But I FEEL SO WELL). (Sobriety makes one manic? had you realized that?—and by the way where IS Bernie?)

The main thing is that my work is coming along. Slowly but surely. I imagine a poem about 2500 lines long. The "working" idea is to have 28 sections, the first word of each beginning with a successive letter of the alphabet, plus two sections between M + N, titled or starting YES and NO, conveying as much as I can of the pros + cons, the ambivalence felt about E. et al. I've only done about 4 at this point, and some of my sense of what's to come is extremely obscure not to say woozy—but as you see I'm excited. Next week I'll have the finished bits xeroxed and send them to you; but don't show them to any of our least-bit <u>literary</u> friends, because it is not in a finished state. If you have suggestions, keep them warm until we're together and can talk. Right now is still a bit too early for that.

Richard comes up tomorrow afternoon for 2 nights: one with G + E, one by ourselves. <u>He</u> isn't drinking either. The anthology with Tom V's photo is out, very elegant and very interesting; his preface recalls how difficult Modern Poetry was for Miss Wickwire his high-school teacher. I sent him a note signed with her name, say that Mod. Poetry was now thanks to him an open book, but oh dear why had Modern <u>Prose</u> become so impenetrable? That's it for today. Another dear letter from Tony—love to him. And to YOU (kiss).

J.

The Yellow Pages Volume of poems not collected in Merrill's other books to that point.
Richard Richard Howard.
Tom V Thomas Victor (d. 1989), American photographer of writers and artists.

To Charlotte Arner   POSTCARD | WUSTL
[March 1974]
[Stonington, CT]

Dear Frau Geliebte—What's left of you, that is! I'm on the eve of more trips (out west, and then to Greece the next month) but David + I will <u>both</u> be here in July—I for at least 5 months—+ perhaps then you can demonstrate for us how to lose weight on "cuisine provinciale." I've stopped smoking <u>and</u> drinking, eat nothing, give off the odor of sanctity, and am altogether extremely dull. Let's hope it's just a phase, and life begins at 48.

> Love to you and Bob always,
> Jimmy

Charlotte Arner Wife of Robert Arner, Merrill's student at Bard.
What's left of you Evidently she had been on a diet. The postcard image is a vintage photo of a luscious young woman, with a loose gown off her bare shoulders.

To Elizabeth Bishop   VASSAR
                                                              19 April 1974
                                                           [Stonington, CT]

Dear Elizabeth—

Thank you for John's note, nothing urgent in it, just thanks for *The Yellow Pages*. I thought—our whole Crowd thought—your reading was a great success; I just wish it had gone on longer. In Washington, I hadn't been able to <u>hear</u> from that seat in the glare on stage; so that it was a special pleasure to have "Crusoe" again—since I also appear not to possess a copy of it. That fact, which will allow you to dismiss the following tentative remark, gives me the courage to make it. (And I wouldn't make it if I hadn't checked my impression with a Practising Critic like DK.) Something strikes me as not quite right about Friday when he appears; about what you do with him. The poem's last line, it's true, gives the full resonance of feeling earlier withheld or deflected into the landscape + fauna. Yet I wondered: why that faintly dismissive tone—"poor boy" and his "prettiness"? Why that, I mean, without some expression of the relation that makes him "dear" as well. A lot will go without saying, and does. But I found I was yearning for, say some lines about <u>how</u> <u>they</u> <u>communicated,</u> Crusoe + Friday: did they make a language? of sounds? of signs? Well, I don't want to press it, and blush for having gone this far; but the poem is so magnificent, and so touching, and so strong (for me) <u>except</u> at this one turning where something seems to wobble unintentionally, that I thought I'd trust your knowing how immensely everything you do matters to me, and blurt out my diffident reservation—since the poem isn't yet between boards.

None of my new ones will be, either, for quite a while, now that I've embarked on a poem whose length and subject (David J's and my experiences at the Ouija Board) have led me to speak of it as "The Divine Comedy"—let me, like Manuelzinho's mistress, apologize "here and now" to Dante. Oddly enough I finished the first third of it on Good Friday; and felt I was seated a few days later next to the Mt of Purgatory itself, in the person of that awful Mrs Mumford. Do you suppose one should write her (him?) a note? I'd give a lot to have the recipe for that entrée—Chicken à la Joker, or whatever . . .

I leave here on the 25th and NY on the 29th, returning June 12 or so. This will be a special summer in Stonington, with daily blasting on Water St, in the interest of the new sewer—more reason than ever, I hope you'll feel, to pay a visit.

Oh dear, I wonder if I'm the least bit right about "Crusoe." I wonder too if you're the least bit like me—who either welcome or ignore such a comment. Please finish the new poems by mid-June!

Love always,
Jimmy

Wasn't it fun at the National Gallery? So good for a painter to see things through "our" eyes for a change. David McI.—who has read and heard about you for years—instantly made a place for you in his Pantheon. Apparently the bearded man with all the books in NY is perfectly all right. David K speaks well of him, and some old, old friends have kept telling me at annual intervals that he is kind, honest, sincere, etc etc etc.

Manuelzinho's mistress She is the speaker in Bishop's poem "Manuelzinho" in *Questions of Travel* (1966).
the first third of it Of "The Book of Ephraim" (*Divine Comedies*, 1976), a long poem that became the first of three books in *The Changing Light at Sandover* (1982) and was later republished in an annotated stand-alone edition edited by Stephen Yenser (2018).

To David McIntosh   WUSTL
                                                                     9 May 1974
                                                                 [Athens, Greece]

David dear,

Your letter all about the red canyon full of wind reached me in New York before I left. It sounds like a marvelous place, but I shall need old automobilists' goggles before going there, or have my eyelids stitched shut like a shrunken head's—well, why not? We've had severe winds here too, why? Has the whole world's climate pattern been upset, as one hears now + then in authoritative tones from people like Daniel? Hot days, cool days, and mostly wind. I was taken <u>at once</u> to see Maria's tomb, a rug-sized marble box full of earth, in which lies an ugly moderne slab of marble with a thin bronze cross in relief. Where the headboard would be if it were a bed rises a marble cross (40 years old?) with her parents' names, and now hers. What saves it is the earth round the flat slab all planted: pansies, columbine, begonias—or am I making it up?—petunias surely, lots of little flowers, and two evergreen footmen flanking their playground. (In fact the entire cemetary is <u>charming</u>—family tombs like houses, all above ground as in New Orleans, dowdy if marble can be dowdy: an armchair of marble; a marble cannon and shells for a general; an angel extending a broken propeller to a helmeted + goggled young pilot; urns to burn; and live cypresses, and views of the sea. I'm not a cemetary buff—I've been to Valéry's grave at Sète but not to Père Lachaise—but felt right at home in this one.) Maria at once began complaining (when we sat at the Ouija Board) about the waste, the nonsense of keeping up a grave; yet didn't sound seriously annoyed. She is at Stage 4—higher than one had expected. Ephraim said, No, she wasn't beautiful; but was like a jewel, her glance shone directly into you. She arrived suffering from what they call "the great sickness"—not cancer, but a longing not to stay, a longing to be reborn. She became instantly famous for saying of Heaven "But it is impossible for me to stay anywhere where I have no little corner of my own." Her patron is St Agatha, she whose breasts were cut off—"the first women's libber" Maria ad libbed—and M helps her, laughing quietly at the absurdity of it,

428 | *A Whole World*

decide on how the ever-expanding Mind of the universe should be channeled. Ephraim said of her that everyone had always fallen in love with her, and that in return she . . . loved them, it's true, but never, never as much as they loved her. We—and Tony—promptly saw the truth of <u>that.</u> All her sufferings (she said) were like a final racking cough, after which—air, air, air! The hour soothed us very much.

Aside from that there's little news. I'm working 4 or 5 hours a day. We saw *The Sting* the other night with Bernie—I adored it—and we went with Margot and Johnny Camp's girl, the clever + delightful Francine, and a taller wonderful trilingual (Greek, English, Hebrew) artist-scholar named Niko Stavroulakis to the reforestation center at Kaisarianí 3 miles from Athens. A locked gate was opened for us, just above the little restored church, and we were suddenly on a hillside ablaze with wildflowers, hundreds of different ones, from microscopic orchids to buttercups big as butterplates, and almond trees already hung with fruit covered in silvergreen flocking, and water flowing, and wild columbine, wild strawberries—too much of a concentration, like a millefleurs tapestry to which the only possible response was "Hang it!"

D + I are grouchy with one another. I must try to remember that he leaves in 12 days, <u>and</u> that the house has been repainted outside (plus assorted rooms—the bathroom is a DREAM) under his supervision.

I love you,
James

The Sting Film (1973) directed by George Roy Hill.
Stavroulakis Nikos Stavroulakis (1932–2017), cofounder and first director of the Jewish Museum of Greece in Athens.

To Judith Moffett   NYPL
                                                    5 November 1974
                                                    [Stonington, CT]

Dear Judy,

Here for this one evening, with your letter which came at noon.
Rather than brood too much, let me make a stab at some answers.
If the numerical scheme or sequence falls away, it will be because I
already suspect that each question in its fashion points to the heart
of the matter.

   1. I got a lot of "nature" as a child, through things I naively could
not believe were what others meant by Nature. (Nature in poetry
meant, clearly, trees and lakes, birds perhaps—but never parrots or
peacocks; plants especially; and feelings of reverence.) At perhaps 9 I
was given custody of a segment of earth, and instructed on the plant-
ing + tending of what turned out to be a great choked hell of zinnias.
How I loathed them! The time I had to spend with them was torture.
But at the same age I had a passion for, say, tropical fish, the blossom
of the columbine, seashells—all, you will notice, pretty "gem-like"
things. [*in the margin*: <u>small</u> things, too. My nearsightedness wasn't
discovered til I'd been a year [in] school.] The dogs I adored were
also, no doubt, part of Nature, though this had never been explained
to me. I spent all my early years—through my teens at least—trying
hopefully to agree with other people's taste: if I could just manage
<u>that</u>, whatever was wrong with me might magically come right. Then,
too, whether I truly liked nature or not, or liked her best when she
most resembled artifice, I understood—especially as I approached
maturity—that she provided images invaluable through being com-
mon currency. Anything in nature could not be wholly private or
subjective. The most peculiar thoughts or feelings were "safe" the
moment they touched the base of whatever natural objects or pro-
cess one might choose in order to describe them. [*in the margin*: cf. 7
below] This grew into an esthetic principle. A certain NY art gallery
used to show in its window, when I was 15 or 16, still-life oils by a
painter—I forget who; no one "great"—wherein all the objects were
themselves supremely rare and valuable: lacquer-work, old porce-
lain, coral beads, etc. I saw how terribly wrong that was—no tension

between medium + subject. Oysters by Manet were the answer. To be sure, I never acquired EB's virtuosity in this regard—her astonishing gift for conferring beauty on the plainest, humblest things, like that fender of dented blue enamel in "The Moose"—but I remain pleased whenever I remember to let these things appear. ("Conferring" is more what I do; she discovers.) Proust must have represented an intermediate stage. One could, I learned from him, write about nature without having to seem brainwashed by correct attitudes. A shrub could be as interesting as a duchess. "Flowers are people . . ."

2. You can see how much of the above is interwoven with my sense of what others expected of me, and my shame over not being the person they wanted me to be. "Charles" became that side of me which could live—or could have lived—or still can live—without tension a Good Life among agreeable surroundings. Not a slave, necessarily, to pleasant manners and well-cooked meals. Able even to work up a touch of irony at their expense. But always self-satisfied, never subversive. I could have been him entirely, perhaps, if who I was at the age of 20 had ever seemed—as it did in so many of the rich young people I grew up among—cause for unreserved self-congratulation.

3. That book seemed too long, and its pieces individually too short, for me to arrive at an unbroken order. The suggestion to divide it up came from my friend Barbara Deming (she wrote *Prison Notes* and *We Cannot Live Without Our Lives*—the latter, out this year, includes a selection of oddly haunting poems), and I think I have followed her arrangement on the whole faithfully. Sections I + II have by + large the earliest-written poems in the book. III may be chiefly "lighter" in spirit, and IV "darker" in the sense that most of the poems can be read as being about death + rebirth. I didn't want all the mythological poems together, or all the "Short Stories" in sequence. Her decisions struck me, at that point, as probably saner than any I could have made myself.

4. Yes, in the sense that "things near to home" were still too ambiguous or inaccessible (emotionally) to use in poetry. Writing *The Seraglio* and the 2 plays did more for this sort of confidence, I rather think, that the first long stay in Europe. Also, I was going to an analyst in Rome—for about 15 months, 5 or 6 days a week. That must have had some effect, sooner or later.

5. Through coming to feel that encrustation was (a) in bad taste—

in most art; and (b) suspect, psychologically, as being . . . overly defensive. The passionate encrustations of Proust are again the exception—every phrase a live organism. In my undergraduate thesis on him, I ventured to account for his sometimes obsessive proliferation of metaphor as a device which "made pain bearable." I may have meant, in those days, the pain of direct self-revelation or confrontation. Later on, it developed that the alternative to the brocaded coat didn't have to be nakedness—an ironic leotard, for instance, did just as well. People were always telling me, even in my teens, to be clear and simple; and I can remember thinking—as I suppose I still do—that such clarity could only come as a reward for having given a lot of obscurity. Put that way, it sounds like the worst kind of chi-chi dialectic. However.

6. Your parenthesis at the end of this question sounds exactly right. Probably I share the feelings about intelligence that came through from my parents + their friends—that, if one had it, it was nicer to conceal the fact. Or: it was for emergency use, like a fire-extinguisher; afterward, the room would have to be redecorated. As you imply, love of wisdom has nothing whatever to do with intelligence; and I am only <u>beginning</u> to think that I might care more deeply for philosophy than I've ever let on till now. Which leads to

7. Reading in Jung how ancient and wide-spread is the resistance to consciousness—how even God, in the matter of Job, found it easier not "to consult His omniscience"—has been helpful lately in reconciling me to my own ambivalent microcosm. There is no consciousness without personality, says Jung, in perhaps those exact words. He further notes that "it is precisely Peter, who lacks self-control and is fickle in character, whom Christ wishes to make the rock + foundation of his Church." I wouldn't like to think that personality is merely anybody's sum of contradictions; what I value more is the tone or style in which these are arrived at, but that tone may no longer be "personality" so much as the key-signature of the next variation. One doesn't want to say "soul"—not being a philosopher <u>yet</u>, or knowing the proper terminologies. Besides, I can already see your Ethics gleefully rubbing their hands in the wings. Do you imagine by the way that Eliot, in his "dictum," meant by personality something like "a facility with masks"? It would have been like him.

It is hours later. Time for a drink. I don't think DK has done his bit on me as yet. Certainly he would balk at your using it before it had appeared—isn't that how all you Professional Critics react? Of course you are free to write him. Kathleen Bonann would be c/o UCLA Eng. Dept. I think you left a whole line out of your letter, which reads—no, I see: just a long parenthesis.

Love,
Jimmy

each question Moffett had sent Merrill a set of questions, answers to which she would draw on when writing about his work. In her book *James Merrill: An Introduction to the Poetry* (1984) she quotes from his response to her fifth question here.
a great choked hell of zinnias See his later poem "Alessio and the Zinnias" in *A Scattering of Salts* (1995).
"Charles" Recurrent figure in Merrill's work, as in "Charles on Fire," *Nights and Days* (1966).
That book *The Country of a Thousand Years of Peace* (1959).
Barbara Deming (1917–84), American writer, feminist, activist, founder of the Money for Women fund in 1975.
Jung For Jung on Job see especially the long essay "Answer to Job" (1952).
DK has done his bit Kalstone's essay on Merrill's poetry appeared in his book *Five Temperaments: Elizabeth Bishop, Robert Lowell, James Merrill, Adrienne Rich, John Ashbery* (1977).
Kathleen Bonann A UCLA student who was cultivating a friendship with Merrill and would much later, as Kathleen Bonann Marshall, write a dissertation titled "Dear Premises: James Merrill and the Domestic Impulse in His Work and in His Life."

To Stephen Yenser

22 November 1974
[Stonington, CT]

Dear Stephen,

Such a good letter from you on returning late yesterday (oops, that double space): the Man called from Yale saying, with abject excuses, that really, even in my case, t-he tiresome administrat-ive people—no he doesn't stutter, this machine has started to—needed more than 2 sentences to describe my "seminar"—so I gassed on for a page, with another between the lines) from the terrible town. Both nights at the opera turned out to be gloriously exciting, especially the Janacek *Jen-*

ufa a masterpiece from the last decade when opera was really opera (t-he 1st of this century). My sister + I were quite transported, and so were Richard + Sandy, ten rows behind us. I may just go again next Saturday afternoon (you can hear the broadcast, but it may only frustrate you). Was your *Pelléas* good? I hope they sang it in French with perfect accent? No? Well, never mind.

That's encouraging about the Fulbright nomination. My going to Yale would delay the removal to Athens only briefly. I couldn't possibly return—if I come back here in May—much before December. But with DJ and Alan and Nelly and Tony and Bernie you won't have time to miss me.

How good you are—how good you have been from the start—about the poor old DC. (How bad I've been about what you send; I realized after we talked that my suggestion made no sense whatever, in the acanthus poem. Your forbearance is exemplary.) I mean to prune away as many jokes as I can bear to (like "Years, idle years") when the poem is done—certainly in the last sections. Anyone who reads that far is bound to be <u>serious</u>. (Alison just called. She wants to spend a week or so in Athens, late February, how about that? I'd called last night, and got Jonathan. He said he was publishing his new book himself. Braziller didn't even want to read it, after his descriptive letter. I asked if he'd seen—been sent by you—the *Mass Review*. No, he said, sounding rather left out of things. There'll only be 250 copies. I asked, might there be an extra one for your admirer SY? He said, "Well, when you've read it, you'll know if he'd still be interested." So like Jonathan.)

Yes, I turn off my hearing aid when John H gets on the subject of, among others, Lac. Practically every character in the poem is <u>clef</u> except The Foot. See p. 100 for a list of "nulls", i.e. purely made-up figures. Ember is Ashbery. Steampump + Tallman, Auden + Spender. Moroz, Frost (I think). Kidd is Richard. Lake is Elizabeth. (Somewhere I have a last message to Image, about a recent suicide of some poor woman deluded into thinking she was an agent. It ends: "I wonder what the chilly Lake said of it.") JH cut through a certain amount of wild surmise on DK's part, saying: "I don't understand, people keep talking to me as if I'd written a poem à clef." I agree, I like the Image sections best. They were charming to receive, from odd cities, on bizarre hotel letter-paper.

Sending you the article about rare books wasn't meant to make you writhe. Just that when the Crash comes, and I am old and poor and have sold my Marianne Moore Egoist Press pamphlet and your letters to me, you may have to help me out—or take me in.

Kilo is Pound. Puritan is TSE.

Wednesday I heard that an old friend had died (a painless embolism): Louise Fitzhugh. I wonder if Mary ever read any of her books—*Harriet the Spy* was famous, also *Suzuki Beane*. She was practically my first student, the year I taught at Bard. We had, I think, one conference—she'd written a clumsy villanelle about a wounded seagull, and my comments scared her so much that she switched from lit. to child psychology and began an affair with the Older Woman who taught it. The next spring we met, high as kites, at the local roadhouse—she was 20, I was 22—and ended up in bed. I was absurdly in love for a month; but it only turned out that I'd scared her yet another time. When the smoke cleared, we liked each other no end. A kind of gamine from Memphis (she was Peter Taylor's niece), sometimes very chic, sometimes a Dead End Kid . . . But I've had 2 large sherries, and it's time to butter my parsnips.

The enclosed finally got developed. I'll phone in the next days "pour prendre congé"—Meanwhile love to you both.

> Yours ever,
> James

the Man called from Yale Merrill had agreed to teach a class in poetry writing at Yale.
the Janacek *Jenufa* Opera (1904) by Czech composer Leoš Janáček (1854–1928).
Richard + Sandy Richard Howard and Sanford Friedman.
your *Pelléas* Yenser had attended a Los Angeles production of Debussy's *Pelléas et Mélisande.*
Fulbright nomination Yenser later received the Fulbright teaching fellowship at the University of Athens for 1975–76.
"Years, idle years" Merrill had momentarily thought to begin section Y of "The Book of Ephraim" with a parodic allusion to Tennyson's lyric beginning "Tears, idle tears."
Alison Alison Lurie.
Jonathan Jonathan Bishop.
the *Mass Review* Yenser had published a poetic sequence entitled "Clos Camardon" in *The Massachusetts Review* that included an epigraph from Bishop's book *Something Else.*
John H. John Hollander.
Lac The code-names Hollander uses for the spies in his long poem *Reflections on*

Espionage (1976) link to contemporary poets and critics; in this sense it is a "poem à clef." For example, Lac is Cal spelled backward, and therefore Robert Lowell, whose nickname it was. Hollander sent Merrill passages addressed to Image, Merrill's code-name in the poem, and incorporated Merrill's verse replies in the poem's notes. "Puritan" refers to Norman Holmes Pearson rather than T. S. Eliot. It was Pearson's actual OSS code name.

Marianne Moore Egoist Press pamphlet The 24-page *Poems*, published in 1921.

Dead End Kid Sidney Kingsley's Broadway play *Dead End* (1935) and its Hollywood adaptation (1937) featured a group of young, street-wise New York actors who became known as the Dead End Kids and made six subsequent films for Warner Bros.

"pour prendre congé" To take leave.

To Claude Fredericks

GETTY
18 January 1975
[Athens, Greece]

Dearest Claude,

A sad occasion for a letter—or not a letter, then, so much as reaching out to press your hand. Chester died in his sleep the night before last. One of the "good" boys, who was staying in the house, found him and called us. It was only the 2nd dead body I'd seen—and even my grandmother was already embaumée + macquillée by the time I got there, while poor C. lay all mottled and askew, clothes undone, on a filthy bed. It was—we'd all been saying for months, for years— what he was bent upon. And yet in the nature of things we blame ourselves. For not insisting on a hospital, for not having made this remark or refused that favor—his needs + demands were unrelenting. Now his old stone-deaf father is flying over. Burial has been arranged (following tomorrow's autopsy) through the Jewish Community. I can't think in sequence. I'd given a reading at the British Council 2 nights before. Walking into the small, brightly-lit auditorium, there he sat, for once sober in a clean shirt and suit. Our eyes met and <u>held</u> together; he sustained a smile full of theatre, understatement, helplessness . . . Before Christmas I'd protested, in a letter to him, against the claims he was making on my time + patience; so there'd been a resultant, not coldness so much as formality between us ever since. On Xmas day one of the boys came staggering under the weight of Wystan's Austrian set of the OED, which he wanted me to have. Oh, it's Margaret I grieve for along with that generous and selfish and spectacularly ruined person babbling out his own tedious splendeurs et misères, the thefts and the blow-jobs, the memoirs and the jokes, bloated and hunched, the empty glass held out with an air both peremptory and supplicating—yet who had been so quick, so glamorous, a mere 30 years ago, as to captivate—ah but we know how little it takes to be captivated; the point is that it lasted, that Wystan all simply <u>adored</u> C. his whole life long. They're doing the *Rake* next month. He couldn't even hang on for that. Remember the curtain calls at la Fenice—only yesterday! And yesterday morning (or 20 years ago) the "good" boy looked seriously into my eyes and said: "Ti einai o anthropos!" What? I couldn't imagine what he was saying, made him repeat it, explain it. Oh. Here today, gone tomorrow, dew on a blade. Oh yes. That.

So everything is upside down. Which in fact allows me to write, whereas the working schedule leaves me with no further wish to use words at the day's end. It has been quiet. I've felt at times—in spite of, or along with, more sex than I need—extremely withdrawn; at least preoccupied. But the end is in sight—of the poem? of the world? If only of the former, I vow to pay more heed to the latter as soon as I'm free to. What "strange and very beautiful" something has happened to you, dear one? Bless you always. Here's David's love, and mine.

Jamie

the "good" boys In contrast to the bad boys who exploited Kallman.
it's Margaret I grieve for Allusion to G. M. Hopkins's poem "Spring and Fall," which begins: "Margaret, are you grieving / Over Goldengrove unleaving?"
the *Rake* *The Rake's Progress* (1951), opera by Igor Stravinsky with a libretto by Auden and Kallman.
la Fenice The Teatro La Fenice in Venice, where Merrill and Fredericks (separately) attended the premiere of *The Rake's Progress*.
"Ti einai o anthropos!" "What is man!" See *Hamlet*, II.2: "What a piece of work is man."
dew on a blade See *Othello*, I.2: "Keep up your bright swords, for the dew will rust 'em."

To John Hollander   YALE
                                                            18 January 1975
                                                          [Athens, Greece]

Dear John,

Ed Mendelson said you might be phoning, but I wanted to write in
any case. Chester had been in spectacularly bad shape, and getting
worse. He had gone to Austria after Xmas, did not return on the
expected day. Frau Ströbl telephoned Alan saying he was too weak
from drink to make the trip. Finally—his doctor there having (with
what naiveté!) said "either you return to Athens and <u>rest</u> or I will
forcibly hospitalize you"—he came back: blue-white, cramped into a
ball, covered with sores, burns, God knows what. We gave him what
advice we could, reminded him how much good the clinic last spring
had done him. But naturally he had found a dangerously mild + per-
missive doctor here, all shifty-eyed doubletalk yesterday (in front of
the Embassy woman) about the psychology of alcoholics—and, in
short . . . Two evenings ago, he had been at home with Alan and the
only two "good" boys he knew—who have never stolen from him or
beaten him up. He had gone downtown at noon as usual, drunk his
endless ouzos, managed to get home. That evening he couldn't eat
anything (besides, the dog in Austria had chewed up his bridge), kept
lying down and struggling up. After Alan left, the boys slept in the
house, and found they couldn't move him the next morning. We got
there before 10. The First Aid people had come and gone saying call
his doctor and the police. Niko and I found a clean sheet to cover
him with. It was Friday, we remembered, and Alan would have gone
out early to shop at the weekly street-market nearby. The other boy
found him there with Rachel and Stavros. Within 3 hours all the offi-
cial people had come, Chester was taken for an autopsy (now <u>there</u> is
a slip), and the apartment was sealed for what promises to be several
months. We are all, as you can imagine, blaming ourselves, up to a
point. Alan "nearly" phoned us that last evening to ask if he shouldn't
take matters into his own hands and call the doctor. I had written, in
mid-December, a stiff letter to C. begging him not to use me as his
banker—he <u>had</u> money, couldn't he spare me going downtown during
my work time, to bring him drachmas which would then be stolen

by the next day?—especially as he went downtown himself every day to drink. The letter hurt him, I know. But there was no end to his demands and needs. There hasn't been one yet, for that matter. He's never made any legal provision for Wystan's mss. etc; let alone a will (though one has the sense of great expectations having been aroused among the local trade). By an unhappy coincidence our house was broken into 3 nights ago, when I was reading at the British Council. At the reception—our last living glimpse of Chester—David told him we suspected one of his friends (who in fact had lifted 14,000 Austrian shillings from C. on his return from Vienna, but nevertheless was found comfortably ensconced chez C. the morning of the reading, and knew just where everyone would be at 8 p.m.). Well, as I say, we all could have shown more imagination or love or forbearance, if only <u>because</u> he would do nothing for himself. On the other hand, there had been for weeks only the faintest glimmer, from him, of living or wanting to. It's a state of mind that can be lived through only so often—to which the autopsy is bound to add a very stark footnote. The burial is set for tomorrow. Through Nikos Stavroulakis' very kind intervention the Jewish Community is making an exception—they like to keep their small plot for local people—and are ready to collect Chester after the autopsy, wash him and dress him [and] bury him, always provided that the ten men can be found. Which no doubt is where Bernie—hitherto sputtering + dancing like water on a stove with eagerness to participate—will emerge from the telephonic wings. (B + Alan haven't spoken for years.)

Chester had wanted (perhaps never in writing) to have his ashes scattered on the grave of his friend "St Yannis" near Olympia. But in Greece there's no cremation. The body would have to go to Switzerland for that. After 3 years it is legal (in the Jewish graveyard too? I wonder) to exhume and do with the remains . . . what one likes. Rachel says the moral is: never die abroad. I can't agree with her. Everything—the arrangements—reactions + behavior of all concerned—has been really quite comfortingly on a human scale. My dear, I'm writing precipitously, I can't find words for what I feel. Here at least are a few of the facts, for what they're worth.

Love to you all—
Jimmy

Ed Mendelson Edward Mendelson (b. 1946), professor of English at Columbia University, Auden's literary executor and editor as well as the author of several books about him.
Frau Ströbl Frau Josefa Ströbl, Auden and Kallman's housekeeper in their farmhouse in Kirchstetten, Austria.
Alan Alan Ansen.

To Elizabeth Bishop

VASSAR
29 January 1975
[Athens, Greece]

Dear Elizabeth,

You'll have left the pelicans and the lime pies these many weeks, I'm afraid, but thank you, however belatedly, for the postcard. We've had a can of condensed milk in Stonington for <u>years</u>—now at last I know what I can do with it!

It's raining today, which seems more like winter. Until now, the weather has been golden and mild, and the air really black with pollution. One wipes off the windshield after a couple of hours—Al Jolson's face has nothing on one's palm.

I've lost all track of time. Through work, on one hand. The "divine comedy" is perilously near if not completion, then a point at which I'll be free to fuss + fuss + fuss over it. It's withdrawn me so from life. What will the world seem like when I slip back into it? Then on the other hand, there was the death of Chester Kallman, only 12 days ago, but it seems like months. You must have met him at some point? He'd been a ruin even since before Wystan died. "He's trying to kill himself," we'd all said so often that I think we'd stopped believing it, so that the fact shocked us more than we understood that first morning, waiting for the doctor, the police, the woman from the Embassy, while poor Chester just lay in the next room, as so often in life, unable to struggle up from bed. He's left a dreadful mess behind. An old, old will names Wystan and me as literary executors. He'd never got round to making any formal provision for what WHA left him—the sole heir. Meanwhile they've finally sealed the apartment (a Greek boy who was staying there returned the following evening from a visit to his village, innocently let himself in, wondered at the silence, Chester's stopped watch, put some eggs on to boil, telephoned Alan Ansen nearby, heard what had happened, rushed out to have it confirmed face-to-face, remembered the eggs, rushed back, and only <u>then</u> was apprehended by the policeman "on guard") and we are waiting for word from the few and singularly uncommunicative relatives. He was buried by the local Jewish Community—a stark little service, beautifully chanted—without a coffin, "nella nuda terra" (in the chilling phrase used by the Italian press describing Stravinsky's funeral)— after which everyone drank coffee and cognac at a centrally located café, so as not to bring death back into their own houses. I didn't set out to go into all this detail—it's only that we've no other news to speak of. Even the cultural pickings—*Amarcord* and the local opera's *Pique Dame*—have been next to nothing. Oh, we have a new cleaning woman, wonderfully efficient, but the price we pay isn't just folding money; she insists on cooking for us, great greasy moussakas and starchy lentil soups which leave me with indigestion and nothing to do with <u>my</u> hands.

David is painting in oils: a portrait of our friend Tony, a view of our friend Nelly in her salon. Lots of trial and error. It reminds me of Robert Morse who, while painting Grace's portrait, kept up a steady murmur about how <u>difficult</u> it all was. Finally Grace asked why he bothered to paint if it was so difficult, and he answered proudly: "Because I can."

I wish we were nearer Lewis Wharf than we are. I'd love to have your news (a new poem?) but fancy you are as always kneedeep in unanswered letters—how well I understand. This is the first one I've written in ten days. <u>Don't answer it.</u> Just give love to Alice and Frank and John and Bill (and to yourself of course) from David and

Jimmy

Al Jolson's face Al Jolson (1886–1950), American actor and singer who performed in blackface.
Amarcord Federico Fellini's film, which won the Best Foreign Film Oscar for 1974.
Pique Dame Tchaikovsky's opera *The Queen of Spades* (1890).
Lewis Wharf Location of the condominium on Boston Harbor where Bishop lived.
Alice and Frank and John and Bill Alice Methfessel, American poet Frank Bidart (b. 1939), and John Brinnin and his partner Bill Read.

To Stephen Yenser   YALE
                                            1 March 1975
                                            Athens, Greece

Dear Stephen,

You will laugh, but these old eyes filled with tears to read your praise. Even if only the least bit of it is deserved, it will do + do + do for a long while. I'm slowly beginning to feel very silly and lightheaded. Connections come + go as in a fever, and as I said in my last letter it's all I can think of—still. Sometimes I fancy that the <u>real</u> creative act comes <u>now</u>, in justifying the ways of, well, god; seeing the connections; wishing them stronger than perhaps they are. What <u>you</u> see in V and Z, say—well, again, if just the least bit of it is <u>there</u>, there to the exclusion of its—who knows—accidental smudging or contradiction in other places, then I can only be immensely relieved.

I by now quite agree with you as to the capitalization of Time. It should stand, perhaps, in <u>A</u>, then not reappear until "in good Time" at the end of W. In fact, wherever possible, I feel the word itself must be deleted or paraphrased—see the enclosed revisions of S and the end of V. The same goes for mirrors—on reflection, they are too numerous; a window is better at the end of V; and in the 1st section of M Ephraim can lead "Her to a spring, or source, oh wonder! in / Whose shining depths . . ." There may be other spots. I'm not pleased with the couplets in U, either, but think the end of M (overleaf) is on the right track. As it stood, it sounded too much like a rehash of the end of I. <u>I</u> don't miss anything I've taken out.

A lovely spoonerism occurs to me for Z: The love that moves the stars has marred the stove. I don't mean to incorporate it, however. But nothing can be final til I'm back at the Selectric.

Yesterday it snowed—the 4th or 5th time this winter—but turned golden by afternoon. There are crimson baby leaves tipping each branch of the rose-bushes: just the color of that gilt blood one imagines on the grooms' faces in *Macbeth*. And après demain the Fiftieth Year begins. Selected Friends are coming for keftédes, deviled eggs, a sandwich bomb from Bocala's—by "selected" I mean, of course, Not Bernie. For a while it seemed as if the senior Jacksons would be here—DJ lashed himself into action, found a lovely 5th floor apartment—4 rooms, huge veranda with awnings—in Ano Ilisia, a 15 minute walk due East—for $110 a month (unfurnished)—and even lined up Taki's mother to <u>live</u> with them; but at present old Mary is too weak to travel, a woman has been found to sleep in the house, and the whole project is delayed for at least a month. The apt. it seemed wisest to let slip through his fingers. That rent saved over a couple of months might just pay for those hour-long phone calls he's had to make. His headaches have come back, and a cold, he's utterly prostrate today.

I'd better lie down myself.

We'll have our *NYRB* before long with Eleanor's letter. One barely legible is here from Grace in Marrakesh today announcing that poor E, returning from a weekend with Mary and Jim, felt worse and worse until she ended up in the American hospital (you knew she was in Paris?) with a burst appendix. Out of danger by now. Too many pearls in those French oysters. Enough, Love to you both. And bless you forever and ever for this whole year in which I can't think what you've been doing <u>except</u> respond to these fortnightly installments. I'm afraid I've been dreadfully demanding in my charming, diffident way. At least you can be sure that nothing on this scale will ever come to you again from this quarter.

Yours ever,
James

V and Z Drafts of "The Book of Ephraim," which is organized in twenty-six sections, one for each letter of the alphabet, as in the mention of A, W, and Z below.
Eleanor's letter Eleanor Perenyi's rebuttal of Robert Craft's negative review of her biography of Franz Liszt appeared along with Craft's reply in *The New York Review of Books*, 6 March 1975.

To Daryl Hine   WUSTL
                                                   7 March 1975
                                              [Athens, Greece]

Dear Heart,

Ten years ago you would probably have written me a letter of
reproach, it's taken me so long to answer. Think how wise you are
now at 39—and how gifted! Your book is here, and exactly what I had
been craving sans le savoir for months. Not, for once, having seen it
assembled in typescript beforehand, it quite bursts upon me: poems
I'd forgotten, poems I'd even imagined belonged to an earlier col-
lection (like "Burnt Out" and "Ego")—my dear, it wouldn't surprise
me if this were your strongest volume to date. Even poems I "don't
care for" like the *Mlle.* editor one, <u>read</u> so well; and the ones I already
did like, like my divine tablets, the breathtaking "Charm"; "On This
Rock"; your B.C. and your Russia, take on the patine, only partly
print-conferred of lasting joys. "Vowel Movements" has now grown
on me to the extent that I wonder at it (far from the loo) 2 or 3 times
a day. If you detect a note of surprise in my response, it's because I'd
been listening to <u>you</u>, silly number, whining about the decline of your
powers—a subject I hereby forbid you ever to broach again, not to
me. It won't wash. This is a marvelous book. (May I only point out,
<u>not</u> <u>for</u> <u>the</u> <u>first</u> <u>time</u>, that the first line of your Wilde anagram lacks
a letter, an <u>e</u>? In the 2nd edition it will have to go something like:
"I? Tried for gain—I? Well, how scales fall!" And while you're on that
page, deitalicize line 3 of Li Po.) I even like Richard's comment!

   As for me, la commedia è finita—virtually. All down if not all done.
(But I will send it to you only after the Selectric in Stonington has
made <u>its</u> final decisions.) It leaves me feeling remote + bemused.
Who will give me a course in regaining touch with reality? There's
daily tinkering ahead for the next month or two—I expect to stay
here (except for a week in Rome starting next Friday) until mid-May.
I don't know, perhaps my uncertainty means that it's <u>not</u> finished;
but doesn't the "creative act" also mean the after-time in which one
rationalizes all those accidental or instinctive twists + turns whereby
the work emerges from the void? It is at present 2550 lines long—that
includes the prose quotations (section Q) however.

Poor Chester—I mean poor us, <u>Chester</u> is young, beautiful and happy at Stage Four; Ephraim says he looks exactly as E. himself did at 20. The flat is still sealed, I am still waiting to hear (there's been no formal notice) whether I'm a literary executor. There was a big article in the *NY Post*, which no one has sent me, about the messy Estate; so you may know more than I do. All I can tell you, I'm afraid, is what terrible condition he was in towards the end—barely able to stir from fetal position, head sagging, arms crossed, only that monstrous liver keeping knees and chin apart. He <u>would</u> <u>not</u> go to a clinic. Every day he somehow got to the downtown bar where Evil Boys threatened him till he gave them money, great piles of it, as he drank his daily halfbottle of ouzo. D + I were the first on the scene after Niko (who'd spent the night) phoned—no the First Aid people had already come, shrugged, and left. His was my 2nd corpse, and I must say my grandmother had been made to look much prettier by the time I saw <u>her</u>. Niko and I found a sheet—"No, Niko, a clean one"—to cover him. And the house filled up, in that funny spirit of elation that precedes any real taking-in of the fact: a woman from the Embassy, the shifty-eyed alcoholic doctor C had combed Athens to find and retain, Nelly, the Police, Alan and Rachel Hadas . . . Three days later the Jewish community buried him, nella nuda terra (as the papers said of Stravinsky) wound in a shroud sickeningly reddened by whatever the autopsy had entailed—nonetheless a service, by comparison with the few Episcopalian ones I've seen, that came very close to meeting what HJ would call the terms of the case. Bernie was one of the Ten Men of course—wearing a silly little Swiss hat by Sally Victor—and disgraced himself by nearly throwing up as soon as he'd cast a womanish fistful of clay, running off to join the women in fact ("Where has the other gentleman gone?" cried the rabbi in vexation) when he should have been helping with the shovels. Un mouvement de gaieté . . . A month later the local opera did the *Rake*, so very well, with a fine black Tom (what else), that we wished him back all over again; as I continue to do, now and then, so that I could kill him for leaving his affairs in such disorder. Though even that has a bright side, one feels, watching the faces of <u>some</u> of his catamites, when they learn what their great expectations have amounted to. Does the heart good.

Gore Vidal was here last night + the night before. DJ sat up with him till 2:30 this morning, enthralled by an absolutely private talk show. "I am greater than America," he said at one point. After about 20 drinks he sounds remarkably like Marius. Claire Bloom was with us for dinner—so pretty. He told a story about yachting through the Aegean with Paul Newman, and being pursued by a police boat for having inadvertently cruised too near one of the prison islands. Early one morning Gore was awakened by shots in his cabin, and suddenly Newman was standing by his bunk, quite hysterical in his robe. "You've never heard," said Gore, "a more faggot reading of this line: They're fffiring at usss!—there was America's hero, in the grand tradition of Franklin Pangborn."

The mag. keeps arriving. I <u>don't</u> think you should let Malanga do any more reviews. D. Halpern may not be much of a poet, but it should be a critic who says so, not a camp-follower. He has No. Mind. At. All. Enough.

> Our love always to you and Sam.
> J.

Your book Hine's poetry collection *Resident Alien* (1975).
Richard's comment Richard Howard's jacket blurb: "How provoked Daryl Hine must be to hear yet again that he is civilized, witty, playful, and urbane! It is a languid catalogue so listed, or enlisted, in the easy cause of *causerie*, unless the further truth is told: the poet Hine is savage, demanding, seriously alive, not dead serious, and besieged."
la commedia è finita Merrill had almost finished "The Book of Ephraim" (*Divine Comedies*, 1976).
Ten Men A minyan, the quorum required by traditional Jewish congregations for certain rituals.
Sally Victor (1905–77), American milliner and ready-to-wear executive.
Marius Marius Bewley (1916–73), British-American literary critic, specialist in Henry James, and professor of English at Rutgers.
Claire Bloom British stage and screen actor (b. 1931), Vidal's close friend for over fifty years.
Franklin Pangborn (1889–1958), Hollywood character actor known for his comically affected manner.
the mag. *Poetry*, which Hine edited.
Malanga Gerard Malanga (b. 1943), poet and artist closely associated with Andy Warhol.
D. Halpern Daniel Halpern (b. 1945), American poet and editor.

To J. D. McClatchy

8 March 1975
Athens, Greece

Dear Sandy,

Your long unanswered letter is all overscribbled with telephone numbers and shopping lists ("eggs, yoghurt, salad, tongue, peanut butter, garbage bags" it says on one side; and on the other, there is DJ's ingenious reply to the boy who makes the mistake of asking in advance how much he is going to get—a system whereby, from a basic 500 drachmas, stringent deductions are made for, as it says on your letter, "not kissing; small cock; no technique; not appearing to enjoy the experience, etc." DJ, who in years past has been known as God's gift to the ugly boy, has in fact of late—but I shan't bore you, with so little space at my disposal, writing about things that happen All Over The World). Your letter, then, gave me great pleasure, as did the card that preceded it, and the birthday telegram, itself nearly a week old. It's touching when friends Remember.

Life here has taken a turn outward. Faces, places. Gore Vidal spent 2 evenings with us—two whole <u>long</u> talk shows absolutely to ourselves (and some starry-eyed prompting by Claire Bloom). I am so slow, I ought to have known years ago that he is mad, yet it took till now . . . Tomorrow there's a picnic to a medical site beginning with A, where in 1962 I caught that facial paralysis; what will it be this time. And next week—just as Alison arrives (her letter went astray)—Tony Parigory + I go to Rome for 6 days. My brother + sister-in-law will be there, so will Grace, and the Vassilikoi who remained mercifully absent from Athens all winter, closing flats and having their teeth seen to, while I peacefully finished the D.C.

Yes, yes! it's finished$_{ii}$—all set down (There'll be months of tinkering, of course, until I'm back at the Selectric which makes all my final decisions) A to Z. It may not be precisely what any of us had in mind, but I'm pleased on the whole, when I'm not merely bemused by how far out of the world it kept me, all these months, and wondering why I'm not more eager at the thought of reentering it. If you thought I was "recessed" the year before last—! If you were just down the road a piece I'd urge you to come over and read it; as it is, I can't send it to you, I really don't want to make a clean copy on this antique Olivetti. I fancy I'll be home in mid-May, and there will be time then (on my side, perhaps not yours).

Letters <u>have</u> been going astray, it's the first year we've noticed; as you know, it doesn't bother me <u>at all</u>.

No cultural news. They did a surprisingly good *Rake* at the local opera—American tenor + soprano, the Tom in fact black (what else)—and the others singing in a whenever intelligible wincingly bad Greek translation; but singing well; the orchestra incandescent under a tiny Chinaman name Mr Chu—comparatively incandescent, I mean, after the sludge of *Pique Dame*. Mr Chu conducts *Falstaff* tomorrow evening—you'll admit the repertoire is ambitious. We'll see how much we can take of that. Poor Chester. It has made a big hole in our lives. Somebody will have to come over soon, unseal his apartment, and dispose of things—but who + when? Ruthven Todd was last week's rumor. These last days have been warm + blue—a hyacinth came up on the terrace (where, for that matter, unlike America, stock is constantly rising, putting forth fragrant dividends). My friend Manoli comes 3 evenings a week. I think we are getting a tiny bit tired of each other—we caught one another downtown a few days ago, each in rather suspicious company—but are much too nice to say so.

Well, my dear, write. Are you happy? (No.) Are you seeing too many people? (Yes.) But let me hear about it anyhow.

Much love,
James

the **Vassilikoi** Greek plural of Vassilikos (i.e., Mimi and Vassilis).
the **D.C.** "The Book of Ephraim" (*Divine Comedies*, 1976).
Falstaff Verdi's final opera (1893).
Ruthven Todd (1914–78), Scottish-born American poet and editor of the works of William Blake.

To Alison Lurie   WUSTL
                                                        24 March 1975
                                                        [Athens, Greece]

Dear Alison,

Your tape is a delight to hear, and marvelously helpful in the bargain.
I saw (or heard) at once that you were right about the meditation bit.
That has been changed, and some clarification added in the section
about E. going underground. I shall listen to it again this week, when
I've assimilated the first wave of reflections it brought me. I do so
value your clear, clear eye—<u>and</u> the time and energy you sacrificed,
surrounded by glories, in order to read so carefully.

Rome was vile. It rained constantly and the Japanese were every-
where, buying leather articles with enormous difficulty—it took
one of them 3 minutes by my watch to explain that something was
too big. <u>They</u>, to be sure, were too small and too young, I thought,
to be so far from home with such bulging wallets. Tony wondered if
they represented the young Catholic element. Grace never arrived.
I caught cold <u>twice</u>, had to spend two feverish evenings in the hotel
room whose phone didn't work; then when I did go out, bought
things I wished I hadn't and ordered dishes I couldn't taste. The air-
port strike that upset your plans kept us there an extra 5 hours—not a
threatened 48, thanks to Tony's going in person to Olympic Airlines
and getting us onto a plane (full of Japanese) and into David's waiting
arms. Now I'm fine, but <u>he</u> received That Telephone Call again—the
old people are coming after all—and has been rushing about in pur-
suit of apartments, housekeepers, a telephone, etc., just as he did a
month ago. He is brim-full of your visit, the delight of it, the things
you saw and said—so that I wish even more that I hadn't had to leave
just as you were starting to hit your stride.

"THEY" told me yesterday (after I'd made the revisions mentioned
above) to make no further changes—that in May FOUR MORE
WORDS would come to me as a final touch. In fact I think I shall
put it aside at least long enough to write a review I promised Barbara
of Keeley's Cavafy translations and Liddell's biography. How one
shrinks from these public displays of ignorance and bias.

Have a lovely time in London, and Scotland. Let's hope for a summer meeting (or summit?) in S'ton or NY or wherever.

> With grateful love always—
> Jimmy

"THEY" Spirits contacted by way of the Ouija board.
Barbara Barbara Epstein (1908–2006), co-founder and editor of *The New York Review of Books.*
Keeley's Cavafy translations *C. P. Cavafy: Collected Poems,* translated by Edmund Keeley and Philip Sherrard and edited by George Savidis (Princeton University Press, 1975).
Liddell's biography *Cavafy* (1974) by Robert Liddell (1908–92), English writer, longtime resident of Athens.

To John Hollander   YALE
8 April 1975
Athens, Greece

Dear John,

I'd have written you this morning (if I'd had time yesterday to finish a long-deferred page to DK)—now I'm glad that I didn't, for noon has brought your letter on Capricorn paper. How deeply I feel for you, with regard to the book's reception. Ever since Louise Bogan's traumatic paragraph on *First Poems* I've been lucky—too lucky, it seems now and then: something must be profoundly wrong about poems that nobody much bothers to attack; but then I remember Ms B's lines—God rest, god <u>roast</u> her soul—which had their tonic ingredient at that stage in my life; but for you, at yours—! If it isn't malice + politics I can't imagine what lies behind it. This new book, in which I read (and have read since Harry gave me the bound proofs in December) several hours every week, is of such surpassing beauty + refinement— well, maybe that's it, after all. The big Destructive Desmond Out There won't stand for it. A refinement, as I was saying, that reaches back preserveringly, renewingly, to everything that is most precious; and allows us to foresee, in spite of evidence that would be crippling but for you, the life of these things in the art to come. Obviously I don't believe we are living now in "post-history" as JA says on the jacket. Nothing can be over and done with that is still able to inspire such animus. (Isn't it the presence of the past in your work & temperament that so vexes Helen V, ignoring how it quickens & changes in your hands?) Well, for what it's worth, I am full of admiration. Long ago I may have felt that your great knowledge had in it something of affectation—long ago none of us had much besides affectation—but it isn't knowledge any more, it is vision. As for Harry, oh yes, he has his mean streak, or his blind one. Just remember that he is usually kind, thoughtful, etc. but that there's something incomplete in his nature. Did I ever quote Chester on Alan Ansen to you?—when Rachel married Stavros (who had lived all those years with Alan) I asked C how Alan was taking it. Chester rolled his eyes and made his Ljuba Welitsch face and said contemptuously almost, "Oh you know Alan—he never lets himself suffer". Meaning—does it follow?—that he wouldn't therefore know what others were likely to feel. It's true of Harry, or somewhat. The way he's always shrugged off any expression of sympathy—at his mother's death, at Elizabeth's. So I think he can't have meant to hurt you, really; he was just being himself. Your last letter, with much about Anne in it, stays in my mind. I can't imagine who thinks you're behaving foolishly by letting her see you or by letting yourself see her. These "clean breaks" date from the dreadful old days of capital punishment as opposed to today's humane & redemptive penitentiaries. Whatever the future, yours & hers, surely the most natural thing is to keep in touch.

I'll be back mid-May, and shall probably spend all summer and fall in Stonington. So of course I'd be glad to read, for only a little more than our marvelous Richard asks. I'm glad Martha is well again—Wagner is Geritol for the young—and look forward to seeing you all very soon. Greece is too beautiful right now; we have lilacs & freesias on the terrace, and in the once-Royal Gardens Queen Amalia's wistaria has achieved its annual satori—800 square feet of it. One shadow looms: the old Jacksons are arriving for good—I mean forever—in about 8 days. D has fixed up a little flat within groaning distance of the house . . . Enough.

Our love,
Jimmy

new book Hollander's poem collection *Tales Told of the Fathers* (1975).
Helen V Helen Vendler.
Harry Harry Ford.
our marvelous Richard Richard Howard.
Martha The Hollanders' daughter.
Geritol Brand name since 1950 for vitamin complexes rich in iron associated with countering the effects of aging and curing "tired blood."

To David Jackson

WUSTL
9 June 1975
[Stonington, CT]

My dear good love,

Your voice is still in my ears, 3 hours later. I feel that Mary will have laughed at our tears in the mirror, and that we can trust Maria to make her at home among the flowerbeds. You know—you must—that it was not a bad death, as deaths go; and much as it shattered you, that moment of recognition is somehow what makes it all right: as if, at the end, she had finally accepted the consciousness resisted so painfully all this time. My mother reminded me that Miss Annie did the same thing—came out of her coma, looked her in the eye, and said "My poor baby"—her last words. That you were there, by her, in order to hear them, must have meant everything to poor Mary; and will mean everything to you, in time to come. I feel so wrenched not to be with you through it all. I thought of getting on a plane—cancelling all these pointlessnesses—except they aren't easily cancelled: my mother's visit, principally. And then I thought, if I don't come, perhaps that will help you to plan on coming here in a couple of months, if old George is in competent hands. We'll see.

Taki and Vaso send much sympathy; so does Rosie Sprague whom I called to get out of going to Amherst today for her parents' party. I'll try presently to reach Grimes and Sewelly. Phyl sounded full of sadness and love for you and Mary and the poor old monster. She said that the Black Hills account "matures" on June 14, and that they will be sending $3000 (plus—imagine—<u>four</u> % interest) to the Sun City Bank; plus I believe whatever may be in a checking acct. She also has the necessary papers to withdraw whatever is in the Crocker Bank (they wouldn't tell her on the phone, but she'll go one day soon in person) and <u>that</u> will then go to the Sun City acct. She sounded ready to get cracking on the house as well.

I've just talked to Sewelly—who said she has almost worn out your last letter, rereading it. She feels very deeply that it's right, the way it happened; as of course it <u>is</u>. And will be writing you today. I asked her to let Grimes know. I also tried to call Fred Bryan (no answer) and would have phoned the Daughterys if I'd had a number. But there's no urgency there, I guess, and a note from you whenever you get round to it would mean more. I've told Edith too, who broke into tears, and said she'd try to phone.

This is one of those Days—a new young cleaning woman, peeping out from under Elaine's wing; and flirting madly with Taki—and in a few hours Madison Morrison (from Oklahoma U, husband of Charlie Curtis's granddaughter) is coming up for the night—so I shan't try to write any more. My heart is so full for you. My love always—

J.

moment of recognition Mary Jackson died in Athens, where she and her husband, George, David's father, had come to be cared for by their son. On the verge of death Mary looked at David and said her last words: "Bye-bye." George died three weeks later.
Phyl Phyllis Jackson, David's sister-in-law, his brother George's widow.
Madison Morrison (1940–2013), American poet, professor at the University of Oklahoma.

To Robin Magowan   YALE
                                                                  24 June 1975
                                                              [Stonington, CT]

Dear Robin,

I've read your letter over and over, with great appreciation and interest. You raise questions that I may be unable to answer except in the tiresome genre of self-justification. I suppose, throughout the poem, I take life (which includes life with Ephraim) as "given"—including as well my own turn of mind on the threshold of 50 having survived all these experiences sufficiently to write about them even in that manner you don't altogether like. It is presumably a certain shallowness that has allowed me to write without succumbing to the dangers of the experience—as when (in H and P and U) I'm seen to turn aside from it. Last summer I dreamed I was in a taxi whose driver I kept urging to make a left turn into a wooded park. When he finally did, there was an accident—which I just barely survived. The last sequence of the dream found me pacing the sidewalk in front of the emergency room, bleeding from the eyes, but still able to see. My compact with the Powers was never total; and the poem for better or worse has to be read as an account of that kind of compact, in which one says Yes with one's fingers crossed. If the result isn't Goethe or Dante, tant pis.

I know that you are right about the rhymes in at least a third of their appearances. But these things are all but impossible to unmake. There are, as you say, infinite possibilities, "an infinity of means"— but here I do disagree with you. To use more than a handful of formal devices in even a work this length is unthinkable to me. What would become of the syllabics in X-2, for instance, if the poem hadn't been metrical up to that point?

Your "gay limbo" made me smile. But I think the point is just as in the world ici-bas: that people are drawn together by common assumptions, life styles, "Tastes." Maya and W Stevens don't particularly lend themselves to the nonsense in U, but neither are they excluded from it—in fact they can be felt as opening the door for the stern voice from Above. For Whom the cocktail party is <u>not</u> the supreme institution.

As for Wendell's art, you must remember that he is 18. His art is nothing I should be able to take very seriously for another 10 or 15 years. Thus far he has technique and promise, but he is still entangled in ideologies, things he feels he <u>must</u> express. When through work he has created a self of his own, that will be time enough to scorn it. I guess I'd thought of the lost novel, really, as being my counter-theme throughout the poem. Its loss (described in "The Will" which will appear earlier in the book—that sonnet sequence you remember, with the ibis and the Egyptian tomb?) sets up an undertow never completely neutralized. I've been working presently at clarifying the figure of "Mrs Smith" who now gets 12 lines in place of Joanna's one (in D), and with any luck will come to mind together with the "woman of the world" on Z-2.

Enfin. This is all very lame. I can't help but feel that the poem is done—Ephraim says it is! But don't fail to send me your annotated copy, after the Burnetts have seen it. There's time for quite a few tiny topical improvements. A big hole is being made in my summer. David's mother died 2 weeks ago (broken hip, pneumonia) and I feel it would help for me to dart over—otherwise I couldn't be with him till December. So I'll be there July 25—Aug 19. I very much want to see your Ling pages. Richard was in Italy these last 6 weeks. I'll try to get some sort of answer out of him. Saw him at lunch 10 days ago and asked head-on if he was still planning to do your book. He said yes, but failed to "enlarge." He wants to come up in July—shall I stall him in the elevator till he signs a firm promise? But do I gather that he <u>still</u> has had no final version of the book from you? This is bad strategy. If you want to make changes, substitutions, etc, isn't it wiser to wait until you hear that the book is going to the printer?—then if need be fly over and <u>make</u> R sit down with you over the Ultimate Text. Sorry this is so scattered a letter, my mother's due here tomorrow, and nothing is as it should be on the housekeeping scene.

Love,
Jimmy

the poem Merrill responds to Robin Magowan's critique of "The Book of Ephraim," and refers below to various characters in the poem (e.g., Maya, Stevens, Wendell).
your Ling pages Robin Magowan had lived with Nancy Ling Perry (1947–74), a member of the radical Symbionese Liberation Army killed in a gunfight with the Los Angeles Police Department. Magowan wrote about their relationship in a longish poem "In Memory of Nancy Ling (Perry)," published in *Poetry* (1975) and later in his *Memoirs of a Minotaur* (1999).

To Rachel Hadas   RUTGERS
                                    19 February 1976
                                     Athens, Greece

Dear Rachel (and Stavros)—

Thank you for your carte postale. The letter you have been clam-
oring for should still by rights go unwritten, there being absolutely
nothing to tell. Two inches of snow last week—what will <u>that</u> mean
in New York or Vermont? I climb to my study, DJ goes to his sketch-
ing class where the two models alternate: a skinny black girl from
Jamaica who won't take off her panties, and keeps shifting so that
the erasers are just as busy as the pencils; and a Junoesque Anglida,
superbly naked, who simply faints away rather than break the pose.
Nelly gives little dinners. Margot has "unwrapped" a new boy-friend
named Dimitri—very mannerly, perfect English, but fat and balding.
Alan came to lunch the other day to meet a most lively man named
Henry Sloss who has come, with wife + kiddies, to spend 4 months
teaching world lit. at the Air Base (first week: "Ghosts") and, while
he lasts, be made use of to supply us with PX whisky and peanutbut-
ter. Oh, and Nelly's landlord tells her she must move out before Sep-
tember, and her latest thought is to "store everything and travel for
a year." Throughout, our telephone rings incessantly. If unanswered,
the callers have been known to pelt David's shutters with pebbles
long after midnight. Autá loipón.

But weren't you planning to fly over last week? You could have seen
it all for yourself . . .

Chester's Niko (sideburns) returned v. healthy-looking from
11 months in Libya. He will have to leave soon again (Iran? Iraq?)
because he had to give all his earnings to his sister's husband—the
father had promised a prika (unknown to poor Niko) 3 years ago. He
says he is fairly fluent in Arabic, English, and Polish by now.

Vassilikos and his wife are here, but it is hard to see them, they
keep such odd hours, and sit around a lot at cafes, which I won't do.
V. + I held forth in an university classroom last week, about the joys
and problems of translating one another. Despite cold bleak filthy
corridors whose every inch of wallspace was covered with left-wing

announcements, the tone of our group was that of a Mallarmé "Tuesday."

And so it will go, I daresay, until early May when we begin a rigidly planned month: visit to Robin Magowan, London rendezvous with my mother, DJ sailing for NY, week in Paris before Ma + I fly home.

Love to you both, "together or apart" (R. Frost)—
Jimmy

Anglida Englishwoman.
Margot Margot Camp.
Henry Sloss (b. 1941), American poet, then resident in Greece.
"Ghosts" Play by Henrik Ibsen (1828–1906).
Autá loipón That's all.
prika Dowry.
a Mallarmé "Tuesday" On Tuesday evenings the French poet Stéphane Mallarmé (1842–98) hosted salons at his home in Paris that were attended by writers and other intellectuals, including such fellow poets as Valéry, Yeats, and Rilke.
"together or apart" The last words of Frost's poem "The Tuft of Flowers."

To Eleanor Perenyi

YALE
25 February 1976
Athens, Greece

Dearest E—

Postscript in a recent letter from McClatchy says you are worried about your health—and so therefore are we. Lacking details, we meanwhile trust it is a not unfamiliar seasonal slump which has often followed the drama of Getting Grace Off. My own horoscope says to beware of attacks of hypochondria whenever I'm not at work. Perhaps that shoe also fits? If only you were landing at the airport in this evening's fairy snowfall, we might be able to clear it all up over dinner. Instead, DJ is off to a tavern with Margot Camp, her new Greek lover no longer "under wraps," and a monumental Belgian bore, and I am staying at home with one of the pleasantest little head-colds I've had in years.

L'heure approche—my mid-century mark, a week from today. I

can't think why the prospect is so exhilarating, unless it has to do with the case of French champagne we procured today through our invaluable new friends' PX cards, at $6 a bottle. We've paid in imponderables a great deal more. I spent hours with <u>him</u> over a long poem he'd written, DJ takes <u>her</u> to his drawing class—but they're actually very bright + datable, so much so that Nelly has had them to dinner, and the young Yensers' noses look a wee bit out of joint. As Alfred Corn's last letter put it, "PX vobiscum." The other night we all went to see a N.Y. group called The Bread + Puppet Theatre— interminable stale Happenings with ideological strings all too visibly attached, every vestige of "place" + "performance" stamped out like meter + rhyme in poetry—and after only 2 acts ("The Stations of the Cross" was one) we removed to a carnival-festooned tavern where DJ pretended to <u>be</u> Waverly Root, or Wavery Route rather, since he collided lightly but decisively with a taxi on our way home at 3 a.m. So you see, we do have <u>some</u> fun.

Plans grow daily more intricate for the May 16 Summit Meeting in London with Mrs Plummer and a <u>frightful</u> couple from Atlanta— whose presence, however, may free us for an evening or 2 with Alison + maybe even <u>Stephen Spender</u> (name to be uttered ecstatically as by Barbara E.) David wisely sails for NY on the 22nd—I don't fly home till June 7, with the others—so you will have him undiluted for those first ten days. He's had far too much Greece these last 2 years—even he admits it.

We met the other day the Ghikas—I'd met him in 1950 with Kimon, David had met her some years ago in Paris at Mary's. Very nice, we thought (she told the ultimate Eddie Gathorne-Hardy story: back in the dawn of Time he took Rosamund Lehmann to the movies; half way through, wordlessly reached over for her purse, opened it, peed in it, + wordlessly returned it to her lap—RL too shy to say or do anything)—then Vassili telephoned the next day: "Jimmy because I love you, I must tell you that a trap is being set for you. Barbara Ghikas is going to invite you for drinks, and Kimon is going to be there." So far, no follow-up. Love to our dear ones—Billy, Hallowells, Cappucino—and <u>write</u>. We miss you + send hugs +

Kisses—
Jimmy

our invaluable new friends Henry and Maggie Sloss.
Alfred Corn (b. 1943), American poet, fiction writer and critic, and soon to become J. D. McClatchy's partner.
"PX Vobiscum" Parody of the Latin phrase "Pax vobiscum": Peace be with you.
The Bread and Puppet Theater A politically radical traveling puppet show, founded in New York City in 1963.
Waverly Root Waverley Root (1903–82), American journalist and writer, author of *The Food of Italy* (1971) and other books on food.
Barbara E. Barbara Epstein.
the Ghikas Nikos Hadjikyriakos-Ghika and his wife, Barbara Hutchinson.
Rosamund Lehmann Rosamond Lehmann (1901–90), English writer in the Bloomsbury group.
Billy Billy Boatwright.

To Stephen Yenser and Mary Bomba   YALE
5/6 July 1976
Stonington, CT

Dear Stephen + Mary—

This will be interrupted any moment by Jonathan Bishop's arrival—at least I hope it will, because it is a hot day + the water at the Point is like chilled mercury (or by now in part <u>is</u>); but let me at least start. I can't recall, nor does your last note say, whether I was going to send you this check to England or wait for your return. But I think you may be counting on it. If you had sent me your acct. no. in California . . . ? No matter. Your calculations are as usual off. You are not buying dollars from me, I am buying drachmes from you, and the rate is different—like, say, 36 to the dollar? Let it then be a difference we split, and make it 37 even, which comes to something closer to $1257. This sum, according to small print in the Kolonaki Convention of April 1976, is discussable <u>only</u> in your favor.

DJ is off to Boston for his I hope only check-up. The operation was a most brilliant success. As a heavy smoker he couldn't be given a general anesthetic, and so was wheeled upstairs from the recovery room still numb from the waist down but quite touchingly conscious, wide-eyed + serious like a child one has awakened after midnight and carried outdoors to see the stars. Our "friends" had promised deep revelations which would recur—be recalled to him, I mean—by his peering into a certain ginger-jar on the sideboard here; all this came to pass and perhaps accounted for his post-op state of mind. By that same evening he was his old self, furious at the prospect of four days on jello + the odd bouillon cube intact in a couple of inches of warm water; ringing for service; switching channels; calling long distance; complaining about no view—these last complaints stopped after Elizabeth B told him that she had spent her 12th birthday in that very hospital in a lovely room overlooking the river and the (no longer standing, but anyhow) BOSTON CASKET CO. The next day I quietly returned to Stonington, meaning to go up and fetch him; but they let him out a day early and he arrived by Yellow Cab instead.

What else? Well, Jim and M*A*R*Y—haven't I written since then, how awful? They loved the Cuisinart quenelles, and the potroast in clarified jelly. 8 people drank as many bottles of Mumm's, plus 2 of good old Bordeaux—But in fact, our hearts aren't in any of this. We are personifications of Neglect. I wouldn't be writing this letter if we were going to have what DK (from Venice) calls Luigi Board this afternoon. The transcript is now some 70 pages (single-space without any paragraphing—hence I find all but impossible to reread) and we have at least 3 more weeks to go before the Revelations are complete, or complete enough for me to have some sense of overall proportions. It is long and awfully didactic in parts, but shot through with golden veins of narrative and just when you think no, no, this is really too dull ZOWIE, a coup de théâtre that turns out to have been perfectly prepared when the smoke clears. I dread the day it dawns on me how long it will have to be. David is absorbed a bit malgré lui, thinks it can't be good to be so withdrawn from Life. I try to persuade him that it will pass, that we'll be set down good as new on the right side of the dark wood. But on the other hand: one doesn't have these experiences without being changed by them. In any case They have said he has 29 more years to live—till 83—so he has time to get over it. I have no exact deadline.

Morning. How this paper has crinkled. Jonathan left a moment ago—a very nice visit actually, in spite of much melancholy content. He + Alison are after all separating, and he still loves her. Aside from that I enjoyed getting a practicing Catholic's view of what's been happening to DJ + me. He took it as seriously as one wished, and saw no trace of "evil" in the experience—as Maria said, NO SMELL OF SULPHUR; Someone, he concluded, must be strongly protecting us.

And there you are in Lontino. After ravishing séjours on Islands. That house not rented will haunt you forever—how vividly we were able to picture the "much agonizing + changing of mind" that preceded your decision. Have a lovely time, telephone when you've caught your breath in Sept.

Our love always,
James

Jim and M*A*R*Y James West and Mary McCarthy.
The transcript The Ouija transcript that would be the basis of *Mirabell: Books of Number* (1978).
Lontino Greek version of London.
That house not rented On the Greek island of Folegandros.

To Elizabeth Bishop

VASSAR
8 August 1976
Stonington, CT

Dear Elizabeth,

A day and evening of torrential rain, which I hope you have been spared. People in town say "hurricane" but surely not. Though if so, surely very good for convalescence, all that extra electrical energy going around begging. I hope in any case, that you are obeying Dr Coué and growing daily stronger on Sabine Farm.

David left the hospital a day early. Before I could even drive up to fetch him, he had arrived back here in a Yellow Cab. He's been back once for a check-up, and must go again. The doctor acted pleased, and the patient in no perceptible discomfort. It nevertheless remains a most peculiar season for us both, as we are in the clutch of a dictée from the Spirits which has been going on every day for 2 months, and promises to end (perforce) only when D sails from Greece on Sept 13. This is evidently the part of the poem that corresponds to Hell + Purgatory combined (if "Ephraim" was mainly Terra). It is dictated by Fallen Angels who are all now obedient computerized atomic-powered slaves of "God Biology"; and their job is to lead us to the great doors beyond which the Angels will address us. Does this strike you as very odd? Well, that makes two—no, three—of us. But neither can I see it as anything to be idly switched off like a TV channel. Under these circumstances, we aren't going anywhere. Mary invites us, and Grace and Eleanor, or any combination of the four, to Castine. Not this year. I can only hope that we will be gently returned to the World when our Dictators have been appeased. A letter the other day says we can expect a call (or visit) from Madison Morrison. Then 20 minutes on the phone with Mary Merrill, safely + happily back from England—she wondered in her wholly un-paranoid way if you had "turned against them", and I assured her that wasn't the least bit like you, and explained the hospital etc.

Yesterday was the village fair. As usual Eleanor skimmed all the goodies from the book sale: *The Garden of Allah* ("Here even Death wore a golden robe and walked with a light foot"), Daisy of Pless's *Memoirs* ("Count X has given me a Venetian vase with orchids in relief. Eighteen of these were shattered before a perfect one emerged—how like Life!"—along with allusions to people one wants to know more about, like Prince "Fairy" Metternich) and so forth. I only picked up Ronald Knox's *Memories of the Future* which, except for the title, is rather tarsome. We had a parade, however, that included 6 or 7 enchanting old cars, with the FORD trademark stamped in blue on their silvery running-boards. And a kilt-and-bagpipe corps.

Oh. You may have had a letter and/or phone call from my good friend at Yale, Sandy McClatchy, who hopes to arrange a reading for you there in September. I hope I didn't do wrong in encouraging him?

Well, have a healthy + peaceful time, and have the new book in final form when you return. I can't tell you how I look forward to it. David turns aside from Telly Savalas (whoever he is) to blow a kiss.

Love always,
Jimmy

Dr Coué Émile Coué de la Châtaigneraie (1857–1926), French physician and pharmacologist who devised supposed cures based on autosuggestion and who invented the placebo effect.
Sabine Farm A house Bishop rented during the summer on North Haven Island in Maine. The name alludes to Horace's villa, given to him by Maecenas, where he

wrote his odes and epodes. The husband of Bishop's North Haven landlady was named Horace.
Castine Harbor town in Maine where West and McCarthy had a summer home.
The Garden of Allah Anecdotal history of the Hollywood hotel (1970) by Sheilah Graham (1904–88), British-American writer and Hollywood gossip columnist, famous in part for her relationship with F. Scott Fitzgerald.
Daisy of Pless's *Memoirs Daisy, Princess of Pless, by Herself* (1929), a memoir by the Edwardian socialite born Mary Theresa Olivia Cornwallis-West (1873–1943).
Prince "Fairy" Metternich Klemens von Metternich (1773–1859), Austrian diplomat.
Ronald Knox's *Memories of the Future* English Catholic priest Ronald Arbuthnott Knox (1888–1957) wrote the satirical *Memories of the Future: Being Memories of the Years 1915–1972, Written in the Year of Grace 1988 by Opal, Lady Porstock* in 1923.
the new book *Geography III*.
Telly Savalas Aristotelis "Telly" Savalas (1922–94), American character actor best known for his title role as television's lollipop-sucking detective *Kojak*.

To David McIntosh

WUSTL
22 April 1977
[Stonington, CT]

Dearest David—

Who would have thought that a Pulitzer prize would leave me so exhilarated? My congressman has telephoned ("Don't know how political you are") also a child from Norwich ("I write poetry too, but the scouts take a lot of my time") plus a whole pack of cub reporters. I know how Mowgli felt. But the new poem (as a result?) positively BLAZES ahead. It's over 2/3 done, so pages since last August.

Now I leave here on Sunday for Syracuse, Chicago, Kalamazoo + a week in Atlanta. Back on the 6th or 7th for a week, to pack + tidy, then to NY + Athens on the 17th. I'm sorry not to have seen you, but perhaps we're both not altogether "ourselves" this year. A local friend (from 15 years past) has resurfaced—in November actually: by now father of 6, his Korean tattoos sadly blurred—yet somehow exactly the sandbag essential to my upward-straining balloon. I long for Greece, I long for everything—it's bewildering to have been so happy these last few weeks . . .

The Reeves came to dinner. They'd been (with Brock) in Greece for a week. F. has a new book of poems—not very good I'm afraid—about to be published.

I'll phone before I leave. Meanwhile a happy birthday to you (+ a by now time-honored unimaginative check)—with love always,

James

a Pulitzer prize For *Divine Comedies* (1976).
Mowgli A "man-cub" with extraordinary skills raised by a wolf pack who finally must deal with his humanity in stories by Rudyard Kipling in *The Jungle Book* (1894) and *The Second Jungle Book* (1895).
the new poem *Mirabell: Books of Number* (1978).
A local friend Peter Tourville (1941–2011).
F. F. D. Reeve.

To David McIntosh

WUSTL
10 May 1977
[Stonington, CT]

Dear David—

This will just be a scrawled page—it's after 10, I'm having a 2nd drink—and I can only say that being with you, those memories, stand between me + some pretty awful subsequent moments. I really don't want to go into it. Peter was nearly killed. He came over Sunday afternoon, out of the hospital, but feverish, a great swollen scar from breastbone to below the navel. He will probably go back to Vermont + look for work on a farm + that's of course what he would have done months ago if I hadn't prevailed upon him to stay nearby. Let him go— I'll do what I can to help with immediate expenses (insurance pays his medical bills)—yet I'd so much counted, I fear, on having him for a couple of years—looking after things around the house, redoing a lot of Taki's work—work that would make an 8 year old blush—but that's not the point. We were fond of each other, we needed each other; but that scar says (in hieroglyphics) what keeps being said over + over these years: It cannot be. Says it to him, but the echo reaches me quite clearly. Forgive me for letting it reach you as well. I've somehow been able to work a few hours + that too is a blessing. But meanwhile Daryl Hine has gone round the bend: seen God in a parking lot + taken off his clothes + been arrested. His vision tallies with Dante's + what I've been merely told, never experienced . . . And I guess I'm lucky after all, between these two violences, to flesh + spirit, to be left with a platter licked clean but still uncracked. The way life reaches in through an opening + shakes us by the neck: as if to remind us.

Let me remind <u>you</u> to send your magic spinach pie recipe. It was so good. Everything was good, those days. Here is love in tatters, and blessings in disguise.

James

Peter Peter Tourville.

To Robin Magowan

WUSTL
3 June 1977
Athens, Greece

Dear Robin,

Clouds, sun through smog, there'll never be any real Greek weather again. No mornings after 3 hours sleep when you wake up tingling— And it's not as if one couldn't use the time.

Extraordinary letter from Suzel, all in French, phrased to what by rights should be a fare-thee-well. I'm very fond of her au fond, but we have this funny pattern. She gets into debt or on the brink of some insane business venture and writes asking me for a sum of money (I had let her have 1 or 2 thousand back in the early fifties) each time larger—the last I think was nearly $2 million. I write or cable back that it is out of the question. Several years of silence follow. Then a perfectly charming letter or meeting "out of the blue", a spate of correspondence about times old + new. Then another whammy, and another cable explaining, etc etc. I trust your impressions are being polished for the mails.

I've been here 16 days or so, seeing hardly anyone. Tony went off to Patmos with his Prince + Princess (Sadruddin + Katy) <u>and</u> Germaine! We had enough time with the P + P not to envy him as much as he would like us to. He'll join us on Samos (Pythagorion) for some days en route back to Athens. (We're there June 11–21.)

Daily swims (for neck) and daily dictation. The first of 3 terms with the angels is behind us—ending wonderfully but also rather upsettingly with God Himself alone in space singing like a humpbacked whale. I felt that a narrative convention had been violated, but am not, mind you, complaining. I'm just about midway through section 7 of the middle vol—2 + a half sections to go, or 1/4 of the whole. Too often it seems to write itself . . .

Bernie is bringing Stewart Perowne for drinks this evening. B is still technically "down" but there are telltale brassgreen shoots coming up through the black loam. You may have heard about Daryl? He was vouchsafed the Ultimate Vision (pinpoint of light surrounded by revolving spheres, as in Dante and Niels Bohr) in an Evanston parking lot one noon; honored it by taking off all his clothes; and was arrested for indecent exp. Also resigned from the mag and gave away his car to a P. Rican taxi driver he'd met the night before. We are all worried, I suppose, but I at least am not repelled—as I would be by something like this in BVW. Daryl is too clever + too . . . creative? Still, one is grateful for one's relative insulation.

Doris's note from London didn't say anything about your last attack. I trust it passed quickly, and am sorry not to have written as soon as I heard from you. Packing and a few last minute emergencies (<u>and</u> a final belch or two from the Public before It turned Its attention to a new meal) made letters difficult in May. I do hope you're all right + that the exercises are beginning to make a difference. Luckily I feel only the merest twinges, pain written in invisible ink—for which I seldom bother to take even an aspirin. Yet the cudgel will probably remain raised for the rest of one's days. Are the boys with you? Carole?

> My love (+ David's) to all or any.
> Jimmy

Prince + Princess (Sadruddin + Katy) Prince Sadruddin Aga Khan (1933–2003), much-decorated humanitarian and connoisseur and collector of Islamic art, and Catherine Aleya Beriketti Sursock (b. 1938), whom he married in 1972.
God Himself alone in space God's song (ten decasyllabic lines) is set down in "The First Lessons: 10" in *Scripts for the Pageant* (1980), the third part of the *Sandover* trilogy.
Stewart Perowne (1901–89), British diplomat, historian, and explorer.
Niels Bohr (1885–1962), Dutch theoretical physicist, proponent of peaceful use of atomic power, awarded the Nobel Prize in 1922 for his work on atomic structure.

your last attack A head injury incurred playing soccer.
belch or two from the Public Congratulations on the Pulitzer Prize.
the boys Robin Magowan's sons.
Carole Robin's wife Carol Wise.

To J. D. McClatchy and Alfred Corn

YALE
27 June 1977
[Athens, Greece]

My dears,

Our darling Robert, as Eleanor's cable called him . . . There simply aren't words for what he meant to us. I'm so glad you "got" him before it was too late. We're getting him now, to be sure, whenever we sit down to the board; but it's just not the same; the golden phrases flake away, and beneath them is a leaden casket. (Need I say that Main Street may assume we're in touch with him, but mustn't, I think, be told outright; it's too soon.) And the week before, George Cotzias! He is joining the seminar with MM +WHA; the 2nd term (of only 5 days) begins on Friday.

Can it be that you still enjoy Stonington? I hate to think how much you've had to cope with—none of it avoidable, I guess. And now we have a new boiler. Was the wine under water??? As long as the water came from a boiler leak, and needn't be rechristened Chateau Night-soil, I suppose it can just be left to dry out. As for Peter, I'm steeling myself—the promised Letter is surely about to arrive. Since it hasn't yet, the issue seems simple enough. I've told him that I'll <u>only</u> send money to his "wife" when I hear from <u>her</u>, and I don't see why I need to change that policy—the $50 DK sent him doesn't break <u>my</u> word. Then when I think of those insufferable Greeks! I ought to have known this would happen. Too busy even to check out the cellar (or do they have a key?) That's what one gets for one's fatal attractions to non-Lab souls.

Sandy's 2 questions. "The School Play" hasn't been published; it took yet another letter to that Shakespeare Org. in London to find that out; anyhow it's mine to do what I like with—probably send to *NYker* after their summer moratorium. "Light of the Street . . ." is a proverb quoted by Oscar Lewis in *The Children of Sanchez* I think. One year Strato had been helling around more than usual, hardly ever here, hardly ever at his parents. I quoted the saying to him and it really struck home—eyes filled with great tears of self-pity—but as for changing him, I should have used sticks and stones.

Jim Boatwright + Harry Pemberton (teaches philosophy at W + L) are now both installed down the street, until just the other day with a sort of dumb blonde baby queen of 22, who reads his lines like the early Lana Turner + of course has no trouble snapping up every one of the beautiful boys H + J have been panting after for years. They rigged up a little peephole + spend hours watching sourly. And the endless hot showers (HP: "The electric bill? Is he going to chip in?") and the empty milk bottles ("He drank my breakfast. I don't have any breakfast!"). Two days ago he was at last shipped off to Mickey-mouse, as some of us call that most popular of Islands, and within 12 hours replaced by <u>another</u> W + L student, better looking but also inflexibly straight ("Jim, he's going to cramp our style!") whose early eviction is already in the air.

Time to go shopping. I've finished 7 and will send a copy along today or whenever. It looks frightful on this typewriter!

Love from us both,

J.

---

darling Robert Robert Morse had died suddenly.
Main Street The Stone and Perenyi household.
George Cotzias He too (as GK, the *C* in his name reverting to the original Greek *K*) had joined those in the spirits' world.
the seminar with MM & WHA Sessions conducted by superior spirits in the other world and attended by select souls there and by Merrill and Jackson by way of the Ouija board.
those insufferable Greeks The Alevras family.
non-Lab souls Souls of inferior quality, not produced in the Research Lab in the other world.
"The School Play" Merrill's poem, collected in *Late Settings* (1985), based on his experience playing First Herald in Shakespeare's *Richard II* at St. Bernard's School.
"Light of the Street . . ." Adopted as the title of a poem by Merrill in *The Fire Screen* (1969).
Oscar Lewis (1914–70), American anthropologist.
Harry Pemberton Harrison J. Pemberton Jr. (1925–2017), professor of philosophy at Washington and Lee University, where Boatwright was also a professor.
Mickeymouse The Greek island of Mykonos.
finished 7 Section 7 of *Mirabell: Books of Number* (1978).

To J. D. McClatchy and Alfred Corn   YALE
                                                11 July 1977
                                            [Athens, Greece]

Boys! (as Robert addresses us on the Board).

A heat wave. I've just watered down the terrace and the roof of my adjoining study, so that now at 3:30 the temperature in here is way down to about 102, but with the little fan whirling, more than tolerable. Two fat envelopes from Sandy today, Alfred's account of village doings last Saturday. One would hardly have realized how much one had longed to be au courant—especially of things like the cellar. I've fired off a grumpy letter to Taki, which won't do any good; but asking him, for instance, to restore their apartment, when they move out, to its <u>original</u> squalor: take down those hideous room divides up to the ceiling, those superfluous doors. Since Peter may well have found a job in Vt, there's no telling whether he'll move in or not. I'll hunt up his address, though, and you can send him a line when the apt. is finally available. Then, if he doesn't want it, Cynthia's old schoolmate, Gorgeous Charlie Muscarella—the nephew, also, of Butcher Joe at the Market—can be called in to paint everything white. The floors may be a problem. One surely doesn't want Taki's red carpet. Dark red deckpaint with sealer? If the place is as appallingly filthy as I fear it will be, just ask Cynthia to contact that place in Mystic who do our top-room tiles twice a year, and see if they can't send a team of rugged studs in Miss Bonami drag. <u>Anything</u> on your list of needed improvements, dear Sandy, is OK with me (just don't replace my divinely comfy mattress). Keep track and I'll send you checks at intervals. I must have said in every letter thus far that I wish you didn't have to cope with so many tiresome emergencies; I'll say it again.

July 4–10 p.m. here. We had been introduced to the Muses that afternoon, and I was still, by evening, quite under the pall of what WHA called that BRILLIANT NASTY FAMILY. Their mother, the QUEEN of Ephraim's phrase, and promised as next day's treat, they had identified, in parting, as Chaos. Imagine our apprehension— and imagine our delight when this radiant, brisk, lightly ironic Lady strode into our midst. Wystan recognized her as BLAKE'S STARRY

FIGURE RAINBOW HUED—an illustration I can't place, if it exists; I settled for memories of Ina Claire. She plans to linger—or "hover"— through the last 10 sessions. MM: SETTING HEAVEN ATREMBLE RUNNING HER WHITE GLOVES OVER ALL THE SHELVES! She has also asked particularly that Robert (WHO IS THAT STRIK-ING BLOND MAN?—and indeed he is the single parent in our crowd) join the seminar before his rebirth, as a very great composer, in Min-nesota. RM: MENDELSSOHN SO AMUSING CHATS AWAY GIV-ING ME A MASTER COURSE IN SUBMERGED TENTHS I'M TO GET NEXT BEETHOVEN (HEARING AID?) Ephraim, those days, had not been ostensibly available; but Maria made a remark about how all the actors seem to be doubling or tripling roles—Nature/Chaos/Psyche is also, somehow St Agatha the gardener—and I am quite prepared to have E. emerge as a tiny facet of glorious Michael himself.

I'm a touch bemused, as always, by your enthusiasm for the pages I keep grinding out; and hope that it won't prevent you, when the time comes, from suggesting passages that could be blue-penciled as trivial or redundant (too much Accident? Density?—topics that in Heaven seem almost to go without saying, beside the point, though at Mirabell's level, of course . . .). 8 is now nearly done, but must include—since he's to figure in the sequel—a passage on Robert, which I've only begun to tackle. Terza rima again? Don't, whatever you do, bruit it about that he's so much with us. It can't be what the Main St houses want to hear at this stage, if ever.

Friend of Daryl's named Gerry Caspary came to dine on the ter-race the other evening. Byzantine historian, uncomely, dressed with that negative flair one finds in certain really dedicated (and success-ful) cruisers—drab, citified. It's Donald Richie's style, and never fails. He also, when laughing, had worked up a really repellent snort, like a hog at Guerlain's, which Tony, in spite of our prayers, imitates relentlessly. He did however give a firsthand report of Daryl's taxi driver friend: "Very animated and, yes, goodlooking—if one likes toothless smiles." Daryl's given him so much, why not his own two front teeth?—though apparently the car hasn't been formally turned over—D "can't find the papers". But he pays the repair bills. Oh yes, and the car isn't insured. And there have been "gifts of jewelry"!!!

By all means stay at 107 till I return. I'm only sorry to turn you out then—or do <u>you</u> want to rent the downstairs flat? Since these months are making you, willy-nilly, such efficient janitors, I might even pay you to stay on. Anyhow, I see getting back on or around Oct 15, time for a course of facials before the Morgan Library reading Nov 2.

Oh, we spoke to Nabokov. Heaven is just as he imagined it, A GRAND HOTEL, and he's learning how to make wonderful moths materialize TICKLINGLY ON MY WRIST. A bit superior still: A WHAT? A REPRESENTATIVE? AM I A DREARY CONSTITUENCY?—but promises to come + drink Hu Kwa with us, once Maria + Wystan return to the Elements. He said he'd like "18 W. 11th ST"—WE MUST PUT THE POLITICAL POLTER IN THE GEIST ROOM. Stage 5.

DJ still free of headaches. I too went to the healer, who "did" my neck and my Plantar's wart. The latter's hard to be sure about—at least until it doesn't hurt any more—but, even after exercises, there are no twinges whatever from the former. After our cures, we took him out to dinner with Margot Camp, who only got to shake hands but felt "an electric thrill" go up her arm. "Is she really an archeologist?" Finbarr asked old Grace Edwards the next day, and shook his head over the reply. Three different people had "dragged" him up to the Acropolis—nothing but old rocks, when rock and roll is what <u>he</u>'s looking for.

> Basta, my dears. And love from DJ
> and
> JM

Robert addresses us Robert Morse had died recently (see preceding letter) and now communicates over the Ouija board.

Cynthia Merrill's housekeeper in Stonington.

Miss Bonami drag Bon Ami is a popular American household cleanser ("No Harsh Chemicals"). In *Mirabell: Books of Number* (1978) the spirit of Chester Kallman ridicules his life to come, in which he will be a straight Jewish woman: "LITTLE MISS BONAMI OOH SO GLAD / TO FIND ARCADIA IN A BRILLO PAD."

the Muses See *Scripts for the Pageant* (1980), section "&," "The Middle Lessons: 4" for the poetic version.

Ina Claire (1893–1985), American stage and film actor.

8 is now nearly done Section 8 of *Mirabell: Books of Number.*

glorious Michael himself The angel of light, one of the four chief angels closest to God Biology (God B), one of the two presiding powers (along with God A) in the universe.

Gerry Caspary Gerard Ernest Caspary (1929–2008), professor of history at UC Berkeley, author of *Politics and Exegesis: Origen and the Two Swords* (1979).
Guerlain's The House of Guerlain, highly regarded Paris parfumerie established in 1828.
107 107 Water Street.
the healer Finbarr Nolan (b. 1952), Irish faith healer, author of *Seventh Son of a Seventh Son: The Life Story of a Healer* (1992), who lived for two years in the United States.

To J. D. McClatchy and Alfred Corn

YALE
15 July 1977
Samos, Greece

Dear S + A—

Here we are on Samos, gathering strength after a very long day's excursion to Ephesus. Too late in the spring, I fear, for the full beauty of the site—only a few last poppies, and thistles into a bank of which I stumbled, hurting my knee. A great bleached boneyard, really, seen in the all too audible company of a tiresome man named Spencer Williams who makes harpsichords in LA after having all his paintings burned in a fire, and deciding that he didn't like sitting down enough to write more than 4 chapters of his first novel. (Wystan + Maria saw the skeleton fleshed out: palanquins, wharves with pleasure rafts, A YOUNG BEAUTY SCREAMING WITH LAUGHTER RAN OUT OF THE GREAT BATHS ON TRAJAN'S STREET—and secured us a brief interview with the Temple architect, to whom the Goddess appeared in a dream, saying "Suckle here and here. This teat is proportion, this teat splendor" etc. Ask Daryl to tell you his clerihew about her.) Two lovely hours on the calm sea going + coming, and pompous mini-formalities at the respective customs. It's the only sensible way to enter Turkey, now that planes are rerouted over Bulgaria.

Pythagoras' village, where we're staying, is packed with small yachts and Scandinavian tourists, and the townspeople have grown perfunctory. Still, the water is lovely and the wine, as of old, delicious. Tony was meant to arrive yesterday noon, but didn't, so DJ, impressing the local operators no end, managed to get a call through to him on Patmos where he is staying with Sadruddin + Katy. Operator (after DJ emerges from the booth): Excuse me, isn't Katy a Greek name? DJ: (Does she think I was talking to the maid? Must correct that) Ah yes, the <u>Princess</u> is Greek. Op: Po-po-po! Anyhow, T is due this noon by caique. We haven't envied him, after seeing how rude the Prince was to a waiter. And they don't drink.

Your two letters, as I think I said, gave us such pleasure. To have Stonington so lovingly described, looked at in ways we have by long + imperceptible degrees renounced—the twilit walks, the piquant argo of the locals—was thrilling beyond even your fluent words. And Ralph N-F!! And the new machinery to play the new music <u>on</u>. Are you going to let him dictate melodies? Or Fauré himself? IT has us quite on tenterhooks, in case we get another musicale after the Strauss/Flagstad hour. Between trying to finish section 7 and taking down the new material I fear I'm rather groggy—the level of this letter proves as much—but the end is almost in sight, though we expect nothing except more surprises. Thanks too for the new tenant's lease. I dreamed that Peter + family had moved in <u>with</u> Taki + Vaso, and woke up in a sweat. If you manage to stay above all that, congratulations. Enter D just now. He thinks he has sighted Tony's black sail. In any case, it's time for my hundred strokes.

Much much love—

J.

Wystan and Maria saw From their otherworldly vantage, the two spirits could see the lively past of the "bleached boneyard" at the archeological site of Ephesus.
interview with the Temple architect For the poetic version, see a passage shortly after the set piece "Samos" early in "&" in *Scripts for the Pageant* (1980).
the Goddess The many-breasted Artemis (Diana) of Ephesus.
Pythagoras' village Now called in his honor Pythagorio.
Op: Po-po-po The operator (Op) responds with a Greek expression that means something like "Big deal!"
T Tony Parigory.
the new machinery A new stereo.
the Strauss/Flagstad hour Richard Strauss, via the Ouija board, creates a "fifth last song," and Kirsten Flagstad (who sang the premiere of his *Four Last Songs* in 1950) performs it, in *Scripts for the Pageant*.

To Stephen Yenser   YALE
                                                        15 July 1977
                                                    [Athens, Greece]

Dear Stephen,

A Friday morning. Coolish for a change—we had a really crashing heat-wave last week that called for frequent immersions in the tepid tub followed by slow evaporations in front of the electric fan. Eleni downstairs ironing while waiting for D to wake up so she can do his room. I at work on the only unwritten section of 8—which must introduce Robert Morse whose subsequent place in the poem can alas no longer be doubted; the dear man died last month. A gall bladder operation which (says Eleanor) revealed advanced liver cancer. His last words to her—she called Bedford the night before he went into the hospital, "What are you doing there all alone, Robert?"— were, "Oh, watching my favorite program: 'As the Stomach Turns' . . ." As often, we are torn between poor worldly grief and the enchanted translation of our dear one to the cup darting from letter to letter; for Robert, and George Cotzias (the scientist, my sister's friend, who died that same week) have joined the Seminar—while it lasts: a final "term" of 10 sessions begins in 2 weeks. I could go on for the rest of the page about <u>that</u>, but maybe you'd like some local color first.

Athens isn't what it was. (How would I know, who never go out? I know.) The air is foul, the beaches jammed and reeking. It's like the 2nd half of *Death in Venice* without the pretty backgrounds. Quite a distance to come for the sake of the 2 or 3 remaining taverns that allow—if one half shuts one's eyes—for the old magic. Samos was nice <u>enough</u>; but the yachts and the Danes, and the huge air-conditioned hotel built smack on the pretty empty beach we'd remembered. Yesterday we took off and drove to Corinth for a swim + lunch (Jim Boatwright is spending a few days in Margot Camp's little whitewashed place there) but only through concerted good will could the hours be looked back on as well spent. It's true, I missed Baryshnikov dancing in *Push Comes to Shove*—and no seats could be had for his *Giselle;* missed too the Lyriki Skini's *Carmen* which Jim walked out of at midnight when the 2nd of 4 acts ended, but "I can't just be imagining." Even DJ is thinking of going to Morocco for 3 months as soon as I leave. People? Bernie's graph heads upward; we don't see him. Tony, each year less animated, but a comfort. Nelly, darting hither + yon— she doesn't see <u>us</u>. Alan, after a high blood-pressure scare, resolutely dieting; we glimpse what's left of him. (And drove him out to Jean Demos' for a dinner with Valerie Eliot, a chiffon-swathed Hera of polychrome pink and gold, whose drying combinations, also pink, in a lavatory thoroughly dusted with her pink face-powder, was itself a study. Wystan says they all used to call her PLUMP PUSS. Perfectly nice, you understand.) Through an odd heavy lame charming woman of 60, Grace Edwards (something of an archeologist, also an ordained minister—who knows of what church?) we visited a young Irish healer named Finbarr Nolan. Before, Grace could hardly get up stairs; now she is positively spry, standing on tiptoe, etc. FN "did" DJ's sinuses and, you know, his headaches have just about disappeared. Or at worst, one will burst into its old apartment, then withdraw after a few minutes, as if realizing that another, far serener tenant is in possession. My neck, by the same token, gives me not a twinge, even though I've resumed last year's somewhat strenuous exercises—which <u>this</u> year always precipitated a crisis; and the loathsome Plantar's wart on my left footsole is slowly slowly sloughing itself into oblivion. This Finbarr is, needless to say, the 7th son of a 7th son; about 24; heart-breakingly "normal" where he isn't unique—loves soccer games and dreams of the "shows" at Las Vegas. He says his cures work about 60% of the time—which when you think about it is staggering. He may well be on his way to the USA right now, under some university auspices in NY State. Finally there's old George Lazaretos, back to goldbricking after a convalescent leave (kidneystone operation, huge scar); and old Manoli whose vast + luxurious Tae Kwon Do Academy has in two months attracted perhaps five students. "We" are not discouraged by that. As soon as several thousand more dollars have been spent on advertising, he'll be turning the crowds away! You now know all.

The shape + content of the 3rd volume (the angels) is already pure fascination. The way I see the entire poem now (as others may have seen it from the start—but as you know, I'm slow to catch on) is as a kind of map of the imagination. (It's a plausible way of looking at Dante, for that matter—or even *The Waste Land*.) The effects, allowing for the day-by-day soap-opera format, are coming to be curiously

Shakespearean—grand scenes that alternate with <u>our</u> low comedy; the three "good" archangels, plus the human shades, pleading with Gabriel who is lord of antimatter; sideshow appearances of The Five in all their splendor; a shattering hour with the Muses—girls nastier or more brilliant you couldn't ask for; followed by—imagine our apprehension <u>and</u> our relief—their Mother (Chaos/Psyche/Nature), a brisk, radiant figure full of sense and wit, to picture whom I had to fall back on old memories of Ina Claire, who plans, for better or worse, to "hover" throughout our final lessons. (Maria: HEAVEN ATREMBLE RUNNING HER WHITE GLOVES OVER ALL THE SHELVES.) But a lot of it is really very scary—glimpses into the Lab—and Gabriel as yet isn't about to relent.

Enough. DJ bounds upstairs—a swim off the rocks at Varkisa? Why not!

Our love to you and Mary; I hope you've shaken off the pall of the term's end; I've been such a bad letter-writer, and can't really promise to reform; but write, won't you? Did I say how much I enjoyed Trudi's article?

James

Eleni Merrill's housekeeper in Athens, following Kleo.
Lyriki Skini Athens opera house.
Jean Demos Formerly on the faculty at the New England Conservatory of Music, and widow of Harvard professor Raphael Demos, she lived in the suburb of Kifissia.
Valerie Eliot (1926–2012), T. S. Eliot's second wife and literary executor.
the 3rd volume (the angels) *Scripts for the Pageant* (1980).
The Five In *Scripts for the Pageant*, "Lesson 5: Meeting the Five," the four archangels introduce an historical avatar of each of the essential five powers, each in this instance associated in turn with one of the five senses, that do the divine "V Work."
Trudi Mary Bomba Yenser's mother, Gertrude Bomba, who had spent some time in Europe the preceding year and had published a travel piece that Yenser had sent to Merrill.

To David McIntosh   WUSTL
                                                    14 August 1977
                                                    Athens, Greece

Dearest David,

Every day, when I'm not thinking about your exploded pyramid, I
wonder when I'll have an hour to write you—and suddenly here it is.
A holiday weekend. Tomorrow (Monday) the Assumption of the Vir-
gin, and thus name-day for 500,000 Marias in Greece alone, we are
invited to Sounion by "Taki"'s niece. It will be my first visit there since
M. died, and I expect to see it with both old eyes and new. The figure
of Maria, in this summer's transcript, has been unfolding like a four-
dimensional rose—I daren't try to paraphrase, it sounds so bizarre;
but in its own words it has a quite sublime logic. Finally our lessons
are over. The archangels, God himself, and his twin Nature (also
known as Psyche, Chaos, and Queen Mab) have all spoken to us and
withdrawn, like their counterparts in Wagner, via a rainbow bridge.
What remains is twofold: a day-by-day reading aloud of the all-but-
finished Vol. II to an audience of interested parties—except for DJ,
all dead of course: Gertrude Stein, Alice Toklas (who provides the
"refreshments"), Wallace Stevens, Yeats, along with Maria + Auden +
Hans + Maya + Marius. They make suggestions—too few, I fear—and
assure me, thus far, that the whole thing is a marvel, while I shake my
head and protest that 3/4 of it was done <u>for</u> me. And then, perhaps
when we return from Venice, will come a ritual hour—reminiscent of
the close of *The Tempest*, when Prospero drowns his Book—of break-
ing a little mirror among the blossoms and sunlight and wind on our
terrace, and releasing even these last dear ones into their new exis-
tences. Looking back, what an experience! One could have been the
Son of Sam; instead, it was a long, safe, blessed journey. With some
odd side-trips. Last month, no, in June we visited a healer named Fin-
barr Nolan, Irish, 24 years old, 7th son of a 7th son. And as a result
DJ has no more headaches—or, at worst, only a fleeting shadow of
the old agony, as it burst into the spaces it had once occupied, found
Something Else in possession, and shrank away foiled like Mr Coffee
Nerves; my neck has given me no trouble, even if I do the exercises
that all Spring instantly precipitated a migraine; and the loathsome

Plantar's wart on my sole has already sloughed away from the size of a nutmeg to that of a coriander seed. If he ever comes your way, go to him! (The only one of our friends he didn't help was Karen Ingle, but her trouble is congenital and naturally long advanced.) And a week from today we sail from Piraeus to Venice! I can't wait. We'll rent a car there and drive, with DK, down to see dear old Umberto Morra near Arezzo, but mainly it will be two weeks of idle bliss. Tony joins us at the end for a few days, and sails back with us on Sept 6. While we're sitting here at the crystal ball, I should add that I'll be back in Stonington, as planned, around mid-October.

Time, needless to say, has slipped by unnoticed. I have only 100–150 lines of the last section to write, and am purposely leaving them for late September. A few swims, a very few evenings "out", and that's been the summer. (DJ, bless his soul, goes swimming nearly every noon and out on the town nearly every night, but—as he represents "Nature" to my "Mind" in the scheme of things, that would be his privilege.) I wonder how you are, how the house is coming, if you've been able to work. You may well have no time for a full letter—just put it into telegraphese on 2 postcards. Then in October we can use the phone! (How is Mary Lou by the way?)

Much love always,
James

"Taki"'s niece Nina Koutsadakis, Maria Mitsotaki's niece ("Taki" here short for "Mitsotaki").
Vol. II *Mirabell: Books of Number* (1978).
the Son of Sam Moniker invented for himself by David Berkowitz (b. 1953), American serial killer who terrorized New York City in 1976 and 1977 and claimed he had been inspired by a demonic dog named Harvey.
Karen Ingle Tom Ingle's daughter was living in Athens.
Mary Lou Mary Lou Aswell.

To David Jackson   WUSTL
                                         24–26 December 1977
                                            [Palm Beach, FL]

My dear,

Your cable from Marrakech arrived yesterday noon. I've felt so happy and relieved ever since, to know that at least you are out of that ghastly resort and into a more authentic (warmer too?) place. I don't know where to send this letter, but if I've not heard anything further, imagine you'll be passing through Torremolinos again en route to meet Sewelly. Tony said he'd forwarded a batch of things to Poste Restante, Torremolinos (though I <u>told</u> him it wasn't a permanent address)—and let's hope they finally fall into your hands.

Here I am in this odd house. It has a funny quality which I put my finger on yesterday only—it was built on spec. As a result nothing in it or about it reflects the least personal consideration: no built-in shelves, no alcove for this or that—just the pure expensive paradigm of what a faceless couple of gracious livers might be expected to snap at. Most of it was furnished in the same spirit too, and it is like living in a perfectly celestial motel, with one's own little heated pool, a TV I can regulate by pressing buttons on my bedside table (Ma + I watched half! of *A Star is Born* last night after the 3 couples who came for dinner left at 9:30—I could hardly blame them; the dullness they drew out of <u>us</u>!!) and across the street the glorious empty beach, the turquoise and fire-opal sea whither I shall presently repair. No sooner here, I joined Ma in the pool for her exercises, and that did it—or the cold I had had before leaving S'ton did. Terrible headaches, <u>face</u>aches that lasted all day. I don't know whether it was neck or sinus, and say "was" only because today's hasn't begun yet. I've got my traction thing set up (had to buy a new one) and that seems to help. It's on its way out, I feel—yesterday I kept it controlled without having to take one of the blockbuster pills—so don't be alarmed.

I'm reading Wordsworth's *Prelude*—a poem longer than Mirabell's. He has a turn of mind rather like Claude—much arrogance and self-congratulation for being so sensitive to grand Natural sublimities. Yet transparent enough to let you glimpse the experiences themselves throughout—and they are often fascinating: a river trip through France in 1793, a monastery left empty by the Terror. Mountebanks in the London slums. A gaga old veteran wandering through the moors. Between doses of that, *The Princess Casamassima*. We must in Athens get <u>all</u> of James and read him every two years the way Gertrude and Alice did. It is so fine, one forgets. The grasp, the detail, the eddying drift towards truths so hairraising one can't quite believe that anyone painted by Sargent <u>knew</u> such things. Also the wonderful narrative simplification: 600 pages but really only a handful of scenes, just so many beads to the necklace . . . Oh and we saw *Close Encounters* the film everyone seems to be praising. About UFOs making contact. Wonderful touches. The hero leans out of his car window for a better view and is promptly sunburned on that side of his face. Household gadgets going crazy as They hover outside. Weird music instead of a dial tone when a phone is lifted. But alas we get to see the spaceships and glimpse the little green bipeds that man them . . . and that won't do, will it? Ma has by now read all of *Mirabell*. We talk about it, clearing up difficult bits—and it may be just as well that no great swan-dive into Truth has been performed. No mention of the bits about sex; probably she's relieved to find the poem so hard to read—her friends will never reach this or that revealing passage.

It's Xmas eve. We're going to the Magowans tonight. Mark will be there. Evidently Eliza, Doris's mother, goes out only in the daytime. Champagne was ordered under my eyes, and there will be (?) caviar from me—if they decide to serve it. I wish I knew what you were doing. Like Xmas eve in Bombay 21 years ago—but at least we were together in that seething "dry" city. Jean de Fevrimont? And Tony— are naked tribesman shaking their spears at him? More later.

25 Dec. KALA CHRISTOUGENNA! Nice evening at Doris + Bob's. The cavvy, the Scotch smoked salmon Mark brought, <u>sweetbreads</u> (cholesterol) + apple tart with hard sauce. Champagne after dinner, and much opening of presents. All <u>I</u> wanted was the young English butler, named James, who moved elegantly from guest to guest, thanking them whenever they accepted something from his tray.

IF YOU SET FOOT IN FRANCE BETWEEN NOW + FEB, REMEMBER MY VIVACIDOL. Check validity date. It should be available now through Nov 78, so get as may boxes as you can—8 or 10.

Another cloudy day. I despair of getting any color—it cleared yesterday only in time for us to go to church, a touching service, carols sung by tiny children, Xmas pageant acted out by the same. Down the aisle came a Donkey, a Cow, a Sheep, and finally a Dove—little girl sashaying wrapped in panel cut from Jean Harlow evening dress—white satin bordered with ostrich plumes.

Ruth Feldman by the way "is" somebody. She translates Italian poetry, one has seen her name everywhere—did you know that? Now to work, or to bed at least, accompanied by the amazing gadget I gave Ma—she's letting me try it out: a little white box that simulates various "white sounds"—surf or rain or waterfall. Every time I woke up in the night it put me right back to sleep—couldn't even watch *The Sting* on TV for very long.

And last night (today is the 26th) it was *I, Claudius* with the same actor as Caligula who played *The Naked Civil Servant*. Ma + I watched riveted. Earlier there had been an open house (noon) at a woman's whom I'd not seen since CEM was alive—widow now of a former partner, rather Guitou in appearance. Then for drinks arrived four people from Atlanta including another recent widow¡—Mrs McGourty!!! She asked for you + Tony + Nelly, and in fact, set in the melon-pink and white highceilinged room of a Palm Beach mansion built on spec, she seemed perfectly OK. But not Athens material. Enormous Marie is starry eyed in the kitchen, dancing all night, oh! so happy! Looking forward to next season. I'm not sure anyone else is. First of all, there may be a question of renting a place, paying for it in m-o-n-e-y; and this house, just to give you an idea, gets $6000 a month in season.

It has turned clear but cold. Infuriating. To work!

Love and happy 1978.
Jim

Torremolinos Port on the Mediterranean in southern Spain.
A Star is Born Probably the 1957 musical version directed by George Cukor.
Close Encounters Stephen Spielberg's *Close Encounters of the Third Kind* (1977).
KALA CHRISTOUGENNA! Merry Christmas!
VIVACIDOL Drug formerly manufactured in France containing amlodipine, a calcium channel blocker used to stimulate blood flow.
Ruth Feldman (1911–2003), American poet and translator.
I, Claudius British television series (1976) adapted from Robert Graves's books *I, Claudius* and *Claudius the God.*
the same actor John Hurt.

The Naked Civil Servant TV film (1975) based on Quentin Crisp's 1968 autobiography.

To David McIntosh

WUSTL
11 April 1978
Stonington, CT

Dearest David,

Thank you for your recipe and the images of your garden—which I hope photographs will soon help me to visualize even more clearly. I've made the pie twice now, the second time with broccoli and iceberg lettuce (both steamed + chopped) in lieu of spinach and chili in lieu of curry, but I think the original with curry is best. It is a most heartening dish. Something has sprouted here for which your garden may be too intemperate, though it may do as a houseplant. Listen to its story:

Years ago Maria and DJ were driving back from Sounion when she spotted, growing wild, a small tree, and thought it was worth digging up for our terrace. You won't remember it, but it stands just to the left as one comes up the iron stair to that top level. I don't know its name, it's really more of a shrub, the trunk and branches black, extremely twiggy, and the whole, whether because of its natural bent or the hardships of its early years, contorted into dramatic zigzags, bending sideways out of the pot toward the flagstones. The leaves are frondlike, suggesting a dwarf ailanthus, which it is not. Come September it blooms—small plump yellow blossoms like double buttercups; then seed-pods form and hang all winter though the leaves have fallen. When the time came in our sessions with the angels to "release" Wystan and Maria back into the world, we were told to do so by breaking a mirror. This seemed right, but also painfully sharp and "final." In the event the ritual was as follows: we broke a small mirror with a marble stylus (it will be the closing episode in the poem), let the pieces fall into a bowl of water, and poured this—quicksilver fragments and all—onto the tree—which for the occasion (DJ's birthday last September) had clothed itself in fantastic luxury, golden trousers like those of a Heian dandy sweeping the terrace floor, muffling its limbs; and to this day in the earth it grows from, splinters of mirror wink up through the branches at the sky. Last month I brought a seed-pod through customs (illegal) and planted it, and now two tiny frond-shoots have appeared, barely an inch high but doing beautifully in a handful of earth borrowed from Eleanor's magic garden. Somebody someday will uncover its Latin name—its photograph in full bloom is too distracting for a sensible opinion.

Oh, what days! I'm up by six, work for four hours or so; then errands, phone calls, what not; something to eat; a nap—a real <u>nap</u> in which I don't sleep but lie on my back with hands crossed like a crusader's effigy, and listen to myself snore—once, twice, three times; get up (40 or 50 minutes have passed) and only then drink the day's one cup of strong filtered coffee, sweetened, with a twist of lemon peel—and back to work for another four hours—five? At 8 o'clock a drink or two; at 9 something to eat—not much (I nibble at things off and on throughout the day: a piece of ginger, a handful of granola, some tollhouse bits)—and in bed by 10:30. The result is that no time whatever seems to have passed for endless months, and yet, like a radiant babe found under a cabbage (my brain?) before me lie already 85 pages, or over half of Vol. III. There have been distractions of course, but these too end by seeming part of the routine: nights at the opera, dinners at Grace's, monthly visits from a hayseed Vermont farmer now nearly 40 (who lived in town 15 years ago)—visits in which we say the same words and smoke the same pot and play the same game of Scrabble and do the same things in bed until Sunday morning when he hitchhikes back home leaving me with the same headcold which I now suspect he carried with him in place of a credit card. A couple of days for recovery, and on with the work! Those who have read the first 50 pages say it is astounding—and, you know, it sort of <u>is</u>. What I don't alas write are letters, one or two a month perhaps, and tipsy postcards to people who must be answered. I've missed writing <u>you</u> more than almost anyone—so here's a letter. I feel our paths are more parallel than not, these years, and look forward to the day when one of us can cross over to the other's for a spell.

With love always—
James

Heian Characteristic of the Japanese Heian era, 794–1185.
its Latin name *Cassia fistula.* The cassia plays a role in the ritual that concludes *Scripts for the Pageant* (1980).
Vol. III *Scripts for the Pageant*, the third part of *The Changing Light at Sandover* (1982).
Vermont farmer Peter Tourville.

To David Jackson

WUSTL
24 May 1978
[Stonington, CT]

Dearest D—

25 years on Tuesday? Flip little verses won't do. Sincere prose, medium of truth, to say how perfectly unimaginable, how dull, how empty, those years—for somewhere, in some Borgesian library, they exist in that form—subtracted of DJ, appear. I think, too, of our first year or so together, or even our first weeks; of other people I had known before you; and the by contrast absolute <u>trust</u> I felt in you from the beginning. Trust in your goodness and honesty, trust in your feeling for me. I don't believe I can have understood at the time how few people there would be, in a whole lifetime, that I could say as much for. If indeed there are any others. A little diagram showing the proportions of base to height in, oh, the Great Pyramid, might express it: one needs that deep + extensive ground plan (58 ruins, 27 serious quarrels, 1001 magic nights) to feed energy and receive it back from the apex. I love you, my dear; you have been the greatest blessing to me—and I hope there haven't been too many days when you couldn't say something of the sort back to me (in silence). Now—25 more???

Crumbling syntax in the above is due to PT's having come down yesterday—two days off from his furniture mnftg. co. (temporarily out of wood). He leaves in an hour or so, but is meanwhile sweeping down the stairs, the studio, etc. He's for once in a cheery mood, thanks to the removal of 8 teeth last week—no more swollen pumpkin faces and body-wide infections. Now <u>that</u> was money well spent—$20 a tooth, plus a mysterious extra $5 (for the tsatsá?).

Sunday—it's Memorial Day weekend—a party here, the first since when??—for the basic 45 people. DK will be here to help, as will nice

Rachel Jacoff. Sandy and Alfred driving up from NH (they leave for a month in England a few days later, but will be back in order to take 107 over from me until whenever Yale starts up—early Sept?). Jean Detre back in town, thin as a râle (winter at Fla fat farm). Well, you can imagine the guest list. Oh, Robin M. called out of the blue, and came up for the night on Monday. He sort of breaks my heart. The vast "autobiography" which is now <u>not</u> being published in England, due perhaps to his not having invested a quarter million in the firm, run by a friend of Suzel's, he has now put in the hands of an ex-alcoholic ex-editor (age 50) who is going to show him how to turn it into one of those sock-it-to-the-public life stories. Also the Braziller poetry series has folded; R got a letter from them, never a word from Richard—to whom I wrote reproachfully and got in return such a page of breezy self-justification as I never hope to read from anyone again. I'm into the Last Ten Lessons, and to my amazement, all kinds of opaque spots in the transcript are coming clear—all that about the Black, Time running backwards, oil etc. So it's marvelous to work on it, slowly, and watch the sense being made, just as they'd promised, under one's very eyes. I hope these letters reach you, and that Crete is divine. Here we have 2 lovely days, then a foggy or windy one. Today's the latter. Edith called. Enough. Time to drop P at Rte 85.

> 25 hugs + kisses, and one to grow
> on.—
>
> J.

PT Peter Tourville.
the tsatsa The madam in a Greek whorehouse.
Rachel Jacoff Dante scholar and editor (b. 1938), professor of comparative literature and Italian at Wellesley College.
the Last Ten Lessons In *Scripts for the Pageant* (1980), section "No."

LEFT: Hellen Plummer and Annie Ingram, Merrill's mother and grandmother

BOTTOM: Frederick Buechner, c. 1948

TOP: Claude Fredericks on top of Mount Equinox near his home in Vermont, 1956

RIGHT: David Jackson in Stonington, c. 1958, with portrait of Jackson by Larry Rivers. Photo by Rollie McKenna

TOP: Merrill on the beach in California, 1955. Photo by David Jackson

LEFT: Merrill carried a typewriter with him around the world in 1956–57. He typed his letters on carbon paper during this period to keep a record of the trip. Here he is in Thailand.

TOP: Irma Brandeis

LEFT: Daryl Hine, 1965

BOTTOM: Louise Fitzhugh at work

TOP: Athens friends Mimi and
Vassili Vassilikos in a taverna
with Jackson and Merrill

LEFT: Probably it was Merrill
who took this photo of Strato
Mouflouzelis

BOTTOM: Judith Moffett

TOP: David McIntosh at El Santuario de Chimayó, New Mexico

RIGHT: Elizabeth Bishop, holding what is probably a miniature ox from *bumba meu boi*, a Brazilian folk festival

BOTTOM: Kalstone and Merrill poolside in Key West, c. 1983

TOP: J. D. McClatchy on the deck at 107 Water Street, 1973

LEFT: Tony Parigory, Jackson, and Maria Mitsotaki in front of a double portrait of Jackson and Merrill in Athens

BOTTOM: Stephen Yenser in front of a painting by Louise Leak

LEFT: Peter Hooten in the living room of Jackson and Merrill's house in Key West

BOTTOM: Merrill in the morning, visiting Stephen Yenser, 1988

To Irma Brandeis
WUSTL
28 June 1978
[Stonington, CT]

Irma my dear (let me still call you that)—

I wish I didn't have to hunt down the grain of truth in your letter. I feel that nothing has changed my affection for you. Yet something clearly—and what, if not my words and actions?—has allowed you to read that affection as one more synonym for neglect. This is almost more than I can accept, but I feel awkward now, and must try to avoid all forms of protestation including the Catalogue Aria of dear ones who have come to share your view.

Reading the *Timaeus*, without any trace of satisfaction I find that I cannot understand it. Is it impatience with any "life of the mind" (including very often my own—why else have its doting angels needed to spoon-feed me?) that drives me to check out the vocabulary, dwell on this or that image, but neglect the sense? It is very much the way I read your piece on Pirandello—a reading which made <u>you</u> howl and me howl <u>back</u> at the rightness of your reproach. You remarked years ago on my preference for mindless company.

Now you unlike Plato have been my friend—I nearly caught myself saying; when, whether in fact or merely in the poem, the final strain on my credulity was to have a friend (Maria) emerge as Plato's latest avatar. So in a way the shaky comparison holds: you and she both send me to a text I can only skim. Is this how the mad reason? Plato might well have thought so.

Maria though is dead and gone, and can't be grieved by my misreadings of her. You can and have been and are, and your letter even puts in three fairytale nutshells the things I'm trying to say: "I know" and "<u>What</u> loss?" and "I'm sorry." If the middle one sounds closest to this evening's truth, it's that your letter, to have been quite fair, wouldn't leave me as it does—admitting that our porch needs repair, though the view from where I sit is in no real danger of being spoiled.

It's too simple a note to end on. Another ten minutes pass, and ten—twelve?—years roll backward. I've sent you a poem that I couldn't possibly find to look at now; but it has offended you in a way that at the time I seemed to understand. Yet at the time I must also the doctor didn't tell them, perhaps rightly, since she could never have agreed to surgery, was that 2 valves in her heart were barely functioning. Had V known, he might have given the show away out of simple strain? Anyhow, they were in Rome. Mimi's last letter to me (June) described a certain white dress she'd bought—so beautiful, so expensive she couldn't yet imagine the occasion on which to wear it. Then 3 weeks ago, Vassili telephoned with the news. "She's wearing the white dress," he added. Six days later he was in Athens, wearing what we presumed to be the old black shirt she'd last seen him in—really in a terrible state, not eating, smoking 4 packs a day. In 20 years they'd been apart exactly 3 nights, two last summer while she was in intensive care, one in 1962 when he had to cover a remote village disaster for the papers. She told him what to write and stood over him while he did so—alas, too often the books read that way. She had died instantly, painlessly, collapsing as she stepped into the flat with him, late at night; in his arms, smiling. A good friend would have been on a plane the next day—not me, but I seem to have made up for it by suggesting he look into that beautiful Protestant cemetary— non-Catholic rather—where in fact (as he put it) like people arriving late at night only to find that everything but the bridal suite has been booked, one last double plot was free, and there she lies—his name already on the stone—"between Shelley and Goethe's son." He stayed here the first night, but talking English exhausted him. Thereafter he'd look in every day or so, always thinner and tenser—until something quite extraordinary happened. We were by then towards the end of a "reading" of the all but completed Vol III—to a spectacular audience that included, along with all the regulars, Proust, Goethe, Dante, Mother Nature herself—dressed "democratically" in a blue schoolgirl's smock—and . . . Mimi. V seemed to want to hear about all this; indeed the only time he'd brightened up was an evening when I urged him to try writing syllabics in Greek, made up a Marianne-type stanza; or else a sestina, showing him "Samos" from the poem. He ended by sitting with us during the reading of the last 10 lessons, followed by some short but very touching exchanges between him and QM as well as poor Mimi moaning in Greek "Don't say it!" when he complained that words had no healing virtue for him any more (QM: MY BLUE SMOCK WET WITH THAT POOR CHILD'S TEARS)—but somehow a wonder was wrought. On one hand he seemed to grasp with perfect ease what the poem was saying, said it was as if he had taken an "interior shower"; and on the other, he began to eat and changed his shirt. Now he's back in Rome. All kinds of awful adjustments lie ahead, to be sure, but it does seem almost as if the worst were behind him.

Otherwise . . . I've written through to the end, and need perhaps 4 more days of typing. Sooner or later I'll send a copy to McClatchy and ask him to xerox one for you. It's right enough to pass as a pen-ultimate draft, I think. Meanwhile the idea of a short (25 pp at most) Epilogue keeps dancing before my venerable beads—something that wouldn't go in the original edition of Vol III, but would fit comfortably enough in the one-volume edition of the Sacred Books (along with the Appendix containing "Words for Maria," "The Will" etc). It would feature the five-day "ceremony" ending with Robert M's rebirth as the marvelous musical child from Minnesota: the Angels and QM came on successive days, each bringing the gift of a sense—hers being smell, of course, the breath of life. But would also provide irresistible glimpses of Maria et al. and the things they're doing, and perhaps end (too *Between the Acts?*) with the Reading about to begin in the old ballroom renovated for that purpose, Alice's buffet spread out, Mimi blinking in her white, Vassili smoking in his black . . . It could be arranged, I think, not to sound too self-congratulatory. That's something I don't yet feel—well, today I don't feel anything; or am letting my back hurt just to keep from understanding that, give or take 100 lines, it's done, done, done, and who would have ever imagined . . . ?

Thank you for your 2 suggestions by the way. The Yeats business (QM's) clearly must be fixed, and the something better for MM to say may come up. We'll be away Sept 15–Oct 1, but maybe Martin McKinsey will turn up before that. Christian Ayoub is here these days. Tony in a deep depression (business deals not so shady that everyone else in Greece doesn't resort to them as a matter of course may catch up with him if old Mezikis dies); Bernie repellently effervescing (starting with his father's death in June). Eleni quite understandably down at the mouth, the Salonika earthquake having all but destroyed the grand apartment building she was putting her savings into. DJ, Manos, George, all much as you remember them. Nelly lives for food. And drink. And excursions. We've sensibly been nowhere, just look sympathetic at horror stories of overcrowded island boats and rat-world accommodations. The Golden Bantam corn D planted at Dorothy's has come up abundantly—we've had two baskets full sent by air from Chania; D is glad you are learning the thrill of eating your own produce. Do send the new poem(s). I'm <u>not</u> tired of the Clos sequence—clearly it has taken a life of its own, for you, had little or nothing any more to do with Lorna, and you must let it have its way. Up to a point, bien sûr. Nothing in excess, said Maria, millennia ago.

Our love to you both—

Love ever,
James

the bakáli Bakery.
Kifissia Expensive and fashionable northern suburb of Athens.
a "reading" . . . Vol III This séance, in which JM read aloud *Scripts for the Pageant* or "Vol III" (1980), is the basis of "The Ballroom at Sandover," the final section of "Coda: The Higher Keys," which completes *The Changing Light at Sandover* (1982).
a sestina . . . "Samos" "Samos," a section in *Scripts for the Pageant*, is a canzone, a repeating form resembling a sestina but longer and more complex.
QM Queen Mother, major figure in the Ouija board's empyrean, also known as Nature and Psyche.
the end Of *Scripts for the Pageant.*
Epilogue This became "Coda: The Higher Keys."
the one-volume edition of the Sacred Books Never compiled in the form described here.
It The "Epilogue" or "Coda."
Between the Acts Virginia Woolf's last novel.
MM Maria Mitsotaki.
Martin McKinsey American scholar, friend of the Yensers, translator and editor of *Clearing the Ground: C. P. Cavafy, Poetry and Prose, 1902–1911.*
Christian Ayoub Christian Ayoub Sinano (1927–89), Alexandrian-born writer who lived in Paris and Montreal.
Dorothy Dorothy Andrews (d. 2008), American painter who lived on Crete.
the Clos sequence Yenser's poem "Clos Camardon" in his collection *The Fire in All Things* (1993).
Nothing in excess, said Maria In *Sandover* it turns out that Maria was an avatar of Plato.

To Judith Moffett   NYPL
                                              13 August 1978
                                            [Athens, Greece]

Dear Judy,

Two letters are now here from you—and not a peep from me. There's
little enough to tell: lovely weather, middays on the beach, work
progressing at a rather reduced pace for various reasons—and Mira-
bell assures us it's all right on schedule. We both thought your letter
about <u>him</u> most sensible. As you imply ("I believe, if not in Mirabell,
in you") the question of belief is twofold—belief in the experience;
belief in the teachings. These last are what are likely to stick in a
reader's throat, as they always begin by doing in our own. As they
might still in mine if I didn't by now know enough to remind myself of
certain connections so simple as to be upstaged by a parade of show-
ier effects. One doesn't believe in God for a lack of proof? Yet if God
is "Biology"—the "word" or principle of life itself—proof abounds,
and who could not believe? Mirabell et al announce themselves as
subatomic particles within ourselves/cells; the R/Lab + its workings
become a dramatization of genetic forces that make weekly head-
lines in this decade's papers. Without keeping in mind something of
these basic connections, it is all bound to seem impossibly baroque.
Not till late in Vol III, by which time one of the creatures of Atlantis
has joined us, do we connect that whole embroidery with the "his-
tory" of a perhaps mythical but "stable" particle coexisting with the
"volatile" or "bat" particle. Such cords hold—or ought to—the gassy
balloon in place [*in the margin:* This, plus a basic paradox: The far-
thest out is the farthest <u>in</u>. The toy spyglass]. *Mirabell*, at any rate,
strikes <u>me</u> as increasingly limpid and orderly; and I can only hope
that the Public will exhibit a capacity similar to those listeners' who,
at first hurt and insulted by *Pelléas* now, fifty years later, drink it in
like *Porgy and Bess*. In short I can't be worried. In the months since
Don Justice's remark made me wince, I've been cloned to withstand
that sort of thing. Beyond all this I can only agree with you: *Mirabell*
<u>is</u> convoluted and anti-human by contrast with Vol III, but had this
not been the case, how on earth to feel the quickening of joy and sim-
plicity when we get to the angels? *Purgatorio* is dry and "moralistic" by

contrast with what follows or even what goes before—and the pity is that most readers settle for the sensational pictures and emotions of Hell and find Dante's heaven as deadly as Milton's, when in fact . . . but this is no criticism of <u>Dante</u>.

Yesterday a telephone call from Crete alerted DJ to pick up something at the downtown Olympic airlines depot. He brought back a sturdy basket with a white cloth sewn across its top, his name marked thereon in purple letters. Inside we found: a jar labeled Mint Chutney, another of Apricot jam, a dozen perfectly ripe green figs (no asp), 3 avocados each perhaps 3 inches long, 3 tiny green peppers, and 15 small ears of Golden Bantam corn—corn he himself had planted in our friend Dorothy's garden 7 weeks ago! The butter ran down our chins.

But you have other questions. And yes, I must admit that "only certain people's opinions are going to matter." No reflection on them, if you like. Have you noticed that I admire you less for being unable to read Proust? I may well end up liking earlier (or later?) poems I've written better than this big affair—as being more recognizably "mine," as being more perfect transmutations of "experience." Ah well. End of page. Be happy on Meadowvale Lane!

Love from DJ + JM

Don Justice Donald Justice (1925–2004), American poet. In a letter to Merrill of 10 August 1977 Moffett had reported that he had called Merrill one of his favorite poets and had found "The Book of Ephraim" an "aberration" that was "baffling."

To Judith Moffett   NYPL
18 February 1979
Stonington, CT

Dear Judy,

This is not a report on your ms. of poems alas (though the Wordsworths arrived yesterday and I've read it through once only—liking it; tasting again that delicious Grasmere gingerbread—Sandy and Alfred brought me some last year—and wondering if those slugs and liver flukes are as symbolic as they seemed to be) but just (and think-ing how nicely it works with the now-much-stronger title poem) to answer your question about sending something to *Field*. Perfectly sensible thing to do, all the more since they turned down some of those diffy poems in *Braving the E.* for reasons akin to yours. I looked over the "Sound Without Sense" pages—which I'm glad to say don't convince me <u>at all</u>. On p. 48 you imply that I'm courting these effects for reasons that have nothing to do with aesthetic theory—so good-bye my long study of Mallarmé. Further down you compare my lines to "obscenities screamed"—really? I who so seldom raise my voice? Perhaps you've tidied that bit up by now, as well as the description of Poirier's perfectly sensible pronouncement as striking a note of "Shrill outrage". . . . when it's you, as you go on to say, who are shrill and outraged where Poirier is in control of what he's saying. Aside from touches like that, though, you make good enough sense on your terms. My final feeling about the whole "Pocatello" question (etymol-ogy: Italo-American, meaning <u>I</u> <u>am</u> <u>reticent</u>) is that you are treating these poems, regardless of their quality good or bad, as if they were products of pop culture that would go forever unread if they aren't read in the pulsing N*O*W, the immediacy of their first few years. Had I ever doubted that the private meaning of "18 W 11" would even-tually be known to a reader who cares, I'd have made up a newspaper clipping as epigraph, or stuck a note in the back of the book; I could still do that, I guess—but why? You're doing it for me in this piece, as Saez did in his. It's only the naive tourists in "Arrival at Santos" who ask for "immediate comprehension" of the novelty. It may be, indeed, that this note of urgent, breathless striving is what made me uncom-fortable in your "Blackout"—is this the moment to make a joke?—He who knows his place doesn't run in it. Anyhow, I'm tempted as I've not been for <u>years</u> to write a really opaque poem, just to watch you turn into an aerosol bomb again. Instead I've spent a fruitless 15 minutes looking through these pp. and the *Mirabell* review—because I thought I'd seen a point where you called Yahya a <u>Turkish</u> prince instead of a Persian or Iranian—but I've evidently mistaken. And have no further quibbles with the review. High time for hot bath.

Love and more soon—
Jimmy

"Sound Without Sense" Moffett's essay "Sound Without Sense: Willful Obscurity in Poetry, with Some Illustrations from James Merrill's Canon" appeared in the *New England Review*, vol. 3, no. 2 (Winter 1980).

"Pocatello" question Shorthand for the issue created by what Moffett understood as passages in Merrill's poems that would defeat average American readers, such as some in Pocatello, Idaho.

Saez Richard Saez, "James Merrill's Oedipal Fire," *Parnassus: Poetry in Review*, vol. 3, no. 1 (1978).

"Arrival at Santos" Poem by Elizabeth Bishop.

your "Blackout" Moffett's poem of that name in her volume *Whinny Moor Crossing* (1984).

the *Mirabell* review Moffett's review essay of *Mirabell: Books of Number*, "What Is Truth?" in *American Poetry Review* 8 (September/October 1979).

To Tony Parigory   WUSTL
                                                          18 February 1979
                                                           Stonington, CT

Tony darling—

I've been back here a week or so; found your letter (and safely received the one to Palm Beach with its shocking enclosures!) and sent on the one to DJ (after reading it—my dear, you haven't lost your touch: Number 5, Number 6, Number 7) who is still in Key West and will not be North until March 1st. I telephoned him on Valentine's Day morning, and was answered by a very seductive voice with a heavy French accent. This was Hervé, of whom you are bound to hear in great detail; at least he sounds better than the previous "conquest"—a black disco-roller-skating star whose last of many unwanted telephone calls was from the local jail, and very coldly answered by our Dear One. In short, it's a coup de foudre: DJ and Key West. And all considered, since he was utterly determined to buy something on this trip South, he has done quite well. Mrs P and I had been appalled when he phoned from Savannah to say that he was about to make a large deposit on a $150,000 house ("reduced from 175,000!") with a 2 acre azalea garden and a floating dock for one's cocktail launch—but luckily the weather turned cold and he realized it would never do for winters. K/W is (as you will see) really very pretty and also great fun. For D there are the discos open till 3 or 4 a.m., amorous consummations on the dancefloor, pits of burning coals (on chilly nights) round which The Boys toast marshmallows. For us both there is divine weather, beaches (not as nice as Palm Beach, the sea colder and shallower, but still . . . fairly divine), beautiful fresh fruit and fish, glorious vegetation overarching little old-fashioned cracking sidewalks and the tin-roofed gingerbread houses. The town is large enough (32,000 permanent; plus, oh, 50,000 pleasure-sikas) so that one can be quite inconspicuous—as if anyone cared except the tattooed bullies who beat up poor Tennessee for singing hymns. The question all this raises is: what about Greece? But it simply can't be answered at this early date. D will be returning after mid-April and I'll follow in late July, if not before. (Meanwhile he's having a POOL put in the garden, and some interior work in the house, closets, bigger bathroom, etc.) (And I can no longer sneer at the Magowans for having four addresses.) Speaking of whom, Mark and Nina are getting married early in May. I'm a trifle distrait these days. My flame Peter has been here this entire week, having left his non-wife upon hearing that two of her three children weren't his. But I expect he'll go back to her, as soon as he's smoked all my last summer's home-grown pot.

Don't in any case tell Manoli, if you talk, about the house (unless I've done so myself in an indiscreet postcard)—he'd leap to conclusions we simply saunter towards; and indeed the likeliest thing is that we give nothing up. Why should we?

I'll attend to your banking when I'm in NY again (March 2)—as it stands your figures seem contradictory. You say you have $1779— ah, I SEE. D'accord, you may expect 720 rosebushes by early next month. I'm sorry I don't know where to reach Harry, else I'd phone him while he's convalescent. Peter DeM finally reached me, and he's met Ed White since, no thanks to me however. The weather has been ZERO (Fahrenheit) for the last 6 days. The harbor is a sheet of ice, yet the calendar Spring is only a month away. Bizarre. I hope you are soon moved and happy in this shop. Wait till late summer for some of your housewarmings.

A kiss to Nellaki and much much love ever—
J.

pleasure-sikas Pleasure seekers, with a pun on "sikas" (see Merrill's letter to Tony Parigory, 18 September 1962).
poor Tennessee Tennessee Williams.

Mark and Nina Mark Magowan, Merrill's nephew, and Mark's fiancée, Nina. Magowan became president and publisher of Vendome Press.
Harry Henry M. Blackmer (1927–88), American expatriate and friend of Tony Parigory's.
Nellaki Nelly Liambey's nickname, the *-aki* being a Greek diminutive.

To Humphrey Carpenter

COLUMBIA
9 April 1979
[Stonington, CT]

Dear Mr Carpenter,

Thank you for your letter. I first knew Chester in the mid-50's, but never intimately until he began coming to Greece, 8 or 10 years later. If he talked about his early life, I simply don't remember the details. I believe he was at the U. of Michigan when Auden taught there. Wystan wrote a faery masque to be acted by Chester and some of his friends; I've heard this spoken of by both Chester and Wystan. I suggested that Mr Anderson get in touch with Alan Ansen in Athens (Dimocharous 53, Athens 601). He is perhaps the most reliable authority—far more so than Caskey whose own "decline" promises to outdo poor Chester's. Ansen is not only extremely bright and cultivated, but the keeper of a detailed journal which no doubt covers a lot of the material you need. He is presently writing up some of his notes on WHA's New School lectures. You may have seen his memorandum on the composition of the *Rake* Libretto (in the *Hudson Review*, early 50's) and a letter setting straight a number of facts in an article in the *Advocate* last year. (He can guide you to the issues in question more easily than I.)

Chester's character. (What follows will be inadequate.) He was first of all extremely intelligent about writing; I should like to second Wystan's endorsement of his ear and his judgment. He was funny and shameless and obsessed by sex. I asked him, a year before the end,—he repeated the question to Wystan who laughed approvingly—when he intended to give it up and start living for pleasure. But by then it was an uncontrollable reflex. He was a brilliant story-teller, though, and could make the most spellbinding monologues out of the often rather limited material of casual pick-ups or recurrent household scenes. (In these, I came to suspect a heavy dose of staircase wit, at least when it came to something devastating he had said in Greek. He knew Greek well enough but his enunciation must have been a problem for the unprepared listener. Which reminds me of a wee vignette: after CK gave a reading in London—1973?—he was given no time to greet a number of friends in the audience. Wystan swept him from backstage into a cab; they were late for dinner. The cab drove in silence for a minute or two. Then WHA: "My dear, if I may say so, your reading could give a little more weight to the unstressed syllables in your line." CK: "Wystan, I never wanted to sound like a calypso singer.") In these stories he presented himself—in every way but literally—as a woman: the cultured matron [*in the margin:* the mother surrounded by pots and pans], the slut with the heart of gold, etc, etc. I wonder if his lifelong passion for opera—especially for the heroines and the sopranos who impersonated them—didn't provide him with a trunkful of what are now called "role models." He seemed often to invite jealousy, betrayal, despair, in order to play that part to the hilt. And the part, alas, was far less often the restrained Marschallin than some suicidal Leonora or Violetta. I can't do justice to the verve and humor of these hours; he wasn't looking for pity—he was sharing his life with you [*in the margin:* a life already half "distanced" by style], and it struck a chord of affection in every kind of listener. I recall a young American who turned up from somewhere—perfectly "straight," entirely unsophisticated—saying, after listening to Chester rant for most of an afternoon, "You know, love does that to people. When my brother's wife left him, he . . ." Well, I've come to the end of my page. And fear that I've given, like Caskey, too lopsided a portrait. Nothing said of his gentleness, his generosity, his deep loyalty to Wystan. Whoever tried to come between them got mangled by the gears. My few days in Kirchstetten (August 1968) gave a glimpse of Chester at peace—if peace is the word for all that cooking, all those guests and excursions. But his beloved Yannis was there—an even-tempered and sensitive young man, by the way—as well as Wystan; and for once all was right with the world.

Yours sincerely,
James Merrill

Humphrey Carpenter (1946–2005), prolific English writer, including *W. H. Auden: A Biography* (1981).
Caskey William Caskey (1921–81), American photographer.
WHA's New School lectures Ansen evidently did not finish writing up those notes. His four notebooks on Auden's lectures on Shakespeare are in the Berg Collection in the New York Public Library. They are the chief source for Arthur Kirsch's edition of W. H. Auden, *Lectures on Shakespeare* (2000).

To Richard Baker

WUSTL
27 April 1979
[Stonington, CT]

Dear Mr. Baker,

Thank you for your invitation to help nominate next year's Pulitzer Prize winner in Poetry.

Again, alas, I must disqualify myself. Not because of a forthcoming book but in widely-shared dismay at the handling of this year's award.

The reversal of a majority opinion by a presumably less knowledgeable committee is not without precedent in your annals. I understand that this may be an embarrassment built into your charter, and applaud the tact that has kept the clause in question from being invoked as a matter of course in other years. When, however, a nomination is overruled without consulting the jury, and the action quite rightly made public, a situation arises that spoils everyone's pleasure in what ought to be a clear chime of acclaim heard throughout the land. Neither the nominated nor the actual winner can rejoice; no more can the jurors; and indeed the honor felt by every past or future recipient is slightly but decisively tarnished.

Sincerely,
James Merrill

the handling of this year's award Mark Strand's *The Late Hour* had been the nominating jury's choice for the Pulitzer Prize in Poetry but the award went to Robert Penn Warren for his *Now and Then: Poems, 1976–1978*.

To Humphrey Carpenter　　　　　　　COLUMBIA
28 April 1979
Stonington, CT

Dear Mr. Carpenter,

In haste, as I shall be away from my desk for the next ten days or so. If there is any chance of your being in New York on May 9th, might we have lunch? I want to get home by that evening, Stonington is another 2 hours, door to door, from New Haven, so I don't recommend your trying to squeeze it in on the 11th. Closer to 3 and a half hours (one way) from New York, but if you were free to come either Saturday or Sunday I'd be delighted to see you. Saturday evening I'm out to dinner, but we could talk in the afternoon—or at any time Sunday. There's plenty of room if you wanted to stay over. Failing all else, there's always the telephone.

Your questions:

(1) You are right, I think, about Chester's reputation. "Real impact" is given to very few poets to make, however, in any generation. Chester's technical skill alone put him in an unfashionable camp. It is perhaps his talent as a librettist that sets him apart (though here I speak with limited authority, all the more since I've not seen his Boccaccio libretto for Chavez, and others I may not know of). In this field he surely, at first, knew more than Wystan. While I never shared their joint enthusiasm for the figure of Baba in the *Rake*, the delicious Epilogue, whatever it may owe to *Don Giovanni*, was entirely Chester's contribution, and for me makes the perfect conclusion to that work.

(2) Jealous of Auden's reputation? I think not. Proud of it, jealous to protect and uphold it, indignant at any slur. This attitude is plausible if you consider how deeply he identified with it—the cuts and changes WHA made eagerly, from the first, at his suggestion. He didn't approve of Auden's late manner, the prosy, workmanlike style more and more cultivated; he regretted the gorgeous feats of language in the earlier work. But let anyone else say so! A scathing retort to the effect that we are dealing after all with the greatest English poet since Milton. I've heard him use that phrase more than once. Indeed, Wystan kept reminding people of C's collaborations because people (in the glow of W's celebrity) tended to forget C.

(3) Almost entirely dependent on Auden for money? Well . . .
The libretti brought in royalties which, together with performance
rights, might have accounted for $2000 a year, for Chester alone. At
least once a foundation (one with which I am associated) gave him
a grant—small but his very own—to write poetry. The rest indeed
would have come from Auden, and where money was concerned, at
least in those last 10 years, Chester was like a child with matches.
Wystan resented the extravagance (mainly the "lavish" presents to
boys, which included far too many involuntary ones—or may I say
unprotested thefts?) but never of course cut off the source of supply.
No doubt there were scenes, reprimands, and all that. It can't have
been easy on either side.

(4) But no: in the years I knew Chester I felt no trace of sexual
jealousy in the air. Here I can speak from experience. It is a phase
eventually reached by many sensible couples—the homosexual ones
at least. It may take a while, but it had passed I should think almost
entirely by the late 1950s. Wystan always struck me as delighted
whenever the rare person turned up who could make Chester even
briefly happy. Chester encouraged Wystan to see the good qualities
in that (to me nameless and faceless) Austrian who became Wystan's
last steady sexual friend. I know no more than you about Wystan's
"fidelity" to Chester, but I can speak for the concern and good will
on both sides in this matter. The three principal Greeks in Chester's
life—two of whom spoke adequate German and so could converse
with Wystan—revered him for his friendly courtesy toward them.
Caskey is dead bang wrong about Yannis Boras. Chester had a taste
for thugs, there <u>were</u> people who periodically beat him up and robbed
him and tormented him. But Yannis was kind and decent and intel-
ligent, with a charming zany streak. A village boy from near Olympia,
who from the start wanted to make something of himself. Chester
told of their first lunch in a nice restaurant; Yannis pretended to
have already eaten so not as to reveal his lack of table manners—"But
how he watched everything we did!" reported C. There were scenes.
<u>Once</u> Yannis slapped Chester's face. Chester telephoned me in hys-
terics to come fetch him in the car. I did; and found Chester already
on his highest dignity, one cheek slightly pinkened, and Yannis still
white with shock at his own outburst—occasioned, I believe, by his
walking in on C in bed with someone else. At Kirchstetten Yannis

fitted beautifully in the household. Part of the time he was taking courses in Vienna—to become what? an accountant? Since Chester didn't drive he could take over part of the time, and spare Wystan the trouble. He liked girls without needing to commit himself. On his Austrian papers he put down "Moslem" for religion—a joke of course; yet when his body was sent back to his village for burial they had placed him in his coffin (open) in the traditional Moslem pose, one hand to his chest; and the Greek priest (I seem to recall—I wasn't there) couldn't bury him in the churchyard. But they crowned him all the same with [the] white wedding wreath worn by those who died unmarried.

How one runs on. I enclose a snapshot of Chester and Yannis—worth 1000 words?—which it would be kind of you to return. And I'll hope to hear from you. If lunch in NY on the 9th suits you, please call me shortly before 12 at YU 8 8953. The night before I'll be in Utica, NY, c/o David Lehman (100 College Hill Rd)—where a note would reach me.

> Sincerely yours,
> James Merrill

his Boccaccio libretto for Chavez The only opera by Mexican composer Carlos Chávez (1899–1978), with its libretto by Kallman, was called *Panfilo and Lauretta* at its premiere in 1957 and *Love Propitiated* and then *The Visitors* in later revisions and revivals.
David Lehman (b. 1948), American poet and editor.

To Eleanor Perenyi   YALE
                                        3 October 1979
                                        Athens, Greece

Dearest E—

Your most welcome letter keeps gathering resonance as we too fling ourselves into Simplifying Action. For the garden on Main St read the House on Ath. Eph. Up bright and early this morning, we ruthlessly stripped every object from the walls (narsty nails and ugly plaster pits), every book and record destined for America [*in the margin:*

from the shelves]; made Babel-like piles of the Unwanted, Vasilikos in triplicate, Evie Dodson's watercolor of the S'ton cemetary. Fat boxes were assembled and filled—heavier than leaden coffins—with Auden's complete *OED*. There's even the question of some furniture to go out in Saturday's shipment on a Miami-bound freighter laden with container-corporation containers into one of which, if I've rightly understood, the Volkswagen is expected to fit. Enter a breathless Messenger: "Why are you packing those cartons so carefully?—since every book will be removed by Customs and examined for smuggled currency—before they go on board." It was then I felt the tears welling up. And after all, when you come to think of it, how often in life is it vouchsafed to move into an absolutely pristine space, furnished only incidentally with beds and some kitchen things, but chiefly with the illusion that one can do without the rest; or, if one can't, that the walls and closets and bureaus will fill up with new things, slowly and wisely chosen for once, not just the dear old junk of a life halfway round the world. In this raw, ghastly state the house has lost 99% of its charm. And the plants? the huge camellia already thick with buds? the fat gardenias, a trio of exquisite sisters still blooming? John and Abby pretend to care about such things but I don't believe them for a minute. So I guess, now that nothing else is on the wall, the writing is. We'll never live here again. I notice by now no analogy whatever with your revisions in the garden—just the spurt of courage and decision that saw you through the painful bit. All changes sound most sensible indeed, and I'm sorry not to have been there to murmur encouragement throughout. What a treat to look forward to next summer's blossoming confirmation.

The Cretan weather did wonders for us, and held until the penultimate day. I'd been expecting to read my proofs which however didn't arrive, leaving me stuck with my Ariel-like sprints along the yellow sands and a paperback of *The Brothers Karamazov* (2/3 of that to go). David missed a horrifying explosion on the docks, savaging 1000 cars, by one day—but we're both safely back and about to drive up to Nelly's cousin Rita's on Euboia for the night tomorrow.

Phone rang the evening I returned. "Hello." (Nervous vocal scurryings.) "Yes?" "Oh J-J-Jimmy it's me. I was trying to get another number." (Yes, that is what he said.) He'd called merrily in early Aug. to say he was back and David had reminded him we were no longer friends. This time he told me about pending lawsuits with his brother ("for alienation of his mother's affections" or some such nonsense) and mother to reclaim the diamonds she gave him and then took back; about his wonderful productivity, forthcoming publications and exhibitions. And how heartbroken he was by our estrangement— "but it will pass." "I daresay. <u>Good</u>-bye." Tony glimpsed him barefoot in Kolonaki—he'd arrived with both feet in airline icebuckets, some hideous infection still purple and pustulent which make shoes out of the question. It makes one so <u>angry</u>. Jimmy Draper was here too, installing a show of Greece-inspired pickies and furnishings from the Met which DJ (I've not been yet) says is heavenly. The left-wing papers are seething. 2 weeks from today we have the opening of Mimi's posthumous pastels in the same gallery that shows Tsarouchis. Oh this country. Well, enough. This is "for" Grace and Billy as well as dearest You. I'll be back around Nov 15, or even before—but no formal appearances for the first 4 or 5 days, just a snuggle in the new elevator, etc. Much much love from both.

Ever—

Jimmy

Main St The street on which Eleanor and her mother lived in Stonington and where Eleanor, an authority on gardens, was revising the plantings.

Ath. Eph. Athinaion Efivon 44, from which Merrill and Jackson were moving after fifteen years.

Evie Dodson Evelyn Dodson and her husband John lived near Merrill and Jackson in Stonington.

Auden's complete *OED* Chester Kallman, shortly before his death, made a gift to Merrill of the 26-volume set.

John and Abby John Camp, director of excavation at the Athenian Agora for the American School of Classical Studies at Athens, and his wife took over the house in Athens, which Merrill's will later gave to the school.

Phone rang The voice on the other end of the line belongs to Bernie Winebaum, identifiable by his stutter.

Jimmy Draper James David Draper (b. 1943), art historian and author, for more than forty years a curator at the Metropolitan Museum of Art, and partner of Robert Isaacson.

Mimi Mimi Vassilikos.

Billy Billy Boatwright.

To Thom Gunn

Dear Thom,

Back from Greece only this month, I'm quite bowled over by your marvelous piece on *Mirabell* in the *SF Review*—impossible to imagine anything more generous or more welcome. After a number of complaints about how "private" and "difficult" the book was, you make it all sound—just as it finally came to seem to David and me—like, well, the second most natural thing in the world. I've mailed a copy down to Key West where I'll be joining him next month; he'll be thrilled! Memories of Elli's Bier-Bar and the reptile house in Berlin . . .

Here also are your *Collected Poems* which I'm reading, as I always do read you, with immense sympathy and admiration. I wanted to write you about *Jack Straw's Castle* when it appeared, but was already too blearily deep in *Mirabell* etc. to do more than think wistfully of letters. Anyhow I got "The Bed" by heart after the first few readings—such perfect phrasing, plus all that truth—then lost that heart to the noble and adorable Yoko. I'm sorry not to find some of those poems reprinted (like "The Geysers"—don't we stand up for our old excesses?) but can see that you didn't want to tip the scales too much in favor of recent work. Since I hanker all too vainly after slim volumes nowadays, I'm not complaining. It's a splendid body of work, and so completely yours.

I mean to be in San Francisco for a few days in April and will make a sign as the time draws near, in hopes that we can get together. Meanwhile endless thanks and congratulations.

Yours,

Jimmy

your marvelous piece Gunn called *Mirabell* "the most convincing description of a gay marriage I know" in his review of the poem titled "A Heroic Enterprise," *San Francisco Review of Books* (August 1979).
Elli's Bier-Bar . . . Berlin See Merrill's letter to John and Anne Hollander, 14 November 1961.
Jack Straw's Castle Title of Gunn's volume of poems published in 1976.
"The Bed" Opening poem in *Jack Straw's Castle.*
Yoko The dog who is the speaker in the eponymous poem in *Jack Straw's Castle.*

To Kimon Friar   WUSTL
                                              24 December 1979
                                               Palm Beach, FL

Dear Kimon,

I fear I've delayed so long in answering your letter that you may receive this only after you've returned from the White House. My invitation duly arrived—a whole little kit, in fact, of things one might want to show one's grandchildren—but my plans were made, and it's (in any case) almost as difficult to get to Washington from Key West as it is from Athens. I don't regret missing the Carters and John Frederick Nims but I'm sorry not to be seeing you—and, of course, meeting Elytis. In your letter you find it odd that I don't write about his prize. Pull yourself together! I was in Athens when the Prize was announced and telephoned you that very day. We then spoke quite a bit about it, you showed me the *Books Abroad* issue devoted to him, etc., etc. In short, I have for once <u>not</u> been silent in a matter that concerns you. As to the *Odyssey*, a new paragraph is required.

I've brought it South with me and am (as of yesterday) into the 7th Book. I'm reading it with the greatest wonder and delight—a response which is precisely the measure of the changes I've undergone in the last 21 years. Time enough for a whole self to be born and reach voting age (or is it 18 by now?). In 1958 I simply could not read this poem—perhaps all the more because <u>you</u> had translated it and dedicated the translation to me. I felt repelled and threatened by its passion, by the (I thought) vulgar heightening of sensation, by the defiant heroics—at least as far as I read; I can now confess that I didn't get beyond Book 4. Even before I knew you I was conscious of a shyness in the face of the Monumental—which coin's obverse was the proud (or mortified) realization that I would never write more than small mannerly poems in a minor key. Thanks to a thousand things, to 20 years of Greece among them, that coin has been melted down and made part of my own Monument. And I find myself reading Kazantzakis, as I said, with wonder and delight, but also with forbearance and affection, as if we were schoolmates reunited after some long estrangement. Alas that it took so long. Alas that <u>you</u> had to live all these years with the (not constant, I'm sure, but whenever the realization crossed your mind) bitterness of having your gift to me made so little of. But the greater pity would have been for me never to see the light that shines from every page of this wonderful book to illuminate everything from the Greece I've known and the Greeks I've loved to the quite different way in which I've confronted, oh, Man and Death and the Gods. My admiration is wholly channeled through your English—though some day I must look carefully [at] at least a few pages of the original. You are writing in what strikes me as a full-blown style of your own devising. The echoes of Chapman and Pope, on one hand, and of the Romantics from Keats to Dowson on the other, invite us to imagine the evidently vaster sources and resources of the original; but these "echoes" fuse into a surface so varied, so beautifully handled throughout, that I've already paused a thousand times in simple pleasure at a line like "sighed deeply, and like light foam danced on thundering foam" or "into my brain's deep forge and thereby turned to flame" where the vowel of "brain" and the f of "forge" make the last word inevitable. I shan't go on now; I want to write again when I've finished the entire poem—and besides, here in Palm Beach, one doesn't write letters of any description. Tomorrow's Christmas. Then on the 28th I proceed to Key West where, according to David, the dream-house is ready and waiting, the pool filled, the mango and guava and papaya trees planted and already hung with fruit. I'll stay till early March, then spend another few days here with my mother, then go North—for bound copies of my book should be ready then and I want to send them out myself.

I hired my own lawyer and managed to escape testifying in the Auden trial. No decision had been reached when I left NY but it sounds as if the Library was winning.

You have the Key West address?—702 Elizabeth St, Key West, Fla 33040. And a telephone number: (305) 294 7109. But if this doesn't reach you in time—well, belated Christmas and New Year greetings.

> And love always,
> Jimmy

My invitation To the ceremony honoring Odysseus Elytis (1911–96), Greek poet, winner of the Nobel Prize in Literature for 1979, whose *The Sovereign Sun: Selected Poems* had been translated into English by Friar.
John Frederick Nims (1913–99), American poet and editor.

the *Books Abroad* issue Vol. 49, no. 4 (Autumn 1975).

Odyssey Friar's translation of Kazantzakis's *The Odyssey: A Modern Sequel* (1958).

or is it 18 The 26th Amendment to the Constitution had become law in 1971 and established the minimum voting age at eighteen.

Chapman George Chapman (1559–1634), English writer and classical scholar, best known for his translations of Homer.

Dowson Ernest Dowson (1867–1900), English writer associated with the Decadents.

the dream-house The house Jackson bought at 702 Elizabeth Street in Key West.

the Auden trial In Manhattan Surrogate Court in December 1979, between Chester Kallman's father, an eighty-six-year-old dentist, and the New York Public Library. The latter was awarded Auden's manuscripts and other papers.

To Eleanor Perenyi   YALE

1 January 1980

Key West, Florida

Dearest E—

On the back of some rejected sketches for a coffee-table to be made by some ironworks on a neighboring Key. (The prices of even shop-worn furniture here . . . !)

D doesn't mention your Christmas gift, perhaps because I haven't christened it yet. But it's here and I'm reading the instructions. You're so right, culture is what we need. Even empty, it's a beautiful object and we thank you lovingly. Yesterday the mercury plunged to about 60 degrees and the garden so lovingly described was left to fend for itself while we crawled under our electric blankets and got out our ski-skins. In the evening we made a dash for the gay disco where they serve a "Sunday night supper" for $1 (beef stew, rice, string beans—delicious) and free marshmallows are toasted over a bed of coals and there's a heated bar for Oldies. One figure in dark glasses, slumped among millionairesses, could have gone ungreeted—but not by Our David: "Tennessee! Jimmy's over there!" So I had to go over and sit between him and somebody named Texas Kate who owns Schweppes, and promise to read the poems he's been writing. Peter Taylor then tried to make friends but TW is so far gone, so egocentric and therefore so bored, that the name meant nothing—just as his own will in another ten years.

The house is really a joy. You have to see the big back room to understand. DK and I imagine you and David driving down together one of these years! I have a large room cleverly made into two by a 7 foot high bookcase—all made of lovely white boards laid horizontally, into which picture hooks and thumbtacks sink easily and don't come loose. Ceiling fans everywhere. The climate reminds me of May or early Oct. in Stonington, brisk, dry, brilliant—except during cloud-bursts of course. Two blocks away, an excellent fishmarket: yellow-tail, kingfish, grouper, crawfish, shrimp. And there you are at Duval St with a good half dozen "elements" to choose from, not unlike the fishmarket: hippie, polyester, macho biker, local black, faggot, Cuban—but turn a corner and they vanish, and you're walking back home past gingerbread houses and astounding banyans.

The day must be drawing near when Grace can be moved home. I think about her twenty times a day, viscerally almost, as if Body English over the miles would make her strong as well. Should there ever develop any financial pinch—I know she broods about this but you seemed to think things were all right for the present—I hope you'll turn to me knowing I'd want to help. You might comfort yourself meanwhile by thinking about using 72nd St next winter (Jan. through March) if Main St is under control; I'll keep it open for you.

Write us all the news!

Love always,
J.

To Robert and Charlotte Arner   POSTCARD | WUSTL
11 January 1980
702 Elizabeth St., Key West, Fla., 33040

Dear Bob and Charlotte,

Your vegetarian card reaches us down here—I was going blind read-ing page proofs up North, and D was going mad with carpenters and garden people down here, so we sent none. He's bought a house at the above address [*in the margin*: Athens is being phased out], small but roomy, with a pool, and everything on one floor; so we are now prepared for the sunset years—and the sunsets are staggering. Hundreds of implausibly garbed young people burst into applause on the docks every afternoon ("Let's hear it for the sun!"). It's my first Florida winter since 1937 and I'm ecstatic. As I must come North after early March (after Geburstag here among floating hibiscus) I'll see some snow. A book will go off to you soon thereafter to conclude my massive work which has made such a hermit of me since January 1974. Strange to be out in the world again; one benefit is to see dear ones too long eclipsed—let's <u>us</u> see each other in May or June (April I must spend in Calif.). Very heartening to know you're together.

Love from both.

J.

postcard On the front, a photo of a grouper in a Key Largo reef. Merrill circles the fish's name and writes "<u>perfect</u> for sashimi."
page proofs For *Scripts for the Pageant* (1980).
"Let's hear it . . ." See Merrill's poem "Clearing the Title" in *Late Settings* (1985).
my first Florida winter since 1937 The winter before his parents divorced. But he had been to Florida in the winter for short visits many times since then.

To David Kalstone

Dear distant One,

The Boats' Memorial Day party for DJ is about to commence—a perfect sparkling afternoon, dry, cool, and both of us atingle from a <u>two</u>-hour Weedj (of which more presently). I hope you are at least half as happy to be in Venice as we are to be here, and that Venice itself looks almost as pretty. The days in NYC were predictably frantic after your departure, but really great fun thanks to having Casa Tua to repair to—DJ I'm afraid felt his style a wee bit cramped in the 72nd St. maid's room. S and I loved seeing the P. Brook Bird play. Ed gave us wine and some yum smoked Swiss meat beforehand, then we took him to Duff's. Monday Stephen spent in a tizzy of for once quite justified apprehension—he had lunched on Sunday ah! so happily with

Lorna (the ex-wife and subject of practically every poem he's written since she walked out on him in 1971) at the insidiously named Nirvana on CPSouth: at last they were on good terms. I had a faint misgiving about his reading all those poems with her and some of their old friends in the audience, but he said she'd "seen" most of them . . . seen but not fully taken in. By the end of the program she was a wreck of rage and hysteria, the "friends" said goodbye with glaring formality, and S was left (with divine One, of course) asking himself where he'd gone wrong. I tried to make him see that this was, for him, like losing the mss. of the novel for me; since his male vanity forbade him to be on bad terms or no terms at all with an ex-love, and since the poet in him was enslaved to this numbing, no longer rewarding subject-matter, some kind of showdown had to be arranged. At least one could pretend it was all as simple as that. Judy <u>ecstatic</u> over her grant. They (S and J) had lunch and most of the afternoon together the next day—chattering away like young lovers—after a morning trip to the Met. (Flash-forward to the Inst. luncheon: Leon Edel's lady-friend from last year came up, reintroduced herself and said: "<u>We</u> were at the Met yesterday morning too. No, I didn't see you, but I heard your <u>beautiful</u> <u>voice</u> and said, That <u>has</u> to be JM.") Tues. evening, the Kenyon reading: Walcott, the Hechts, Mr Doctorow, obsequious Philip Schultz, Judy, the Taylors (they'll go anywhere, to anything), the Fords (who slipped out without saying hello, as if they were Guermantes), <u>odd</u> Fred Turner and FAT Ron Sharp. Dinner beforehand at the Minetta Tavern, after which DJ darted off to the rival reading (Ed's). At the party afterwards Stephen at last got through to Lorna who hadn't been answering her phone all day, and got his ear nicely charred—then we walked to 22nd St and drank your Kriter and declared our chaste and boundless love for one another with many a crust-dry kiss; and then it was morning and off we separately went, leaving not too much of a mess for Patrick I hope. (I've spoken to him, he's all primed for his briefing from John Myers.) I'll leave the luncheon for DJ to describe. It's Party Time! Sandy and Alfred are coming up, and the table's laid for a spaghetti all'aglio and fruit din.

Tuesday. Party sheer heaven. M*a*r*k served. He's started smoking again after 11 years, so I've asked him to come up some evening and (m) "listen to my cassette." Grace and Isabel in rival chairs. The

Potters, both their sons and daughters-in-law, the Thatchers with-out Anne (Heard about her rape? DJ, you tell him), the Wimpfs—everybody in short. DJ naively beforehand: It'll be over, what, around 9:30? We were home at 8:15 hearing all about the Hollanders' party for Martha's graduation. Anne was there, too gorgeous for words at the side of her daughter—while Natalie kept her distance at the side of her dainty little mother.

Today a man from *Newsweek* is coming up to interview—where will it end? Mirabell says never, and has given us the first of 5 lessons on THE WORLD OR THE BIG BUFFET or LET IT (the world) COME IN, AND WHEN NOT TO BE THERE TO GREET IT or: HOW TO AVOID POISONOUS FATTY JUNK FOODS such as LUNATIC FRINGERS, SCEPTICS and IMITATORS. He says we must get a private telephone, keeping our old number hooked up to a squawk box like yours (". . . I'll call you back. If you're a stranger would you mind saying why you're calling?")—and get a local secretary, and have the bank pay the bills. We're thrilled and eager to comply. In the audi-ence at Amherst was a shy premedical student named Ralph whom I'll meet in a few years through David Merrill (the union organizer) and who will, as a raging anarchist 12 years hence, play a protective role in my life—more thrills! Finally Michael at his grandest and grav-est took over and said that with these radical forthcoming changes in the world YOUR TEXTS WILL BECOME SCRIPTURE TO MORE THAN WE HAD ANTICIPATED . . . FORGIVE US COMING NOW WITH THIS LARGE BILL TO BE PAID. THERE WILL BE REWARDS, THE EVILS OF OLD AGE WILL BE LIGHTENED BY THE VERY BURDENS OF FAME LAID ON YOU. ABOVE ALL RESIST DESPISING THE WORLD. ITS DESSERTS ARE MEA-GRE, YOUR SWEET NATURES AMPLE IF RATIONED, OUR LOVE A BOUNDLESS (au?) RESERVOIR.

So don't mention the extra telephone to anyone when we get round to it—less than 10 people will have the number: my mother and brother, Y*O*U, Harry F, DMc, and Peter T. I'll leave the rest of this page for DJ. Longing to have novità. Abbraciamenti caldissimi a te ed a Giuliano. Velvet paws!

xxx

J.

the P. Brook Bird play Peter Brook's production of *The Conference of the Birds* at La MaMa.
Ed Edmund White.
his reading Yenser had read with others at the 92nd Street YMHA.
Walcott, et al., Derek Walcott (1930–2017), Santa Lucian poet and playwright; E. L. Doctorow (1931–2015), American novelist; Philip Schultz (b. 1945), American poet; Judy: Judy Moffett; the Taylors: Peter Taylor (1917–94), American short story writer and novelist, and his wife Eleanor Ross Taylor (1920–2011), American poet; the Fords: Harry Ford and his wife Kathleen Ford; Fred Turner: Frederick Turner (b. 1943), American poet and editor of *The Kenyon Review;* Ron Sharp: Ronald A. Sharp, American academic, literary critic, and Acting President of Kenyon College.
22nd St Location of Kalstone's apartment.
Patrick Patrick Merla, American writer and editor, prominent in the early promotion of gay literature, who was to stay in Kalstone's apartment; later secretary of the Ingram Merrill Foundation and assistant to Merrill.
M*a*r*k Mark Strand (1934–2014), American poet.
(m) For "metaphor."
Martha Martha Hollander (b. 1959), who graduated from Yale in 1980.
Anne John and Anne Hollander divorced in 1977.
Natalie Natalie Charkow, American sculptor, who married John Hollander in 1981.

To Claude Fredericks

GETTY
23 October 1980
[Stonington, CT]

Dearest Claude—

I'm just back from the South, Atlanta and Key West, and your birthday has slipped past. Only without a sign from me because everything was driven from my head by an unexpected toothache, which in turn led to 21 unexpected hours at my mother's dentist and the founding, at their end, of a little dynasty of crowns on the upper left side of my mouth—just about where the Opera Club used to be as you faced the stage in the old Met. It didn't end there, though—I reached Key West only to have the same terrible pain come back, and another dentist said I had an abcess, and gave me penicillin and pain-killers; a third dentist up here said THAT TOOTH MUST GO! with the result that tomorrow Dentist Number 4 will forcibly remove the tiny backmost monarch—less than nine days a Queen!—and I will have a glamorous hollow in my old cheek and no more pain for a while I hope. I hope too that your celebrations were unclouded by anything of the sort. MANY HAPPY RETURNS!

My mother has sold her house and bought an only proportionately smaller condominium a few blocks away. So I spent as much time as I could helping her decide what to keep ("You'll be grateful to me for getting rid of all these things <u>now</u>")—which meant I'm afraid that boxes of my letters to her are presently lying about this house unopened. The few I looked at—from ages 7 or 8—gave me a turn, I must say. For instance, "Thank you for always being so kind to me." Does one say that to anyone but a jailor? (Meanwhile I was writing passionate ones to Mademoiselle: "I want you for my Mother.") Also, a document reveals that she's 2 years older than I thought: 82. Knowing which, I see clearer than ever those pitiful yet blessed signs of decline, uncertainty, fatigue—and my heart can go out to her as never before, knowing there can't be more than—dear God? FIFTEEN more years?

And now there's the Fall to look ahead to. I'm reading in New Haven next week, in Montreal (where I've never been) in November, Chicago in early December, and finally H*O*U*S*T*O*N. <u>Everybody</u> is going to be there, not just DK and Sandy and Stephen Yenser but, oh, John Hollander and Rachel Hadas and Ed White. Now don't you get cold feet and decide to stay in the East. Some of us—practically a charter flight—are arriving Dec 27 in the late afternoon. I have to read the following evening, and the "session" on me is the next morning (all this at the Hyatt Regency where I presume we'll all be staying). DK and I fly to Key West on the 30th. Perhaps on the 28th or 29th I could slip off for a little lunch with you and Vira? I'd love to see her—it's been so long. Well, there are weeks and weeks to plan it.

These days I'm at last typing up the summer transcripts, and will send you and David yours in due time. Right now I'm groggy from a beer and red cabbage on top of my penicillin and aspirin—and leave you with a sloppy kiss.

Ever,
Jamey

H*O*U*S*T*O*N The site in 1981 of the Modern Language Association conference, which included a panel about Merrill's work.
Vira Fredericks's mother, who lived in Houston.
the summer transcripts Dictations from the Ouija board.

To Robert Arner

WUSTL
19 January 1981
Key West, FL

Dear Bob,

I'd had an idea we could have given you a small award without putting you through the trouble of applying. Our lawyer says no—this only works in the case of "well-known figures." But others on the committee have seen at least your pictures in Stonington + are well disposed. Can you get this application to us by March 1st? It would help if one or two people wrote for you (this for our files mainly). These letters needn't be exhaustive [*in the margin:* perhaps a dozen or so slides, too?]. I'd suggest that you ask for 5 to 8 thousand at most, as we operate on a smallish scale.

Key West is glacial. We can sit bundled up in a sunny corner (like shipboard elevenses) but no question of a dip in the pool. What a swindle!

Here's love from us both to you + Charlotte.

Ever,

Jimmy

P.S. Mail application direct to: Harry Ford, C⁄o Atheneum, 597 Fifth Ave, NYC 10017

Mail application The Ingram Merrill Foundation gave Arner a grant for $8,000 in 1981.

To Kimon Friar

WUSTL
4 February 1981
Key West, FL

Dear Kimon,

The mails are really terrible. Your January 8th letter reached me only two days ago—forwarded from Stonington, it's true (as I surely wrote you, I'm here until March 20) but even so . . . A second letter (Jan 16) came yesterday. Both very welcome. And the points you raise are often crucial, though (to me) of less weight than your general approval. I'm glad that you felt the joy in Vol III. At the time it seemed that our hearts would break with it—or with the cumulative beauty of the transcripts and their implications. Of course I recall the passage where Odysseus blesses his senses—one of the more startling connections between our two poems.

Let me try to answer your questions about *Ephraim*. The initial letters it is true, do not spell out a message, but neither are they all as random as they appear. Section H (beginning "High . . .") is about the experience of hypnosis. Section I (beginning "I . . .") is about my chat with my psychiatrist, the ego in danger, or whatever. Section T ("The . . .") is the one in which Time speaks. W has the meeting with Wendell. I took care, perhaps mistakenly, to avoid this relentless relevance in every case. *Ephraim* wasn't written in sequence. After the first hour in which I'd made a few notes for each letter of the alphabet—a scheme I kept before me throughout the year of writing—I began with A and B, then jumped to V(enice), then N (the novel) and F, and so forth. Y and Z were the last to be composed, however. I saw no reason to put everyone's name in the Dramatis Personae—which I call a "partial list." An illusion of thoroughness at that stage seemed sufficient.

The patrons see their reps. through every important experience— birth and death and also unforeseeable emergencies. They are indispensable for the great mass of humanity—less so for the "Lab souls." See *Mirabell* p 51. "Prole" (a slang derivation, by Orwell I think, from "proletarian")—Wystan in heaven assumes a young "ideal" appearance, evidently featuring a more muscular build than he had on Earth. The woman in Maya's dream is simply the former tenant of her apartment. Maya died of a stroke—I was not at her side, but we heard details from others. I did visit Hans 10 days before he died, in Lausanne, summer 1950. Farmetton is JM's previous incarnation. RF lived in South Africa, was in love with Peter, whose aunt Hedwig perhaps made trouble. JM says "my" in this passage speaking of himself as Rufus [*in the margin:* so it's Rufus that "I" see in the mirror]. I've made some changes here, for clarity, which will be in the complete edition. Ghédé is the Haitian god of the dead; I'd hoped the title of Maya's book would help a reader understand that he's a god. Gopping is a place name. This particular baby is given no name in the poem; soon dies; is reborn as Virginia West's baby (DJ's belated realization is that the mother <u>he</u>'d had in mind isn't named Virginia at all); and eventually as Wendell. I ought (I fancy) to have recognized in Wendell's eyes the influence of his patron, Ephraim. Nana is CM's mother. No I'd forgotten the dragon-mother in *F6*. Sergei is probably a projection of myself as an old man. He loves Leo but (perforce) without consummation. He's based on the character of Ken in "The Summer People" (in *The Fire Screen;* "The Will" by the way can be found right there in *Divine Comedies*). I had a clear enough groundplan for the lost novel, without entirely knowing how it wd work itself out. The pueblo, landscape etc are local color. Leo and the other soldiers either tortured or raped the adolescent spy in Vietnam. Mrs Smith is more complicated. She is an early version of Nature in the trilogy— the "woman of the world" on the last page of *Ephraim*, and her withdrawal from Sergei's life, leaving him a house and an income, while <u>she</u> goes off to Venice and a titled husband, I privately feel foreshadows the sudden "distancing" of Maria when she is revealed as one of Plato's many incarnations. I'll bring you this spring a wonderful 30 page essay by an ex-student, Stephen Yenser, which says nearly everything I can imagine worth saying about *Ephraim*. I must confess that I didn't especially want clarity in handling the lost novel etc—rather a kind of cubist abstraction of a novel, enough to "represent" a volume of life, and its rendering into language. This is the residual poison of my long infatuation with the likes of Mallarmé, and no doubt less appropriate in a long poem than in a tiny lyric. Still . . . As I say at the start of *Mirabell* I <u>never</u> imagined the poem would turn into a trilogy. I thought it had ended with *Ephraim*. Yes, we don't see the spirits; they see us in reflecting surfaces. I'll bring you the 2 books you're missing. I should get to Athens in the first 10 days of May.

Yes, that's old John Myers. He's been our (increasingly inefficient) sec'y for over 20 years now. Poor dear, he had cancer of the bladder 4 years ago, but after chemotherapy was very hopeful until just last month they found something else and had to remove a kidney. I think your grant is taxable—alas. I'd better stop. It's cold down here but today the sun is out and so shall I be five minutes hence. David was so pleased by what you wrote about his part in it all. Any books you send should always go to S'ton where I'll be sure to find them sooner or later. I'm afraid much of this is hasty and off the top of my mind—enough.

Love,
Jimmy

Odysseus blesses his senses In Friar's translation of Kazantzakis's *Odyssey.*
Maya's book *Divine Horsemen: The Voodoo Gods of Haiti* (1953).
F6 *The Ascent of F6: A Tragedy in Two Acts* by W. H. Auden and Christopher Isherwood.
30 page essay Published in *Canto* magazine, much of it eventually incorporated in Yenser's annotated edition of *The Book of Ephraim* (2018).
our . . . sec'y Secretary of the Ingram Merrill Foundation.

To J. D. McClatchy

YALE
25 February 1981
[Stonington, CT]

Dearest S—

What a link you are with the real world. Thank you for the piece on Irving, the Dante clipping, and more than I can ever hope to say for all your trouble in the matter of these tapes. Check enclosed for them and the gr*ss. God the parties. To go one afternoon to the Wilburs' bash at a smart new beachfront club (3 barmen, lobster-brandy-and-cream dip kept hot over a gemlike flame, Tennessee looking Grace straight into her unseeing eyes and declaring: "I think you are a very great lady") and the next evening to dinner at Alison's (prepared by Ted: egg salad with peanuts in it, garnished with crisp bacon and accompanied by two breads, all followed by an Entenmann coffee-cake, DJ murmuring "I hadn't realized you wanted us for breakfast") gives you some sense of the range. Our next regime is scheduled for March 10, just after the last foreseeable party.

Judy—I dread seeing that piece. I've been trying to tell her for some time that she's making a huge mistake in every quarter of her life by sweeping her real motives under the carpet. That whole business of her mother and father not knowing that she's ever published a book! Secretly of course she wants them to find out, and have it be a humiliation for them, made infinitely greater by the deception. She's really Oedipus in Scene I. But I fear that by the day the earth opens at Colonus it will simply be a bargain basement to which she descends. Basta. Here's my "latest"—it's sort of about her.

STREETLAMP

By day unlit, the magic helmet keeping
Its lord invisible, now at dusk leaps forth,
Air darkens round, less after all (despite
Ambit and atomies magnesium-bright)
A person than a presence of sheer mind
Which, in itself however logical,
Brought once more to bear upon the scene—
Glassglint, palmetto, crabgrass between cracks,
And, glowering feebly at its pale, five shacks—
Arrays our poor old crossroads in a dread
Exceeding dark's own. This discourager
Alike of stealth and star has come to do
By night. The dog it dusts asleep or dead.
Wings battering the naught it makes to shine.

¡Viva Mexico!

Much love to you and A from both—
J.

Irving Irving Lavin.
hot over a gemlike flame Allusion to Walter Pater's "to burn always with this hard, gemlike flame" in the "Conclusion" to *The Renaissance: Studies in Art and Poetry*.
Ted Edward Hower (b. 1941), American writer, Alison Lurie's second husband.
next regime Merrill and Jackson periodically stopped drinking and smoking.
that piece See letter to Moffett, 18 February 1979.
Streetlamp A slightly revised version appears as "Arclight" in *Late Settings* (1985).

To Robert Isaacson   MORGAN LIBRARY
                                        3 January 1982
                                        [Athens, Greece]

Dear Robert,

I meant to call you at the time, but one thing or another kept putting
me off. Maybe you've heard by now: Umberto died. On November
5th, at home. The news reached Stonington (in a packet of clippings
sent to Grace from Rome) about 3 weeks later. It had remained for
the servants to put a black-edged announcement in the papers—la
famiglia Vincioni, which I assume to be Mario's name; at least I wrote
a little letter addressed that way. The other clippings were a couple
of memorials or evocations or whatever, touching the high points,
the friendship with BB, the family connections, the end-of-war
adventure, and on what it was like to be received at Metelliano . . .
He was 84. I think I told you that I spent a night there in early May.
He seemed fine, ate heartily, talked wonderfully. Then in June, when
I called from Venice, he was in hospital after collapsing from some
kind of abdominal haemorrhage. In July and August I received three
identical letters from him—a typed page and 2 carbons, sent vari-
ously to Stonington, Athens, and Key West—asking for information
about Helen Vendler. Someone had sent him the review of her book,
clipped from Barbara's rag, and he wanted a copy. There had been,
he explained, a Frau Vendler who looked after him for a few years
when he was little—a Czech, he thought—and he wondered if by any
chance there might be a connection. I wrote telling him that Vendler
was Helen's married name, and suggested that he phone David Kal-
stone in Venice, since D had actually known the husband, for fur-
ther info. In <u>early</u> <u>December</u> a final letter arrived from Umberto
(mailed late Sept.)—a scrawl thanking me for HV's book, saying he
was "improving slowly", and asking how he could reach my "friend
in Padova" for information as to Vendler's origins. Do you remem-
ber, from the Painter biography how Proust hallucinates, in the days
before he dies, a severe, rather terrible woman, all in black at his bed-
side? Let's hope this Frau Vendler was a kinder figure, for I fancy she
must have been the Angel of our old friend's death—to judge by his

obsession with her during these last months. Well. I wanted to tell you all this as carefully as I could. He was a father we shared.

Glorious hot weather down here, plus our usual nest of singing nerds. I'm staying till the last week of March. Happy 1982 and much love to you and JD from DJ and

Jimmy

Mario Umberto Morra's longtime butler.
BB Bernard Berenson.
the end-of-war adventure Merrill gives a version of it in his poem "Bronze" in *Late Settings* (1985).
Metalliano Italian village in the province of Arezzo in Tuscany, site of Morra's villa.
review of her book . . . Barbara's rag "The Powers of Sympathy," Irvin Ehrenpreis's review of Vendler's *Part of Nature, Part of Us: Modern American Poets* in *The New York Review of Books* (May 29, 1980), where Barbara Epstein was one of the editors.
the Painter biography George D. Painter, *Marcel Proust: A Biography* (vol. 1, 1959; vol. 2, 1965).
JD James Draper.

To Stephen Yenser   YALE
                                                   6 May 1982
                                              [Stonington, CT]

Dear Stephen,

How good to have your letter—and the floor plan: now I can follow you around. Obviously that apricot tree just hated Mme Boy and her flocked wallpaper. Either that or QM has spoken to it. I long to see the place in three dimensions. We've been putting out some flowers on the deck—a rose-bush, white impatiens, a salmony begonia (in memory of the American lady in Italy, poking her gardener at work on the borders: "Bisogna bigonia!") and some hanging geraniums, one in its 3rd year. You'll have gathered that DJ's back, green thumb and all, having had a rather good time, and looking well.

Friday before last DK and I drove John Ashbery up to his house in Hudson (NY)—a staggering belle époche affair set on a small lot and right on Courthouse Square. You've never seen so much golden oak and stained glass, so many pantries and cupboards. His dining table (came with the house) makes yours look like something one unfolds for a TV dinner. Not that we dined off his. He gave us a drink, himself abstaining, and out we dashed to a Swiss restaurant. Home rather late, but JA wanted to try the Board. Little came through, mainly the alphabet, and at one point, rather feebly: JA KNOWS. Next morning David Kermani's tires were found slashed, not ours luckily, and off we went with John to Vassar for EB day. Lovely weather. About 80 people for lunch at the President's house: Rollie, Brinnin, Moss, U.T. Summers, John Myers (who'd been invited to the ceremony but decided to crash the lunch with Arthur anyhow). We took a quick look at a little exhibit in the library—photographs, notebooks, EB's battered old primer, its cover stamped with a shield largely filled by "an enormous fish" (herring)—then sat on a hot platform under the still shadeless trees for readings and talks. I have a poster I'll send you one of these days. An hour's nap at Alumnae House, then back to La Presidentessa for dinner. Guest-list drastically mutilated by Alice. Poor U.T. had to eat in a restaurant—bad judgement, considering that she has (as she pointed out) some 80 letters from Elizabeth. Flashbulbs and undergraduate gospel singers before we sat down, Founder's Day fireworks we all ran out to see between courses. I sat next to Nancy Milford (author of *Zelda*—why was she there?) and the unamuseable librarian hired not long before to tend the hoard. We were in NY around noon the next day—just time for some errands and a quiet dinner (DK, Sandy and Alfred, and Brad Leithauser) to fortify us for the next day's party given by Maxine Groffsky for Balanchine's star, Suzanne Farrell. Very glamorous, both the party and Miss F—though I fear most of "us" didn't know what to say to her (as she perfectly realized: she told Bobby Fizdale, "These people seem to think I can't talk."). By 9 your tireless chronicler was on his stool backstage at The Little Players' final NY performance. They're moving home to Ohio. Not a dry eye in the house. June 16 they'll be on TV—quite a wonderful film you must try not to miss (PBS or whatever, cross-country). That same day John Ashbery (whom we'd not seen since Vassar) had a pain in his neck which got so bad by Thursday that he went into hospital. Friday he was in a coma, and saved only by a lot of quick thinking. It turned out to be a staph infection which had caused a huge abscess on his spinal column. He's still in intensive care, but out of the respirator, and David Kermani sounded optimistic. You can imagine what resonance that Ouija message has taken on, in some quarters. I got the feeling from Kermani that he doesn't want this talked about until the outcome is more positive, so Discretion. Well, I feel debriefed though wondering, just now, what's duller than a newsy letter. Oh, one nice touch. DK and I, both awake and groaning in the guestroom at Hudson, had the following exchange—JM: If this were only tomorrow we could just tiptoe downstairs and drive back to NY. DK: Why don't we anyhow? Elizabeth would have! Our love to you and Mary.

Yours ever,
James

Mme Boy Yenser and his wife Mary Bomba, helped by a loan from Merrill, had just bought a house in Los Angeles previously owned by a Swiss woman named Boy de la Tour, which had flocked wallpaper in two rooms and an apricot tree that had borne fruit for the first time in years.
QM According to the Ouija board, the goddess Nature/Psyche/Chaos, also known as Queen Mother.
Bisogna bigonia! You need begonia!
David Kermani John Ashbery's partner and later his husband.
"an enormous fish" Merrill quotes Bishop's poem "The Fish."
Brad Leithauser (b. 1953), American poet and literary critic.
Maxine Groffsky Literary agent, and Paris editor of *The Paris Review* during the George Plimpton era.

To Samuel Lock

WUSTL
19 August 1982
[Stonington, CT]

Dear Samuel—

Here is your 2nd card (a six-horse village sounds like perfection) and I'm covered with shame for my months of silence. Let me quickly reassure you that all is well—if "well" can also mean . . . (here should follow a half dozen adjectives that don't present themselves to me, this lovely clear morning, while the radio's Brahms sextet and Mrs

Woodrow's vacuum cleaner fight it out two rooms away). We've seen too many people, as usual. Also it's been a very frustrating season with my publisher. The 2 volumes were scheduled for May, then July, now—November? Little wavelets of proof come in at absurdly long intervals. I must keep reminding myself how lucky we are to have found a printer at all, since for a while it seemed that the original typeface had followed the printer of the last 3 books into retirement. Well, enough of that—except that I've spent all spring + summer on tenterhooks, to no particular avail. We had one magical evening at the kabuki in New York. Various "living national treasures" starred in the plays, and a hamamichi (that ramp on which actors enter + leave through the audience) had been constructed, and Faubion Bowers translated discreetly over the earphones. The texts themselves are poor stuff,—homily, farce, melodrama—but that could easily be the point, just as the scenery looks like nothing so much as painted flats. Yet it is against this scenery and out of this unsubtle language that, in each play, an extraordinary thing happens: musicians change positions, the central character(s) sheds a layer of clothing, reappears with new + frightening make-up. What had been mere linear "talk" in "action" now becomes a cat's cradle of howls + poses struck, or dance-figures reiterated. One could imagine *Oedipus Rex* staged this way, or *Lear*. The actors constantly manage to move like puppets— but puppets of themselves, not manipulated by "the gods"—well, it's very exciting to watch. My Greek friend Manoli spent all of July here. His obsession this year is jogging; we spent hours retracing the day's course in the car, and turning miles into kilometers on my pocket calculator. I suspect he hopes to become a living National Treasure, and perhaps he will if places high enough in the "over forty" category (which he enters 5 years hence) of the Marathon. I also spent a week in Santa Fe, staying with the friend who traveled with me to Italy + Istanbul last year, and seeing as much as I could of an old friend now in torture—she's losing her skin, it flakes away day + night—but still a fount of high spirits. It's a landscape for which I thirst: high, parched, dazzled, and always a relief to come home from, like recovering from a fit of "inspiration".

We're going to Montreal for a week in early September—+ will see Christian of course (assuming he's there—the phone didn't answer last Sunday). David's never been. I loved it 2 years ago. Now I must start writing postcards to alert those whose hospitality we have designs on—I hope this finds you + Adrian refreshed + at work.

All love to you both—
James

Samuel Lock (1926–2016), British novelist and playwright, partner of painter Adrien de Menasce (1925–95), who was a member of the Alexandrian group of friends that included Tony Parigory, Christian Ayoub Sinano, and Bernard de Zogheb.
Faubion Bowers (1917–99), an aide-de-camp for General Douglas MacArthur during the Allied occupation of Japan, became a scholar of Japanese theater, especially Kabuki, and wrote the definitive biography of the Russian composer Alexander Scriabin.
Christian Christian Ayoub Sinano.

To Samuel Lock

WUSTL
4 February 1983
Key West, Fl

Dear Samuel,

Your account of that party! Actually it's been so long since the days when I stayed up willingly beyond midnight, or even eleven o'clock, that given the choice between attending the party and reading your description of it, I wouldn't hesitate to pick the latter. Its being a party that you didn't go to either, gives it a doubly remote beauty, a reflection seen in a second mirror; whereas at the function itself your shoe might have pinched or the lobster salad disagreed with me—wonderful to be spared all that! In the terms of your analogy, of course, those pains become the very ones I cherish, even as their memory fades, when I try to relive my spells of working on the long poem. All I know is that it was the single most thrilling episode in my life, and I'm very touched by the magical image you found to explain, somehow, its effect upon us both.

Our winter has been most peculiar so far. I had to go North for ten days last month, where it was mild and bright as Springtime. On my return the Miami–Key West plane couldn't land: fog and rain sent us back to the mainland for a "complimentary" night in a nasty motel. And as soon as we flew in the next morning the skies opened and <u>22</u> inches of rain fell in that single weekend. Something of the sort happens every few days. I must be an optimist because I always expect rain to clear up and bright days to repeat themselves forever. Yesterday was perfect, dry and blazingly cool. As I bicycled down Duval St. what should I see but a little green parrot—untethered, "free as a bird"—perched atop one of the benches (those same benches Christian likes to hold court from, all night long sometimes). A shopkeeper emerged as I watched, and proceeded to give the parrot a mist-bath with an atomizer: one very pleased parrot, even from half a block away.

We've clearly reached a certain age—the grand events of the season have been on TV. They showed what we <u>had</u> gone to see last fall in NY, a glorious *Idomeneo*, and in the same week the *Rheingold* of that famous, rather Marxist production of the *Ring* that they've only now withdrawn from Bayreuth, with gods like decadent magnates out of *Buddenbrooks* and a passionately lyrical Alberich in a sleazy business suit. You must be used to such treats, but over here they're few and far between. Meanwhile the usual writers have gathered, and we give or go to parties whose purpose, if not their settings, might as well be draped in cobwebs. A line is being drawn with ever greater clarity between those who "write" and those who use word-processors; only the most naive hostess still fancies that the two camps will enjoy each other's company. I'm secretly curious to see one of the w-ps at work. If a single button can change "Millicent" to "Emily" on every page of a long manuscript, why couldn't another change Millicent's age, say, from 21 to 79, so that automatically "peach-petal" would become "wrinkled" and "glided" to "hobbled", and so on through all the details of background (Paris landmarks replaced by those of Pittsburgh) and plot (spy ring to football team)? Hackwork without tears. The temperature has dropped 15 degrees since I began this letter. Time to bundle up and pour a drink. David joins in fondest wishes to you and Adrian.

Ever,
James

Idomeneo Mozart opera.
Marxist production of the *Ring* Patrice Chéreau's controversial 1976 production of Wagner's four-opera *Der Ring des Nibelungen,* conducted by Pierre Boulez and celebrating the centenary of the Bayreuth Festival, was captured live on video in 1980 and telecast by PBS in seven installments over six months in 1983.
Buddenbrooks Novel by Thomas Mann (1875–1955).

To Samuel Lock

WUSTL
22 February 1983
Key West, FL

Samuel—

I'm writing in the euphoria of having finished answering all the letters accumulating since last Fall: a clean desk ready to receive today's mail. And here is your card with its dulcet impeachment—oh dear, I <u>am</u> sorry. But the truth is sorrier yet: I seem unable to advise anyone as to getting their poems published in this country. I had a letter a few weeks back from a poet's <u>wife</u> asking me please to read his work and do something about it because (she went on) "a word from you to a New York publisher . . ." She is dead bang wrong, la pauvre. It's true, 2 or 3 times in the past years, I've written a note on behalf of this or that younger poet whom I admire very much. But nothing has ever come of it beyond months of expectancy followed by a polite rejection. There are smaller presses, to be sure, but these are (a) regional affairs specializing in the frogs of that particular pond, or (b) in it for the money, and printing deluxe pamphlets by established people, which they can then sell for $60 or $100 apiece. So I remain at a loss. True, a position of Power has lately been offered me—the judgeship of the Yale Younger Poets—thanks to which I can select the only one of those abovementioned 3 I admire who is still under 40. But it seems as if poetry were harder now to publish than ever before in my memory at least. It's even hard to get in the magazines, those with more than a circulation of 500 copies. Atheneum, I meant to say earlier, hasn't added to its poetry list in, oh, fifteen years. Harry Ford simply shudders when the question comes up. So now you see why I "forgot" to respond to your inquiry.

The sun came out today after another long spell of clouds and torrents. The lizards are now fullgrown, striking attitudes with scarlet throat outpuffed on the ramparts of brick around the petunia bed; you'd think these were the walls of Troy. And we have a pair of zebra butterflies, yellow stripes on black, whose flutterings could probably bring on an epileptic fit in the right person. Three Sapphic friends from Montreal have arrived and want to be taken to the dog track tonight. I wish we were going to see Adrian's hats instead. This in haste.

But with love to you both from D and
J.

To Alice Notley

7 July 1983
Stonington, CT

Dear Alice Notley—

Word just now reaches me (from Jane Freilicher via John Myers) of your great misfortune. Please accept this check, and with it all my sympathy.

Sincerely,
James Merrill

Alice Notley (b. 1945), American poet.
Jane Freilicher (1924–2014), American painter associated with the New York school of poets and painters.
great misfortune The death of Notley's husband, the poet Ted Berrigan (1934–83), occurred the day before this note was sent.

To David Tacium

NYPL

28 November 1983
[Stonington, CT]

Dear David,

Your letter made it here in only 5 days, and this unseemly prompt response is due to my leaving tomorrow morning for NYC—I'll be back here barely long enough to have my teeth cleaned and flash a goodbye smile to Grace and Eleanor before heading for KW on the 15th. I can't recall at exactly what point on the cliff of my narrative I left you hanging, but things (as they usually do) have eased up a good deal since then. After all our respective ages, Peter's and mine, will total a century sometime in mid-January and with all the good will and affection in the world there's a limit to what 2 people can ask of one another at that great age.

Far more interesting is your new attachment. Odd how you manage to make yourself, over and over, sound like the young men in 19th century novels. That must be part of the fun. Of course in <u>this</u> century it's a touch harder to drive the Older Woman to suicide or to "ruin" the ingénue—but I did feel, for the length of several sentences, that I was back in *Les Liaisons Dangereuses*. I hope it's keeping you off the streets—or more exactly, off the Mountain. When Daryl told me about <u>that</u>, I shook my old head. For purely medical reasons, believe me. Promiscuity has been my tried and true friend for long spells, but now there is this new Disease, and until they've found a cure for it everyone who's not suicidal will have to be very very careful, not to say monogamous. The symptoms don't show up for two years, after which your chances of living more than another two are slimissimi. Anything you've heard to the contrary is wishful thinking, according to the gay doctors we've heard on the subject. Even a lovely wet kiss may do the trick . . . <u>in</u>. And the cases keep doubling each year. So when, borne up on the endocrine wave, your eyes brim over as you tell Sylvie "Belle âme, c'est toi qui me sauveras de moi-même," you will be stating—of all things!—the simple truth.

Well, I've been all over the country, seen cowboy ballroom-dancing in Dallas, and Tony Hecht mastering ceremonies in the Capital. The days with Daryl were divinely restful and fun. The dog, entre nous, couldn't be more "me." I read great swatches of the new poem, with even more pleasure than I'd anticipated. Will came to dinner one night—we played bridge afterwards, for which W showed considerable talent, while poor Daryl simply (and why not, given his nature) went down. He (Daryl) is one of the entirely adorable souls on earth, and I'd have gone on to say if only he could do some serious teaching— except that he called 2 days ago thrilled by an offer from his "enemy" Mary Kinzie to take a prosody course this spring at Northwestern. This may lead to a 2nd course and he's overjoyed as you can imagine.

I've had a series of colds and am only up and dressed today for the first time since Friday—3 days in bed with the phone unplugged, "weak as a flower" as old Eddy Gathorne-Hardy loved to say, and listening to *The Bartered Bride*, surely the sweetest and sanest opera since *Figaros Hochzeit*. The NY calendar has filled up hideously meanwhile—nothing that can't be canceled if I enjoy a relapse—but it looks unlikely that we'll see each other before next year. Or will you come to Key West under Christian's partridge wing? I gather you think everyone's down on you. This isn't true (Daryl isn't and I'm not, to begin with) but if it <u>were</u> you'd need only to bear in mind that even the fogeys at the top of the heap like to be asked after and (if the occasion arises) thanked. It didn't escape DK's gimlet eye that, after some days as his guest, you made no sign until it was a question of getting the Hechts' address. Tiny, trivial things (said quite without irony) like that. With which bittersweet lozenge for the toe of your stocking, and in hopes that it has already fallen through the hole, je te souhaite tante belle chose and eagerly await the next installment at 702 Elizabeth St (zip 33040). I hope the family Xmas isn't too awful. Pretend that you're Byron making up for the exiguous amenities of an Albanian <u>qusht</u>.

Love,
James

David Tacium Montreal-based author, actor, and teacher, friend of Daryl Hine's.
Peter's Peter Tourville's.
the Mountain Mount Royal Park, designed by Frederick Law Olmsted, close to downtown Montreal; here referred to as a site for gay cruising.
Les Liaisons Dangereuses Epistolary novel by French writer and army officer Pierre Chaderos de Laclos (1741–1803).

this new Disease HIV/AIDS. The latter term was first used by the Center for Disease Control in 1982, and by the end of 1983 over three thousand cases had been diagnosed in the United States.
Mary Kinzie (b. 1944), American poet, critic, and professor at Northwestern University, where Hine also taught.
The Bartered Bride Opera by Czech composer Bedrich Smetana (1824–1884).
Belle âme . . . moi-même Darling, it is you who will save me from myself!

To David McIntosh

WUSTL
1 March 1984
Key West, FL

Dearest David—

Your letter came just today—a wonderful one. I know <u>exactly</u> what you mean about the "inner content" of a work revealing itself at the very end, only hours away from completion. Nothing's more thrilling or more mysterious. I long to see the painting that gave you those hours. Will you bring slides? And Andrea's watch! And Gerry's Christmas decorations! How <u>lively</u> the world grows when we're exhilarated and can take it in.

My body has been nagging at me the last couple of weeks. Dr. says it's a mild prostate infection. I've arranged for a 2nd opinion during the days (March 6–12) I go north. (Then I return here for a week— then to my mother—then north again on March 27.) Otherwise I've been happier than I can easily say. Someone has come into my life. He's 33, lives in NYC with a lover—so there are difficulties on both sides, but aren't there always? You'll meet him when you come East, and will like him I hope. His friend collects and restores Puerto Rican Santos. He himself, it had better be said at the start, is an actor.

Let me leave it at that for the time being. I look forward very much to your visit. After March 27, I'll be between S'ton + NY—you have that phone, don't you? 988 8953.

Love always,
James

Someone Peter Hooten. See Biographies.
His friend Alan Moss (aka Alan Moss Reverón), Manhattan collector and dealer of decorative art. See Merrill's poem "Santo" in *Late Settings* (1985).

To Claude Fredericks

GETTY
13 March 1984
Key West, FL

Dearest Claude,

Your phone call made me even happier than I mostly am, these days; and to return yesterday from a week up north, and find those pages from 1950 makes me—touched and bemused and grateful to a degree you may have an inkling of by the end of this page. First of all, so much LIFE flooding back, preserved uncannily; never "lost" per-haps, but transmuted beyond even painstaking recall into whoever we've become. My muse, I suppose, asks that a lot be forgotten, as part of (self-) forgiveness, or the conventions of the kind of work I needed to do—so that to find here our flowers pressed whole, past crumbling, is a great wonder. I must ask myself—and can't answer—what I'd have felt if this packet had reached me even 30 days ago. As it is, an extraordinary coincidence, the Valentine's Day of <u>this</u> year, has turned me again into a lover—a bond so sudden, so longed-for, so miraculously mutual—that here again are those looks and words and perambulations you recorded, and which, much as I dreamed, I truly didn't dream would ever come to me again. Our affective selves don't age, do they? A lifelong dial set at 18? 22? much earlier? The same headlong pony one may have somewhat learned to guide more wisely. It's been years and years since I've felt like this, long before David McI appeared bringing the indissoluble gladness and torment you perhaps put in your diary 14 years ago. No torment now. Even the folly of knowing myself a full quarter century older than my dear one sleeps like a nymph among flowers, as do the "problems" to be faced together—his friend, his career; DJ and mine. If I said to you in 1950 that I wanted it "to cost everything," what could I say today?—except that love costs nothing, that the cost isn't counted as the corner is turned and the rainbow entered. I don't see my life changing outwardly. For better or worse David and I have what we have. And Peter Tourville? I don't plan to throw <u>him</u> any further off-kilter than he already is by breaking a pattern of—what—15 meetings a year? My Valentine's Day Peter doesn't appear worried by any of that: if anything, grateful that we both have anchors to keep us from scudding too far too swiftly. This isn't altogether your way, I know. But I needn't explain to you the crazy geometry whereby one offers at best limited seating on the periphery of one's life, while the room held in readiness at the heart is boundless.

You'll meet Peter in New York, where he lives. His friend Alan thinks of me as an adored mentor, e basta. (How long will <u>that</u> last?) I met them at a reading 2 Novembers ago. Just a few words exchanged, then a week later a photograph in the mail: a still, if you can believe it, from a film made on Mykonos in 1973, in which he played a Greek fisherman in love with Bo Derek. A party in town, a dinner, a day in Stonington last summer. Finally a week by himself down here last month, in whose course . . . He was born and raised not far from my father's birthplace in central Florida. In 1978 he heard me read at UCLA, and knew. Well, enough for now. Dear Claude, come back soon!

With love always—
Jamey

a film made on Mykonos *Fantasies*, made in 1973 but not released until 1981, directed by John Derek.
my father's birthplace Green Cove Springs, Florida, in 1885.

To Peter Hooten

Dear Peter Hooten,

I am JM's new typewriter, and want to thank you for those minutes in your arms yesterday. They, far more than the extension cord found in a drawer this morning, account for the electric current flowing through me. Please come back again soon and hold me. If you can't write a poem <u>to</u> me, write one <u>with</u> me. The touch of your fingers in the shop—but don't let me go on this way. I must be Institutional, Brusque, Modest; Impersonal, Big-time, Monotonous; an Invincibly Bachelorette Machine—as befits my monogram. JM loves you. That's enough. I wish you joy.

Sincerely,
Ida Belle Morgenstern

Ida Belle Morgenstern Her initials are of course IBM. The letter's uncharacteristically specific address at the outset ensures that the recipient can find her easily.

To Tony Parigory

Tony dearest,

Your Easter gift arrived last weekend. Two days later, an impromptu phone call from Vassilikos brought <u>him</u> to the house for an hour, along with his Maria's brother (adelphara!) and a very grand Cavafy album published last year in Athens, photos, documents, texts—which you've surely seen—so I am wallowing in the good gay poet. A thousand thanks! V. said he sees you in Kolonaki now and then and that you look well. I hope he's right; and that appearances don't deceive.

I'm afraid the rest of this letter will be entirely about ME, but I can't help it. I'm in love! It's been so long that I'm bemused, not to say astonished and, oh my dear, so wildly happy—! But let me tell it in sequence. In November 1982 I have a reading in a NY bookshop: a small packed space—and kept encountering a beautiful face in the 1st row gazing raptly at me for the whole hour. He brought a book for me to sign afterwards, we spoke a bit, and I told him where he could write me. Ten days later came a letter <u>and</u> a photograph, a still from a film (can you imagine) made on Mykonos in 1973, starring Bo Derek and Peter Hooten. His name is Peter Hooten, and he played a Greek sailor, though he doesn't look particularly Greek—blazing blue eyes, ruddy skin, curly brown hair. He was 23 then. Nothing quite that glamorous has happened to him since (he played in something called *Orca* about a savage whale) until 1978 when he found *Divine Comedies* in a Los Angeles bookstore, and heard me give a reading at UCLA. Well, the next Spring (1983) I asked him and his friend (of course there's a friend—who runs a shop of "modern antiques" in SoHo) to a party on 72nd St. We talked quite a bit. He's from central Florida, still has a trace of a lovely Southern accent. As he left I gave him a hug and said "Let's not lose each other" and he said "Don't worry." Last summer he came up here for a day and a night, to a full house of DJ, Jim Boatwright and his Chinese lover Lee Toy. In the fall I had him and Alan (the friend) for dinner, and a lunch or two alone with him. By then it seemed rather hopeless, yet he was so charming, why not just add him to my little list of dear young men, like Sandy and Stephen Yenser and the rest. Then, lo and behold, he followed up on an idle invitation to spend a week in KW last February, and on Valentine's Day Eve it happened! There had been a big party 2 days earlier, at which brazen Mrs Wilbur sat him down and said "Jimmy seems to be interested in you, how nice if you could come to mean something to each other, if only for a while"—whereupon P burst into tears! Well, staggering declarations were put into words over the following days; and after he went north, phone calls, letters. Alan chooses to see me as a kind of "platonic mentor," and the surface of neither P's nor my life is very much changed, except that we spend hours or days together whenever possible. David "knows" and seems to be taking it with a sort of wry goodwill. What has me reeling with gratitude and delight is the extraordinary <u>trust</u> P. makes me feel. Nothing ambiguous or secretive in his feeling, just pure, committed devotion. For me, he is everybody I've ever loved in my life rolled into one. There are even moments when he looks like Strato, other touches of DJ, DMc, somebody else back in 1949 . . . It's too uncanny for easy description. Voila. Be a bit discreet in your letters—DJ is back in the Dominican Rep. but should be here by month's end. Peter and I plan some weeks abroad—London and Venice (he's never been to the latter) and <u>not</u> Greece, tempted though I am. Another time. That would be in June. Meanwhile, light candles for me, and write to tell me how you are, and that I'm not entirely an idiot.

> Love to Nellaki and to heavenly You—
> Jimmy

adelphara! Sisters!
Mrs Wilbur Richard Wilbur's wife, Mary Charlotte ("Charlee") (1922–2007).
Nellaki Nelly Liambey.

To Peter Hooten

HOOTEN
29 April 1984
[Stonington, CT]

My Beloved Peter,

Your letters are pretty hard to stop rereading, and I have to admit that mine are by and large a touch "tame" next to them. Perhaps that's all right?—since we haven't, by a long shot, reached the point where we can say sensible things face to face. Did you see the interview with Kundera (the Czech novelist) in today's Book Section? He says, "I think you have to write about love with supreme skepticism. . . . The language of 'love' is a language about feelings that justify bad behavior." And then: "Whatever is left over after you apply skepticism to feeling—that's love." Which is the view of the Lady of Sandover as well, and we must be sure to make that crossing safely in the months and years ahead. For the time being it is pure sympathetic magic to idealize one another. Yet I'm [so] conscious of my limitations that I can't repress a little nervous headshake (<u>or</u>, to be sure, the golden waves of wonder and gratitude) when I read how great I am in your eyes. It must be the same for you, no? You wouldn't otherwise keep worrying about being "worthy" of me. Remember, then, that I feel the same. Perhaps feeling (for the beloved) and skepticism (for the feeling) can coexist to mutual advantage? Illustration: Driving at sunset down crowded Massachusetts Ave. into Cambridge the other day, we stopped for a light within view of a big, angry red brick building just ahead. It had turrets and crenellations and almost a portcullis instead of a door. White letters partly obscured by the corner tower (from where we sat) said:

RAGE WAREHOUSE
IRE PROOF.

—as if some stronghold of bad feeling were also protection against it. Of course the next slide I want to show is that one I mentioned, of the river at night, still as glass, doubling all the lights of the city: all the greed and careless planning, everything random and rushed and wretched, turned by a single stroke into perfect, festive tranquility. So that is possible too.

By the time you get this it will be only an hour before we're in each other's arms—time standing still, or seeming to.

> I love you—
> JM

Kundera Milan Kundera (b.1929), Czech-born French writer and citizen.
the Lady of Sandover Nature, aka Psyche and Queen Mum, or QM.

To David McIntosh

WUSTL
10 May 1984
[Stonington, CT]

Dear David,

Herewith are 2 things I'd have given you in New York next week. The pamphlet was done as a birthday surprise by Sandy McClatchy and Alfred Corn—they were in touch with you, now that I think of it; or have we already spoken of that? "Bronze" I began shortly after your trip in '81; kept abandoning, then resuming, to finish finally only about two months ago. I know, from the letter you wrote me about Who's poem, how you view these poems that involve you. Indeed, the torturous "history" of its composition hints at my reluctance to confront yet again those old frustrations. Let's hope that this is the last word on the subject! You understand, of course, that (even though the poem briefly addresses you) it's in fact addressed to that tangle of feelings I've had, over the years, no real way of facing except through writing, and which would have been, if not crippling, at least wasteful to disregard. Looking at it now, in the light of unforeseen happiness, I like the way it coheres and radiates, even though I can't envy its author.

The happiness grows, fills and bewilders me—him as well. It's what I'd given up expecting, except as the idlest of day-dreams. Even David seems to approve, when he forgets to be crusty and disgruntled. I'd hope you and Peter (DJ has much to say about the economy of <u>names</u> in my "love-life") would meet next week. His friend (what <u>he</u> knows and feels is another question; for the present that bond works as a stabilizer, much as DJ's and mine does) collects santos from Puerto Rico, and had looked forward to giving you a candlelit display of his favorites. Another season.

We leave for a month—Amsterdam, London, Cornwall, Venice, a few final days in the Alps—on June 1. As yet no firm word about Mexico. I'll let you know when it comes. If it doesn't I'll still count on seeing you in August.

With love always,
James

The pamphlet *Occasions & Inscriptions*, a collection of thirty-three such, some never printed elsewhere, edited by Corn and McClatchy and published in a limited edition on Merrill's birthday in 1984 by Jordan Davies.
"Bronze" A limited edition of Merrill's poem published by Nadja in 1984. The poem appeared in *Late Settings* (1985). McIntosh ("David the Fair") figures in the first stanza.
"Who's poem" Merrill's "Ginger Beef," in which McIntosh's dog Who is featured, appeared in *The Inner Room* (1988). See notes to Merrill's letters to McIntosh of 2 August 1971 and 12 July 1984.

To Donald Windham

Dear Don,

You're abroad now, and I <u>shall</u> be by the time you return; better that this page wait for you than you for it. We've been enthralled by "Truman and others" these last days. The way you show what time can do without ever talking about <u>it</u>—as Proust does for instance, to the point where it virtually becomes the God of a world grown coherent, if only as a result—strikes to the marrow. It's nearly 30 years since T. spent his summer in our little village. Where have they flown? Into us all, I suppose, bringing about the changes you describe with such terrible plainness. Your readers (or DJ and I at least) put down the book wishing you'd been spared those bitter outcomes, and gasping as one does after a narrow escape. Well, friendships fade. All one asks is that they do so decently, bequeathing their chemicals to the compost heap instead of to that awful afterlife of pulp and tabloid. What madness to have sought that <u>kind</u> of celebrity in the first place;—and how easy for the likes of me to say so, who never had to fret about money. I wish some day you'd take up what I sensed hovering in the background as I read: the hostility implicit between those two "camps," as dramatized by Auden's refusal to meet Tennessee—"He won't do." Is this merely some bizarre highbrow/lowbrow delusion? a question of gay etiquette? of class? We've all felt the sting of those nettles in one way or another. What savagery here below, eh? Enough. Endless thanks for writing yet one more book that keeps me <u>thinking</u>.

> Our love always to you and Sandy—
> Jimmy

Dear Donald,

Just to add, since I reviewed, 1000 years ago?, *Emblems* for the V.V. You've remained in my Pantheon of American Writers. But that was Atlanta! Why not these more recent years? The Truman book is Testimony to that "why not" above, I suppose. Thank you for it. Love to Sandy,

Yrs,
David

"Truman and others" *Lost Friendships: A Memoir of Truman Capote, Tennessee Williams, and Others* (1986) by Donald Windham (1920–2010).
Emblems *Emblems of Conduct* (1964), Windham's memoir.
the V.V. *The Village Voice.*
Sandy Sandy Campbell (1922–88), American actor and writer, Windham's longtime lover.

To David McIntosh

WUSTL
12 July 1984
[Stonington, CT]

Dear David,

I returned about 12 days ago, but the splashdown has been less tidy than usual—largely because of some sort of virus I left with (along with a course of antibiotics) but which resurfaced in Venice and Lucerne (a second course) luckily never longer than 36 hours at a time, and which (following course 3) I trust has departed forever. It didn't really spoil the trip. Nothing, I think, <u>could</u> have spoiled those heavenly, happy days. Walking the cliffs of Cornwall, on or along a deep thatch of tiny blossoming things, wigs of pink-orange hair worn by strange dwarf shrubs, then rocks swinging into view seamed like Auden's face. From London to the Palazzo Barbaro. An hour in which everyone put on a white beauty mask out of a tube and posed, like carnival figures, for the camera. A day in Ravenna. A day in the meadows above Lake Lucerne, air full of constant cowbell gamelan orchestra. And always hours when Peter and I could be alone. I can't think when I've been so happy. We saw in the British Museum one of those Mughal or Hindu miniatures of an elephant entirely made up of interlocking figures, gods, avatars, bodhisattvas; it's the way I feel about him—traits and attributes I found to love in others, brought together in an entirely new amalgam. Not unexpectedly there's something of you—a sweet serenity longed-for and sustained, a feeling for solitary places. So that there are reasons to feel that I've known him much much longer than a handful of months. Well, I hope you'll meet soon: you'll like each other.

It's taken me these 12 days to clear my desk, write the preface for <u>next</u> year's Yale Younger Poet, and decide (taking a leaf out of your last Spring's calendar) not to go anywhere for the rest of the summer. My reasons are the same as yours: I <u>must</u> get something done, and if I have to start packing 20 days hence—! The famous Mexican Poetry conference fell into angry 3rd-world hands. My desk was covered with letters imploring me not to accept the invitation which, for its part, remained purely hypothetical. I'd have come without that, as you know; the point was to see you, and ML and Agi. I still want to, but not this summer. DJ's plans for California are under way; he'll stay a few days longer there instead of getting off at Lamy—again, no reflection on Santa Fe, but on <u>me</u>, I suppose, for backing out. Obviously there've been certain tensions between us recently. He likes Peter, and P thinks the world of him, but a few wrinkles in the 3 of us being together still need ironing out. So—another reason for staying here in August—P and I can have some time together while he's away.

All of this strikes me at times as very odd. I must stop acting like an orphan gobbling cookies in fear of the plate's being taken away. For oddest of all is there being no shadow of a cause for that particular fear. Still, it's going to take a while to adjust to, and I can only beg your understanding and patience.

"Bronze" will be going in the new book, so I'm pleased you like it. The Who/Nambé poem <u>won't</u> go in. That's another thing I must do between now and Labor Day: decide on a title and contents.

Drink time!

I'm glad that you enjoyed Rob's visit. He <u>is</u> good company, even in the crowded city. I mean to call him soon.

Do break my news gently to ML. I'll do my best to come see her before too long.

With love always,
James

<u>next</u> **year's Yale Younger Poet** Pamela Alexander, *Navigable Waterways* (1985).
ML and Agi Mary Lou Aswell and Agnes Sims.
the new book "Bronze," which describes Merrill's trip to Italy with McIntosh in 1981, was published in *Late Settings* (1985).
Rob Robert Perkins (b. 1949), writer, independent filmmaker, and collaborator with poets, including Elizabeth Bishop, Octavio Paz, Seamus Heaney, and Merrill, in his series "The Written Image."
break my news gently That he will not be going as planned to New Mexico.

To Peter Hooten

HOOTEN
11 September 1984
[Stonington, CT]

My Beloved Peter,

I've had this cassette several years now, and with me in the car these last days. It's your turn to get it by heart. The text (if memory serves) is made up of six "Chinese" poems translated rather pantingly into German—with, I mean, a lot of very un-Chinese rhetorical appeals to Life and Beauty and The World. Song I invites us to drink, then says "Wait"—and presents some very gloomy reasons to drain, at last, the goblet to the lees: "Dark is life, dark is death" goes the refrain. Song II: loneliness among falling autumn leaves. Towards the end, a passionate phrase: "Ah Sun of Love, will you nevermore shine upon me!" Song III describes a little green-and-white porcelain pavilion mirrored in water. Smartly robed friends sit drinking and chatting, some of them writing verses. It's "all upside-down," this view of life. Song IV: a young woman wandering by a stream is startled by a bunch of boys on horseback. That handsomest catches her eye, and she responds. V: "The Drunkard in Spring"—a bird laughing on the bough, but what does <u>he</u> care? The last song describes two friends parting—male friends: Mahler allowed for the performance of this cycle by tenor and baritone instead of tenor and alto. Why are you leaving and where are you going? the narrator asks. Home says the other. Life has been bitter. I'm going back to my homeland, wrapped forever in distant blue light, forever, forever . . . It may help if you think of Klimt. It is art that essentially looks back at the past rather than forward toward stark new forms. Just as Klimt's hieratic, friezelike figures would be unthinkable without some memory of classicism, so you'll hear in Mahler (for instance in the last sung phrase of song IV) the very bones of early music under the gold leaf and begemmings in the orchestra. He adored Mozart, and was responsible for the first Vienna production of *Così fan Tutte* (which you and I are going to hear in rehearsal on December 7, by the way—a little Pearl Harbor celebration) in nearly 100 years. Keeping that in mind you can hear the perfect sugar glazes of the rococo crystallizing, as it were, into glittering granular pangs by the end of that century. Or hear the kind of scarcely melodic rhythmical motif that keeps the momentum in a piece by Bach in that obsessive figure (——— ÷——— —) from the orchestral interlude in the 6th song. Bach also would be responsible for the ravishing play of solo instruments. There's even, along with everything else, a mandolin in the last song. Well, perhaps I'm telling you nothing you don't know. You've seen from the start that this is a love letter, right? If only I were kissing you instead, in wide-eyed silence!

I love you!
JM

this cassette *Das Lied von der Erde*, song cycle by Gustav Mahler.
Klimt Gustav Klimt (1862–1918), Austrian painter.
the orchestral interlude It precedes the third and final section of the long sixth movement, entitled "Der Abschied" (The Farewell).

To David McIntosh

WUSTL
6 May 1985
Stonington, CT

Dearest David,

Ouf! an evening alone. I put Peter on an early afternoon train—by now DK has taken him to a party for Suzanne Farrell—and spent the remaining daylight hours <u>working</u>: not reading the Yale Younger Poets, but right here at my <u>desk</u>. As you know I can't take much solitude, but after 5 weeks of none, and much as I cherish my young friend, it is bliss. A little dinner of asparagus and rice, a drink or two, and this long-postponed letter. In lieu of a birthday present (I still blush) please take this check to help with your physiotherapy. It sounds as though progress were being made. Thank Goodness. You have sufficient bodily problems not to have to deal with falls in airports.

In St Louis I saw Ann McGarrell several times. She took us to the Museum where a smallish room is filled with 5 of her husband's enormous paintings. Lots of intense primary color, rather in the style of the Tchelitchew *Hide and Seek,* thinly painted on inspection, and (aside from the oddly inept figures that dominate or punctuate these picture-window panels) a whole anthology of effects out of Italian painting, Piero to Caravaggio, plus touches of Max Ernst—bits of landscape made out of emerald or fuchsia fur, and so forth; and the windowframes studded with grisaille postcards of those and other masters. Nicer than in reproduction or, for that matter, than this account of them. Then to her flat for dinner. Mr McG is in New York, but we saw rather too much of the child, Flora, doing high kicks in her nightie, at ten a dangerous little piece of jailbait. Then she and some friends gave a non-academic cocktail party, with delicious food, which I ought to have enjoyed more than I did (nowhere to sit down). Karen may be coming over this summer, and within reach of Stonington for part of the time; and the translation . . . proceeds.

What by the way (if anything) have you heard from your gallery lady in NY?? Then there was a huge to-do the other night, first at the Guggenheim Museum, later at an apartment on upper Fifth Ave (full of Soutine and De Stael) in connection with some Awards. I got one, George Rochberg (Rochman?) got another. He is the composer, as you'll recall, of *The Confidence Man* and I'm only glad you weren't there to hear me praising it to him. I even praised the libretto. "Oh," he cried, "you must tell my wife!"—who wrote the awful libretto, as I remembered too late. Nothing for it: I was led over to her and had to start in—but she was luckily a great chatterbox and didn't quiz me on my favorite episodes.

Something I can tell no one else—only 6 people in the world know—has darkened these last weeks more than I can possibly say. You will keep it to yourself, I know. I told you DK had been in hospital with a terrible case of pneumonia. My dear, it's a strain of AIDS. Of all people. He fancies—perhaps rightly, it's anyone's guess—that he got it in the Mt. Sinai hospital 2 summers ago [*in the margin*: There were a couple of cases on his floor.], when his retina had slipped for the 2nd time. He rallied, as I told you—luckily his white corpuscle count is still quite high—but faces what we've all learned to imagine. Of course there are "programs," and "treatments" from France or Sweden which, through his very good young doctor, will soon be available to him here. He is wonderfully sane and stubborn about the whole thing, plans to go to Venice as usual, and mercifully, thanks to a Guggenheim Fellowship, has the whole coming year off from teaching. But so shattering. He's the first person I <u>know</u> to be stricken. Peter Hooten was wonderful. The first 2 nights, when nobody thought in time to book a night nurse, he stayed in David's hospital room, sponging his brow, making scenes when the IV slipped out—12 hours of this each night—and I can well believe that his sunny positivism, in those first dangerous hours, made the difference between life and death. David has also, in the last 6 months, come very close to a fine young man (21) graduating this June from Rutgers. It's pretty scary for <u>him</u>, evidently, but he's been a brick so far. There's no question of telling gossipy DJ, or fifty other people, and I feel awfully self-indulgent dumping it like this into your lap. I suppose I wanted to see if I could <u>begin</u> to write it down. Well—tuck it away and forgive me for clouding your sky with it. If you want to send him a line, say only that you'd heard he was ill and are glad he's better. He <u>is</u> better, after all. (Address: 471 West 22, NYC 10011)

(Pause.) It's cold and rainy, but very beautiful here. Cherry and dogwood at their fullest—the latter achieving a raspberry sherbet hue I can't recall in other seasons or places. The beach at the point littered with Christmas trees, perhaps to keep the expensive imported sand from blowing away. We went to a greenhouse in Westerly, and now the terrace pots are planted with lupin, anemones, arugula, parsley, begonias, a red-and-mauve petunia with a holly leaf, morning glories, and a Golden Rain Tree, 4 inches high, brought from New Harmony, Indiana, where the leaflet described it almost like a household pet, a tree that abandoned the wilderness in order to be a friend to man. We'll see.

My love always—
James

Ann McGarrell (1933–2016), writer and translator.
her husband's James McGarrell (1930–2020), painter and printmaker on the faculty
at Washington University.
Tchelitchew Pavel Tchelitchew (1898–1957), Russian-born painter who worked in
Germany, France, and the United States, partner of Charles Henri Ford.
the child, Flora Flo McGarrell (1974–2010), born female; son of Ann and James,
he was an agri-sculptor and filmmaker who died in an earthquake in Haiti in 2010.
Karen Karen Pennau Fronduti, one of three translators (Ann McGarrell was
another) of *Mirabell: Books of Number* into Italian.
George Rochberg (1919–2005), American composer, whose opera *The Confidence
Man* (1982) was based on Melville's novel.

To Peter Hooten

HOOTEN
10 September 1985
Athens, Greece

Peter, dearest Heart—

Your letter was waiting when I walked downhill to Tony's shop this
morning. What joy to have a word from you, such ardent loving words
that I'm still all aglow. I don't think I know, myself, how to write love
letters! From your example and judging from how much pleasure
yours gives me, I ought to cover this whole page with assurances that
you are the wonder who spreads happiness throughout the world
(at least this corner of it), for that's how I see you, my Sunshine, and
myself a mere dry kernel sprouting feebly in your beams. Instead I
just give you—not even "news" alas, just schedules and qualms and a
vignette or two. Is it that I'm shy? or that I've spent a lifetime testing
the double edge, the duplicity of language? Hurry up and turn that
corner on Mt Lykabettos, and I'll show you what I mean!

I really needn't have come all this way to spend a couple of hours
every day watching four kittens and their mother. But I do. They are
enthralling—she so proud, so concerned, so sure of her role; they so
inventive, such victims of whim and imperfect motor control. Off
and on a big disreputable "father" turns up, long enough to drop his
street-smart mask and—who knows? borrow a few bucks from the
"kitty" for his night on the town? They're enough to make me long
for a litter of my own and a life of no more travel so as to be sure
they're cared for properly. You didn't tell me where you'd thought of

our going, before the Paris hotel came through. Well, take me there blindfold one day . . .

The mother cat and her most intrepid kitten, the black, blue-eyed one, actually set foot inside the kitchen this morning. I stroked her and held the little one's eye for a bit. The civilizing force is <u>food</u>, as you might imagine. Cheese. Something called "Friskies" (there was a box in the house). But her mind is henceforth divided. She nurses sitting up, head swiveled imploringly in my direction. "Take my beautiful children if you must. Only see that they get a better life. Table manners, piano lessons . . ." All of that is in her look. I hear her calling me even now . . .

We had a drink with Alan down the street, Alan Ansen that is, and took him to dinner nearby. Poor DJ had <u>gone out</u> the night before, to a gay bar whose proprietress shrieked with joy at the sight of him, then even had a last half bottle of wine somewhere else—and was barely functional all day, left in the middle of dinner, and probably won't get up until I give him a vitamin shot. We're lunching at Nelly's but first I want to see a show in the newly-restored Schliemann mansion downtown. Octavio tonight . . . A letter from Robin says that he'd independently reached the same conclusion about Bali, and is all <u>for</u> Kyoto, Japanese natural beauties, theatre, food, etc. So we shall be a family of kittens ourselves, it would seem.

Dearest PH,

Octavio flies to NY tomorrow—I'll give him this to mail—+ your number to call you. <u>I</u>'ll call you tomorrow also. This brings all my love to wonderful <u>you</u>. We have our reservation at the Grand Victoria on <u>Oct 1</u>—Tuesday—but I hope we'll be together long before then.

I love you! I love you!

JM

---

watching four kittens They are featured in Merrill's poem "Nine Lives" (*A Scattering of Salts*, 1995).
Schliemann mansion Designed for the archaeologist Heinrich Schliemann by his friend the Saxon-Greek architect Ernst Ziller and completed in 1881; now the home of the Numismatic Museum.
Octavio Octavio Ciano, Stephen Magowan's partner.
conclusion about Bali That it was not the right place for the parties to meet.

To Stephen Yenser   YALE
                                                    12 September 1985
                                                       Athens, Greece

Dear Stephen,

Just like old times to receive a long letter from you all the way to Ath-
ens. I'm still fussing with my "marbles" as the enclosed pages will
show. DK thought the 2nd section (in the draft you wrote about at
such kind length) drew overmuch upon the imagery of "Time"—and
indeed, most of it had been written years ago; I used it shamefacedly,
faute de mieux. I don't presume to think we now have a finished ver-
sion, but hope it's pretty much on the right track. It's no joke when I
say I find it almost impossible any longer to hold in my mind a poem
this long—the way I held, say, "The 1002nd Night" in its day. This
makes for terrible uncertainties—of the kind that obliged Matisse to
give up the brush and palette (no longer trusting his eye or hand or
both) in favor of scissors and colored paper. You take a benign view
of the results—"interloopings and interlopings"—but I'm afraid that
what was once "composition" is turning into "motif" without the
inner dynamics (whatever that means) I could call upon 20 years ago.
I'm not writing you this in order to make you spend even a minute
refuting it, rather just so you'll know how these things strike me.

Peter will have phoned you about the trip—not to Bali now, but
Japan—and how my reading date in Seattle obliges us not to postpone
it more than a few days. Maybe it's wiser to wait until Fall—though
poor Peter is so depressed career-wise that he shouldn't have to wait
any longer than absolutely necessary for a little round of applause.

We're settled in our house, I in the basement apartment whence
Despoinis Elli was taken feet-first a year or two ago—or four by now.
If we'd had this extra space in the old days we might well still <u>be</u> in
Athens: 3 and a half little rooms, plus bath and kitchen. Out in back,
a family of 4 kittens not yet quite weaned. Cool, much quieter than
upstairs—perhaps even warmer in winter? I adore it. (My bedroom is
now a little parlor opening into the entrance hall, and of course DJ is
upstairs with the dust and the racket and the telephone.) The terrace
is a mess, but the house is freshly prettily painted inside and out.

This morning the phone rang, then the doorbell, both by appointment and presently I was sitting over coffee with Strato—my first glimpse of him since 1971. He's a wreck, it's really horrifying—fat, quite bald, <u>lame</u>. He returned from nearly 10 years in Canada with such bad lower back trouble that he had no sensation from the hips down. The drier climate here has been of some help, but he refuses to have an operation and is in constant pain. They're all but penniless. The son (18) took the car without permission (or a license) and wrecked it (much as his father came close to doing every time he borrowed a car of ours—never returned without a dent, or a bent axle, or <u>something</u>—as of course I didn't fail to point out). Now he and his brother Costa have a kiosk together, and Vaso is making shirts. He gets a small pension from Canada, where if he would return for an operation he'd from then on receive at least $300 a month . . . There's a 12 year old daughter, too. But he is still full of jokes, and one of these days I'll tell you a few from this morning's hour.

Manos returned from Mytilyne (or wherever those I's and y's go) yesterday. <u>His</u> life isn't so wonderful either. People <u>will</u> do things their own way—thank goodness! Otherwise, at least in these two cases, they'd have done them <u>my</u> way and I'd be faced with that mistake instead of—what? These genre portraits by Time? These lives displayed so . . . openly, without vanity or complacency, as part of what simply <u>is</u>, and in as much detail as I have heart or patience for. How easy to forget, at our desks, that Tony is OK (drinks too much, repeats himself worse than ever), George smokes too much and works 5 mornings a week for Tony. Nelly is in full bloom. She now has a "chauffeur"—an old village man who drives her car a couple of mornings a week. She took me to Plaka yesterday to see a new Byzantine museum installed in the "old university"—Plaka itself is getting a lot of restoration, the earsplitting boites are out, etc—it will be lovely in a few years. After that, to Piraeus to see a huge pointless exhibit "Ellada kai Thalassa" installed in a vast customs shed. Melina's brother's idea—cost: a half million$$.

Vassili and Maria turned up for 5 minutes. Grace Edwards joined us for dinner one evening. Kimon will appear next week—as will, if the Board's to be believed, over tea in Kolonaki Square, with his mother and nurse (while the father is at the ministry, discussing some Trade agreement between the 2 countries), a little 8 year old from Bombay. His hat will blow in our direction. The prospect has discovered undreamed-of depths of scepticism in yours truly, and reduced David to terminal jitters. But what if—?

Everyone has asked for you, and to be remembered.

> Love to you and Mary from us both.
> James

my "marbles" Merrill's poem "Losing the Marbles" in *The Inner Room* (1988). "Time" appeared in *Nights and Days* (1966).
our house Athinaion Efivon 44.
Despoinis Elli Miss Elli, the elderly former tenant of the lower part of Athinaion Efivon 44.
a new Byzantine museum In the National and Kapodistrian University of Athens.
Melina's brother Spiros Mercouri (d. 2018).
"Ellada kai Thalassa" The title of the exhibit: *Greece and the Sea.*
if the Board's to be believed The Ouija board had instructed JM and DJ to expect to encounter the reincarnated Maria in Kolonaki Square; see Merrill's poem "Nine Lives" in *A Scattering of Salts* (1995).

To Mary McCarthy

VASSAR
5 March 1986
Key West, FL

Dear Mary,

I've just put down your *Vanity Fair* piece, which is a joy from start to finish. So interesting, and so beautifully turned; those morals like fish eyes "between stones in the depths of clear water." The book itself should be coming out this year? I can hardly wait.

Your complicity in the Birthday Book (presented to me 2 days ago) gives me even greater pleasure. One never has that many readers, and I've noticed that most of my "senior" friends—anyone over 40 or 50—don't read as carefully as they once did. Or is the word avidly? Your letter proves what an exception you are, not that proof is necessary. Your questions flatter me more than someone else's compliments would. May I try to answer a few, just to show my gratitude?

In "Santorini": Empedocles isn't really transported to this Aegean island, just because both turn up in the same poem. The stanza personifies Earth (Gaia) as an explosive mother. Her child (mankind, if you like) loves her, if you like, according to his bond, in a relatively normal Oedipal way. When she erupts, however, his fascination changes into something else—an Empedocles complex, it might be called, or at least a form of merging in keeping with her new, violent aspect.

Our "Friend" in the penultimate stanza is the Sun, who indeed burns a hole through the film.

In "Lenses" part 3, the pivot-word (as Haiku writers call it) is "pointer": both hound and telescope. The erratic itinerary of either Odysseus or Orion (the Hunter) ends in recognition by the dog/lens. (This image I stole from Lampedusa. The prince's telescopes are capped by day, and wait patiently "like animals who know they will not be fed until evening.") The swineherd doesn't tell the story. The subject of "begin the retelling" is "one of their company." <u>Maggiore</u>. <u>Lento</u>. are conventional usage in musical scores, especially variations. Mozart has lots of movements (in his piano sonatas) where a <u>Minore</u> variation is followed by a <u>Maggiore</u>, and the set is seldom complete without a slow, richly ornamented variation towards the end.

Finally, "Think Tank": The poem is spoken, if you can bear it, by a tank full of tropical fish, some species of which actually do move in little schools (hence "scholar"). I remember my boyhood guppies would eat their young unless promptly removed from temptation. <u>Ich</u> is a common disease afflicting tropical fish (short for a long term, but the abbreviation has its own entry in my dictionary). Its similarity to the German pronoun was hard to resist, so I didn't. The little society struck me (at least for a short poem's purpose) as analogous to this or that human community—even one of thinkers, hence the ready-made phrase of the title. The dechlorinated crystal slab is the aquarium itself. Now the Snail: there's always one in a good aquarium. It cleans up after the fish, washes the glass walls from within, prevents the build-up of algae. In that sense a servant. Huge from the perspective of the smaller fish. As an emblem of forgetfulness, ominously blind, for (thanks to its offices) the fish will be free to repeat—or "condemned to repeat"—their past of cannibalism, narcissism, the shudderings of ich, etc . . .

Not that any of the above answers your real question, which has to do with my reasons for attempting such precarious effects. Nor shall I venture so much as a sentence in that direction. Yet I'm truly very grateful for your letter, and recognize in it the constant, ambiguous companion of my life as writer: forever leading me to reconsider how much I can get away with not saying, as if Experience were an oasis who goes to the party dressed as a mirage . . .

We had a fine birthday party. Friends came from far places, New York, Los Angeles, St Louis. The last couple left only this afternoon, so I've begun to feel my age. Enclosed is a little party favor. David joins in much love, dearest Mary, to you and Jim.

> Always,
> Jimmy

your *Vanity Fair* piece *Vanity Fair* published McCarthy's memoir "How I Grew" in its March 1986 issue; her book of the same title appeared in 1987.
Birthday Book *James Merrill: A Tribute*, a collection of contributions by Merrill's friends on the occasion of his sixtieth birthday, solicited by McClatchy and Corn and published as a limited edition by Jordan Davies.
Your questions About poems in Merrill's *Late Settings* (1985).
"Santorini" "Santorini: Stopping the Leak" (*Late Settings*).
"Friend" In the penultimate stanza of "Santorini: Stopping the Leak."
Lampedusa Giuseppe Tomasi di Lampedusa (1896–1957), the last prince of Lampedusa, Italian literary critic and author of one famous, posthumously published novel, *Il Gattopardo* (*The Leopard*, 1958), to which Merrill alludes.
party favor A copy of *James Merrill: A Tribute*.

To Tony Parigory

WUSTL
6 March 1986
Key West, FL

Tonaki darling,

The last of our out-of-town guests left yesterday afternoon. In the evening we saw the local theatre's production of *As Is*—a tearjerker about AIDS—and today, aside from my long-deferred visit to the gym—we are lapsing into grateful silence. It was all really very pleasant, if a bit much, and only the absence of two very dear friends— you and David Kalstone—cast a shadow on the festivities. (Poor DK, he's been in hospital again: much deterioration in the last month or so, and nothing that can be treated, you understand. It is more than his young friend can cope with, and both have lapsed into a slough of infantilism, clothes unwashed, bills unpaid, hours spent sleeping. Finally they're in touch with one of those support systems, and will have a Gay Men's Crisis Buddy to come and do housework, run errands, and so forth.) Of course you both <u>were</u> present in the pages of my birthday book, which is seldom out of my hands, and puts me to sleep at night more smilingly than do my collected poems. I love your contribution, and devoutly hope that it will encourage you to set about those MEMOIRS we all expect from you. Now that you're past sixty, Primrose, what else is there to do, just answer me that? One cannot live nuit et zour in Baluchistan.

In eight days I must head north, and things will be fast and furious for the next ten weeks: Palm Beach, Stonington, NYC, Los Angeles, Frisco, Japan, Peking, and (on the way back) Hawaii, Seattle, and again LA. Donald has made us a lovely itinerary, not too hectic on paper, and I'm looking forward to it very much indeed. Unfortunately I've not made the strides I'd fancied I might in my very serious Japanese grammar. Key West of course is crawling with Jap tourists, but I daren't address them. What if I were to lose face??? David I think stays on, perhaps until early or mid-May, then plans to come out to LA for a week or so—even though Bob Grimes will be in England—to see Peter and Mary (Yenser) act my little playlet—two performances in one evening.

He and I aren't on awfully good terms most of the time. That's nothing new, I know. Still . . . Peter irritates him, and his endless parade of black "indigents" (as he calls them in company) drive <u>me</u> up the wall. Peter too has revealed himself just a touch less than perfect. He has a frightful temper! He went up to NYC for 2 nights in the flat and a day's shooting on his film in New Jersey—yes, they've started up the film again. Eleanor was using it for a fortnight, but naturally agreed to let him sleep in the maid's room. Apparently when she came in from her dinner party she didn't ask how he was, just began on the cockroaches and the mess in the fridge, as if these were his fault. He left her a note that was just barely not insulting, then on his return blew up at me. But blew UP. It lasted 48 hours and didn't stop until I pushed him fully clothed into the pool in mid-shout. We talked a little about it afterwards. It is clearly the tip of the iceberg of quite a different problem—to wit, I suspect, a certain amount of sexual molestation in childhood at the hands of an older sister, which is known to be a classic source of rage in an adult man. But it alarms me—and him, too. Keep all of this to yourself. He is still the answer to a prayer. (Now he's back in Santo Domingo. We'll not meet until early April—no, March 31—in Los Angeles.)

Please tell George that I was delighted by his card. I'll send Nellaki one of the enclosed—little party favors, nothing more. And one will be on the way, plus a letter, for Bernard in the next few days. Christian is very much here, looking better than last year, even slimmer (though this last is, I fear, mainly thanks to his modish wardrobe of clothes several sizes too large—even for him!)

> All love to you, dearest, and write
> soon—
> Jimmy

No word from Strato as yet—thank heavens. This rapprochement must not be overdone.

As Is Play by William Hoffman (1939–2017), playwright, librettist, director, and editor.
AIDS Merrill was diagnosed on April 31, 1986, with ARC (AIDS-related complex).
Gay Men's Crisis Buddy The Gay Men's Health Crisis, nonprofit and volunteer-staffed, was created in January 1982 by writer and activist Larry Kramer and friends "to end the AIDs epidemic and uplift the lives of all affected."
zour Imitation of the Greek pronunciation of "jour."
Baluchistan Among the antiques Parigory sold in his shop were Baluchi carpets.
Donald Donald Richie.
my little playlet *The Image Maker,* included in *The Inner Room* (1988).
Peter Peter Hooten.
Santo Domingo Where Hooten's film took him.

To Tony Parigory   WUSTL
                                            16 June 1986
                                          Stonington, CT

Dearest Tony—

I'd planned to write you this morning—looked forward all week to writing you—and indeed <u>am</u> writing you. But not the letter I'd imagined, about Japan + China. Sandy McClatchy phoned while we were at table last night: David K. had just died. It had been foreseen for weeks—months—+ finally his days + hours were numbered. The virus had gone to his brain. He <u>knew</u> us, but grew vaguer + vaguer, like a kind of galloping senility. He was bedridden + mercifully tended by a very lively + cheerful Haitian named Jacques (DK was his 4th case) who left him only an hour or so a day. The poor lovaire Christopher grew more childish + ineffectual even than he <u>had</u> been at the start. Big scenes took place (with D. perfectly able to hear but not to intervene) about the will etc. Peter + I went to see him a couple of times as soon as we got to NY—but it was too late for any closeness. He lay with eyes shut + squeezed our hands. Toward the end—a thousand times worse—he lay with eyes <u>open</u>, day + night, as if to shut them would extinguish him for good. Oh my dear, I saw it coming. Yet I can't stop breaking into sobs every 30 minutes—all morning. He was such a friend—never a misunderstanding or quarrel—like having a 2nd <u>self</u> one could reach by telephone or walking into the next room. He wants his ashes scattered from the Palazzo Barbaro— Mrs Curtis won't go for <u>that</u>, you can be sure! Earlier this week dear Kay Keast (Bill Meredith's sister) died of cancer, + I leave tomorrow for NY + Southampton where there's a memorial service for Bobby Magowan—who by now seems to have died FIVE times in the last 6 months—so koukla, all is death + darkness in this ravishing bright day. Please tell Nelly—I had a lovely letter from her, plus card (with kitty) from Rome. Love to George.

Mille baci—

J.

The virus HIV.
Palazzo Barbaro Splendid house on the Grand Canal in Venice, built in 1425, where Henry James, Robert Browning, John Singer Sargent, Claude Monet, and other writers and painters visited in the late nineteenth century; the inspiration for Milly Theale's palazzo in *The Wings of the Dove*, and the model for the Isabella Stewart Gardner Museum in Boston. See the passage from Kalstone's journal quoted in Merrill's letter to David McIntosh of 12 September 1986.
Mrs Curtis Patricia Curtis, American owner of most of the Palazzo Barbaro.
Bobby Magowan Robert Magowan, Merrill's brother-in-law, died on December 19, 1985.
koukla Doll (Greek), an affectionate term.

To David McIntosh

Dear David,

You've probably given up on me by now. Here is a letter in hopes that you haven't. I came back yesterday from a not very eventful (and dreadfully muggy) week in New York. Saw a few friends, and went through DK's papers—there weren't many, he was a model of tidiness next to me—with Richard Poirier, the co-literary-executor. We decided it was most fitting to return letters to those correspondents who were close to David; and so here are the few cards and pages from you that he had filed away. There were also 6 or 8 notebooks, some of them little more than engagement books, but others with dreams and thoughts and sketches for the Venetian novel he always wanted to write. These I've arranged to go to Washington U. in St Louis. Finally there were 3 big boxes of drafts, xeroxes, etc, pertaining to the book he was at work on—about Elizabeth B and Marianne Moore and Lowell. Most of that material is also on his floppy disks, and the good news is that there is already about 7/8 of a finished book—all but a concluding chapter. The editor at Farrar Straus who's made a preliminary [review] of this material is very excited by it.

While Maxine Groffsky was consigning a pill-box-full of our dear one to the Grand Canal, Peter and I took Rollie's dinghy—have I told you this?—out a hundred yards or so, on a diamond-clear morning. With tears simply bursting out of my eyes, an hour earlier, I'd written a few lines which we burned and mixed with the "cremains." By the time the plastic bag with all of this in it had been turned inside-out under water, and the mansize cloud of white revolved once like one of Balanchine's dancers before dispersing, I felt so strong and grateful—and hoped, when my time comes, for nothing better than to be given back to the elements at the hand of a friend. This was selfish perhaps, in that so many of D's other friends were excluded from that moment, but one can't have everything. I'd reserved a last teaspoon to go at the base of Eleanor's apple tree, and as DJ and a couple of others stood around, I read a couple of Philip Sidney poems.

Meanwhile I've been working with increasing assurance on a

sequence of short prose pieces, in which notes and memories of Japan are put together with fears and fantasies involving David. (This page has one of them on its other side.) The end is in sight—mostly polishing—perhaps another couple of weeks.

I'm so happy about your painting and wish I could see the new works. I'm <u>sure</u> they are wonderful, and come to you—as everything in your work has for the last year or two—as a bountiful reward for a life of faith and dedication. These qualities don't ensure the reward, but they sweeten it if it comes.

I'm glad you met Peter and Barbara. (I agree with you about his poems.) <u>They</u> are certainly a dedicated pair, and Peter is an inspired traveler. Get him to tell you about Ladakh!

Peter Hooten is off to Jugoslavia next month to make a movie in or near Sarajevo. He's accumulated these millions of lire in Italy, which he wants me to come over and help him use up; so I'm more or less planning to go for 2 or 3 weeks in early October. Rome, perhaps Capri, Paestum. A nice old folks' tour.

It's now Friday morning, and I must get cracking.

My love always—
James

Richard Poirier (1925–2009), American literary scholar and critic, a founder of the Library of America and founding editor of the journal *Raritan;* Kalstone's colleague in the English department at Rutgers.

concluding chapter Merrill wrote the Afterword for Kalstone's *Becoming a Poet: Elizabeth Bishop with Marianne Moore and Robert Lowell,* edited by Robert Hemenway and published in 1989.

Rollie's dinghy See Merrill's poem "Farewell Performance" in *The Inner Room* (1988).

a sequence of short prose pieces "Prose of Departure" in *The Inner Room.*

Peter and Barbara Peter Sacks (b. 1950), South African–born American poet, literary scholar, and later painter, and his wife at the time, Barbara Kassel (b. 1952), American painter.

Ladakh "Land of High Passes," geographically fascinating and culturally rich region in the present-day Indian state of Jammu and Kashmir, inhabited since the Neolithic period, and a key point on the Silk Road.

To David McIntosh

CAREFUL: A GLOOMY LETTER, BY AND LARGE

Dear David,

Time canters by, kicking up dust as we squint vainly after it. DK's memorial service is only a week or so away. I'm not going to do anything so self-centered as to read this poem (over) but I mean to try to paraphrase it in the simplest terms, adding Maxine's midnight moment in Venice (consigning from a gondola the little vial she'd smuggled from NY, just under the Palazzo windows), and our final minutes in Eleanor's garden, reading Sidney's translation of the 23rd Psalm after putting the last teaspoonful among the lilies-of-the-valley under her apple tree. The program ends with the 5th Ruckert song by Mahler—do you know it? instant tears—but I'll let David himself have the last unsung words, by reading this paragraph from his Venetian journal, dated 28.vii.84. You can be with us in spirit all the better if I copy it out for you:

> Tonight, standing at the Barbaro window, I think must be the
> most beautiful night in the world. Cool. Soft vanishing sunlight
> and slow shadows on the Grand Canal. One deep sun spot. Being
> alone. Oh, to open my heart as I have not in years—Venice, my
> beautiful Venice. The heart aches as the light passes. The town
> is full of beacons, each with its own hour. I have never known
> it so beguiling as this summer—the lightning and hail the other
> evening . . . Oh never <u>not</u> to return!

Well, maybe after that some of the grieving can be put aside. Rollie just called. She's in NY for the night, and coming up tomorrow in order to go to John Brinnin's "surprise" 70th birthday party at a friend's house near his home in Duxbury. On Monday, though, she goes back to NY for the better part of a week in hospital—a battery of tests to do with her heart. She's been taken off medication to prepare, and is already feeling weak and sluggish. If you'd not heard this you'll want to send her a word. I should be able to call you midweek with her hospital-room phone number. David and I will go into town on Thursday (18th).

Meanwhile I seem to have come down with a mercifully light case of shingles—a couple of big patches on the temple, one on the eyebrow, another on the eyelid; but the eye is untouched, and the much-publicized AGONY is a matter of trivial twinges. Even so, an unwelcome visitor. Peter flew off to Yugoslavia ten days ago, to star in a film about the Liberation there. He plays a USMC Captain—a promotion, he having played nothing higher than a sergeant up to now. He bubbles over on the phone. The plan—forgive me if I've told you this—is that I fly over in about a month, to spend 2 or 3 weeks with him. Maybe in Rome, with a few days on Capri and a look at the temples at Paestum.

Oh, and Eleanor lost a breast: a small, wholly "contained" malignancy. She's recovering her customary animus, but feels a bit unbalanced, and no wonder: the breast weighed 19 pounds. Grace reigns on, serene if not supreme, at the nursing home.

We spoke of my visiting you next Spring. My dates at Tucson—where they give me a little guest-house—are the week ending April 4. I'm due in Houston on the 14th. I know that's a blustery season, but we might even meet in Tucson and spend part of those days looking around there—beautiful mountains, they say, and at that time of the year a blooming desert. Peter may be with me, it's too soon to be sure. Reflect upon it.

Your last letter had nothing about your work. I hope this isn't a bad phase?

My love always—
James

this poem "Farewell Performance," published in *The Inner Room* (1988).
5th Ruckert song Gustav Mahler's *Rückert-Lieder* are a group of songs set to poems by Friedrich Rückert (1788–1866). They were written independently and appear in different orders. This one begins "Ich bin der Welt abhanden gekommen."
Rollie McKenna and McIntosh were friends. He first visited Stonington, and met Merrill as a consequence, on her recommendation.
Tucson . . . Houston Merrill had been invited to read his poetry at the University of Arizona and at the University of Houston.

To Irma Brandeis   WUSTL
                                          23 September 1986
                                          [Stonington, CT]

Dearest Irma,

This program (enclosed) made for a very impressive hour. I can't tell you how beautifully the young woman sang, with her plain pink face and big lowered eyes—and, for the Mahler, her hands slightly clenched resting on the piano's lid. We were <u>all</u>, in fact, just fine. It was left to me to describe what happened to the remains. One of these poems tells half the story—not, of course, that I read it. The other half described Maxine Groffsky emptying a little vial she'd smuggled into Italy into the starlit waters of the Grand Canal. There were perhaps 300 people present—rather an eyeopener for the relatives, who we all felt hadn't until this year thought David especially remarkable.

I'm relieved to have it behind me. His end has been with me every day all summer. As of this morning it's Fall. David and I—you'll remember—had been planning to propose ourselves for a day or so in Annandale before he goes south. But I've been set back by a little case of shingles (mercifully mild) and told to stay fairly quiet if I'm to be well enough to go to Rome. That is a new development: Peter Hooten went off to Yugoslavia to make another of his "spaghetti Army" movies, by whose end he'll have amassed lots and lots of lire. He asked me to fly over and help him spend them, so I think I shall. May I then come up for a day or night (or both) in November? (I'd be gone maybe 3 weeks at most.)

Otherwise all's well [*in the margin:* And you??]. David has nearly finished the sorting-out of decades of letters, which has taken him nearly five summers. Some lovely things came to light, like a letter from Alfred Corn about meeting our Stonington friends for the first time, in 1973. Naturally they were all showing off for a new face. Mrs Stone talked about the Yangtze gorges, Robert Morse about smoking opium in Thailand. Not to be outdone in sophistication, Grace then said: "But Robert, it's a well-known fact, isn't it, that opium and sex don't mix?" Robert smiled and said, "Poppycock!"

Let me close now. I'll phone in a week or so.

Love always,
Jamie

This program For David Kalstone's memorial service at the New York Public Library, September 20, 1986.
the young woman Dawn Upshaw (b. 1960), American soprano.

To Stephen Yenser   YALE
                                                    12 January 1987
                                                    Key West, FL

Dear Stephen,

What a day! About 11 this morning, a knock on the door. Nondescript lady, says she lives in the next block, hands me your Christmas Package: "You all weren't in, the postman left it with me, I promised to bring it round—then we went up to Orlando to spend the holidays, and I clean forgot until just this minute." I didn't know whether to cut her throat (for causing you all that nuisance of forms to be filled out) or hug her to my heart: here was my Wand! Lifted from its beautiful wrapping, wound in slender black-on-white verses, it is the magician's, or the sedentary cogitator's, version of the Malika (Makila?): never to be dipped, like the latter, in red clay, just waved over the heads of an imaginary orchestra, or laid on a beaded divan next to a shrugged-off cape and a pair of white kid gloves. It is the most enchanting and least useful present I've had in Heaven knows how long. And to think that it nearly ended up in someone else's hands!

That Peter was due to arrive at 2 o'clock made, in conjunction with that morning incident, for a day already too rich. But where the pennies from heaven are concerned, it evidently never rains but it pours. Minutes before I left for the airport came the BOOK (by overnight mail from Harvard—did you put them up to it?). It is so hefty and so handsome, I can barely put it aside to write this page. Then David snatches it up, then Peter does—you would think it was an eye or a tooth we shared, the three Weird Sisters here at the End of the World. You can't know, now or ever, how I've yearned for its coming; or how long. Long before it was written or conceived, almost before <u>you</u> were, there'd been this fantasy (like Enoch Soames's in Beerbohm) of reading about myself from a kind of astral perspective, pages of starlike sympathy and intelligence. Now here they are, 331 of them, and I feel this afternoon as if I shall never need to open another book of any description for the rest of my life. (Once I get it away from my housemates, that is.) Mona and Jarvis will be over shortly, and there's a bottle of Mumm's on ice to toast it and you.

David, by the way, is thrilled by his illustration, and the index entry: 217–318, <u>passim</u>. That's practically a record, I've assured him, for sustained reference. And Peter is thrilled by having the text end with a line of the Santero's.

We'll probably phone you this evening, at any rate long before you get these words. But something had to spill over into writing. Thank you and Mary for a present all the more beautiful for arriving after I'd given up hope. As for *The Consuming Myth*, may it earn you laurels on Earth and a crown in Heaven. Now perhaps somebody will let <u>me</u> have another go at it!

Yours ever,
James

my Wand A conductor's baton, a gift.

Malika (Makila?) The latter: a Basque walking stick, a gift mentioned in the fourth sonnet in Merrill's sequence "Days of 1971" (*Braving the Elements*, 1972).

the BOOK Yenser's *The Consuming Myth: The Work of James Merrill* had just been published.

Enoch Soames's in Beerbohm Soames is the eponymous character in a 1916 story by the parodist Max Beerbohm (1872–1956) that combines elements of historical fact, science fiction, and fantasy.

his illustration Yenser's book reproduces Jackson's drawing of their house in Athens.

a line of the Santero's Manuel, the santero (maker of religious images in Santeria), in Merrill's short drama *The Image Maker* (*The Inner Room*, 1988), tells his mother: "My work, Mamá. That's *my* whole life."

To Peter Hooten

HOOTEN
20 February 1987
Key West, FL

Precious John Peter,

It's the morning after Liz Lear's garden party. Same format as last year, but among the sixty guests were some new faces (and at least one beloved one absent). Leonard Bernstein, who is staying in John Brinnin's empty apartment, was there: sonorous, emotional, looking frightful—fat and ravaged—drinking and smoking as if his life depended upon it; but charming, too—he said he's been reading *Sandover* again, and spoke with such understanding of its <u>techniques</u> that I was transported into a kind of Arcadia full of inspired denizens piping and scribbling under trellises in perfect harmony. Meanwhile a great buffet was being decimated, so I took my tray and joined Jimbo and Bill Wright, since my place at a dim corner table in the depths of the garden had already been filled. But before long the Lashes went home and I slipped over to Join the Wilburs, DJ, and Rust. It was very dark and uncertain underfoot. Charlee had already fallen, as shards of a flowerpot underfoot testified. When they got up to leave, I followed DJ to fill our glasses at the bar (wine and soda respectively) and stumbled on one of the fragments, lurching forward until the side of my face collided with a heavy stone urn on a plinth all of which then, including me, crashed into the shrubbery. (Moral: it is dangerous to drink too little or not at all.) Later, when my bloody ear had been swabbed, and Joy Williams joined us at the same table, she caught her silver heel between the bricks and nearly went sprawling herself. We have dubbed that corner of Liz's garden "The Bermuda Triangle." But it was a good party. We stayed until 11:15. Many asked for you. Joy and Tom Sanchez were having an enthralling drunken talk about their writing. Joy (at great length): "I really, really believe that short stories are the most demanding, the most subtle, the richest of forms you can work with. Poetry's <u>nothing</u> compared to a short story"—and so forth. Finally I reached into the next chair and took her hand. "Joy, I'm just going to forget that I heard you say that." You're right, she is adorable. So am I.

Tonight we're serving the HAM to nine people, so I mustn't go on.

An overnight packet arrived with photographs of Barbara Kassel's new work; she wants me to write something for her catalogue—the show opens April 28 (write it down)—along with snapshots of two paintings "in progress" that might do for my jacket. I wish you were here to look at them with me. But there's time.

We'll have talked on the phone before you read this. But in case the birds have ears, LET ME WHISPER ON PAPER THAT I LOVE YOU. And hope so much that the professional clouds will part, and a beam of pure gold—fame and money, that is—falls on your by then naturally colored ringlets.

Bless you, my dear one—
JM

Liz Lear Key West resident, on the board of the Key West Literary Seminars.
Jimbo Peter Hooten's younger brother.
Bill Wright William Wright (1930–2016), biographer and nonfiction writer.
Rust L. Rust Hills (1924–2008), writer and fiction editor of *Esquire* magazine, husband of Joy Williams (b. 1944), fiction writer and essayist.
Tom Sanchez (b. 1943), novelist and film director.
something for her catalogue "New Paintings," reprinted in Merrill's *Collected Prose* (2004) as "Barbara Kassel."
my jacket Merrill bought one of Kassel's paintings and had it reproduced on the dust jacket of *The Inner Room*.

To Stephen Yenser   YALE
19 October 1987
Stonington, CT

Dear Stephen,

After the pleasure your cards from Greece have given me, I want to make sure that something other than bills and junk mail awaits your return. It sounds like a lovely trip, if I may say so when you are only (by today's card) five days into your stay on Folegandros, and I regret that Peter and I haven't been able to saunter up to your table in the local tavern unexpectedly. I drove up this afternoon after a few days in NY. DJ took the train last Friday and reports that all's well in Florida. (What about those earthquakes out your way? That must have given you a scare. My mother sent me a letter from one of her now elderly "Red Cross girls"—a woman who'd come to see "The Image Maker"— describing the horror of days without air-conditioning or TV.) Times are changing everywhere. One used to go to the theater in New York, or to cocktail parties—not this year. This year it's memorial services. There was an evening at the Guggenheim museum to commemorate the 10th anniversary of Lowell's death. Wm. Alfred, Bidart, Heaney, Peter Taylor, and Helen V. (among others!) spoke. We sat within chatting distance of Lizzie and Harriet, and Penny Fitzgerald; and mingled vinously in the lobby afterwards. The program ended with his own voice reading "Skunk Hour"—sounding very Southern in the mid-Sixties, and causing gooseflesh nonetheless. The next day we went down to a Washington Square gallery for John Myers' service, a minefield of half-recognized faces. Speakers: Hilton Kramer (saying at tiresome length that J hadn't been in it for the money), Grace Hartigan (wonderfully sincere and funny), and me, with just a page to read, and feeling its utter inadequacy. A harpist we'd all slightly known—Daphne Hellman—played on her madly amplified instrument bits of Couperin and Scarlatti from her student days, all the while staring in consternation as her fingers flew and flew, mostly missing the strings. We skipped the uptown party and went straight home with Luly and Dorothea Tanning (who brought us a jack-o-lantern she'd carved most unoriginally) for a cozy dinner. Howard Moss's service has mercifully been put off until next year, but there's many a slip. A call this morning says that Rollie checked into the hospital in NY yesterday, and was going to see a new doctor; I know no further details, but she must have had a scare . . .

I finally typed out a penultimate draft of my concluding pages for DK's book—not pleased with them, either—and collecting impressions from the people who've seen the whole text. Dick Poirier thinks it's fine, but I put my faith in Robt. Hemenway out in Tucson whose involvement and meticulousness I would have no comparison for, if I'd never seen how you work. I'll wait to incorporate his suggestions, then let you see a tidy copy. Also I'm still fussing, of course, with the table of contents for the new book. For a while I thought the Japan prose should go out, but now . . . ? I'm afraid my objection boils down to the number of different places visited. Do I want readers to realize that I all but live in a 747?

Luly returned to dinner on Saturday with Peter Sacks and Barbara Kassel. I gather you'll be seeing them before long. I like them better all the time. Luly is in fine shape and looks forward to seeing you <u>as do we all</u>. Everyone is excited over John's sex-change. Peter even found a round- and pink-faced young woman by Mary Cassatt whom he'd decided looks like "Joan," but I think the actress and <u>our</u> Mary will have to settle between themselves which of them is to wear the pants, so to speak. I seem to recall that was an issue in the '50's. Frank Bidart wanted me to read his pages in the David Lehman *Ecstatic Occasions* volume, which I'd not seen (it may be in KW). So I saw your page making simple sense after <u>such</u> dizzy entries—! FB's piece carries a lot of weight, though, don't you think? I'm glad I'm a mayfly!

Peter and DJ (with whom I've just been separately on the phone) both join in love. We'll talk soon.

Yours ever,

James

"Red Cross girls" Friends of Merrill's mother from her work with the Red Cross in the Pacific during World War II.

Lizzie and Harriet Elizabeth Hardwick and her daughter with Lowell, Harriet Winslow Lowell (b. 1957), whose names are in the title of his volume of poems *For Lizzie and Harriet* (1973).

Penny Fitzgerald Penelope Laurans Fitzgerald (b. 1945), widow of the poet and translator Robert Fitzgerald (1910–85), had a four-decade association with Yale, as faculty member, administrator, college master, and associate editor of *The Yale Review*.

Hilton Kramer (1928–2012), art critic and founding editor of *The New Criterion*.

Grace Hartigan (1922–2008), painter associated with the New York school of poets and painters.

Luly Luly Hamlin, friend of Dorothea Tanning.

Dorothea Tanning (1910–2012), painter, sculptor, printmaker, poet, and memoirist. See letter to her of 26 November 1994.

the new book *The Inner Room* (1988).

the Japan prose "Prose of Departure."

John's sex-change When Merrill revised his play *The Bait* in 1988, he changed the sex of one of the lovers, and the original version's John became Jan, a woman, Julie's lover. Both versions are in the *Collected Novels and Plays* (2002).

our Mary Mary Bomba, who played Julie in *The Bait*.

the David Lehman *Ecstatic Occasions* Lehman edited *Ecstatic Occasions, Expedient Forms* (1978), an anthology of poems accompanied by the poets' contextualizing remarks on the pertinent forms.

To Alfred Corn and J. D. McClatchy

YALE
29 October 1987
[Stonington, CT]

Dear Alfred,

This isn't really an <u>answer</u> to your letter, just to your question about those lines in "After the Fire." The lover's ghost in question is myself—a survivor of the erotic conflagration, or "sheet of flame" ("ma flamme" as they like to say in Racine) (cf. the "sports shirt of flame" in "Friend of the 4th Decade"). I see the old colors just as I feel the outlived love—in memory. Thus everything has changed, and nothing has, these past things being so present still.

Dear A and S—

Very amusing about Jeremy Reed. I couldn't have begun to imagine he'd be like that. Peter went to a reading by Harry Mathews at Books and Co. and saw John Ash lounging far from the crowd; pierced his incognito with a mild phrase, and glided on, leaving JA staring after him. The real JA was there too, and Maxine looking sinfully beautiful with her newly bobbed hair. It has emerged over the Board that DK was especially jealous of that hair . . .

I drove the Splendors and Eleanor down to John and Natalie's. Aunt Eve and Andrew Forge filled out the table. I'm not sure it was a great evening, and poor Natalie <u>knows</u> it wasn't. My suspicion is that the S's in tandem cast something of a blight, though individually and tête-à-tête each is quite rewarding. At 10:30 he instigated a move to drive back—even though the change back to EST gave us another hour. In the car he told a very eerie story about James Lord (whom Eleanor persists in liking, as does SS). While it is not true that JL is an international art thief (that is the <u>other</u> James Lord) he did long ago in the 40's steal—no, borrow a little Bonnard from a Paris gallery. He took it back to his hotel room, hung it on the wall, then went into the bathroom and with a razor cut a fine hairline gash horizontally across his brow. Blood fell and was stanched, the wound healed, and the next week he took Bonnard back to the gallery—where it had not been missed (?!)—and explained what he had done. End of story. Frances Tanning must wish he had thought up that twist!

Speaking of which, there's a review (sent by Stephen Y) of *The Seraglio* by David Leavitt on the front page (bottom 5th) of the *LA Times* last Sunday. He squirms a bit unconvincingly over the self-mutilation, but the rest is glowing. SS had heard over the telephone that <u>I</u> had said they were happily installed, etc. in Stonington. I said, oh from David Plante? I know my correspondents are seeing a lot of him and Nikos. But we've none of us had courage to ask if he associates you with a certain review of his collected poems in *Poetry*.

The John Myers and Robt Lowell memorial services on 2 successive evenings—perhaps I've told you about them; yes. There's a very busy November ahead. I'll be in town for about 15 days of it—in two shifts. Peter does his Robert Frost evening on the 20th, at an odd little theater-church-soupkitchen in the West 70's. There's the Harry Ford gala on the 3rd, followed by a "small reception" at Lyn Chase's; also readings by Merwin-and-Bradley, Mona-and-Herbert Morris, the Marianne Moore centenary. You are well out of it—you'd be in wet sheets by month's end—just stick to your lovely music and soothing theatricals and disappointing food. Oops—nearly noon!

Love,

J.

"After the Fire" In *Braving the Elements* (1972).
"Friend of the 4th Decade" In *The Fire Screen* (1969).
Jeremy Reed (b. 1951), English poet, novelist, and critic.
Harry Mathews (1930–2017), poet and translator.
John Ash (1948–2019), English poet and travel writer.
The real JA John Ashbery.
the Splendors Stephen Spender and his second wife, Natasha.
John and Natalie John Hollander and Natalie Charkow.
Andrew Forge (1923–2002), English painter and art critic, professor of painting and dean of the School of Art at Yale.
James Lord (1922–2009), writer, biographer of his friend Alberto Giacometti.
Frances Tanning Francis Tanning is Merrill's surrogate in *The Seraglio*. The novel opens when a young girl slashes a portrait of her mother. Later, Francis castrates himself with a razor, the "self-mutilation" over which David Leavitt squirms.
David Plante (b. 1940), writer, novelist, memoirist, diarist.
Nikos Nikos Stangos (1936–2004), David Plante's partner, chief subject in Plante's memoir *The Pure Lover* (2009).
Robert Frost evening Peter Hooten performed readings of poems by Frost and Elizabeth Bishop.
Lyn Chase President of the Academy of American Poets.
readings Sponsored by the Academy of American Poets.
Bradley George Bradley (b. 1953), poet, whose *Terms to Be Met* was Merrill's choice for the Yale Younger Poets Award in 1986.

Herbert Morris (1928–2001), American poet, the "H.M." of Merrill's dedication of "From the Cupola" in *Nights and Days* (1966) and the basis of "the writer" in that poem's third line.

To Brian Walker

WALKER
17–18 April 1989
Stonington, CT

Dearest Brian,

Back in the old house. For the first few days I always have the sense of its looking at me through narrowed eyes—rather as I look at <u>it</u>: appraisingly, calculating what another winter has done to us, and how long the new paint job can be deferred. But its gaze this year is curiously innocent, sun shines on the painted chairs under the dome, a little three year-old plant—named, I think, Viola—is actually in bloom, and I realize only now, writing the phrase "new paint job" that this in fact took place last December. Nothing total, mind you, just some cosmetic work on the windowframes and in the big room upstairs. Today I sit with my heart in my mouth, waiting for my builder—the original builder's <u>son</u>, I should say, who long ago took over from his father—to come and tell me what it will cost to conform to the revised Fire Code. If I comply there will be no possible way for us and our guests to go up in flames. Funny how poets are encouraged to "take risks"—at least, that's what all the blurbs praise us for doing—when these are increasingly outlawed for the householder.

I was so happy to talk with you the other evening, and you must try to overlook those moments when I'm thrown off course by self-consciousness in one form or another. It's exactly as when, driving on ice, you brake and the car skids. The "ice" would be those patches from which, oh, the difference in age between us, or a rift in my wits flashes up at me and I say something I couldn't possibly mean about Carolyn Forché, or tease you about needing an audience in order to write. Face to face in a room one could be silent at such times, but that gets unnerving over the telephone. Still, I never want to make you wince. <u>Your</u> happiness shone through everything you said, and I bask in it even now. Stephen in California had made my heart sink (on your behalf) by saying how it grew harder every year to get into a good graduate school—but here you are, brilliantly vindicated, your dish heaped with plums after the threat of bread and water. It reminds me of William Empson's gloss on the "Full many a flower is born to blush unseen" stanza; he says that this simply means that, in 18th century England, there were no government scholarships for the talented. Nice way of starching a too-palpitating image.

California excited us all. Hours of rehearsal (most technical) left everyone gasping at the polish of our performance. Unfortunately you won't, if you come to New York, hear Roger Bourland's music. (Instead you will hear Bruce Saylor's.) But the synthesizer is surely Sandover's totem instrument, and Roger gave us the chitter of bats, a baroque dance, a whiff of bouzouki, as well as grave strings from outer space. These days I'm making a few little changes in the text, as after every performance, so <u>that</u> at least will be "better" next month. We reached LA in a heat wave that (for April) left the town unnerved, but it was dry, and blazing blue, like Greece in the old days, and cooled off at night. Our only experience of local culture was a visit to a new Japanese adjunct to the Museum—2nd rate 19th century scrolls and screens in a building so mindlessly and expensively curved and pleated, with interior penny-splattered pools, carpets and lucite everywhere, that Stephen asked at the desk if he could get a leaflet with the architect's explanation (or Apology). "Only in Japanese," the lady told him.

Now I am going out to the gym, in order to be strong when I meet my builder. (Why shouldn't the house develop some muscles too?)

On Thursday an old (thoroughly extinguished) flame is coming down, as he does once or twice a year, from an apple orchard I settled upon him in New Hampshire. You can read about him in *Late Settings* (a poem titled "Peter," for that is <u>his</u> name, too). He used to live in Stonington. We met him when he was 20 or so, just back from a long stint in Korea. He used to hang around the house until we had time for him, getting in the mood by means of a joint and a dirty book—not unlike the local kids you'll be entertaining next month? Now his beard is white and his girth is enormous. Luckily he no longer drinks or smokes; as it is, he gets pneumonia three times a year. What did I see in him? I suppose it was the side of me that falls not for individuals but types, though the distinction keeps blurring. I never seem to want the same type twice, which somewhat reassures me—like those articles explaining that there are countless germs that give you a cold but once you've had it you'll never get <u>that</u> one again. His first wife died last year, his second wife left just before Christmas, leaving three untamed kids on his hands, yet he remains loyal (I mean to me), amusable, and mildly zonked. He and the other Peter have yet to meet, a fact my dear one views with the greatest suspicion. I must take greater pains not to play upon his jealousy. Will these lines addressed to him (regarding "our" situation) help to minimize it—?:

> One cloudless evening last February
> Lightning struck. My dry wit caught. Within
> Seconds there you were with the wet blanket.
> Smoke-blackened, shivering, I have to grin.

The builder was reassuring. Perhaps the stairwell doesn't, after all, need to be lined with slow-burning material. Mainly it's a question of a couple of outdoor staircases being made to sprout, like Hasidic curls, down either cheek—that and an extensive alarm system costing more than psychoanalysis. Best of all, he will placate the company office in Hartford until the work gets done. Those are the telephone calls that simply undo me.

Christian is back in Montreal, but ill. He began vomiting blood the night of his return from Switzerland, and has been in the Queen Elizabeth hospital ever since. We spoke to him last week, on hearing the news. He sounded crisp if none too sanguine. Diagnosis: les varices de l'ésophage, but somehow allied to a liver disorder. I still hope you will meet him some day.

I listened to Pärt's part of the tape yesterday. My ears aren't as receptive as they once were, but they liked very much what they heard: a kind of tzigane austerity, meditative and charged with feeling. Nothing that intimidates—an especially welcome quality, even if it happens to be politically correct in his part of the world. Lithuania? Do you know anything about him, like a birthdate? If I ever replace my Meiji period tapedeck I'll send you some Maggie Teyte in return.

Do you know that voice?—singing your favorite composer's "Nell" or "Lydia" or the song that ends "Tes yeux levés au ciel, si tristes et si doux." Well, this is all the letter either of us has time for—you settling into your loft, I with a dozen others to write. Bless your good heart. I count on it so much, you know, and on your good sense too.

Yours ever,
James

Brian Walker Canadian native Brian Esparza Walker (b. 1962), later a professor of political science at UCLA.
Carolyn Forché (b. 1950), American poet.
Stephen in California Stephen Yenser.
William Empson's gloss On the fourteenth stanza of Thomas Gray's "Elegy Written in a Country Churchyard" in the opening chapter of *Some Versions of Pastoral* (1935).
Hours of rehearsal Of Merrill's *Voices from Sandover* (1988), a theatrical adaptation of parts of *The Changing Light at Sandover* (1982).
Bruce Saylor (b. 1946), American composer.
Japanese adjunct to the Museum The Pavilion for Japanese Art, designed by the American architect Bruce Goff (1904–82) for the Los Angeles County Museum of Art.
an old . . . flame Peter Tourville.
Christian Christian Ayoub Sinano.
Pärt Arvo Pärt (b. 1935), Estonian minimalist composer and inventor of tintinnabuli.
Meiji period Japanese era that extended from 1868 to 1912.
your favorite composer Gabriel Fauré.

To Edmund White   YALE
18 April 1989
Stonington, CT

Dear Ed,

I'm just back from California where we did our *Sandover* evening at UCLA. A charming and talented young man on the music faculty came up with some musical cues on his synthesizer that left us sighing with pleasure. On hearing that he's off to France (for the first time) this summer I thought you might enjoy each other—if only socially—and have given him your address and phone. Or will you be at the seaside? His name in Roger Bourland.

Before that there was the "usual" winter in Key West. <u>So</u> many parties, so many passers-through. Peter hated it. We did at least drive up to Marathon and swim with the dolphins—a really peak experience, not unlike one's first dance. During the preliminary lecture by the chaperone the two sexes (species, that is) ogled each other lubriciously, everyone hoping to get the partner of his choice. "Under no circumstances touch the dolphin in the genital area," said the girl, "it excites them too much." Finally the four of us who'd paid more than the other got in the water with <u>five</u> dolphins (no wallflowers) who gave us wet kisses, flipper handshakes, and rides at top speed while we grasped their dorsal fins and felt our trunks slipping down to our ankles. Lester Lanin was never like that.

David is now in Tucson for April. He stays in a Deco hotel across from the Station, meets with the Gay Writers Group, and is generally made much of. He'll be back in a couple of weeks. We have 3 more *Sandovers* this spring, one at a kind of grass roots poetry festival in Detroit, and two at the Guggenheim.

No one talks of anything but Alfred and Sandy. For a while I thought I wouldn't need to take sides, but A's behavior has been so callous and sanctimonious that I don't care if I ever lay eyes on him again. I know you're his old friend, but entre nous I've always liked Sandy better. Correction: Eleanor <u>did</u> talk of nothing but S and A, but now she has been to Russia, followed by 3 weeks in Poznan where her son is Consul, so we hear about all the scenes she made—at least the successful ones. On an excursion they found themselves having tea with that radical priest <u>and</u> Lech Walesa. The latter <u>kissed</u> <u>her</u> <u>hand</u>!

David—<u>our</u> David—'s book should be going to press soon. His brother for once didn't answer my Christmas card. Such a relief. And that is just about all the news I can give you. Do make a sign if you come this way.

Much love,
Jimmy

our *Sandover* evening Performance of *Voices from Sandover.*
Lester Lanin (1907–2004), bandleader.
David—our David—'s book Kalstone's *Becoming a Poet*. Kalstone and White had been close friends.

To Brian Walker   WALKER
                                                         14 June 1989
                                                      Stonington, CT

Dearest Brian,

If you can write me from a tent in a downpour may I not write you
from bed? I've read your page over + over about braving the river in
your kayak: almost Homeric in its verve + horror. Give me a nice de-
gree or two of fever any day. (I think it's a uremic infection—I had
one 15 months ago and the symptoms are the same. I'll see our local
doctor—the grandson of HG Wells + Rebecca West—tomorrow.) I
got up this morning after a restless night in which I seemed to be re-
creating word by word, like a character in Borges, a (mercifully) short
Richard Wilbur poem entitled "Insomnia"—:

  All night the headland
  Lunges into the nimble
  Capework of the wind.

—got up and went right back to bed, realizing that something was
terribly wrong, not with me so much as with the "larger commu-
nity," as RW calls it. Over the radio came Sousa marches, George M.
Cohan, finally Marilyn Horne backed up by a male chorus in "It's a
Grand Old Flag" (from Rossini's otherwise forgotten *L'Americana in
Delirio*)—well, it was FLAG DAY, and you must know that 45 years
ago today I was inducted into the U.S. Army. I left our NY apart-
ment, making my mother promise to write me every day (as she did,
poor thing—luckily I was once more a civilian seven months later)
and proceeded to Fort Dix in New Jersey. Within 24 hours I had
been issued fatigues + dog-tags, peeled my first potato in this vale of
tears, and been given the kind of haircut reserved (after the war) for
French women who took up with German officers. On the whole I
rather liked the Army. While I can't pretend it "made a man of me,"
it showed that I was at least as tough and adaptable as the others. I
too have slept in a tent—though not for 12 hours at a stretch. And I
had my first "experience" with a corporal—outranked!—in the boiler
room of our barracks. Instead of being sent into combat I was made a

clerk, and spent my evenings at the Recreation Center turning pages while one of my colleagues accompanied himself in Wotan's "Fare-well" or "Zaza, piccola zingara." Enfin: dozens of memories danced through my head before the program ended . . .

John Brinnin called this morning. He's off to Europe, briefly, in a few weeks, then will be housesitting in Maine during August. That is when he plans a few days in NB. I gave him your number and explained about the times. He cheapened himself by wondering "if Brian will remember me." (It's the obverse of that noble letter Karen Blixen receives from her Swahili servant: "We hold you in such esteem that it is inconceivable that you forget us"—or words to that effect. The same correspondent once addressed her as Honourable Lioness.) Well, if Darlings Island comes through we may have to plan a house party!

I beam to think you are enjoying *The Ambassadors*. When I read it last—a year ago—I came to see it as (almost) an allegory of the Novelist. Strether's famous "Live all you can" speech—isn't that what the author always exhorts his characters to do? And its pendant—when Mme de Vionnet breaks down + sobs "It's how you see us—!" shows the characters, as it were, reciprocating, fulfilling their end of the miraculous compact. Do you want to read more of HJ? *The Euro-peans* is an enchantment, very light + funny. *The Wings of the Dove*, though not as rich + perfect as *The Ambassadors* is quite a tearjerker. Then there's the collection of sketches called *The American Scene* written when he returned from England for the 1st time in Decades. Here, freed from the gilded cage of plot, his famous late style really takes wing. It may be his best book and every word of it is pertinent right now.

An hour later. (What was I about to say? No matter.) Remember that I have seen what happens to you in a thrift shop, if only for 5 minutes. I can even imagine—though a line got dropped from your letter at just that point—the shade of yellow of that cracked bowl. (When you read *The Golden Bowl* by HJ you'll recognize the original of your scene of discovery.) You'll wear your new shoes to Stonington, I hope. Yes, Rilke must be the patron saint of fripiers. Do read a piece by Hofmannsthal (in something of the same vein)—"The Letter of Lord Chandos." You can read it in the Ursprache.

I'm running down. I'm not used to longhand + the sun has set, and

DJ gone out to dinner. I'll be more myself in a day or two, but even now, weak as a flower, send you all the fragrance I can muster.

Love,
James

15.vi.89 Bloomsday, + the insufferable radio is playing jigs + ballads. The doctor confirms my diagnosis, + I'm off in a spurt of germs to fill his prescription. That New Moon soup: I hope it is served to you someday! Remember the Cavafy poem about the bloodstained bandage a boy leaves in his wastebasket? Of course now that "100 year old eggs" can be made in a day, we can expect an "instant" New Moon Soup to turn up in the novelty shops, or at Ferragamo's. Basta. Love—J.
—ah, now comes some Pärt on the radio . . .

"Insomnia" Merrill misquotes Wilbur's "Sleepless at Crown Point" in *The Mind-Reader: New Poems* (1976).
"It's a Grand Old Flag" "Grand Old Flag," a 1906 song by the aforementioned George M. Cohan.
L'Americana in Delirio Merrill, in pseudo-delirium, invents the opera, parodying the title of Rossini's *L'italiana in Algeri,* a specialty of Horne's.
Wotan's "Farewell" The finale of Wagner's *Die Walküre.*
"Zaza, piccola zingara" Baritone aria from Leoncavallo's opera *Zazà.*
NB New Brunswick, Canada, where Walker was visiting that summer.
Karen Blixen Better known under her pen name as Isak Dinesen (1885–1962), Danish writer.
Darlings Island In Hampton Parish, New Brunswick, Canada.
Strether . . . Mme de Vionnet Characters in Henry James's novel *The Ambassadors.*
the Cavafy poem "The Bandaged Shoulder."
"100 year old eggs" Preserved eggs, Chinese delicacies. Walker was studying Chinese culture.
New Moon Soup Traditional soup served at Chinese New Year reunion dinner.

To Stephen Yenser   YALE
4 July 1989
Stonington, CT

Dear Stephen,

This is one of a whole selection of stationery designed for me by Tom Bolt, whose job allows him long evening hours at play with a computer and a fancy printer. One page has the Ouija Board's arc of letters at the top, YES and NO in the corners, and the numerals at the bottom. Now if my letters could only be written by the Powers, while I do something else . . . (But what do you think about this? Can I get away with it?—once the sigma of POIHTHS is made terminal.) There's also a perfectly plain one, with just my name and address, which I can use for the people I don't want to frighten off.

It's the 4th of July. John and Natalie drove up for dinner (and the night) at Eleanor's with Rollie, us, and Sandy who arrived on Saturday and after 2 nights in our hall bedroom moved, as planned, to E's. Day begins here with a lot of hammering. Yesterday we moved poor David at 8 in the morning into Sandy's bed, still warm, where he "slept" for another five hours.

I feel, wrongly no doubt, that you are the least bit incommunicado. Yet I keep thinking of you and <u>at</u> you, and chafing, and aching. Mary and I talked twice on her birthday, which may or may not have helped her. The statistics certainly are on your side: 51% current marriages won't last. What I keep thinking, though, is colored perhaps by that Greek alphabet at the top of the page: that love is a tyrannical power, a fever, a wreaker of havoc. We in its power think we have never been more ourselves, and wake in amazement with a beloved severed head in our arms. There is always, of course, the exultation attendant upon possession by any god; and the creative surge, and sense of endless possibility—for a caricature of this state we have only to recall Bernie's manic spells. I suppose I'm urging you to keep in mind the degree to which you don't know what you're doing, something not at all incompatible with the subject's sense of heightened lucidity. Mary said that she had suggested a therapist or counselor (just as I did) but that you had said it hardly seemed worthwhile, since you could imagine so clearly what this person would have to say. Now that has seldom been my impression of a therapist. True, in the months or first year after extended therapy, one's intimate link with the doctor prolongs his tone of voice and turn of mind; but this doesn't really take care of the inevitable pile-up of dirty linen over a decade or so. Isn't the question partly whether you <u>want</u>, at this point, an analytic voice? The other question, which I also know from deep inside, is: why should it be necessary to turn so many lives upside-down in order, when the smoke clears, to have moved only a few inches from one's starting place? This is a real toughie, and you mustn't expect me either to answer or to illustrate it; but it corresponds to a sneaking impression I've had more than once.

Remember, finally, that I'm a child of the Broken Home, and that situations like your present one take me back to inconsolable nights— Mademoiselle and cough syrup, etc. Without those memories I might very possibly have put an end to life with DJ—and he by the same token might have found an alternative to chainsmoking in front of his TV set all day and all night. These are points at which Experience deludes quite as much as it teaches. The Voltaire in me wants to say that what-ever happens is for the best; the mind is inventive and supple enough to make sure of that; it's only in movies that lives are "wrecked", and so forth. Melissa may continue to make you very happy, or proceed to make you very unhappy. Either way, it will be exactly what you deserve—as you know already in the thrilling clutches of the goddess. You see by now, dear friend, that these are just idle thoughts, not an argument at all. But entertain them, for old times' sake.

There's bound to be some "news". I sent off my introduction to Yale, and am FOREVER FREE! My love to you. Take care.

> Yours ever,
> James

This . . . stationery Merrill wrote his letter on a page of letterhead stationery with Greek typography specially designed for him by Thomas Bolt (b. 1959), whose vol-ume *Out of the Woods* Merrill had selected for the Yale Younger Poets series in 1988.
the sigma of POIHTHS The capitalized word spells the Greek word "poet," but the concluding letter should be a capital sigma: Σ.
I sent off my introduction His last introduction to a Yale Younger Poets volume, *Hermit with Landscape* by Daniel Hall in 1989.

To Francis Peschka and Gordon Murdock

WUSTL
6 July 1989
Stonington, CT

My dears,

A friend with access to a computer designed this paper for me and my dormant letter-writing self leaps dewy-eyed from its bed. If I cannot adorn my pages with floral water-colours, perhaps this alphabet will sugar the pill?

Goodness, it has been forever since I wrote. We ought at least to have sent you a postcard from DeTrop—Detroit, that is—but that leg of our tour was simply too grueling. We played in the Majestic Theater, where Houdini once appeared (or maybe disappeared), but it had since then become a cinema, before finally being gutted and turned into a disco run by the owner of the Gnome Restaurant, which now fronts the theater. It was loud and filthy, the technical people were inept, our stools weren't the right height. But you would have been proud of us. Troupers to the last! By the time we got to the Guggenheim for our 2 performances in late May, we all but sank back into the expert hands of a lighting man who flung sunsets and starbursts, thunderheads and banks of flowers onto a scrim behind which were (intermittently visible) 5 musicians—3 strings, flute, and harp—and our composer, Bruce Saylor. Unfortunately the young braggadocio we hired to videotape it botched the job, or at least came up with something very inferior. Still, in a few weeks I'd love to lend you the tape, so you can see for yourselves what we've been up to.

Since then, things have been duller. Peter's out in LA, making contacts and hoping for stardom. I've been here, with David, trying to tidy up my desk, write the last of my introductions for the Yale Younger Poets series, work on a few poems. Once every 10 days we give a dinner party (we owe everyone in town) but it's too exhausting and, now that I hardly ever drink so much as a glass of wine, not much fun. Our strategy is to <u>deserve</u> a week or two in Canada in August, and my trip (with Peter) to Athens and Istanbul in late September.

I guess I haven't written since P and I went to a *Ring* cycle. It was my first since 1939, though I must surely have heard the individual operas once or twice each since then. It got bad reviews on the whole, but <u>we</u> were thrilled by nearly everything—the direction, the lighting, the wonderful "effects". Fafner and his cave were somehow one; the hollow cluttered with old gold sprouted crablike pincers, opened a great wet pink mouth, and sang. At the very end, foolishly, a dozen people walked onto stage and stood in silhouette staring out at the Light of Love over the receding waters. It would have been more fun, I thought, if they had been recognizable—Franck, Chabrier, Debussy, Schoenberg, etc. The basso roles were sung electrifyingly well, and Behrens quite won my heart from her first moment onstage when, in her eagerness for battle, she simply, with her russet mane, butts Wotan in the solar plexus, like a little pony. As with Callas, there was no explanation for how she "did" certain things unless it was by <u>thinking</u> them with the utmost concentration. Now we have something quite different ahead of us next week: the Peter Sellars *Don Giovanni* and *Cosi*. We went to his *Figaro* last year and were enraptured against all our advance prejudice.

Well, I'm sorry we didn't make it to H*U*R*O*N while we were at it. How lovely it would be to see you! This brings hugs from us all to all of you.

Ever,
Jimmy

Frank Peschka and Gordon Murdock The puppeteers who created The Little Players.
our tour Merrill and Hooten's reading tour of the playscript *Voices from Sandover.*
a *Ring* cycle The Metropolitan Opera's *Ring*, produced by Otto Schenk and conducted by James Levine. See Merrill's poem "The Ring Cycle" in *A Scattering of Salts* (1995).
Behrens Hildegard Behrens (1937–2009), German soprano.
Peter Sellars American theater and opera director (b. 1957), known for his provocative contemporary stagings.
H*U*R*O*N Peschka and Murdock lived in Huron, Ohio.

To Brian Walker   WALKER
12 July 1989
Stonington, CT

Dearest Brian,

(Stationery courtesy of a friend who works nights with a computer—)
Your letter on melon-colored paper took only five days to arrive, and I made haste to answer—all the more gratefully for not having been sure, before today, whether you were planning a return to St John, or where, in that event, I could with any soupçon of confidence, write to you. I wanted first of all to thank you again for your trouble in the matter of Darlings Island. I <u>am</u> disappointed, as well as embar-

rassed to have enlisted you unnecessarily. It's plain from this and similar instances that I'm turning into the kind of elderly fussbudget who keeps forever changing his plans. The look on poor Joyce's face whenever I enter her travel agency down the street has long since told me the worst; and now I shall have deserved—¡ay de mi!—that same waxen smile of forbearance from you. If Peter were happier this season than he sounds over the telephone we should perhaps by now have come to terms with Square Peg. As it stands, I'm setting up only a couple of nights in Montreal and three in Quebec—at which point we'll either improvise or head back home. Do I need to add that one source of P's insecurity is the light he knows would shine from my eyes at the sight of you. It shocked him when he saw it first, and while I've tried to persuade him that to be charmed by or drawn to a new friend oughtn't in itself to count as a betrayal, he remains unconvinced. (Reading your letter, with its kaleidoscopic disunities of place and action, in the light of our austere, sublimated Triangle, is to re-experience the contrast between Shakespeare and Racine.) It goes without saying, surely, that it's exactly as we are that you and I have the best of one another, an intimacy without claims or quicksands. Not that I haven't imagined something further, but even my second adolescence is long behind me—I no longer crow with anticipation of the untried and untrue. Is that too baldly put? HJ could have conveyed it, as you say, "wonderfully". And in so <u>many</u> words.

With somebody named Darius at the wheel I too might drive to Oregon, but my body English flings itself to the balance on the side of your book. Time flies, and these are such crucial years for you. Since the work is going well, give yourself to it. Imagine an *Ambassadors* in which the garden party is given not by a sculptor but an old, much-modeled piece of human clay. The keen-eyed American sits down next to the youngest guest and begins: "<u>Don't</u>, whatever you do, live more than you have to! . . ." But you know best, as the squirrel in Central Park knows just how many nuts are needed to see him through the long New York winter. I like how you write about HJ—as if his effects weren't after all wholly incompatible with Philosophy. I also look forward to ongoing demonstrations, by you, that New York bears any slightest resemblance to "Society." To that end, my address book is <u>your</u> address book. And a vignette: Decades ago, when your enchanting compatriot Charles Ritchie—whom we in Stonington met as Elizabeth Bowen's lover—was Ambassador to Paris, he went to his first dinner party. Twelve or sixteen Parisians at table, all totally ignoring him and his wife. Finally, at a change of course, the large woman to his left recollected herself and, interrupting an anecdote she was telling someone across the table, addressed him. "Alors, Monsieur, vous venez du Canada?" "Oui, Madame." "C'est un très grand pays!" "Oui, Madame." "Il doit faire très froid l'hiver!" "Oui, Madame." Whereupon, back to her friend: ". . . puis le lendemain, Marie-Bismuth, sans aucune idée, bla-bla-bla—"

We're having a few ravishing days. The Sound sparkles. I've even climbed down the ladder (of the dock across the street) and dipped into it—very bracing. Our terrace is a mass of nasturtiums, whose blossoms do everything for a salad. (In NY these edible flowers cost, by weight, as much as caviar.) Eleanor had us to dinner with Sandy and the Hollanders. The garden was at its greenest, the tiny skulls of fallen crabapples cracked underfoot, and the roses rambled almost as compulsively as DJ. He had a recurrence of his Problem (diverticulitis) yesterday, so Eleanor and I went by ourselves to dine at the coveside house of two married writers. But they know only American literature, and very little before 1920—we kept biting our tongues so as not to mortify them by too many allusions to Tolstoy and Proust. The pickings here are slim. Once or twice a week the deathly stillness of 10 p.m. is broken by convivial voices heading home after a late evening, but all in all we might be a community of hardworking peasants. Giving dinners is hard work. So is going to them.

I go to New York tomorrow for a full week. My darling nephew Stephen (43 and gay) is having a kidney removed—they found a cancer—and so far I'm the only one in the family who's been told. His mother, all unknowing, returns from a pleasure trip on the day of the operation. (She's my half-sister, 12 years older.) S's lover Octavio is at his best at such times, guided poor Stephen through cat scans and 2nd opinions, has mantras and homeopathy at his fingertips, etc. Our doctor (George Cotzias, up in the Lab) says not to worry. On the bright side Peter and I are going to *Don Giovanni* and *Così Fan Tutte* directed by the miraculous Peter Sellars, who staged last year's *Figaro* as if in a duplex in Trump Tower. (For the wedding music, Figaro himself slipped a glittering CD onto its turntable.) And maybe we'll get to see *Batman*.

This is far too short a letter—perhaps I'll try calling you this evening—but for the moment (8:30 in the morning) let us go back to our desks—

Love,
James

Charles Ritchie Canadian diplomat (1906–95), Elizabeth Bowen's longtime lover, known for his diaries *The Siren Years: A Canadian Diplomat Abroad 1937–1945* and its sequels.
Elizabeth Bowen (1899–1973), Anglo-Irish novelist and short-story writer.
Batman Film (1989) directed by Tim Burton.

To Stephen Yenser

YALE
22 July 1989
Stonington, CT

Dear Stephen,

I got back from my week in NY about 48 hours ago (in a plane that sat shuddering on the LaGuardia runway for an hour and a half— "We're 60th in line for takeoff," announced the pilot cheerfully once the doors were shut). While I was away Grace had a tiny setback which resulted in the following conversation:

> GSZ: Why am I in this hospital? Is my husband a doctor?
> Harriet: No, you're a widow, Mrs Stone. Your husband was a
> Navy man.
> GSZ: Oh yes . . . Then tell me, who am I having an affair with?

In NY we drove out on two successive days to see the Peter Sellars *Don Giovanni* and *Così Fan Tutte*—neither as uniformly good as last year's *Figaro* but full of memorable moments. The Don and Leporello were sung by pale black identical twins, both stoned out of their heads when the time comes to change clothes (identical leather jackets). Don G then sings a stanza of his serenade, and falls flat on his face for the 2nd stanza. Donna Anna shoots up before her ecstatic cabaletta in "Non mi dir." The final banquet is a bag full of Burger King's best. But I may have told you that already in my note.

Peter says he went to see Stephen Magowan in hospital today, recovering quickly and cheerfully. He's the only one of those boys with the authentic sunshine gene.

I was glad to find your letter—and to receive, today, the newspaper photo of that cast at Glyndebourne. It didn't "tell" very much and probably wasn't meant to. Sandy said you'd phoned him sounding unhappy and put-upon, but without saying why; I didn't elucidate. Are you seeing a shrink? Is anything coming of that? I don't know if anyone (Kelly? Jonathan?) has given you a talking-to. Talkings-to aren't my style, goodness knows. But I'm getting darker and darker vibes as the situation begins to sink in. I don't even know how to be specific. Something in your account of your little flat started me thinking: that's how you might have to live for a long, long time, if things follow their course. And while I understand the attraction of the wee love-nest—an attraction that partakes of a clean sweep made in a number of directions—I'm old enough to wonder if there's not an element of self-punishment involved. To wonder also if, to any least extent, you simply want OUT of life with Mary and have found the most plausible way of accomplishing the break. Peter said you were drinking a lot. Sandy says your sleeping-patterns are upside-down. Can I say, without sounding like a fogey, that these aren't good signs? Can I say that at least part of you must be perfectly miserable? (I know, I'm thinking of my father at a similar juncture; and of his telling me, years later, that it was the biggest mistake of his life.) I don't suggest that Mary will necessarily turn vindictive. My mother nearly forewent all alimony in favor of a settlement that, though seemingly generous, would have turned into a pittance with the changing economy. These are among the consequences you'll have to consider. Of course Eros has given you the energy to face them hundred-fold but who knows? You don't. I don't. I just worry about it. It's the question you and I hoped the shrink might have an answer to: are you mad or sane? *(over)

It's not "like" me to raise such issues. Do understand one reason I'm upset: this is the first time in 22 years that I've failed to identify with you. Despite certain similarities (my age-difference with

P, yours with Melissa), the rest is too close to (the broken) home. I hate to add even a shadow of "disapproval" to your load of worries, and have to smile at seeing myself—of all people—even tentatively ranged against "antisocial" behavior. But there, I've said it. End of letter. And my love for you is unchanged.

Yours ever,
James

*I still hope a time might come (or is it too late for that?) when you and Mary could have some joint sessions with shrink or counselor. There must be a lot to say to a 3rd person. And better that it be said that way than to save it all for the courtroom. The courtroom can be avoided, as you know; but the circumstances are hardly those of your first divorce.
On reflection I guess I <u>do</u> suggest that Mary could "turn vindictive." It is one of the conventions of female psychology, analogous perhaps to our male euphoria on the threshold of a new love . . .

(Kelly? Jonathan?) Yenser's younger brother and his friend Jonathan Post (b. 1947), professor of English at UCLA.
Melissa Melissa Berton (b. 1967), who was to become Yenser's third wife.

To Rachel Hadas

Dear Rachel—

I finished your book yesterday, reading always more slowly, the more it sank in how very much I was liking it, + how moved I was (am) to feel a part of it in so many ways. I shan't reread it in this format, but look forward to doing so as soon as it reaches me in print. The poem I think "works" very nicely both on its own and offsetting the prose. As a reader I find it hard to handle more than one short line at a time, + still feel the pentameter sustaining one—but this is the smallest of objections. I also doubt that I served rabbit <u>liver</u> paté, more likely a paté of minced rabbit meat. (Those were days when Strato <u>looked</u> like a rabbit, red eyes + all . . .) Your elegant division of chapters makes me feel quite foolish to be writing "chronologically." Yet the impulse behind both is the same. Most of all, it seems to me that you've managed to present yourself as a quite adorable person— without airs or coyness—and that this is, of course, far more than a merely literary victory. (Much of it must be Jonathan's doing—the way the Japanese load themselves with quiet towards their parents and <u>only</u> when a child is born does the burden begin to lift.) Well, as I say, I'm touched as well as admiring. And now for my camomile.

Love,
Jimmy

your book Hadas's *Living in Time* (1990), combining prose and poetry, included memories of her years in Greece and her friendship with Merrill.
Jonathan's doing Jonathan Hadas Edwards (b. 1984), Hadas's son.

To Peter Moore

MOORE
24 August 1990
Cambridge, MA

Dear Peter Moore,

Your very welcome letter reaches me here—our "cast" has been given the day off, a reward for knowing our lines so well. Tomorrow we say them before an audience, and Sunday the filming begins—a week of 10 hour days: make-up, costumes, the works! I must say it's as absorbing—almost—as getting up each morning to write the poem was. Peter Hooten + I are in a friend's apartment a couple of miles from Harvard Sq. where everyone else is being housed. We have a view of the Charles, a dripping tap, our clutter everywhere. I read Peter your account of reciting "The Moose" in Wales; he loved it. He has staged (minimally) an evening of 2 actresses reading EB to one another, but you already know how well she goes over at whatever level of sophistication. You might enjoy David Kalstone's *Becoming a*

Poet—out last fall (Farrar Straus), a book both critical + biographical—
and supremely tactful to boot. DK was a dear dear friend, who died
in 1986 of AIDS. You asked me to recommend some younger poets
+ novelists. The 1st name that comes to mind is Jeffrey Harrison—a
book of poems called *The Singing Underneath* (Dutton?—I can't
recall . . .) He's indebted to EB but no one can fake that perfect,
natural note. I read his poems the way a dog eats grass. Richard Ken-
ney? More baroque, but very likeable. Mary Jo Salter's latest book
(*Unfinished Portrait*) delighted me. I like Sandra MacPherson too.
Novelists . . . hmm. I liked *Housekeeping* (Marilynne Robinson) even
though it was made into a movie. There are other titles, but they
elude me.

I've been—yet again—invited to that Harborfront poetry Festival,
next April—and this time may be able to accept. Do you ever attend?
Is it pleasantly arranged?

You won't easily find a copy of *Sandover*—not from the publish-
ers. Atheneum, as part of its ongoing drive to self-destruction, has
returned my copyright to me, rather than trouble themselves to
reprint. Knopf may bring it out again, but it will take a couple of
years. We've not even been able to rustle up copies enough to give our
actors. When the smoke clears I may have one or 2 left over + would
be happy to send you one, if you've been unable to find it through
other channels. Let me know in a month or two.

I'm ashamed to say I don't know wildflowers very well. Peter + I
looked up the ones we saw in Cornwall. EB took it upon herself to
"educate" poor sedentary night-blooming Frank Bidart when he vis-
ited her Maine Island—till then he'd only known the rose + the daisy.
His obsession with punctuation inspired her to make him a lovely
present. She collected oddly shaped bits from a black shingle beach,
glued them onto a board so that they took the aspect of commas,
dashes, exclamation points etc. + had it framed with a label in her spi-
dery hand: "Examples of Pleistocene punctuation for FB from EB."

Now I must leave you. Fondest wishes to you (+ Jeffrey)
James

Peter Moore Dr. Peter Moore (1934–2019), Canadian psychologist based in
Toronto, author of " 'Homosexual': The Label that Damns," *Canadian Medical Asso-
ciation Journal*, vol. 106 (1972).

Jeffrey Harrison (b. 1957); Merrill chose his volume as a winner of the National Poetry Series in 1988.
Richard Kenney (b. 1948); Merrill chose his *The Evolution of the Flightless Bird* for the 1983 Yale Series of Younger Poets.

To Claude Fredericks

GETTY
29 May 1991
Stonington, CT

Dearest Claude,

Oh dear, I had no notion that you'd been nursing a grievance!—though even as I write, something tells me not to be too surprised. You've written me that same page (more or less) at least twice a decade since the Beginning of Time—and the problem is never what you think it is (i.e. some imagined coldness towards you, whom I love and revere) but rather the very thing you put your finger on in those journal pages from March of 1950: the (to your philosophical eye) absurd claims I allow just about anybody to make upon my time; claims that leave me exhausted and cross with myself. I can't remember exactly when I was less than satisfactory on the phone—was I calling from Key West? from New York?—but I can be sure, and so can you, that I couldn't foresee having any greater leisure, for weeks to come, for the kind of communion we both deserve from each other. Overextension of the social or domestic web is, <u>as you know</u>, the lifelong rack I've been stretched upon, to the point where my dear ones sometimes don't know me. This last year it has all been made worse by the projects that took me from my desk to Cambridge and Los Angeles; and by the increased contrary pull of my Double Life—David's slide into apathy leaving me feeling just as guilty as does Peter's quite maniac form of self-destructiveness—so you see, I can (like you) take personally things I perhaps shouldn't. . . . Dear friend, let's not labor the point any longer. It's how I've chosen to live, not how I feel about you. As you surely, surely, surely know.

I'm glad that some of the shutters fit. Eleanor swears that the recalcitrant ones will respond to immersion for 2 or 3 days in paint remover—but what does she know? (Of course new shutters might be cheaper than that much paint remover.) . . . This is only my second guestless day on Water Street. First we had a Dutch friend (not seen since 1959 when he was studying psychiatry at Johns Hopkins). Then Peter came with Rob Perkins (as a buffer against the ubiquitous "phonies" of our defenseless little village) and we showed the completed videotape to about 25 people. Many a fence was mended that evening. Peter and Eleanor spoke pleasantly to each other for the first time since 1987; Sewelly and old Philip Stapp, after a much longer coldness, were cordial; as were our tenant Ray Izbicki and our hostess, nice Mrs Riordan, whom he'd been reviling for 20 months. The healing "Good Friday music" of *Sandover*? Not really: halfway through the screening P. transferred his hostility to poor drunk Louise Wimpfheimer who wasn't understanding a word and saying as much to her neighbor, and the next day precipitated something Too Awful from the offended grocer's still smouldering doxy—if you recall that old story. . . . But, yes, the tape is finished and I hope that we can show it to you and Todd very soon. (I'll try to think when, when I've had a little more time to catch my breath.)

In New York Andrew Harvey came to lunch—in a smart white suit and black shirt—and spoke with such pleasure of his time with you. He took you to a party? Who was there? Have you read his new book? I have a little stack of novels to get through; I'm not sure they stick in the mind—which may be the ultimate kindness to one's reader. Anyhow it's fun to turn the scented pages. He is in certain ways an avatar of Tony Harwood: much improved, to be sure. One day the Great Casting Director will finally get it right.

I've got a lot of little changes to make in the Memoir, but have for the moment turned to other things. Harry's sending me a contract for *Sandover* (at last!!—it's been o.p. for 2 years) as well as a new selected poems; and I'm trying to write a poem about my new windbreaker whose weightless fabric is imprinted with a colorful map of the world.

Surely Todd is back by now? Is he with his mother or at home where he belongs (Pawlet)? Please give him love and sympathy, from Peter too. And love to you from us all,

> Especially
> Jamey

completed videotape A version of *Voices from Sandover*, produced by Peter Hooten and directed by Joan Darling, that had been shot at the Agassiz Theater, Harvard University.

Philip Stapp (1908–2003), artist and video animator, Stonington resident.

Ray Izbicki Rev. Raymond A. Izbicki (1921–2007), Merrill's longtime tenant in the second-floor flat at 107 Water Street, who was ordained in the Anglican (Old Catholic) Church.

offended grocer Offended, that is, by Merrill's poem "November Ode" that lampooned the lone remaining "dear dim local grocery" in Stonington that had been "shut down by the State." The poem was published in the 27 October 1988 issue of *The New York Review of Books* and is reprinted in *Collected Poems* (2001).

Andrew Harvey (b. 1952), British religious scholar, author of many books on mysticism, founding director of the Institute for Sacred Activism.

the Memoir *A Different Person* (1993).

new selected poems *Selected Poems 1946–1985* (1992).

a poem about my new windbreaker "Self-Portrait in Tyvek™ Windbreaker" (*A Scattering of Salts*, 1995).

To Stephen Yenser   YALE
                                              16 July 1991
                                          Stonington, CT

Dear Stephen:

After listening to Sandy, who thought that last asterisk-placed stanza too reminiscent of a section from "Losing the Marbles" and suggested that "Sing our final air." made for a crisp enough conclusion, I tried to rewrite accordingly. Out went the original stanza 12 in favor of what you'll read (below), followed by these lines in part thriftily versified from a recent paragraph added to the Memoir:

At first it hurt in such a crush of others
To be oneself. But the years pass. You and I've ex-
hausted the subjective. True to type?
Why not? For Type is tops in Nature's book
And ourselves, gladly suffered to the extent
That we embody (or refine) it. Tyvek's
Motley of countries lighter than money spent
Visiting them's our uniform, and "Brothers,
Earth's all we got!" our message, though by week's end—

As breaker after breaker pounds on the beach,
The swell of fashion cresting to collapse—
Who wants to be caught dead [etc.]

. . . In this new version you'll be reading I've restored the original last stanza and somewhat accommodated the intermediate draft to this arrangement. I don't greatly mourn the life-class stanza, do you? What do you think of Sandy's point (resemblance to "Losing the Marbles") and the ending he suggested? I don't mean to play one mentor off against the other, but the poem is now like those hands in Canasta (awful game) that get so full of cards that you can't see what you've got. You'll also notice that I've adopted nearly all your little suggestions—all but de-personifying the jacket; I sort of like that touch. Thank you—as ALWAYS—for your marvelous attention.

Thank you too for your report on David Marinoff. I hope Peter and I can put our heads together with him in September. Our calendar is as usual v. complex from now until Sept 14. (We're off to Cooperstown next weekend, then to Claude, then to my brother's in NH. And the following week to Minneapolis for a reading AND the premier of Marjorie Hess's opera *Mirabell* which has been in the works 2–3 years now.) At least I have Atlanta behind me. Reading excerpts from the memoir to Mrs P was not such a good idea: "I've prayed twice a day for nearly 50 years that none of this would ever come to light . . . In fact I'd just been praying when I slipped and broke my hip in church, so I guess God got tired of hearing that particular prayer." JM: Did you never in all those years pray to have your embarrassment and shame taken away? HP: Never. Oh well (a sweet smile) I may be gone by the time it's published. I hope I am. . . . I've left the ms. with her at her request, but God is now making her eyes burn too severely to read more than a page a day. "And of course I can't ask anyone else to read it to me." I must say I gobbled up a *Newsweek* cover story on Halcion with just a teensy trace of envy. Did you see it? Lizard-faced woman (59) crazed by popular sleeping pill shoots her old mother and is so successfully defended that the case gets thrown out of court; whereupon she and her lawyer sue Upjohn for 21 million—to be split, no doubt, with the judge.

Meanwhile Peter doesn't sound too good. He stays sober, I think, but our therapist has added a small (?) dose of lithium to his Prozac. Then he was felled by a nasty big abscess in his backside . . . We took Elzbieta (who goes to Brazil with the Robert Wilson troupe in October) to an avant garde dance recital. The longest number was done by David Neumann's company which (for this particular dance) featured a midget agile enough to keep pace with the fullgrown dancers as they scampered about the stage and small enough to be picked up and cradled like a baby by the women. Afterwards we four had dinner. That morning's *Times* had printed Bill Ball's obituary (with a charming young photograph of him). It seems he took pills, having repeatedly threatened to do so over the years: a periodic depressive. So no one now has a word left to say against him and we all hope he was buried in the Auden hairpiece he refused to give back.

I didn't find the latest "Vertumnal" in your packet (won't you send it along?) but am grateful for the *Yale Review* and *Poetry* (both of which I'd seen). The prose section of "Vertumnal" is helped immensely, I think, by the weeding out of punctuation. You've certainly done your best for those poets, most of whom seem to deserve it. I was even won over to Galway K for the first time in ages by that wonderful line about the bluets. Thanks too for the *Times* piece mentioning Eleanor. She had no good to say of its author—a shameless plagiarist of *Green Thoughts* as she has told him in crushing terms. She was meant, by the way, to go to the Southwest for ten days with David & Pam Leeming (lively newish couple in town) but, on top of a bout of walking pneumonia, missed her connection at Penn Station (having allowed a mere hour between trains) and of course everything was booked solid for the weeks ahead. The poor Leemings had to cancel a whole string of reservations, air-conditioned "kneeling" van, etc., but at least they were spared E conking out at 7000 feet after her first kir. This trip was meant to be a dry run for next year's jaunt to Cappadocia (the L's know Turkey very well). Now it is dawning on her that she can never travel anywhere again. (Speaking of travel, Sandy gave me a book on travelers to Greece which quotes this wonderful line on Byron: "a shark for sensations, when he had lost velocity he could not feed, or function"—Frederic Raphael.)

I'll walk down to the P.O. with this. I'm sure you could dine out on your wedding plans, but don't give them away—I'll see for myself in February.

> Love to M. Yours ever,
> James

tried to rewrite The poem being revised is "Self-Portrait in Tyvek™ Windbreaker." Merrill did not use the stanza quoted here and kept a version of what he previously had as a conclusion.
David Marinoff Yenser's former student and friend.
Marjorie Hess's opera *Mirabell* Marjorie Ann Hess (b. 1958), aka Maura Bosch, wrote the music for an opera based on *Mirabell: Books of Number* and collaborated with Merrill on the libretto.
Mrs P Hellen Plummer.
Elzbieta Elzbieta Czyzewska (1938–2010), Polish actor who played Maria Mitsotaki in the video *Voices from Sandover* and whose life was the basis for the film *Anna* (1987), directed by Yurek Bogayevicz.
Robert Wilson (b. 1941), avant-garde theater artist, director, designer, playwright.
David Neumann (b. 1965), choreographer, dancer, actor who played 741/Mirabell in the video *Voices from Sandover*.
Bill Ball William Ball (1931–91), stage director and founder of the American Conservatory Theater, who played W. H. Auden in the video *Voices from Sandover*.
"Vertumnal" A poem by Yenser in his volume *The Fire in All Things* (1993).
those poets In Yenser's review in the June 1991 issue of *Poetry* of books by Henri Coulette, Galway Kinnell, Marilyn Hacker, Elizabeth Spires, Medbh McGuckian, Elizabeth Alexander, and Edgar Bowers.
David and Pam Leeming David Leeming (b. 1937), professor of English and comparative literature at the University of Connecticut, whose books include *James Baldwin: A Biography* (1994), and his wife, Pamela.
a book on travelers to Greece Robert Eisner's *Travelers to an Antique Land* (1991), which quotes Frederic Raphael's *Byron* (1982).

To Craig Poile

POILE
24 September 1991
Stonington, CT

Dear Mr Poile,

Those are hard questions. Mercifully you are looking for answers provided by the poem, not by life. I suppose I would look to QM's words for a clue: her injunction as to "JUDGMENT DAY" (p. 487) and her scolding for the witch Feeling on the next page; her warning (p. 438) about trust in Feeling as a destructive idea; her, or somebody's distinction between this kind of feeling (allied to Chaos) and "clear-eyed devotion" personified by Maria. Compare, in Ephraim's book, the threat that DJ and JM will be separated in the afterlife; but recall his emphasis upon DEVOTION as THE MAIN IMPETUS. Note also the identification of the Bats with feeling & Chaos, and of Uni (p. 461) with something stabler, where "love" fits in this scheme will be up to you to further define and evaluate. . . . Maybe you'll have to read Jung after all.

Robert Polito is working on an index of the whole, which one day will make essays like yours, and letters like this, easier to write.

It seems to me that DJ and JM have become not just mates but soul-mates by the poem's end. I'd say—since you seem to be wondering—that the "revelations" of the poem accomplish this, just as surely as their "folie a deux" (another handy definition of love?) brings the poem into being.

I hope this is some help.

Sincerely,
James Merrill

Craig Poile (b. 1967), Canadian poet.
Robert Polito (b. 1951), literary critic and professor at the New School, author of *A Reader's Guide to James Merrill's "The Changing Light at Sandover"* (1994).

To David McIntosh

Dear David,

I'm so glad to have your letter; sorry, too, of course, for the griefs and grimnesses you've been facing. In "charmed Stonington" nobody as yet has died of AIDS, and we don't see people like the old Albuquerque woman underfoot. Grace died, though, about two weeks ago. There was a service of sorts last Saturday before her ashes were consigned to the really very pretty and spacious cemetery which I'd somehow never before visited, although to judge by the stones it is full of old friends. Peter Perenyi flew back from his arms talks in Geneva, Sandy McClatchy read a beautiful page out of Colette about a "black rose," and I read the Keats "Ode to Autumn"—every word of which spoke to me of Grace and what I felt for her. "Close bosom friend of the maturing sun" ("maturing son," to the degree that she was the mother of my grown-up years). Or those bleating "full-grown lambs" that brought back the story of some childish disobedience on her part which ended with her asking her nurse, "Am I still your little baby lamb?" Eleanor coped very nicely. Now when the phone rings (she said) she'll know it isn't <u>that call</u>.

Let me talk to you a moment about my problems. After about a year and a half on-and-off the wagon, not to mention pot and cocaine, Peter checked himself into a detox unit at Roosevelt Hospital last week. Today he moved to their rehabilitation center—a marble mansion on East 93rd St—where he will stay, I hope, the full 28 days of the course. It's tough but has a high recovery rate. "All the baseball players go there," somebody said (whatever that means). I'm relieved that he's taken this step, but pretty much wrung out from the months that led up to it. This is where my double life takes its toll. Between the time I feel I owe DJ and the time I feel I owe Peter (never enough from either's viewpoint) I positively gasp for privacy and solitude. That's the main reason I've been unable thus far to take you up on your dear suggestion that we meet somewhere for a few days. In principle this would be an ideal month, but of course it's full up with things arranged with P. in mind—people coming to stay, a small part for me in a real movie (5 days in Pittsburgh), etc.—and I'm unable to see a clearing. A visit to Fla. wouldn't be the worst idea. We have a guestroom, so does Rollie, and there are some quite nice B & B places, sometimes with individual units, that might give you more privacy yet. But first I'll want to see how much time I'll have to spend back in NY if Peter needs support. From all the above you understand—in case you hadn't before—that I have a kind of nursemaid vocation. Or as the counselor is bound to point out, my four most consuming lovers have been addicts, whether I knew it or not: not until 1985, when I saw him for the first time in 13 years, did Strato tell me about his gambling; whereupon all our mysterious troubles made perfect and horrible sense in retrospect. The meeting I've just come back from, where a counselor talks to the families, was a lesson in how the shoe fits . . .

It's too late to countermand the *NYRB*—they send out their Xmas order forms in August—so you'll just have to bear with it another year. As Jane Bowles said when thanking some New York friends for airmailing at vast expense to Tangier a year's subscription to the Sunday *Times*, "There's nothing like it for the cat's box." But life isn't all gloom—I'm off to the opera in ten minutes and to St Louis (for 2 days) tomorrow.

Love,
James

a marble mansion on East 93rd St The William Goadby Loew House, known at the time as the Smithers Alcoholism Center and currently part of the Spence School. **real movie** Merrill had a cameo role as a doctor in the film *Lorenzo's Oil* (1992), directed by George Miller, about a child with a rare disease.

To Peter Moore MOORE

25 November/6 December 1991
[Stonington, CT]

Dear Peter,

Your letter awaited my arrival—prompt flights, smooth connections— yesterday just after dark, from Tucson. DJ was at the airport, as usual too thinly dressed for the little cold snap we're enjoying, and perhaps a bit too thin in any case. (The fridge is empty except for some bacon and junk food.) I spent an hour or two fussing about and unpacking, [*in the margin*: the printer chose to emphasize this, why?] then, over dinner at a place we like, began trying to tell him about Sierra Tucson. Two hours later he made the unsolicited observation that I seemed changed. I think so too, and (if you don't mind being a sounding board) thought I might strum out some of these new tunes—both because you dance so well to them and I need to set my thoughts in order for the inevitable Poem.

It's Pop Psychotherapy. Now that nobody can afford that hand-made underwear from Vienna, along comes Benetton to let it all hang out in. Groups in circles, friendly but utterly non-directive counselors, who say "That's OK, you don't have to share if you don't feel like it." No caffeine or desserts on the menu. The patients live in dorms named for the local cacti. I had friends to stay with in Tucson, 25 mile drive each way, but worth it, because it was an emotional week and, after Pittsburgh, I'd broken into tears in a hotel room once too often.

After visiting hours on Sunday a ban on communication (word or glance) with your patient goes into effect. Rather like *The Magic Flute*. The exception is the highly ritualized hour in the afternoon group at which you give your patient a list of grievances, or vice versa; or tell each other your "boundaries" or what you love about each other. At those times you are looking deeply into each other's eyes while the counselors voyeuristically study your faces for telltale signs of Anger, Fear, Shame, Guilt, Sadness, Hurt, or Loneliness.

Those seven words are, by and large, what we are given to work with. Like the child's first watercolor box. (You may also say "happy" or "glad" but then you wouldn't be in that particular room if that's what you were feeling!)

Dear Peter,

That was all ten, no, twelve days ago; I had thought to give it to you blow-by-blow but—not that I have better things to do—<u>other</u> things than letters are taking precedence. Suffice it to say that the week was a "success," culminating in P's getting a 9-hour pass, during which we went to the famous Desert Museum, stood in a cage full of humming-birds, looked into the eyes of the Mountain Lion (perhaps the most beautiful face made by God), and had a lovely dinner tete-a-tete, feeling quite rededicated to each other. There had been one moment I wanted you to know about. Peter "acted up" in the afternoon group one day, and stormed out of the room. The blank-faced counselor said, "When Peter behaves like this, I feel <u>afraid</u>," and everyone else felt <u>afraid</u>, too. I especially did, thinking, "Oh dear, he's resisting the therapy, and if <u>this</u> doesn't work, what hope have we?"—and drove back to Tucson in a Brown Study. The next day, entering that same room, I was surprised by a new Peter, popping out from behind a door, wearing a black eyeshade and a sign on his sweater; CONFRONT ME IF I TRY TO CONTROL. The eyeshade, which he had been wearing all day, had been imposed by his morning group, to teach him dependence on others. I was really tickled by the efficacy of such light, symbolic devices. Anyhow, he is now in—are you ready?—a Trappist monastery outside of Atlanta. They've taken him for a whole month—it turns out the Abbot is gay, and must have found P's forthright letter of application irresistible—which means that he and I can meet in NYC on Jan 4th and start getting to know each other again.

Part of that reeducation is going to be painful. We've idealized each other so! And I'm going to have to learn in some detail about a lot of compulsive sexual behavior which will remind me of how I lived at his age—and I will both hate and envy him for it. But I have been busily revising my own life in the light of co-dependency, reading books about male incest survivors (P's central problem, as he sees it, is his dreadful older sister who made a kind of bedizened sexual doll of him, and even tried, when he was 18, to get him into bed with her and her husband), and trying on, like an unbecoming jacket, the possibility that I too have been twisted, more than I realize, by early experience. One morning a lecturer put on a cassette of New Age music and regressed us. We walked through a tunnel in the light at whose end we'd all be under 12. Tears began <u>streaming</u> down my face. There's your house, go in, smell the smells, it's supper time—and I was standing by the bare mirror table in Palm Beach, and nobody else was there, mother and father (whose last year together this was) mere shadows at either end of the room. The tears only stopped at the elderly mouth of the tunnel. So I guess I'm ready to spend a season or two "in recovery" myself, not just to keep P. company.

I'd best ring off—the day's phone calls have begun. But your welcoming letter was better than a dozen hugs, and I hope to have another one early in 1992, with a snapshot of you and a 36-year old Jeffrey grinning by this year's tree.

Love always,
James

Sierra Tucson Residential treatment center for drug addiction, alcohol abuse, and mental health concerns. Merrill's poem about his experience there is "Family Week at Oracle Ranch" in *A Scattering of Salts* (1995).
Desert Museum Arizona-Sonora Desert Museum, a zoo, aquarium, botanical garden, natural history museum, and art gallery.

To Alice Quinn   NYPL
22 January 1992
[Stonington, CT]

Dear Alice—

I'm surprised that all this legal paranoia is laid at my feet without anybody's having sent out a feeler to DuPont. If <u>they</u> don't care, then we have no problem, right? I suggest that your lawyer do this <u>right now</u>.

To "breathe" means, I've always thought, the full transaction: inhale/exhale. Since Tyvek can't inhale, can it fairly be said to breathe at all? The point is important to the poem, where so much depends on airlessness—the ozone layer breaking down—the "final air" at the close, etc.

If DuPont <u>should</u> prove fussy, here's a possible solution: change the name of the product to Skyvex & rewrite lines 2 and 3 as follows:

> Science contributed the seeming frail
> Unrippable stuff first used for Hermetic Mail.
> (Hermes??)

Maybe your lawyer will think Skyvex is too close to Tyvek, but I like it as a name—and it works with the essential rhyme in the last stanza.

My big question: what happened to Poetic License??

I'll be back in NY this evening. Give me a call (988 8953) about any part of all of this.

Yours,
James

this legal paranoia Alice Quinn was the poetry editor at *The New Yorker* (1987–2007), and the magazine was concerned that mention of "Tyvek" in "Self-Portrait in a Tyvek™ Windbreaker" might expose the magazine to a suit. The trademark was added to address the issue.

To Bernard de Zogheb NYPL
12 April 1992
Stonington, CT

Dear Bernard,

Delicious to have a long green letter from you—despite the sand-grains that beset you on the road to Cairo—and to read about the Rare Book Library, and to learn by heart, on a first reading, the exquisite "Ramadam-dam" which is now sweeping New York. I'm afraid Prof Rodenback is wrong: I never translated "Le Testament de Pola"—just "Pola Diva"—so somebody else is to blame for its loss of "spontaneous charm." How nice that Christinette and Shawn are there. Keep feeding them material <u>slowly</u> and they will have to stay until it runs out.

I am sitting in my study in Stonington—no longer quite the bone-yard it had become a few years ago, what with the deaths of Robert and Isabel, and Grace's removal to a rest home. She died last October—aged over 100—while having a body rub and listening to a cassette of harp music. But recently people we know have been buying houses: Bishop Moore (the tall handsome radical Episcopalian who espouses gay marriages—as well he might, having fathered eight children); a tiresome and peremptory Mrs Lang who also has a house in Key West and whose parties no one can either endure or refuse; and best of all, Sandy McClatchy whom you may recall (I'm not sure if you met)—now a charming 45 year old man of letters and editor of the *Yale Review*. With Grace's demise, Eleanor has come into a popularity all her own. . . . I've been in New York much of the winter and spring. Perhaps Tony told you that Peter had a bad spell—2 months in rehabilitation (drinks and drugs) followed by a month, which he adored, in a Trappist monastery. He has been "clean" since early October, and getting quite a bit of therapy, but there are still lots of ups and downs. We plan 3 weeks in Holland, Denmark, and Scotland, beginning mid-June; and hope to visit Tony in Athens after 15th of October (when David heads south). This will perhaps make up for my not having set foot off the North American continent for two and one half years.

Before leaving for Holland I shall submit (to Knopf) the memoir I've been working on during that time. I picked the period of my first expatriation (March 1950—November 1952) and have tried to let the part stand for the whole. Each chapter has a postscript in italics, carrying some of the stories and themes outside my time frame. My mother begs me to wait "till she's gone" before publishing it; it is, I admit, full of things she knows but doesn't want her friends to. But as I pointed out to her she is only 92 and likely to live another 10 years, while I could drop dead tomorrow. Besides, my word-processor wrote the book, not I.

Well, it would be lovely if you found yourself in Athens in October. Or in Key West next winter! Please forgive my long silence. It's such a pleasure to be in touch.

Love always,
Dzimmy

"Ramadam-dam" Song by de Zogheb.
Prof Rodenbeck John Rodenbeck, translator, publisher, and professor who specialized in the literature of Alexandria, including the work of de Zogheb.
"Le Testament de Pola" The final poem in the set preceding the prose pieces in *Pola de Péra suivi de Proses pour Pola* (1964) by (Christian) Ayoub Sinano.
"Pola Diva" Merrill's poem "Pola Diva" is a translation of the second poem in the collection. Pola, a courtesan, was once a diva at the opera house in Pera in Istanbul.
Christinette Christine Ayoub, daughter of Christian Ayoub Sinano and the philosopher Josiane Boulade Ayoub.
Bishop Moore Paul Moore Jr. (1919–2003), Episcopal bishop of New York from 1972 to 1989.

To Agha Shahid Ali

HAMILTON
30 October 1992
New York, NY

Dearest Shahid—

I'm leaving for Atlanta in about 12 hours + want to send you a line about your "dissolutions." It <u>is</u> a lovely font, isn't it? I like how the poem moves from start to finish. But, you ask me to be FRANK; and I must scold you for your irresponsible rhymes. In these terminal seasons of human artistry you must—we all must—be especially careful <u>never</u> to rhyme damp—can—grand—telegram; or scream—scene et. al. Get off the fence + decide what your rhyme word [is] and stick to it. [*In the margin:* I wd prefer you not to rely on "dream," as much as you do. Too facile.] My dear—do you have a rhyming dictionary? The poem leads me to think that you don't. I myself would never dream of undertaking such a form without one. (I've probably reduced 4 or 5 to tatters in my long life.) Let me know. I will be happy to send you one + it can remain "our little secret." Now don't pout. Nothing is more welcome than an incentive to ever harder work. And while you can't do very much about Bosnia, you <u>can</u> improve this poem.

Peter is getting a puppy—a Jack Russell Toby—dog who will be old enough to leave its mother in 2 weeks. They're circus dogs, and in fact this one's grandfather is a celebrated drag queen—hardly even out of spangled hat + ruffled skirt. Entre nous, I hope we can raise P's puppy to be <u>all dog</u>.

Horrors! Nearly 10 pm + I've not even begun assembling my toilet articles. I'll be at it till midnight.

Love to you dear heart always—
James

Agha Shahid Ali (1949–2001), Kashmiri-American poet, whom Merrill befriended when he visited the University of Arizona, where Ali was studying.
your "dissolutions" Ali's poem "The Correspondent" uses *rimas dissoulutas*, a troubadour form in which the end words of one stanza rhyme with the end words of the next stanza rather than with each other. The revised poem was collected in Ali's *The Country Without a Post Office* (1997).
a puppy To be named Cosmo and commemorated in poem of that name in *A Scattering of Salts* (1995).

To Agha Shahid Ali

POSTCARD | HAMILTON
6 November 1992
New York, NY

Dearest S—

What a darling you are. Only a true artist would respond to criticism with a lovely letter like yours. I'm sure the Muse is <u>all</u> <u>abeam</u>. I returned from Atlanta just now; jaw aching from 10 hours at the dentist. My gum is <u>mincemeat</u>.

xxx from Peter + James

To Allan Gurganus

DUKE
11 January 1993
Key West, FL

Dear Heart—

Harry Mathews told me a story I must pass on to you. He heard it from an English woman with Trollopian name, whose grandfather might well have been there:

The late 1880's. A dinner party. The table is dominated by a shaggy white hayrick in evening clothes: Lord Tennyson. As he does not speak, the other guests [*in the margin*: All in their giddy 50s or 60s] drag the level of conversation down to <u>limericks</u>. Many are quoted, some even improper ones. All agree that the form is essentially comic, a <u>serious</u> limerick unthinkable. At length a silence falls and the cobwebbed lips of the Laureate part. Out comes this:

There are people now living in Eareth
Whom nobody seeth nor heareth
And there by the marge
Of the River a barge
Which nobody roweth nor steereth.

It's awful, the number of friends we have here. I miss New York where people have better things to do than to see <u>one</u>. Peter says when I whistle over the phone, Cosmo licks the receiver. Perhaps it's worth getting a 900 number + placing an ad in a dog magazine? I miss you too.

Love,
James

Allan Gurganus American writer and painter (b. 1947), whose works include the novel *Oldest Living Confederate Widow Tells All* (1989) and the collection of short stories *White People* (1991).

To Allan Gurganus

DUKE
21 February 1993
New York, NY

Dear Heart—

I was searching for a book yesterday and lo! there on the shelf sat my Pleïade Tolstoy (*Souvenirs et Recits*) with "Le Bonheur Conjugal." I imagine the little volume simpering, with burning ears, as we talked about it. Equally strange, from its pages fluttered the enclosed, which I must have typed out at least 20 years ago. It's a stanza from "Beppo," + I have long imagined that the last 4 lines described a person I might grow to resemble. Reading them now I hear a dry little voice deep inside: Dream on!

My nephew took me to an all-Chopin recital by the prodigy Yevgeny Kissen. Tall, a bit gangling, a cloud of dark hair, face like a water-lily, and <u>hands</u> like a whole ballet company. You've never seen such pas de deux, such pliés and leaps, + descants. (I'd better look up those terms; isn't <u>ballon</u> what they call the ability to "leap and pause" as Nijinsky put it?) Everyone cheering + swooning—And to think that the outside world simply will not believe that one has never attended a rock concert.

It's Sunday. Snow, etc. I'm about to spend an hour with Peter (visitor's day). He has another week, after which—? Every time he phones it's a different person from the last. But when I return, Tolstoy will be waiting.

Thank you for our evening. You are one in ten million (don't ask me how I know: I know) and on that note I go out into the Great Flakiness.

Yours ever,
James

Then he was faithful too, as well as amorous;
So that no sort of female could complain,
Although they're now and then a little clamorous,
He never put the pretty souls in pain;
His heart was one of those which most enamour us,
Wax to receive and marble to retain:
He was a lover of the good old school,
Who still become more constant as they cool.

"Le Bonheur Conjugal" Or "Le Bonheur familial" (1859), French title of Tolstoy's short story, usually translated into English as "Family Happiness."
Then he was faithful too Merrill quotes, as he does elsewhere, but more fully here, the 34th stanza of Byron's *Beppo*.
My nephew Stephen Magowan.
Yevgeny Kissen Evgeny Kissin (b. 1971), Russian pianist.

To Peter Moore

MOORE
28 February 1993
New York, NY

Dear Peter,

I've been on the point of writing again and again, and now from you comes a page so head-turning that I can't but fling myself upon keyboard and screen, and begin. I don't think my machine does graphics, outsize capitals, etc. (If it does, I'd rather not know about it.) But I'm properly impressed by yours.

This last month has been wonderful—all by myself in New York, neither in DJ's fire nor PH's frying pan. The former is safely glued to his TV set in Key West, the latter (following, alas, a Major Relapse) emerges from rehab tomorrow. I very much hope that we can amicably live apart, if only as a trial, for six months. All my friends are "horrified" by what I've been "put through," which of course is largely nonsense. I recently read the following sentence and think it is true: "Suffering warms the coldness of life." Without that suffering, I mean, I would have turned into an old wrinkled nut and never written those recent poems you are good enough to praise. As far as our health goes, things seem to be holding their own. We're not taking any of the antiviral drugs; so toxic, says our nutritionist. Instead the latter has started me on a kind of peroxide therapy (1% food grade peroxide to 99% pure water, aloe vera, etc.). The fascinating point—upheld by many European doctors—is that cancer and viral cells need very little oxygen, indeed are killed by high levels of oxygen in the blood. Not unlike the effect of Interferon, only harmless. You probably know about it; what do you think?

Just before P. went round the bend we got a puppy—a little self-willed Jack Russell named Cosmo. (He is too much for me to handle alone, and has been boarding where he was born, surrounded by sisters and cousins and aunts. Awful to miss any stage in his puppyhood.) He is highly pedigree'd—nothing but the best for the young master: his grandfather is a highly-paid transvestite known in art-directing circles as One-Take Toby, always happiest in his spangled tutu and silly hat. We noticed Cosmo's immediate interest in our closets and despaired of his growing up to be All Dog . . . You will have seen that a poem is coming out of the foregoing. Its epigraph will be from Howard Moss: "People who love animals once loved people."

I'm glad the new hip's a success. So many friends who've had it done in the last year or so are dancing in the streets. I've begun to feel envious twinges, especially after walking 30 blocks, so maybe I'll be joining the club. I also rather envy you that 39 year old patient with a wiry body. Not that he'd ever look at me: I saw myself undressed in the mirror 2 weeks ago and thought it was Larry Rivers' mother-in-law. So no more sweets for a while. Now for my lovely Aveeno oatmeal bath. Love to you and Jeffrey as ever—

James

recent poems "Self-Portrait in a Tyvek™ Windbreaker," "Family Week at Oracle Ranch," and perhaps other poems collected in *A Scattering of Salts* (1995).

antiviral drugs To treat HIV infection.
"People who love animals . . ." Howard Moss, "From a Notebook," *Whatever Is Moving: Essays* (1981).

To Bernard de Zogheb

NYPL
28 February 1993
New York, NY

Dear Bernard,

Again a long silence from me, but I have been delighted (and indirectly rebuked in the most civilized fashion) to have TWO from you, and shall do my best to fill you in.

The recent telephone calls to Tony have been very encouraging. He sounds like his old self—voice strong & clear, laughing & alert. God knows how long it will last. There is often such a year of grace before the virus does its victim in. Luckily Tony is concentrating on recovery from his heart attack, and one can only worry about one thing at a time. En tout cas I am planning to be in Athens in the last days of April—arriving the 26th or 27th, and staying until about the 12th of May. I see that we may miss each other, but my trip depends partly on attending a little poetry conference in Sweden (where I've never been), which begins May 13. Also I shouldn't spend more than a month away for a dozen reasons. Peter's addictions (there has been a Major Relapse of late), David's helplessness, and so forth. It is exciting about your Exposition, and I quite see that your plans are even less flexible than mine. But we'll hope for a reunion in Key West.

David perhaps isn't as out of it as I make him sound. The following conversazione, which Germaine might enjoy too, proves that he can not only follow but contribute to what goes on around him. Scena: the living room in Key West. Personaggi: JM & DJ, Harry Mathews (a novelist) and his French wife Marie. Another Frenchwoman, Denise. And an octogenarian Mrs Lash who came to the States from Germany sixty years ago. Curtain up. Harry: . . . and now it appears that doctors recommend an aspirin a day against heart trouble. This is because even one aspirin produces countless microscopic lesions in the stomach, and by losing a bit of blood our blood-pressure is reduced.

> JM: Like being bled by an 18th century barber.
> Denise: Or leeches. I remember my Perpignan grandmother with a leech attached to each earlobe, like earrings. By the evening's end they were so fat that they fell to the floor. She would put on a new pair the next afternoon.
> Tutti: Ugh!
> Marie: Leech, ca veut dire sangsue?
> Harry: Oui.
> JM: Trude, how do you say leech in German?
> Mrs Lash: Oh my god, it's been so long . . . wait . . . it will come . . .
> David (suddenly): BLUTSUCKER! (General hilarity.)
> Mrs L: But he's right. <u>Blutsauger</u> is the word. Bravo, David!

So you see, dear Bernard, what glittering company awaits you. En principe I am there from late December until about March 10, spending Christmas as always with my mother. One can never be absolutely sure. I simply don't know where Peter and I will stand six months from now. I've told him he should find a place of his own, but he has suffered so much—as, let me say, have I—that we may either want to be together more closely than ever or not want to be together at all. En principe, if you came in very late February and stayed through the first 10 days of March, we could then fly to NYC together, or make our separate visits in Florida before meeting in New York. Reflect upon it.

What else? My memoir is coming out in September. We have—or had, until P went to the clinic—a PUPPY, a strong-willed Jack Russell terrier named Cosmo. Too much of a handful for me to look after unassisted. He is impeccably pedigreed. His grandfather is a highly paid transvestite known in art-directing circles as One-Take Toby (never had to shoot a scene twice), dressed always in spangled tutu and Hedda Hopper hat. We have viewed with dismay Cosmo's interest in our closets. Of course we want him to grow up to be All Dog, the way our parents wanted us to grow up to be All Boy. But now if he's to be the child of a Broken Home—no, it doesn't bode well. The last time I walked him (a month ago) I could tell from an air of furtive self-congratulation that he had something forbidden in his mouth. I removed a frozen turd. . . .

Thrilling that you're at work on a new opera, and what a panoramic subject! I wouldn't worry, myself, about using a tune more than once in the course of your vast oeuvre. But these arbitrary restrictions a great artist imposes upon himself are inevitably fruitful. Vas-y! And if you do get a telephone, please let me be among the first to have the number.

Now, a lovely Aveeno oatmeal bath, and on with the hazards of an icy Sunday in New York. Have you seen a movie called *The Crying Game*—it's all anyone talks of at dinner parties (as if I'd know . . .) Love to Germaine. How I would adore to see her.

And to you, dear heart, always—

J.

the virus HIV.
Hedda Hopper (1885–1966), American actor and gossip columnist known for her extravagant headgear.
a new opera *La Vita Alessandrina* (1996), finished after Merrill's death and dedicated to him and Robert Liddell.
The Crying Game (1993), directed by Neil Jordan.

To Allan Gurganus

DUKE
1 March 1993
New York, NY

Dear Heart,

Shirley Temple's favorite poems? What a treasure! So young in 1936, and so well-read withal. A remark of Mr Tate's comes to mind: he and a young teacher are crossing a campus after a less than satisfactory interview with the Dean.

The young man (breaking a silence): The Dean's favorite poet is Emily Dickinson.

Mr Tate: The Dean hasn't read enough to have a favorite poet.

. . . You should also know that David Jackson gave Shirley Temple her first kiss. Or says he did. At a dance for Hollywood youngsters, some of whom he went to school with. Her arms were <u>so short</u>, said the kisser-and-teller, they barely reached round his neck.

And this leads to a reference by Daryl Hine, decades ago, through clenched teeth, to his "deformity". What deformity? cried Virgil and Anne. Oh don't pretend you don't know, said Daryl sulkily; I mean the ludicrous shortness of my arms.—But they weren't short, his friends protested; rather they were (if not nobly) elegantly proportioned. Where did so bizarre a notion come from?—Daryl: Hmpf. Why then do the cuffs of every shirt I buy come down to my fingertips? . . . And thus he learned, better late than never, what the <u>other</u> measurement on the label inside his collars meant.

Two days later—a new month. Peter walked in this morning, sprung from Smithers, with his dreadful doormat beard, but mild and bent on being a good boy. To him "work" means showbiz or things literary—jobs that more often than not entail after-hours receptions with waiters and drinks and irresistible people all on their drug of choice. So the parting word of advice from his counselor was: "Oh, <u>Peter</u>, get a job in a <u>hardware store</u> for a year." It suddenly makes him seem potentially mysterious and attractive all over again, getting his "bearings" in that world of no-longer-metaphorical nuts and screws and what not. There must be courses in how to handle a sales slip. I'm still nipping up to Stonington on Thursday, staying about ten days. I'll phone you from there.

I finished "Le Bonheur Conjugal"—whew. Very close to home; but so is everything T. wrote. Oldest story in the world, of course. How did Adam and Eve feel about each other after the first weeks? The beauty of this young Tolstoy is how his world keeps recovering its sweetness, and it's a great boon of a verity after those rancid ones he's just led us through. I'm a bit distratto—overlook it, please—and take this letter merely as an occasion to fill out your set of postcard silhouettes.

> With love always—
> James

Shirley Temple's favorite poems *Shirley Temple's Favorite Poems*, illustrated by Binnie Brueggeman (1936).
Mr Tate Allen Tate (1899–1979), American poet and literary critic.
Virgil and Anne The Burnetts.

To Frederick Buechner WHEATON
14 June 1993
Stonington, CT

Dear Freddy,

Fans with access to fancy computers make gifts unshowable except to Old Friends. I loved your rapid tour of L '43 names, but frankly it doesn't make me envious. It's <u>you</u> I wanted to see, and I hope one doesn't need a Reunion (while hundreds cheer) to bring that off. I'm still in a restless phase—unable to work, trying a new antidepressant: my sympathy with Judy grows month by month—and have arranged to keep on the move this summer. Two trips to Atlanta, a S'hampton weekend, my brother's birthday, a visit to old Tom Detre in Maine, opera in Cooperstown, usw.

How splendid about Dinah and Katherine! You'll be cooing as never before. Keep me posted, won't you. Just between us, if there is any one thing on earth that makes me feel my age, it is K's magazine. Heavens . . . Peter, though, thinks it very stylish.

He is doing OK. He's moved 3/4s of his things out of 72nd St, and taken a year's lease on a funny little house in Lakeville Ct, where he works happily all day in the garden, then gives in to <u>his</u> depression. Cosmo the terrier is company even entertainment. I could have watched him and the neighbors' cat play "Tracy & Hepburn" all day.

David is almost beyond change. Chain smoking, <u>cartoons</u> on TV, all day in bed, ebbing away. Either I have a disastrous effect on my loved ones or I fall for people with the bad seed already sewn in them.

Kimon died: a 2nd stroke, in Athens, age 82. I'd spent an hour with him in late April, a sad shuffling husk in pajamas and robe, but fairly lucid. And a few days later, Conway Twitty . . .

I do want to see you and we can plan something. Love always to Judy and TOI.

Ever,
Jimmy

L '43 The Lawrenceville School's class of 1943 fiftieth reunion, which Buechner attended.

Dinah and Katherine Buechner's daughters. Katherine founded *South Beach*, a magazine of fashion and the arts in Miami.
Conway Twitty (1933–93), American country-and-western singer.

To David Jackson

WUSTL
16 January 1994
[Key West, FL]

David—

I hate to write so formally, but when we talk it's in one ear & out the other.

My feeling is that you have become a very selfish + inconsiderate person. There's, for one thing, the ongoing TV noise which, combined with your refusal to use earphones, makes life hell for anyone within earshot. Ray has talked <u>seriously</u> of moving. If he does, it's over: I close up the house and move to NYC. You can go wherever you feel at home.

Then last night at Sandy's—after the fiasco of going from store to store for cigarettes—you were asked not to smoke at table: it irritated Hubert (who is dying). You sat next to H, and surprise!—dessert wasn't even over when you lit up. Hubert quietly moved to the sofa in the first room. Within 5 minutes you moved in, sat down next to him, and lit a cigarette.

So all that matters—right?—is <u>your</u> gratification. I doubt that I have the strength to live under the same roof with you <u>ever again</u>.

Love,

J.

to write so formally Merrill and Jackson were both in Key West, in the same house, when this letter was written and hand-delivered.
Hubert Hubert Sorin (1962–94), Edmund White's lover, a French architect, who had AIDS.

To Allan Gurganus

DUKE
11 March 1994
New York, NY

Dearest Heart,

This is my first half-hour at the computer since my return to NY. It took a young expert (I think he's a priest, he and his lover wear matching wedding bands) no time at all to perceive that the missing length of large intestine had been put in <u>backwards</u>—a mistake I believe Nature Herself has been known to make. Well I was so pleased that I paid him and he was gone before I remembered some other things I wanted him to do. But now what?—beyond of course writing you.

(24 hours pass.) A sort of horrified uncertainty possesses me these days. On the advice of nearly everyone I took a hard line with David and told him not to dream of coming north next month—to spend 6 months, presumably "being of help" to me—but to plan on six <u>weeks</u> around the 1st of September. Was this the right thing to do? Is that how you treat someone who's given you his life? whom you love and look after (albeit at an ever-increasing distance)? I'm afraid this is no case of "tough love"; dictated rather by fear & fatigue <u>and</u> by well-wishing friends, like Ray downstairs, and Sandy, neither of whom has enjoyed the splendeurs et misères of a lifelong relationship. David's wife, who lives in Mystic and whom I adore, is on my side, but she has learned her strengths in AA. . . . Where are the people who really <u>know</u>? The horror stems mostly for having sworn for the last half-century that I WOULD NEVER [TREAT] ANYONE THE WAY MY FATHER DID TO MY MOTHER, or I WILL NEVER MAKE ANYONE SUFFER THE WAY X'S BEHAVIOR IS MAKING ME SUFFER TODAY. And now I'm doing all those things, and indeed have done them regularly throughout my life, like the yearly purges one goes to Roumania for. So . . .

But I feel stronger, and my mind has cleared up. By tomorrow I shall be able to do neighborhood errands without clinging to good sluggish black Mary whom Peter got from an agency. <u>He</u> is justifiably ecstatic over this improvement which is after all largely his doing;

and so am I, even if it is also due to a lethal medication. Anything's better than the Living Death I was slipping into. I can't believe I'm inflicting on you a letter like this. But you understand how it helps the writer, if no one else. One thing we love and marvel at in you is how you have room in your heart for all of us. (I judge from a privileged position, but still . . .) Peter said so, a few 100 pages into *Confederate Widow*, which he declares the best book he can remember reading, ever. Yes, we are all in your heart & what could be a greater comfort?

And you? Shouting orders, sword drawn, at a regiment of work-men?

So. Off to my acupuncture.

> Love & blessings—
> James

large intestine The computer's.
Confederate Widow Gurganus's first novel, *Oldest Living Confederate Widow Tells All* (1989), was on the *New York Times* Best Sellers list for eight months.
a lethal medication AZT, the antiretroviral drug used to treat HIV/AIDS.

To Frederick Buechner

Dearest Freddy,

Such a joy to see you, sit with you at Hulot's, talk, etc. There are at least a dozen things I wanted to say, but they slipped my "mind" or there wasn't time. Thank you for Annie D's book, which is quite extraordinary, the first time around (there'll be another). Much of it seems to be written by her cat—lucid, implacable, utterly strange. Mostly she seems to be speaking as a member of another species, on better terms with light and water, insects and islands, than with her fellow humans. I felt her terrible eyes on me as I read. This gave off—except in her really supreme moments, like the burning moth, the face of the child, and how both of these fuse into Christ at the close—a faint air of . . . self-congratulation? Where one might have welcomed humility. But then, it is hard to be both humble and capable of writing that well. We aren't all Chinese sages.

I can see that the months or years ahead are going to be a dream of Trial & Error. The hemoglobin count has just fallen impressively, due (we think) to the AZT I've been taking. This drug is now thought far less of than at first, I'm glad to add my voice to its detractors. So I'm off it now and giving myself a daily shot of Epogen, which is so expensive I might as well develop a cocaine habit and get it all over with ($800 a week). But it presumably stimulates the bone marrow to produce new cells—little do they know what awaits them—and raises the spirits wonderfully. Thus I can hardly get up a flight of stairs, but my mind tap-dances up and down them throughout the day, and very little upsets or frightens me.

I can't recall if I spoke to you about Peter during these last months. I might easily, without him, [have] slipped through the cracks, life had grown so bleak. But with his love and his astounding caregiving talent, here I am to tell the tale. I don't think I've ever felt such love before, and I see it as a kind of miracle. Lord knows, he has his troubles, which often show in loud scenes, etc. These, however, pass within hours, and incidentally remind me of love as an emotion, a fire at the heart of life. This side of Peter—who when he's uneasy talks too much, blurts things out—has turned many of my friends slightly but perceptibly against him; this dismays me (though I see why) all the more because he has so few friends of his own. For better or worse I seem to be his life, his fate if you will. Nothing much has helped, neither AA or psychotherapy—until the Church came along (first that Cistercian monastery outside of Atlanta, now a funny little Episcopalian affair in Lyme Rock CT, whose rector is a Virginian named Mitzi Noble) and caught his imagination. As an actor he throws himself into genuflecting, kissing the chalice he mustn't drink from; but I see it, with fingers crossed, as the role of a lifetime and only hope he will play it through to the end. The one thing, Old Friend, that does upset and frighten me is what will become of him should I die first, as would seem wholly probable irrespective of health. He'll be well enough taken care of, but that's not what I mean. I don't ask you to take him under your wing or even make a friend of him. Just now and then to let him know he's in your prayers and that you will always bless him for the sweetness and vividness he brought to (already!)

these past ten years. Now my old eyes are wet. Time for Epogen! (All this, I trust, very much entre nous.)

I'm counting on a triplet to Vermont, but first I may have to go to my world-class dentist in Atlanta. Decay under two crowns? It sounds like a pre-WWI central European principality. Enough. We'll not lose touch. Love always to you and Judy.

Jimmy

Annie D's book Annie Dillard's *Pilgrim at Tinker Creek* (1974).
Epogen Epoetin alfa, medication used in treatment of anemia caused by chronic kidney disease.

To David Jackson

WUSTL
12 July 1994
[New York, NY]

David:

I've figured it out about Bobek and Dr "Oz." Remember, three weeks ago you said you'd heard of this great healer from someone you'd met down there at a party. And assured me that my name never entered the conversation. But of course (according to the other day's truthful version) the "stranger" was Bobek.

How did he know I was ill? Who on earth could have told him . . . except you. Whether you remember doing so or not. (You managed to never remember telling John Hohnsbeen, at your jazz club, that Peter had AIDS.) You are fully capable of betraying me to Bobek. Whom I think you know I despise—of <u>all</u> the people to tell!

Actually it's a betrayal either way. Supposing you didn't tell him, the obvious line would have been to deny it stoutly. Funny how many lies you can tell on your own behalf—but not one for me! Instead your silence gave consent to Bobek's hypothesis.

Either of the two versions is almost too painful to contemplate. It's easy to blame your behavior on the combination of wine and Xanax that every evening turns you into the parody of a slack-jawed old man. But years before this lethal medication began you were a great improviser. We all thought it was charming. We were wrong.

You'll say that I'm overreacting? That is not <u>for</u> you to say. I don't think you understand any longer what people feel. Keeping my secret is the one <u>serious</u> thing I've asked of you in the past ten years. And you've blown it twice now. From where I sit you are a live grenade with the pin pulled out, and I mean to stay as far beyond your range as I possibly can.

Whether or not you know it, Bobek's friend Kevin is a pal of the terrible Janice (my mortal enemy since that market poem appeared). Think what <u>she</u> could do to me here in the Village. Unlikely? Perhaps. But your indiscretion opens the possibility.

Try, <u>try</u>, TRY to think what you've been doing, and how horribly it upsets me.

J.

my secret That he has AIDS.
the market poem "November Ode" (1988) in *Collected Poems* (2001).

To Claude Fredericks

GETTY
6 August 1994
[Stonington, CT]

Dearest Claude—

Here is the new book. I think you'll have seen some—perhaps many—of these already; but who knows?

We had <u>such</u> a pleasant & happy time in Pawlet. You give yourself so easily, so fully—perhaps that's what "being a Buddhist" means, but I suspect it's really just "being you." Anyhow, we lapped it up like cream, a crème bavarois.

Oh and we realized, in the car, that we'd left behind a white face-cloth stiff with calamine lotion. This was a cloth we'd brought with us (one of those you sent a year or so ago), <u>not</u> one of the House Face-cloths which of course we'd not have left so grossly stained.

Now I'm off to have an oxygenating I.V. drip. It takes about 90 minutes, with a needle in a wrist vein. But I seem to be in better shape than the others in the dr's office. We'll talk when I return from

La Mamma—much love meanwhile & again bless you for your kind-
ness to Peter & Cosmo &

Jamey

the new book Galleys for *A Scattering of Salts* (1995).
a crème bavarois One of Fredericks's specialties.
La Mamma His mother, in Atlanta.

To Claude Fredericks

GETTY
14 September 1994
Stonington, CT

Dearest Claude—

This is what happens when you have nutty friends with access to a
fancy computer . . .

The photos you sent of P. & moi are beyond praise: pure delight,
pure gratitude—or impure, rather, to the degree that I must pes-
ter you for extra copies—perhaps 5 of each? For him, for our Polish
actress, for Cesar, for the Natl. Portrait Gallery . . . While your vis-
ible virtues will, in the long run, win out over my giddy attitudes, you
must remember that in those early years when you saw yourself as
the young Pindar or Plotinus io <u>invece</u> was studying Irene Dunne
& Katharine Hepburn. Next time we're together we'll have Peter
supervise the poses + the powder-puffery.

He left for a monastery on the Henry Luce estate (!) near
Charleston—near also to his brother whose little son he's being God-
father to. Then to Fla (sister having a baby). Then back here. Cosmo
yawning attendance . . .

S'ton is quite denuded. Sandy, Eleanor, <u>and</u> Bishop Moore + wife are
all in Turkey. David is here, but how would one know—aside from the
reek + sprinkling of his cigarettes in every corner, + the stupid voices
of his TV at every hour. With him is our KW gardener, an angelic
Mexican-American with a pigtail who means to become a Franciscan
brother. (<u>He</u> is admiring yr photographs even as I write this.)

So: we're off Oct 2, returning the 23rd. I'll be in NY (minus a day in

Pittsburgh) from Monday the 19th (Sept) until the Departure. David + Rolando head south about the 23rd, so there'll be more leisure to call you then. My health seems to be good, aside from a miniplague of boils right out of Job, + the yo-yo drop of my cell count. But it has risen + dropped before this so I don't greatly fret. There is a sense I'd have at this age, regardless of any "condition"—of wanting things tidied up, new Will signed, etc. Most of these are coming to pass. One of John Hersey's last visitors said "Your friends are concerned." John (smiling): "Tell them I bask in their concern." Exactly.

Love always dear friend—

J.

This An arrow points to Tom Bolt's Ouija board letterhead.
our Polish actress Elzbieta Czyzewska.
Cesar Peter Hooten's friend Cesar Rotundi.
a monastery Mepkin Abbey.
our KW gardener Rolando Rodriguez, who worked for Jackson and Merrill in Key West.
John Hersey (1914–93), American journalist and novelist, a Key West friend of Merrill's and Jackson's.

To Torren Blair   BLAIR
19 September 1994
New York, NY

Dear Torren,

Here I am in New York, with nothing to do but switch on my "Kundry" (name of the soulless leman in *Parsifal* who knows only to serve & seduce & obey). I'd been cudgeling my wits in the car this afternoon for some way to amuse you while I'm gone—and then it came to me: I would ask you a favor! (That usually does the trick—knowing that someone thinks well enough of us to impose.) But here is what I had in mind:

Everyone I might have asked in the past is presently either in Europe or (my elderly cleaning lady's case) laid up with a cracked rib; so that I need YOU to look in twice a week and water the plants.

You'll find a set of keys by making a hairpin turn to the left when you reach my floor; thence following a hip-high bookcase to its end. You are now in almost total darkness, but by feeling an inch or so down the narrow further end of the case you must come upon a nail from which the fake Oreo cookie of a keyring depends. One of those keys turns the lock built into my doorknob. (There is another bolt-type lock just above, but <u>that</u> set of keys has been mislaid, unless nice white-haired Ray from downstairs has found them between now and <u>his</u> departure for Europe.)

Once inside the apartment, you'll see the plants. The succulents, "living stones" or <u>lithops</u> ("stone eyes") as a botanist would call them, need only a scant teaspoon. Be more generous toward the hanging fern and the upstairs orange tree. But they'll all be grateful for your attention. My chiropractor was telling me how well plants have been found to respond to Mozart—"and only Mozart," he stressed. Perhaps; but I can picture (can't you?) a relatively unsophisticated young thing benefiting from even Telemann.

Now that you have done your first of several good deeds (through 12 October when Ray returns) I hope you will "hang out" for a while each time, if you <u>have</u> time—drink in the view, make a cup of tea, take a beer from one of the bottom drawers of the fridge; look at the books upstairs or in my awful mess of a study. Feel at home there; I should like that. You might even, from the apartment, telephone this number in town; I'll be here until 2 October: (212) 988 8953. And when I get back it will be your turn to ask a favor.

Meanwhile I'm grateful for yesterday's talk. Take very good care of yourself. Yours,

*

*P.S. Will you call me James? Or if that is too precipitous, "JM"? That is how I mostly think of myself. . . .
PPS. The 2nd set of keys (both locks) have been found & will be on the nail (so forget the chocolate cookie)

Torren Blair Stonington resident and high-school senior interested in literature, to whom Merrill was introduced by Billy Boatwright.
my "Kundry" His IBM word processor. See *A Different Person* (1993) and "Scrapping the Computer" in *A Scattering of Salts* (1995).

To Torren Blair

Virginia WOOLF: *To the Lighthouse*. Stream of consciousness but without the mythical/erudite Joycean rocks to impel (and impede) the current. Very beautiful. It ends, "I have had my vision," and she is entitled to say so.

Nigel DENNIS: *Cards of Identity*. Very funny & provocative novel about the malleability of the self. One chapter is a 5-act parody of Shakespeare.

Sybille BEDFORD: *A Legacy*. Bourgeois stuffiness vs. easy-going Impressionism, bracingly written. Agonizing glimpses of military school. Donkey-ex-machina as finale.

Donald SUTHERLAND: *On, Romanticism*. Perhaps the most stylish and convincing book about art that I know. Poetry mainly, but some splendid chapters on opera and Pompeian painting. Hard to find: If you ever see a copy snap it up.

The nice thing about the last three is that you needn't read more by the same author. If VW appeals to you, go on to *Mrs Dalloway, The Waves, Between the Acts*, etc.

If you like Dostoevsky you might enjoy DICKENS. Dostoevsky learned from him. *Great Expectations* or *David Copperfield* (early) and *Bleak House* or *Our Mutual Friend* (late). I hadn't liked *A Christmas Carol* when I was little, so never read anything else till age 30. Such joy when the time came. Other great English novels: *Emma* (Jane AUSTEN), *Middlemarch* (G. ELIOT).

French prose. You might do well to wait a few years before tackling PROUST. Or if overcome by temptation, try the self-contained *Un Amour de Swann* at the end of *Swann's Way*. Or a strange wonderful book of essays & "sketches" *Contre Sainte-Beuve*. STENDHAL: *Chartreuse de Parme* & *Le Rouge et le Noir*. I have a weakness for the short *De l'Amour* (note especially the little story "Le Rameau de Salzbourg"). RADIGUET: *Le Bal du Comte d'Orgel* (a deliberate 1920's copy of the 17th cent. masterpiece *La Princesse de Clèves*).

Here follows a list that almost anyone might make. But I am happiest on the beaten path.
Poetry (English & French):

Thomas WYATT: Sonnet—"Who list to hunt, I know where is a hind . . ." This is rumored to have lost poor Wyatt his head, for it describes his love for Anne Boleyn; "Caesar" being Henry VIII.

"They flee from me who sometime did me seek . . ." I began one day to put this into contemporary English but got no farther than line 1: "They turn me down who used to call me up . . ."

SHAKESPEARE: *Sonnets*, selected plays—certainly *The Tempest, Lear, Hamlet, As You Like It, Antony & Cleo, Richard II,*—but why stop there?

John DONNE: "The Relic" (what do you suppose he means by "a something else"?); "A Valediction Forbidding Mourning"; "The Ecstasie"; from the *Elegies*, "To his Mistress on Going to Bed," and "Nature's lay Idiot . . ." Sonnet, "Batter my heart, three-personed God . . ."

George HERBERT: "The Collar," "Love," "The Flower," "The Rose," "Love Unknown" (cf. Eliz. Bishop's "The Weed"). Browse in him—I don't have his works in NY. It's the natural speaking tone you want to catch, remarkable for his time.

Andrew MARVELL: "The Garden," "Horatian Ode"; poems spoken by a mower to "Julia"—scythes, glowworms, pastoral images;

Alex. POPE: *The Rape of the Lock;* to (name?—or just "A Young Lady") with the works of Voltaire; "Epistle to Miss Blount on her Leaving London." If you like him as much as I do, "Epistle to Dr Arbuthnot" . . .

MILTON: *Lycidas*; "Hymn on Christ's Nativity."

William BLAKE: *Songs of Innocence & Experience; The Book of Thel.*

Wm WORDSWORTH: Sonnet "Upon Westminster Bridge"; Ode ("Intimations of Immortality"); "Lines Composed near Tintern Abbey."

I marked the poems in your little KEATS.

SHELLEY: "Adonais"; "Ode to the West Wind."

BYRON: Beppo, "We'll Go no more a-roving . . ." If you get into the spirit of "Don Juan" go with it. (Cf. Auden's "Letter to Lord B.")

R BROWNING: "The Englishman in Italy"; the dramatic monologues? I don't know. "The Bishop of St Praxed's Orders his Tomb" . . . maybe. "A Toccata of Galuppi's."

COLERIDGE: "Ancient Mariner," "Dejection," "Frost at Midnight."

TENNYSON. "The Lady of Shalott"? *In Memoriam* is marvelous. We read it in college in a course that also included Darwin & Cardinal Newman.

G M HOPKINS: "The Starlit Night." The so-called "Terrible Sonnets." "The Windhover"; "Felix Randall." "Glory be to God for dappled things . . ."

As for the 20th century, look around. Of course I'm partial to <u>all</u> of E Bishop, poetry and prose. There's not that much. Don't miss "Cirque d'Hiver," "The Shampoo," "The Riverman," "From the Country to the City," "The Bight," "At the Fishhouses," "Florida," "Crusoe in England," "One Art," "Sonnet"—her last poem.

Hart Crane: "Royal Palm"; opening section of *The Bridge*, more if it grabs you.

Eliot: Obviously *The Waste Land*. "Sweeney Agonistes," "Sweeney among the Nightingales." Poem about child & Xmas tree. Beautiful diction in the *Four Quartets*, but all that dogma . . .

Stevens I've marked for you.

May Swenson, John Crowe Ransom, Randall Jarrell ("At the Washington Zoo") . . . I find Lowell hard to take, but there are some wonderful things ("Skunk Hour," "The Quaker Graveyard"—much of it apparently lifted from Melville).

In French:

Baudelaire: "Recueillement," "L'Invitation au Voyage"; "Le Vin"; "Spleen"; "La vieille servante dont vous etiez jalouse" (1st line); "La Chevelure," etc, etc.

Verlaine: "Clair de Lune"

La Fontaine: get the tone of the *Fables*. (I said for you the last
  lines of "Les Deux Pigeons.")
Mallarmé: very difficult but, to me, irresistible. Sonnet, "Le
  vierge, le vivace, et le bel aujourd'hui"—every line ending
  with the same vowel sound. "Herodiade." "Prose pour des
  Esseintes"; "L'Après-midi d'un Faune," "Cantique de St Jean
  Baptiste."
Paul Valéry: "Le Cimitière Marin," "Palme," lighter sonnets
  like "Grenades," a sonnet to Mallarmé in his "yole" (yawl?)
  at Valvins, "trainant quelques soleils ardemment situés"—
  that last word rhyming with "si tu es" a couple of lines
  above.
Apollinaire: La Chanson du Mal-Aimé (lovely to memmorize
  bits of). He uses a habit-forming 5-line stanza. Also "Cor de
  Chasse" if that's the title; it begins "Notre histoire est noble
  et tragique . . ."

Beyond that in French I don't go—except for Ponge (essay in <u>Rec-
itative</u>). Racine would fit in this list as a poet but you'd probably do
well to read *Phèdre* in the light of the Euripides *Hippolytos*. The famous
line in *Bajazet*—Nourri dans le serail, j'en connais les detours—made
for a merry moment years ago in Athens. I misquoted it "Elevé
dans le sérail" only to be corrected humorously by Maria: "Pourri
dans le sérail"—which Tony in turn promptly topped: "Souris dans
le sérail . . ." But *Phèdre* is in a class by itself, even though it didn't
make Harold Bloom's Canon. (As we have grazed Greek drama,
be sure you read *The Bacchae*—also Euripides—if nothing else for a
while.)

Forgive me for going on at such length. More will follow less
promptly. If you are happy to have a mentor I am overjoyed to have a
pupil. I await your letter!

JM

---

lost poor Wyatt his head Wyatt was imprisoned in 1536 but released and returned
to royal favor before he died of natural causes in 1542.
Poem about child & Xmas tree Eliot's "The Cultivation of Christmas Trees."
a sonnet to Mallarmé . . . Valvins The poem is "Valvins," in Valéry's *Album de vers*

anciens, in which Valéry calls Mallarmé's canoe a "yole," a term usually designating a small, canoe-shaped craft with a sail.
Harold Bloom's Canon Harold Bloom, *The Western Canon: The Books and School of the Ages* (1994).

To Peter Moore

MOORE
22 September 1994
New York, NY
underlining + check marks by me

Dear Peter,

Your lovely letter—it would be a reminder (if one were needed) that I've all but stopped writing them myself! An androgynous person comes in every week or so, & I <u>dictate</u> letters to him. Without being Henry James I'm getting rather good at this vaudeville. But it's not the same. The main difficulty is a <u>cataract</u> ripening on my right eye. I'll have it attended to within the next 6–8 months. (Nihil obstat, says my M.D.)

But all's well. I could easily have slipped through the cracks last winter: depression, anemia, even hallucinations (did that paw on my knee belong to the little white dog who loved me, or to the dog's <u>dark twin</u> who wished me ill?). I can't tell you how ardently <u>Peter</u> looked after me. He has a genius for care-giving—and saw to everything. Largely thanks to him (& some judicious medication) I am close to being myself once more. The doctors think I'll last for a while! But as I was saying P. & I have grown amazingly close—it's like the 1st year of knowing each other—except that we've gone through terrible time[s], <u>through</u> them & into a kind of light—lightness? Confidence? Serenity? Pourvu que ça dure. We're leaving Oct 2 for 3 weeks in Prague <u>&</u> Vienna.

There are still touchy subjects between us—<u>you</u> are one of them I think, but I'm not putting it to the test. You know how fond I am of you, but P. is just beginning to make his peace with "my friends." An astonishing breakthrough: one day he said "I don't want to be buried in the family plot in Florida. I want to be buried at your side in

Stonington. Let's get [a plot] big enough for DJ [whom he's resented almost from the start] etc." [*The remainder of the letter is illegible.*]

To Torren Blair   POSTCARD | BLAIR
                                          24 September 1994
                                             New York, NY

Dear Torren,

You may not have had my letter—sent to <u>18</u> Cutler, while the [illegible] are listed in the phone book at <u>11</u>. If the letter turns up please don't worry about the plans. Mrs Woodrow just today rose from her bed + looked in (as you are still welcome to do). Solitude in NY! I've even written most of a poem. Despite this morning's major stumble & this afternoon's arrowhead of a split tooth, <u>whatever is, is right!</u> Yours, JM If you get a chance to call before I leave—evening of Oct 23—<u>by all means do.</u>

Postcard On the front, the Buddhist temple in Kyoto, the "Silver Pavilion," which Merrill visited in 1957 and 1986.
Whatever is See Alexander Pope, "An Essay on Man," Epistle I.

To Frederick Buechner   WHEATON
                                        [c. November 7, 1994]
                                             New York, NY

Dear Freddy,

Sharmy sent me a photo-announcement of little Benjamin—only I can't read the name of her <u>street</u> in order to respond directly. His pumpkin is of the same phenomenological sphere as that boulder in Burma wrapped in gold leaf. Both elicit cries of delight from the visitor. So please send on the enclosed to S. and David.

We're back only long enough to start repacking for Chicago and St. Louis. Then in late Dec, we'll drive out to Tucson (where I went to First Grade)—back in 1933, so as to avoid being another Lindbergh Baby, says my mother <u>now</u>; I was told it was because I was "delicate." We'll stay for the Three Worst Months, and I can't say how I look forward to being where I know only a couple of people. Like 1st Georgetown summer. I'm feeling well; the drs. comment on my good color, energy, etc., preferring to dwell on appearances rather than blood-counts etc. Cheerful withal . . .

Much love to you & Judy. We'll talk on the phone after T'giving.

Always,

J.

Sharmy Sharman Buechner, Buechner's daughter, was Merrill's goddaughter. Her son Benjamin was born August 25, 1994.
boulder in Burma Kyaiktiyo Pagoda, Burma, also known as the Golden Rock, is a small pagoda perched on a cliff atop a rock covered in gold-painted leaves.
back long enough In October 1994, Merrill and Hooten took a short trip to Prague. See his poem "Rhapsody on Czech Themes" in *Collected Poems* (2001).
Chicago and St. Louis Reading at the Art Institute of Chicago, followed by a symposium with a poetry reading by Merrill and papers about his work by Richard Kenney, Rachel Hadas, Stephen Yenser, and Helen Vendler, hosted by Special Collections at Washington University.
Lindbergh Baby During the Depression, Merrill's parents worried that he might be kidnapped by the people who took Charles Lindbergh's son, or by copycat criminals.
1st Georgetown summer The summer of 1948, which Merrill and Buechner spent together on Georgetown Island, Maine.

To Dorothea Tanning

WUSTL
26 November 1994
New York, NY

Dear Dorothea,

I would dread writing you this letter if I didn't hope to be doing a kindness to both myself and to you, for you will now have time to find a replacement. I cannot do the preface. Let me beg your indulgence by giving you a few reasons. First and foremost this kind of piece is simply not my métier. For seven years I wrote prefaces of one thousand words each for the talented young poets I had picked as judge of the Yale Younger Poets Series. These were people whose work I admired, in whose powers I had faith, about whom as fellow poets I should have had a great deal to say—and yet it was all I could do to come up with that annual piece of . . . something <u>more</u> than fluency. A dark cloud lay over me for sometimes as long as three months until the manuscript had been selected and the preface written. I thought it might have been different to write about you but on returning from Europe a month ago and finding that for one reason or another what I had written was unsuitable the same cloud took shape and I have been lying under it with my face turned to the wall.

I wish I were one of those Protean artists whose daily life is a sparkling fountain of variety and <u>trouvailles</u>—like you, my dear. But the mortifying truth is that if I write five poems in the course of a year I consider that year well spent. I cannot work without as much time to myself as possible, time not only to "create" but to give to the process of revision which to me is the vital and truly stimulating part of my labors. I need that time more and more and at the risk of giving rise to puzzlement or hurt feelings find myself less and less able to take on anything like a commission, even for a dear and valued friend whose work I love; I mean you.

When the smoke cleared I saw the three bits of my preface of which I thought truly well would not do, given your publisher's vision of the book. (I mean Room 202, the Scotch-tape Sleeper and the two acrostic poems.) You can see how this left me back at Square One. Please feel free to use the little acrostics in any way you like. I could even write a <u>third</u> one if that would help because this <u>is</u> my métier. But as for the rest as a whole let's just forget about it. I tried my best and cannot go any further. (Had you thought of asking Harry Mathews? I think he would fill the bill handsomely and without fuss.)

We look forward to seeing you on the ninth but let's by all means talk between now and then.

> With love always from your abject but adoring
> James

Dorothea Tanning Merrill encouraged her poems. His close friend in his last years, Tanning selected three lines from Merrill's "Declaration Day" (*The Inner Room*, 1988) so that he would be included in her book *Another Language of Flowers*, which paired her canvases with poems by various poets, otherwise written for the occasion, and which was published after his death.
the preface To *Dorothea Tanning*, text by Jean Christophe Bailly, trans. Richard Howard (George Braziller, 1995). The publisher wanted Merrill to write a preface to

this "comprehensive overview" of the artist's work, but in the end, Braziller settled for the "little acrostics" Merrill mentions, which frame the foldout work on paper "Encyclopedia" (plate 269).

little acrostics Along with a quatrain on "Room Two Hundred and Two" and a sonnet-length "Masquerade" for her, Merrill had written two acrostics that he sent to Tanning on November 26, 1994. The first: "Designs upon us / Ommatidia / Roving a kind of / Ottoman Empire / Tirade and hookah / Hot poppy smoke / Exhaling youngest / Ancient of days." And the second: "Doom-lit door-haunted / Odalisque / Rigors of disorder / Open fire opal / Thighs fetish-full / Halloween's here / Even the littlest / Amoebas dress up."

[*The following short letter was sent with two separate messages enclosed. These are printed after the text of the letter.*]

To Torren Blair

BLAIR
30 November 1994
[New York, NY]

Dear Torren—

I'd hoped we'd see each other these last days, but I've been busier than expected (the Czech poem grows & grows) and so, I imagine, have you. I'll surely have a couple of days here between now & Christmas, but won't know until my minisurgery (cataract) can be scheduled. I'm seeing Dr A. tomorrow, he will refer me to Dr B, & so forth . . .

My rain checks don't usually bounce, but looking closely at my calendar it seems best not to try for the Opera on Dec 23. Peter & I will be dismantling the tree that day, and heading for Tucson the next. I still very much want to take you to something splendid like the Britten; and one of these days, shall. I'll get word to you when my crystal ball unclouds, + hope we can have an hour or 2 later in Dec.

Yours,
JM

P.S. Never hesitate to call me in NY if you feel like talking, 988 8953

*

"The mind has added nothing to human nature. It is a violence from within that protects us from a violence without. It is the imagination pressing back against the pressure of reality. It seems . . . to have something to do with our self-preservation, and that, no doubt, is why the expression of it, the sound of its words, helps us to live our lives."—Wallace Stevens

*

A thought for today: As a relief from these terrible martyrdoms that fill museums in the western world, why not Einstein or Mozart on a crucifix? or Chekhov? or Vermeer? It's them I pray to, don't you?

Czech poem "Rhapsody on Czech Themes" in *Collected Poems* (2001).
the Britten Benjamin Britten's opera *Peter Grimes.* Merrill had hoped to take Blair to the Metropolitan Opera to hear it on December 23.
"The mind" From the last paragraph of Stevens's essay "The Noble Rider and the Sound of Words." Copied on a postcard showing a black-and-white photo of the interior of the Basilica of San Vitale in Ravenna. On a visit there in 1952, Merrill was dazzled by the sixth-century mosaics. See his memoir, *A Different Person.*

To Torren Blair   BLAIR
                                                    4 December 1994
                                                      New York, NY

Dear Torren,

A Sunday in the City. Morning putting the latest "finishing touches" on the by now too long, too packed with goodies (a Xmas fruit cake) poem I came back from Czechoslovakia eager to begin. Its equivalent—a Christmas tree of excessive beauty, which Peter hung with lights & baubles—stands in the next room. It's been years since I've had one like this: a major tree. Already doomed, of course, kept functioning, looking its best, entirely thanks to an IV system discreetly out of sight . . .

This is mainly to say that I'll be in S'ton on the 19 December, probably till the morning of the 21st; and hope we had have even a little time together. If not, let's at least talk on the phone. I have a few CDs for your Christmas. You've complained of not knowing much about music—and you seemed not displeased by my bit of unaccompanied Berlioz—so I want you to get to know a few things that have at odd times meant the world to me. Maybe I'm tipping the scale overmuch in favor of song, but you are after all, like me, partial to words. And perhaps I can take for granted that you already know enough to seek out the Mozart piano concertos (not forgetting that early one— K. 271—where the closing rondo breaks off to encompass a minuet of the greatest poignance and restraint, before resuming its headlong race to the finish line); the late Beethoven piano sonatas (Op. 53, Op. 111) and quartets (Op. 131 is my favorite, as it was his) which remain more "demanding", or at least more intimate, than the Symphonies. Well, enough about music. . . .

The poem you sent. I take it as a hopeful sign that you are writing about sex, a great subject at 16 (or indeed at 60 if one is still so disposed). Were you ever warned against what they once called the Sentimental Fallacy? I was. It's when you project your feelings onto something usually in nature (not your own, but of course it is all one). Despite the warnings, I believe it is a great & natural resource. (Elizabeth Bishop does it to perfection—her lichens in "The Shampoo," her "tall, uncertain palms" in "Arrival at Santos.") You are doing it here. Watch out, though, for editorial language ("so terribly pitiful") which interrupts your vision. Any chance to keep the scale small, since you are ostensibly writing about water-drops, will be welcome. "Shriek" in the penultimate line might work better than "scream." Also I'd consider taking out "into the street" and not let <u>us</u> reach the street till the end. You'll tell me if these are helpful comments. (Or aren't.)

My cataract "procedure" (as they now call minor surgery) is set for Dec. 14. I expect it will go well, and that I'll not be prevented from coming up to Stonington. Where I hope to see you.

Yours,

JM

poem I came back . . . eager to begin See "Rhapsody on Czech Themes" in Merrill's *Collected Poems* (2001).
a Christmas tree See Merrill's "Christmas Tree" in *Collected Poems*.

To Torren Blair   POSTCARD | BLAIR
                                    6 December 1994
                                    New York, NY

"François de Séreuse avait exactement son age. De toutes les saisons de la vie humaine le printemps est la plus seyante et la plus difficile à porter."—from *Le Bal du Comte d'Orgel*, a short masterpiece by a 20 year old (Raymond Radiguet). Don't be cowed by Competition. If you can't lick 'em, join 'em!

JM

"François de Séreuse avait" "François de Séreuse was the same age exactly. Of all the seasons of human life, spring is the most becoming, and the most difficult to carry off."
Raymond Radiguet (1903–23), French novelist, poet, and playwright who died at age twenty and whose second novel, *Le Bal du Comte d'Orgel,* was published posthumously in 1924.

To Torren Blair   POSTCARD | BLAIR
                                    [6 December 1994]
                                    [New York, NY]

Dear Torren—

I'd understood (wrongly?) that recent views of Chaos show her to be a mistress of extraordinary & subtle <u>patterns</u>. So the last word is never spoken? I should like to believe that and so (as an optimist) should you!

Yours
JM

postcard Image of painting of American flamingo by James Audubon.
Chaos Reference to chaos theory. Chaos is also another name for Psyche in *The Changing Light at Sandover* (1982).

To Stephen Yenser

POSTCARD | YALE
4 January 1995
Tucson, AZ

Sir:

I have been much distressed by the gradual lowering of the hemline in the shorts worn by basketball players. Some of them now resemble those baggy knee-lengths worn by overweight youths on NYC streets. In shorts like that, even a goodlooking dude becomes a NERD. I am writing you in hopes that you will encourage your favorite teams not to accept this awful new fashion.

Sincerely,
Mrs Jemmer Lal (Tucson)

postcard The photo is of a basketball game at the McHale Center, University of Arizona.
Mrs Jemmer Lal A near anagram for "James Merrill."

To Torren Blair

BLAIR
5 January 1995
Tucson, AZ

Dear Torren,

This recently came out in paperback & I want you to have a copy (small but vexing errors in the original edition now set right). It's with some degree of presumption that I offer it—on the grounds, that is, that you aren't interested just in my taste and tone and turn of mind but also in <u>how I got that way.</u> Which is, I suppose, the subject of these pages. The callow protagonist seen in the sunset glow of the home stretch. . . . Reading Joyce you'll have felt how the poorest particulars are of a piece with the grandest universals. And it is your business, and mine, to bring about that meeting in as seamless & distinctive a way as possible. Is this what you want to learn from Rimbaud? Fine. Get the <u>feel</u> of self-destruction, of a mind hurt into vision. Just don't force it. I've known these to come of themselves, without <u>dérèglement</u> or conscious invitation.

We're delighted with our arrangements here. It's the largest house I've lived in since childhood. Not many rooms, but big ones: the scale all but cinematic, the taste likewise. Great views, dwarf daffodils in bloom, a pool of manycolored koi. Cosmo, already a junk sculpture of spines & burrs, is nonetheless ecstatic—or was until some neighbors warned us about coyotes, who are famous for carrying off a small privileged dog in the blink of an eye, just like the Lindbergh baby. So it's back to the leash. Right now we're enjoying a couple of days of rain, to thirst for when the much-advertised sun returns.

Now, more for your list. You understand, these are names (almost) anyone could furnish. Don't above all feel confined to the books or poems I suggest: strike out cross-country.

For a short piece about poetry you can't do better than to look up Howard NEMEROV on a 2-line epigram by Kipling. There's bound to be a Nemerov Miscellany or collection of his essays in the Conn College library. Otherwise Sandy McClatchy could point you to it. (Feel free to call him—535 9131.) HN's style is very engaging and his mind of an enviable clarity. This perhaps works against many of his poems—not enough left to "accident"? [*in the margin*: chaos?] Still, he's someone you should know about.

Two more writers ending in –OV. CHEKHOV: <u>all</u> of his plays are wonders of the world. My favorite is probably *Three Sisters*. Short stories as well, though it's not a form I readily give myself to.

NABOKOV: *Lolita* made him famous, and it is quite a triumph. But I prefer 2 other novels, one early and one late. *Bend Sinister* is a terrible, terrible story immaculately written, about life under Stalin. And a paranoid fantasy in the guise of notes to the last, 1001-line poem by a famous old Frost-like American. VN knows how to keep you in the palm of his hand.

I hope all's well. Yours,
JM

This *A Different Person* (1993).
NEMEROV . . . Kipling See the section entitled "Form in Poetry" in Nemerov's essay "The Protean Encounter," collected in his *Reflexions on Poetry & Poetics*.

Kipling's couplet, from "The Coward" (*The Years Between*), an epitaph for "a soldier shot by his comrades for cowardice in battle," goes as follows: "I could not look on Death, which being known, / Men led me to him, blindfold and alone."
a paranoid fantasy Nabokov's *Pale Fire,* which includes a 999-line poem.

To Torren Blair

BLAIR
14/16 January 1995
Tucson, AZ

Dear Torren,

Thank you for your phonecall. The letter is bound to come today. (It did!—see below.)

Such a pity when people phase out the idea of apprenticeship. It happens most among writers, the line of reasoning being "Well, I've been using language ever since I was 18 months old, and am never without things to say. Surely that entitles me to write some of it down and call it a poem?" Or you go no further than to imitate a friend's work, like those spiders in the dome of Hagia Sophia, and take that for sufficient training. Painters do the same thing, but they still go to museums. (Don't they?) Music <u>can</u> be written imitatively—pop music mostly—though it helps to know some theory, what a chord is, how chords progress, how harmony works, etc. Listen, by the way, attentively several times to the closing movement of the Mozart K 271, in which the almost manic rondo encapsulates a sad & exquisite minuet. But to resume: words are fair game for the whole world.

On the car radio the other day we heard a musical talk show that was to culminate in the studio performance of a difficult string quartet. The talkers, aside from the unspeakable host, were the composer (named Erb) and the four young musicians. They talked all right, in "our" common language; but spoke so clumsily. Inarticulate, begging for laughs, self-deprecating. "American" manners, designed to win over the listener—"You wouldn't kick me, I'm just a puppy!" Never to be mistaken for that "plain dull charm" attributed by a worldweary grownup to the 10 year old heroine of *What Maisie Knew* (Henry James. On our list for 1999). The talk show had no sentence worth chewing on. No variety of tone, tune, modulation; it was to my ears the insult it would have been, to theirs, had I sat down at the piano and begun to slap the keys, cheerful as a child—afterwards looking round with a goofy grin: "Hey, I just made that up!"

Not that I'm happy with how I speak. It's too late to change, but my "mature" choice would have been a voice more at home in the world, one that suggested neither privilege nor disadvantage. (Hard not to run on too long when you feel strongly about something . . .)

(FLASH) Yes—a Red-Letter Day! Mailed Wednesday, here Saturday. Peter lit up at the mention of Ed Sanders, whom he knew as having once been married to Ellen Geer. She is the daughter of the late Will Geer, a rather famous and definitely versatile actor—tonight Appalachia, tomorrow Lear on the heath. Peter toured with the company 20 years ago; he recited the youthful Robert Frost, Geer the crochety old one. They all slept in the bus. P. recalls seeing Poetry in Motion and fully agrees with your autopsy, nor does he hold any special brief for Sanders. The name brought back memories, is all. Thanks for explaining CD Rom. A letter came not a word of which I understood. Internet? modems? I instinctively shrink from those terms—like Cosmo the other day from our young yoga teacher's eerie imitation of the noise a rattlesnake makes.

Conrad? We read *Victory* in school and didn't think it was very good. I once taught *Lord Jim* (this was back when I <u>did</u> teach every now & then; I am seldom credited with the invention of the Reverse Sabbatical—a year of instruction followed by six of repose) and admired it. The character of Marlow is a most useful & likeable device. The much praised late novel *Nostromo* took me a long time to tune in to, but I remember my pleasure when I did. Conrad here gives the impression of having invented cinematic techniques before the movies did. Aerial views, dolly & zoom . . . Like Nabokov he writes amazingly well, considering that English wasn't his native tongue.

I hope to have reread *Ulysses* before our next meeting. The bit you quote is lovely. Peter freaked out when he first saw me take food from a knife (a piece of cheese or smear of jam). I guess he's insufficiently Irish.

You ask me to enlarge upon "pushing meaning into acts of nature." I don't claim the phrase as mine. But perhaps the subject would be the pros & cons of letting an image out of nature—skylark or volcano or witty remark—speak for itself. Not automatically needing to nudge your reader: this stands for Ecstasy or Anger or the godgiven Play of Mind.

The point, I believe, is to feel your feelings in the presence of something in the "outside world"—a tree, a portrait, the hood of a car, an article about a new scientific discovery—which will reflect your heightened state of mind <u>back</u> to you. You will not have to say "I". This will become 2nd nature, if you wish it to. [*In the margin*: You may already know this. Trust the <u>knowledge</u>.]

One of your present advantages is a relative immaturity that gives you time to focus on your craft. Of course ideas & metaphors will come your way, but the chances are that they will be sources of embarrassment even a few years hence. What will not embarrass you is the fulfilling of formal problems, whether set by older models or contrived by yourself. Am I urging you to write sestinas, villanelles, sonnets? I am. Because to have done so implies a level of skill you may one day go far beyond, but which meanwhile will not turn to ashes in your mouth like This Season's Deep Thought. Live 40 more years and you'll find those TSDTs resurfacing, encrusted with rare submarine textures for your own personal use. So there's no hurry, at least where Content is involved. Now's the time to surrender to the Craft. At your age you can learn quickly & lastingly. Learn the full expressiveness of your medium, the forms, the meters, the joys of syntax direct <u>and</u> devious. If a friend or teacher should read this page and say "What utter shit!" remember that he has my sympathy, not my envy. Of course you deplore Ginsberg, as I do those arid acres in Pound's *Cantos* (or in my own *Mirabell* for that matter). Yet I remain <u>glad</u> that modernism "happened" and "animal movements" like the Beats brought fresh air, offered new approaches. Best of all made a disturbance behind which we could get on with our own work without having to enroll in a School, or (in WC Williams' horrible phrase) breaking the back of the pentameter . . .

Tell me if I'm putting things not plainly enough—or too plainly. That's one reason I need my pupil's letters: to find a tone that reaches him with reasonable dispatch. This is such a delight for me—to be writing "real" letters, that is, to someone who'll read them with corresponding delight. (Where to start your reading list? Anywhere. Reality, says A R Ammons, is abob with centers.)

Auden's rationale for formal "constraints"—which ideally set free more than they constrain—was that your conscious mind would be so occupied with finding a rhyme or an amphibrach (look it up) that your subconscious filled enough of the gap to supply things you could never have come up with on your own. Consider in this light any quatrain from WHA's "The Fall of Rome":

> Fantastic grow the evening gowns.
> As agents of the Fisc pursue
> Absconding tax-defaulters through
> The sewers of provincial towns.

or (again from memory):

> Caesar's double bed is warm
> But an unimportant clerk
> Writes <u>I do not like my work</u>
> On a pink official form.

(How much prose would it take to make the connections in those 4 lines.) A plausible exercise: translate this poem into our late 20th century Workshop Idiom—unrhymed, unmetered, "natural word order," lines measured, if at all, by their length, and so forth. How much will you lose? how much gain? Is it even <u>do-able</u> in the first place?

16.i.1995

From FLASH to C*R*A*S*H, so to speak. Yesterday on the road to Bisbee, pretty town once famous for its copper mines, a woman in a powder-blue van pulled slowly and unwisely onto the 2-lane highway. For half a second her horrified eyes met P's horrified eyes. No choice but to swerve to the right, skid on gravel provided by a thoughtful State, and plow into the red car behind the van. It broke their axle, squashed our engine whose budding holocaust the radiator's gush promptly discouraged. Now arrived: police, tow-truck, ambulance into which the two women from the red car disappeared, taped to their stretchers like mummies (both suffering from whiplash)—well, as you said of your exam, I shall leave the rest to your imagination. We, at least, weren't hurt, beyond the sprained finger with which I mean to show Arizona drivers what I think of them. Cosmo set a high standard for Cool, giving his version to each of the officers in turn, frowning over "reports." Only hours later came the shock, and we had to stop on the road & hold hands. I assure you this isn't the kind of thing Peter & I are known for doing. I mean the collision.

Of course all the returns aren't in. But that's it for today.

Yours,
JM

TIP: Sign letters in your own hand, not the WP keyboard.

the composer Erb Donald Erb (1927–2008).
Ed Sanders (b. 1939), American writer and social activist.
Ellen Geer American actor and director (b. 1941).
Will Geer American actor and social activist (1902–78).
Poetry in Motion Documentary feature film (1982) directed by Ron Mann, featuring Sanders and other contemporary poets reading and performing their work.
to feel . . . back to you Merrill discusses the subject in "On 'Yánnina': An Interview with David Kalstone" in *Collected Prose* (2004).
breaking . . . pentameter Merrill mixes up Williams and Ezra Pound. See Pound, "*Canto LXXXI*": "(To break the pentameter, that was the first heave)."
says A R Ammons (1926–2001), in his poem "Essay on Poetics" (*Collected Poems: 1951–71*, 1972).
W.H.A.'s "The Fall of Rome" Merrill slightly misquotes each of the stanzas.

To Torren Blair

BLAIR
17–20 January 1995
Tucson, AZ

Dear Torren,

Another opera I'll take you to if I may. (Better luck this time?) I have a pair of tickets to *Pelléas et Mélisande* on April 13, in New York. This seems even more desirable for your first opera than *Peter Grimes* would have been. The (French) text is of high quality, by Maurice Maeterlinck, first staged as a play, then set to music by Debussy. It's one of the high points of Symbolism, a fin-de-siècle movement that had a great effect for a short time. In Proust's day you could listen to plays & concerts over your telephone (imagine), and this he liked doing—lest he trigger an attack of asthma, or mar his image as a recluse—with *Pelléas*. It's more a "music-drama" than an opera: no "numbers" to bring down the house, just an ebb-and-flow of superb textures, and a vocal line that owes more to plainsong than to what we think of as overt melody, counterpoint, etc. The obvious antecedent is Wagner—as he is in Berlioz—but a Wagner whose deep Rhine-gold has been "to airy thinness beat" (Donne's "Valediction," on your list). Ideally I'd like you to get to the apartment <u>in time for your nap</u>—3 or 4 p.m.? The opera's at 8, and the mean little chambre de bonne there is at your disposal. (Easiest would be to leave your wheels in the RR garage at New Haven, and take Metro North to Grand Central.) The next day I would keep you company back to Stonington, where I shan't have been since last December. See if your calendar permits this. Even if the date falls outside your Easter break, couldn't a class be cut? If it's not a week of exams. . . .

Consider this a formal invitation. "The favor of a reply" is requested before 21 March.

Another date—not as vital—is 16 May, when I have 2 whole hours to fill up in a "hall" in the Village. I'll read poems, Peter & his young friend Katherine Pew—her parents live almost next door out here—will do my little play *The Image Maker.* And if all else fails I can answer questions from the audience. I'd be happy if you were there. And a 3rd date, should you not yet have left for Ireland: the young poet I spoke of, Jeffrey Harrison, is reading in that Farmington garden on July 5. I've agreed to introduce him.

This letter adds nothing to your burden of future reading. Yet the other day's near-fatal episode leaves me with a sense that it is vital—to me, to us both—that I tell you whatever I can while I'm still around. My impulse is to write to you for an hour or two every day. I fight the impulse, remembering the law of diminishing returns. The cistern needs time to fill.

Today, snow—the first, they say, in seven years—and as much of a blizzard as this mild climate can muster. Big flakes, field of Queen Anne's Lace. Last night: big stars, clouds tinted by the urban gempool to the south. The clouds are exactly the color of the white patches on our harlequin koi—a white ever so faintly suffused by blood and gold.

At intervals, into the upturned face drop the soft, soft pinpricks of dew. Seeing my high-&-dry human silhouette the fish have clustered to be fed, and Cosmo barking like mad falls into their pond.

Have you ever tried haiku? It's not a form we can properly use in English, but that doesn't stem the tide. Richard Howard, speaking as a poetry editor, said that reading 500 haiku a month was like being nibbled to death by goldfish. Be that as it may, the lesson they teach is small but valuable. With only 17 syllables you are forced to consider what's essential. For instance (while Peter drives I like to sit with pen poised above a notebook), here speaks a giant saguaro cactus:

> Hail daybreak. Summon
> From the deep wound in my side
> This Gilded Flicker.

This after some 20 variants. The form (three lines—5/7/5) needs specificity or it slides away. Thus I had to jettison the too-familiar "idea" of Pain Becoming Song, and baldly name the resident woodpecker, leaving the rest for a reader at home with overtones. "Gilded," without saying so, shows the bird answering to dawn, while its full name might describe the 3-line poem. (Another still unresolved problem: the articles. Should it be a deep wound & the flicker—as if there were no wound without a bird in it—or a flicker, making its emergence more of a surprise—and so on into an infinite gloaming of revision . . .) The subject needn't be Nature. After massage & yoga out here, an all-but-chronic condition that's kept me popping Advil for the last 4 months uttered this (regional) sigh of relief:

> Upper-back "hot points"—
> Last week a searing gunfight,
> Today a ghost town.

—the setting, you see, even in something so tiny, miming back to you what you feel.

Our yoga instructor and his housemate (Professor of Classics at local State U.) has us to dinner for Young Gordon's 32nd birthday. We brought him some 60's-style comic books. He was thrilled! He'd never read a comic book growing up. In fact he'd never read a book of any description, so busy was he living the life of the Body. He is a dear soul, friendly & talkative, saying whatever comes into his head—a blessed prelapsarian condition—and every day more deeply given to the Yoruba gods & their disciplines. Yoruba, you may know, is the religion brought here by the slave trade and grafted upon Christianity (the world of my playlet mentioned above). So a hybrid faith comes into being, very "primitive," with animal sacrifice, divine possession etc. In carefully chosen corners of the house are G's wee gods, whom we were taken to meet. I will have to look at them more closely when my cataracts are gone. Can it be that one of them was a blob of soft whitish wax, crowned with beads? Another (the Path-Clearer) is a small metal bucket full of toy tools, shovels & rakes, a ladder. Offerings of food and flowers, on big occasions a lighted cigar. I am treated with respect by Gordon and his friends, as a kind of honorary Yoruban. This is thanks to my long friendship with Maya Deren who after becoming known for her experimental films went to Haiti to study voodoo. She wrote a book (*Divine Horsemen*) about the experience which led to her possession by Erzulie, the Haitian equivalent of Aphrodite and the BVM. Anyhow, Maya is among the few white votaries. Her name opens doors, and I have slipped through this one, at least in the eyes of the Believers. Maya both alive & dead figures throughout *Sandover*. (Much self-advertisement in this letter—sorry about that.)

See the attached poem. This can be the result when you let yourself go in a letter. It requires an indulgent reader, like you—like me as well. "Having something to say" needn't account for all the motive for & rewards of Correspondence.

I picked up a copy of *Ulysses* today. And am reading a book about Gertrude Stein. Here is the full if not exactly riveting account of her one meeting with Joyce at a reception in Paris: She allowed herself to be led to Joyce's side and . . . said "we have never met and he said no although our names are always together, and then we talked of Paris and where we lived and why we lived where we lived and that was all . . ."

Pour prendre congé let me tell you that Venice is well-known as the Sorbet Capital of Europe. The summer of 1984 added to the usual 24 or 30 flavors something never before—or after, I believe—tasted: a watermelon ice complete with wholly convincing seeds of dark chocolate. Or don't you have a sweet tooth?

Yours,
JM

Katherine Pew (b. 1968), American writer.
near-fatal episode Hooten and Merrill's car accident.
Our yoga instructor and his housemate Gordon Sieveke and Norman Austin, professor of classics at the University of Arizona.
the attached poem "Koi" (*Collected Poems*, 2001).
a book about Gertrude Stein *Gertrude Stein Remembered*, ed. Linda Simon (1994).
Pour prendre congé To take leave.

To Torren Blair

BLAIR
28–30 January 1995
Tucson, AZ

Dear Torren,

Who? What? Where? Why? When?
Time for you to write again.

Your mother wrote—a short lovely letter—and sent me your piece in *The Day*. It's not easy to address that kind of audience, and you do it extremely well. I'm talking about tone, and inwardly comparing your handling of the subject with a 5-page letter written by the Bishop of Connecticut on the Sin of Racism. This, the author hoped, was to be read aloud in Ct. churches; and so it came to pass, in Peter's little northwestern parish, that he & I and a 3rd reader intoned the Bishop's truly deadly language. No feeling behind it, just throat-clearing and corporate flatulence. Someone is bound to speak up saying that the issues matter more than the language does, but as I see it they rise or fall together. One reason Darwin had such an impact must have been the beauty and sufficiency of his style.

As for racism, my brother (Memoir XVI) is certainly part of the solution. His school in Boston (he was headmaster 1960–90) featured immediate seating for black & foreign students. His daughter Amy in fact married one of her black classmates after each had outgrown the original color-coordinated spouse. We are all proud of them; it can't have been easy. In my different sphere, as a "creative" gay man, I feel I too am part of the solution, though never quite persuaded that it helps to know this. Our sister, amazing at 80—with her foursquare life in four Lovely Homes like the discreet letterings in gold on a plateglass shop-window: NEW YORK, SOUTHAMPTON, PALM BEACH, SAN FRANCISCO—remains transparently part of the problem.

Anyhow, I was delighted to have a word from your mother, and look forward to meeting the entire cast in April.

I've been in rather gloomed-over this week. So many obstacles to my cataract "procedure"—tests, examinations, stimuli to raise my platelet count—when I'd pictured it as a simple conveyor-belt operation—but no. There were bad moments: to think of Joyce and his ever thicker glasses, of Milton and his ever thinner daughters, was no consolation. Happily it's "nihil obstat" at present. By 10 Feb unless something <u>else</u> goes wrong, I shall be wearing (without, let's hope, having become in the process "ugly & venomous" like Shakespeare's toad) a "precious jewel in my head"—the newly implanted lens.

About 150 pages into *Ulysses* I find a completely different book from the one I prided myself on having read at 20—when I fancied from the opening that I was meant to <u>like</u> Buck Mulligan, and pictured Bloom as a horrid little man trapped in his libidinous jail. All is different now. The finest tweezers put each least detail in place and I am enthralled. Bloom's misremembering of the words from *Don Giovanni*—thinking <u>voglio</u> instead of <u>vorrei</u> would merely have been autocratic carelessness in a book by Miss Stein; here, though, we trust that some distinction is coming alive between active & subjunctive modes, or wishing & willing—and to that tiniest degree our eyes are peeled for what JJ will "do" with this. To command that kind of attention is part of what we mean by mastery. Thus far along I don't see the Homeric correlative as being much to the point. Yes of course Stephen "is looking for a father" but then so are hundreds of thousands of young men. My book on Gertrude Stein quotes

Picasso (of all people) saying "Joyce has written an obscure book which the whole world understands." What a shocker it must have been when it appeared! One reward of a long life is to approach these early ground-breaking works from the Other Side, nodding wisely & approvingly at their iconoclastic verve. I never got far into *Moby-Dick* until I was past 50. (Melville wrote it at 37?) Finally taking it as a breathtaking performance by a starry-eyed verbal Baryshnikov, I couldn't put it down.

In church this morning the minister asked: Why is today a Holy Day? And in one voice the congregation chortled back: The Super Bowl!—or as Robert Morse, late of Main St, liked to call it, the Superb Owl.

Monday Peter came in from his one-day computer course, flushed with skills & projects. You've never seen a more dashing Nerd / And for the sake of rhyme, Send Word!

Yours,
JM

—and a sprig of Arizona rosemary for your mother

The Day New London, CT, newspaper.
Memoir XVI Sixteenth chapter in *A Different Person* (1993).
His school in Boston Charles Merrill founded the progressive Commonwealth School.
"ugly & venomous" See the speech by the Duke in *As You Like It*, II.1.
"precious jewel" From the same speech.
<u>voglio</u> **instead of** <u>vorrei</u> *"I want"* instead of *"I would like."*

To André Aciman   ACIMAN
                                                      1 February 1995
                                                         Tucson, AZ

Dear André Aciman,

I can only begin to tell you how touched and delighted I am by *Out of Egypt*. Thanks to Christian Ayoub's friendship and his two little books, to the kitchen-Italian libretti of Bernard de Zogheb, to the anecdotes of my irreplaceable Tony Parigory in Athens (where I lived for a number of years), and not to mention Cavafy, Alexandria has permanently colored my days. To find it now in your pages, all rosy and clear-eyed from the tonic of your telling, is the greatest imaginable gift. That whole world of the trivial & the tragic, interwoven as in Chekhov, and underscored as in opera, is for me the very best life has to offer, and as close to a "real" home as I've ever come. No reflection on my parents, that the Stork delivered me to West Eleventh Street instead of the Corniche. But here I am. What do you do with so much blue, once you've seen it? (Terrible things await us before the book ends. Meanwhile, just a long sigh of relief . . .)

Well, I could spin this all out at greater length—you can't be averse to praise. Most of all, though, I want to go back to the beginning and read it through a second time.

Sincerely,
James Merrill

André Aciman (b. 1951), born and raised in Alexandria, writer of fiction and nonfiction and professor of comparative literature at the City University of New York.
Out of Egypt Aciman's memoir (1994) won a Whiting Award in 1995.
the Corniche Alexandria's waterfront promenade.

Chronology

1926 On March 3rd, born in New York City to Charles Edward Merrill and Hellen Ingram Merrill. The family lived in Manhattan, in Southampton on Long Island in a grand house called The Orchard, and in Palm Beach, Florida, on a property called Merrill's Landing. Merrill's half siblings, Charles and Doris, children of Charles Merrill's first marriage, lived with their mother.

1936–38 Attended St. Bernard's School in Manhattan.

1939–42 His parents concluded a bitter divorce in 1939. After the divorce, lived with his mother in the Carlyle Hotel, in a Manhattan town house, and later in a house in New Canaan, Connecticut. Attended Lawrenceville School in New Jersey and started writing poetry. In 1942, as a sixteenth-birthday gift, his father published his poetry and prose in a limited edition called *Jim's Book*. Close friendship and literary collaboration at Lawrenceville with Frederick Buechner.

1943–44 Graduated from Lawrenceville in 1943 and enrolled at Amherst College, his father's alma mater. Majored in English, while studying French and Ancient Greek literature, among other subjects.

1944–45 Inducted into the US Army in June, and served eight months in training camps. Re-enrolled at Amherst in September and fell in love with Kimon Friar, a temporary instructor at the college. Introduced by Friar to W. H. Auden; the filmmaker, dancer, and anthropologist Maya Deren; and the writer Anaïs Nin. Played the lead role in a college production of Jean Cocteau's *Orphée*. His mother's discovery of his love affair led to conflict and melodrama.

1946–47 Treated by a psychoanalyst at his mother's direction. To Mexico City in the summer with his brother, Charles, and Charles's wife, Mary: his first trip outside the US. Friar arranged for publication in Athens of Merrill's short volume of poems *The Black Swan*, in an edition of one hundred copies. First publications in *Poetry* magazine. Met Dutch poet Hans Lodeizen. His verse play *The Birthday* performed at Amherst. Completed honors thesis on Marcel Proust supervised by Ruben Brower ("*À la recherche du temps perdu*: Impressionism in Literature"). In June, awarded his BA *summa cum laude* from Amherst. Moved to Manhattan after graduation.

1948–49 With Buechner, spent the summer on Georgetown Island on the Maine coast. Taught at Bard College for the academic year. Met Elizabeth Bishop. Won *Poetry*'s Levinson Prize. Befriended Irma Brandeis. To Paris. Brief affair with his student Louise Fitzhugh.

1950–52 Met and fell in love with Claude Fredericks. Read poetry with Richard Wilbur at Amherst and was dissatisfied with his voice and his poems. With Friar in Athens and on Poros and Rhodes, and hospitalized briefly in Athens. With Fredericks in France, Switzerland (to see Lodeizen, who was suffering from leukemia and died shortly afterward), Austria, and Italy. Mother remarried to William Plummer. With Fredericks on Mallorca. *First Poems*, dedicated to Buechner, published by Knopf. In Rome, separated from Fredericks, undertook psychoanalytic treatment with Dr. Thomas Detre. Love affair with Robert Isaacson, with whom he travels to Greece and Istanbul. In Rome, friendships with Umberto Morra, Marilyn Lavin, and Guitou Knoop. Returned to New York in December 1952.

1953 Living in an apartment on West Tenth Street. In Barbados with his father, and in Atlanta with his mother. For his birthday, Buechner gave him a Ouija board. His play *The Bait* produced in

New York. Fell in love with David Jackson. With Jackson, first experiments with the Ouija board.

1954 With Jackson, rented rooms for the summer in a commercial building at 107 Water Street in Stonington, Connecticut. Met Wallace Stevens at Stevens's seventy-fifth birthday party, hosted by the Knopfs in connection with the publication of Stevens's *Collected Poems*.

1955 Ingram Merrill Foundation established; the foundation supported writers, artists, and various cultural organizations and charities through annual grants until Merrill's death. His chapbook of poems *Short Stories* published by Fredericks's Banyan Press. His play *The Immortal Husband* produced in New York to mixed reviews. Drove with Jackson to Los Angeles, where he met Jackson's family and his wife Doris Sewell ("Sewelly") Jackson. In Stonington, with Jackson, made contact on the Ouija board with the spirit Ephraim. Read Yeats's letters and *A Vision*. Taught at Amherst through the academic year 1955–56. Writing *The Seraglio*. Adopted a kitten, Maisie.

1956–57 Purchased 107 Water Street and began renovations. Read at the Poetry Center in San Francisco, and met Allen Ginsberg and Gregory Corso. Round-the-world trip with Jackson, beginning in Japan, where he befriended Donald Richie. On hearing that his father had died, decided not to return to the US for the funeral. In Hong Kong, Thailand, Ceylon, India, Turkey, Switzerland, West Germany, Italy, France, and England. *The Seraglio* published by Knopf to mixed reviews.

1958 Spent winter in Santa Fe with Jackson, finishing his collection of poems, *The Country of a Thousand Years of Peace*, published the next year by Knopf.

1959 With Jackson, to Paris, Munich, Tangier, Morocco, Spain, Athens. In Stonington, friendships with his neighbors Robert and Isabel Morse and Grace Stone and Eleanor Perenyi; the clique called itself the Surly Temple.

1960–61 With Jackson, to Paris (where he met Daryl Hine), Berlin, Munich, Venice, Alexandria (where he met Christian Ayoub Sinano), Athens.

1962 With Jackson, to Paris, Yugoslavia, and Greece. Friendships with Tony Parigory, Maria Mitsotaki, and Nelly Liambey in Athens. In Athens, afflicted with Bell's palsy. Visited by Robin and Betty Magowan and Grace Stone. His book of poems *Water Street* published by Atheneum, where his editor, Harry Ford, had moved from Knopf. Break with Friar.

1963 To Istanbul with his mother and Greece with Jackson. With Parigory, to Chicago, Seattle, San Francisco, and Santa Fe. At Mona Van Duyn's request, began donating his papers to Special Collections, Washington University St. Louis.

1964 In May, purchased a house in Athens at Athinaion Efivon 44, near Kolonaki Square, with views of Mount Lycabettos. Friendships in Athens with Alan Ansen, Chester Kallman, and Mimi and Vassilis Vassilikos. Began a passionate affair with Strato Mouflouzelis.

1965 Returned to Stonington in January. *The (Diblos) Notebook*, an experimental novel based on his experience in Greece and his relationship with Friar, published by Atheneum, then nominated for the National Book Award. Returned to Greece in July, where he spent most of the next year and a half.

1966 Deteriorating relationship with Mouflouzelis. To Iran with Donald Richie, and to Rome. Met Kostas Tympakianakis. *Nights and Days* published by Atheneum.

1967 Won the National Book Award for *Nights and Days*, judged by Auden, James Dickey, and Howard Nemerov. Returned to New York to receive the award. Taught a poetry writing course at the University of Wisconsin in Madison, where his students included Stephen Yenser and Judith Moffett. Read his poems at the University of California at Berkeley. Affair with Mouflouzelis ending. Summer in Stonington. Visited Mary McCarthy, also Robert Lowell and Elizabeth Hardwick, in Maine. Briefly in Greece. Visited Tympakianakis on Crete, then Mimi and Vassilis Vassilikos in Paris. In Chicago to see Hine and read at *Poetry* magazine's Poetry Day. Readings at the University of Virginia, the 92nd Street YMHA, and Princeton. Awarded honorary LittD degree by Amherst.

1968 In February, met David McIntosh. Visited his mother in Atlanta and the Morses in Jamaica. With McIntosh for nine days in Wyoming. In Greece, with Jackson. Visited Auden and Kallman in Kirchstetten, Austria. Served as Fanny Hurst Visiting Poet at Washington University St. Louis in the fall. With McIntosh in Nambé Pueblo, near Santa Fe.

1969 Attended Elizabeth Bishop's reading at the Guggenheim Museum. Jackson's parents and Parigory visited Merrill and Jackson in Stonington. Staying with McIntosh in Nambé Pueblo. Attended stepfather William Plummer's funeral in Atlanta. To Rome and then to Athens to visit Jackson. *The Fire Screen*, dedicated to Jackson, published by Atheneum.

1970 Christos Alevras and his family moved from Greece into the second-floor apartment at 107 Water Street. Alevras worked as a handyman for Merrill, who sponsored his and his family's immigration. Hosted McIntosh in Stonington. In summer, visited Peru with Charles and Mary Merrill, and then Bishop in Brazil. With McIntosh, in Vermont and New Hampshire, and then Greece. Hosted Bishop in Stonington in December. Elected to the National Institute of Arts and Letters.

1971 In March, visiting Mary Lou Aswell and McIntosh in New Mexico. Meetings in Stonington with Dr. Albert Rothenberg, who used Merrill as a case study in his research on the psychology of creativity. Met Mouflouzelis in Paris, and drove with him through France (visiting Yenser) and Italy (visiting Umberto Morra) to Greece. Went to Yannina with Yenser, who spent the summer in

Greece. Returned as Fanny Hurst Visiting Professor to Washington University St. Louis in November.

1972 Visited Yenser in Los Angeles and McIntosh in Santa Fe. Introduced to Transcendental Meditation. Returned to Greece, with David Kalstone. *Braving the Elements*, dedicated to Hellen Plummer, published by Atheneum. Helen Vendler reviewed the book positively in September in *The New York Times Book Review*. Began friendship with J. D. McClatchy. To Istanbul. Awarded Bollingen Prize for *Braving the Elements*.

1973 To Paris, visiting Mimi and Vassilis Vassilikos, and Mary McCarthy. Spent birthday in Atlanta with his mother. With McIntosh in Santa Fe. Attended Yenser's wedding to Mary Bomba in Los Angeles. Read with Bishop at the 92nd Street YMHA. To Venice with Kalstone, and Greece, where he saw Truman Capote and met William Burroughs. Friendship with Manos Karastefanis. Mother visited Greece for the first and only time; Judith Moffett in Athens too. Auden died in September. Hosted Yenser and Bomba in Stonington.

1974 Maria Mitsotaki died. Abandoned attempts to write a novel about the Ouija board and began writing "The Book of Ephraim" in Stonington. *The Yellow Pages* published by Temple Bar Bookshop, Cambridge, Massachusetts. Introduced to the doctor and medical researcher George Cotzias by his sister, Doris.

1975 Chester Kallman died. Visited Rome with Parigory. Finished "The Book of Ephraim." Jackson's parents came to Athens to be cared for. After Merrill returned to Stonington, they died, first his mother, then his father. Merrill returned to Athens briefly that summer, then taught a fall-semester poetry writing course at Yale.

1976 In Greece visited Poros with Yenser in April and later in the month traveled with him and Bomba to Istanbul. Tony Harwood died. *Divine Comedies* published by Atheneum. Jackson hospitalized for minor surgery in Boston. Daily Ouija board sessions in Stonington. After Jackson returned to Greece, Merrill visited

Fredericks in Vermont, Charles and Mary Merrill in New Hampshire, and Harry Pemberton and James Boatwright in Virginia. Relationship with Peter Tourville.

1977 Won Pulitzer Prize for *Divine Comedies*. To San Francisco, Los Angeles, Syracuse, Chicago, and Kalamazoo for readings. George Cotzias and Robert Morse died. On the island of Samos with Jackson and Parigory. Daily Ouija board sessions in Athens. Finished *Mirabell: Books of Number* in Greece. Christmas with his mother in Atlanta.

1978 Celebrated twenty-fifth anniversary with Jackson in May. Traveled to Crete and Athens. Mimi Vassilikos died suddenly. *Mirabell*, second volume of the Ouija board trilogy, published by Atheneum, won Merrill a second National Book Award, and was hailed by judges as "nothing less than monumental in scale and execution."

1979 With Jackson, bought a house in Key West at 702 Elizabeth Street. Began spending winters there, where his friends included John Malcolm Brinnin, John Ciardi, John and Barbara Hersey, Harry Mathews, Alison Lurie, and Richard and Charlee Wilbur. Bishop died suddenly in October. In fall, with Jackson, permanently moved out of Athinaion Efivon 44.

1980 Readings at Stanford, the New School, Harvard, UCLA, in San Francisco, and at Yale, Bard, and Princeton. *Scripts for the Pageant* published by Atheneum in April.

1981 With McIntosh to Italy, hosted by Umberto Morra, and to Greece. October in Key West.

1982 With Kalstone, visited John Ashbery in Hudson, New York. At Vassar, celebrated the college's purchase of Bishop's papers. At Fredericks's home in Vermont, burned Ouija board transcripts. *The Changing Light at Sandover* and *From the First Nine: Poems 1946–1976* published by Atheneum. *Sandover*, gathering the Ouija board trilogy and a coda, won the National Book Critics Circle Award.

Interviewed by McClatchy for *The Paris Review*. Awarded honorary LittD by Yale.

1983 Judged Bollingen Prize (awarded to Anthony Hecht and John Hollander). Spent winter in Key West. Met Peter Hooten. Began judging the Yale Series of Younger Poets prize. With Friar in Athens, Kalstone in Venice, and Perenyi in Italy and Holland. Canoe trip on the Connecticut River with Peter Tourville.

1984 Hooten and Merrill became lovers when Hooten visited Key West in February. Read at Harvard with Seamus Heaney in April. With Hooten, to Europe in May (Amsterdam, London, Cornwall, Venice), and travels in New England during the summer. With McIntosh and Mary Lou Aswell in Santa Fe in September. Readings at the Iowa Writers Workshop and UCLA.

1985 Winter in Key West, with Hooten living next door to Merrill and Jackson. Visited Green Cove Springs, Florida, his father's birthplace, with Hooten. Writer-in-residence at Washington University St. Louis. Kalstone diagnosed with AIDS. With Jackson, saw Kalstone in Venice, then visited Athens (the last time for Jackson). Met Hooten in Paris. In New York, attended a Merrill Lynch–sponsored party for the firm's cofounder Charles Merrill's birth. *Late Settings* published by Atheneum. Robert Magowan died.

1986 Party for his sixtieth birthday in Key West. Named first Connecticut State Poet Laureate. At the Mayo Clinic, diagnosed with HIV infection, which he kept secret from most people. To Japan with Hooten and Robin and Stephen Magowan and Stephen's partner Octavio Ciano, hosted by Richie. Verse play *The Image Maker* produced at UCLA in May, and the next year at Seton Hall University. Kalstone died of AIDS in June. *Recitative: Prose*, a book of essays and interviews, edited by McClatchy, published by North Point. With Hooten, to Switzerland, Rome, and Capri in the fall.

1987 In summer, to Martha's Vineyard with Jackson, to New Hampshire and Montreal with Hooten, and to Atlanta to see his mother. Read at a memorial service for Lowell in New York and at a centenary celebration of Marianne Moore. Harry Ford returned to Knopf, which published Merrill's next collection, *The Inner Room*.

1988 With Hooten to Hawaii, where they visited W. S. Merwin. *Voices from Sandover*, a staged reading adapted from *The Changing Light at Sandover*, performed in Cambridge, Massachusetts, at UCLA, and at the Guggenheim Museum, with Merrill and Hooten as actors. Celebrated his mother's ninetieth birthday in Atlanta. In September, to England with Hooten. James Boatwright died of AIDS.

1989 With Hooten to Bishop's childhood home in Nova Scotia, and then to Athens, Istanbul, and Vienna. Read at the 92nd St YMHA in a program for the ten-year anniversary of Bishop's death. Inducted into the American Academy of Arts and Letters in December.

1990 A new version of *Voices from Sandover*, with eight actors, including Merrill, videotaped in August at the Agassiz Theater at Harvard. To Los Angeles to edit the videotape. Conflicts with Hooten. In October, won the first Bobbitt National Prize for Poetry, awarded by the Library of Congress, for *The Inner Room*. Christmas with his mother in Atlanta.

1991 In Los Angeles for further editing of *Voices from Sandover*. Grace Stone died. Hooten admitted to the Smithers Clinic in New York for addiction treatment, then moved to Sierra Tucson, where Merrill visited. Parigory suffering with AIDS.

1992 With Hooten to Rotterdam for Poetry International Festival, and to Copenhagen and Scotland. With Hooten, chose a Jack Russell terrier as a pet and named him Cosmo. Hosted Jackson's seventieth birthday party in Stonington. Visit from Parigory. *Selected Poems 1946–1985* published by Knopf. Christmas with his mother in Atlanta.

1993 Alone, increasingly ill, and in Greece for the last time, seeing Parigory and Friar. Both Parigory and Friar died later that year.

To Sweden for a poetry festival. To his mother in Atlanta, and his brother in New Hampshire. In summer, told McClatchy he had AIDS and asked him to help keep his condition private. Reading at Yale. *A Different Person: A Memoir* published by Knopf. Treated for HIV by doctors in New York and Pittsburgh.

1994 Ill, isolated, and depressed in Key West. In New York, resided in his grandmother Mis' Annie's former apartment at 164 East Seventy-Second Street, while Hooten lived in Lakeville, Connecticut. With Hooten, stayed with Fredericks in Vermont in summer, and toured Prague and Vienna in fall. Friendship with Torren Blair. Reading at the Art Institute of Chicago and a celebration of his work at Olin Library, Washington University St. Louis, with Yenser, Vendler, and others speaking about his poetry.

1995 With Hooten, in Tucson for the winter. While hospitalized for pancreatitis, died of a heart attack on February 6. On February 13, after a burial service in Stonington, his ashes were interred in the Stonington Cemetery. *A Scattering of Salts*, his final book of poems, published by Knopf in March. A memorial tribute was held at the New York Public Library on May 13.

Biographies

Elizabeth Bishop (1911–79), poet, born in Worcester, Massachusetts. Member of a class at Vassar that included Mary McCarthy. Marianne Moore's protégée and a close friend of Robert Lowell. Merrill, who met her in 1948, admired her work more than that of any other living poet. Lived in Brazil from 1951 to 1967 and for short periods after that. By the time she received the Neustadt International Prize for Literature for *Geography III* (1976) was widely recognized as a contemporary master. Merrill visited her in Brazil, saw her often in the 1970s in Boston and Stonington, and wrote several brief prose pieces in homage to her, as well as the elegiac poem "Overdue Pilgrimage to Nova Scotia" (*A Scattering of Salts*, 1995).

Irma Brandeis (1905–90), scholar of Italian language and literature, and Merrill's colleague when he taught at Bard, where she taught for thirty-five years. Author of *The Ladder of Vision: A Study of Dante's Comedy* (1961). A friend of the Italian poet Eugenio Montale and the original of the figure of Clizia in his poems, especially those in *Le occasioni,* and in his *Lettere a Clizia*. Served on the board of the Ingram Merrill Foundation from its beginning until her death. Merrill endowed the Irma Brandeis Chair at Bard in her memory.

Louise Fitzhugh (1928–74), writer and illustrator of books for children and teens. Merrill's student at Bard, where they briefly had a romantic relationship. Her career began when she illustrated Sandra Scoppettone's *Suzuki Beane* (1961). The first book entirely her own was *Harriet the Spy* (1964), which has never been out of print. Her second was a sequel, *The Long Secret* (1965), perhaps the first children's book to address the subject of menstruation. She later cowrote with Scoppettone, and illustrated, the antiwar text *Bang Bang You're Dead* (1969). Died suddenly of a cerebral aneurysm.

Claude Fredericks (1923–2013), writer, publisher of the Banyan Press, which printed hand-set limited editions of works by Merrill, Gertrude Stein, Stephen Spender, and other writers. Also a professor of ancient Greek, Italian, and Japanese language and literature at Bennington College. In 1947, bought a farmhouse in Pawlet, Vermont, and lived there the rest of his life. "The love of my life," Merrill considered him in 1950–51, and lifelong friend afterward. Inspiration for Julian Morrow, a character in his student Donna Tartt's novel *The Secret History* (1992). His diary *The Journal of Claude Fredericks*, held at the Getty Research Center, documents his life between the ages of 8 and 89.

Kimon Friar (1911–93), translator, editor, and critic born to Greek parents on an island now part of Turkey. Became an American citizen as a child. Exponent of modern Greek poetry for Anglophone readers. His works include the translation, with its author, of Nikos Kazantzakis's *The Odyssey: A Modern Sequel* (1958), dedicated to Merrill, and Odysseus Elytis's *The Sovereign Sun: Selected Poems* (1974). Director of the 92nd Street YMHA Poetry Center 1943–46. While hired to teach returning GIs at Amherst in 1945, became Merrill's mentor and first lover.

Daryl Hine (1936–2012), Canadian poet, translator, and editor. Merrill's friend and protégé after their meeting in Paris in 1960. Translated Hesiod, Theocritus, and other classical poets while composing a dozen volumes of polished traditional verse of his own inspiration on occasionally risqué themes. Editor of *Poetry* magazine from 1968 to 1978. **Samuel Todes** (1927–94), a philosopher, was his partner, whose Harvard dissertation was posthumously published as *Body and World* (2001).

John Hollander (1929–2013), literary scholar and critic, teacher, anthologist, and prolific, technically expert, and inventive poet, whose first book was selected by W. H. Auden for the Yale Younger

Poets series. His art and literary acumen converged in unique works such as *Types of Shape* (1969), a book of shaped poems dedicated to Merrill, and *Rhyme's Reason* (1981), a self-exemplifying guide to poetic forms common and esoteric. He and his first wife, **Anne Loesser Hollander** (1930–2014), were friends of Merrill's and Jackson's beginning in 1959, when he taught at Connecticut College. Later, when he taught at Yale as Sterling Professor of English, and married the sculptor **Natalie Charkow** (b. 1933), saw Merrill regularly. Served on the Ingram Merrill Foundation board for forty years. Merrill's poem "Dreams of Clothes" in *Braving the Elements* (1972) is dedicated to John and Anne Hollander, and "Home Fires," in *A Scattering of Salts* (1995), is dedicated to John.

Peter Hooten (b. 1950), actor and producer. A Floridian by birth, attended Ithaca College. Toured the US with the actor Will Geer, reciting poetry by Robert Frost and other literary texts in a program of Americana. Acted in popular TV shows such as *Marcus Welby, M.D.* and *The Waltons*, and with actors such as Bo Derek, Charlotte Rampling, Richard Harris, and Sir John Mills in a variety of movies. Attended Merrill's reading at UCLA in 1980, met him in 1983, and was his lover from 1984 until the poet's death. Mounted productions of *The Image Maker* and *The Bait* and produced the video of *Voices from Sandover*, the theatrical adaptation of *The Changing Light at Sandover*.

Richard Howard (b. 1929), poet, translator, literary critic, and editor. Howard's many volumes of verse, which feature dramatic monologues, include *Untitled Subjects* (1969), for which he won the Pulitzer Prize. Merrill's dedication of "Lost in Translation" to his friend comports with the latter's preeminence as a translator from modern and contemporary French prose and poetry, indicated by assorted honors, including the National Book Award for his version of Charles Baudelaire's *Les Fleurs du mal* (1983).

David Jackson (1922–2001) met Merrill in May 1953, and became his lifelong partner. Born in South Dakota, grew up in Los Angeles. As a student at UCLA in 1947, married the graphic artist Doris "Sewelly" Sewell. (She remained his wife and his and Merrill's friend, and lived near them in Mystic, Connecticut.) Author of a prize-winning short story, "The English Gardens," in *Partisan Review* (March–April 1961), but unsuccessful in his efforts to publish novels commercially. Also a self-taught painter who depicted scenes of daily life. Primary residence in Athens 1965–79, and after 1979 in Key West. Long relationship in Greece with George Lazaretos, a career navy officer. From 1953 on, was Merrill's collaborator on the Ouija board, including the occult communications that were the basis for Merrill's epic poem *The Changing Light at Sandover* (1982), in which, with Merrill, he is one of the primary characters.

David Kalstone (1933–86), literary critic, who studied at Harvard with Merrill's friend and teacher Reuben Brower, and became a professor of English at Rutgers. Merrill's close friend from the 1960s until his death from AIDS, he is the dedicatee of "Investiture at Cecconi's" and the elegy "Farewell Performance," and a tutelary spirit behind "Prose of Departure," all in *The Inner Room* (1988). In the 1970s and 1980s, Merrill visited him in the summer in Venice, where he rented rooms in the Palazzo Barbaro. Author of *Sidney's Poetry: Contexts and Interpretations* (1965), *Five Temperaments: Elizabeth Bishop, Robert Lowell, James Merrill, Adrienne Rich, John Ashbery* (1977), and, posthumously, *Becoming a Poet: Elizabeth Bishop with Marianne Moore and Robert Lowell* (1989), which Merrill completed by writing a coda.

Hans Lodeizen (1924–50), Dutch poet, author of one innovative volume of poems, *Het innerlijk behang en andere gedichten* (*The Inner Wallpaper and Other Poems*, 1950). Merrill's friend during Merrill's senior year at Amherst, where, as a visiting student, Lodeizen studied biology. Died in a sanatorium in Lausanne, Switzerland, shortly after Merrill visited him. The subject of Merrill's elegy "The Country of a Thousand Years of Peace." As a spirit contacted via the Ouija board, became a character in *The Changing Light at Sandover* (1982). See also Merrill's portrait of him in *A Different Person* (1993).

Doris Merrill Magowan (1914–2001), first child of Charles E. Merrill and Eliza Church Merrill, and James Merrill's half sister.

Lived with her mother and her brother Charles after her parents' divorce in 1925, while remaining close to her father. Married **Robert Magowan** (1903–85) in 1935, in a grand wedding on Charles Merrill's Southampton estate, The Orchard. Robert Magowan was a Merrill Lynch executive and the CEO of Safeway (1955–70), the West Coast supermarket chain, which expanded through a merger led by Charles Merrill in 1926. Based in San Francisco, with houses in Palm Beach and Southampton, the Magowans had five sons, Robin, Merrill, Peter, Stephen, and Mark. Doris became an expert collector of antiques, a gardener, and a noted philanthropist.

Robin Magowan (b. 1936), Merrill's nephew, oldest son of Doris and Robert Magowan. As a professor of English, taught at the University of Washington and the University of California at Berkeley before moving to France, and then England, where he founded the transatlantic review *Margin*. Author of many books, including the poetry collection *Lilac Cigarette in a Wish Cathedral* (1998) and *Memoirs of a Minotaur: Adventures Among the Powerful and Gifted from Merrill Lynch to Patty Hearst* (2000), a revised edition of an autobiography he first published in 1999.

J. D. McClatchy (1946–2018), poet, librettist, translator, editor, critic, teacher. As a graduate student at Yale in 1972, introduced himself to Merrill by a fan letter, and became his close friend. Merrill dedicated *A Different Person* (1993) to him. Published sixteen opera libretti, in addition to eight volumes of verse, three collections of critical essays, and numerous anthologies. Taught creative writing at Columbia, Princeton, and Yale, and served as editor of *The Yale Review* for twenty-five years. Chancellor of the Academy of American Poets, president of the American Academy of Arts and Letters. With Stephen Yenser, Merrill's co–literary executor and coeditor of five of Merrill's posthumously published works.

David McIntosh (b. 1938), painter with an interest in abstraction and an affinity for Japanese aesthetics, born in Wyoming and based in northern New Mexico, who met Merrill in 1968 and traveled extensively with him in the Rocky Mountains, New Mexico, New England, Italy, and Greece. Many poems in *Braving the Elements*

(1972) refer to experiences they shared. See also "Bronze" in *Late Settings* (1985) and "Ginger Beef" in *The Inner Room* (1988).

Charles E. Merrill (1885–1956), father of James Merrill. Son of a country doctor in Florida, attended Amherst College and the University of Michigan before working in finance. With Edmund Lynch, founded the firm Merrill Lynch, which encouraged middle-class investment in the stock market across the US and "brought Wall Street to Main Street." Led chain-store mergers for McCrory's, Kresge's, and Safeway, making the latter the largest grocery chain in the western United States. A philanthropist known for his lavish lifestyle, owned splendid homes including The Orchard, a thirty-acre estate in Southampton on Long Island, and Merrill's Landing, a compound stretching from the Atlantic to Lake Worth Lagoon in Palm Beach, Florida. Married to and divorced from Eliza Church Merrill (mother of his children Doris and Charles), Hellen Ingram Merrill (mother of James), and Kinta Des Mares. Troubled by heart disease from the 1940s onward. Represented as Benjamin Tanning in his son James's novel *The Seraglio* (1957).

Charles Merrill Jr. (1920–2017), second child of Charles E. Merrill and Eliza Church Merrill, and James Merrill's half brother. Cofounded the Thomas Jefferson School in Saint Louis and founded the Commonwealth School in Boston, in 1958, which he directed until his retirement in 1981. Advocate for racial justice and equal access to education in the United States, with a lifelong sympathy for the political struggles of Eastern European people. In 1941, married Mary Klohr, with whom he had five children: Catherine, David, Bruce, Amy, and Paul. Mary, a talented weaver, with whom James was close, died in 1999. In 2010, married Julie Boudreaux.

Judith Moffett (b. 1942), writer, literary critic, and translator from the Swedish. Merrill's student at the University of Wisconsin in 1967. Her work includes three volumes of poems and several books of science fiction, as well as *James Merrill: An Introduction to the Poetry* (1984) and the memoir *Unlikely Friends: James Merrill and Judith Moffett* (2019).

Umberto Morra (1897–1981), Italian journalist, cultural ambassador, and an active antifascist during World War II. Reputedly the out-of-wedlock son of King Umberto I. Merrill met him in 1951 and for the next thirty years frequently visited him at his family estate in Cortona. See Merrill's portraits of him in *A Different Person* (1993) and in "Bronze" in *Late Settings* (1985).

Strato Mouflouzelis (b. 1942) met Merrill in September 1964, and became his lover in a circle of friends that included Mimi and Vassilis Vassilikos, Tony Parigory, and George Lazaretos, David Jackson's lover. During the period of his closeness with Merrill, was also involved, without Merrill's knowledge, with Vaso, a woman whom he later married and with whom he had a son and a daughter. Serving in the Greek Air Force as a mechanic when he met Merrill; later worked as a taxi driver and builder. With his family, moved for work to Canada during the 1970s, before returning to live in Athens.

Tony Parigory (1926?–93), born in Alexandria, Egypt, the son of a Greek stockbroker, was a fine antiques dealer in Athens. With Maria Mitsotaki and Nelly Liambey, became close friends with Merrill in the early 1960s. Member of a circle of Alexandrian expatriates that included the French-Greek writer Christian Ayoub Sinano and the puppet-show librettist Bernard de Zogheb. Traveled in the United States with Merrill. Died of AIDS. See Merrill's elegy "Tony: Ending the Life" in *A Scattering of Salts* (1995).

Hellen Ingram Plummer (1898–2000), James Merrill's mother. Born in Jacksonville, Florida, the only child of James Wilmot Ingram, a businessman, and **Annie Hill Ingram**, who was known in the family as "Mis' Annie," and with whom Hellen was close. Popular and successful in local schools, became society editor of a Jacksonville newspaper, then writer and publisher of her own society report, *Silhouette*. While taking journalism and fiction writing courses at Columbia University, befriended the publisher Condé Nast. In New York, met Charles E. Merrill and, after he divorced his first wife, married him in 1925. Their marriage ended in divorce in 1939. During the Second World War, served as a Red Cross volunteer in the Pacific. In 1950, married **William L. Plummer** (1896–1969), a Floridian by birth who served as a brigadier general in the United States Air Force during the Second World War, and became a businessman in Atlanta after the war. He had one child by a first marriage, Betty Plummer Potts Woodruff, James Merrill's stepsister. Hellen was known for her philanthropy in Atlanta, Jacksonville, and Palm Beach.

Donald Richie (1924–2013), American expatriate in Japan from 1947 on, writer in many genres and experimental filmmaker, a connoisseur of and guide to contemporary Japanese culture, especially its cinema, and expert on the directors Yasujiro Ozu and Akira Kurosawa in particular. Among his many works is *The Inland Sea* (1971), a travel memoir made into a documentary he narrated for PBS. Met Merrill in Tokyo in 1956, and hosted him on his second visit to Japan in 1986, which prompted "Prose of Departure" in *The Inner Room* (1988), a *haibun* series of travel notes (a Japanese genre) which Merrill dedicated to him.

Grace Zaring Stone (1891–1991), American novelist who also wrote under the pseudonym Ethel Vance, three of whose novels became films. Mother of **Eleanor Perenyi** (1918–2009), American writer, whose books include *Liszt: The Artist as Romantic Hero* (1974) and *Green Thoughts: A Writer in the Garden* (1981). The two were friends and neighbors of Merrill and Jackson in Stonington for many years and the bases for characters in Merrill's ballad "The Summer People" (*The Fire Screen*, 1969).

Vassilis Vassilikos (b. 1934), Greek novelist, playwright, poet, diplomat, politician. He and his wife, **Mimí Vassilikos** (d. 1978), a painter, became Merrill's friends in Athens in 1964. Famous for his novel Z (1966), based on the assassination of the Greek pacifist and politician Grigoris Lambrakis and source of the film of the same name by Costa-Gavras, Vassilikos was exiled under the dictatorial regime of the Greek "colonels." Vassilikos and Merrill translated some of each other's writing. Mimí's death and Vassilis's mourning figure prominently at the close of *The Changing Light at Sandover* (1982).

Stephen Yenser (b. 1941), poet, literary critic, and, with J. D. McClatchy, Merrill's co–literary executor and coeditor of five of his posthumously published works. Met Merrill while a PhD student at the University of Wisconsin during the poet's teaching stint there in 1967 and was a close friend thereafter. Saw Merrill in Greece in the 1970s. As professor at UCLA, hosted Merrill for poetry readings in Los Angeles. In addition to three books of poems and two other books of criticism, wrote *The Consuming Myth: The Work of James Merrill* (1987) and edited and annotated *The Book of Ephraim* (2018). Merrill dedicated "Yánnina" (*Divine Comedies*, 1976) and *A Scattering of Salts* (1995) to him.

Acknowledgments

In the 1980s, James Merrill asked his friends to give his letters in their possession to Special Collections at Washington University in St. Louis, where he had been depositing his papers since 1964, when he had been invited by poet and faculty member Mona Van Duyn to establish an archive there. He made arrangements for specific correspondence—including his letters to Strato Mouflouzelis and David McIntosh—to be collected along with his papers. He made other provisions so that his letters to and from Elizabeth Bishop, over a period of thirty years, would be part of Bishop's archive at Vassar College, where his letters to Mary McCarthy are also held.

J. D. McClatchy, acting with Stephen Yenser as a co-executor of James Merrill's literary estate, was instrumental in gathering additional Merrill letters after his death in 1995. McClatchy used Merrill's address book to contact friends and family, who made their letters from Merrill available to the executors for potential publication. McClatchy and Yenser deposited their own letters from Merrill and other relevant material at the Beinecke Rare Book and Manuscript Library at Yale University, where the poet's letters to John Hollander, Robin Magowan, and other friends are also preserved. McClatchy read hundreds of Merrill's letters in the process of selecting correspondence for publication, and discussed editorial principles with his partner editors, before illness made it impossible for him to continue work on the book.

Timothy Young, Curator of Modern Books and Manuscripts at the Beinecke, carefully tracked the disposition of original documents and oversaw the compiling, copying, filing, and posting to the editors of many weighty boxes of correspondence.

Joel Minor, Curator, Modern Literature Collection / Manuscripts of the Julian Edison Department of Special Collections at Washington University Libraries, cheerfully collaborated with the editors over a long period of time to facilitate this book, which his predecessor, John Hodge, had helped to get off the ground. Sarah Schnuriger, Special Collections Assistant, recovered and catalogued crucial documents.

Chelsie Malyszek energetically assisted the editors in the preparation of the text at every stage, from corresponding with archivists, through transcribing and proofreading the letters selected, to researching material for the notes. Stathis Gourgouris generously translated Merrill's letters composed in Greek, provided annotations for those texts, and gave advice about other matters pertaining to Greek. Susan Bianconi maintained McClatchy's archive of letter copies, with assistance from Kamran Javadizadeh and Oana Marian. Forrester Hammer evaluated and winnowed undated correspondence.

We could not have completed this selection without the help in diverse ways of Leslie Brody, Frederick Buechner, Lynn Callahan, Henri Cole, Rachel Hadas, Marc Harrington, Patrick Kurp, the Lodeizen family, Sylvia Lynch, Robin Magowan, David McIntosh, Judith Moffett, Regan Morse, Jeffrey Posternak at the Wylie Agency, Alice Quinn, Sam Shea, Ricardo Sternberg, Brian Walker, and Wick York.

Throughout the project, the editors have counted on Deborah Garrison, our editor at Alfred A. Knopf, who has been a source of inspiration, encouragement, and good judgment. We are also indebted to her colleagues at Knopf, including Todd Portnowitz, Pei Koay, Anne Achenbaum, and Lisa Montebello. Patrick Dillon was an exemplary copyeditor. The late Sonny Mehta warmly supported the posthumous publication of five volumes of Merrill's work, the last of which is this volume. We are grateful to Reagan Arthur, his successor, for shoring up his legacy and for her commitment to publishing writers' correspondence.

Chip Kidd designed the cover for this volume, as he has for all Merrill books edited by McClatchy and Yenser, as well as Langdon Hammer's biography of the poet.

The editors are particularly grateful to the Hellen Plummer Foundation, directed by Mark Magowan and Amy Merrill, for supporting the preparation of the manuscript over several years. UCLA's COR Faculty Research Grants have been vital.

The institutions listed below made copies of Merrill's letters available to the editors. We provide in parentheses the abbreviations we use when indicating where particular letters are housed.

Archives & Special Collections, Robert Frost Library, Amherst College (Amherst)

Rare Books and Literary Manuscripts, Bancroft Library, University of California, Berkeley (Berkeley)

Special Collections, Rare Book & Manuscript Library, Columbia University (Columbia)

David M. Rubenstein Rare Book & Manuscript Library, Duke University (Duke)

Stuart A. Rose Manuscript, Archives, and Rare Book Library, Emory University (Emory)

Special Collections, Getty Research Institute (Getty)

Special Collections, Hamilton College Library, Hamilton College (Hamilton)

Special Collections and Archives, Houghton Library, Harvard University (Harvard)

Archives, Literatuurmuseum at the Hague (Literatuurmuseum)

Mississippi Department of Archives and History (Mississippi)

Literary and Historical Manuscripts, The Morgan Library & Museum (Morgan Library)

Henry W. and Albert A. Berg Collection of English and American Literature, The New York Public Library (NYPL)

Manuscripts and Archives Division, The New York Public Library (NYPL Archives)

American Literature Collection, The Rosenbach Library (Rosenbach)

Special Collections and University Archives, Archibald S. Alexander Library, Rutgers University (Rutgers)

Harry Ransom Center, University of Texas at Austin (Texas)

Archives and Special Collections Library, Vassar College (Vassar)

Special Collections, Buswell Library, Wheaton College (Wheaton)

Modern Literature Collection / Manuscripts of the Julian Edison
Department of Special Collections at Washington University
Libraries Olin Library, Washington University St. Louis
(WUSTL)
Beinecke Rare Book & Manuscript Library, Yale University (Yale)

Others who made correspondence available to us include André
Aciman (Aciman); Torren Blair (Blair); The Louise Fitzhugh Estate
(Fitzhugh); Peter Hooten (Hooten); Richard Howard (Howard);
Marilyn Lavin (Lavin); Peter Moore (Moore); Alice Notley (Notley);
Craig Poile (Poile); and Brian Walker (Walker).

Index

JM refers to James Merrill

James Merrill, an eminent figure in late-twentieth-century American poetry, won virtually all of the pertinent honors, including the Bollingen Prize, the inaugural Bobbitt Prize, the National Book Award (twice), and the Pulitzer Prize. In addition to his twelve volumes of poems, beginning with *The Black Swan* (1946) and ending with the posthumous *A Scattering of Salts* (1995), he wrote the epic verse trilogy *The Changing Light at Sandover* (1982); two plays, *The Immortal Husband* (1956) and *The Bait* (1960); two novels, *The Seraglio* (1957) and *The (Diblos) Notebook* (1965); and the memoir *A Different Person* (1993). His *Collected Poems* appeared in 2001; his *Collected Prose* (which includes critical and occasional essays and interviews) was published in 2004. A chancellor of the Academy of American Poets, a member of the American Academy of Arts and Letters, and the founder of the Ingram Merrill Foundation, he traveled widely and had homes in Athens, Greece, and Key West, Florida, while his chief residence for the last forty years of his life was in Stonington, Connecticut. In 2017 that building was designated a National Historic Landmark.

Langdon Hammer is the Niel Gray Jr. Professor of English at Yale University. His books include *James Merrill: Life and Art* and *Hart Crane and Allen Tate: Janus-Faced Modernism,* and he edited the Library of America volumes *Hart Crane: Complete Poetry and Selected Letters* and *May Swenson: Collected Poems.* A former Guggenheim fellow, he writes about poetry for *The New York Review of Books, The Yale Review,* and *The American Scholar,* where he has been the poetry editor since 2004. He is writing a critical biography of Elizabeth Bishop.

Stephen Yenser's volumes of poems are *The Fire in All Things,* awarded the Walt Whitman Award by the Academy of American Poets; *Blue Guide*; and *Stone Fruit.* Distinguished Research Professor at UCLA and curator of the poetry series at the Hammer Museum, he has written three books of criticism, including *The Consuming Myth: The Work of James Merrill;* coedited with J. D. McClatchy five volumes of Merrill's work; and annotated a stand-alone edition of Merrill's *The Book of Ephraim.*

A NOTE ABOUT THE TYPE

This book was set in Hoefler Text, a family of fonts designed by Jonathan Hoefler, who was born in 1970. First designed in 1991, Hoefler Text was intended as an advancement on existing desk- top computer typography, including as it does an exponentially larger number of glyphs than previous fonts. In form, Hoefler Text looks to the old-style fonts of the seventeenth century, but it is wholly of its time, employing a precision and sophisti- cation only available to the late twentieth century.

Composed by North Market Street Graphics
Lancaster, Pennsylvania

Printed and bound by Sheridan Books, Inc.
Versailles, Kentucky